Britain's War

DANIEL TODMAN

Britain's War

Into Battle, 1937–1941

OXFORD
UNIVERSITY PRESS

OXFORD

UNIVERSITY PRESS

Oxford University Press is a department of the University of Oxford. It furthers the University's objective of excellence in research, scholarship, and education by publishing worldwide. Oxford is a registered trade mark of Oxford University Press in the UK and certain other countries.

Published in the United States of America by Oxford University Press
198 Madison Avenue, New York, NY 10016, United States of America.

© Daniel Todman 2016

First published in Great Britain by Allen Lane.

Library of Congress Cataloging-in-Publication Data

Names: Todman, Daniel, author.
Title: Britain's war / Daniel Todman.
Description: New York, NY : Oxford University Press, 2016– | "First published in Great Britain by Allen Lane"—Title page verso. | Includes bibliographical references and index. Contents: Volume I. Into Battle, 1937–1941.
Identifiers: LCCN 2016004416 | ISBN 9780190621803
(volume 1 : hardback : acid-free paper)
Subjects: LCSH: World War, 1939–1945—Great Britain. | World War, 1939–1945—Campaigns—Great Britain. | World War, 1939–1945—Social aspects—Great Britain. | BISAC: HISTORY / Military / World War II. | HISTORY / General.
Classification: LCC D759 .T59 2016 | DDC 940.53/41—dc23
LC record available at https://lccn.loc.gov/2016004416

1 3 5 7 9 8 6 4 2

Printed by Sheridan Books, Inc., United States of America

For Alex and Agatha

Contents

List of Illustrations

List of Maps

List of Tables

A Note on Money, Weights and Measures and Military Formations

MONEY

For the whole period covered by this book, the UK system of money was based on pounds (£), shillings (s.) and pence (d.). Twelve pence equalled one shilling, and twenty shillings equalled a pound.

The sums of money referred to here are always those of the time – unless otherwise noted, they are not adjusted into constant terms to take account of inflation. There are several ways of translating these sums to put them into the context of the early twenty-first century. Which one is best to use depends on the context.[1]

In terms of household income and consumption, for example, £1 in 1937 bought goods and services worth £56.30 at 2013 prices.* Since, however, most people's earnings and standards of living were relatively much lower in the 1930s than they are eight decades later it would be misleading to see an annual income of £250 as the equivalent of £14,080 – which is the value of goods that such an income would have purchased in 2013. In terms of social status, earning £250 a year in 1937 was worth about £61,330 in 2013 money. It's important to bear in mind that during the war, both inflation and working-class earnings increased very rapidly. By 1941, the value of what you could buy with £1 had fallen to £42.24 in 2013 terms, and an annual income of £250 was the equivalent to earning £38,540 in 2013.

A lot of the expenditures discussed in this book are those of the state, rather than of individuals. To get a sense of their significance in historical context, it's better to consider these in terms of their relative share of overall economic output. This rose significantly after the

---

* 2013 rather than 2016 because this is the latest point for which all the data are available.

outbreak of war. To get a sense of government expenditure in contemporary terms, multiply figures from the late 1930s by 350, and those from 1940–41 by 250 or 200.

Readers who want to compute what any amount they find in this book is worth, using these measures and others, should make use of the wonderful calculator at the website www.measuringworth.com/ukcompare.

WEIGHTS AND MEASURES

Weights are given in ounces (oz), pounds (lb), and tons; 16oz = 1lb, 14lb = 1 stone, 112lb = 1 hundredweight, 2,240lb = 1 ton. To convert to metric, 2.2lbs = 1 kg, 1,016kg = 1 ton.

Lengths are given in inches, feet, yards and miles; 12 inches = 1 foot, 3 feet = 1 yard, 1,760 yards = 1 mile. Area is given in square footage and acres; 640 acres = 1 square mile. To convert to metric, 1.61km = 1 mile.

Ship sizes are given in gross tons: a measurement of the total volume of all the internal enclosed spaces of a ship calculated on the basis one gross ton = 100 cubic feet. This is a different way of calculating ship size to the deadweight tonnage, which is the number of tons of 2,240lb that a ship can carry at its summer loading level. Ship movements through ports are given in net tons, which are defined as gross tonnage minus space not used for cargo.[2]

MILITARY FORMATIONS

Unit strengths and organizations varied during the war, but to get a sense of the numbers involved when British military formations are discussed, it can be taken that at full strength in 1940–41:

An infantry division = about 18,000 soldiers
An armoured division = 250 tanks
A squadron = 12–16 operational aircraft, plus 4 or more in reserve

Figures for divisions, squadrons or warships conceal a large number of base troops who were required to keep the complex machinery of war supplied and maintained. At the start of 1941, it was calculated that each division of 18,000 men required another 23,000 soldiers behind the lines, working in the maintenance and supply units that kept the fighting troops in the field.[3]

Introduction: War Stories

Tucked at the back of my desk drawer, in an old hearing-aid box, are the medals that could have belonged to my grandfather. The War and Defence Medals and the 1939–45 and France and Germany Stars were the sort awarded for service, rather than valour – and they match the three years that Charles Todman spent driving tanks and trucks in the UK before, transferred to a machine-gun battalion, he was sent out to North-west Europe at the start of September 1944. Their metal shines and their ribbons are unfaded. These are medals that have never been worn.

For most of the time that I knew him, Grandad showed no sign of thinking of himself as a veteran. He never went to the Royal British Legion, or belonged to a regimental association, or went to ceremonies on Remembrance Sunday. As a child, I was not regaled with his war stories. Only with reluctance could he be persuaded to name the guns wielded by my Airfix plastic soldiers, and when the film *A Bridge Too Far* made one of its frequent appearances on television, my grandmother, Nanny, told me to turn it off because it was too noisy. The medals he had actually received for his wartime service had been lost: given to his sons to play with, they had disappeared into the cracks that had opened up in the sun-baked garden of their Metroland house one summer in the 1950s. That seemed to sum up how he had decided to treat the war. Judging by the pictures they kept on their walls, he and Nanny were much keener on celebrating their post-retirement holidays, their grandsons, and the awards given to their home-made wine than on marking their participation in the Second World War.

Yet the war had been the defining moment of their lives. How else would a trainee accountant from London and a miner's daughter from

Tyneside ever have met, if military service hadn't brought them both to a dance in the sergeants' mess at the army camp at Barnard Castle? They first met when he picked her up after she fell on the floor, but in their wedding photos, Grandad in his uniform looks like the one who might be about to topple over. Her father had drunk him and his mates under the table the night before. Husband and wife obviously made good use of the last moments before he was sent to Europe, because their first child, my father, was born exactly nine months after his embarkation leave, at the start of May 1945. The Russians were in Berlin, the war in Europe was in its final days, and the midwife insisted that the boy would have to be called Victor to mark the occasion, thus ensuring that he would spend the rest of his life as a war memorial.

His parents never used that name in my hearing: they always called him Bill, his second name, instead. This was probably not just a matter of preference. Years later, Grandad was still angry that, although the fighting had finished, he had not been allowed home to see his new son. Instead, he was stuck in a recently surrendered Hamburg with his unit, waiting for further service in the Far East. The end of the war with Japan saved him from that, but he didn't get a leave long enough to come home again until the end of October 1945. Unlike a lot of families, they didn't have to deal with bereavement or disability, but the anxiety and the pain of separation – during the pregnancy, then during the first year of my father's life, because Grandad wasn't demobbed until May 1946 – must have been terrible. When he returned home, they put the war behind them and got on with their lives.

Yet they were also interested in, and proud of, their grandsons. After my first book was published, Grandad decided that it might be nice if I could have his medals. When the Ministry of Defence explained that they didn't issue replacements, he bought new ones from a dealer to pass on to me. In a letter, he recalled some of what he had experienced during that final, bitter campaign, including the terrifying day that rocket-firing Hawker Typhoons mistook the target marking and attacked his unit rather than the Germans. My brother and I bought him a copy of the regimental history for his birthday, and he read it with apparent interest. After all these years, he said, it was good to know what had actually been going on.

In contrast to Grandad Todman, as I was growing up my maternal grandfather, Frederick Spackman, seemed to talk about the war every time we saw him. Fred had been a fitter with the London Transport Passenger Board and, having joined the Territorial Army in 1938, he spent the war repairing vehicles in workshops in Britain and Egypt. It was without doubt the most exotic thing that ever happened to him. The studio portraits taken by a wartime photographer in Cairo show Fred doing his best to look like Errol Flynn, but there wasn't much swashbuckling in his stories. They were always the same. The motor-bike accident that had put him in hospital, as one of the war's first British casualties, on 3 September 1939. The time he knew more than the officer who had to test his mechanical knowledge. Keeping a chameleon, learning to repair watches and counting to ten in Arabic. The working of the Wilson epicyclic gearbox in the Daimler Armoured Car.

These tales were so familiar that we could repeat them word for word and, to us if not to him, they became something of a joke. Only at the end of his life did it become apparent that he could have told a different set of stories. The hasty first marriage conducted in the shadow of impending war. The wife who then told him that she was carrying a child and that she was not sure if he was the father. The belated divorce. All this had been written out of the family's history: the strength of the taboo such that my mother, his daughter by his second marriage, had known nothing about it at all. While Fred was abroad, his estranged wife continued to draw an allowance from his pay, his father died and all his possessions were sold. On demobilization, he had to rebuild his life completely from scratch. Like most men of his generation, he did not enjoy unrestrained displays of emotion. Perhaps it was not surprising that he liked to keep his memories of the war closely controlled.

I tell these anecdotes not just as a means of paying tribute or claiming inherited authority, but also to make a point about the complexity and fluidity of our relationship with the past. What we put in and leave out of our history matters, but what we think we know can always be subject to change. Eighty years on from 1939, with the war disappearing over the boundary of lived memory, we can still question and rework the stories we tell about it, finding new meanings and turning the familiar strange.

This is the first of a two-part history of Britain's Second World War, running from 1937 to 1947. In a way no other book has done, these two volumes join together histories that are usually told separately – strategic, political and economic, military, cultural and social – to build a broad and coherent picture of the country as it prepared for, fought and emerged from a total war. The books are written on the principle that if we want to understand the war, we have to grasp that fighting and home fronts, strategic decisions and economic effects, military contingencies and political opportunities were all interconnected. Only by linking them together can we start to understand the course and consequences of the war. Exploring the conflict from these different angles also allows us to follow its story at different levels: from the high politics of grand strategic decision-making, via the statistics of production, inflation and infant mortality, to the myriad of individual experiences that give a sense of what it was like to be caught up in (or left out of) great events as they happened. In so doing, we can see how some of the stories that were told to make sense of the conflict at the time continue to influence how we think about the war.

This is a history centred on the United Kingdom, but it is not just a British history. The Britain of the 1930s and 1940s was an imperial country, and the Empire was crucial to why and how Britain fought. The history of the Empire at war is not just one of shared service, but of exploitation, resistance, repression and the hope of liberation. The fate of the British Empire is one of the great stories of the war. In some ways, this is also an international history. What happened to Britain during these years only makes sense if it is seen as part of a global system. The plunge into war, and the course of the violence that followed, were shaped by the actions and reactions of the great powers. The vast extent of Britain's economic and strategic interests meant that, from its outset, the consequences of the conflict stretched across the world. Perhaps most importantly, it's important to put Britain's experience of war into international context in order to understand how distinct it was, and just how lightly the British managed to escape from their second encounter with a modern total war.

To comprehend the course of the war, we need to have a sense of why battles were won or lost – and how people understood victory and defeat at the time – but wars consist mainly of things other than fighting. While the experience of combat and the history of military operations have their place in both these books, they spend more time on other aspects of the conflict: the factory, the food queue, the Whitehall office, the dockyard and the broadcasting studio. Putting combat in its place is a significant part of understanding what really mattered to the outcome of the war: the colossal mobilization of modern industrial economies to produce the weapons, food and equipment with which victory would be pursued. This was also a crucial factor in determining individual experience: for all the drama of the Battle of Britain and the Blitz in 1940–41, their impact on British life was marginal compared to the full employment, rising wages and increasing prices that resulted from the expansion of munitions production to meet the demands of the war.

In reconstructing history we have constantly to remember that people at the time could only guess at a future that to us is plainly known. No one in 1939 knew that the war would end in 1945. For this reason, both volumes of *Britain's War* tell the story as it went along, rather than following each separate theme across the whole course of the war. This serves to emphasize just how much the conflict changed – for strategists, service personnel and civilians – as it went on. 'Wartime' was not an invariant condition. Two great changes – the Fall of France and Germany's attack on the Soviet Union – bookend the year-long struggle to defend the United Kingdom which forms the centrepiece of this volume. Another – the entries of Japan and America into the conflict – forms the dividing line between this book and its sequel, which carries the story of the conflict past the eventual Allied victory to the moment of Indian independence in 1947.

This volume, *Into Battle*, tells the story from the descent into a European war during the 1930s to the explosion of a more global conflict at the end of 1941. At its heart is an argument about viewing 1940 not as a 'Finest Hour', but as the decisive year in twentieth-century British history. Ironically, even as the resilience of Britain and its empire vindicated at least some of the strategies adopted by the governments of the 1930s, the combination of Westminster machination, military defeat and economic escalation swept in a new political order that would shape British life for the next three decades. Meanwhile, by ensuring that Germany was unable to capitalize on its victory over France, British strength determined, for the last time, the future of the world. As Britain held out against a Nazi-occupied Europe, and Germany failed to subdue its sea-girt enemy, both combatants were driven to find the resources they needed to secure a decisive victory. Their desperation would turn the conflict into a bigger, more global war that neither was able to win. By December 1941, the beginning of the Second World War was coming to an end, but the real war was only just beginning.

PART ONE
Prelude

I

Studies in Celebration

Deep in the Underground station, the crush was growing worse. With the platforms already crammed, new arrivals kept pressing in. All but overwhelmed, railway staff and policemen tried to maintain calm. As the newcomers descended, the air grew thicker: the heat of close packed bodies creating an almost suffocating fug. Grumpy indignation and humorous resignation, however, eclipsed panic. On the packed platform, someone was trying to persuade their neighbours into another round of song.

Then a train rumbled in, and a fresh wave of passengers emerged. As their bedraggled replacements took the chance of escape, the newcomers pressed towards the exits, desperate to get outside and join in the fun. It was just after 6 p.m. on 12 May 1937. London was celebrating the crowning of a new king. And outside, the rain was pouring down.

'I'M PATRIOTIC ALL RIGHT'

The momentum of excitement had been building for some time. The previous weekend had seen the largest traffic jams London had ever known as sightseers flocked into the decorated streets. With the capital's busmen on strike for shorter hours, gridlock had descended when thousands of visitors from the suburbs came in their own cars. Over the days that followed, spectators began to camp out in the most favourable spots to see the royal family on their way to and from Westminster Abbey. In the early hours of coronation morning, their slumbers were broken by the growing crowds, the testing of the public address system and the stamp of marching troops. Inside Buckingham Palace, the noise woke the king, who fretted that the archbishop of Canterbury might put the great crown of England on him back to front.[1]

The vast parade to the abbey got under way at half past ten. Twenty-seven thousand servicemen lined the route. The archbishop and the king having managed their respective duties well enough, the royal family returned home, accompanied by another 6,000 troops, drawn from every part of the armed forces and every corner of His Majesty's realms – from the Life Guards, via the Bermuda Militia and the Royal Canadian Mounted Police, to the Army Dental Corps. The rest of the abbey congregation, among them the Conservative MP Henry 'Chips' Channon, faced a long wait before they could emerge. Fortunately, some had brought provisions. 'Chocolates were munched, and flasks slyly produced,' Channon recorded, and he fell into a fawning reverie over the highlights of the ceremony: 'the shaft of sunlight, catching the King's golden tunic as he sat for the crowning; the kneeling Bishops drawn up like a flight of geese in deploy position; and then the loveliest moment of all, the swirl when the Peeresses put on their coronets'.[2]

Outside, 570 miles of steel scaffolding and 1,400 tons of timber had been used to construct viewing stands (covered and uncovered, depending on the status of the intended occupants) in which were seated 90,000 official and paying spectators. On Victoria Embankment, the London County Council had assembled 37,000 schoolchildren – sustained by the donation to each of a half-pint of milk and a packet of crisps by the Milk and Potato Marketing Boards – to pay shrill homage.[3] Crowds packed the space between the stands. Over the forty-six hours of continuous service before and after the coronation, a record 5,669,000 passenger journeys were made on the London Underground – a number somewhat inflated by the continuing bus strike.[4] Twenty thousand policemen were on duty, connected by a combination of wireless and telephones to three 'nerve centres' from which they could be directed to the points of greatest need. Despite the revelry, the total number of offences dealt with by Bow Street police court over the period of the coronation was rather less than normal for a weekday.[5]

Perhaps that was because it was so wet. The sun briefly pierced the drizzle as the royals made their way to the abbey, but as they returned the heavens opened. Nonetheless, the next day's newspapers reported an enthusiastic reception from the crowds: loudest – as measured by the

Daily Express 'cheerometer' – for, in order, Queen Mary (the king's mother), the king and queen, and the street cleaners who picked up the horses' dung from behind the cavalry and carriages.[6]

Some people weren't sure for whom they were shouting. Three people back from the barrier on Great Marlborough Street, the balconies of the buildings opposite could be seen but not the road itself. A nineteen-year-old secretarial student from Kent who had come up to watch the big day therefore found herself at something of a loss when, at five past three, cheering began: 'at procession we can't see . . . Constant rumours as to who passes. Violet says she can lip-read people's mouths on balconies . . . but seems to get same people twice. Much cheering on balconies for King. Not much cheering from behind barricades.'[7]

Once the parade finished, the barriers came down and the streets were turned over to the public, who now slid across carriageways coated in 'a sort of papier-maché paste of old newspapers, bags, flags, pieces of cloth, etc, well mixed with a mud basis'.[8] The more exhausted spectators departed, but the rest surged on in search of pubs and cafés to refresh themselves for further celebrations. Some gathered outside the palace, on the balcony of which the king and queen made three appearances to great acclamation. In Oxford Street, someone set up a radio, and ballroom dancing began in the middle of the road. Near Trafalgar Square, a woman stopped to look at photographs of the procession that had already been posted outside a news cinema:

> Two working class men are also looking and they are making remarks about the people in the picture – 'Look at the old girl, she looks as if she's got toothache' and at another picture of the actual crowning: 'Look, they're just putting it on his nut'. I said to one of them: 'You're not very loyal, are you?' 'Oh I'm patriotic all right, I've been up all night waiting to see the procession.'[9]

Across the UK, cities, towns, villages, streets and houses had been decorated and castles, cathedrals and council buildings floodlit. The street parties for which many poorer areas of London had been saving were rained off, as were the planned parades in Southend, Lincoln and Hull, but elsewhere a mixture of better weather and persistence won out. In Cardiff, there was a pageant illustrating the industrial and municipal progress of the city over the previous century, an air rally, a coronation ball, concerts and fireworks in the parks, a procession of boats on the River Taff, a military parade and a twenty-one gun salute. In Southport, the morning's procession and civic service of thanks were followed by a display of tableaux, physical exercises and dancing by 3,000 schoolchildren at the ground of the local football club. In Liverpool docks, the great ocean-going ships were decorated with flags and lights. A civic procession made its way to the city's cathedral, outside which, after the service, a 'King's Champion' (in fact a local police inspector on horseback in replica medieval armour) led the crowds in affirmations of allegiance. Then came a flypast by No. 611 (West Lancashire) Bomber Squadron. In Glasgow, the Corporation paid for teas for thousands of schoolchildren, pensioners, invalids, poor mothers and the unemployed. Four thousand troops paraded the streets; 80,000 people went to Hampden Park to watch a display of physical drill and dancing by 1,500 children, followed first by daylight fireworks, then, that evening, by a sports carnival featuring an exhibition football match, a demonstration of air-raid rescue methods by a specially trained squad of police officers, and the massed skirl of 800 pipers.[10]

The writer J. B. Priestley watched the celebrations in pessimistic mood. By the late 1930s, Priestley was a multimedia celebrity with a string of successful novels and plays to his name. Progressive in his politics but averse to political parties, Priestley usually turned his fears about the modern world into a celebration of good humour, honesty and family loyalty. In the crowds below his window, however, he could see little hope for the future:

> They had wandered away from religion but had not even arrived yet at science. Great music, drama, art, they knew little or nothing of these. They had lost the fields and the woods but had not exchanged them for a truly civilised urban life. Most of them probably did not know how to make love or even to eat and drink properly ... So much wealth, so much time, so much energy could be spared for the crowning of a king ... But to crown at last these people themselves, where were the wealth and time and energy for this task? Who would, after taking down the bunting and the lights, tear down the streets themselves and build a nobler, happier, beautiful Britain?[11]

'REALLY QUITE HUMAN'

The summer of royal occasions did not end with the coronation. The next day, the king and queen staged an unannounced drive through North London to see the street decorations for themselves. On 20 May, there was a full naval review off Portsmouth, in which the king inspected a procession of vessels six miles long, including the ten battleships and battlecruisers and four aircraft carriers of the Royal Navy's Home, Mediterranean and Reserve Fleets, as well as the American USS *New York* and the German battleship *Admiral Graf Spee*. That evening, the whole armada was illuminated by a forest of lamps and cascading fireworks. Three days later, the royal family joined the representatives of the Dominions, India and the colonies to celebrate Empire Day with a service of thanksgiving at St Paul's, and in July, the king and queen paid state visits to Scotland and Northern Ireland.

Official celebrations throughout the Empire mirrored those in the UK. On coronation day itself, Sydney Harbour Bridge was illuminated, first by lamps, then by a huge firework display. Brisbane floodlit its city centre and held church services, a ceremonial parade, a military sports show and a concert by massed choirs. Ottowans attended a parade of the military garrison, war veterans, scouts, guides and schoolchildren. Jamaica spent £5,000 on decorations and entertainment for children, the aged and infirm. In India, the viceroy processed through the Simla bazaar and attended the feeding of hundreds of the local poor.[12]

A British coronation was an international event. The *New York Sun* congratulated the British authorities for their success in labouring 'loyally . . . to safeguard and buttress democracy in a period when its enemies at both extremes of political fanaticism bitterly assail its philosophy, belittle its accomplishments, emphasize its shortcomings, and unite in demanding its destruction'. Yet there was also a message from Adolf Hitler, sending his best wishes for 'a long and happy reign for the welfare of Great Britain, Ireland, the oversea British Dominions, and India, as well as in the interest of the preservation of the peace of the world'.[13]

All this celebration could easily have been being held for someone else. The new king's elder brother, formerly Edward VIII, now the duke of Windsor, had assumed the throne on their father's death in January 1936, only to be forced into abdication that December because he was determined to marry the American divorcée Wallis Simpson. Edward's insistence on a union that went against the teaching of the church of which he was head offended the morals of senior politicians in Britain and the Dominions. It also confirmed their suspicions of irresponsibility in a monarch whose charisma won popular acclaim but who was too ready to voice his own feelings on such sensitive issues as friendship with Germany or the condition of the unemployed. For almost the whole of 1936, the king's affair with Simpson and the constitutional wranglings that resulted had gone unreported in the British press. When the news finally broke, it briefly appeared that public support might be rallied behind Edward. By the end of the year, however, he had gone, to be replaced by his brother – safely married and the embodiment of dutiful service.

Abdication in fact exacerbated Edward's selfishness and lack of political acumen. Effectively exiled to the continent, and egged on by his wife-to-be, he was now embroiled in a bitter argument with his brother over money and titles. In the study of a French château, he became the first British monarch to hear his successor being crowned.[14]

He could do that because this was the first coronation to be broadcast on radio. The former king was far from the only listener. By the time of the coronation about 8 million British households had a radio licence, and in that week's programming the coronation was inescapable. On the previous Sunday, for example, alongside the fairly normal Sabbath schedule – religious services from the chapel of St John's College, Cambridge, and the Bethesda Methodist Chapel, Old Colwyn, a selection of light classical works played by the Bournemouth Municipal Orchestra and a celebration of William Barnes, the early nineteenth-century Dorset poet – listeners to the BBC's National Programme would also have been treated to a discussion of the religious significance of the coronation, a special service led by the archbishop of Canterbury, and a performance of the 1902 operetta *Merrie England*. For those who wanted something a little more modern there was the commercial competition: Radio Luxembourg had the 'Ovaltine Programme of Melody and Swing' and the 'Kraft Show with Billy Cotton and Jack Doyle', before a special talk on the coronation by the Conservative MP and former minister Winston Churchill – a programme provided by the broadcaster devoid of sponsorship as a marker of the solemnity of the occasion.[15]

On the day of the coronation, the radio meant that most people could listen in live. For such a national occasion, the BBC – with a plethora of commentators and radio personalities interviewing members of the crowd – was the only choice, and no local celebration was complete without a loudspeaker relaying the service from Westminster Abbey. In a Cambridge college, a young man: 'Listened in to part of commentary on ceremony in common room with 9 people (4 conservatives, 3 liberals, 1 fascist, 1 fabian). General reaction: embarrassed grins, and outright laughter when the commentator was outstandingly loyal. Fascist stood for National Anthem. Conservative remarked "bloody fool!".' Nonetheless, they all 'agreed that the Coronation was a good thing because it improved trade, gave ruling class prestige and broke down class barriers'.[16]

The wireless also allowed the king to address the peoples of his empire. At eight o'clock in the evening of the great day, after much practice and with considerable determination, the king took to the airwaves. His themes were family, duty and imperial fellowship:

> Those of you who are children now will, I hope, retain memories of a day of carefree happiness . . . In years to come, some of you will travel from one part of the Commonwealth to another, and moving thus within the family circle will meet others . . . whose hearts are united in devotion to our common heritage. You will learn, I hope, how much our free association means to us, how much our friendship with each other and with all the nations upon earth can help the cause of peace and progress.[17]

Newsreel cameras had been positioned alongside the radio microphones, and their footage was rushed to cinemas where it was slotted into the normal programme. At a screening of the spy film *Second Bureau* in Carshalton, Surrey, that evening, for example, the main feature was stopped in the middle to show the first newsreel of the coronation. The audience clapped vigorously at every appearance of the king and queen. Then it stopped again for the radio broadcast of the king's speech, starting with the national anthem:

> Everyone stood up, uncertainly and at slightly different times, as they always do, with that rumbling noise of a crowd getting to its feet, and

then sat down again for the King's speech. The whole audience was silent and almost motionless throughout. We noticed the hesitation in the King's voice, and his inability to pronounce his r's properly. After the speech the national anthem again, everybody stood again, and a good part of the audience sang, gathering strength by the time they came to 'send him victorious'.[18]

The coronation was also broadcast on a new television service, inaugurated only at the very end of 1936. Approximately 60,000 people, living within a maximum distance of 63 miles of the transmitter at Alexandra Palace and wealthy or well-connected enough to have access to one of the early sets, watched the procession live. Among them was the same Cambridge scholar who had listened to the abbey ceremony on the radio:

> Saw televised procession in home of local tradesman. His wife and parents-in-law constantly remarked: 'Isn't it all wonderful,' 'After all, it just shows all this socialist nonsense up, doesn't it?' 'This is the only country where you could have a ceremony like this, without fear of someone throwing a bomb'. They also exchanged anecdotes about the Royal Family, all of which had the same point – that the Windsors are really quite human.[19]

So human, in fact, that in private discussions with the BBC before the coronation, the archbishop of Canterbury had vetoed the broadcast of live television images from inside Westminster Abbey itself, lest they catch the king's face spasming as he tried to overcome his stammer.[20]

OBSERVING THE CORONATION

Television was not the only way in which this coronation was being seen in a new light.[21] It was also investigated by a recently created group called Mass-Observation, whose members hoped that the close study of everyday life might make the world a better place. From across the country, forty-three volunteers sent in detailed descriptions of their experiences and emotions on coronation day to the group's London headquarters in Blackheath, while a team of twelve specially trained observers had mingled with the crowds in the capital. Thousands of copies of a questionnaire about the day had also been distributed, of which just under eighty found their way back to Blackheath. These eye-witness reports have peppered this account of the coronation. The material collected was published a few months later as a book, *May the Twelfth*.

Mass-Observation had begun as a mixture of artistic endeavour, political project and social scientific exploration. It germinated among a group of surrealist writers and artists gathered around the poet, journalist and sometime Communist Charles Madge. In his day job on the *Daily Mirror*, Madge had seen during the abdication crisis the gap between what the public actually knew and the ways that press and government talked about 'public opinion'. He thought that a network of observers who recorded their day-to-day experiences and emotions might provide the evidence to increase understanding of how popular attitudes were formed.

At the start of 1937, a letter from Madge to the left-wing weekly magazine the *New Statesman* explaining this plan brought him into contact with Tom Harrisson – an ornithologist turned anthropologist, who had recently published an account of his time living among tribespeople in the New Hebrides and was now engaged on a similar investigation into the working-class inhabitants of Bolton. A talented self-publicist with a rising profile as a writer and broadcaster, Harrisson saw an explicitly political rationale for working out what people actually thought. Strengthening the connection between leaders and led was meant to bolster democracy. Together, Madge and Harrisson composed a letter to the *New Statesman* announcing the formation of Mass-Observation.

Although ostensibly allied, their projects remained separate. Harrisson led a rather chaotic team of observers who scrutinized what Boltonians did but seldom asked how they felt. Madge attempted to assemble a national panel of correspondents who wrote, strictly anonymously, detailed reflections on one day of their own lives each month. He edited *May the Twelfth* with his friend Humphrey Jennings, another poet and a film-maker. The book's emphasis on bizarre juxtapositions showed more of Mass-Observation's surrealist roots than its social scientific aspirations. On publication, it sparked fierce arguments with modernist writers who thought it too light-hearted and academics who condemned its lack of intellectual rigour.

Although the mass enfranchisement that followed the Great War had made 'public opinion' a political touchstone, the new science of opinion polling was still regarded with distrust by most professional politicians as a form of special pleading. Mass-Observation's project left many reviewers uncomfortable at the idea of being observed by, as the right-wing weekly the *Spectator* put it, 'busybodies of the left'. Harrisson, who was always keener on making arguments than art-works, later wrote off *May the Twelfth* as a 'crazy idea' edited by 'a whole bunch of intellectual poets'.[22] Priced at an expensive 12/6, the book was a commercial flop.[23]

Running through *May the Twelfth* was a tension between its celebration of ordinary people's individuality and the observers' sense of alienation. Madge's recruits – disproportionately young and politically left-of-centre – were often suspicious of patriotism and the status quo, but also conscious of how unusual this made them. As a female typist explained, she had become 'very bored with the word Coronation', which she felt was being 'artificially bumped up'. As the celebrations went on, however:

> I was surprised how much I responded to the atmosphere of the crowd, the cheering, etc. I felt a definite pride and thrill in belonging to the Empire, which in ordinary life, with my political bias, is just the opposite of my true feelings.
>
> Yet I felt a definite sense of relief that I could experience this emotion and be in and of the crowd. One becomes very weary of always being in the minority, thinking things silly which other people care about; one must always be arguing, or repressing oneself, and it is psychologically very bad . . .
>
> Reviewing it all calmly afterwards, one sees how very dangerous all this is – the beliefs and convictions of a lifetime can be set aside so easily. Therefore, although people will probably always like pageantry, colour, little princesses, etc., and it seems a pity to rob them of this colourful make-believe element – nevertheless because it make it in the end harder for us to think and behave as rational beings when we are exposed to this strain and tension – I would definitely vote agin it. It is too dangerous a weapon to be in the hands of the people at present in power in this country.[24]

So what sort of country was it?

2

Ancient and Modern

It might seem strange to begin the story of Britain's Second World War with the hubbub of the coronation rather than a siren's wail. Neither the nation nor its people, however, sprang into existence on the declaration of war.

WEALTH AND TECHNOLOGY

When George VI came to the throne, the UK was still distinguished internationally by its industrial and trading wealth.[1] Very few Britons worked the land. Instead, they lived in and around huge cities – most of them in seven great conurbations: London, Glasgow, Manchester, Leeds, Birmingham, Liverpool and Sheffield – where they worked in factories, offices and shops. In the rest of the world, only Belgium was as heavily urbanized as the UK. When it came to sucking in food and raw material imports from abroad and churning out manufactured goods for export, Britain still led the world. The UK also remained central to the machinery of international commerce, with British banks and insurance houses holding colossal overseas assets and the British-registered merchant fleet dwarfing any other.

The period between the wars saw a rapid expansion of new forms of manufacturing driven on by growing domestic consumption, including motor cars, household electrical goods, manmade cloth and processed foods. Modern industries depended on their interaction with cutting-edge science, and the years between the wars saw the rise, industrially and culturally, of the scientific expert as a key figure in British life. In contrast, the older 'staple' export industries – coalmining, iron and

19

steel-making, heavy engineering, cotton weaving – struggled in the face of economic vicissitude and foreign competition. But they too were adopting modern production techniques, and they remained a vital part of the economy, employing huge numbers of workers and defining the cities in which they were based. Across industry, this was also a period of conglomeration, with a trend towards larger, shareholder-owned companies. Huge multinationals based in Britain – Vickers-Armstrong in engineering, ICI in chemical production and Courtaulds in synthetic fibres – had interests spread across the world.

The global nature of the British economy, the rise of new science and industry and the consequent changes in the work Britons did, the clothes they put on their backs and the food in their mouths meant that this already felt like a very modern society. But perhaps the most obvious herald of the modern age was a wide-ranging revolution in communications. Since the end of the Great War, motor transport had become the norm. Horse-drawn vehicles had all but disappeared from the roads. Car ownership was mostly the preserve of the better off, but from 1930 onwards, more passenger miles were travelled every year in cars, buses and on motorcycles than in railway carriages.[2] At the end of the decade, the UK had the largest automobile industry in Europe. Air travel was only for the very wealthy, but the 1930s saw the aerial linkage of the Empire, with a new network of routes between the UK, Africa, Asia and Australia operated by Imperial Airways, and a popular though troubled scheme of imperial airmail. Both on land and in the skies, the achievements of British pioneers of speed and distance, including Sir Malcolm Campbell and Amy Johnson, occasioned great excitement and celebrity.

Alongside this transformation of physical movement came the birth of a modern mass media society. The inter-war period saw both a booming national press start to overtake the circulation of local newspapers and the rise of the cheap paperback – in the emergence of the Left Book Club and the Penguin Special, a location for serious information and political discussion as well as popular entertainment.[3] Still more striking was the advance of film and the onward march of radio. By the late 1930s, the UK had about 5,000 cinemas, now showing with sound and, for the very first time, some films in colour as well as in black and white. Each week a nation of 48 million inhabitants bought about 20 million cinema tickets.[4] Newsreel programmes shown alongside or instead of main screenings presented audiences with a mixture of big events, exotic oddities and matters of local interest, all with a familiarly non-controversial commentary. Since the late 1920s, radio had been transformed from a hobbyist's interest to a consumer staple. By the mid-1930s, more than three-quarters of British households had access to a wireless.[5] British society was connected as it had never been before by its simultaneous listening in to the great ceremonial and sporting events of inter-war life. The new mass media turned film actors and singers into celebrities, but it also ennobled a new sort of public expert – the commentator on matters social, spiritual and scientific, like J. B. Priestley, who communicated with their audience via broadcast talks, newspaper columns and books as well as public appearances.

WAR AND DEPRESSION

For all its modernity, however, the United Kingdom was no longer – as it had been within living memory – the singular great power in the world economy. Since the late nineteenth century, the country's relative global economic position had been eroded by larger, more recently industrialized competitors with bigger home markets – in particular, America and Germany. That erosion was much hastened by the loss of export markets, sales of foreign holdings, the accumulation of dollar debt and wage increases that resulted from the First World War. In the course of that conflict, New York displaced London as the main well-spring of global finance. The war had also broken a pre-1914 network of international free trade from which the UK had for generations benefitted. During the 1920s, attempts to restore it, including the return of the pound to the international Gold Standard at its pre-war rate, helped the City of London, but left British businesses less competitive than their overseas rivals and struggling with a ruinously high bank rate. A rapid boom and catastrophic bust at the start of the decade had been followed by a prolonged period of low growth.

From the end of the 1920s, the onset of a global economic and political crisis (now remembered as the Great Depression, but in Britain at the time more usually called the 'slump') broke the precariously reconstructed framework of post-war world trade. In the UK, unemployment soared to a peak of 23 per cent of the insured workforce, sterling was forced off the Gold Standard, and the spectre of total financial collapse loomed.[6] The British government reacted to this catastrophe by raising tariff barriers, with advantageous rates, known as 'imperial preference', for goods imported from the Empire. After the widespread abandonment of the Gold Standard, a new trading group formed around the sterling bloc, made up of countries which based their currencies on the pound and held their reserves in London. As well as most of the British Empire, this included Egypt, Argentina and all of Scandinavia – nations dependent on trade with the UK and with whom similar agreements on tariffs were negotiated. These countries also wanted access to London's capital markets, which were easier to access than those in America. Other countries were also adopting protectionist measures, but the UK's retreat from free trade was particularly damaging because of its place within the international economy. While it encouraged a shift towards more imperial trade, however, the adoption of imperial preference did not – indeed, given Britain's need for high value markets, could not – signal a withdrawal into autarchy. In the mid-1930s, two-thirds of British imports and well over half its export trade were with countries outside the Empire.[7]

Internationally, the UK's departure from the Gold Standard ended hopes of rebuilding the pre-1914 economic order. Domestically, however, it made possible a reduction in the bank rate, removing one of the constraints on industrial growth during the previous decade and sparking a boom in private housebuilding that helped to drive recovery. Compared to America, Germany and – rather later – France, the British great slump was relatively swift and shallow. Nationally, after 1932 unemployment fell, if only back to 9 per cent of the workforce by the time that George VI was crowned.[8] Improving efficiency in mass production and an ongoing global expansion of agricultural production led to positive terms of trade, and for those in employment, disposable incomes grew. By 1937 they were about 10 per cent higher than they had been a decade before.[9] The new industries in particular bounced back relatively quickly and, in the Midlands and south-east England, where they were concentrated, prosperity rapidly returned.

With world trade still depressed, however, exports did not return even to the level of the late 1920s. In south Wales, the central belt of Scotland and northern England, in communities built around mining, shipbuilding and weaving, rates of long-term joblessness therefore remained extremely high. Meanwhile, the deficit between imports and exports grew so pronounced that it could no longer be covered by the UK's reduced invisible earnings on investments and shipping. The country's balance of payments was pushed narrowly but persistently into the red. By the start of 1937, the post-crash boom was beginning to overheat as rising government spending on rearmament fuelled inflation, and another cyclical slump seemed to be just around the corner.

DEMOCRACY, RELIGION AND RESPECTABILITY

The UK of the 1930s was therefore a distinctly modern place, in ways that marked it out from both its past and its future. It was also a more democratic place than it had been a generation before, its people less obedient, less jingoist and less religious than their forebears. Observed from the twenty-first century, on the other hand, it was strikingly hierarchical, Christian, patriotic and dutiful. Wealth and property were very unevenly divided across society, but, in striking contrast to the situation in the UK of the 2010s, the level of inequality was decreasing.

It was still in some ways a very young democracy. For all Westminster's reputation as the mother of parliaments, the country had only recently moved to a universal adult franchise, with two great extensions of the vote in 1918 and 1928 expanding the electorate to include all men and women on a more or less equal basis for the first time.[10] At the 1910 general election, the last before the Great War, 7.7 million people cast a vote. Nineteen years later, that number had increased three-and-a-half fold, to just under 29 million people.[11]

The expansion of democracy raised hopes of a better world, but also deep anxieties. The lingering aftermath of the war included the consolidation of the Bolshevik regime in Russia, outbreaks of violence at home and in the Empire (above all in Ireland, which was both), the return of millions of demobilized servicemen, high levels of industrial unrest and the emergence of the Labour Party as a new political entity committed to achieving a socialist commonwealth. Although the unemployment of the post-war slump diminished union power, fears of wage cuts after Britain's return to the Gold Standard sparked a brief general strike in 1926. Simultaneously, the growth of the mass media raised fears that the new electorate would be led astray by demagogues or distracted by mass-produced thrills.

Fears of social disintegration were misplaced. The experience of victory did not encourage a separation between servicemen and civilians: in the mainland UK the war ennobled peace, not violence. Post-war cuts wrecked the hopes of 'homes fit for heroes', but wartime wage rises and the provision of a Treasury-supported dole for the unemployed took the edge off discontent. Income tax remained much higher than it had been before the conflict, allowing all governments to increase social spending slightly even while sticking to the contemporary orthodoxy that the budget must be balanced.

Meanwhile, the political system adapted. A series of three-way party fights between Conservatives, Labour and a declining Liberal Party yielded brief opportunities for Labour to exercise minority government, from the second of which it was toppled by the maelstrom of the Great Depression. The 'National' coalition that replaced it shaped a new form of party politics, but also brought a political stability legitimized by electoral successes and the country's fortuitous avoidance of the worst of the slump.

The mid-1930s therefore seemed in some ways much calmer than the early 1920s. There was little argument that Britain was now a democracy of some sort, even if politicians disagreed about what exactly democracy meant. There was scant support for those who proposed more dictatorial systems of government. Britons' successful transition to a mass franchise was celebrated as evidence of their peculiar genius for moderation.

Part of that political stability came from the fact that the UK was also more nationally united than it had ever been before. Since the late nineteenth century, the question of Irish Home Rule had divided British politics, but following the formation of the Irish Free State, and with Northern Ireland awarded its own, Unionist-dominated devolved parliament, separatist nationalism effectively vanished from the domestic agenda. A tiny Irish Republican Army sought to reunify an independent Ireland, but it had few adherents and in 1937 had just been proscribed by the Free State. Small separatist movements existed in Scotland and Wales, where the leader of the Welsh National Party, Saunders Lewis, achieved some celebrity following his prosecution for setting fire to an RAF training school at Penyberth in December 1936. But the poets and dreamers who now espoused Welsh independence struggled to agree among themselves, let alone to gather any popular following. Scottish nationalism enjoyed a more respectable status but its strongest strand wanted not independence but greater recognition within the Union. Being Scottish, Welsh or Northern Irish was possible within, rather than without, a broader Britishness that had regional variety at its cornerstones.

The UK might have been united nationally, but it was still run locally. Since the start of the century, central government had increasingly taken on responsibility for organizing public welfare, handing out central grants through which local authorities could deliver national policies. Between 1900 and 1930, the proportion of English and Welsh local authority expenditure made up by central grants increased from 12 to 26 per cent. Even so, most of what local authorities did was paid for by local ratepayers, not from central taxation, and principles of local autonomy and accountability were still generally accepted as fundamental to the functioning of the British state. Health, education and fire and police services were all locally administered, and municipal provision of public transport and utilities was on the increase. Every local authority had its own fire brigade – 1,668 in the UK overall. At the start of the 1930s, more than a third of mains gas production and one in eight buses in England and Wales were owned by municipal authorities.[12]

When George VI began his reign with a radio broadcast emphasizing peace and progress, he was articulating a specifically 1930s version of national identity. The bombastic imperialism present before 1914 had been left mired in the mud of the Western Front; aggressive nationalism was now viewed with suspicion. Patriotism had, however, been quietened, not eliminated. In an era when race, rather than culture, remained the standard reference point for explanations of human difference, Britons were presumed not just to be white, but also civilized and in control of their emotions in a way that marked them out from other European peoples, let alone those born in Africa or Asia. Such assumptions seemed self-evident in the UK's wealth, imperial power and political stability. So it was perhaps unsurprising that even the most internationally minded Briton tended to regard the rest of the planet with a feeling of innate superiority.

That sense of a natural hierarchy reflected in part the abiding influence of Christianity, not just as a faith but also as a lens through which to view the world. The UK of the 1930s was a less obviously religious place than it had been at the start of the century. Protestant church attendances had declined as religious devotions competed with new leisure opportunities. Nonconformist denominations in particular struggled to add younger members to their ageing congregations. The great denominational debates of a generation before – state control of education, temperance, keeping the Sabbath – no longer illuminated national politics. Catholicism was the religion of a growing minority, thanks principally to immigration from Ireland, but while a fierce sectarian divide was apparent in Liverpool, Glasgow and Northern Ireland, nationally the trend was towards greater ecumenism in the face of diminishing religiosity.

The UK remained, however, a Christian country: constitutionally and ceremonially, but also more fundamentally in terms of patterns of belief. The desire to reinvigorate Anglicanism sparked its own brief revivalist moment in the later 1930s. Young churchmen shifted increasingly away from their traditional Toryism towards enthusiasm for social progress as a means of spiritual regeneration. The chapels may have found it difficult to recruit new members, but older generations of worshippers remained. Christian belief, as opposed to church attendance, remained very strong, as did a Christian culture passed on through Sunday schools, communal singalongs, public ceremonials and religious broadcasting. This was more than just knowing the words to hymns. The abiding presence of Christianity shaped perceptions of good and evil, charity and forbearance, and sacrifice redeemed – above all, the sacrifice of those fallen in the last war, who had died that others might live.

Christianity was also the key component in a public morality in which abortion and male homosexuality were illegal and divorce was extremely difficult and costly (even after a liberalization of the law, just too late for Edward VIII, in 1937–38). Illegitimacy was a source of shame, and sex in general remained a topic of ignorance, embarrassment and fear. Pre-marital intercourse was relatively common, at least once marriage had been agreed, but the young woman who displayed sexual knowledge, let alone experience, risked lasting damage to her reputation.

As this indicated, an older version of 'respectable' behaviour – chaste, sober, thrifty, self-improving – persisted, as part of a wider set of social virtues – duty, deference – in which wives were presumed to owe obedience to husbands, children to adults, workers to bosses, and in which satisfaction was meant to come from knowing your place and respecting your betters. By the late 1930s, such attitudes were being challenged from a number of different directions: pressure from women for a more equal role within marriage; economic change, including the growth in employment for young workers; a new consumerism encouraged by mass production and the mass media; and a growing interest – with the popularization of Freudian psychology – in the self as a site of understanding and fulfilment. These trends, many of which would come to define 'modern' Britain, had not yet displaced older notions of faith, service and the importance of sublimating individual contentment to social obligation.[13]

THE APOGEE OF THE MIDDLE CLASSES

When Mass-Observers recounted the coronation, they talked about class to describe the differences within their society.[14] Like many Britons, they could place themselves and others easily within three categories – upper, middle and working – by using speech, dress and behaviour as indicators of income, occupation and family background.

Since the end of the previous century, the landed aristocrats who traditionally comprised the upper class had been assailed by high death duties, rising democracy and prolonged agricultural depression. As the court balls and swirling peeresses of the coronation indicated, however, they were not yet extinct. Numerically tiny and socially concentrated, in an era before widespread home ownership the upper class remained at the end of the 1930s extremely rich relative to the rest of the population: the best-off 1 per cent of the population retained well over half of the nation's wealth.[15]

The Windsors, the wealthiest aristocrats of the lot, had been carefully rebranded by the new king's father, George V, as paradigms of familial virtue, political stability and charitable endeavour. They remained in place as constitutional monarchs. Below them, the poorer gentry had to sell up and find work, but the most extensively landed peers, having lost decisive political power, managed to keep their great estates and their place in the upper ranks of the Tory party, the army and rural local government. These ancient families had become intermingled with a rising plutocracy of globalized commerce, ennobled in recent decades for services to party funds. The press's obsession with high society linked bright young aristocrats to the new stars of the gramophone record, the radio broadcast and the cinema screen, so the social cachet of the upper class remained high – even if it now rested as much on clothes-horsing expensive fashion as on inherited prestige.

For all its public prominence, the upper class was less and less politically influential. Locally and nationally, public life was dominated by middle-class men. The middle classes, the widest sector of society in terms of range of income, made up about a quarter of the population. They included rich business owners whose fortunes carried them to the edge of an upper-class lifestyle and the lawyers, doctors, clergymen and military officers who had traditionally made up the professional middle class. The changes in the economy since the start of the century had greatly increased the number of clerks and salesmen then generally identified as making up the 'lower middle class'. The middle classes were therefore growing, and the most striking development of the 1930s was the emergence of a new stratum of salaried technicians – the engineers, managers, draughtsmen and scientists required in up-to-the minute industries.

The successful businessman, making a few thousand pounds a year, with a big detached house, live-in servants, telephone, car and two children at public school, had a very different life from the draughtsman on an income ten times smaller, with a mortgaged suburban villa, a daily help, a season ticket for the train and a boy at grammar school. What they had in common was an obsession with home ownership, payment for secondary education and private insurance for pensions and medical treatment (although 1937 saw state coverage extended for the first time to the 'black-coated workers' of the lower middle class), a bank account for savings, and liability for local rates and income tax. In an era when local authorities exercised such an important role relative to central government, leading local society was a key part of what it meant to be middle class.

For the middle classes, the economic slump meant business failure and a paucity of promotion, but seldom long-term joblessness. As a result, they benefitted particularly from falling prices, the boom in private house construction and the burgeoning supply of new consumer goods. The domesticity this encouraged was matched with a growing idealization among the middle classes of 'companionate' marriage, in which husband and wife spent time and took decisions together – not least to limit the number of children they had, since middle-class families were relatively small and getting smaller.

Women were now legally entitled to enter the professions, and paid work was relatively common for young middle-class women, who had largely replaced men in secretarial work. Almost all employers, however, operated a marriage bar requiring women to resign after they wed. The resulting division between a predominantly male world of work and a female world of the home was replicated politically, despite the extension of universal adult suffrage. A few women MPs were now in Parliament, but their voices were heard disproportionately on matters of motherhood and welfare. For women of reasonable means and some education, voluntary efforts to improve the lot of the less fortunate – within the conventional boundaries of feminine expertise – offered the opportunity of a public role.

In important ways, the middle classes of inter-war Britain were more unified than they had been before. Middle-class voices dominated the radio airwaves and cinema soundtracks. The advent of the automobile had made some of them much more geographically mobile. As Labour rose and the chapels declined between the wars, the long-running separation of the English middle classes between Anglican Tories and nonconformist Liberals began to be replaced by a shared antipathy to socialism. As opposition to socialism became part of middle-class identity, so the widening of democracy also encouraged a host of non-partisan civic associations – including the Women's Institute, the Townswoman's Guild and the League of Nations Union – that sought to guide the newly enfranchised masses along the path of sound citizenship.[16] These efforts reflected the broad swathe of progressive middle-class opinion that came together around a belief in democracy, education and better social provision.

The intersection of this improving impulse with enduring fears of popular immorality shaped the new media in distinctive ways. On the airwaves, fears for the susceptible audience underpinned the setting up of the BBC as a public corporation with a determinedly non-commercial remit. Initially, this meant a fairly dour diet of religion and serious-minded talks. By the late 1930s, however, in the face of competition from commercial broadcasters on the continent, the BBC had adapted its schedules to provide more 'variety' shows and popular music, even amid its famously sober Sunday schedules. The Corporation nonetheless remained guided by the dictum of its original director-general, Sir John Reith, that it should 'give the audience slightly better than it now thinks it likes': a version of good taste rooted in light classical music, choral singing and organ recitals, educative lectures and domestic dramas peopled almost exclusively by the middle class. Reith's insistence that the BBC be seen as impartial easily translated into a refusal to allow airtime to voices that dissented from the government line. Indeed, the Corporation's enthusiasm for broadcasting national ceremonies, combined with its preternatural reverence for royalty, made it a powerful agent in promoting the status quo.[17]

The sometimes uncomfortable fit between new forms of communication and old attitudes fed into one of the defining tensions of the age. This was the gap within the middle class between the self-consciously modern, up and coming new professionals, with their belief in progress through technology, and what they perceived as the outdated, conventional inefficiency of their more traditional counterparts. The theme of modernization impeded was central to the bestselling work of fiction of the 1930s, *The Citadel*, by A. J. Cronin.[18] Published in July 1937, *The Citadel* catalogued the struggles of a young doctor amid an outdated and venal system. The novel's climax featured a peroration by its hero, Dr Andrew Manson, which encapsulated the frustrations of the new techno-professionals:

> It's high time we started to put our own house in order, and I don't mean the superficial things either ... our whole organisation is rotten. We ought to be arranged in scientific units ... There ought to be attempts to bring science into the front line ... The whole profession is far too intolerant and smug. Structurally, we're static. We never think of advancing, altering our system. We say we'll do things and we don't.[19]

TURNED OUT NICE? WORKING-CLASS BRITONS

Although the middle classes were expanding and dominant, the UK remained an overwhelmingly working-class country.[20] Three-quarters of the population depended on the income earned in waged labour. In terms of numbers, it was a nation of factory hands, machinists, transport workers, dockers, shop assistants, farm labourers and domestic servants. The working classes too were changing as a result of alterations in the economy. The percentage of the workforce employed in the staple industries fell during the 1930s, as younger miners, shipwrights and millworkers left their home towns for more certain jobs in the new manufacturing sectors. Across industry, the proportion of skilled workers was slowly declining, as production-line technology replaced artisanal aptitude.

At the time of the coronation, working-class living standards had increased dramatically in the space of a generation. Wages had risen swiftly during and after the First World War, while working hours fell and the state's provision of welfare for the least well off improved. Wages fell more than middle-class salaries during the inter-war slumps, but they did so less steeply than prices, so disposable incomes nonetheless increased. That was seldom sufficient to afford the cars or labour-saving devices then gracing middle-class households, but it did mean more money to spend on food, clothes, home furnishings, cigarettes and bus rides, as well as radios, bicycles and rent. Even within the 1930s, a mix of better food, better housing and advances in medical treatment made for improving health. The rate of infant mortality fell nationally, from 76 per thousand live births in 1929 to 55 per thousand in 1938, although the rate of maternal mortality in the early 1930s was higher than it had been at the start of the century.[21] Most workers did not, in 1937, enjoy a statutory right to a holiday, but the fall in working hours had meant a boom in leisure pursuits, both public – the cinema, the dance hall, greyhound racing and motorcycle speedway – and private – pools coupons, illegal betting slips and carefully tended gardens and allotments.

Even such minor distractions left little over from a weekly household income probably somewhere under £4 a week. Having a bank account, like earning enough to be eligible for income tax, was relatively unusual, and the most frequent form of working-class saving was payments into friendly societies and life insurance policies whose collectors made their rounds each week. In contrast to the concentration of wealth in the hands of the very rich, and at a point when £250 a year was widely considered the bare minimum to maintain a middle-class lifestyle, two-thirds of the adults who died in the UK in 1934 left total assets worth less than £100.[22]

Nationally, working-class home ownership remained extremely rare.[23] Only the better paid could afford the rents on one of the new suburban estates on which a million new council houses had gone up since 1918. The majority of working-class families still lived in easily identifiable urban heartlands: thousands of densely packed houses, close to mills and factories, clustered along streets full of the social life for which there wasn't room indoors, with proximity encouraging a neighbourliness that was as supportive as it was intrusive and was much missed by emigrants to the new estates. Not least in reaction to this proximity, privacy was as important an aspiration of working-class life as public activity was for the middle classes.

Most working-class women worked before marriage, and the new industries' thirst for cheap, non-unionized labour offered some young women increased spending power and an alternative to domestic service. Made up and dressed up, they were eager customers for the dance halls and cinemas that dotted the urban landscape between the wars. Marriage and motherhood meant withdrawal from the formal economy to the hard toil of washing, cooking, cleaning and child-rearing. The time that allowed middle-class women to volunteer their efforts to good causes was won for them by their employment of working-class cooks and maids.

Working-class families were smaller than they had been a generation before, but they remained typically larger than those of the middle class. Relatively few working-class children were educated beyond the senior classes of elementary school. The declining number who won a grammar-school scholarship, in competition against the offspring of the sharp-elbowed lower middle class, gained a passport to the ranks of clerkdom or industrial expertise, but most families thought it better for their children to get jobs rather than ideas above their station.

The decline of traditional industries encouraged internal migration from the old manufacturing heartlands towards the new factories in central and southern England, but working-class life remained much more local than that of the middle classes. Nationally, there were significant differences in the patterns of health and housing between the different parts of the United Kingdom. In Scotland and Northern Ireland, improvements in infant mortality and life expectancy lagged behind those in England and Wales, thanks largely to a lower starting point in terms of working-class diet and accommodation relative to the average elsewhere in the UK. A Scottish preference for communal housing was apparent in the greater effort that went into slum clearance and the construction of new council accommodation during the 1930s.

Regionally, working lives differed dramatically between the long-apprenticed, highly skilled pits, factories and slipways of the traditional staple industries; the more antiseptic assembly lines of the new industries, with fewer skilled workers; and the most rustic countryside, where an ageing population was isolated both from the hum of city life and the boon of mains water and electricity. Locally, working-class neighbourhoods were often separated by distinctions between the self-consciously respectable – church- or chapel-going, sober and law-abiding – and those they thought rough – poorer, less observant, harder drinking and probably headed for a bad end.

The two most important divides within the working classes, however, were the extent of unionization and of unemployment. The trade unions were the iconic form of working-class political organization, but they were also important social organisms – a vehicle, at their strongest, for education, leisure and welfare as well as workplace representation. They formed a key part of a wider Labour movement alongside, and sharing membership with, constituency Labour parties and branches of the Co-operative movement. The great union leaders, above all Sir Walter Citrine, the general secretary of the Trades Union Congress, and Ernest Bevin, head of the Transport and General Workers' Union (TGWU), were important national figures, not least because of the power of the bloc votes they controlled at Labour's annual party conferences.

In some sectors of the economy – docking, transport, mining, shipbuilding – industrial relations were fractious. In 1936–37 there was a long-running dispute over union recognition at the Harworth colliery in Nottinghamshire as well as the London busmen's strike that marked the coronation. The growth of big business and the state's pursuit of social peace, however, both encouraged a growing acceptance that free collective bargaining was a legitimate, even necessary, tool for setting pay and conditions. The combination of wider union recognition, high unemployment and rising real wages discouraged industrial militancy during the 1930s: the seven years after 1933 saw fewer days lost to strike action than any equivalent period between 1900 and 1990.[24]

The majority of workers did not, however, belong to a union. Having peaked at over 8 million after the First World War, trade-union membership fell during the 1920s, and fell again as a result of the 1929–32 slump. As the recovery got under way it rose, from 4.4 million in 1933 to 5.3 million in 1937, just under a third of the insured workforce.[25] Membership was densest among male manual workers in the traditional industries, and very much weaker among women workers throughout the country.

Like trade-union membership, long-term unemployment was almost entirely a working-class phenomenon, but did not afflict the whole of the working class. Indeed, the longer it went on, the more joblessness developed its own distinct culture. Poor, bored and often hungry, reliant on benefits set at a breadline level, their family finances and readiness to work subject to close bureaucratic scrutiny, and lacking the work that had defined their lives, unemployed men developed particular patterns of life: talking on the streets, standing outside factories, or sitting in the library or cinema for warmth as much as distraction.

The suffering of those who spent most of the decade unemployed stood in contrast to the majority who kept their jobs throughout the slump – with the starkest relief between those regions in the north and west where most working men were not in fact in work, and the incipient affluence of the best paid in the boom towns of the Midlands and south-east England. In 1933, J. B. Priestley visited one of the hardest-hit places, the north-eastern shipbuilding town of Jarrow:

There is no escape anywhere in Jarrow from its prevailing misery, for it is entirely a working class town. One little street may be rather more wretched than another, but to the outsider they all look alike. One of every two shops appeared to be permanently closed. Wherever we went there were men hanging about, not scores but hundreds and thousands

34

of them. The whole town looked as if it had entered a perpetual penni-less bleak Sabbath. The men wore the drawn masks of prisoners of war.[26]

Three years later, with about 60 per cent of the workforce in Jarrow still unemployed, shipwrights from the town staged a subsequently much celebrated march to London, accompanied by the local Labour MP, 'Red' Ellen Wilkinson. It was peaceful, well supported and, ultim-ately, totally fruitless. Ironically, the cohesion displayed by such communities, under the assault of frustration and impoverishment, decreased the likelihood that the unemployed would risk the insecurity of departure in search of uncertain work elsewhere. But the geographi-cal concentration of unemployment also militated against any radical solution. There was much sympathy for Jarrow – but its suffering was particular, not universal.

Working-class voices were rare on the BBC's regional stations and all but unheard on its National Programme, but they were present in the cinema, thanks above all to the Lancashire accents of Gracie Fields and George Formby, the two most successful British film entertainers of the decade. Blessed with musical skill and comic timing, both actors played similar characters in all their films: accident-prone everywoman and everyman for whom things 'turned out nice again' (in Formby's famous catchphrase), not because they were better or stronger than anyone else, but because they played fair and kept smiling. Fields starred in roles that mirrored her own rags-to-riches tale as a former mill-girl – including appearances as a maid and a shipwright's daughter – whereas Formby appeared as a skilled tradesman in nondescript suburban settings which carefully separated him from the traditions of heavy industry. A roll-call of their films might stand as an account of a more optimistic 1930s: *Looking on the Bright Side* (1932), *Look Up and Laugh* and *Off the Dole* (both 1935), *Keep Your Seats Please* (1936), *Feather Your Nest* and *Keep Fit* (both 1937), *We're Going to be Rich* (1938).[27]

These films were funny, with some mildly smutty songs, non-realistic (not least because George always ended up with a girl whose accent marked her out as upper middle class) and politically uncontentious. The Fields vehicle *Sing as We Go* (1934), scripted by Priestley, featured mill closures and unemployment. Its resolution, however – a singalong followed by a return to work – was not really a practical policy for the long-term jobless. Other attempts to represent working-class lives – including the documentary film movement and the artistic impulses behind Mass-Observation – struggled to escape an essentially middle-class national culture which did not now exclude or vilify the working classes, but did tend to relegate them to the role of supporting actors, comedy sidekicks, and subjects for study and instruction.

CLASSES AND CONFLICT

At the end of the 1930s, Mass-Observation asked its members to consider the topic of class.[28] One, far from untypical response, was that marrying 'out of one's "class"' was 'a mistake, as the different degrees of education both in the arts and (for want of a better word) "breeding" will mitigate [sic] against success'.[29] Such comments illustrated the degree of cultural separation that persisted between Britons despite the boom in mass communications. Their country remained a deeply unequal place, not only in terms of wealth but also in terms of the status attributed to different layers of society.

Notwithstanding the social mobility consequent on the expansion of the middle class, the career trajectory of those without the right accent, table manners and connections was fairly limited. At the right time and in particular settings – the pub, the regimental reunion, the works outing, the League of Nations Union meeting – encounters across the boundaries of class were not just possible but celebrated. While the mood was democratic, however, a set of fairly strong class prejudices was still easily discerned: aristocratic disdain for the 'middle class monsters' who had taken over politics; industrial workers' distrust of clerks in the factory office; their bosses' suspicion of trade unionists as work-shy troublemakers; and suburban homeowners' appalled reaction at the construction of neighbouring council estates. Yet preconceptions about the fecklessness of the poor and jobless and the aggressive selfishness of the trade unions were also common among the majority of the working class who were neither unemployed nor unionized. Those middle-class progressives who were most keen on creating a fairer society also struggled to escape the belief that the working class – with whom they often had little actual contact – were apathetic, witless and dirty; and that the trade unions were part of the established inertia against which they were fighting, not part of the solution. The absence of a revolution on the Russian model had convinced the intelligentsia that British workers were passive and vulnerable. Most of them had little idea of the complex and cunning strategies that the working classes had had to develop in order to navigate their daily lives.

The differences between the classes formed a series of cultural watersheds, rather than a set of social fault lines. By the end of the decade, the country was commonly depicted and widely understood not as a powder-keg of class conflict, but rather as a collection of different types united by a national talent for co-existence, orderly progress and loyalty to the crown. That might not accurately have represented the profound gaps in wealth and power that remained, but it did reflect a country in which the most significant separation for national politics lay not between the classes, but rather between the unemployed, for whom it seemed that work might never return, and everyone else, who could still realistically aspire to a moderately more prosperous future.

3
Politics and the Slump

British politics during the 1930s was different from that of the 1920s largely as a result of domestic reactions to the great slump. These recast the political landscape, but they did not lead, as elsewhere in Europe, to the destruction of democracy.

THE SEARCH FOR STABILITY

In the years after the First World War, British politics was shaped by the emergence of the Labour Party as an independent force, backed by the trade unions and explicitly committed to socialism.[1] In 1918, fear of Labour's potential kept the Conservatives in the coalition formed to win the war under the Liberal prime minister David Lloyd George. In 1922, distaste for his personality and disgust at his policies led to a backbench revolt that broke the coalition and reconstituted the pre-war battle between the Liberals and Conservatives into a three-corner fight with Labour.

This in itself turned out to be a moderating contest. With the Liberals fractured by the war, visibly declining but not yet finished, both Labour and Conservative politicians saw a realistic route to power in attracting former Liberal voters, rather than pandering to their own extremists, and strove to capture the middle ground. Despite its opponents' fears, the Labour movement was never a transmission vector for international Bolshevism. Revolutionary Marxism had little sway, either among the middle-class Fabians and socialists who made up the party's intellectual wing, or among the great trade union leaders, who combined a determination to defend their members' interests with a deep patriotism, belief in tradition and respect for the constitution. Since this mirrored Liberal and Conservative attachment to parliamentary democracy, the dominant trend on all sides was to work within the existing system, rather than to break it.

The Labour leader, Ramsay MacDonald, matched a faith in a socialist paradise with a trust that gradual progress was the best way to get there: Labour must demonstrate its fitness for power by working within the rules. The Conservative leader, Stanley Baldwin, who had played a leading role in destroying the Lloyd George coalition, spent the rest of the 1920s house-training his party against the inclinations of its more reactionary members. Baldwin's Conservatism was run by and for middle-class businessmen, but staged an appeal to all Britons as the guarantor of social peace.

Like many of his colleagues, Baldwin was deeply worried about whether a newly democratic Britain could cope with the challenges of the post-war era. As he put it privately in June 1929: 'Democracy has arrived at a gallop . . . and I feel all the time that it is a race for life; can we educate them before the crash comes?'[2] Unlike more pessimistic Conservatives, however, Baldwin retained a belief in the fundamental moderation and good sense of the British people, provided they were given the appropriate lead. As a counter to the dangers of the new democracy, Baldwin summoned up an invented tradition of idyllic national tranquillity. Together, he and MacDonald did more than any other two individuals to ensure that the UK successfully navigated the transition to mass democracy.

The Conservatives dominated 1920s politics, winning general elections in 1922 and 1924 by promoting themselves as a better bet to stop Labour than the still squabbling Liberals, but losing in 1923 when they campaigned on tariffs, reunited Liberal supporters, and split the anti-socialist vote. At that point, vitally, Baldwin and George V accepted Labour's right to form a minority government, which tried to build a reputation for responsibility with an orthodox mixture of balanced budgets and free trade. When the Conservatives returned to power less than a year later, the desire to inoculate voters against the temptations of socialism ensured that their domestic agenda also included welfare and health reforms. Baldwin continued to speak the language of social unity despite the upheaval of the General Strike. At the 1929 election, however, the Conservatives' failure to tackle the rising problem of unemployment and a brief revival of Liberal support meant that, as in 1923, no party gained an outright majority. Since Labour had more seats than either of its opponents, it now formed its second minority government.

THE NATIONAL GOVERNMENT

Labour was therefore in power when the country was hit by the full impact of the slump.[3] As banks collapsed and tariff walls went up abroad, and tax receipts plunged and unemployment skyrocketed at home, Labour was held – not least by its own leaders – to the economic conventions of the 1920s: balanced budgets, free trade and the Gold Standard as prerequisites of international confidence in the pound. But balancing the budget meant cutting unemployment benefit and hitting the very men the Labour Party had been created to help. In 1931, in the midst of an apparently cataclysmic financial crisis, this tension split the government and led to its collapse. MacDonald formed a new 'National' coalition – initially intended only as an emergency measure to escape the immediate crisis – backed by the Conservatives, Liberals and a rump of Labour members. It passed the cuts but was still forced to leave the Gold Standard and devalue sterling, and soon implemented the protectionist measures long favoured by the Conservatives. Those Liberal and Labour members who remained devoted to free trade now left the government.

In retrospect, the shock inflicted by the UK's adoption of tariffs deepened and prolonged the global depression. In the meantime, however, the National coalition won a crushing election victory as the responsible choice to save the economy. Labour, in contrast, had swung sharply to the left, mythologized its departure from office as the result of a conspiracy of international financiers rather than its own incompetence, and fought on a radical platform of nationalization and central economic controls. When the votes were counted in December 1931, 554 National MPs were returned, 470 of them Conservative. Labour was reduced to fifty-two MPs.

The National Government therefore endured well beyond the crisis that had brought it into existence. MacDonald remained as prime minister until 1935. He was an influential figure in the first years of the administration, but a declining and increasingly pathetic presence as the years went on. Bereft after the death of his wife, he was expelled and demonized by the party he had helped to found, and retained as premier on Conservative sufferance as a signifier of the government's 'National' status. Baldwin, in contrast, who had been no great enthusiast for this new coalition at its start, found in it his political apotheosis. After 1929 he had only narrowly survived attempts to oust him as party leader. Now, he used the 'National' tag to outflank the right of his own party and to pursue his moderate brand of Conservatism. As lord president of the council, he set the political agenda while MacDonald remained in the spotlight, and in June 1935, he swapped places with the outgoing premier to become prime minister for the third time.

As a leader, Baldwin tended to avoid confrontation and compass the middle ground. Many of his rivals took this as evidence of lassitude and lack of intellectual depth, but his imprecision on policy was to prove his greatest weapon in retaining power. Instantly recognizable – his pipe as strong a trademark as Thatcher's handbag would be for a later generation – Baldwin commanded immense public prestige. In speeches that reached a huge audience via newspapers, pamphlet reprints, newsreels and radio broadcasts, he preached the same comforting tale – that Britons were peaceful and reasonable individuals and should vote accordingly in the face of Labour's aggressive egalitarianism. His repeated emphasis on personal freedom and Christian morality played a vital part in bringing nonconformist former Liberal voters round to the idea of supporting – or at least not actively opposing – a government dominated by Conservatives.

Behind these figureheads, much of the policy direction within the government came – as he himself was not shy of pointing out – from the chancellor, Neville Chamberlain. The younger son of Joseph, the Liberal Unionist who had lit up Edwardian politics with his campaign for tariff reform, and the half-brother of Austen, who had led the Conservative Party in the early 1920s and remained an influential backbencher – Neville Chamberlain had come late to the family trade after cutting his teeth on municipal politics in Birmingham. His first entry onto a larger stage was as director of national service, with responsibility for mobilizing industrial labour, in the wartime coalition. This was an ignominious failure: the post had a huge potential remit but minimal actual power, and caused such controversy that Lloyd George rapidly dismissed him.

During the 1920s, however, Chamberlain's political career accelerated. He established a formidable reputation as a reforming minister of health in Baldwin's second government. An administrative dynamo with an immense capacity for work, he scorned Baldwin's vagueness but admired his political abilities. As he put it in 1935, although he supplied the 'policy and the drive':

> S.B. does also supply something that is even more valuable in retaining the floating vote. I suppose we may never get back to the old days when every little boy and girl was either a little liberal or a little conservative. And if that is so it will be the non-party men & women who will decide the nature of the Government and the S.B.s, if there are any, will capture them.[4]

Chamberlain lacked this conciliatory touch. In contrast to his leader's emollient hopes that, in troubled times, everyone would find it within themselves to get on, the chancellor's remorseless logic and disdain for his opponents gave the impression that he had been, as one of them put it, 'weaned on a pickle'.[5]

After he arrived at the Treasury in 1931, Chamberlain concentrated on restoring business confidence, first by tight restrictions on spending to rebalance the budget and secondly by the imposition of a general tariff on imports and imperial preference. The bank rate was set low to allow the renegotiation of domestic First World War debts (a major drain on expenditure well into the 1930s), and left low as it became apparent that cheap money was driving the boom in house construction. Controlling expenditure and inhibiting the dumping of foreign-made goods probably did make British businessmen feel more confident and help to secure a recovery, but the most important factors in the UK's escape from the slump – devaluation and low interest rates – came either despite the government's best efforts or as the side effect of its policies. This was no obstacle to its taking the credit as prospects improved.

Even as the economy recuperated, Chamberlain kept a tight rein on government spending. The benefit cuts introduced in 1931 were maintained until 1935, when in anticipation of a general election the chancellor restored benefits to their previous level and reduced taxes.

He steadfastly rejected calls for public investment to provide work for the unemployed, who therefore bore the brunt of the pain of the slump. This was no great political problem, however, for a government whose claim to power was rooted in its determination – unlike its predecessor – not to allow the plight of the jobless to endanger the interests of the nation.

THE FAILURE OF EXTREMISM

During the early 1930s, British politics was affected by some of the same extremist tendencies that afflicted other countries hit by the disaster of the Great Depression.[6] The strong sense of imminent collapse and its impact on the new electorate encouraged critics of parliamentary democracy and heightened fears for its future. The nature of the National Government's birth and subsequent dominance and the Labour Party's swing to the left meant that both were happy to portray the other as a danger to democracy. Through the National Unemployed Workers' Movement, the Communist Party of Great Britain (CPGB) sought to mobilize the jobless. The maverick politician Sir Oswald Mosley – first a Conservative, then a Labour minister – broke away to form a 'New Party', which promised strong leadership to solve the economic difficulties. When that failed to attract support at the 1931 election, Mosley formed the British Union of Fascists (BUF), a movement which initially attracted much interest, notably from Lord Rothermere, the owner of the *Daily Mail*. Neither Communism nor Fascism, however, was able to build a base of mass support in the United Kingdom.

The CPGB could not persuade the unemployed to revolt. A surge in recruitment in 1931 still left it with only 9,000 members, a number that fell back during the mid-1930s before recovering to a then record 12,500 members in May 1937.[7] Mosley's BUF was initially more successful. With the *Daily Mail*'s help, it had around 50,000 members in 1934, before the beatings meted out to protestors at a Fascist rally at Olympia demonstrated the movement's brutal undercurrent. Membership slumped. When the Fascists then concentrated their efforts on an anti-Semitic campaign in London's East End, they achieved a local revival in recruitment, but also became more violent. Following a confrontation between Fascist and anti-Fascist demonstrators at the 'Battle of Cable Street' in October 1936, the government pushed through a Public Order Act which forbade the wearing of political uniforms and gave the police the right to prohibit marches. During 1937, the BUF was in decline everywhere outside East London – losing members, splintering among extremists, and short of funds.[8]

At their strongest during the 1930s, Britain's leading anti-democratic parties therefore collectively managed memberships only in the low tens of thousands. In contrast, the Labour Party had almost 447,000 individual members in 1937. Another 2 million were 'affiliated' members through the trade unions. The Conservatives kept no national membership figures at this point, but where Labour thought its local branches were doing well if they had more than a thousand members, local Conservative Associations often had three or four times that. The youth wing of the party, the Junior Imperial League, alone had 100,000 members in 1939. When the Conservatives aggregated national figures in 1946 – after a period of significant decline – they still had almost a million members.[9] Both major parties – and even, in their traditional strongholds, the struggling Liberals – were highly successful mass movements, based on strong local organizations built around members who lived in the constituency. The cultural life of the Labour activist – an all-enveloping round of party committees, discussion groups and summer schools, all based on achieving a better understanding of socialism – was very different from the 'non-political' mix of garden parties and charity fêtes that engaged their Conservative counterparts, but what really animated both of them was the excitement of getting out the vote when they had to fight an election.

The results of these contests reflected the strong preference for the mainstream. Faced with governments struggling to deal with massive economic problems at home and dynamic dictatorships abroad, British electors voted in huge numbers for moderation in a parliamentary democracy. The explanation might have been that they were an innately placid but independently minded people, ill-suited to totalitarianism. This was certainly how they had been schooled to think of themselves over the previous two decades. Yet the failure of extremism had less to do with national character than national circumstance. In Britain, the worst of the depression was relatively brief or regionally concentrated. The government maintained a welfare system that, however inadequate, allowed the unemployed enough support to survive. The National administration had many faults, but it did create a feeling of political stability that limited the attractions of more radical alternatives. The British experience of the 1930s was not a fertile breeding ground for Fascism or Communism. In international comparison, this was a very fortunate escape.

4

Politics and the Empire

The colonial troops who marched through London for the coronation embodied the continuing strength and scope of the British Empire. When George VI was crowned, it encompassed a quarter of the world's land mass and had a population of more than 500 million. It too had been stricken by recurrent crises since the end of the last war, but here too, by the late 1930s, a route to stability seemed to have been found.

A NEW IMPERIALISM?

The British Empire had emerged from the Great War larger than it had ever been. In the Middle East in particular, Britain's presence had significantly expanded as it sought to secure the route to India through the Suez Canal and guarantee access to the increasingly important supply of oil from the Persian Gulf. The Empire too, however, had been caught up in that great moment of revolution, instability and democracy that grew out of the war. In Australia, Canada, New Zealand and South Africa, Dominion governments had become increasingly assertive. The war resulted in an upsurge of nationalist unrest in Ireland, India and Egypt. Britain, with its vast war debts, faced a choice between garrisoning expanded and restless territories abroad and increasing social spending at home. The violent repression of colonial protest was criticized in Parliament and the press as unsuited to the new era of peaceful progress.

Together, these created a fresh trend in imperial policy. Dominion autonomy was acknowledged and accepted. Concessions were made to nationalist movements, with India promised government reforms and eventual self-rule in 1919, and Egypt and the Irish Free State granted independence in 1922. Territorial aggrandizement was abandoned, the Empire withdrew from its furthest-flung conquests in the Middle East, and 'air policing' by the RAF was welcomed as a cheaper option to placing soldiers' boots on the ground. Greater emphasis came to be placed on the Empire as an exercise in trusteeship, in which, rather than taking on their inviolable right to perpetual rule, the enlightened British guided less developed peoples along the path to eventual – often far distant – self-government within a Commonwealth of nations which shared common values and systems derived from the 'mother of parliaments' at Westminster.

The Empire was an important element of British national identity, but its reality was very distant from most British lives. It was nonetheless an inescapable part of popular culture: in plays and novels, and above all on cinema screens, it offered an exotic location for adventures in which white Britons exercised a natural rule over darker-skinned locals who were loyal or treacherous according to the needs of the plot. British imperial enthusiasts, eager to educate the new electorate, spent much of the period worried about how little the public knew or cared about the patches of pink on schoolroom maps. The result was a stepping up of pro-Empire propaganda, including the annual celebration of Empire Day (24 May, Queen Victoria's birthday) and two enormous Empire exhibitions – at Wembley in 1924 and Glasgow in 1938. Significantly, the first was all about the Empire's proud traditions, the second about its bright, technologically advanced future. They attracted millions of visitors, but never as many as their organizers had hoped.

In practice, the Empire remained much the same racist, exploitative, brutal institution that it had always been, which was why it continued to arouse so much animosity and opposition from nationalist movements. There was no great set of legislation committing Britain to building the basis for self-rule throughout the colonial lands, nor enough money and political intent to address issues of welfare and economic development. Meanwhile, the liberal repurposing of Empire aroused antagonism from a more aggressive tradition – particularly strong among older colonial administrators and settlers and the right wing of the Conservative Party – that saw giving in to peripheral nationalism as evidence of metropolitan decline.

The British Empire, 1937

COMMONWEALTH AND CONFLICT

For the Dominions, the years between the wars were ones of increasing independence. Under the Balfour Declaration of 1926, which was confirmed by the Statute of Westminster in 1931, they were permitted to formulate their own domestic and foreign policies as members of the British Commonwealth with equal status to the United Kingdom. They retained the monarch as their head of state, and George VI was the first king to be crowned monarch of each of them and of the UK separately, rather than of the Empire as a whole. When the Irish Free State was formed in 1922, it too had been a Dominion. But having spent most of the 1930s waging a trade war with the UK, the president of the Irish Executive Council, Éamon de Valera, took the opportunity of the abdication to rewrite his country's constitution. By the end of 1937, the Irish Free State had become Ireland, a country with its own president as head of state, but with the British monarch still written into statute. It remained a member of the Commonwealth.

The implementation of imperial preference in response to the global economic crisis linked the Commonwealth together economically as never before. But when the tariff system was worked out at the Ottawa Conference of 1932, the hard bargaining of the Dominion leaders left little doubt that they attached more weight to their own country's interests than to those of the UK. British politicians comforted themselves that they had kept the Commonwealth together, but it was Dominion farmers rather than British consumers who benefitted most directly from preferential tariffs.

While the Dominions were keen on setting their own foreign policies, they were much less eager to share the burden of imperial defence: instead, they relied on Britain to bear the lion's share of spending on the military forces necessary to ensure their security. When Commonwealth leaders, in London for the coronation, held a conference on imperial defence in 1937, their perceptions of international dangers differed widely depending on their geographical position. All were willing to come to Britain's aid if the country were attacked. None wanted to be involved in other people's wars. As at Ottawa, the British preferred to keep the Commonwealth together rather than push disagreements to breaking point, so the conference communiqué simply reaffirmed that it

was the 'sole responsibility of the several Parliaments of the British Commonwealth to decide the nature and scope of their own defence policy'.[1]

The changing nature of the Dominions' relationship with the United
Kingdom provided part of the context for the great argument about
India that took place within the British Conservative Party during the
first half of the 1930s. It was not surprising that the Empire became the
subject of an intra-Conservative fight. Liberal and Labour critics of
colonialism had been denatured by the recasting of the imperial project
as an exercise in education and development. Much though they might
hate imperialism as a cause of conflict and an embodiment of privilege,
few on the left wanted the immediate dissolution of a British Empire
that was popularly regarded as a responsible force for international
good, though there was widespread support for Indian independence.
For the Conservatives, in contrast, belief in the Empire was a much
more complex issue, simultaneously a shibboleth of party membership
and the site for fierce disagreement over policy.[2]

During the 1920s, the fighting had focused on proposals for preferential tariffs for imperial trade. These were popular with Conservative
supporters but not with the rest of the electorate. At the end of the decade, Baldwin only just saw off a campaign by the newspaper barons,
Lords Rothermere and Beaverbrook, to force the Tories to adopt
'imperial preference'. This battle, and Baldwin's condemnation, in a
March 1931 speech, of the newspaper men for seeking 'power without
responsibility – the prerogative of the harlot throughout the ages',
opened a gap between the National Government and the popular press
that was never fully to be healed. The economic crisis won the argument for protectionism, but a small group of MPs around the vocal
Conservative backbencher Leo Amery continued to advocate still
tighter trade links with the Commonwealth as a means of forging
imperial cohesion. By then, however, the Conservatives were embroiled
in another dispute over India.

IRWIN AND INDIA

Between the wars, India was still the great centrepiece of the British
Empire. It was divided into the eleven major provinces of British India
(in which lived about two-thirds of the Indian population), which were

governed directly by British administrators, and more than five hundred princely states. These were ruled by Indian rajas who pledged their allegiance to the king emperor, as represented in India by the British viceroy. The viceroy's writ ran over the whole Raj, but the Indian princes were allowed a lot of freedom in their domestic policy. In turn, they provided units for the Indian army and a conservative bulwark for British rule.

British India was run by just over a thousand British civil servants, backed up by a legion of Indian bureaucrats. British authority was supported by the threat of force from the army and an Indian police force that was 200,000 strong. Given, however, the small number of Britons in the Raj, it always depended on maintaining the consent of the ruled. To do this, the British had long consulted with those Indians who they judged to be the leaders of communal opinion. In the process, they had categorized and confirmed already-existing divisions of religion, race and class, and helped to create a society in which politics became communally defined. India's Muslims made up about 20 per cent of the population of the predominantly Hindu country. In most of the provinces of British India, they were in the minority, but in Bengal and the northwest, they made up the majority of the population. In 1906, worried by the first signs that Britain was devolving power into Indian hands, Muslim leaders in northern India formed a party to protect their interests, the Muslim League. They also persuaded the British to recognize their right to separate representation in the provincial elections that took place – on a very limited franchise – after 1909.

The Indian National Congress, founded in 1885, was in contrast the first party to claim to represent all Indians. It started off, however, as a party of a narrow, well-educated Hindu elite, and though it would succeed in transforming itself into something approaching a mass movement by the end of the 1930s, it remained dominated by Hindus. The Congress was frequently divided by arguments between moderate and extremist factions, who disagreed over whether to co-operate with the British, as well as by disputes between those who favoured and abjured violence in pursuit of independence.

The First World War supercharged Indian nationalism. The reforms promised by the British under the 1919 Government of India Act were not sufficient to forestall the onset of unrest. From 1919 to 1922, a new Congress leader, Mohandas Gandhi, led a campaign against British rule that temporarily united Congress and Muslim nationalists in common cause. Though never encompassing the whole of India, it put the British authorities under considerable pressure. Gandhi's approach was based on non-violent civil disobedience, but – not for the last time – the campaign rapidly ran out of his control and violence broke out. At that point, Gandhi called an abrupt halt to it. This led to a rupture with the Muslims who had previously been willing to work with him.

In March 1926, a new viceroy arrived in India.[3] Lord Irwin (later Lord Halifax) was the embodiment of the British establishment: a tall, vulpine-featured High Church Anglican, even in temper and circumlocutory in speech. As a young MP in the years after the war, he had combined aristocratic confidence with the political moderation of the modern Conservative – which was probably why Baldwin asked him to take up the post. Publicly and privately, Irwin drew on a deep well of religious faith and assumed a stance of high morality. Like many British liberals, he believed that national self-determination could not be opposed indefinitely, and that Britain would have to accept and adapt to nationalist demands in order to maintain its power. He also believed that India had become a sectarian powder keg. Communal violence, usually the result of economic tensions, had grown more frequent during the 1920s, and Irwin feared a catastrophic social breakdown. He thought that he could give the lead that would allow reason to prevail.

In 1929, Irwin was faced with the threat of a new campaign of civil disobedience from the Congress following the appointment of an all-British commission, under Sir John Simon, to review India's constitutional future. The viceroy's response was a dramatic intervention in the hope of peace. The Simon Commission had already decided that India was not ready for self-government, but Irwin fixed the commission's report. He made sure that it would recommend further talks on a federal constitution that would safeguard the position of India's Muslims and the British viceroy. Then, Irwin unilaterally issued a statement committing the British government to giving India Dominion status. Though he had bounced both of them into this policy, MacDonald and Baldwin gave him their support.

Irwin hoped that he could rally moderate opinion to a progressive compromise that kept India within the Commonwealth and guaranteed British influence. Since rallying moderate opinion meant splitting the Congress, Gandhi was understandably unimpressed with this repetition of the well-worn British tactic of divide and rule. He too was desperate to avoid a violent disintegration of India. Ghandi had his own strategy for keeping control of Congress and encouraging moderation by emphasizing his position as a spiritual leader. This fitted with his own faith – that India must choose a path away from Western materialism – but since it involved adopting the trappings of a Hindu saint, it also served to alienate Muslims.

Gandhi now launched his next campaign of civil disobedience. He was arrested. As the Indian police beat non-violent protestors, the jails filled and violent riots and disorder broke out. Once more, the Raj came under severe strain. Irwin continued his efforts to seek a compromise. On 5 March 1931, he and Gandhi agreed a truce. Both the disobedience campaign and the British efforts to suppress Congress would stop, while Gandhi was released from prison and travelled to London to take part in the constitutional talks. These failed to resolve the question of how to handle the position of India's minorities in any future federation. Since the Indians couldn't agree, the British announced, they would have to settle a new constitution for themselves.

In December 1931, Gandhi returned to India. Irwin had now finished his time as viceroy. When the protests started again, the British authorities responded with a harsh nationwide crackdown that stopped the campaign in its tracks, but cost even more of their legitimacy in the eyes of most Congress supporters.

CHURCHILL AND THE DIEHARDS

From its start, Irwin's attempt to build a bridge over India's troubled waters aroused a furious reaction from the right wing of the Conservative Party. The so-called 'diehards', who had earned their name opposing Irish independence, now chose India for a doomed battle against the tide of post-war politics. For these older, more traditional Tories, concessions to Indian nationalism were not a route to imperial salvation, but rather an abdication of responsibility, typical of a country that had gone to the dogs since 1914. The diehards were only a minority of Conservative MPs, but they threatened to stir up a revolt in the party after the 1929 election defeat.

One of those who offered to lead the diehards into battle was Winston Churchill.[4] Like Chamberlain, Churchill was the inheritor of a family legacy of unfulfilled political promise. He had dallied as a soldier and journalist before becoming a Conservative MP. In 1904, he crossed the floor to join the Liberal Party in opposition to Joseph Chamberlain's campaign for tariff reform. In the years before the First World War, he had risen rapidly to the Liberal front bench. Churchill began the conflict as first lord of the admiralty, lost his job after the disastrous expedition to the Dardanelles, served briefly in the trenches, and then returned to high office as minister for munitions in the Lloyd George coalition. After the war, he played a leading role in negotiating the departure of southern Ireland from the Union.

Churchill was passionately opposed to socialism and hostile to mass democracy. When the coalition collapsed, he returned to the Conservatives because they seemed the only party capable of stopping Labour. His track record in office and continued faith in free trade made this an uncomfortable fit, but also encouraged Baldwin to rescue his political career by appointing him chancellor in 1924. There, Churchill oversaw the calamitous return of sterling to the Gold Standard at its pre-war rate, cut back on military spending, and initiated a reform of local government finance that was itself widely implicated in the Conservative failure at the 1929 election.

Churchill was a man of great ambition, given to following his instincts and nearly always up for a fight. His confrontational style was ill-suited to the new era of political caution, and he had little time for Baldwin's remorseless pursuit of the centre. On India, he shared the diehards' belief that negotiating with the nationalists was wrong. This was partly because, even by the standards of the time, Churchill was a savage racist. When he looked towards the Raj, he still saw it through the mess windows of the 4th Hussars, with whom he had travelled to Bangalore during his brief stint as a junior subaltern in 1896. He distrusted Indians in general, and hated Hinduism in particular, and he had little sense of the ways in which India was changing or sympathy for the challenges facing Indian politicians. In 1930, as he launched an attack on the government's India policy, seeking the leadership of the Conservative Party with the support of Rothermere and Beaverbrook, Churchill gave his prejudices free rein in political speeches and press columns, conjuring up images of wild-eyed Indians massacring white women and children. For more modern Tories, it was bad enough that Churchill thought these things; even worse that he was willing to say them in public in order to advance his own political position, and in the process stir up the sort of violent passions that would make any peaceful solution still harder to find.

Churchill's racism was inseparable from his passionate patriotism and belief in Britain's imperial duty. Because he believed the worst of Indians, he rejected Irwin's position – that the only way to defuse the time bomb of Indian nationalism and communal politics was to offer a moral lead to the middle ground. Churchill argued that if Indians were left to govern themselves, the result would be bloody chaos: so it was Britain's job to stay in India, crack down on any dissent and hold the line against politicians who claimed to represent the nation but were really just angling for sectarian advantage. He did not countenance the idea that this might make things worse.

Many Conservatives were suspicious of Churchill. He was always a slightly strange fit with the diehards. After all, he was personally implicated in many of the developments that made them most angry, above all the retreat from Ireland. Where they felt that Lloyd George had wrecked politics, Churchill looked back longingly to the days when such political strongmen had really made a difference. Not for the first or last time, he was widely suspected of having put his convictions at the service of unscrupulous ambition. Yet at the start of 1931, his appeals to racial stereotypes and national pride touched off just enough atavistic enthusiasm among Conservatives for it to look like Baldwin was in serious trouble. Then Irwin negotiated his pact with Gandhi, and the apparent achievement of a compromise wrecked Churchill's push on the leadership.

'A MONSTROUS MONUMENT OF SHAM'

When the National Government was formed there was, unsurprisingly, no room for Churchill. He was too troublesome, too anti-socialist, and too out of touch with the spirit of the times. Despite the failure of the constitutional talks, MacDonald and Baldwin were determined to press on with Indian reforms. Baldwin not only believed that adaptation was the only way to preserve British rule: he was also determined that India should not become a running sore in domestic politics in the same way that Ireland had been a generation before. He gave the responsibility to a new secretary of state for India, Sir Samuel Hoare.

Another moderate, modernizing Conservative who saw his life's work as establishing social peace, Hoare was always slightly too cunning for his own good.[5] He now drew up a plan that was designed to build Indian political support for a British-designed constitution. By devolving power to elected assemblies in the provinces as part of the process of reform, the British would tempt more Indians into government and outflank Congress's claim to represent an all-India nationalism. Hoare accurately judged the lure of potential power. In 1934, Gandhi had to accept demands from Congress moderates to be allowed to stand in the provincial elections, where their burgeoning support seemed likely to assure them the chance of office. Disappointed by their enthusiasm for earthly advancement over spiritual regeneration, and keen to reassert his moral authority, he withdrew from the Congress altogether.

In Britain, Churchill and the diehards fought a prolonged rearguard action against the Indian reforms. They tried their best to raise the constituency faithful against Baldwin, particularly in Lancashire, where competition from Indian textiles was devastating the local cotton industry. In Parliament, the battle culminated in a prolonged struggle against the Government of India Bill as it moved onto the statute books during the first half of 1935. Support for the government among Conservative MPs was marshalled by the chief whip, David Margesson.[6] Though capable of great charm, Margesson developed a reputation as a terrifying enforcer who 'put the fear of God into new members' as he loomed over them in his black morning coat.[7] The brutal skill with which he kept the government's troops in line made him an influential figure behind the political scenes.

The new Bill allowed elected assemblies in the provinces of British India to form autonomous regional governments, significantly extended the franchise while keeping separate Hindu, Muslim and Sikh electorates, and laid out plans for a federal assembly that would form the basis for a transition to Dominion status. It expanded the electorate to include about a sixth of India's population, bringing a form of mass democracy to the subcontinent for the first time, and gave Indians extensive powers of self-government. Burma, which had its own nationalist movement, was separated from the Raj and given limited powers of self-government of its own. Compared to what any other European empire was doing during the 1930s, all this showed a remarkable willingness to reach an accommodation with nationalism.[8]

It was also designed to safeguard British power. British governors would continue to preside over the provincial assemblies, and the British viceroy would retain control of India's defence, security and foreign policies. In the new federal assembly, a third of the members would be appointed by the Indian princes, and the rest elected from the provinces, where a third of the seats would be reserved for Muslims. The Indian National Congress had spent the previous two decades trying to prove that it spoke for all Indians. Now if it accepted federation it could at best win only a minority of seats in the assembly. Hoare counted on two things: first, that the majority of Indian princes could be made to participate in a national democratic body, and second, that the extension of the franchise would limit Congress's electoral support and make it glad to take up its place in the federal assembly.

When Churchill called the Government of India Bill 'a monstrous monument of sham', he was therefore in some ways right, if for the wrong reasons.[9] His passionate denunciations of reform did not convince Conservative MPs that he was acting out of anything other than self-interest. What he depicted as a disastrous dereliction of national duty, they saw as a pragmatic adaptation to realities. The diehards' rejection of compromise seemed like a relic of a bygone age. The Bill passed its final reading in the Commons on 4 June 1935.

The Indian National Congress opposed the Government of India Act. So did the Muslim League, now under the leadership of Mohammad Ali Jinnah, because although the new constitution protected Muslim political rights, it also promised to restrict them to a permanent (if powerful) minority who would never be able to choose their own path in a federal India. Yet both parties now prepared to contest the first elections for the provincial assemblies to be held under the new franchise, scheduled for the winter of 1936–37. Victory here would be the way to demonstrate their support and impose their will as the British moved towards a transfer of power.

The election results were announced in February 1937. Congress had won an impressive victory. It had developed into an effectively organized political party that proved well able to win over newly enfranchised voters among the wealthy peasants of India's rural areas. The Congress won seats across the country, and was able to form governments in seven out of the eleven provinces. To the mainstream of political opinion in Britain – including the majority of Conservatives and the Labour Party – Congress's electoral success demonstrated its legitimacy in a way that the great agitational campaigns never had. It could obviously call on support throughout the country, and it would have to be included in any future constitutional settlement. Indian independence had been brought significantly closer. In any case, by the late 1930s, India had lost much of its economic appeal for the British. Even the Indian army was becoming increasingly expensive for the British Exchequer. Almost the only great tie remaining was India's substantial debt to Britain. Increasingly, loosening Britain's hold on the subcontinent looked like it made sense.[10]

In India, meanwhile, senior British officials also accepted the results of the 1937 elections. They stopped trying to divide the nationalists, and instead started working with them in provincial government in the hope that they could guide what was now the dominant force in Indian politics. Both parties soon found they were happy with this collaboration: the British because in office, provincial Congress politicians proved to be less radical than expected in attacking the apparatus of the Raj; the Congressmen because they were finally in power with a victory that allowed them to call the shots, and because they could look forward – after another election victory and, if necessary, another campaign of civil disobedience – to winning independence on their own terms.

In some ways, this represented a remarkable success for British policy, in the sense that it promoted moderation over revolution and brought the Congress at a provincial level into co-operation with the British government. Yet the scale of the Congress victory also helped to doom progress towards the Indian federation envisaged in the 1935 Government of India Act. It was probably a lost cause in any case. From 1936 a new viceroy, Lord Linlithgow, did everything he could to persuade the Indian princes to accede to the federation. Yet the British could never bring enough of them round to the idea of submitting themselves to a federal assembly in which the majority of members would be democratically elected. After 1937, meanwhile, Congress had won such a substantial mandate that it could easily refuse to accept a constitution designed to limit its power. A new settlement would have to be found.

In contrast to the Indian National Congress, the Muslim League did very badly at the 1937 elections. It secured less than a quarter of the seats reserved for Muslims and was unable to form a government in any of the provinces. Yet the Congress victory served to reinvigorate Muslim politics. Suddenly, Congress politicians were in power, re-directing the benefits of influence towards their own communities and away from the Muslims who had long worked alongside the British. Worse, the Congress high command encouraged its party workers to celebrate their victory in terms that struck Muslim politicians as asser-tions of Hindu dominance. Independence on Congress terms looked like a profound threat to Muslim interests. All this helped Jinnah in his goal of making the Muslim League the sole voice of India's Muslims.[11]

Despite his withdrawal from politics, Gandhi remained the guiding light of the Indian National Congress, but much of the running would now be made by a generation of leaders who had come up through the struggles of the 1920s and 1930s. Jawaharlal Nehru, the Congress president in 1937, had set himself up as Gandhi's successor, but he was cut from a very different cloth: industrially produced rather than home-spun. A Harrow-educated socialist who was very much at home with the left wing of the British Labour Party, Nehru looked forward to an Indian future of social and physical, rather than spiritual, reconstruc-tion, with a strong modern state building success on a Soviet-style centrally planned economy. Nehru had always been keener on confron-tation rather than co-operation with the British, and he had initially opposed the entry into provincial government. He also saw the issue of communal politics in class terms. As far as he was concerned, the Mus-lim League were feudal oppressors keeping decent peasants down. When Jinnah approached him with plans to share power after the Brit-ish had gone, Nehru waved him away. Gandhi was unwilling to contradict him and risk splitting the party. Now, therefore, Jinnah started talking of Muslims achieving their 'national goal' and building up their own power. There would be further struggles to come.

As for Churchill, his intransigence over India was one of the things that would keep him out of office for the rest of the 1930s. Though he was deeply upset and disappointed when it became obvious that the Government of India Bill was going to pass, he was not a man to be downhearted for long. Even as he went down fighting over India, he had already started to wage a new campaign on a much less divisive front: the need for national security.

5

Peace and War

The economic collapse which caused the Great Depression was inter-twined with a global security crisis rooted in anticipation and apprehension of another worldwide war. Reactions to this crisis not only affected British foreign and defence policy: they also became an important factor in domestic politics.

THE LAST WAR?

During the 1920s, British foreign policy had been guided by two interconnected concerns: the protection of the UK and the Empire, and the promotion of peace and prevention of another global war.[1] There were, broadly speaking, two different perspectives on how these might be achieved. Both had their roots in the nineteenth century and their tendrils trained by the Great War. One – common among but not confined to the Liberals and Labour – was internationalist; placing hope in the League of Nations, the new global body set up at the end of the First World War to promote open diplomacy, eventual multilateral disarmament and mutual security. The other – more frequently but not definitively Conservative – was isolationist; it was anxious to avoid foreign entanglements of the sort that had precipitated the last conflict, worried about the safety of the Empire, and doubted the utility of the new League.

In practice, both viewpoints shared some common assumptions: that military alliances and an arms race had helped to create the last war; that a needless repetition of the bloodletting of 1914–18 would be a fundamental evil; and that Germany had been too harshly treated at the war's end. In office, politicians also had to cope with the world as it was: Britain's distinctive place as a naval great power with wide-ranging imperial commitments; the increasing cost of modern weaponry and the demand for increased social spending at home; the advent of the Soviet Union; the rise of Japan; and the isolationism of the United States, which never joined the League of Nations. As a result, foreign policy followed a fairly consistent line despite changes in government. Public commitments to the principles of the League were matched with multilateral security agreements, rather than the construction of the alliance blocs that had characterized Europe before 1914. The need to guarantee imperial security led to programmes of rearmament while the international situation remained fraught during the first half of the 1920s, followed by retrenchment during its quieter second half.

In the Far East, Britain's ally Japan emerged from the First World War as an aggressive Asian power that might pose a threat to the Empire in the future. To guard against this, the decision was taken to build a new naval base at Singapore. This was meant to provide the infrastructure to allow a British fleet to operate in the Far East. Since Britain did not want to pay the price of keeping two fleets – one to protect the UK, the other stationed permanently in eastern waters – Singapore became the keystone of a naval strategy based on transferring force to where it was needed. Normally, the Royal Navy would keep all its capital ships at home, but if hostilities threatened in eastern waters, a powerful fleet would be sent to Singapore.

At the Washington Conference of 1921–22, the British abandoned the increasingly dysfunctional alliance with Japan in favour of a four-power agreement to maintain the status quo in the Pacific and a naval treaty which limited major ship construction and fixed the maximum number of US and Japanese battleships as equal to, and 60 per cent of, respectively, the number possessed by the UK. This conceded in principle the possibility that someone else could have as large a fleet as the Royal Navy: in practice, American isolationism helped to ensure that the British remained the world's largest naval power. It also ensured that Britain had enough ships to deal with any European enemy and still send the fleet east to confront Japan. Almost immediately, however, the Singapore base became a political football: postponed by the first Labour government of 1924, then restarted (at a very slow pace) by their Conservative successors.

In Europe, the Paris peace conference in 1919 had carved out from the wreckage of former empires a new set of Eastern and Central European nation states. The Versailles treaty left Germany paying heavy reparations to its former enemies, with parts of its territory broken off and others demilitarized, and strict limitations placed on its armed forces. Unlike other national groups, European populations who were considered ethnically German were not given the opportunity of self-determination. All of these elements formed the basis for German nationalist complaint and subversion of the treaty, while France, having paid the price in blood for previous German aggression, was determined to enforce the terms agreed at Versailles. As a result, the early 1920s were a period of tension and repeated crises. Since the British hoped to rehabilitate Germany as a trading partner, they were much more willing than the French to moderate the post-war settlement. Having withdrawn its garrisons from Germany, the UK did not renew its military alliance with France. Indeed, British governments saw French revanchism rather than German revisionism as the greater threat to European stability, and the strength of the French air force was used as the justification for a substantial British programme of aerial rearmament.

In 1925, in an effort to restore European stability, France, Germany, Belgium, the UK and Italy signed the Locarno Pact, guaranteeing the first three nations' shared borders against any aggression from each other. Significantly, Eastern Europe was not covered by the treaty: an indication of British diplomats' willingness to accept modifications to Germany's borders in a region far removed from the UK, and their hope that a reassured France could be convinced to abandon its attempts to build an alliance bloc on the far side of its former opponent.

European tensions eased after Locarno, and it appeared possible that hopes of a lasting peace might be fulfilled. In the second half of the 1920s, British military spending was cut back, and the rearmament programmes of the first part of the decade were not completed. Reductions in defence spending did not, however, put Britain out of the major league: taking the 1920s as a whole, it spent at least as much on its armed forces as any other country on earth.[2]

As chancellor in the 1924–29 Conservative government, Churchill had fought a fierce battle to restrain the Royal Navy's demands for continued expansion. He was a supporter of the navy, but unlike the admirals, he argued that Britain did not need to be preparing for an inevitable war with Japan. On the contrary, a cautious, rational people like the Japanese were unlikely to start a fight they were bound to lose. Even if Britain was occupied with a major European war, Japanese aggression would inevitably bring America in on Britain's side: another reason for the Japanese not to open hostilities in the first place. Under Churchill, the Treasury authorized the resumption of work on the base at Singapore, but on a much-reduced scheme that could not support the size of fleet necessary to take on the Japanese navy ship-for-ship. If this always lent an air of unreality to the Admiralty's planning for a future war, the Singapore base nonetheless became a powerful symbol of Britain's commitment to defending the Empire, particularly to Australia and New Zealand, which based their defence policies on the fact that the British navy would protect them from the Japanese.

From 1925, the British participated in drawn out preparations for a world disarmament conference that many hoped would remove a cause of war. As part of these preparations, when the Labour Party returned to office in 1929, it suspended work on the Singapore base again. In 1930, Ramsay MacDonald agreed to cut the Royal Navy's cruiser fleet (a type of vessel not covered by previous naval accords, and in which the British had built heavily during the 1920s), but only in order to secure American agreement to a naval treaty, signed in London that summer, which placed a renewed moratorium on the construction of new battleships and was meant to help lay the groundwork for the disarmament conference, now finally scheduled to start in Geneva in 1932.

THE NEXT WAR?

Even as it began, however, the conference's chances of success were being placed in doubt by the onset of the most profound crisis of the years between the wars.[3] The Great Depression resulted in a breakdown in international economic co-operation, as the major liberal democracies – the USA, the UK and France – blamed each other for their economic woes and retreated into protectionism. The apparent collapse of capitalism spurred on the Soviet Union's military and industrial expansion. Fear of Soviet power played a key role in the Japanese army's efforts to expand its empire on the East Asian mainland, starting with the invasion of Manchuria in 1931. In Germany, the rise of the Nazi party resulted in the appointment of Adolf Hitler as Chancellor in January 1933. The Nazis crushed democratic institutions, spoke aggressively of the need to redraw borders to re-unite the German peoples of Europe, and massively increased spending on the armed forces. Alarmed by these developments, by the mid-1930s the French would also begin to rearm.

In the UK, MacDonald, a determined internationalist, was unable to impose his perspective on colleagues whose attention was focused on avoiding economic catastrophe. Under a new foreign secretary, Sir John Simon, the leader of the National Liberals, Britain condemned, but did nothing to oppose, Japanese aggression in Manchuria. The League of Nations, after a lengthy investigation, criticized the Japanese, prompting their departure from the League but not from their newly acquired territory. No other action was taken against them. The British delegation arrived at the World Disarmament Conference ready to accept German demands for the right to rearm, in the hope of a broader settlement, but they would not offer the military alliance to the French that might have reconciled the latter to a German revival. With no agreement possible, Hitler, newly arrived in power, had the pretext to remove his country from both the disarmament conference and the League of Nations in October 1933. The conference stumbled on, but without German participation it was already effectively defunct.

These episodes caused British leaders some anxiety but were not seen to require a resort to arms. Japanese aggression offended internationalists and raised concerns about the safety of the Empire. Such concerns militated against any attempt to protect Manchuria, although they did lead to a review of British defences and the abandonment of the planning presumption that there would be no major war within the next decade. Like all government departments, the armed forces' budgets had been cut in an effort to eliminate the deficit. Given the country's economic problems and the need not to be seen to be disrupting international efforts at disarmament, the Cabinet now decided for the present not to revive military spending. As Baldwin summed up for his fellow ministers: 'At the moment the financial position governed the whole situation, but clearly the efficiency of the Defence Services would have to be considered as soon as the results of the Disarmament Conference are known.'[4]

The British blamed French intransigence for the collapse of the disarmament talks, but during 1933 and 1934, they also became increasingly aware of the dramatic increase in German armaments spending since Hitler's arrival in power. During the first two years of his chancellorship, German expenditure on the military as a proportion of national income jumped from 1 to almost 10 per cent.[5] During 1934, in an effort to fund this expansion, Germany tried to default on its repayment of UK loans, and took advantage of the resulting collapse in bond prices to buy back overseas debt. Previous German governments had explored ways of rebuilding their armed forces. Now, the Nazis had actually begun a massive, but still surreptitious, reconstruction of military power, including a nascent air force that, it was feared, might soon directly threaten the UK with a 'knock-out blow' – a devastating aerial attack on its great cities that would instantly fracture any ability to resist.

The fear of air attack was the ugly sister of the communications revolution of the inter-war period – the evil counterpart to the excitement of speed and the freedom of the skies. It grew out of the shocking experiences of the last war – the terrible destruction that could be unleashed by modern weapons, and the impact of the bombing raids on London by German airships and aircraft from 1915 – and was magnified by the rapidity of scientific and technological development in the years after the war. Of particular relevance to the UK was the way in which air power eroded the traditional island security from surprise attack. Warnings of an aerial knock-out blow – usually accompanied by dreadful descriptions of mass death and popular panic – gained wide currency in Britain during the 1920s. In 1924, for example, the military commentator Basil Liddell Hart asked his readers to:

Imagine for a moment London, Manchester, Birmingham and half a dozen other great cities simultaneously attacked, the business localities and Fleet Street wrecked, Whitehall a heap of ruins, the slum districts maddened into the impulse to break loose and maraud, the railways cut, factories destroyed. Would not the general will to resist vanish, and what use would be the still determined factions of the nation, without organisation and direction?[6]

As the world became increasingly unstable in the early 1930s, the expectation that any future war would be accompanied by mass death and social breakdown was deployed both by those who wanted to promote the cause of peace and by advocates of additional investment in British defences.

It was in the context of Germany's illicit revival of its military strength that the National Government allowed British strategists to move from managing disarmament to planning rearmament. Over the winter of 1933–34, a new Defence Requirements Committee brought together the professional heads of the military and senior civil servants to consider how to make up the armed forces' deficiencies. In contemplating the threat from Japan and Germany, they faced two very different military dangers. Fighting Japan would require an even more powerful Royal Navy, equipped with the ships, bases and stockpiled supplies to defend British possessions on the other side of the world. A rearmed Germany, on the other hand, might launch a land war which would force Britain to send an expeditionary army – a 'Field Force' – to the aid of France, but could also threaten the home islands with aerial attack.

How these threats were assessed would determine who got the lion's share of resources, so these discussions were matters of service politics as well as strategic appreciation. In practice, the committee's members could not agree on the greatest danger and fudged their final report, presenting the Japanese as the most imminent threat, but Germany as the 'ultimate enemy', against which the UK must be prepared by the end of the 1930s (a fortuitous choice of target date, based on the time thought necessary to construct new arms manufacturing capacity). To guarantee security, the report proposed a wide-ranging programme of rearmament that would build up all the services over the next five years.

Now the chancellor intervened. Chamberlain was horrified by the prospect that untrammelled military spending would wreck the fragile economic recovery. He argued instead for a focus on deterring Germany from any rash attack by building a large, UK-based bomber air force. This would provide domestic security, avoid the expense and provocation of an across-the-board arms race and demonstrate that the government was committed to protecting the country from a 'knock-out blow'. An aerial deterrent would also allow the British to sidestep the binding commitment to send an army to support the French, thus reducing the risk of repeating the slaughter of the last war. Although Chamberlain was persuaded to restart work on the base at Singapore, he believed that Britain could reach a diplomatic settlement with Japan to reduce tensions in the Far East. He therefore insisted that decisions on naval construction (not coincidentally, the most expensive and longest-term spending commitment) could be put off until after the next round of international naval negotiations, due to take place in London in 1935. These arguments, presented with the chancellor's customary bureaucratic heft, fundamentally altered the programme of rearmament, reducing total defence expenditure by a third and concentrating on the RAF at the expense of the army and navy.

This revised plan formed the basis for the first public announcement of British rearmament: a scheme of air force expansion that was approved by Parliament on 18 July 1934. But during the second half of 1934, revelations about the rapid growth of the German air force required the government to increase its own plans to build up the RAF, although the aim was still to deter a confrontation rather than win an inevitable war. The British therefore continued their diplomatic attempts to legitimize German rearmament and reduce European tensions. At the start of 1935, these led briefly to discussions of a continent-wide air pact in which everyone would have an air force and agree collectively to bomb any aggressor.

Such proposals did not halt what looked increasingly like an arms race. In March 1935, the British government laid out its whole programme of rearmament in a White Paper on defence designed to educate the public in the need for military spending. The Nazi regime, counting on revelations of its growing power to deter any outside intervention until it could actually defend itself, responded by officially announcing the existence of a German air force, which it falsely claimed to be as large as the British and still growing. It then reintroduced military conscription as part of a major enlargement of its army. In turn, the British government decided to accelerate plans for RAF expansion.

To ensure that the Royal Navy was not out-built by its potential opponents, the British happily signed a bilateral naval agreement with Germany, which allowed the Germans a fleet, but fixed it at a third of the size of the Royal Navy. This breach of the Versailles treaty greatly annoyed the French, but meant that, provided everyone stuck to their existing agreements, the British would be able to match the number of potential enemy vessels in European and Far Eastern waters. In fact, Japan's determination to build more battleships would shortly lead to its abandonment of the 1930 naval accords. Britain's senior sailors were already planning a massive new programme of warship construction that would enable them to outpace all comers during the second half of the decade. As the British looked to guarantee their maritime power, the French looked to reinforce their continental strength. In March 1935, they signed a defence pact with the Soviet Union, agreeing mutual aid in case of a war with Germany. If the Germans were going to build their army, the French would threaten them with a conflict on two fronts. To the British, this looked like exactly the sort of alliance building that had led to the last war.

WAR AND DICTATORSHIP

It might be argued that the early 1930s actually saw no great change in the underlying nature of the UK's foreign policy.[7] Throughout the 1920s, after all, British ministers had consistently placed national and imperial interests ahead of selfless international co-operation and adapted defence expenditure to the changing threat of conflict. The shift from the pursuit of disarmament as a route to global peace to the acceptance of rearmament in a world divided between nations certainly, however, looked significant. That helps to explain both public reactions and the political consequences.

Less than two decades after 1918, there were few Britons who believed that another 'great' war would be anything less than a disaster for humanity. The meaning of the last conflict remained hotly contested, but two things on which everybody agreed were that it had been horrific, and that a future repeat would be worse – above all because the new technology of air warfare would unleash the gas, fire and high explosive of the front-line trench upon civilians at home. The result would be not just physical destruction but moral degradation. Baldwin's comment, in a Commons debate on international affairs in 1932, that 'the bomber will always get through' is often quoted; less well remembered is his brutal description of the strategic consequence: 'The only defence is in offence, which means that you have to kill more women and children more quickly than the enemy if you want to save yourselves.'[8]

The general apprehension of another great war both spurred on and was encouraged by a variety of peace movements which had, by the end of the 1920s, attracted considerable support. These included absolute pacifist organizations that opposed any use of force and wanted total unilateral disarmament. Some were rooted in nonconformist Christian sects with a long history of non-violence, such as the Quaker Friends Peace Committee. Others, such as the No More War Movement, came from a radical socialist tradition, and saw opposition to war as part of a revolutionary reordering of society on the way to a better, fairer world. Such pacifism had substantial support within the Labour Party: Labour's first post-1931 leader, George Lansbury, was a Christian socialist pacifist. On the left of British politics, thanks largely to the work of J. A. Hobson, war was seen as the product of imperialist capitalism, and therefore not only avoidable but immoral.

Absolute pacifists were, however, always only a small but vocal minority. A much larger, liberal constituency, which hoped that international co-operation might eliminate the causes of war but did not want a revolution or unilateral disarmament, was embodied in the League of Nations Union. Created to promote the League's work and to encourage a more democratic foreign policy, the LNU was a deliberately broad body, led by a Conservative peer, Lord Cecil, supported by a Liberal academic, Gilbert Murray, and a Labour MP, Philip Noel-Baker. In 1931, it had about 400,000 paying subscribers, held together in a national network of nearly 3,000 branches and further sustained by a web of public meetings, pamphlets and congregational affiliations – strongest among Methodists but with a significant Anglican component.[9]

The LNU's leadership shared more absolute pacifists' suspicion that private arms manufacturers – the *Merchants of Death*, in the title of a 1934 tract – were themselves a cause of war. They strongly supported multilateral disarmament. Significantly, however, they did not completely abjure the use of force in international affairs. Although happy to assert the vital necessity of peace – not least as a means to win the support of outright pacifists – Cecil in particular believed that Britain should maintain its armed forces, partly because it needed to manage the Empire and protect its nationals abroad, but also because he hoped that it would take the lead in organizing intervention, if necessary backed by military might, against any international aggressor.

This opposition to war intersected with anxieties about the global rise of extremism. Although neither Fascists nor Communists gained much support in the UK, their manifestations overseas attracted huge public interest, not least because they raised fears of an ideological conflict that would presage a descent into international chaos.

Perceptions of foreign extremism divided broadly on ideological lines. Those on the right were more sensitive to the threats posed to national and imperial security by Germany and Japan, and were converted more quickly to rearmament as a result. British Conservatives were largely antipathetic to Nazism. Thuggish, radical, populist – the Nazis embodied everything that more traditional Tories thought was wrong with modern politics. The British right was also, however, generally antagonistic to the Soviet Union, and therefore willing to accept Hitler's regime if it created a bulwark against Bolshevism rather than a danger to Western European stability.

For the left, in contrast, a fundamental opposition to Fascism conflicted for most of the decade with a disgust for arms races and a reluctance to defend a world of nations and empires. Whereas the right saw Soviet and Nazi tyranny as essentially the same thing, the British left – though often anti-Communist – idealized the USSR as an example of the progress that could be made when a country was run by and for the people. Enthusiasm for popular democracy and industrial modernity tended to drown out the cries of the collectivized and the purged. As a result, the strand of opinion that held up the Soviet system as a positive vision for humanity was much stronger than any equivalent advocacy for Nazism.

At the same time as bolstering a particular view of progress, the example of totalitarian regimes abroad also served to encourage the affirmation of a set of more traditional liberal values. Freedom, tolerance and a worldview built on compromise rather than dogma were held up as archetypally British by Conservatives and Liberals as well as by socialists eager to separate themselves from Communism. Baldwin – its most politically successful exponent – used this vision to define a broad centre ground of British politics which, while sympathetic to the desire for social improvement, asserted a fundamental incompatibility between a national desire for individualism and compromise and an essentially foreign trend towards greater state control.

As this suggested, understandings of international affairs were conditioned not only by political ideologies but also by a set of stereotypes about character and inheritance. Nazi violence – the furore surrounding the Reichstag fire of 1933, the persecution of opposition politicians and the exodus of Jewish academics forced out of German universities – all stirred up the spectres of the last war: Hunnish barbarians once again battering on the walls of civilization. A suspicion of past propaganda also encouraged a desire to believe that there was a good Germany – rational, cultured, almost Anglo-Saxon – that might reassert itself if only the Versailles settlement could be reworked. Conceptions of the Soviet Union similarly fed off a dual vision of despotic Slavs and romantic Russians, although of course the USSR did not have Germany's form in instigating global conflict.

In the early 1930s, the danger of war was simultaneously terrifying and vague. Within Whitehall, there was time to debate what the best strategy for rearmament would be, and to select a solution based on deterring a possibility rather than preparing for the certainty of war. For peace activists, divisive questions about the use of force could still be subsumed within the hope that international agreement would preclude the need for violence. And far from being a vital part of defending democracy, war itself seemed the greatest threat to democracy's survival, unleashing as it would forces that were feared in different ways across the political spectrum – social strife, widened state control and heightened popular emotion.

6

Peace and Progress

All this had important implications for British politics, and set the conditions for the second half of the 1930s in the same way that the economic crisis had done since 1931.

THE POLITICS OF PEACE

Although Conservatives generally supported rearmament, there were significant differences within the party about how best to proceed.[1] The imperialist wing demanded that the government pay greater attention, in both foreign and defence policy, to the protection of the Empire and Dominions. Another strand of concern, in which Churchill took a prominent part, latched onto public concerns about bombing and pressed for more rapid aerial rearmament. From late 1932, before Hitler became Chancellor, Churchill warned, in explicitly power-political terms, of the dangers posed by a resurgent Germany, denigrated efforts at disarmament while the international situation remained uncertain, and stressed the importance of British backing for France's attempts to build a framework for European security. During 1934 and 1935, making use of information secretly supplied to him by civil servants, he argued publicly that government assertions about British air superiority were based on serious underestimates of Germany's position. In so doing, he conjured up not only the catastrophic human damage that would be done by a future war, but also the prospect of a mortal danger to national security from 'the only form of war that we have seen in the world in which complete predominance gives no opportunity of recovery'.[2]

Inevitably, such warnings were regarded with some cynicism by those who knew that Churchill had reduced military spending during his time at the Treasury in the 1920s. In fact, he took care to warn Baldwin in advance of his interventions on defence. Such pressure was not entirely unwelcome to a government trying to win the political argument for rearmament. It did, however, help to increase the pressure to prioritize spending on the RAF over the other armed forces, particularly after Hitler's revelation of the Luftwaffe's apparent strength in March 1935. Churchill's campaign for more rapid rearmament allowed him to rebuild links with senior backbenchers, including Leo Amery and Austen Chamberlain, who had opposed his position over Indian reforms. It brought him back within the corridors of power, with an invitation from Baldwin to join a new committee looking into air defence research. He remained, however, too dangerous a figure for this to presage a return to actual office.

In contrast, both the Liberal and Labour parties initially opposed rearmament. The diminishing band of Liberals accused the government of warmongering because it had abandoned too quickly the collective measures that alone might guarantee peace. Labour warned not only that new weapons would make more likely another war, but that they might also be turned against socialists, perhaps in the Soviet Union, maybe even at home.

In October 1933, the Labour candidate in a by-election in East Fulham added to a litany of complaints about the government's domestic shortcomings the charge that it had forced Germany out of the disarmament conference. He won a dramatic victory, with a 29.2 per cent swing of the vote compared to 1931. Shortly afterwards, Labour's annual conference in Hastings passed by acclamation a motion that it should take no part in any future war. This swing towards a more isolationist stance, and Labour members' demands for unilateral disarmament, did not prevent the party winning control of the London County Council in 1934. Tensions then arose, however, between Lansbury's rather other-worldly pacifism and the growing conviction of senior trade unionists – well aware of the fate of their brethren in Germany – that Fascism must be opposed, if necessary, by force of arms.

For Baldwin, who took charge of presenting the government's rearmament policy, the different ways in which Britons viewed the world posed not only political difficulties but also a strategic challenge. From its outset, the UK's rearmament programme – like that in every other country – was conditioned by the memory of the colossal industrial and social demands of the last war. Fighting another such conflict would, it was plain, require public consent, but the costs even of repairing Britain's defences sufficiently to ward off another war would demand sacrifices that might be more than a democracy could bear. Even after East Fulham, it was unlikely that disagreements over rearmament would allow Labour to return to office. But they might lead to a departure of Liberal voters that would erode the government's claim to 'National' credentials just when they were most necessary.

From the summer of 1933, therefore, Baldwin attempted to seize the centre ground in international as well as domestic policy. He did this not, like Churchill, by proclaiming British military weakness. In Baldwin's view, this risked simply paralysing a terrified electorate into inaction. Instead, he came at the problem obliquely, by asserting the importance of British democracy as a bulwark against totalitarianism. Left to himself, Baldwin thought Fascism marginally preferable to Communism, but he saw both as part of the same problem – a contagion of dictatorship that, even if it did not infect the UK, might still result in a deadly global fever. He also, however, knew that he needed to temper his message to appeal to that part of public opinion that might not otherwise support the government. As he put it privately in early 1934, it was time to tell the public 'that we are the only defenders left of liberty in a world of Fascists'. Here was a stick with which to beat domestic extremists, but also a trumpet through which to sound a clarion call to liberal opinion.

THE PEACE BALLOT

As it turned out, it was the LNU that set the underlying tempo for Baldwin's tune.[3] The Union had been thrown into turmoil by the events of the early 1930s, taking no strong stance over Manchuria, and struggling to explain the League's inaction against Japan. Rising fears that internationalist hopes had been misplaced were reinforced by the long drawn out death of the World Disarmament Conference. The prospect of an actual war, which tended to exacerbate differences between the degrees of pacifism within the movement, and the threat that public

75

opinion was shifting away from collective action and towards isolationism, encouraged the LNU to take a strong stand to reunite itself
and to reaffirm the importance of international co-operation. In late
1934, it launched the 'National Declaration' – better known as the
'Peace Ballot' – a nationwide plebiscite in which respondents were
asked to offer their views on membership of the League, disarmament
and action against international aggressors.

Carried out between that winter and the early summer of 1935, the
ballot was a remarkable logistic achievement. Half a million volunteers
collected responses from 11½ million Britons. The ballot attracted the
support of many left-wing peace activists, but it also enthused the
residuum of nonconformist voters who were still moved by the notion
of a moral foreign policy. It was opposed, and in some places boy-
cotted, by Conservatives who feared that the ballot would be rigged to
provide ammunition against the government. Isolationists attacked it
as the slippery slope into other people's wars: Lord Beaverbrook's
papers therefore called it 'the ballot of blood'.

The results, announced in July 1935, indicated overwhelming
support among respondents for British membership of the League of
Nations (96 per cent in favour), multilateral disarmament (91 per cent),
the abolition of military aircraft (83 per cent) and the prohibition of
private arms sales (90 per cent). The use of economic sanctions by
League members against an aggressor was supported by 87 per cent of
those who replied. Fifty-nine per cent believed that military measures
would also be justified. The chapel-going areas of England and Wales,
where response rates were highest, showed the least enthusiasm for the
use of armed force.

As an exercise in political influence, the 'Peace Ballot' therefore
demonstrated huge, if uneven, support for the LNU's moderate internationalism. As an attempt to educate the public, it had studiously
avoided the question of what would happen if Britain's commitment to
the League led it into a war. Collective security was positioned as an
alternative to, not a justification for, rearmament. Above all, however,
it was another indication of the survival into the 1930s of another
essentially Victorian ideal: a remarkable confidence that the UK could,
by setting an example, exercise moral suasion over the rest of the world.
It was a forlorn hope.

During the early 1930s, Italy, under the Fascist regime led by Benito

Mussolini, had seemed to offer a vital European counterweight to German aggression. Italian pressure helped to see off a German threat to absorb Austria in 1934, and in April 1935, in response to Germany's military expansion, the Italians signed an agreement with France and Britain to uphold the Locarno treaties and prevent further breaches of the Treaty of Versailles. Mussolini was, however, driven by the same sense of impending conflagration that was coming to dominate world affairs. That meant building Italy's overseas possessions, and from the end of the 1920s, Italy's forces prepared to expand its East African empire by attacking Abyssinia – a slave-owning autocracy but also an independent member of the League of Nations.

As Italian threats to Abyssinia became increasingly bellicose in the summer of 1935, British ministers faced the prospect that the 'left and middle wing of public opinion' embodied in the Peace Ballot would expect the UK to stick by its responsibilities to a fellow member of the League. Using the Royal Navy to enforce economic sanctions against Italy in a bid to guarantee collective security, however, might trigger a military confrontation in the Mediterranean. Despite their lack of preparation, this was not a fight that Britain's sailors were likely to lose, but the losses suffered in the process might cripple their long-term preparations against Germany and Japan. Meanwhile, Italy would also be lost as a European ally. The government's attempt to square this strategic circle consisted of promising 'collective resistance to all acts of unprovoked aggression' (as Hoare, now foreign secretary, put it in Geneva that September), but in fact preparing the mildest of sanctions, in the knowledge that they would be as unprovocative as they were ineffective, and insisting on co-operation with the French, who were expected to demand that Britain give up on Abyssinia in the hope of securing Italian support against Germany.

In October, the Italians finally launched their much-threatened invasion and quickly overran Abyssinia. The British implemented their minimal sanctions, and Hoare convinced his colleagues to hold back from further action until he had settled matters with the French. Baldwin, meanwhile, took the opportunity to call a general election for November. The anger occasioned by Italian colonial misdemeanours allowed him to crowbar support behind a policy of rearmament designed to deter Germany. Baldwin's promise to the electorate was that the government was rebuilding the armed forces to fulfil its continuing commitment to world peace through the covenant of the League of Nations. He reassured them that this was not an arms race – there would be, he said, 'no great armaments' – but rather a responsible policy to guarantee national security in an unstable age. The linkage between 'arms and the covenant' was eagerly taken up by Conservative candidates: in their election addresses they made even more frequent reference to the League of Nations than they did to the government's economic record. The government's 1935 manifesto explicitly linked challenges at home and overseas to conclude that: 'In present circumstances, it is more than ever necessary that the British Government should not only be united amongst themselves, but that they should represent that spirit of national cooperation which will best secure the confidence and respect of the world.'[4]

Meanwhile, the tension between Lansbury's principled pacifism and the growing desire of the right of his party to do something more practical about the looming international catastrophe was about to snap. At Labour's 1935 party conference in October, Ernest Bevin launched a devastating attack on Lansbury and those who were trying to take the party further to the left.

By 1935, Bevin had become a man who was used to getting what he wanted. He was the orphaned son of a maid, who had worked as a farm labourer and delivery driver before becoming a trade union organizer. Union work taught him how to persuade men and wield power. Bevin's role in organizing dock labour during the First World War turned him into a national figure. Like most of the older trade union bosses, Bevin had no problem combining socialism and patriotism, and with his own secure support base in the TGWU, he had little time for the machinations of Labour's political wing.[5] Now he delivered a brutal bludgeoning to Lansbury's presumption of moral authority, accusing him of 'hawking your conscience round from body to body asking to be told what to do with it'. Lansbury resigned. With his deputy, Clement Attlee, having taken his place (but Lansbury's face still on the party's leaflets), Labour fought the election in disarray. In foreign affairs, it now revived its support for collective security – even backed by military sanctions – but opposed the government's defence programme as 'a danger to the peace of the world and the security of the country'.[6]

THE VERDICT OF 1935

The government got another crushing victory that set a parliamentary balance that would endure, though no one then knew it, until 1945.[7] Four hundred and twenty-nine National Government MPs were returned. Three hundred and eighty-seven of them were Conservatives, but vestigial traces of a coalition remained in the form of eight representatives of 'National Labour' (who had put economic stability ahead of remodelling society) and forty-four 'Liberal Nationals' (who had put keeping out socialism ahead of defending free trade). On the opposition benches, the Liberals were reduced to a mere twenty-one MPs. Labour, despite its travails, recovered to win 154 seats. Another four MPs sat for the Independent Labour Party, which had split from Labour in 1931 because it was insufficiently socialist, and one Communist MP, Willie Gallacher, was finally elected (after five unsuccessful attempts since 1922), for the Scottish constituency of West Fife.

This parliamentary pie chart reflected the strength of the National Government's position as a coalition of the moderate right and Baldwin's success in positioning his administration as the responsible choice for domestic stability and international security. The government rallied to its support not only the middle classes, who had benefitted most from its economic policies, but also a majority of working-class electors, mainly by presenting 'National' as the rational, non-denominationally Christian and unifying opposite of a Labour Party portrayed as ideological, atheistic and sectional. With MPs elected in every part of the UK, and special attention paid in the election manifesto to nationalist feeling in Scotland (with proposals to return the Scottish Office to Edinburgh), a Conservative-dominated government could really claim to have made a successfully 'national' appeal. The Conservative MPs in the 1935 intake also changed the nature of the party in the Commons. It became less diehard and less aristocratic, and more interested in issues such as the efficiency of business. That also meant that it drew further away, in style and substance, from the sort of politics represented by Winston Churchill.

In contrast to the government's success, Labour's recovery could not conceal another electoral failure. It had not recovered the reputation for responsibility so painstakingly gathered during the 1920s but destroyed by the events of 1931. Whereas the government proffered more of the same economically – gradual recovery, increasing prosperity – Labour offered a much more radical alternative. Proposals for taking the holdings of the joint stock banks into public ownership had been quietly abandoned since 1931, but the party still proposed nationalizing the commanding heights of heavy industry, the Bank of England, fuel and power, and imposing central economic planning to direct resources towards the construction of a more equal society. The resultant promise of expropriation and social strife served to alienate the party from the middle classes and from female voters. Labour's plans to increase welfare spending had wider appeal, but did little to restore its reputation for budgetary prudence or to dispel its opponents' charge that it was the party of the unemployed. Internationally, meanwhile, Baldwin's electoral strategy had cast Labour's uncertainty and rejection of rearmament as further examples of its idealistic irrationality.

Labour would have struggled anyway, but the party's chances were further hit by the decline of the Liberals as a third force in politics. With fewer Liberals standing, voters who were determined, after 1931, not to allow Labour back into office, now tended either to support the National Government or to withhold their ballots. The electoral consequences were grim. In 1935, Labour won a slightly higher percentage of the total votes than in 1929, but in the new bipolar political landscape forged by the economic crash, this got it only just over half as many seats as it had six years before. Its parliamentary position might partially have recovered from the hiding of 1931, and it was certainly the only major party of opposition, but it had little prospect of forming another government while Baldwin's National alliance endured.

The election of Clement Attlee as Labour leader after the election did not seem likely to improve the party's chances of returning to office. The son of a well-to-do solicitor, Attlee had been educated at Haileybury, the public school that trained the men who ran the British Empire. Mission work in the East End had helped to convert Attlee to socialism, and he joined the Labour Party in 1908. During the First World War, he served as an infantry officer at Gallipoli, in Mesopotamia and on the Western Front. After the war, he rose through the ranks of local politics, becoming mayor of the London borough of Stepney, then MP for Limehouse. His military experience led to his being appointed under-secretary for war in the 1924 Labour government. He was one of the few Labour MPs who retained his seat after 1931.

Attlee was not a charismatic figure. He was physically small, didn't say much, and seemed reluctant to impose himself on people. This led a lot of his opponents to underestimate his ruthless drive and skill at operating the levers of power. Like most of the rest of the Labour leadership, Attlee's time in local politics and experience of the party's own Byzantine bureaucracy had given him a lengthy training in how to get what he wanted from a committee. These were, however, skills that looked more impressive in office than in opposition, where Attlee seemed indecisive and hesitant. His hard work in the House won the loyalty of the few Labour MPs who remained after 1931, but many of those who supported him for the leadership in 1935 did so because they thought he would follow the Labour Party rather than direct it. After MacDonald's departure, Labour had its suspicions of leaders who might follow their own path.[8]

This was one reason why Attlee's greatest rival, Herbert Morrison, was not elected leader in his place. Morrison was the son of a South London policeman, and had been a shop boy and a brewery clerk before becoming a full-time socialist activist. He was blind in one eye, but chose to refuse military service during the First World War on the grounds of conscientious objection rather than disability. After the war, Morrison was elected as a Labour mayor and MP, and as a London County Councillor. He served as transport minister in the Labour government, but lost his seat in 1931.

London, however, was Labour's one great success story of the mid-1930s. The party won control of the London County Council (LCC) in 1934, and Morrison became the leader of the world's greatest metropolis. Apart from the trade union bosses, this made him the most powerful Labour politician in the country. As leader of the LCC, he introduced a green belt for the city, began new schemes of slum clearance and fought for the money to build a new bridge across the Thames. He also oversaw the introduction of the London Passenger Transport Board, a public corporation to run the capital's underground railways, trams and buses. Moreover, he managed to do all of this without adding too much to the rates, a key achievement for a party seeking to rebuild its reputation for financial respectability.[9]

Morrison was a very modern politician. He understood the need for a give-and-take relationship with journalists, set up press releases and press conferences and loved playing up to his image as a cheeky Cockney barrow boy made good. He also grasped the importance of modern advertising and publicity techniques when it came to broadcasting Labour's message to the electorate. Having been re-elected as an MP in 1935, he immediately set about making a run for the leadership. The strength of his image as a little London superman, however, meant that he was seen as out of touch with Labour's roots in the industrial areas. Morrison was also on the conservative, gradualist wing of the Labour movement, and his battles against Communist infiltration brought him into conflict with the Labour left, which backed Attlee instead. For all his grasp of how to communicate with the public, Morrison was not a subtle political operator, and his attempts to win supporters made him look untrustworthy. He had clashed with Ernest Bevin about transport workers' rights, and the union leader maintained a lasting hatred of the city boss. After Morrison was defeated over the party leadership, he refused to accept the nomination as Attlee's deputy. Instead, that place went to the former schoolteacher Arthur Greenwood. Morrison spent most of the rest of the 1930s concentrating on running London, but he had not given up his ambition of leading his party.[10]

7

State and Society

The result of the 1935 election confirmed the triumph of a particular version of democracy. Labour's espousal of a democratic socialism – constitutionally achieved but egalitarian, collective and in which the state would transform society – proved unavailing in the face of the liberal democracy represented by Baldwin – individualist, ecumenical and replete with freedoms responsibly enjoyed, including the freedom to be jobless, hungry and poor. These fundamentally different visions reflected a broader set of debates about the place of the state, which had been set off by the crises of the 1930s and the rise of totalitarian regimes overseas.

PLANNING AND PROTECTION

In the UK, as throughout the world, the great slump had encouraged calls for greater government intervention.[1] The urgent activity of the dictatorships, above all the Soviet Union's massive programmes of industrialization under the Five Year Plans, seemed to provide potent examples of the improving power of central direction. This sparked an enthusiasm for planning as a panacea across the British political spectrum. Labour's economists, for example, promoted planning as the only route to socialism. In contrast, the intellectual pressure group Political and Economic Planning saw state involvement as a means to preserve, rather than to supersede, capitalism. The Next Five Years Group – among whose members was the dissident Conservative MP Harold Macmillan – argued for a mix of public and private enterprise in an economy planned by and for industrial federations: a corporatist vision similar to that favoured by Oswald Mosley. As this suggested, not only did the 'planomaniacs' diverge widely in their aims, but some of them also posed their own threat to democratic politics.[2] And while planning attracted some support on the fringes, it never became the accepted wisdom among academic economists.

Some cheerleaders for planning were influenced by another economic outlier, John Maynard Keynes. An academic, former civil servant and sometime Liberal, Keynes was also a public intellectual, already widely acknowledged as one of his generation's most provocative minds. Keynes was no friend of planning, and his analyses of market irrationality offered little hope to those who were. Rather, he believed that improved management of economies could be undertaken to enhance the general good.

From the late 1920s, Keynes advocated state investment in public works as a means to ameliorate the effects of the slump – an approach that underpinned the 1929 Liberal manifesto. Keynes' pursuit of a novel middle ground that would address economic problems without recourse to more revolutionary forms of state intervention interested moderate figures across all the major parties.

In 1936, the publishing house run by Macmillan's brother brought out Keynes' *General Theory of Employment, Interest and Money*, in which he argued that governments should take responsibility for minimizing unemployment by using a mixture of interest rates and capital investment funded by borrowing to manage demand. As its author recognized, however, the *General Theory* was a rather technical treatise that had little immediate impact. More striking to contemporaries was the New Deal then taking shape in America under President Roosevelt. This was conceived without Keynesian influence, but it could be taken as a dramatic example of what he suggested might work: massive government spending on infrastructure to relieve unemployment. In Britain, similar ideas had emerged in the Liberals' 1929 electoral manifesto, and were put forward again by David Lloyd George as he tried to stage a political comeback in spring 1935.

Unsurprisingly, given its champions, to most supporters of the National Government planning looked like a fundamentally un-British threat to private enterprise and individual freedom, the preserve of the ideologically extreme and the politically unscrupulous. In the Treasury, Keynes was regarded as bright but impractical. Borrowing to fund public works would expand the national debt, increase the demand for imports, worsen the balance of trade, erode business confidence, and therefore worsen the economic crisis. In 1934, to meet charges that it was doing too little to help the unemployed, the government did introduce 'special areas' legislation to encourage investment in the depressed industrial heartlands. These measures were, however, poorly resourced, ineffectual and publicly criticized even by some of those responsible for making them work.

In Neville Chamberlain's view, there was simply no quick fix to the issue of regional industrial decline. As he told the Commons:

> There is one thing I do detest in politics, and it is humbug. I have never, therefore, attempted to mislead the public into an expectation that there was any speedy way out of our trouble. I have said from the beginning . . . that while there are many ways of dealing with this problem that one could think of, we shall only solve it by degrees and steady progress towards a restoration of normal conditions.[3]

Or, as he had put it privately in November 1936, discussing south Wales: 'when all is said and done, there must remain a large number of people for whom we can find no work . . . and who must either move, or stagnate there for the rest of their lives'.[4]

The pursuit of 'normal conditions', however, had in fact involved the chancellor in several innovative interventions by the state. As well as the tariffs imposed from 1931, Chamberlain's time at the Exchequer also saw the inauguration of the Bank of England Exchange Equalization Account, which, in default of a return to a fixed standard against gold, bought and sold currency to iron out fluctuations in the value of the pound. In 1936, to forestall a new crisis brought about by a devaluation of the franc, the British, French and Americans agreed a new tripartite scheme to fix their currencies against each other: a much delayed restoration of the international co-operation that had broken down as they blamed each other for the slump. The National Government also supported schemes to rationalize production in depressed industries, maintained the farm subsidies introduced by the previous Labour administration, introduced new agricultural marketing boards to promote British produce, and brought to fruition its predecessor's plans for the London Passenger Transport Board, in the process taking private assets into public ownership. During 1937, it extended the provision for 'special areas' and nationalized the revenue from land under which coal was mined. By that point, there was even a more sympathetic reception from the Treasury for Keynes' suggestion that, with the boom beginning to overheat, the government should delay capital expenditure in order to reduce inflation and stimulate future demand. None of these measures was given the fanfare of the New Deal, nor were they connected by any great overarching plan, but they did demonstrate Chamberlain's pragmatic willingness to use state action to bolster economic stability.

WELFARE, HEALTH AND EDUCATION

The government's inability to solve the problem of mass unemployment meant that the welfare of the jobless remained a major issue of social policy throughout the 1930s.[5] It posed significant challenges to the system of unemployment relief established over the previous two decades. Most manual workers paid national insurance against periods of temporary unemployment. Those who had exhausted their contributions or lacked insurance had recourse either to a dole funded by the Treasury or to payments from local Public Assistance Committees, funded by the rates. Under Labour, rising joblessness had bankrupted the national insurance fund and threatened budgetary deficits. The National Government cut benefits, reintroduced the requirement for claimants to prove they were seeking work, and brought in a stringent household means test, much detested by the unemployed for its humiliating scrutiny of family finances. In so doing, it demonstrated its determination to balance the budget without permanently increasing tax and to halt what many senior Conservatives, including Baldwin, feared was a slide into unlimited spending by politicians buying the votes of a venal electorate.

Characteristically, Chamberlain responded to a big problem by seeking a complex and overarching solution. Over the winter of 1934, he pursued an overhaul of the entire unemployment benefit system, re-establishing the national insurance fund on an actuarially sound basis and replacing local committees with a single Unemployment Assistance Board which would set welfare payments for the whole country. This would, he hoped, take the issue out of politics, thus

avoiding both unrestrained future spending and negating local challenges to the paucity of provision from Westminster. In the short term,
however, many of the long-term unemployed were left getting less
money than they had before. Well-supported demonstrations erupted
across the UK. With an election looming, the government backed
down, delaying the new scheme's implementation until 1937 and fixing
the basic rate of payment to ensure that nobody lost out.

The episode confirmed Chamberlain's reputation among his opponents as a callous despot with little regard for the unfortunate. The
chancellor's vision of himself could not have been more different.
Chamberlain thought, with good reason, that he was one of the great
social reformers, far more set than most of his colleagues on bettering
the condition of the people as a moral as well as a political duty. As
he noted with amusement, this meant that many Conservatives saw
him (alongside Hoare) as one of the only two real 'socialists' in the
Cabinet.

As the recovery continued, Chamberlain started to turn his ambitions into reality. The government supported slum clearance (though
always privileging private housebuilding over council construction)
and extended national insurance to new categories of workers. New
legislation improved factory conditions and forced local authorities to
employ more midwives. From the middle of the decade, Chamberlain
sought to tie these initiatives together in a wide-ranging campaign to
improve the nation's health. During the first half of 1937, this found
expression in a new Physical Training and Recreation Act, which aimed
to improve the 'national physique' by promoting group exercise, better
diets and voluntary summer camps. This was, if not exactly strength
through joy, then at least health through physical jerks, porridge and
fresh air.[6]

As Chamberlain's proposals indicated, this was a period when
concerns about social inequality combined with longer-running fears
about the decline of the British racial stock to encourage demands for
more active improvements to the nation's health. The 1936 study *Food,
Health and Income*, by Sir John Boyd Orr, an expert in the new science
of nutrition, for instance, suggested that half the population had an
inadequate diet and that a fifth of British children were chronically
malnourished. Boyd Orr left a furious account in his memoirs of a
clash with Sir Kingsley Wood, the Conservative minister of health, in

which the latter insisted that there was no real poverty left in Britain because no one now died of starvation. Whatever the truth of the tale, the confrontation was instructive: the National politician concerned with relative improvement and unwilling to see personal diet as the responsibility of the state; the campaigning technocrat eager to meet the nutritional needs of the people whether they wanted it or not.[7]

By the late 1930s, the system of medical care was also the subject of significant political debate.[8] As with unemployment benefit, most but not all workers were covered by a contributory national scheme of medical insurance. This was administered by insurance companies and friendly societies, and entitled members to be seen by a 'panel' doctor, a general practitioner paid per patient and thereby discouraged from specialism. Measures of public health, including school health and midwives, were under local authority control. So too were some public hospitals, others being funded by voluntary donation. There were wide discrepancies in provision across the country depending on what local ratepayers would stand, with the most economically deprived and least healthy areas least able to meet their inhabitants' medical needs. Hospital care was not covered by national insurance and had to be paid for by anybody whose income exceeded the minimal level set by the means test.

Working-class patients – particularly parents prioritizing their children's needs – therefore often ended up enduring debilitating but not terminal ailments that could not be treated by inexpert panel doctors. Middle-class Britons, meanwhile, had to arrange their own health insurance and complained increasingly about its high cost as the decade went on. Here then was another inefficient system comprised of incremental accretions from previous partial reforms. It was ripe for another dose of the massive bureaucratic redesign in which Chamberlain specialized. And indeed, when the Conservatives started to think about how they would win the general election due before the end of 1940, one of the policies under consideration was a nationwide restructuring of medical provision within the existing insurance framework.[9]

Like the health system, Britain's schools were also widely seen as in need of reform. Here too, the traditions of localism and voluntarism, as well as continuing sectarian suspicions and piecemeal reforms, had produced a pattern of infinite local variation but very limited attainment, in which most people's education consisted of elementary schooling that stopped at fourteen. Earlier attempts to overhaul education and to strengthen secondary provision had floundered in the face of concerns about cost and the consequences of expanding state provision for the autonomy of church schools. The Education Act of 1936 was a cautious attempt to get through more limited reforms: it aimed to raise the school leaving age to fifteen by 1 September 1939, but put in place such widespread exemptions that seven-eighths of children would not have been compelled to stay at school past fourteen.[10]

Starting in 1933, the Board of Education's Consultative Committee (chaired from 1934 by Sir William Spens, a natural scientist and master of Corpus Christi College, Cambridge) deliberated at length over the structure of secondary education. The committee's report, published at the very end of 1938, set out much more dramatic suggestions for reform. The school leaving age would be raised to sixteen, and from eleven, pupils would enter a tripartite system of grammar, modern and technical schools, to which they would be allocated on the basis of their performance in written tests. There they would study specific and complete curricula (a departure both from the extra years that had been tacked onto the elementary school programme, and from the grammar schools' existing focus on preparing students solely for university), which would be designed to meet their different aptitudes. The Spens report rejected the widespread use of comprehensive schools – in which children of different abilities would be taught in the same institution – but it emphasized the importance of achieving parity of staffing levels and esteem across the secondary system: the 'modern' schools should not be seen as the poorer cousins of the grammars.[11] All this was too much for the Board of Education, which was still working on extending the leaving age to fifteen and was well aware of the cost and controversy that would be involved in the Spens proposals. The report was carefully shelved: perhaps its recommendations might come in useful in the future.

As discussions of welfare, health and education indicated, the National Government was eager to improve the condition of Britain, and that meant that it was open to pressure – political and practical – to increase and centralize the role of the state. The measures it enacted, however, involved a distinct conception of the nation and its citizens, with the emphasis on individual responsibility and a reluctance to take on any great new spending commitments of uncertain size and duration. Among a large part of the electorate – including the many working-class voters, even in areas of high unemployment, who disdained overreliance on the dole – such limitations were not flaws but rather demonstrations that this was a more practical administration than the Labour alternative. To a significant proportion of progressive opinion, however, the government's policies fell well short of their hopes for social improvement. Ironically, however, for all the concern about national welfare during the 1930s, it was national security that would drive on the greatest expansion of the state.

8

Division and Unity

In the year following the 1935 election, a series of events overseas – the continuing conflict in Abyssinia, Hitler's reoccupation of the Rhineland and the opening of the Spanish Civil War – exercised a heavy influence on British politics. Their effect was fissiparous: in some cases intensifying divisions between right and left, but also splintering political parties and the peace movement among themselves. British politics might have been polarized by the crumbling of peace, but the political system of the 1930s did not fracture. The resolution of a further crisis, this time over the Abdication, allowed Baldwin to stage a remarkable comeback in the twilight of his premiership.

'THE REALISATION OF WHAT SANCTIONS MEAN'

No sooner had the government been returned to office on the basis of its commitment to collective security than it was revealed that Hoare had in the meantime agreed a secret deal with his counterpart, the French foreign minister Pierre Laval, to acquiesce in the Italian seizure of Abyssinia.[1] Amid outrage from all sides, Baldwin disclaimed all knowledge of the scheme, temporarily removed Hoare from office, and appointed Anthony Eden in his stead.

Although he was a son of the landed gentry, Eden was a progressive politician who appealed to people who weren't diehard Conservatives. He was young – just thirty-eight when he became foreign secretary – and good-looking, with a matinee idol's moustache. He had served as a junior officer in the First World War, in which both his brothers died.

Like many younger Conservatives, Eden came back from the trenches convinced that something needed to be done to improve the lot of the working class. In the aftermath of the slaughter, he had also become convinced that nations ought to work together to end the scourge of war. As a junior minister at the Foreign Office in the 1920s, he had established a reputation as an enthusiast for the League of Nations. Despite the fact that he had initially supported Hoare's plan, he was seen as the moral alternative, and was hence the ideal man to restore the government's reputation. It was an extremely popular appointment. In a government of old men, Anthony Eden looked like the future.[2]

Attempts to placate Italy were now abandoned in favour of slightly more stringent sanctions. In practice, however, the League of Nations proved unable to forge, let alone enforce, the international economic embargo that might have made Italy disgorge its conquests. Without French, American or German participation, British economic sanctions had little effect, and by the end of April 1936 the Abyssinian forces had been completely defeated.

Meanwhile, Hitler used the ratification of the Franco-Soviet pact in Paris in February as a justification for another long-planned act of aggression. On 7 March, with the world's eyes still on Abyssinia, his troops marched back into the Rhineland – a key industrial area in western Germany, demilitarized after 1918 to allow the French an easy invasion route into their old enemy in the event of another war. Here was another direct challenge to the terms of Versailles, but one that neither the French nor the British government was minded to oppose by force of arms.

France, previously apparently immune to the worst of the Depression, was now tumbling into a series of financial and political crises that were worsened by the prospect of war. French ministers and generals did not want to fight, but they were quite happy to emphasize their bellicosity in order that the British would take the blame for not confronting Hitler. The British government, in turn, was not about to fight for a concession they had been willing to cede in any case. Hitler was left to incorporate a remilitarized Rhineland, a success that emboldened him to open the question of a return of Germany's former colonies. What seemed, in retrospect, like the most clear-cut moment at which Hitler could have been 'stopped' passed almost without comment. Hitler was astonished at the French and British passivity.

From the end of 1935, the failure of collective action over Abyssinia and the rise of German power ensured that foreign policy remained a key topic of political debate. Conservative MPs shared in and responded to the public outrage at the revelation of the Hoare–Laval discussions. For Conservative supporters of the League, Hoare had betrayed Britain's international obligations. Eden thought that Italy was a bigger threat than Germany. Even the majority of Conservatives who lacked faith in the Geneva organization were conscious of the weight of pro-League sentiment in their constituency postbags. From the backbenches, Sir Austen Chamberlain pressurized the government to get rid of Hoare and to try to assert Britain's global authority, but was encouraged to muffle his attacks by a veiled – and ultimately unfulfilled – promise of a return to the Foreign Office.

The imperialist wing of the party, meanwhile, had fewer concerns about Abyssinia's right to independence, but feared that Hoare's conniving had undermined Britain's international reputation and status. Once he was gone, however, they became worried, as before, that a confrontation with Italy in the Mediterranean would threaten imperial security. Their sense that the Empire was at risk was heightened when it appeared that the government was in fact ready to discuss German demands to return the colonies ceded at Versailles.

For all Conservatives, Hitler's incursion into the Rhineland strengthened the belief that unnecessary and ineffective sanctions were pushing Germany and Italy into alliance and weakening Britain's position in Europe. The Rhineland crisis also brought out Conservatives' Francophobia. Since the mechanisms of collective security were broken – as most presumed they were after Abyssinia – the UK should not tie itself into any firmer system of continental alliances of the kind that had proved ruinous in 1914.

This was also Baldwin's view. As he pointed out in private, the effect of the Abyssinian crisis was to make an anti-League argument for him: 'One thundering good thing we have got out of it is the realisation of what sanctions mean. They mean that we have got to be much more self-contained. Europe had to be rearmed and to be ready, that is the conclusion that follows upon collective security.'[3] The prime minister's hands-off approach to foreign policy created a strong impression in his own party that he was letting policy drift just when what was needed was decisive action. Those Conservatives who wanted rapprochement with Italy worried that his unwillingness to take a stand would carry the country into an unnecessary war.

Neville Chamberlain was convinced that sanctions were illogical. At the end of May, he pressed the Cabinet to abandon them. When a decision was delayed, he made a widely reported speech stating that collective security as practised by the League had 'failed to prevent war, failed to stop war, failed to save the victims of aggression'. Continuing sanctions in the current circumstances would be 'the very midsummer of madness'. This deliberate attempt to force through his preferred policy worked. On 18 June 1936, Eden announced the end of sanctions.

In late July, Baldwin submitted to backbench pressure and met a delegation of senior Conservatives, who offered him two days' worth of advice on strategy and foreign affairs. The prime minister made it clear that if Hitler went 'stark mad' and attacked France or Belgium, Britain would have to go to their aid. He was, however, certainly 'not going to get this country into a war with anybody for the League of Nations or anybody else or for anything else'. To that end, he hoped that German ambitions might now be directed eastwards, on the basis that if there had to be a war, it should be between 'Bolshies' and 'Nazis'.[4] This more explicitly isolationist approach at least provided a policy direction around which the bulk of Conservatives could rally.

By August 1936, Baldwin was exhausted. His health broken, he was ordered to take a prolonged rest, during which Chamberlain effectively took charge of the government. Baldwin had already resolved that he would resign as soon as Edward VIII, brought to the throne by his father's death in January, was safely crowned.

ARMS AND THE MEN

Meanwhile, fed by repeated revelations of German strength, Britain's rearmament programme had continued to grow.[5] In February 1936, the Cabinet approved a new scheme for the period 1937–42 that included the construction of seven battleships and four aircraft carriers, and the expansion of the RAF's UK-based squadrons to at least 1,500 aircraft – more if the German air force kept getting larger. For all Baldwin's earlier promises that there would be no arms race, this was a programme designed to ensure that the UK maintained the world's most powerful fleet and developed one of its strongest air forces, but the point was still to deter a war, not to fight one.

The price of rearmament also kept growing. Defence spending for the financial year 1935–36 was £137 million pounds: higher, as a proportion of GDP, than it had been since the early 1920s. At the start of 1936, it was estimated that the new programme would cost at least another £1,000 million by the early 1940s.[6] To start to meet these costs, Chamberlain increased the basic rate of income tax in his April 1936 budget by 1¼ per cent and introduced a controversial levy on sugar, while Treasury officials prepared to raise a defence loan to cover future expenditure. In striking contrast to their attitude to deficit spending on public works to reduce unemployment, borrowing for defence was seen as an acceptable short-term solution to the problem of national security.

As it turned out, increases in revenue made a loan unnecessary in 1936. The Treasury tried to retain a leash on spending, but its key aim was less to hold back rearmament than to match it to strategic priorities, as the key debates revolved around industrial rather than financial capacity.

The last war had educated a generation of strategists in the importance of mass production. Throughout the inter-war period, military contracts were placed to try to maintain munitions-building capacity, and it was generally acknowledged that another major conflict would see massive government intervention to expand and direct armaments production. Everybody knew that this would have to happen in the event of another war, but how far it should happen in peace was a different matter. Intervening to escalate munitions production would be an expensive and economically disruptive process. It would also be politically costly, not least because, in the era of dictatorship and central planning, it carried overtones of the state suborning private enterprise. Since the aim of British strategy was still deterrence, defence programmes targeted increases in front-line strength that would put off potential opponents, not the wholesale shifting over of industry towards a wartime level of munitions output.

Even this more limited approach to rearmament, however, posed its own set of problems. The UK had at this time no single Ministry of Defence, but rather separate service ministries – the Admiralty,

War Office and Air Ministry – to represent each of the armed services. While the government owned some munitions factories and dockyards, the bulk of military equipment was bought from private contractors with which the individual service ministries negotiated design briefs and orders. As the forces all entered into their expansion programmes, their demands competed for limited industrial capacity without regard for strategic priority. They competed not only with each other, but also with purchasers from overseas and the demands of civilian consumption at home. During 1936, instances increased of rearmament being delayed by bottlenecks in production. By the end of the year it was apparent that aircraft deliveries in particular were well down on the targets laid out that spring. As the government spent more, however, suspicions also grew about the healthy profits being made by the arms industry. Together, these provided the context for a debate about whether to step up state control.

In January 1936, Lord Weir – a Scottish industrialist who had overseen an exponential increase in aircraft output during the last war, and was now advising the government on future arms production – sounded a warning to ministers about the demands of the expanded rearmament programme. Its completion, he wrote, would require either a 'semi-war organisation' of industrial controls or a reduction in 'normal civil activity and our export trade'. Weir opposed the first as a concession to socialism and the second as a threat to the economic recovery. When the Cabinet approved the programme the following month, it therefore decided not to instruct industry to prioritize defence orders, but did agree to invest more money in increasing capacity. This would happen through a 'shadow factory' scheme, under which automobile companies agreed to build new plants on the government's account to mass-produce planes and aero-engines designed by aircraft manufacturers. In two years' time, when these factories came on line, they would help to ensure the completion of Britain's deterrent air force.

Experts such as Weir were convinced that the limited availability of skilled workers in the engineering sector would be a critical obstacle to expanding arms production. In the last war, this obstacle had been overcome by 'diluting' the workforce – breaking down manufacturing processes into simpler operations that could be performed by less qualified workers while paying skilled engineers more to oversee their new colleagues. Such schemes could only be put in place with the agreement of trade unionists with their own set of concerns: a desire to see jobs brought to their members who were still unemployed; an insistence that they too should benefit from fat arms contracts; and a fear that, if no war came, the current boom in arms production would be followed by a slump that would leave skilled workers on the streets. The government shied away from intervening in questions of industrial relations, worried that discussions at a national level with trade union leaders would be encumbered by its ideological differences with Labour. Instead, 'dilution' was left to be settled at a local level by negotiation in individual factories.

In early 1936, under parliamentary pressure over problems in production, Baldwin created the new post of minister for co-ordination of defence. Churchill held back in his criticisms of the government in the hope that he might be given the job. It would offer a dynamic leader the chance to invigorate industry, drive on rearmament and increase his political capital. For precisely these reasons, Baldwin and Chamberlain had no intention of giving it to him. Instead, the post went to the former attorney general, Sir Thomas Inskip. His role was not to instruct industry, but rather to align competing demands for scarce industrial resources. Churchill's cronies caricatured Inskip as an incapable yes-man, and called his appointment 'the most cynical . . . since Caligula made his horse a pro-consul'. Unlike their man, Inskip's equine qualities tended more to the cart-horse than the show pony, but this was no disadvantage in his efforts to achieve compromises that would square the circle of genuine strategic difficulty.

Disappointed, Churchill now ramped up his attacks on the government. In the budget debate in April, he argued that peacetime standards were insufficient to the defence crisis now facing the nation: 'we must substitute other conditions – not necessarily war conditions, but conditions which would impinge upon the ordinary daily life and business of this country'.[7] When he went with other backbenchers to visit Baldwin at the end of July, he put a figure on that sacrifice: 25 to 30 per cent of the key engineering industries must be devoted to the manufacture of arms.

From the moment he arrived in his new job, Inskip too had pondered whether the government ought to intervene in industrial production. As Weir, Chamberlain and the Treasury all made plain, such interference would come at a cost: a reduction in engineering exports that would 'lose a large part of our world market not merely temporarily but probably forever', and an impingement on domestic consumption requiring 'a degree of forbearance on the part of the community which would only be forthcoming in the face of grave and imminent emergency'.[8] As Chamberlain explained:

> I do not believe that it *is* imminent. By careful diplomacy I believe we can stave it off, perhaps indefinitely, but if we were now to follow Winston's advice and sacrifice our commerce to the manufacture of arms we should inflict a certain injury on our trade from which it would take generations to recover, we should destroy the confidence which now happily exists and we should cripple the revenue.[9]

Inskip was duly persuaded against greater measures of compulsion.

Churchill was not mollified. Since Inskip was not controlling industry, he returned to demands for the formation of a Ministry of Supply to direct the provision of materiel. In mid-November 1936, when Liberal MPs tabled an amendment to the King's Speech calling for the nationalization of the defence industries, in the hope that eliminating profit would halt the arms race, Churchill took the opportunity to accuse the government of wasting time in a period of 'procrastination, of half measures, of soothing and baffling expedients, of delays'. Whatever its ambitious programmes for the future, he charged, for the next eighteen months the armed forces would be dangerously weak in the face of a revitalized Germany.[10]

Defending himself, Baldwin blamed past public opinion for current deficiencies in defence. Looking back to 1933 and 1934, he argued that there had been a 'stronger pacifist feeling running through this country than at any time since the war'. Nonetheless he had managed, during the 1935 election, to secure public support for rearmament, something which would not have been possible if he had spoken out more ardently at an earlier date. The result, however, was that democratic Britain was lagging two years behind dictatorial Germany in its military preparations.[11]

At the time, the prime minister's colleagues thought this a poor performance: 'a terrible confession of weakness and an unnecessary gift to the opposition'.[12] Ever since, Baldwin's words have been turned against him to accuse him of putting party interests ahead of national security. The charge is inaccurate: the government had certainly shaped its presentation of rearmament for electoral effect, but a fear of the political implications of popular pacifism had not slowed down rearmament. What Baldwin omitted, however, was the prolonged process of official negotiation between the decision to re-arm in 1933 and the actual inauguration of a new defence programme in 1934–35.

The lack of urgency in these discussions might have delayed the start of rearmament, but it did not necessarily leave Britain less well prepared for the conflict that eventually developed in 1939. In the aircraft industry – the key concern for politicians living under the shadow of the bomber – the issue impeding production for the moment was not a shortage of labour, finance or official direction, but rather the need to adapt to a period of dramatic change in aircraft design, as the fabric-covered, open-cockpit biplanes of an earlier era gave way to a new generation of enclosed monoplanes, metal skinned, tubular strutted and capable of dramatically improved performance. These aircraft required not only new skills and new assembly lines for their manufacture, but also, since they were being pressed into development more quickly, more modifications – and concomitant delays – as they moved from prototypes into mass production. This was the reason that the deliveries of the most modern aircraft ordered during 1936 were initially so disappointing.

This was a problem that would only be solved by the accumulation of industrial experience. Throwing a Churchillian supply supremo into the mix would probably have generated more confusion than progress. Quite aside from its possible economic consequences, an all-out programme of military expansion in the mid-1930s would have lumbered Britain with a fleet of immediately out-dated aircraft. Since Churchill's predictions of an imminent attack proved wrong, Britain's cautious start to rearmament actually left it better prepared than it would otherwise have been for the war that actually began at the end of the decade.

These debates around the co-ordination, direction and control of military supplies would rumble on throughout the years that followed. They got to the heart of the dilemma facing democratic politicians in the second half of the 1930s: how far should they subordinate freedom and prosperity to security? It was typical of the age that these debates focused on military technology, the profit motive and the role of the state. Yet they also developed into a thoroughfare for political ambition. In the era of total war, the man who controlled munitions production would exert unparalleled powers over national life.

DEFENDING THE EMPIRE

The proliferation of Britain's potential maritime opponents, the belated start to naval rearmament and the furore over the threat from the air all meanwhile had implications for the defence of the Far East.[13] The launch of powerful new German commerce raiders (armed merchant vessels) and the risk of a war with Italy in the Mediterranean both required the Royal Navy to commit its capital ships to European waters. Though the Admiralty was now embarking on a major new programme of construction, battleships and aircraft carriers took time to build. Older ships were taken out of action as they were refitted to bring them up to date. Yet the commitment to send a fleet to Singapore in the event of hostilities with Japan remained the centrepiece of defence planning in the Far East. As the base at Singapore approached completion, the gap between commitments and resources was reflected in the drawing out of the 'period before relief' – the time that it was expected to take to assemble and despatch a fleet, and for it to then reach Singapore – from six weeks to seventy days in 1937. Privately, the Admiralty already thought that six months would be more likely. In that length of time, a Japanese attack might do serious damage to the British Empire.

As the 'period before relief' elongated over the final years of the 1930s, the governments of Australia and New Zealand repeatedly sought confirmation from the British that they intended to live up to their promises to defend the Empire. As they prioritized the more imminent dangers in Europe, the British authorities became increasingly slippery about how they expressed their determination. Everyone concerned studiously avoided the sort of showdown that might have exposed the redundancy of the 'Singapore strategy'. The British did not want an argument that would threaten Commonwealth unity – not least because Canada and South Africa did not share the same defence priorities as the Pacific Dominions. The Australians and New Zealanders wanted to stick with their existing defence plans – which did not include bearing the full financial burden of protecting themselves against Japan. No one wanted to make a public admission of imperial weakness that would only encourage the Germans, Italians and Japanese.

Meanwhile, plans for the defence of Singapore were overhauled. Originally, the naval base had been defended only against an attack from the sea, since the Malayan peninsula was presumed to be effectively impassable. Since the 1920s, however, the economic development of Malaya had resulted in a good network of roads and ports. Not only would the fleet take longer to arrive, but the base was now exposed to an attack from the north. From the late 1920s, the RAF, ever keen to demonstrate the importance of an independent air force, had angled to take over the strategic burden in the Far East. In 1936, the chiefs of staff agreed that the air force should assume responsibility for the immediate defence of the Far Eastern theatre, although still with the aim of protecting Singapore as a base for the fleet, and the RAF started work on constructing the airfields in Malaya from which British planes were meant to dominate the surrounding area. By now, however, its main focus was on building up its strength in the UK, rather than in the Empire. Just as with the naval base, the British built the facilities for a future war and hoped that they could find the forces to fight it.

The new airfields were built without reference to the army, but they had important implications for the soldiers who would have to fight for Malaya on the ground. If the airfields could not be protected, then an invader would be gifted positions from which to control the skies. To make the most use of aircraft range, some of these airfields were in the north of Malaya. In order to protect them, and to guard against the risk of being outflanked by an invasion further south, the army would have to defend the whole of the peninsula at the same time. The only way to make the new strategy for defending Singapore work was through massive reinforcements of planes and soldiers. As the European crisis remained unresolved, the defence of the Far East became even more a matter of bluff.

In the Middle East, meanwhile, the rise of tensions with Italy had made the British increasingly concerned to protect their position in case of a future war. Although Britain had formally granted Egypt its independence in 1922, the British maintained a substantial military garrison in the country. This enabled them to protect the Suez Canal, but it was also one of the means by which the British could influence Egyptian politics. Egypt was notionally a constitutional monarchy, and politics between the wars had been a three-way struggle between the king, the British and the Wafd – a well-organized nationalist party which usually did well at the ballot box. Since the Egyptians had never accepted the terms on which they had been granted independence, the British military occupation remained without legal basis. During the first half of 1936, however, the threat from Italy made both the Egyptian nationalist government and the British eager to come to an agreement that would bolster their security. On 22 August, they signed a twenty-year treaty that gave Egypt more control of its own armed forces and eliminated the extraterritorial privileges previously enjoyed by Europeans in Egypt. In turn, the British kept their military bases close to the Canal, and accepted a limitation of the garrison to a maximum of 10,000 troops.[14]

That limitation only increased the strategic importance to Britain of Palestine, which had been mandated to the UK by the League of Nations in 1922, and would provide a crucial assembly point for imperial troops in the event of a European war. Yet in Palestine, the British were now facing the consequences of the conflicting promises that they had made to Arab and Jewish nationalists at the height of the Great War. Under the Balfour Declaration of 1917, a White Paper of 1922 and the terms of the League of Nations' Mandate, the British were committed to facilitating Jewish immigration and the creation of a Jewish national home. In Britain, there was substantial political support for Zionism, which was seen as a means to further Palestine's economic development and secure the position of the British Empire. The same documents, however, also bound the British to protect the rights of the existing Palestinian population, the majority of whom were Arab, and to develop representative government within the Mandate.[15]

During the 1920s, Palestinian Arabs began to organize themselves politically for the first time. In London, proposals for greater self-government were repeatedly blocked because it was feared that if the Arabs were given control of their own affairs, they would ban further Jewish immigration. In turn, the Arabs lost faith in British claims to impartiality. These tensions in the Mandate were turned into a crisis by the influx of Jewish refugees after Hitler came to power in Germany in 1933. At a point where most countries maintained strict border controls, Palestine was one place that Jews escaping persecution in Europe could enter fairly easily.

Concerned that they would eventually be turned into a minority,

Arab leaders wanted Jewish immigration to stop. Violence flared over the winter of 1935, and in April 1936 Arab workers began a well-supported general strike. During the summer, Arab guerrillas attacked Jewish settlements and cut the oil pipeline that ran across the north of Palestine. The British responded with a tough security crackdown that embraced collective punishment, including the destruction of houses, for communities thought to be harbouring insurgents. The colonial authorities and the military disagreed about how much force could be used to repress the uprising but, as the revolt continued over the summer, the military won out. The British brought in more soldiers and threatened to introduce martial law if the strike was not brought to an end. In October 1936, a ceasefire was negotiated while a British royal commission considered Palestine's future.

POPULAR FRONTS

During 1936, France and Spain elected Popular Front governments composed of broad spectra of left-wing parties.[16] This encouraged similar efforts in Britain to forge political alliances that could challenge the National Government. They came from two different directions.

The first derived from moves to align Labour, Liberals and dissident Conservatives in a progressive partnership to unseat Baldwin's coalition of the moderate right. The Next Five Years Group began exploring such ideas in 1935, although it took until the end of 1936 to launch a campaign for a 'People's Front'. It received support from the rebel Tories Harold Macmillan and Robert Boothby, but also from Liberals, including Sir Walter Layton, the editorial director of the *News Chronicle* (which advocated such an alliance in its pages), and the newly elected MP for Barnstaple, Richard Acland, who saw much common ground between Liberal aspirations and Labour's socialism. The People's Front was also backed by the Communist writer John Strachey, and G. D. H. Cole, the Labour intellectual. Cole argued that, given the swing that would be needed to transform the party's 1935 performance into an outright victory, such an alliance was the only way of achieving power in the next decade.

The second driver towards co-operation on the left originated from the key shift in international Communist strategy. In 1935, Moscow instructed Communist parties around the world to abandon class war in favour of constructing 'united fronts' of all working-class organizations, which would then build tactical alliances with other left-wing parties. This change underpinned the creation of Popular Front governments elsewhere in Europe. From 1936, the Communist Party of Great Britain campaigned to be allowed to affiliate with Labour.

A third impetus came from the maverick King's Counsel, Sir Stafford Cripps. Cripps the son of a rich lawyer, had trained as a chemist before becoming a barrister. He had run one of the biggest munitions factories in Britain for the Ministry of Munitions during the last war, before carving out a sparkling career at the Bar. Herbert Morrison encouraged him to join the Labour Party, and in 1930 he was made solicitor-general in the Labour government and found a safe parliamentary seat in Bristol. Having retained his seat in 1931, he was left as one of Labour's leading lights in the Commons.

Cripps was a man of faiths, and in the early 1930s he embraced Marxism with an ardent fervour. Through a new organization, the Socialist League, he tried to push Labour further left, against the moderation of the unions, and he spoke of class war and revolution. He was also a man of wealth, who was funding the League, paid the set up and running costs of the left-wing newspaper *Tribune* and had provided funds to relieve the financial strain on Attlee when he was acting as deputy leader. More moderate Labour figures groaned at the way that Cripps' extremist views kept giving ammunition to the Tory-supporting press, but he remained a star turn in the Commons (even though he loathed its boozy atmosphere, which encouraged him to become teetotal), and he did not stage his own bid for the leadership. Cripps denounced sanctions against Italy and rearmament on the basis that they were policies put forward by politicians who were the enemies of the working class. Since war and Fascism were the product of capitalism and imperialism, the only hope was working-class solidarity at home and internationally, and the Socialist League called for a united front with the ILP and the Communists.[17]

The different 'fronts' that arose after 1935 were connected by the growing sense of a Manichaean struggle with Fascism and a rising disgust at the government's foreign policy. Many of those who sought to form popular fronts believed, like Cripps and A. J. Cummings, the *News Chronicle*'s editor, that they were the only alternative to a 'boiled-shirt fascism' incipient in the National Government and which would be brought to the surface in the event of war.[18] Even those who did not think like this might be persuaded of the need for electoral alliances to displace an administration that was fatally mishandling world events. During 1936, the Liberal Party recognized the need for rearmament, and its leader, Sir Archibald Sinclair, furiously attacked the government for its abandonment of Abyssinia. Sinclair's conviction that a change of government was a precondition of effective rearmament and a moral foreign policy made him more sympathetic to the idea of a progressive pact.

By the end of 1936, anxieties about the rising tide of Fascism had been further stoked by the Spanish Civil War. On 17 July, an attempted Nationalist coup led by General Francisco Franco, against the government of the Republican Popular Front, sparked off a ferocious three-year conflict. Germany and Italy swiftly intervened to help the Nationalists, transporting soldiers from Spain's North African colonies, supplying weapons and before long sending 'volunteers' to join in the fighting.

In Britain, ministers and officials worried that the conflagration of ideological extremes in Spain would engulf the whole of Europe. Their primary concern was not, therefore, to protect the democratically elected Spanish government but rather, as Eden told the House of Commons at the start of 1937, to make sure that: 'the conflict shall not spread beyond the boundaries of Spain'. The British government pressured the French Popular Front to minimize any aid to their comrades across the Pyrenees: instead, the two governments set up an international agreement on non-intervention, backed up by naval patrols and a supervisory committee in London. This did nothing in practice to reduce German and Italian involvement, but it did leave the Republic dependent on Soviet military aid for its survival. Until the end of 1936, a swift Nationalist victory appeared certain, but the Republicans managed to hold out, and after a year of war a military stalemate had set in across central Spain with Republican garrisons besieged along the northern coast.

British public interest in the Spanish Civil War took time to get going. Spain was little considered before the conflict broke out, its politics complicated by factors – extremist factionalism and the place of the Catholic Church – that seemed very foreign to most Britons. The wave of violent atrocities on both sides at the start of the war aroused wide-spread condemnation and further alienated British commentators.[19]

The situation changed, however, over the winter of 1936–37. First, as the Republic's military and political situation stabilized, the conflict could be understood more easily as a two-way fight rather than a descent into anarchy. Secondly, British involvement increased. Disregarding official attempts to limit involvement, British volunteers arrived in Spain and found their way to the front line. The majority of the several thousand British volunteers served with Republican forces, most of them as part of the British battalion of the International Brigade, which saw action for the first time in the early months of 1937. Most were young working-class men, although a cohort of middle-class intellectuals linked the war directly to progressive opinion at home. Many had been politically active, and the CPGB played a significant role in recruiting, but while most were set on socialism, for many the rationale for fighting was to defend democracy rather than to inspire world revolution. A smaller, less celebrated number of volunteers – a mix of zealous Catholics, aristocratic adventurers and Fascist fellow travellers – also journeyed to Spain, to fight for the Nationalists. At the same time, a British home front developed in this foreign war as a result of efforts to aid its refugees. Local welfare campaigns sprang up across the country, co-ordinated from the start of 1937 by a National Joint Committee for Spanish Relief. That spring, the arrival of boatloads of child evacuees from the Basque ports provided dramatic evidence of the war's victims and elicited much sympathy.

Few Britons were fully conversant with the labyrinthine complexities of Spanish politics, but from the end of 1936 the war provided an easily accessible arena in which to play out their own anxieties about violence, democracy and dictatorship. In terms of public debate, it tended to polarize existing party political positions. Most Conservatives backed the government and accepted its argument about the need to contain the contagion. Imperialist fears about the implications of German or Italian influence for Gibraltar were less significant than the desire to avoid a Communist takeover, and a significant minority of Tories actively supported the Nationalists as opponents of international Bolshevism.

In contrast, the majority of the British left, convinced that this was part of a wider fight to save democracy, became increasingly committed to the Republican cause and antagonized by the unequal effects of non-intervention. The government's refusal to help the Republic was seen as the equivalent of its abandonment of the unemployed and evidence of its underlying support for Fascism. Criticism from Labour and Liberal MPs became increasingly vituperative, and demands rose for the supply of arms in order at least to level the playing field of non-intervention. The role played by the Communist Party in mobilizing direct support for Spain was the principal factor in a significant rise in its membership during the late 1930s: it did particularly well in appealing to potential recruits from the ancient universities who wanted actively to oppose Fascism. Surveys published by the *News Chronicle* also suggested that the weight of public opinion was increasingly siding with the Republic, probably because, outside Britain's Catholic communities, it was perceived as an embodiment of organized labour or as the fairly elected underdog. Here too, it seemed, was fertile ground for the formation of a centre-left front that linked progressive aspirations at home with the defence of democracy abroad.[20]

Some fronts did form. In the two years after its formation, as 'a sort of reading "Popular Front"' by the publisher Victor Gollancz, the Left Book Club, which made available cheap copies of key books with a left-wing perspective on current affairs, had 50,000 members. Its big print runs meant that it could claim plausibly to have reached beyond party confines and tapped into a broader body of public opinion that was worried by war, Fascism and the state of British society and sought more radical reforms than the National Government was ready to offer.[21] That this was a cause with potentially wide appeal, particularly when couched in less partisan terms than those favoured by the quasi-Communist Gollancz, was evidenced by the success of the Penguin Specials published by Allen Lane in the last years of the 1930s. A list curated to provide quality opinion at a reasonable price included works on ballet, literary taste and modern German art, but was dominated by works that took an anti-Fascist stance on international affairs, which sold in the hundreds of thousands. The sense that, in the face of a looming threat to civilization, progressive people should work together in the cause of democracy was also central to the ethos and early work of Mass-Observation, with its central alliance between a Communist, Madge, and a lapsed Liberal, Harrisson.

At a local level, there were also instances of successful co-operation on the basis of opposition to the government's foreign policy. In practice, any 'front' had little chance of unseating the government constitutionally until the next general election, which was due at the latest by 1940. By-elections, however, provided an opportunity for local alliances. At Derby in July 1936, and in three West Country constituencies in summer 1937, Liberal and Labour activists worked together against National candidates. In the former, the increased turnout probably played a major role in a Labour victory.

There were, however, insuperable obstacles to a Popular Front ever becoming an effective nationwide political force. The greatest of these was the Labour leadership. After its partial recovery in 1935, Labour would have been central to any successful alliance but, despite the enthusiasm of some party members, their leaders remained firmly opposed. Senior Labour politicians and trade union bosses regarded such suggestions from the left as attempts at a parasitic takeover. Quite aside from their personal loathing for Communists, they also recognized the electoral risks if they were to be tarred with the brush of political extremism. They vigorously challenged and threatened with expulsion anyone who promoted a 'front' that might include the CPGB. Cripps only avoided being expelled from the party by shutting down the Socialist League and the campaign for a united front.

Labour's leaders also saw more harm than good in an alliance towards the political centre. Whatever common ground they shared over the means of state intervention, they profoundly disagreed with progressive Liberals and Conservatives about the ends of achieving socialism and empowering the unions. Differences also remained over foreign policy. The Liberals came round during 1936 to supporting rearmament, but Labour MPs continued to vote against the defence budget to demonstrate their disapproval of the arms race.

With the memory of 1931 still fresh, any suggestion of a move towards the middle ground would have been easily cast as a betrayal of Labour's principles. More than that, a tactical realignment of Labour's position was strategically unnecessary. Unlike their counterparts in France and Spain, Labour's leaders did not believe that they faced an imminent threat to the democratic process from domestic Fascism. Citrine and Bevin in particular, the most powerful figures within the Labour movement as a whole, might have loathed the National

Government, but they did not believe that it was about to try, like the Nazis, to smash trade unionism.[22]

Rather than forming an emergency front, Labour could therefore play a longer game – avoiding any dilution of its party's values with political alliances, attempting to influence government policy as re-armament required greater co-operation with the unions, and hoping that future events would bring it to power on its own terms, if not at the next election then at least by the one after that.

It is hard to say whether this belief was well founded. Opinion polling in the later 1930s suggested simultaneously the popularity of Labour's proposed policies on health and welfare, and that very few people would vote differently to get them. The middle-class progressives who made up much of the audience for the Left Book Club and the Penguin Specials might have formed a 'reading popular front', but that did not mean that they were going to support a party still seen as economically and politically incompetent and overcommitted to the organized working class.

On Spain, Labour's policy was cautious, a position shaped primarily by Citrine and Bevin. In practice, neither had much love for the more extreme elements on the Republican side, and they tended to see Labour activists' desire to provide military aid as Communist-inspired threats to their authority. Along with a few right-wing Labour MPs, they had come round much earlier than the bulk of the party to supporting re-armament, but their belief that the UK needed to be protected from German aggression militated against sending weapons to the Republicans. Aware as they were of the shortfalls in production for the forces, Britain's leading trade unionists thought that those arms that were available probably ought to be used to defend the UK. They were also, however, sensitive to the risks that would be posed by a Fascist victory to Britain's position in the Mediterranean. As Bevin pointed out in August 1936: 'it would be a strange thing that it would fall to the lot of the Labour Party to save the British Empire'.[23]

Eager to avoid any equivalent fracture in British society – not least with their Catholic members, antagonized by Republican attacks on the Church – Citrine and Bevin preferred the equitable enforcement of an arms embargo to any actual embroilment in the Spanish Civil War. They tried to warn the government off policies that were too pro-Nationalist, but they also carefully diverted trade unionists' energies away from demands for military intervention and towards campaigns to provide welfare and medical aid for refugees. As Labour politicians struggled to define their own distinctive position beyond criticizing government policy, the party's apparent inactivity disappointed those who demanded 'arms for Spain' and allowed the Communists to make much of the running in actually assisting the Republic. The trade unions' stance, however, helped to ensure that reactions to the new Spanish ulcer were much less destructive in the UK than they were in France, where left and right were now at daggers drawn.[24]

Nonetheless, the threat of international conflict and the political polarization occasioned by the war in Spain made any cross-party political grouping much harder to maintain. During 1936, both tendencies afflicted the anti-war movement. The upsurge in international aggression raised divisive questions about the best response from those who wanted peace. One radical answer was a reassertion of absolute pacifism, as embodied in the Peace Pledge Union (PPU), inaugurated in 1936 by the Reverend Dick Sheppard – the charismatic former vicar of St-Martin-in-the-Fields, and now canon of St Paul's – who asked young men to promise that they would take no part in any future war. The messianic tone of Sheppard's crusade separated it from those who continued to espouse absolute pacifism on political, rather than religious, grounds, and who now worked to expand their own national network of peace councils to support local resistance to war. By autumn 1937, although wracked by internal disputes, the PPU had attracted considerable publicity and 120,000 members.[25]

In contrast, less extreme opponents of war drew the lesson from international inaction over Abyssinia that more concrete measures of collective security now needed to be put in place. That meant rebuilt defences and more formal alliances: an uncomfortably traditional form of power politics but one now increasingly at odds with government policy. The disagreement between pacifists and those willing to fight to preserve the peace opened up divisions within the League of Nations Union as it struggled with the League's embarrassing ineffectiveness in restraining Italy. Although it lost members during the second half of the decade, the LNU was still a significant organization, with a quarter of a million members in 1938, but it too was wracked by political differences. Over the summer of 1936, in an effort to rebuild the movement's popular foundations, Lord Cecil became involved with a new International Peace Campaign. This was a Europe-wide movement, which was particularly strong in France. Most of the LNU's staff regarded it as a front for Communism. This apparent move to the left made it much harder for the Union to stage its appeal to the public or government on the basis of being non-partisan. At the same time, however, the moderate stance of most of the LNU's remaining members also left it seeming boring and out of touch to the ardent young supporters of the Peace Pledge Union or the Communist Party of Great Britain. By the end of 1936, it was becoming increasingly difficult to occupy the political middle ground.[26]

'PREMIER TAKES STOCK, FINDS BRITAIN BEST'

Remarkably, given these foreign and domestic vicissitudes and his faltering health, Baldwin managed to re-forge his own popular front.[27] The prime minister's sense that he was building a moral case for resisting a global slide towards catastrophe exacerbated his distress when Edward VIII refused to place duty over pleasure. The grappling over Edward's fate also, however, afforded Baldwin an opportunity for political recovery as he performed once more his favourite role of national conciliator. As he reassured the country in a newsreel address issued in the middle of the discussions that led to Edward's abdication, and tellingly entitled 'Premier Takes Stock, Finds Britain Best': 'True to our traditions, we have avoided all extremes. We have steered clear of fascism, communism, dictatorship, and we have shown the world that democratic government, constitutional methods and ordered liberty are not inconsistent with progress and prosperity.'[28] While Margesson, the chief whip, made sure that Conservative MPs backed the government, Baldwin was able once more to turn the issue into one of responsibility. With a faulty king removed and a safer one put in his place, Baldwin retired straight after George VI's coronation, in a glow of non-partisan affection.

In contrast, the Abdication wrecked Churchill's efforts to secure a return to power. He too had sought during 1936 to construct an alliance of opinion on international affairs that would reach beyond party.

He tried to direct the League of Nations Union's attention to the danger from Germany. He also met with anti-Nazis – including Tories, Liberals, Citrine and leading Jewish businessmen – as part of a new group which titularly declared itself for the Defence of Freedom and Peace (also known as 'The Focus'). By the end of the year, these private meetings had transmuted into a public movement that held a great rally under the auspices of the LNU at the Albert Hall on 3 December. Speakers demanded a recommitment to the covenant of the League of Nations, greater rearmament and the incorporation of the USSR into a security framework designed to restrain Germany. Churchill's commitment to the latter point indicated an unusually continental perception of strategy. This marked him out from other Conservative dissidents on defence, such as Leo Amery, who preferred imperial isolation. Despite the suspicions aroused by his participation, this mobilization of internationalist opinion temporarily seemed to have the potential to propel Churchill back into cabinet orbit.

All this was ruined by the Abdication. Having established a friendship with the monarch when he was Prince of Wales, Churchill was seen to have a key position as the king's advisor. He argued that Baldwin's lining up of political opinion to force the king's hand was unconstitutional, and he hoped that, given time, Edward could be persuaded to give up his romantic attachment without renouncing the throne.

Lining up to protect the king alongside Churchill was his old friend Max Aitken, Lord Beaverbrook. A Canadian businessman who had left his homeland under a cloud of corruption allegations before the Great War, Aitken had become, after his arrival in Britain, a Conservative MP, a press magnate, a peer and then minister of information in 1918. His ascent had been much aided by a generous chequebook: Beaverbrook liked to put others in his debt.[29]

After the war, Beaverbrook had overseen the transformation of the *Daily Express* into the country's leading national daily. By the late 1930s, it had a circulation of 2.4 million. Determinedly opposed to the 'socialists' – as it called the Labour Party – the *Express* also set itself against unearned privilege and waste in high office, and for the 'little man' with aspirations to do well for himself. Although Beaverbrook let his editors, writers and cartoonists put across their own views where it was good for business, he used the *Express* as a megaphone for his own political opinions, and its leader writers soon learned to follow their master's strident, exhortatory style. Beaverbrook's deep pockets and influence with his fellow press lords gave him a power that he loved to exert, not only for personal and political gain but also for mischief and spite.

An outsider who desperately wanted to be on the inside, Beaverbrook had been very much at home in the dynamic world of the Lloyd George governments, but was left out of the 'responsible' politics of the 1930s. He and Baldwin loathed each other with a passion stoked by their confrontation over Empire Free Trade. Beaverbrook and Churchill, on the other hand, who had been friends since the former entered the Commons in 1911, remained on good terms even though they had differed over issues including the return to the gold standard, Indian constitutional reform and Beaverbrook's Empire Crusade. Their relationship became more distant during the 1930s because Beaverbrook thought Churchill's career was over and he would be no more use to him politically, but they were reunited by the debates over Edward VIII's love affair with Wallis Simpson. Both Churchill and Beaverbrook saw themselves as loyalists, who were sticking by a king betrayed by the unscrupulous Baldwin.

Initially, Beaverbrook followed the king's request to keep the affair out of the papers, and on Edward's behalf he lobbied his fellow press lords to do the same thing. From a modern perspective, what is astonishing is how easy it was to keep the story out of the public sphere. The press, the newsreels and the output of the BBC were controlled by a relatively small group of people who were interconnected by their own network of privilege and power, and who were strongly susceptible to appeals to propriety and the national interest. If they all decided that a story should be suppressed, then a conspiracy of silence could be very effectively maintained.[30]

Like everyone else, Beaverbrook had presumed that, eventually, Edward would be persuaded to give up his attachment to Wallis. Once the story broke, however, he threw the whole weight of his newspapers behind the monarch. 'We cannot afford to lose the King,' trumpeted the *Daily Express*. 'We cannot let him give up the throne.'[31] On this, as with pretty much everything else on which its master took a stand in the late 1930s, the paper was soon proved wrong.

Whatever Beaverbrook's motivation was for defending the king, most of the British political elite presumed that he had done so only in order to have another go at Baldwin. That only confirmed the widespread view of Beaverbrook's irresponsibility. Beaverbrook blamed the government chief whip for thwarting his ambitions: he never forgave Margesson.[32] Churchill's motives were regarded with similar suspicion. Most people at Westminster thought that he had tried to exploit a national tragedy to advance his own position. When he tried to speak up for Edward in the Commons, fellow MPs shouted him down. The collapse in his political stock doomed the always-unstable coalition around his Defence of Freedom and Peace Union, which swiftly disintegrated. It was one more episode to add to Churchill's record of adventurous failures.

'NO-ONE IS MORE CONVINCED THAN I AM OF THE NECESSITY FOR REARMAMENT'

There had never been much doubt that Neville Chamberlain would replace Baldwin. During the autumn of 1936, he had taken an even greater role in the formation of policy, including the reformulation of strategy away from a military commitment to mainland Europe and towards an even more substantial role for the RAF. He was widely seen as the prime-minister- and Conservative-leader-in-waiting. At the last moment, however, there was a minor but inauspicious stumble that reflected both the growing difficulties posed by rearmament and Chamberlain's continued devotion to grand solutions.

In early 1937, the chancellor announced that the government would take out a loan of up to £400 million to cover some of the £1,500 million it now expected to spend on defence over the next five years. This unlocking of further funds posed two problems. The first was that further resources would only increase the armed forces' demands. The second was the domestic impact as the scale of defence expenditure drove up inflation and allowed private arms manufacturers to build up huge profits. As he complained to his sister that spring: 'No-one is more convinced than I am of the necessity for rearmament & for speed in making ourselves safe', but the tensions thus created could all too easily result in

a series of crippling strikes, ruining our programme, a sharp steepening
of costs due to wage increases, leading to the loss of our export trade, a
feverish and artificial boom followed by a disastrous slump and finally
the defeat of the Government and the advent of an ignorant unprepared & heavily pledged Opposition to handle a crisis as severe as that
of 1931.[33]

In the April 1937 budget, his last as chancellor, Chamberlain therefore
put a further three pence on income tax, but also announced a new
National Defence Contribution – a tax on the growth in business profits during the period of rearmament, graduated according to a highly
complex formula so that those who had done best out of the international crisis would pay the most. This was intended to raise funds for
defence, demonstrate to the armed services that public resources were
finite and emphasize to the electorate not only that security came at a
price, but also that the government intended to spread that cost fairly.

Swiftly, however, the new tax ran into a storm of criticism. Almost
everyone believed that it was too complicated. For Labour it did too
little to control profiteering by private arms manufacturers. Conservative backbenchers saw it as an assault on business. Meanwhile share
prices fell as they had not done since the dark days of 1931, in turn
reducing the government's ability to borrow money for rearmament. In
the face of such opposition, as the budget passed through the Commons in May, the defence contribution was transmuted into a fixed rate
5 per cent tax on business profits. The mis-step did nothing to halt
Chamberlain's ascent to 10 Downing Street, but once again his desire
to deliver an interconnected cure-all had outreached his capacity for
political leadership.[34]

Nonetheless, when he succeeded Baldwin on 28 May 1937, Chamberlain was welcomed by the Conservative-supporting press as a
political strong man. He was the same age as Baldwin, and his Cabinet
had no one in it to do the administrative heavy lifting for him as he had
done for his predecessor. It was, however, precisely the new premier's
determination and drive that seemed set to reinvigorate the National
administration.

When Chamberlain came to construct his Cabinet, Margesson suggested that it might be a good idea to find a ministerial place for
Churchill. The new prime minister quickly dismissed the idea. He was

too busy to go to the coronation fleet review, but he noted with amusement that his wife, Annie, who went in his stead, had been 'fortunate in finding Winston', who proved only too 'delighted to show her how admirably he would fill the office' of first lord of the admiralty by talking her through the ships on display.[35] Chamberlain, however, had no intention of offering a ministerial position to a potential rival of unpredictable temperament, dubious loyalty and proven poor judgement. As he told his new secretary of state for war, Leslie Hore-Belisha, when the latter canvassed Churchill's inclusion, 'He won't give the others a chance of even talking.'[36] For all his naval ambitions, in the early summer of 1937, Churchill was marooned on the backbenches, his chances of seizing the tiller as distant as Labour's of winning the next election.

PART TWO

From Peace to War

9

'More sufferings to come'

A few seconds after eleven o'clock on 11 November 1937, the two minutes' silence of the Armistice Day ceremony at the Cenotaph in London was shockingly disrupted. A 'thick-set, fair-headed man, bare-headed, and wearing a mackintosh' broke through the line of sailors at the edge of the crowd. His shouts, 'in a high tormented voice', just audible to those listening to the ceremony on the wireless as well as those closest to the Cenotaph, protested against 'All this hypocrisy!': 'You are deliberately conniving at another war.' Several policemen – all remaining strictly silent – jumped on the lone protestor and subdued him. Aside from a few turned heads to see the cause of the noise, the king, his senior officers and ministers remained absolutely still.

Once the two minutes were up, the man who had broken the silence was removed. It was subsequently announced that he was Stanley Storey, a forty-three-year-old veteran who had recently escaped from the asylum to which he had been committed the previous February. His sense of upset, if not his accusation, aroused a widespread sympathy. As the *Manchester Guardian*'s reporter explained, his shout had not seemed the outburst of a lunatic, but rather:

> the agonised cry of one who had found the strain of the moment and of his own convictions too much to be borne. As such it heightened one's own feelings almost intolerably. There must be few people who can attend the celebrations of Armistice Day without having to thrust into the background of their minds the fear that all the suffering of twenty years ago has not prevented more sufferings to come.

During the final years of the 1930s, the sense that another world war was coming grew increasingly strong. The prolonged anticipation of this second cataclysm was one of the key differences from the outbreak of its predecessor, which had come as a total shock to Britons in the summer of 1914. In 1937, however, it did still seem that more sufferings might yet be averted.[1]

'FAR REACHING PLANS . . . FOR THE APPEASEMENT OF EUROPE & ASIA'

Neville Chamberlain arrived at 10 Downing Street determined to sort out a potentially disastrous international situation. Britain now faced the threat of three wars at the same time: with Germany in Europe, with Italy in the Mediterranean and with Japan in the Far East. As far as Chamberlain was concerned, collective security was dead and the League of Nations defunct. Of Britain's potential allies, France was politically unstable, the USSR was ideologically antipathetic and the USA was unreliably isolationist. Until Britain's rearmament programmes were more complete, it was in a vulnerable position, but the scale of those programmes themselves now threatened the economic revival. In this hazardous environment, keeping the British Empire safe would require a balancing act of global scope and epic complexity.

This was exactly the sort of problem that Chamberlain liked to solve. Five months into his premiership, he was already able to inform his sister that he had in mind 'far reaching plans . . . for the appeasement of Europe & Asia and for the ultimate check of the mad arms race, which if continued must involve us all in ruin'.[2] At the base of these plans were two presumptions. The first was that a war was in nobody's interest. The second was that it should be possible to resolve all the aggressor powers' grievances by a process of interlinked negotiation rather than ad hoc reaction. Being strong enough to make violence look unattractive was a key part of Chamberlain's approach, but he saw no point in making threats that the UK could not back up, nor in constructing alliances that might precipitate an unnecessary war.

Chamberlain found a welcome ally in the senior civil servant Sir Horace Wilson, already installed in Number 10 as a special advisor to the prime minister. Wilson was a self-made man. The son of a furniture maker, he had entered the civil service in 1900 as a boy clerk, then taken a part-time degree at the London School of Economics. Having established a reputation for settling difficult industrial disputes during the Great War, in 1921 he was appointed permanent secretary at the Ministry of Labour, where he played an important part in ending the General Strike. Although the unions resented him for his skill in unpicking their position before negotiations began, in 1930 the second Labour government made Wilson its chief industrial advisor, a title he retained for the rest of the decade. When Baldwin returned to Downing Street in 1935, he needed someone else to keep an overview of the business of government as it passed through the prime minister's office. Wilson was brought in to take up the job, and Chamberlain kept him on.[3]

The two men had got to know each other well during the Ottawa trade talks in 1932. They were both hardworking, seemingly humourless figures with a strong grip on administration. Chamberlain's personality meant that his colleagues seldom became his comrades, and of the people he worked with, Wilson became probably the closest thing that he had to a friend. Sir Horace's position was powerful: all the papers coming in and out of 10 Downing Street passed through his office, and Chamberlain valued his advice on economic policy and the composition of his cabinet. On 20 May 1939, Wilson was made permanent secretary of the Treasury and head of the civil service, which put him in charge of the appointment of all the senior officials in Whitehall.

Wilson's enemies saw him as a Cardinal Richelieu-like figure, pulling the strings of power behind the throne. Wilson maintained that he was servant, not master: he supported Chamberlain, but he did not control him.[4] Before long, however, Chamberlain would come to rely on Wilson as a diplomatic go-between as well as a domestic political fixer. This reflected not only their shared belief that the international problem could be solved by finding grounds for reasonable agreement, but also Chamberlain's desire, unlike his predecessor, to take firm control of foreign policy.

The new prime minister's determination to solve the European situation himself put him at loggerheads with the Foreign Office. His willingness to appease Hitler aroused shrill opposition from the Foreign Office's senior civil servant, Sir Robert Vansittart, a long-term Cassandra of the dangers of German revival. Chamberlain also found himself in disagreement with the foreign secretary, Anthony Eden, who had grown used to doing what he wanted while Baldwin was prime minister.

Over the rights and wrongs of German expansion in Central and Eastern Europe, Eden differed little from the prime minister, although given his liberal reputation he was anxious not to be seen to be giving in to dictators. Like Chamberlain, Eden also found Vansittart's incessant harping on the German threat unhelpful, and he had already lined up a possible replacement: Sir Alexander Cadogan, an aristocratic career diplomat whom Eden had got to know on Britain's delegation to the League of Nations. As soon as Baldwin had appointed him, Eden had invited Cadogan to return from his posting as ambassador to China so that he could serve as Vansittart's deputy and future successor. Where Vansittart was volatile, spiky and increasingly given to writing interminable memoranda on the need to stand up to Hitler, Cadogan was calm, smooth and pragmatic in his desire to match Britain's foreign policies with what it could actually do. For the moment, he was also more optimistic about the prospect of arranging a settlement with Germany.[5]

The thing that really set Chamberlain and Eden apart was the foreign secretary's hatred of Mussolini. The Italian dictator's broken promises about non-intervention in Spain had left Eden deeply suspicious of any rapprochement. Compared to Chamberlain, Eden was much less worried about the risk of the Empire being attacked simultaneously by Germany, Italy and Japan. That meant he had much more room to insist on a firm stance with the Duce.[6]

Chamberlain, however, saw an improvement of relations with Italy as a stepping-stone to a general European settlement. During the summer of 1937, he proffered recognition of Italy's conquest of Abyssinia in the hope of reducing tensions in the Mediterranean and severing the developing connection between Rome and Berlin. When Italy joined Germany and Japan in the Anti-Comintern Pact that November, he saw it as further evidence of the need to bring Mussolini back on side. For Eden, on the other hand, it was proof of the uselessness of relying on Italian promises.

In July 1937, a military scuffle between Chinese and Japanese forces in northern China escalated rapidly into a full-blown, but undeclared, war. As the Japanese armies advanced rapidly in the north, and fierce fighting raged all around the international settlement in Shanghai, China's Nationalist government sought international support. Eager to tie the Japanese down in China, the Soviet Union sent arms and military advisors, but would not sign an alliance that would drag the Red Army into the conflict. In the West, the Nationalists aimed their diplomatic efforts at the United Kingdom – supposedly the other major power in East Asia. Aware as they were of the weakness of their defences in the Far East, the British did not do much to help.

No British minister wanted to be dragged into a repeat of the Abyssinian debacle, with the League of Nations imposing sanctions and the Royal Navy forced into a naval confrontation with Japan as a result. London therefore carefully defused China's appeal to the League, removing any mention of a 'war', which would have compelled action from the signatories of the Washington Treaty, and condemning Japan's actions without binding the UK to do anything about them.

The brutal nature of Japan's assault outraged liberal opinion in Britain. Yet China was a long way away, and had been wracked by conflict for decades: in practice, the war there never quite engaged public sympathies in the same way as the struggle in Spain. In contrast, a combination of a missionary tradition, concern at Japanese expansionism and a desire to maintain a commercial open door all meant that there was a stronger pro-China lobby in the United States. The US president, Franklin Roosevelt, took the opportunity to try to educate American public opinion away from isolationism. On 5 October 1937, he gave a speech in which he called for the 'quarantine' of the nations that were spreading the 'disease' of 'world lawlessness'. Though the nations were not named, many listeners interpreted this as floating the prospect of economic sanctions against Japan.[7]

Chamberlain was sceptical. He suspected that Roosevelt wouldn't stick by his words, but there was also the awful prospect that he would – and that Britain would then have to reject sanctions because, with the European situation as yet unresolved, it could not bear the danger of a war in the Far East. The prime minister believed that Japan too could be appeased, and he did not want American idealism disrupting his own pragmatic pursuit of peace. Again, Eden disagreed. He shared Chamberlain's concerns, but he argued that any opportunity for Anglo-American co-operation must be pursued. Precarious as Britain's position in the Far East was, what it really needed now was a closer relationship with the United States. When it turned out that Roosevelt had never intended to initiate any sort of embargo, Chamberlain was vindicated. As he had always thought, America might be the 'power that had the greatest strength', but 'it would be a rash man who based his calculations on help from that quarter'.[8]

In January 1938, Roosevelt put out secret feelers about a possible world conference, in which the democracies would offer greater access to raw materials in return for the dictators acting less aggressively. Chamberlain rebuffed them. That snub occasioned another fight with his foreign secretary. Once more, Roosevelt's proposals came to nothing, but the gap between the prime minister and his foreign secretary continued to grow.

Chamberlain was not, however, averse to closer co-operation with the United States. Economic relations offered one avenue for a better transatlantic relationship. In the course of 1937, he convinced the Cabinet and Dominion ministers that the UK should accept a request from the US secretary of state, Cordell Hull, for negotiations about reducing trade barriers between the USA and the British Empire. For Hull, the liberalization of world trade was the only route to restoring global peace. For Chamberlain, the discussions were a way to educate Americans in the fundamental soundness of British diplomacy. To that end, he was willing to concede reductions in imperial preference.[9]

In the early months of 1938, as the US trade negotiations rumbled on, Chamberlain also tried to improve Anglo-Irish relations. Here too, Chamberlain was willing to offer up concessions in the hope of an improvement in atmosphere. Controversially, this included ceding control of the 'treaty ports' – three harbours on the western Irish coast from which naval power could be projected far out into the Atlantic, which had been retained by the British after 1921. Since, realistically, they could not have been defended against a hostile hinterland in time of war, Chamberlain thought they were better returned to Irish hands in the hope of friendship in the future. When the prime minister managed to settle the deal himself in direct talks with the Irish taoiseach, Éamon de Valera, it confirmed his faith in the power of personal negotiation.[10]

'IF YOU CAN GET THEM BY PEACEFUL MEANS'

Bereft of formal opportunities to establish communications with Hitler, Chamberlain seized on the chance of a social invitation in November 1937 to the lord president of the council, Lord Halifax, to attend an international sporting exhibition in Berlin. During his visit, Halifax dropped in on the Führer to try to establish his intentions.

Eight years before, as Lord Irwin, Halifax had sought to rally moderate opinion by offering India Dominion status. After returning to the UK in 1931, he had served as a minister for education and for the army. In 1934, he succeeded to his father's peerage and became the third Viscount Halifax.[11] By now, his moral authority was such that he could be regarded, as one observer put it, as more 'a Prince of the Church' than 'a politician'.[12] In foreign affairs, he started from the same point as the prime minister: a reasonable treatment of German demands must be the route to a lasting peace.

Arriving at his first meeting with Hitler, Halifax narrowly avoided mistaking him for a footman.[13] He left unsure as to whether the Nazi leader could grasp the concept of a 'general settlement'. Nonetheless, they had talked over territorial revisions in Central Europe. Hitler wanted to incorporate the German-speaking peoples of the old Habsburg Empire – which had never been part of Germany – into his new Reich. That included a German union with Austria – the *Anschluss* – and the annexation from Czechoslovakia of the Sudetenland – a region where the majority German-speaking population was mixed up with a Czech-speaking minority. Halifax reported back to the Cabinet that these issues could be resolved by negotiation. For Chamberlain, it was the only sensible solution. Why not, he wondered, just tell the Germans: 'Give us satisfactory assurances that you won't use force to deal with Austrians & Czecho-slovakians & we will give you similar assurances that we won't use force to prevent the changes you want if you can get them by peaceful means.'[14]

As 1938 began, the prime minister and the lord president explored a variety of means of improving Anglo-German relations. Vansittart was kicked upstairs to a new post as 'chief diplomatic advisor'. Although comparisons were drawn with Sir Horace Wilson's place as chief industrial advisor, in this case the intention was to sideline Vansittart. Cadogan took his place as permanent under-secretary at the Foreign Office: a place he would occupy for the next eight years. Plans were drawn up for colonial restitution that would give Germany a new say in the running of a huge strip of Central Africa, largely at the expense of the Portuguese, French and Belgian empires. Pressure was exerted on editors to tone down British press and radio criticisms of the Nazis. None of this had any impact at all on Hitler's behaviour.

Instead, German pronouncements on Austria became increasingly aggressive. In turn, Chamberlain reached out more urgently to Italy. The personal lead he took in these discussions, and his determination to offer recognition that Abyssinia now belonged to Italy, precipitated a climactic confrontation with Eden. The foreign secretary did not believe that this was the right means or moment for negotiation. For Chamberlain, on the other hand, the time had come to take decisive action, not least to subordinate a minister whose moral outrage was getting in the way of his policy. On 20 February, Eden resigned, along with his junior ministers, J. P. L. Thomas and Lord Cranborne.[15] Cadogan confessed to the diary in which he vented the emotions that were seldom otherwise on show, that he had spent the day with 'feelings lacerated and one's judgement torn in two'.[16] He liked Eden personally, but he thought that Chamberlain had the more sensible foreign policy.

Chamberlain appointed Halifax to take Eden's place as foreign secretary. As under-secretary of state, he selected a thirty-six-year-old Conservative called 'Rab' Butler. The son of a successful administrator in the Indian Civil Service, Butler was a dedicated believer in the sort of modern, moderately reforming Conservatism espoused by Baldwin and pursued by Chamberlain. His marriage to the daughter of the industrialist Samuel Courtauld had both given Butler a guaranteed income and helped to kick-start his rapid political ascent. As parliamentary private secretary to Samuel Hoare, he had played a significant role in defending the Government of India Bill against the attacks of the diehards. It said a lot for Butler's ability to get on with people that he had nonetheless managed to stay on good terms with Churchill. With Halifax in the Lords, Butler would take on the duty of representing the Foreign Office in the Commons. He fully agreed with Chamberlain's policy of appeasement.[17]

No sooner had the new team at the Foreign Office taken up their posts than the Germans staged their long-threatened occupation of Austria. On 11 March, Hitler pre-empted a referendum on the *Anschluss* by launching an unopposed invasion. The majority of Austrians celebrated this union with the Reich. Given such popular endorsement, there was no demand in Britain for a military response, although there was much disgust at the violent suppression of democracy and persecution of the Jewish population that followed.

Instead, the *Anschluss* focused attention on what would happen next. Through the spring and into summer, the fear that German threats to Czechoslovakia would spark a general war dominated European diplomacy. They also occasioned a significant shift in the nature of British rearmament.

'TO WITHSTAND THE STRAIN'

By the end of 1937, the tension between the rising cost of the armed forces' plans for expansion and the preservation of Britain's economic strength looked like it was about to become unsustainable. Over the next five years, the military wanted to spend up to £1,884 million on defence, but the Treasury thought that the maximum available from revenue and loans would be £1,500 million.[18] During the winter of 1937–38, Sir Thomas Inskip, the minister for the co-ordination of defence, undertook a review of policy to try to bridge this gap.

Inskip's review took as its starting point the fact that the economy mattered. Rearmament required the import of raw materials and manufactured goods. These could only be purchased if the balance of payments was maintained by healthy exports. Britain's ability to spend and borrow would be adversely affected by any reduction in the export trade, but excessive borrowing would in turn lead to inflation, which would make exports less competitive. In peacetime, the government's ability to impose economic controls or to increase taxation was limited by the need to maintain financial stability and public support. Britain's economic power also needed to be preserved because it was itself 'the fourth arm of defence'. Winning any future conflict would require the UK to enter it 'with sufficient economic strength to enable us to make the fullest uses of resources overseas, and to withstand the strain'.[19]

Difficult choices therefore had to be made about priorities. Inskip laid out a hierarchy of British strategic interests: first the defence of the UK and its trade routes; then the security of the Empire (since imperial possessions could be recaptured provided the home islands remained more or less intact); and lastly the territory of any British ally. This was an order heavily influenced by Sir Maurice Hankey, secretary of the

Committee for Imperial Defence, and Lord Chatfield, chief of the naval staff and chairman of the chiefs of staff, both strong advocates of imperial defence and naval expansion.[20]

Putting Britain's allies last – adopting a strategy of 'limited liability' to mainland Europe, as opposed to making a 'continental commitment' – had crucial implications for the army. It was told to concentrate on anti-aircraft defence at home and small-scale expeditionary warfare in the Empire, rather than on the provision of substantial land forces for a European war. In contrast, the Royal Navy was allowed to continue with its current building programme. Much to Chatfield's disappointment, Inskip would not mandate an even larger 'new standard' fleet, however, intended to restore global superiority in the face of a new generation of Japanese battleships. The RAF, in turn, was told to concentrate on building up its UK-based squadrons. Its plans for fighter construction should be maintained, but the aim of matching Germany's bomber force with an equal number of British aircraft was now abandoned in favour of building more aircraft factories. The emphasis on fighters rather than bomber parity marked an important shift from deterrence to defence.

Despite all this, Inskip's final conclusion, presented in early February 1938, was that in the medium term there was no way to limit spending and to guarantee security. Given the worsening international situation, Britain must not appear irresolute. Inskip suggested a compromise to see the country through the period of greatest danger. Total defence spending in the period until March 1942 would be set at £1,650 million, the most the Treasury now thought the country could afford. Spending would, however, be front-loaded, with as many orders placed in the next two years as possible. If there had been no easing of global tensions by that point, the UK would be faced with 'a choice between defence programmes that we cannot afford and a failure to make defence preparations on an adequate scale', for the 'plain fact which cannot be obscured is that it is beyond the resources of this country to make proper provision in peace for defence of the British Empire against three major Powers in three different theatres of war'.[21]

Inskip's task had been much eased by Sir Horace Wilson's advice that the Treasury's estimates of the finance available for defence spending in 1942 were too pessimistic. If the international situation demanded a bigger military budget, Wilson argued, the chancellor would be able

to cut back spending elsewhere.[22] Inskip's subsequent recommendations matched the prime minister's belief that a mixture of rearmament
and negotiation was the route to a general settlement that would be the
best solution for Britain. The spending restrictions that Inskip kept in
place were less good news for senior officers worried about falling
behind potential totalitarian opponents. As his review worked its way
through Whitehall at the beginning of 1938, they argued that their
existing programmes would only be fulfilled if the government took
greater charge of the economy.[23]

Then came the German annexation of Austria. Germany's willingness to use military force strengthened calls to improve Britain's
defences, particularly against a potential aerial knock-out blow. It also
heightened more general fears about the imminence of a European war.
Would preparing for battle destroy the very values for which the country would be fighting? In the aftermath of the *Anschluss*, the chancellor,
Sir John Simon, tried to insist on sticking to the limits set by Inskip.
Simon told his colleagues that no democracy could match Germany's
level of commitment: increasing munitions production in peacetime
would require the sort of controls that would turn Britain into 'a different kind of nation'. During the last war, Simon had resigned from the
Home Office over the introduction of conscription. Now his liberal
principles were once more being challenged by the relentless logic of
military mobilization.[24]

In fact, the government responded to the *Anschluss* with a significant escalation of rearmament and an unprecedented intervention in
the economy. On 23 March, after Sir Horace Wilson had cleared the
ground with Sir Walter Citrine, Chamberlain staged a well-publicized
meeting with the TUC to ask for assistance in easing the supply of
labour for the arms sector.[25] Union leaders happily promised to help.
On the same day, he announced in the Commons that industry must
now prioritize munitions over civil production. In his April budget, to
the theatrical gasps of MPs, Simon raised the basic rate of income tax
to 5s. 6d. in the pound – the same level at which it had been at the
height of the Great War.[26]

The chancellor fought successfully for the retention of the five-year
target of £1,650 million for defence expenditure, but the deteriorating
international situation made it difficult to turn down demands for even
higher spending in the short term. At the end of April, the Cabinet

approved a new RAF scheme that increased the target strength of UK-based squadrons by more than a third, with fighter numbers increased by half again. To achieve this new plan, Britain would have to produce 12,000 aircraft over the next two years, although total output in 1937 had been only about 3,500 planes. More significantly, freed from the need to achieve numerical parity with the Luftwaffe, the Air Ministry now worked to maximize potential wartime production with a co-ordinated programme of industrial expansion.[27]

For all that, the *Anschluss* did not alter Chamberlain and Halifax's conviction that Germany's complaints about the Sudetenland could be peacefully resolved. Czechoslovakia was a much more dangerous flashpoint than Austria. The Czechs had treaties of mutual assistance with France and Russia. If Hitler attacked, he might trigger a Europe-wide war. Britain was bound by no such agreement to Czechoslovakia, but would be dragged in by any attack on France. With British rearmament barely begun, no one in Whitehall thought the country was in a good position to pick a fight. On 16 March, Alec Cadogan described in his diary the conclusions he had come to after an evening spent grappling with 'the situation and what we are to do about it'. Britain must not, he recommended, offer a territorial guarantee to Czechoslovakia:

> I shall be called 'cowardly' but after days and nights of thinking, I have come to the conclusion that is the least bad. We *must* not precipitate a conflict now – we shall be smashed. It *may* not be better later, but anything may happen (I recognise the Micawber strain) . . . Rearm, above *all* in the Air. That is the policy of least resistance, which the Cabinet will probably take. But I am convinced it is the lesser evil.[28]

Bolstered by a depressing report from the chiefs of staff about the state of Britain's armed forces, the prime minister and foreign secretary both agreed that a war would be pointless. France, Britain and Russia were all too weak to defeat Germany quickly. Opposing Nazi aggression with force of arms would not save Czechoslovakia, but merely start a long war in which Hitler would initially have the advantage. Britain could count on Dominion support if it were itself attacked, but the same would not necessarily be true if it intervened in a dispute about Germany's eastern borders.

This pessimistic view overestimated German power, partly because it underestimated the damage the Czechs would do to any invader, but it accurately reflected Chamberlain's desire to avoid a war. The prime minister was also, however, reluctant to encourage Hitler by simply giving in to his demands. During the spring of 1938 therefore, he and Halifax decided to leave Britain's diplomatic position deliberately unclear. The withholding of any firm commitment of support would control French impetuosity, while the threat of a potential Franco-Russo-British alliance would restrain German aggression.[29]

This strategy achieved the first aim but not the second. Since Hitler did not think that Britain and France would fight, his campaign of threats against Czechoslovakia continued. British vagueness did, however, decide the position of France. In Paris, the first quarter of 1938 had seen three changes of government as successive administrations struggled with industrial and economic difficulties amid bitter tensions between right and left. After the *Anschluss*, a new conservative coalition under Premier Édouard Daladier had massively increased defence expenditure. When resultant fears of inflation led to a flight of foreign capital, Daladier devalued the franc and was rewarded with a surge in international investment. France's generals were worried about the state of their country's defences. With Daladier in charge, they hoped that another couple of years of peace would allow them to catch up with Germany. They would only contemplate fighting for Czechoslovakia with a guarantee of help from the RAF. The French foreign minister, Georges Bonnet, was also desperate to avoid war. Unlike Chamberlain, Daladier saw Nazism as a fundamental threat to European peace, but uncertainty about Britain's position left him unable to stand up to Hitler.[30]

In late May 1938, false rumours circulated of an imminent German assault on Czechoslovakia. Lord Halifax told Berlin and Paris that in this case Britain might well be forced to intervene. When the scare passed, Anglo-French firmness was reported to have won the day. For Hitler, this was more than a humiliation: it was a warning. If his opponents gained heart, how would they behave once their rearmament programmes had really got going? He told his generals to get ready for a swift invasion of Czechoslovakia and to begin planning for a war with Britain and France by the mid-1940s. The scene was set for the most drastic international crisis since the Great Depression.

'OUR COUNTRY MUST
BE POWERFULLY ARMED'

Events overseas also had implications for the National Government's domestic opponents. Between 1936 and 1937, Labour's official position on alliances and rearmament had been reconfigured by a powerful coalition of trade unionists, led by Citrine and Bevin, and MPs on the right of the party, including William Gillies (international secretary to Labour from 1920 to 1945) and Hugh Dalton (Labour's principal spokesman on foreign issues during the second half of the 1930s and party chairman 1936–37). They were motivated by their fear of the existential threat from Nazism, a desire to improve Labour's electoral chances by giving it a more coherent foreign policy, and a visceral Germanophobia that was exacerbated by Hitler's accession to power.[31] In spring 1933, Dalton returned from a brief visit to the country aghast at Nazi brutality and convinced that 'Germany is horrible' and that a 'European war must be counted now among the probabilities of the next ten years'.[32]

Against much opposition from pacifists who wanted no truck with violence, internationalists who were more concerned with the war in Spain than British security, and the extreme left who saw the re-equipment of the armed forces as a capitalist conspiracy, these more conservative Labour figures pushed through a new policy of support for rearmament and a strong League of Nations, built around co-ordinated action against aggressors by France, Britain and the USSR. In July 1937, for the first time since 1934, Labour MPs did not oppose the annual vote on military spending. That October, Dalton laid out the shift in stance to the overwhelming approval of the party conference in Bournemouth:

> In this most grim situation, not of the Labour Party's making, our country must be powerfully armed. Otherwise we run risks immediate and immeasurable. Otherwise, a British Labour Government, coming into power tomorrow, would be in danger of humiliation, intimidation and acts of foreign intervention in our national affairs.[33]

By the start of 1938, the official policies of Labour and the Liberals were more or less in line: critical of the new, more active approach to

appeasement, in favour of rearmament and eager for greater international co-operation. No British politician of any stripe wanted to
precipitate another world war, and Labour and Liberal defence policies
shared the government's strategic logic: a large air force and navy, a
reliance on economic power, and no great army to be sucked into the
trenches of another Western Front. During 1938, the major areas for
debate were not whether and how Britain should fight, but rather how
to manage rearmament and whether a greater commitment to collective security would deter war or make it more likely.

With conflicts raging in Spain and China and Hitler becoming more
aggressive, Chamberlain faced a much more difficult situation than his
predecessor. His political position was further worsened by a personality that tended to exacerbate division. Publicly, as well as privately, he
was dismissive of people like the Liberal leader, Sir Archibald Sinclair, who he thought abounded 'in "uplift" and declarations of his
devotion to high moral standards but who if he had his way would have
plunged us into a bloody and ruinous war long ago'.[34] The prime minister was not a man to suffer fools gladly, and his pitiless treatment
of his opponents contributed to the bitter tone of politics in the late
1930s.[35]

Within a year of his accession to the premiership, Chamberlain was
being warned by the Conservative Party chairman that while his strong
leadership was uniting the Tories, his 'outspokenness and precision
had probably frightened the rather weak-kneed Liberals who felt safe
with S.[tanley] B.[aldwin]'.[36] The former prime minister himself, now
elevated to the House of Lords, was also critical of his successor's
inability to build consensus:

> He is a far better debater than I: he hits his opponents hard and our
> backbenches are enthusiastic. All good as far as it goes. But the Labour
> fellows say 'We are back to the Party Dog fight . . . And there never can
> be a national foreign policy as long as he is there.'[37]

As Baldwin recognized, the importance of appearing 'national' would
only increase as the prospects of peace declined. A prime minister who
could so easily be made to look divisive would struggle if he had to rally
the nation in time of war.

The hatred that Chamberlain aroused on the opposition benches
reinforced the suspicion that his government was sympathetic to

Fascism. Levelled at the prime minister, this was an unjust accusation, but his more active approach to appeasement did encourage a minority of Conservatives, including the former air minister Lord Londonderry, into foolish and ultimately unavailing attempts to extend the hand of friendship to Nazism.[38]

The belief that the government was on the wrong side in a coming global cataclysm spurred on supporters of a Popular Front. The spring of 1938 saw fresh instances of local Liberals backing Labour candidates in by-elections, like that of West Fulham in April, where they had more chance of winning the seat. As befitted the majority party of opposition, however, Labour insisted on putting up candidates in constituencies the Liberals hoped to win, splitting the anti-government vote and undermining hopes for a progressive alliance.[39]

Even without this continued party intransigence on the left, however, a Popular Front faced insuperable problems to the right. The next general election was still two years away, and in the meantime the government had a huge parliamentary majority. It would only be displaced with the assistance of Chamberlain's Conservative opponents. In the Commons in early May, Tory critics and opposition leaders did combine for an attack on RAF rearmament which forced the resignation of the hard-working air minister, Lord Swinton, and his incompetent deputy Lord Winterton. For the most part, however, Conservative dissenters proved wary of any outright challenge to the government. The overwhelming bulk of the party supported the broad principles of Chamberlain's approach to Europe. For all that they would later cling to their status as 'anti-appeasers', the few who disagreed with the prime minister's policies in detail could not settle on an alternative approach, and almost all were wary of the career-crippling consequences of disloyalty in an unsuccessful cause.[40]

Churchill's attacks on the supposedly slow pace of rearmament continued, but for the time being he commanded little support inside or outside Parliament. Instead it was Eden who was seen as a potential leader for a new sort of government. Eden had been marked out as a Conservative rising star when Baldwin made him foreign secretary at the age of thirty-eight. As a leading light of moderate Conservatism, he was already touted as a probable successor to Chamberlain. His internationalist credentials made him an attractive figure for Liberals and supporters of the League of Nations, and his apparent refusal to make further concessions to the Italians received widespread public approval.

Once out of office, Eden became a figurehead for a group of younger backbenchers, some of them rather ahead of the former foreign secretary in their opposition to appeasement. In early 1938, he might have been able to lead a wider rebellion among Conservatives disgruntled at giving in to Mussolini. Eden held back, however. His hopes of leading the Conservative Party were not going to be best served by helping Labour to attack the prime minister. For all his antagonism towards Mussolini, he did not actually have a different policy to put forward on Austria or Czechoslovakia. His solution was to keep quiet in the Commons but make public speeches on domestic issues, focusing, as befitted a man who hoped to inherit Baldwin's consensual crown, on the hopes of 'Democracy and Young England'. Even his supporters, however, saw this as a 'flabby' response to the growing international crisis. In trying to walk the line between promoting his career and looking disloyal, Eden managed to avoid both. Chamberlain, in contrast, was freed by the foreign secretary's departure to be more explicit about his loss of faith in the League of Nations, offering the sort of decisive leadership that won over doubting Conservative MPs.[41]

As the spring of 1938 drew to a close, therefore, the prime minister's position remained secure. Even more than before, however, his political future had become tied up with events overseas. In May, his confidence was reinforced by the apparently successful aversion of a German attack on Czechoslovakia. By the end of September, however, it seemed certain that Europe was going to plunge into war.

10

Czechoslovakia to Poland

Between the middle of 1938 and the middle of 1939, Britain teetered between peace and war. The prolonged period of tension created an unstoppable strategic pressure to escalate the arms race, but it also started to change the political landscape.

'A MAN WHO COULD BE RELIED UPON'

During the summer of 1938, tensions over Czechoslovakia continued. British strategy remained the same: keep Germany and France guessing while pressing a peaceful resolution on the Czechs. On 12 September, Hitler gave a much-anticipated speech in Nuremberg in which he denounced the oppression of ethnic Germans. Shortly afterwards, pre-orchestrated riots broke out across the Sudetenland. Hitler now stood ready to give the order for an armed invasion. He was forestalled by a dramatic intervention from Chamberlain.[1]

Since the end of August, Chamberlain and Sir Horace Wilson had been plotting a top-secret diplomatic coup. Wilson hoped that the drama of a sudden personal mission would unlock the route to a negotiated settlement. On 13 September, Chamberlain offered to fly to Germany to talk directly with Hitler. Two days later, accompanied by Wilson, he was in the air bound for Berchtesgaden. It was a brave, innovatory and remarkably modern step: the era of shuttle diplomacy inaugurated by a man born in 1869. At their first meeting, Chamberlain got Hitler to agree to hold back any military action while further attempts were made to secure self-determination for the Sudetenland. The prime minister returned unimpressed by the Führer's physical presence ('the commonest little dog he had ever seen',[2] he told the Cabinet), but convinced that he could avert war and that, for all his 'ruthlessness', Hitler was a 'man who could be relied upon when he had given his word'. While Chamberlain and Hitler were talking, Wilson spoke with German diplomats. They assured him that the prime minister was making a great impression as a strong man. Taking these comments at face value, Wilson relayed them to a suitably gratified Chamberlain.[3]

If arranging for the Sudeten Germans to decide their own form of government seemed uncomfortably like giving in to Hitler's threats, it also appeared to be the only lasting solution to the problem. It certainly seemed preferable to military action to defend their continued government by the Czechoslovak state. On this basis, Chamberlain was able, on his return to London, to secure the support of the Cabinet and of the French, who now joined with the British in telling Prague to acquiesce to a German takeover.

Convinced that he could use force without any immediate risk of outside intervention, Hitler became more aggressive. When Chamberlain flew to meet him for a second time, at Bad Godesberg, on 22 September, he rejected plans for the Sudetenlanders to choose their own government. Instead he insisted that German troops would occupy the disputed area, no matter what and by force if necessary, by the end of September.

Gravely disappointed as he was by this belligerence, Chamberlain was willing to accede. Hitler, after all, assured him that this was the final sticking point in the way of that long-hoped-for European settlement. Back in London, Hitler's demands pushed Cadogan, in his measured diplomatic way, over the edge. Previously, as he explained to his diary on 24 September, he had been able to salve his concerns at 'ceding people to Nazi Germany' with the belief that there would be 'an "orderly" cession' of power under careful international control. Now, Hitler was 'throwing away every last safeguard that we had'. Worse, when leading Cabinet ministers met that afternoon, he found that Chamberlain

> was quite calmly for total surrender . . . Hitler has evidently hypnotised him to a point. Still more horrified to find PM had hypnotised H.[alifax] who capitulates totally. PM took nearly an hour to make his report, and

there was practically no discussion. J.[ohn] S.[imon], see which way the cat was jumping – said that after all it was a question of 'modalities', whether the Germans went in now or later! Ye Gods![4]

Having tried, apparently unsuccessfully, to make Halifax change his mind, Cadogan thought that a disastrous decision was about to be made. He knew, he wrote, that Britain and France were

> in no condition to fight; but I'd rather be beat than dishonoured. How can we look any foreigner in the face after this? How can we hold Egypt, India and the rest?
>
> Above all, *if* we have to capitulate, let's be honest. Let's say we're caught napping: that we can't fight now, but that we remain true to our principles, put ourselves straight into war conditions and *rearm*. Don't – above all – let us pretend we think Hitler's plan is a *good* one! I've never had such a shattering day, or been so depressed and dispirited. I can only hope for a revolt in the Cabinet and Parliament.[5]

The next day, he got what he wished for. After pondering Cadogan's advice, Halifax had spent a sleepless night grappling with his conscience. Now he told the Cabinet that he thought the British should reject Hitler's terms, even if it meant war. In a note passed down the Cabinet table, Chamberlain told him that this was 'a horrible blow to me', and that he did not think that he could accept responsibility if the French dragged Britain into war. When Halifax explained his night of torment, Chamberlain wrote back that 'Night conclusions are seldom taken in the right perspective.'[6] As far as the prime minister was concerned, he was, as usual, the only one who was keeping his head.

A point of fundamental difference had opened up between the foreign secretary and the prime minister. Where Chamberlain still believed he could negotiate a lasting peace, Halifax told colleagues that he could see only one long-term solution: the 'destruction of Nazi-ism'.[7] Other British ministers joined Halifax in opposing any further concessions to Hitler. The French also felt that they had reached the limits of what they could yield. Their intransigence seemed certain to end in war.

On 26 September, Chamberlain sent Wilson to talk to Hitler, begging for some sign that he was open to negotiation. After the German leader proved obdurate, the next day Wilson delivered a personal message from the prime minister, warning that Britain would have to stand by France if hostilities began. In best conciliatory mode, Wilson hedged the threat round with compromises and suggestions of the ways in which both sides could still find a way out. This tactic worked less well with the Führer than it had done with British trade unionists. Shortly after their meeting, Hitler ordered the German army units that would lead the invasion to take up their positions on the frontier.[8]

A European conflict now seemed unstoppable. In Britain, the Fleet was mobilized, and naval and air reservists told to report for duty. Fifty thousand Territorial Army soldiers were called up to position their anti-aircraft and coastal defence guns against a German surprise attack. Gas masks were issued to civilians, trenches dug in parks for shelters, and sirens warmed up, ready to warn the populace of the coming assault.

This sudden mobilization revealed a range of military shortcomings. The Royal Navy was short of escort vessels and minesweepers, and had no secure onshore storage space for its ammunition reserves. The army had only about a third of the guns and searchlights it thought it needed to protect London. Most of the weapons it did have were relics of 1914–18, and all its anti-aircraft batteries lacked key ranging and communications equipment.[9] Of the twenty-six fighter squadrons then available to the RAF for home defence, only six had been equipped with the most modern aircraft. Five of those had Hurricanes whose guns froze up over 15,000 feet, and the other had only just received new Spitfires.[10] If it came to striking back, a shortage of parts meant that only half of Britain's front-line bombers could actually be put into the air.[11]

In terms of air-raid precautions (ARP), preparations were equally inadequate. In 1935, the government had told local authorities to prepare precautionary schemes, but progress had been very limited, first because it was not clear where the funding for ARP would come from, and secondly because many Labour-controlled councils viewed preparing for a war as tantamount to starting one. The 1937 ARP Act, which came into force on 1 January 1938, required local authorities to submit detailed plans to the Home Office, for which the government provided three-quarters of the necessary finance with grants-in-aid. Nine months later, many councils hadn't even begun putting their plans together. Some were ready to issue gas masks to adults (none were as yet available for children); others had only just started to survey how many masks they might need. Plans to evacuate more vulnerable civilians – particularly children – from the most at-risk urban areas were still embryonic: it was not until the second half of September that the London County Council and the Home Office began to improvise schemes to get people out of the capital. Perhaps unsurprisingly, a major preoccupation for officials planning how to implement these ad hoc schemes was how they would deal with the panic that was expected to result.[12]

How serious would any of these deficiencies have been had Britain gone to war? Although the timing was bad, since the process of re-equipping the RAF with modern planes actually left squadrons ineffective for several months, the British, French and Czech air forces outnumbered their potential Luftwaffe opponents. British air production and schemes for wartime aircraft output were in the course of catching up with their enemy equivalents: a point concealed from British analysts by their habit of overestimating the quality of German preparations. Not only was there no Luftwaffe plan for an immediate air attack on London: such an operation was at this point well beyond the capability of the German air force. If the British military could have done little in the short term to aid the Czechs, in retrospect it is clear that they would have been perfectly capable of defending the UK against any threat their enemies could muster while the Royal Navy steamed into place to blockade the German economy. None of this, however, would have offered a quick or easy victory.[13]

At the time, it was the dangers to the UK that seemed more obvious. The chiefs of staff, eager to avoid a war until rearmament was more advanced, backed up their prime minister's reluctance to resort to arms by emphasizing how unprepared the armed forces were. The sense of unreadiness leaked out to, and was shared by, ordinary people as they heard rumours from their relatives in the forces, wondered what their local council was doing, or examined their own inadequate plans for what to do in the event of war. This terrifying moment of collective insecurity was articulated in Chamberlain's mournful radio address to the nation on 27 September 1938, in which he lamented how 'horrible fantastic, incredible' it was to be gearing up for an assault on British cities 'because of a quarrel in a faraway country between people of whom we know nothing'.[14]

The following morning, Wilson, now back in London, met with a representative of the German Foreign Office and made it clear that, while the British were still willing to compromise on the Sudetenland, if Hitler invaded Czechoslovakia, public opinion would force the government to declare war.[15] An hour later, Chamberlain sent a final offer of talks to Hitler, then went to explain events to the Commons. The Chamber was packed with MPs sombrely anticipating the outbreak of war. In the middle of his speech, Chamberlain was suddenly informed that Hitler had agreed to another meeting. When he announced to the House that he was going to fly to Germany once more in search of peace, all sides erupted in rejoicing.

The next day, the prime minister set off to Munich for a four-power conference between the British, the French, the Germans and the Italians. This essentially agreed to everything that Hitler had demanded at Bad Godesberg while denying him a war and guaranteeing the borders of the reduced Czech state. Chamberlain could therefore present it as the outcome of negotiation rather than capitulation. He had also got the German dictator to sign, in the course of a private meeting, an Anglo-German agreement committing both countries to work to resolve differences and secure peace in Europe.

With this step towards a general settlement made, Chamberlain returned, physically exhausted but emotionally elated, to London. He was greeted by cheering crowds: first at the airport, then at Buckingham Palace (where he joined the royal family on the balcony), then at Downing Street. Describing the scene to his sister, Chamberlain wrote that the streets 'were lined from one end to the other with people of every class, shouting themselves hoarse, leaping on the running board, banging on the windows & thrusting their hands into the car to be shaken'. Caught up in the moment, and rather against his better judgement, the prime minister told the crowd that he had secured not only 'peace with honour', but also 'peace for our time'.[16]

'A PUTTING OFF OF EVIL DAYS'

The outpouring of emotion when it appeared that war had been averted was, however, only one facet of a complex and fluctuating range of reactions. By the spring of 1938, Mass-Observation was applying itself to the question of what exactly Britons thought about the international situation. It was now engaged in two area studies: one in Bolton and the other in West Fulham, where it was paid to provide research support for Labour in the by-election.[17] In both places, Tom Harrisson claimed to discern the same pattern. More or less equal proportions of people had already made up their minds for or against the government's foreign policy, but in the middle was a large group who were left 'uncertain, ignorant, bewildered'.[18] Their confusion only increased as the onrush of global events encouraged a sort of self-protective apathy.

Later, looking back on the drawn-out crises of March to September 1938, Harrisson argued that they demonstrated the disconnection between politicians, the media and the people. Since no one really knew what the public was thinking, anyone could claim that their preferred policy was the one that represented the weight of popular opinion. With newspapers concentrating on the evidence that backed up their editorial stance, it was very difficult accurately to discern public attitudes that were, in any case, changing as quickly as the international situation itself.[19]

Even people who had already adopted a party line found it difficult to know what to make of international events that seemed to be leading inexorably to war. Some lacked the time, information or interest to discuss events in Central Europe; as one Bolton barmaid responded to an investigator's question about the *Anschluss*: 'Oh, I'm not fussy.'[20] A third of those interviewed on the streets of west Fulham in March 1938 simply did not answer questions about foreign policy. Although they might have been wary of talking about it in depth, many of those who did respond plainly had an opinion, even if Harrisson might have classified them as 'bewildered': 'I can't understand it properly, but it doesn't seem too good to me', or, more tersely: 'It's a f—ing mess, ain't it?', which seems as accurate a description of European diplomacy in the late 1930s as any.[21]

Unlike the *Anschluss*, the Sudeten crisis clearly held the potential to spark a European war. For this reason, even Chamberlain's political opponents welcomed his dramatic intervention in mid-September. The Labour-owned *Daily Herald* declared that his flight to Berchtesgaden 'must win the sympathy of opinion everywhere, irrespective of party'.[22] Shortly afterwards, when Mass-Observation interviewed inhabitants of a working-class, Labour-supporting street in West Fulham, every other person said something positive about the prime minister. As a fifty-five-year-old woman explained:

> Oh, mister, it scared my wits out, thinking of the last war. They said it was going to be this week, and I heard the milkman say this morning that we can say the worst has passed now. He's a Conservative, he says Mr Chamberlain's done it by going in an aeroplane to Hitler. It was all over the paper. It's a good thing we have men like that isn't it?[23]

After the prime minister's return, however, suspicions grew about his intended solution to the crisis. On Sunday 18 September, a large demonstration, organized by the International Peace Campaign, assembled in Trafalgar Square, where the Labour MP Ellen Wilkinson told them what to say to Chamberlain: 'We don't trust you. We believe that you went to Germany to fix up a sale of the liberties of Czecho-Slovakia.' When Chamberlain arrived at Bad Godesberg he told Hitler that he had been booed on his way to the airport.[24]

The news that the Bad Godesberg talks had broken down dramatically escalated antipathy to Hitler. The 350 interviews that Mass-Observation conducted between Chamberlain's second and third flights revealed growing opposition to any further appeasement. A forty-five-year-old woman had 'Not thought about it much. If the men were in they'd talk about it a lot. They're always saying as Chamberlain has swindled them, but I think he's for peace.' A younger woman explained:

> If there's one thing we want, it's no more war. But I can't see what we are going to do when he keeps on wanting things that he says, like that Czechoslovakia. I know what I'd do if I had him. My husband says, and I agree, that we will have a bigger war now sooner or later for this.

A painter expostulated: 'I used to feel proud to be British but now I am ashamed of my own race', while a thirty-five-year-old man declared: 'it's the bloody limit when we give what's not ours away. Besides, they seem to think we are cowards now. Chamberlain's to blame for this, and we'll not let him forget it either.'[25] These were expressions not of ideological antipathy to Nazism, but rather of injured national pride. In that, they differed little from the growing opposition to further concessions from inside the Cabinet. When rebellious ministers said that the limit of public acceptance had been reached, they were right

to argue as if their gut reactions reflected a wider mood. Yet the looming prospect of war was terrifying, particularly to those who could
look back to the suffering of the last great conflict. The horrific
sense that a war would shortly crash over an unprepared country helps
to explain the outpouring of relief at Chamberlain's final flight to
Munich.

Orchestrating press reaction to the negotiations was an important
part of the government's diplomatic strategy. Unusually for a Conservative prime minister, Chamberlain did not maintain close relations
with the newspaper barons who still controlled a lot of the British
press. He was only really on good terms with Lord Kemsley, the owner
of the *Sunday Times* and the *Daily Sketch*. By the late 1930s, however,
the National Government had developed quite a sophisticated news
management machine, and assisted by Sir Joseph Ball – a former
MI5 officer who had been using his intelligence skills for the Conservative Party since 1924 and was now head of the Conservative Research
Department – Chamberlain gave special briefings to reporters from the
Kemsley papers, as well as for Lord Rothermere's *Daily Mail*.[26] The
Mail's headlines during the Munich crisis told their own story about
the need to manufacture national unity. Having instructed readers to
'Trust Chamberlain' on 19 September, four days later it had to insist
that 'Those who hurl bitter accusations at this time' were 'attacking his
noble project at its foundations'.[27]

In practice, however, a mix of personal lobbying, prior preference
and appeals to the national interest meant that most newspapers backed
the government throughout the crisis. *The Times*, which had the most
influence with the political elite and on other journalists, generally
took it as a matter of policy to support the government of the day.
Its owner, Lord Astor of Hever, did not interfere with the paper's
editorial line, and its editor, Geoffrey Dawson, had backed appeasement since the days of the Baldwin government and continued to do so
during the Munich crisis. Dawson got on well with Lord Halifax: like
the foreign secretary, he was a High Anglican North Yorkshireman
who had been schooled at Eton and Oxford. Baron Astor's brother,
Viscount Astor, who owned the right-wing Sunday weekly the *Observer*, had also backed Chamberlain's brand of progressive Conservatism
during the 1930s. The *Observer* too supported the government's foreign policy.[28]

While Chamberlain was negotiating with Hitler, Sir Samuel Hoare held daily meetings with editors and proprietors, urging them not to criticize any concessions to Hitler lest they derail the pursuit of peace. Hoare was particularly well placed to discuss tactics with Beaverbrook because the press lord was secretly giving him financial support. Beaverbrook had identified Hoare as a man he wanted to champion at the start of the 1930s, and he gave him at least three gifts of £2,000 in order to sustain his political career. Hoare was unsuccessful in his attempts to persuade Chamberlain to give Beaverbrook a ministerial office, but the press lord – who believed in appeasement in any case – was attracted for the moment by the idea of working alongside the government to promote peace.[29] The *Daily Express* lauded Chamberlain's achievements at Munich, insisting that the prime minister had guaranteed the happiness of millions by ensuring that there would be 'no war this year or the next'.

Yet journalists who did not enjoy the same cosy relationship that Beaverbrook had with Hoare accepted the argument that the press had a responsibility not to rock the international boat and rejoiced in the avoidance of war. Both the Liberal-supporting *News Chronicle* and Labour's paper, the *Daily Herald*, criticized the abandonment of the Czechs, but they also recorded their gratitude that peace had been preserved. Meanwhile, the BBC publicized popular expressions of relief and excluded critical commentators from the airwaves, and Halifax leant on the newsreel company, Paramount, to ensure that it did not screen footage of Ellen Wilkinson attacking the government during the rally in Trafalgar Square. In the immediate aftermath of Munich, the voices of those who supported the government sounded much louder than those who opposed it.[30]

The joyful crowds that slowed the prime minister's journey back from Heston airport to Downing Street were, however, a spontaneous assembly, not a journalist's fabrication or the concoction of an official propagandist. Chamberlain had become the unlikely hero of those who prized peace above all else. The ILP MP James Maxton insisted that he had fulfilled the wishes of 'the mass of the common people of the world'.[31] Yet even at its apogee, relief was not the sole emotion. For many Britons, gratitude at the preservation of peace was mixed with worries about the future and a lingering sense of doubt about whether Britain had done the right thing. As a country schoolteacher, who had spent the crisis awaiting the arrival of refugee children from London, wrote to his family at the start of October:

> I wonder how you are all feeling after this nightmarish week. Immensely relieved and thankful and hoping like all of us that it really is the beginning of better things and not just a putting off of the evil days. Perhaps Hitler will keep his word and is quite genuine that he doesn't want anything more in Europe, but I'm afraid I don't trust that lad one inch, not me. Still, Chamberlain seems to and after all he has met the man face to face and has talked to him, so I gather he must know a little more about him than does the mere man in the street.[32]

Beneath a hum of resolutions lauding the prime minister, some local Conservative activists also expressed concerns about concessions to Hitler and deficiencies in defence. They were comforted by the prospect that, as the backbench Tory MP Sir John Wardlaw-Milne put it: 'there can be very little doubt that we shall be considerably better off a year or two hence than we are today. Germany's rearmament has gone very far; ours still has a long way to go.'[33] Here was the start of the myth that Chamberlain had avoided war in order to give the country the chance to be better prepared the next time round.

Like the rest of the country, the Cabinet was in the end grateful that war had been avoided. Unlike Chamberlain, Halifax was downcast, rather than elated, at what he explained to the Lords had been a 'hideous choice of evils'.[34] For all his shame at the outcome, he had no intention of resigning. Rather he would drive on rearmament and insist on a firmer stand against the dictators in the future. Of the ministers who had challenged Chamberlain to oppose Hitler, only one, the first lord of the admiralty, Alfred Duff Cooper, resigned.

Parliament debated the Munich settlement over four days at the start of October. Duff Cooper's resignation speech was couched in terms of personal conscience calculated to do the least possible damage to the government. Chamberlain's justification of his policy was confident: the 'real triumph' of Munich was that it had shown that the great powers could 'agree on a way of carrying out a difficult and delicate operation by discussion instead of by force of arms, and thereby they have averted a catastrophe which would have ended civilisation as we have known it'.[35] Labour and Liberal MPs attacked the government's isolationism and the inefficiency of rearmament, but they could not claim that they would ultimately have gone to war to save the Sudetenland. Loyal Conservatives rallied behind a prime minister whose 'high courage', 'deep faith' and 'grand humanity' had, as one put it, 'drag[ged] us back from that abyss into which we were so nearly being hurled', 'the maddest war with which a reluctant people has ever been faced – to fight over a method of implementing an agreement which had already been reached by all concerned'.[36]

Conservative critics of appeasement found it difficult to align themselves, let alone persuade their colleagues. Eden made another speech advocating a 'revival of our national spirit'.[37] Leo Amery – who disagreed more with the practice than the principle of Chamberlain's policy – demanded the introduction of national service. Churchill crowned a denunciation of past errors in defence and foreign policy by rejecting peaceful coexistence with a Nazi regime 'which vaunts the spirit of aggression and conquest, which derives strength and perverted pleasure from persecution, and uses . . . with pitiless brutality the threat of murderous force'.[38] Winding up for the government, Rab Butler responded that:

> we have two choices, either to settle our differences with Germany by consultation, or to face the inevitability of a clash between the two systems of democracy and dictatorship. In considering this, I must emphatically give my opinion as one of the younger generation. War settles nothing, and I see no alternative to the policy upon which the Prime Minister has so courageously set himself – the construction of peace . . . There is no other country that can achieve this, and . . . in our efforts to understand, to consult with and, if possible, to get friendship with Germany, we do not abandon by one jot or tittle the democratic beliefs which are the very core of our whole being and system.[39]

In the final division, no Conservative voted against the government and only twenty-five abstained. Churchill was one of the few who publicized their iconoclasm by remaining seated in the Chamber while the votes were counted.[40]

'WE MUST DO SOMETHING'

Munich left a political quagmire. A by-election in Oxford, already under way as the crisis reached its peak, demonstrated some of the issues involved. The seat had been held by the Conservatives at the 1935 election. This time round, it was contested for the party by Quintin Hogg, a brilliant young barrister and son of a Tory grandee and former lord chancellor, Lord Hailsham. There was local support for the idea of a Popular Front, and in mid-September the Liberal candidate stood down to allow a single opposition figure to run. After a lengthy debate, a month later the Labour Party also agreed not to contest the seat, and its candidate, Patrick Gordon Walker, withdrew in favour of the philosophy don A. D. Lindsay, master of Balliol College, who ran against Hogg as an 'Independent Progressive'. Lindsay was in fact a member of the Labour Party – an allegiance that aroused some Liberal suspicions – but received support from dissident Conservatives, including Eden, Churchill and Macmillan.

Emotions ran high on both sides during the campaign. Lindsay's supporters insisted that 'A vote for Hogg is a vote for Hitler.' Their man was better suited to debating academic points in the cloister than kissing babies on the doorstep, and Gordon Walker rightly suspected that he would struggle to bring out the working-class vote. When the by-election took place, on 27 October, the turnout rose to 76 per cent (from 67 per cent in 1935) but Conservative support remained secure. Hogg won with a much-reduced majority.[41]

Writing in his diary a few days before the election, an aggrieved Gordon Walker explained the tensions created within the opposition by reactions to Munich:

> An hysterical state of mind was created largely in middle class and University circles . . . The hysteria took the form of 'We must *do* something', 'We must have something that can be successful.' It concentrated itself on the worst, most obvious fault – namely hostility to Chamberlain himself. People persuaded themselves that this was important. 'We only have six months – if we don't beat Chamberlain there'll be no trade unions to preserve'. Quite ludicrous ideas about the importance of Lindsay's victory were evolved. That it would check Chamberlain, lead him to alter his policy, frighten Hitler etc.
>
> Any talk of the importance of holding the Labour movement together, of building up its strength, of looking not only to Oxford but to the whole series of by-elections and to the General Election – all these were swept away by the argument that nothing else mattered but the

next 6 months – and some defeat of Chamberlain, however achieved – in Oxford.[42]

The tensions between the desire of many local activists to 'do something' and their own determination to keep control of strategy and play a longer game, posed challenges to the Labour leaders throughout the last year of peace.

Barely a week after the Oxford by-election, another Nazi outrage confirmed the anxieties raised by the Sudeten crisis. On the night of 9 November 1938, the Nazis unleashed a wave of violence against German Jews. The *Kristallnacht* pogrom – named for the shattered glass of looted Jewish businesses – was followed up by the passing of further anti-Semitic legislation. In Britain, *Kristallnacht* was reported as a shocking abandonment of civilized norms.[43] Sympathy for the victims as Jews was outweighed by alarm at this evidence of the atavistic aggression that made Germany an international danger. For the moment, Chamberlain stopped talking in public about any further discussions with Berlin. He was disgusted by Nazi violence and ready to allow Jewish refugees into Britain, but he was also determined that revulsion at German brutality should not get in the way of peace. For Halifax, in contrast, *Kristallnacht* was further evidence that Hitler represented an existential evil to which the only solution was confrontation, not negotiation.[44]

On 17 November, another significant by-election took place, this time in the Somerset constituency of Bridgwater. Richard Acland, the Liberal MP for a neighbouring constituency, had carefully co-ordinated a campaign to build up backing from local Liberal and Labour supporters for the journalist Vernon Bartlett, a long-time opponent of Fascism. Like Lindsay, Bartlett stood as an 'Independent Progressive'; unlike Lindsay, he was suspected of being a crypto-Liberal. Labour's prospects were much worse than in Oxford, so the party's decision not to fight Bridgwater caused fewer internal ructions. Acland avoided the presence of divisive national figures, such as Lloyd George or Stafford Cripps, who might have aroused partisan allegiances, and received no support from Conservative anti-appeasers. If no more experienced as a politician than Lindsay, Bartlett was a much better campaigner. In a predominantly rural constituency, he reckoned that his willingness to talk corn and cattle (despite an almost total ignorance of agriculture) was at least as important as his stance on foreign affairs. The Conservative vote again held up, but this time an increased turnout gave Bartlett more votes than the Liberals and Labour had managed together in 1935, and he took the seat with a 2,000-strong majority. The Bridgwater result could be taken as evidence of how far public opinion had swung against the Munich settlement in the aftermath of *Kristallnacht*, but there were plainly large numbers of people who, whether because they loved peace or were loyal to their party, continued to vote for the government candidate.[45]

That December, another by-election, at West Perth and Kinross, demonstrated that victory for the anti-appeasers was by no means inevitable. It was sparked by the decision of the sitting Tory MP, Katharine Stewart-Murray, the duchess of Atholl (known as the 'Red Duchess' because of her support for Republican Spain), to resign her seat in protest at the Munich agreement.[46] Stewart-Murray's criticisms of the government had already led to her being de-selected by the constituency party, and she subsequently stood as an Independent without co-ordinating her position with the opposition. In a straight fight with an official Conservative candidate, heavily supported by Conservative Central Office, she was defeated on a much-reduced turnout by 1,300 votes.[47]

Here was a potent warning to dissident Conservatives of the consequences of disloyalty. Like several other rebels over the winter of 1938–39, Churchill had to face down de-selection challenges from Conservative activists in his constituency. While the weight of public attitudes and the fate of Chamberlain's foreign policy remained in the balance, no Conservative could hope to survive if they launched a full-blown challenge against their party leader. What they could do was to keep up their demands for military expansion and its inevitable concomitant – increased government controls. During the autumn of 1938, backbench advocates of rearmament called not only for a Ministry of Supply with powers to direct industry, but also for the immediate introduction of national service. Since the co-operation of organized labour would be essential to controlling manpower in this way, such calls were coupled with suggestions for widening the coalition to create a more 'national' government. Accepting the need for such an expansion posed an implicit question about the position of such a partisan prime minister.[48]

Chamberlain's position was just as difficult as that of his critics. He was safe for the moment from any rebellion or opposition assault, but the ambiguous reaction to the Sudeten crisis did not allow him to seek a new public mandate. In the aftermath of Munich, Conservative Central Office did moot plans to capitalize on his popularity with an immediate general election, but the risk of seeming to take advantage of a national crisis was too great. The by-election results that followed convinced Conservative strategists that 'the uncertainties of the international situation and national defence ... aggravated by the strong feeling aroused by the Jewish persecutions'[49] had left the public mood too unpredictable for them to go to the country. There was no room for Chamberlain to replicate Baldwin's success in 1935, and reconfigure the presentation of policy to capture the centre ground on foreign policy. On the contrary, his political fate now rested even more squarely on the success of his dealings with the dictators.

'THE CONNECTION BETWEEN DIPLOMACY AND STRATEGIC STRENGTH'

Certain as he was of the possibilities of negotiating with Hitler from a position of strength, the prime minister returned from Munich convinced that, as he informed his Cabinet colleagues at the start of October, it was right to make maximum efforts to repair defence deficiencies, but wrong to think 'that as a thanks offering for the *détente*, we should at once embark on a great increase in our armaments programme'.[50] This line was increasingly difficult to hold against those ministers who wanted a more active response, not least because concessions over the Sudetenland had been justified in terms of British weakness. In the month after Munich, Chamberlain's service ministers demanded increases in rearmament.

The greatest pressure came from the Air Ministry, where a new Conservative secretary of state, Sir Kingsley Wood, had been appointed in May 1938. A lawyer drawn into politics through his specialism in industrial insurance, Wood was sustained by a deep Methodist faith. The soft lines of his face, replicated in his circular spectacles, belied a sharp intelligence and an eagle eye for political advantage. Wood had become an ally of Chamberlain's after serving under him at the Ministry of Health in the 1920s. He had no experience of running a forces department and happily admitted that he 'did not know one end of an aircraft from the other': he was made secretary of state for air because he could be relied upon to defend government policy in the Commons. At the end of October, however, he presented a plan for aerial expansion that took a very different line to the prime minister's.[51]

Wood in turn was being pressed by Air Marshal Sir Wilfrid Freeman, a senior RAF officer who played a crucial role in the development of British air power in the decade after 1935. Freeman also had a razor-like mind, a cynical sense of humour, and little tolerance for other people's inefficiency. To a degree matched by few others, he understood the process by which aircraft were designed, ordered and made. Although Freeman had been marked out as one the RAF's rising stars after the last war, his progress had been brought to a halt in 1935 when he divorced his wife. In the 1930s, even a self-consciously 'modern' organization like the RAF regarded this as beyond the pale, and Freeman prepared to leave the service.[52]

Hitler saved Freeman's career. Rather than retiring, in April 1936 Freeman was put in charge of research and development at the Air Ministry. Designing new aircraft was one of the most expensive and failure-fraught things that armed forces around the world did in this period. With aircraft technology changing rapidly, Freeman had to balance the need for the most advanced equipment possible with the danger of picking unproven aircraft designs. He learned to work with the aircraft industry, guiding the aircraft firms to come up with new planes and aero-engines from which the Air Ministry could pick the best. Among other things, Freeman signed the first production order for the Spitfire fighter, and encouraged the development of the heavy bombers with which the RAF hoped to carry the fight to Britain's enemies.

In June 1938, Freeman was made responsible for aircraft production as well as research and development. That meant grappling with the bigger issues of manufacturing and supply as well as the specifics of aircraft design. Under Freeman, the Air Ministry developed a much larger production department that dealt with issues including subcontracting, materials and factory construction as well as airframes and aero-engines. Freeman's reaction to the Munich crisis was simple:

'Peace in our time . . . that means we have a few more months to get ready. How can we increase our programme?' Through Wood, Freeman pressed the Cabinet for decisions.[53]

Convinced that only they could win a coming war, the air staff had drawn up an even larger scheme for RAF expansion. Newly aware that a German decision to concentrate on medium-sized bombers gave them the chance to seize the lead in heavier aircraft, they proposed a fresh concentration on constructing British bombers. As Wood made plain to his colleagues, the scale of these plans would require controls on industry and manpower. When they came before the Cabinet at the start of November, Wood justified these steps by arguing that it was only by 'strengthening our air position that we could give our diplomacy the help which it required. From the domestic point of view, our weakness in the air was the cause of great anxiety in the country.'[54]

The chancellor and the prime minister both opposed such a dramatic escalation in the arms programme. Simon warned that well before it was complete, the new air force scheme would threaten domestic stability:

> The damage which I apprehend is not of the sort which can be got over by calling for 'sacrifices'; it would consist of weakening our economic and financial strength as no increase in taxation could remedy. Excessive borrowing entails risk of higher costs, higher wages, and almost certainly higher interest rates so that the burden on the country even if tolerable at first becomes progressively worse. Moreover, it means substantially increased imports and substantially reduced exports. Our balance of payments – already a serious problem – will become more and more serious. In the end our monetary reserves (which have already been heavily depleted since the crisis by withdrawal of foreign capital from this country) might be still more rapidly exhausted and we should have lost the means of carrying on a long struggle altogether.[55]

Chamberlain highlighted the gap between his attempts to match diplomacy and deterrence and Wood's proposals, which would escalate the arms race. In the aftermath of Munich, however, it was impossible to dismiss the importance of aerial security. The Cabinet would not agree to let the RAF expand as if it were already at war, but it did approve the formation of twelve new fighter squadrons and the gradual re-equipment of Britain's bomber forces with heavy aircraft. It also

sanctioned efforts to build industrial capacity so that aircraft production could be further accelerated after war broke out. The aim was for
Britain to be able to manufacture 17,000 aircraft in the first year of a
conflict that began in October 1939, and 2,000 aircraft a month by the
end of 1941.[56]

In France too, the response to Munich was a dramatic escalation of
rearmament. Unable politically to get agreement on new controls on
industry, Daladier instead placed the defence burden on French workers. Non-military public spending was slashed, laws on working
conditions set aside and fresh investment promised to the arms industry. The French left now split between those who wanted to improve
the country's defences and those who fell back more resolutely on
pacifism. When the trade unions met Daladier's new approach with a
general strike, the response was a violent crackdown. But though they
exacerbated political divisions, the new measures did achieve an
increase in munitions output.

Back in Britain, discussions of defence preparations were cast in
a new light in mid-November by the events of *Kristallnacht*. Reports
came from inside Germany that Hitler's aggression was being egged
on by Nazi extremists who would be happy to accept a war against a
declining British Empire. A month before, Lord Halifax had told
Chamberlain that he approved of Eden's calls for a widening of the
government to bolster 'national unity'. Now, convinced that only the
language of force would turn the tide, he told the prime minister that
Britain must increase air rearmament still further and institute a compulsory national register of men fit for military service or industrial
labour – a prerequisite for conscription.[57]

Chamberlain disagreed with Halifax's remedies, but he could not
ignore this pressure. Over the autumn and winter, he brought in new
expert ministers to bolster his 'national' credentials without threatening his grip on power. Sir John Anderson (an eminent civil servant
turned independent MP) became lord privy seal with a particular
responsibility for air-raid precautions. With the prime minister's support, Anderson rapidly pushed through attempts to improve provision
of shelters, gas masks, emergency services and evacuation. Lord Chatfield (formerly first lord of the admiralty) replaced Inskip as minister
for the co-ordination of defence.

Chamberlain was not willing to concede either a Ministry of Supply or military conscription, but he did now start discussions of a national register that would direct enthusiastic volunteers into the right areas and encourage others to offer their service. Voluntary measures also had the advantage that they would be more easily reversed once peace had been secured. With the TUC – no more eager than the prime minister to see the current government conscripting its members but determined to resist Fascism – lending its support, a huge campaign for voluntary national service was launched with much fanfare during January 1939. In a radio broadcast, Chamberlain informed listeners that 'Compulsion is not in accordance with the democratic system under which we live, or consistent with the tradition of freedom which we have always striven to maintain. We are confident that we shall get all the volunteers we want without recourse to compulsion.'[58]

As 1938 turned into 1939, the prime minister was depressed by the sense that peace remained as distant as ever. The final conclusion of the Anglo-American trade treaty offered some hope of transatlantic co-operation, but the pursuit of an agreement with the Italians had been endangered by their aggressive demands for the cession of territory from France.[59]

Over the winter, rumours from Germany, assiduously passed on by French intelligence, suggested that Hitler might, in a fit of fury, launch an attack westwards against Holland, France or even the UK. The threat greatly strengthened the hand of those, including the foreign secretary, who wanted Britain to make a more concrete commitment to French security. It was a decisive moment. On 6 February, having agreed that British generals could begin full staff talks with their opposite numbers across the Channel, Chamberlain told the Commons that any attack on French vital interests would 'evoke the immediate cooperation of Great Britain'.[60]

This was an acceptance of the continental commitment that had been rejected under Inskip's review a year before. As far as Chamberlain was concerned, however, this was not a U-turn. He was just adapting the same approach he had used all along. Previously such firm demonstrations of his determination had been impossible because Britain had been too weak to make them plausible; now that rearmament had strengthened his hand, he could shift the balance in his quest for peace between concession and deterrence. Characteristically, he lamented to his sister that he was the only one clever enough to understand: his 'firmer line in public' had been 'applauded' as a change in policy by critics who lacked any understanding of 'the connection between diplomacy and strategic strength'.[61]

Meanwhile, debates about a Popular Front were once again occupying the Labour Party. In January 1939, Sir Stafford Cripps launched a new campaign for a broader alliance between 'everyone to the left of Neville Chamberlain'. As Cripps explained to readers of *Tribune*, this front could still not include Conservatives, since even the 'best intentioned Tory Democrats will be driven into fascism when the economic circumstances call for that type of repression'. Labour's National Executive rejected Cripps' proposals as politically naive. Undeterred, Cripps publicized his message in an attempt to raise Labour supporters against the leadership. He could not win over the majority of the party, but his message of urgent action did appeal to many frightened by the danger of Fascism. The internecine struggle was only resolved in May 1939 with his formal expulsion from the Labour Party. It was to prove one of the most important events of his political career.[62]

As winter turned to spring, with the prospect of a united opposition receding still further into the distance, the prime minister's political future looked rosy once more. Providing his plans for a European settlement came off, by the autumn he would finally be able to fight an election that would capitalize on his status as peacemaker to secure another term in government. With peace secured, he would be able to return to his true calling: improving the well-being of the British people. All that was needed was for Hitler to live up to the promises he had made at Munich.

'THE UTMOST OF ITS POWER IN RESISTING SUCH A CHALLENGE'

On 15 March 1939, German troops marched into what was left of Czechoslovakia. Announcing the German invasion to the Commons, Chamberlain concentrated not on Hitler's betrayal or the consequences for the Czechs, but rather on the need to keep working for peace. Given time to consider events, and following an anxious reaction from his supporters, he offered a very different face two days later, when he made a broadcast speech to the Birmingham Unionist Association.

Now he wondered aloud whether there were any limits to Hitler's aims, or whether this was, 'in fact, a step in the direction of an attempt to dominate the world by force?' If it was, he cautioned, Britain would 'take part to the utmost of its power in resisting such a challenge'.[63]

During the second half of March, rumours abounded that the Germans were going to seize further territory in Eastern Europe. One possible target was the northern part of Romania. Another lay between East Prussia and the rest of Germany, where a narrow corridor of German land leading to the free port of Danzig had been allocated to a newly independent Poland at the end of the First World War. Polish fear of the Soviet Union (with which it had fought a war in 1920) had encouraged it to sign a non-aggression pact with Germany in 1934. When negotiations on the future of the 'Polish Corridor' broke down, however, it found itself the target of Hitler's threats.

As a military dictatorship that had taken the opportunity of Hitler's assault on Czechoslovakia to expand its own borders, Poland was not a natural object for British sympathies. It was, however, a means for Chamberlain and Halifax to demonstrate their determination to brook no further smash-and-land grabs by the Nazis. After a hurried period of negotiation, they quickly pushed through an Anglo-French guarantee to Poland, which was announced in the Commons, to cheers from MPs, on 31 March.

For the first time, Sir Horace Wilson seriously disagreed with the prime minister's foreign policy. Keen as ever to seek conciliation, he thought that the commitment to Poland would restrict Britain's room for manoeuvre and drag it into a war for Danzig.[64] Chamberlain thought he had surmounted this problem by guaranteeing Poland's independence, rather than its borders. His aim was to make it clear to Hitler that further international aggression would be met with force, not to rule out the peaceful reallocation of territory after negotiation. A week later, Italy annexed Albania. Now Chamberlain could not stop Halifax when he argued that the best response was to offer further British guarantees to Greece and Romania, the countries that might be next on the dictators' hit list. In turn, on 22 May, Germany and Italy signed a 'Pact of Steel' to co-ordinate their economic and military preparations for war.

Hitler's attack on the rump Czech state also marked the start of a turn against Chamberlain by parts of the Conservative-supporting press. The prime minister's continued willingness to negotiate with Hitler encouraged his Conservative critics to call for a reconstruction of the government. At the end of June, Viscount Astor and Lord Camrose, the owners of the *Observer* and the *Daily Telegraph* – both influential Conservative papers – met with Anthony Eden to discuss how pressure could be brought to bear against Chamberlain. The *Telegraph* then launched a campaign to force the prime minister to give Camrose's friend Churchill ministerial office, in the hope that he would stiffen the government's determination to fight. It was soon taken up by the *Observer*, the *Manchester Guardian* and the *Yorkshire Post* – the two most important regional dailies – the *Daily Mirror* and even the *Daily Worker*. Chamberlain ignored these calls, but Sir Joseph Ball – the director of the Conservative Research Department – was very active in defending the prime minister's position. As well as bugging the Eden Group's phones in order to stay abreast of their machinations, Ball also used the pages of *Truth* – a radical right-wing newssheet with a small circulation, which the Conservatives had secretly acquired in 1936 in order to counteract Rothermere and Beaverbrook's grip on the press – to run a virulent series of anti-Churchill articles during the summer of 1939.[65]

Meanwhile, the promises Britain was making had to be backed up. At the end of March, it was announced that the Territorial Army would double in size. A new shadow factory scheme for aircraft production was instituted. At the end of April, for the first time in modern British history, the government introduced peacetime military conscription. Young men of twenty and twenty-one now became eligible for six months' compulsory training as 'militia men', followed by a period in the reserves. The need to make a big international impression – rather than any pressing demand from Britain's generals – resulted in an annual recruitment target of a quarter of a million men. This would allow Britain not only to keep its anti-aircraft defences in a state of readiness, but also to prepare an expeditionary force to support the French in the event of war. In a few months, the scale of Britain's proposed commitment to a future land war in Europe had been transformed. At the time of Munich, the British had planned to send two divisions to fight alongside the French: by April 1939, they were planning to build an army thirty-two divisions strong.[66]

A rapidly expanding army would require immense supplies of

weapons, equipment and accommodation, but these could not be allowed to interfere with existing plans for the rearmament of the navy and air force. On 20 April, therefore, Chamberlain finally announced the creation of a Ministry of Supply. It would provide munitions for the army in co-ordination with the other service ministries, but also had powers to direct industrial capacity and control reserves of strategic raw materials.

This was not a total takeover of private industry, nor a single organizing body for all the armed forces headed by an arms supremo. Chamberlain's first appointment to be minister of supply was not a dynamic figure such as Churchill or Lloyd George, but rather the unassuming National Liberal MP Leslie Burgin. It was, however, a huge step for a government that had so long resisted dictatorial controls on the economy. As Burgin noted, his new post gave him 'very drastic powers to require supplies to be delivered and work to be done'.[67]

British defence spending accelerated rapidly during the first half of 1939. A White Paper that February laid out expenditure on the armed forces for the coming year of approximately £580 million, compared to £265.5 million in 1937. With the economy outside the arms sector struggling, and unemployment back up to 14 per cent, this was not an increase that could be funded through taxation. The government was also unwilling to countenance a reduction in social spending. Instead, Chamberlain announced a doubling of the Defence Loan to £800 million.

By the time Sir John Simon presented his second budget, on 25 April, estimated defence expenditure had already risen further, to £630 million. Warning that, even without a war, uncontrolled spending might spark another financial crisis, Simon now struggled desperately to enforce limits on the service ministries. His attempts were undermined by the threat of hostilities. As Halifax had already told his colleagues, it was better to 'be bankrupt in peace than beaten in a war against Germany'.[68] By the time the budget was debated for the third time, in mid-July, estimates of defence expenditure for 1939 had risen to £730 million: a sum that for the moment could only be met by further government borrowing.[69]

Having helped the government with its scheme of national registration, the trade unions felt betrayed by the sudden change of policy on conscription. They worried that the introduction of compulsory service in the forces presaged a similar scheme for industrial work. Sir Walter Citrine – himself long convinced that conscription was a necessary part of preparing the country for war – carefully directed protests away from strike action and towards attempts to improve conditions for servicemen and the treatment of conscientious objectors. Eighty-five per cent of Labour MPs voted against the Military Training Bill when it passed through the House of Commons at the end of April, but the party leadership had already decided that, given its own determination to improve the nation's defences, this was not an issue on which the party should fight. Similarly, business opposition to the extension of controls through the Ministry of Supply was limited, and concentrated on setting a time limit for its regulations rather than opposing their introduction.[70]

In contrast to France, in Britain the solution to the problem of economic mobilization was based on a compromise between government, business and labour that helped to preserve the relative stability of the 1930s. In part this was a political difference. The lack of a mass Communist party meant that British conservatives, unlike their French counterparts, concentrated on external rather than internal threats. The British labour movement was better controlled by its leaders and more cohesive. It also reflected a different structure of industrial relations. The National Government was instinctively more comfortable dealing with business federations than with trade unionists, but from the *Anschluss* on, both were actively involved in rearmament. By the start of 1939, both were willing to accept greater government controls in the cause of national defence – provided, on the one hand, that the trade unions got some restrictions on prices and profits, and on the other, that business owners were given the means to keep making money from official contracts. The Treasury's continued preference for an essentially capitalist solution to increasing production – as embodied by Lord Stamp, the economic expert brought in by Chamberlain to review war preparations in summer 1939 – ensured that the restrictions the unions wanted were not implemented before the outbreak of war. The basis for an accommodation between state, capital and labour had, however, already been reached before the fighting began.[71]

The importance of trade unions to the mobilization of industrial manpower meant that the continental commitment posed a danger to

Chamberlain's position. It also made it harder for him to resist demands for an alliance with the Soviet Union. This had long been a complaint of the National Government's parliamentary critics, and their clamour rose after the Polish guarantee. The case for co-operation with the Soviets was strong. Not only could they provide immediate military intervention against a Nazi drive to the east, but their involvement would confront Germany with the prospect of dividing its forces in a two-front war. Whether Soviet co-operation was ever actually achievable was another matter: Stalin probably had no intention of going to war. As far as Chamberlain was concerned, the prospect was so unlikely it was not worth urgently pursuing. Chamberlain suspected that the Soviets actually wanted to set Britain, France and Germany at each other's throats while themselves staying out of any conflict. He also doubted the military capacities of the Red Army, and emphasized the practical difficulties of Eastern and Central European diplomacy where all the small states whose liberty Britain was meant to be defending were as concerned about Stalin's ambitions as they were about those of Hitler.

Chamberlain's position left him isolated as, during April and May 1939, the dangers of involvement in a European war persuaded almost all of his ministerial colleagues that the advantages of a Soviet alliance outweighed its difficulties. With obvious dissatisfaction, he submitted to their will, and on 24 May the Cabinet agreed to pursue a mutual defence pact between France, Britain and the USSR. As the ensuing negotiations stumbled on through July and August, it became apparent that there was an unbridgeable gap between what the Soviets wanted – a binding alliance, plus a free hand to deploy their troops in smaller Eastern European states – what the French and British would offer – more mealy-mouthed definitions that would leave them free to stand back from a Nazi-Soviet fight – and the Western powers' unwillingness to compel the Poles and Romanians to open their borders to the Red Army. Having helped to confirm Soviet suspicions of Anglo-French dilatoriness, Chamberlain was proved correct when the talks broke down. He rebutted suggestions that in the absence of an alliance with the democracies, the USSR might find a way to work with Hitler instead.[72]

'LET US OFFEND THE JEWS
RATHER THAN THE ARABS'

The deteriorating situation in Europe had crucial consequences in the Middle East. In July 1937, the Royal Commission into the future of Palestine had reported that a single state was no longer workable, and that the only solution was to partition the country between Jews and Arabs. Furious Arab leaders accused the British of going back on their promises, and in September 1937, the Arab revolt broke forth with renewed force. One thing the British thought they had learned from the disturbances of the year before was that they needed to crack down quickly. The men who had led the Arab general strike in 1936 were immediately arrested. Only one escaped: the mufti of Jerusalem, Amin al-Husayni, who found sanctuary across the border in the Lebanon. A powerful Sunni cleric and member of one of Palestine's most prominent political families, al-Husayni had originally been appointed by the British. Now, he appealed to other Arabs and other Muslims to help him fight against the British and the Jews.[73]

Back in Palestine, the British effort to decapitate the rebellion did not halt the violence, but it made it less well co-ordinated and moved its focus out of the cities and into the countryside. This time, the British moved more quickly through the repressive repertoire they had learned elsewhere in the Empire. Parts of the Mandate were effectively placed under martial law. The British built a border fence, backed by fortified watchtowers, to stop the flow of supplies over the Syria–Lebanon border. British police and army units swept through rural areas, searching Arab villages, destroying food and houses and imposing collective fines, all in an effort to turn the population against the insurgents.[74]

It was a brutal campaign on both sides. Facing an elusive foe, and encouraged by their commanders to deal roughly with the Arabs, British troops used torture to extract information, beat suspects to death and forced prisoners to ride on the front of their trucks or trains when they travelled on routes that might be mined.[75] When they were attacked, they fired back freely: anyone in the vicinity became a target. Meanwhile, as well as attacking Jewish settlements, security forces and communications, the guerrillas also carried out a campaign of terror against other Arabs, killing politicians who opposed the revolt and farmers who sold land to the Jews. They also extorted money from the same villagers whom the British were fining for backing the rebellion.

During 1938, the violence escalated, and from the summer onwards, the British lost control of substantial portions of Palestine. Short of troops, they came to rely extensively on auxiliary policemen recruited from among the Jewish population. At the peak of the revolt there were about 14,000 of these armed 'supernumeraries'. When it looked like the Czech crisis might result in a European war, the Colonial Office considered using a Jewish army to hold down Palestine while the British concentrated on Germany.[76]

British commanders appealed to London for reinforcements and approval for even tougher policies. With the threat of war rising in Europe, the British government wanted stability. Palestine was seen as crucial to British strategy – an integral part of the defences of the Middle East, and the intended base for Britain's imperial reserve – and the revolt showed dangerous signs of affecting other parts of the Empire – not just among the predominantly Arab populations of Iraq and Egypt, but also, because of the mufti's appeal to Muslim opinion, in parts of India as well.[77]

British ministers were willing to make concessions to get peace in Palestine, but not until the revolt had been beaten. In pursuit of quick results, they sanctioned the military's demands.[78] In the autumn of 1938, after the Munich agreement gave them a breathing space in Europe, the British were able to deploy a second infantry division to Palestine. By the end of the year, their garrison had doubled to 25,000 soldiers and two RAF squadrons. These reinforcements allowed them to take the offensive against the rebels throughout the Mandate. Their commanders included men whose names would become very familiar over the next six years, including Lieutenant General Bernard Montgomery and Air Commodore Arthur Harris. Unlike most of his RAF colleagues, Harris argued that air attacks on Arab villages would be a good way to cripple the guerrillas' morale.

As the British continued their campaign over the winter of 1938–39, the rebels had nowhere to go. Exhausted, the rural population increasingly withdrew their support. The campaign consisted increasingly of internecine warfare between the guerrillas and Arab 'peace bands', organized by pro-negotiation nationalists and armed by the British. Though the violence dragged on, by the spring it was already clear that the revolt had been defeated. By the time the fighting finished, more than 300 Jews and 262 Britons had been killed, but so had more than 5,000 Arabs (approximately 3,800 of them by the security forces: most of the rest by other Arabs). The total number of Arab dead was about 0.5 per cent of the non-Jewish population of Palestine in 1939. Translated into British terms, that would have meant the death of about 200,000 people: or to put it another way, deaths as a result of conflict among the Palestine Arabs were proportionately higher in the three years before September 1939 than they were among Britons in the three years afterwards.[79] The political consequences of the revolt were just as devastating: the urban elite who had led the Palestinian nationalist movement were either imprisoned, in exile, or had fled, and those who were left had no energy or interest in another battle for independence. Yet the need to quieten the Middle East was about to result in a dramatic reversal of British government policy.

During 1938, the colonial secretary, Malcolm MacDonald, had already moved to set up British-Jewish-Arab negotiations on Palestine's future.[80] The conference got under way on 7 February 1939, but no one in Whitehall, including MacDonald, actually thought that a compromise was going to be achieved. Their main aim was to placate the Arab states around the Mandate in order to restore the security of the British Empire in the Middle East. As Chamberlain, supporting MacDonald, explained: 'we are now compelled to consider the Palestine problem mainly from the point of view of the international situation . . . if we must offend one side, let us offend the Jews rather than the Arabs'.[81]

After talks duly broke down at the end of February, the government developed its own policy. On 17 May 1939, the British published a new White Paper on Palestine. This abandoned partition, renounced the idea of creating a Jewish state, and promised that a united Palestine would be made independent within the next ten years. It also placed significant restrictions on Jewish land purchases, and limited Jewish immigration to a maximum of 75,000 over the next five years, with any immigration after that time permitted only with Arab consent. The implication was that the Jews would remain in a minority as Palestine moved towards a system of representative government. The commitments were very conditional: the White Paper stated that a future independence treaty would depend not only on the strategic situation, but also on the participation of all the different communities in Palestine.

This was the same policy that the National Government had pursued over Indian self-government, the Irish treaty ports, or Czechoslovakia – calculated concessions to avoid conflict and safeguard the Empire. Since, however offended they were, the Jews were unlikely to make common cause with Hitler, the shift in official stance made a lot of strategic sense. The restrictions on immigration also meant, however, that just when more Jews than ever were trying to flee from Europe, the British government made it harder for them to leave. There was little other official British help to allow the majority of Jewish refugees to escape.

Unsurprisingly, the Zionist leaders rejected the White Paper. Its publication was greeted by a Jewish general strike and violent demonstrations in Jerusalem and Tel Aviv. By the summer of 1939, Zionist extremists in the Irgun terrorist group stepped up a bombing campaign against the Arabs and prepared for a future rebellion against the British. Meanwhile, the mainstream Jewish defence organization, the Haganah, secretly stockpiled guns and concentrated on organizing illegal immigration. In terms of the future of the Mandate, this was the more significant development: although the Jews were divided politically, the one thing they could all agree on was that more of their people needed to be saved. That would bring them into direct confrontation with the British government.

On the Arab side, Amin al-Husayni also opposed the White Paper. He argued that the measures it set out would neither end Jewish immigration nor lead to any genuine independence for Palestine, since the British would simply use Jewish non-cooperation as an excuse to maintain control. Yet his attempts to re-ignite the rebellion failed. In October 1939, after paying a bribe to the French chief of police, al-Husayni was allowed to escape from Lebanon to Baghdad.[82] His war against the British and the Jews was not over yet.

Back in London, the government's opponents held up the White Paper as another example of its weakness. When the new policy was debated in the Commons on 22 and 23 May 1939, Herbert Morrison told MPs that the Jews were going to be 'sacrificed' to the government's 'inability to govern ... to its apparent fear of, if not, indeed, its sympathy with, violence ... sacrificed to the ... preoccupation with exclusively Imperialist rather than human considerations'.[83] Churchill, a committed Zionist who believed a Jewish state would bulwark the Empire, condemned what he called a 'petition in moral and physical bankruptcy':[84]

> Never was the need for fidelity and firmness more urgent than now. You are not going to found and forge the fabric of a grand alliance to resist aggression, except by showing continued examples of your firmness in carrying out . . . the obligations into which you have entered. I warn the Conservative party . . . that by committing themselves to this lamentable act of default, they will cast our country, and all that it stands for, one more step downward in its fortunes . . .[85]

In the subsequent vote, the government's usual majority of more than two hundred was reduced to just eighty-nine.[86]

'THE LONGER THE WAR IS PUT OFF THE LESS LIKELY IT IS TO COME'

As 1939 went on, Britain and France became increasingly confident about their prospects in a war with Germany. Britain was far from perfectly battle-ready though. Its original programmes of rearmament would not be complete until 1942. Battleships were still on slipways, aircraft still unbuilt, and the army's plans in mid-gear change from an imperial expeditionary force to a continental leviathan. Air-raid precautions provision remained inconsistent, as were preparations to mobilize the economy for war. Ration books were already printed, but there was no realistic plan about how to maintain the flow of supplies through Britain's ports in the event of German air attack.[87]

Nonetheless, by the summer of 1939 Britain was much better prepared to withstand an immediate assault than it had been a year before. In the aircraft industry in particular, there had been a step change in production as factories solved the problems of adapting to modern aircraft construction, laid out their assembly lines and expanded their workforce. A mix of expansion, dilution and subcontracting meant that between June 1938 and June 1939, the workforce in aircraft factories doubled, while the structure weight of aircraft produced increased three-fold. The number of aircraft built in Britain in the first half of 1939 was nearly four times greater than in the equivalent period of 1938, and only slightly less than the total figure for all of 1936 and 1937 combined. In the course of the year as a whole, Britain produced almost as many planes as Germany for the first time since the start of the arms race. British monthly aircraft production exceeded the equivalent German figure for the first time in September 1939. By then, twenty-six of the RAF's thirty-nine fighter squadrons had been re-equipped with the most modern aircraft. Critically, these were now incorporated into an air defence system with an operational set of radar stations that would provide early warning of incoming raids.[88]

Meanwhile, Sir Wilfrid Freeman had been putting in place measures to expand production still further in the future. These included concentrating the manufacture of the most advanced planes among groups of aircraft firms and subcontractors in the same areas; securing funds from the Treasury for new factories to make the aero-engines and aluminium alloys needed to build the new planes, and laying the basis for a repair organization that would get damaged aircraft and engines back into action. By 1939, the total productive floorspace in use by the air industry totalled 8 million square feet. The Air Ministry planned to see that expand to 19 million square feet by 1941. Not only was Britain better protected than it had been in 1938, but it was also going to get even stronger in the years to come.[89]

France too had seen its position transformed. As the labour controls implemented the previous year took effect, military production surged: tank output doubled and aircraft output quadrupled between 1938 and 1939. Major new investment programmes were put in place to expand munitions production still further in the coming years.[90] Now, for the first time in twenty years, French generals were talking in detail with their British counterparts about how the two countries could work together to defeat Germany.

The British and French general staffs were optimistic. Intelligence from Germany suggested that its rearmament programme was creating such economic problems that it was already past its peak: in contrast, British and French programmes were accelerating. This in itself might deter the Germans. If it did not, it would decide the war. Germany and its allies might try to use their temporary advantage on land and in the air, but they would be unable to challenge Anglo-French command of the seas. It now looked as if the British and French would be able to withstand any initial attack, and as any conflict went on, they would mobilize the full weight of their global empires to unstoppable effect. Meanwhile Germany, blocked from obtaining crucial resources, would grind to a halt and be forced to admit defeat. In turn, this belief in a prolonged test of military-economic power encouraged a tough line on Germany's eastward expansion – it should not be allowed to ameliorate its position by grabbing resources from the Balkans and Eastern Europe.[91]

In contrast, the British Treasury remained much less sanguine about the country's long-term strength. Expenditure on defence had breached all limits. Although the arms industries were booming, the rest of the economy seemed primed for another recession just as the surge in government spending ramped up inflation. The huge quantity of imports required for rearmament, including steel from German-controlled Czechoslovakia, was devastating the balance of payments. International investors, spooked by the crises of 1938–39, were withdrawing their money from the City of London. That exerted a downward pressure on sterling, but the US Treasury made it clear that it expected the Bank of England to abide by the 1936 tripartite currency agreement, and sell gold and foreign currency reserves in order to prop up the pound.

Concerned by the international situation, President Roosevelt had now initiated America's own programme of rearmament, and despite the continued strength of isolationist opinion, he had sought to bolster resistance to the dictators by privately reassuring Chamberlain that he would do his best to put US industrial strength behind Britain if war broke out. By the spring of 1939, however, suspicions were growing in the US that, under the guise of the pressures on sterling caused by rearmament, the British were allowing a depreciation of their currency to gain a competitive advantage over American exporters. Despite his words of support, moreover, Roosevelt had not revised the Neutrality Acts that prohibited sales of US arms to nations that were at war.[92] Aware of the need to keep America on side, and given the alternative of attempting to impose at short notice currency controls across the whole Sterling Area, the British complied for as long as they could. Between March 1938 and 25 August 1939, when the attempt was finally abandoned, maintaining exchange rates cost the UK £300 million in gold, 40 per cent of the reserves on which it was counting if it proved necessary to fight a long war. As the chancellor laid out to the Cabinet in July, with the limited measures available to control the economy in peacetime, Britain would be able to maintain its current level of military effort for only about another nine months. The economic pressures created by preparing for battle were such that they could only be mastered with far-reaching controls that would be politically acceptable only once hostilities had actually begun.[93]

The problem of diminishing British currency reserves was as nothing, however, to the difficulties facing Germany and Italy as they struggled to keep up with the Anglo-French rearmament surge. By mid-1939, German plans to increase aircraft and munitions production were being hamstrung by shortages of raw materials. Balance of payments and inflation crises loomed. Spending increased, but production slumped. Meanwhile, the Japanese decided not to join the Pact of Steel: they were more concerned about tensions with the USSR than being dragged into a European war. The Italian government also voiced anxieties as it realized how far it had fallen behind in the arms race and how little chance it would have in the face of British and French naval blockades. British policy seemed to be working.[94]

Hitler understood that the combination of Britain, France and America – which he always presumed would fight on the side of the democracies – would eventually win a prolonged arms race. He still believed, however, that he had a couple of years to get ready for this defining war in the west. One preliminary was to secure his eastern flank. When the Poles not only refused to enter into an alliance with Germany but instead secured Anglo-French security guarantees, he was infuriated. Britain and France were, he was sure, playing the same game they had over the Sudetenland. They would try to coerce him with threats, but if he called their bluff they would not ultimately be willing to fight. Happy as he was to accept the risk of battle, he reassured his generals that British and French threats of action were empty. Now was the moment to destroy Poland.

Chamberlain, having read the reports of Germany's economic problems, believed that Hitler must finally understand the logic of his situation. In late July he told his sister that it was now clear that the Führer

has concluded that we mean business and that the time is not right for the major war. Therein he is fulfilling my expectations. Unlike some of

my critics I go further and say the longer the war is put off the less likely
it is to come at all as we go on perfecting our defences, and building up
the defences of our allies. That is what Winston and co never seem to
realise. You don't need offensive forces sufficient to win a smashing
victory. What you want are defensive forces sufficiently strong to make it
impossible for the other side to win except at such a cost as to make it
not worthwhile.[95]

Convinced that peace could still be achieved but unable to pursue it too
openly, during the summer Chamberlain kept up secret contacts with
German leaders through British pro-Nazi sympathizers and European
businessmen. He wanted to make clear that, if Germany could prove it
did not want war, room was still open for negotiation. None of these
contacts came to anything, but by their nature they demonstrated how
difficult the prime minister's position had now become. However much
he believed that his long-term strategy was reaching fruition, his opponents cast every strengthening of Britain's stance as proof of his earlier
failure. Where he looked for opportunities to make a final grasp for peace,
they raised the fear that he was planning to give in to Hitler again.[96]

At the start of August, the Commons debated whether to adjourn, as
the government proposed, for its normal summer recess. Labour tabled
an amendment suggesting that, given the international situation, the
parliamentary break should be shortened to just three weeks. Eden
remained silent; Churchill attacked the government for avoiding debate
and calling any criticism unpatriotic. Determined to demonstrate his
control, Chamberlain made the issue a motion of confidence. In the
vote that followed, forty rebellious government MPs abstained, but the
rest, including Eden, rallied behind Chamberlain. The Labour motion
was defeated. MPs departed for what was supposed to be a long
vacation.

'ORIENTALS CAN INSULT
ENGLISHMEN WITH IMPUNITY'

Just over a week after Britain issued its guarantee of Polish independence, Cheng Lien-shih, a Chinese banker who worked for the Japanese,
went to the theatre in the British concession in the town of Tientsin, in

the Japanese-controlled zone of northern China. There, he was assassinated by Chinese nationalists. The fate of the suspects in Cheng's murder would spark a crisis that laid bare just how vulnerable Britain's position in the Far East had become.[97]

When the war with China started in summer 1937, Japanese generals had expected a quick victory that would allow them to concentrate on building up their strength for a future struggle with the Soviet Union and the Western empires. Instead, they got bogged down in a seemingly unendable conflict that absorbed men and money without conclusive result. The Japanese were better equipped and trained than their Chinese opponents, and by the end of 1938 they had captured most of northern China and the eastern seaboard. The Nationalist government had been forced to retreat to the south-western stronghold of Chongqing, while a Communist enclave waged a guerrilla war against the Japanese in the north. Yet during 1938, while the eyes of the world were on Austria and Czechoslovakia, Nationalist troops had shown that they could fight long campaigns against the Japanese – and even sometimes beat them – without allowing themselves to be destroyed. By the start of 1939, there were about a million Japanese soldiers in China. That year, the war would cost Japan almost half its national budget. It seemed no closer to a conclusion.[98]

The new British base at Singapore had been opened – with work still going on to complete it – in February 1938. With the threat of war looming in Europe, however, the British had neither the ships to despatch a fleet to Singapore, nor the planes to spare to defend Malaya. Given the weakness of their defences, the British were far from unhappy to see the Japanese stuck in China. Notwithstanding Chamberlain's desire for a rapprochement, British ministers and officials often had the feeling that they ought to be standing up to the Japanese more – and that they would do so, as soon as matters in Europe had been resolved. Though often contemptuous of the corruption and inefficiency that plagued the Nationalist war effort, British observers were confident that Chiang Kai-shek's regime would survive, and the British did what they could to support China – all the while carefully trying to avoid any confrontation with the Japanese.[99]

It was little enough. Britain provided the Nationalists with a paltry amount of financial aid to stabilize the Chinese currency, and by recognizing them as the legitimate government, undermined Japan's argument that it was imposing order on a lawless state. More importantly, the British also allowed military supplies for the Nationalists to travel through their territory. In the year after the war broke out, 60,000 tons of munitions a month moved through the British treaty port of Hong Kong. In February 1938, the British allowed the construction of the Burma Road, a 700-mile route snaking north through mountainous terrain from Lashio in Burma to the Chinese city of Kunming. It was completed in October 1938 (at which point the British loaned the Chinese £500,000 to buy trucks to run along it).[100] It was ready only just in time: in the same month, the Japanese advance to Guangzhou surrounded Hong Kong. Alongside a rail line from the port of Hai Phong in French Indochina, the Burma Road would provide a vital supply link from the outside world to Chongqing.

Even the very limited help that the British government was giving to the Nationalist regime infuriated the Japanese army. It also, however, offered it an opportunity to explain to the Japanese home front why it was failing to win the war. During the spring of 1939, ultranationalist propagandists in Japan, some funded by the army, whipped up a storm of public anger against the duplicitous British imperialists who were exploiting the Chinese in order to hold Japan back from its rightful destiny as a great power.

In Britain's South-East Asian colonies, meanwhile, the war mobilized the sympathies of the Chinese diaspora, including the wealthy merchants of Singapore. Just as in China, a temporary alliance was formed between Nationalist and Communist leaders, who organized door-to-door collections and boycotts of Japanese businesses. Between 1937 and 1942, Chinese communities in South-East Asia remitted home the equivalent of about £80 million – perhaps a third of the war expenditure of the Nationalist government. During the first two years of the war, Japanese exports to Malaya fell by 75 per cent. Violent demonstrations against Japanese interests made the British colonial authorities nervous: who knew what the next target might be of all this anti-imperialist angst?[101]

At the start of 1939, as conflict in Europe grew more imminent, a debate took place within Whitehall about whether to adapt British strategy. A war with three opponents – Germany, Italy and Japan – seemed as likely as ever. Everyone agreed that it would be beyond the Empire's resources to fight all three at once. The answer seemed to be to despatch the weakest one first. In the event of such a war, therefore, the admirals wanted to concentrate their efforts initially on beating the Italians in the Mediterranean. This would mean abandoning the existing pledge to send a strong fleet to the newly opened base at Singapore.

The question was whether to recognize this by changing the plans about how to defend the Empire. If Britain accepted that the Singapore strategy was now unachievable, it could plan instead to send out a 'flying squadron' of just two capital ships to the Far East. If these ships could avoid being brought to battle, they might just be enough to make things difficult for the Japanese until more forces became available. Such a drastic change of plan was, however, bound to lead to a confrontation with the Dominions. For that reason, the 'flying squadron' proposal was rejected. Instead, the British now dropped the Singapore strategy in practice, but retained it in principle. At the start of July, the 'period before relief' was raised from seventy to ninety days. In a three-front war, the Royal Navy was not now going to forsake the Mediterranean to sail out to the Far East, yet planning for a conflict with Japan remained predicated on the commitment that it would do exactly that.[102]

Overstretched as they were, the British had little choice but to look to the United States to assume the burden of being the dominant Western power in the Pacific and East Asia. As yet, it was still far from certain that they would take up the load. By the spring of 1939, the Americans were taking more of an interest in the fate of China. They arranged a loan of $25 million to the Chinese government and issued a 'moral embargo' on the sale of aircraft parts to Japan.

Not least because of their work together on the China station, relations between the British and American navies improved from the fierce rivalry that had existed in the 1920s to a closer co-operation and sharing of information. In March 1939, Roosevelt welcomed an inquiry from Lord Halifax about the resumption of talks on naval strategy. They eventually took place – in conditions of extraordinary secrecy – that June, at the home of the American chief of naval operations (and Roosevelt's trusted friend) Admiral William Leahy. A single British officer handed over signal and code books that would allow the two navies to work together if a war broke out. He also explained – with much more honesty than the British showed to the Pacific

Dominions – that Britain's European commitments meant that it was for the moment unable to send a fleet worthy of the name to Singapore. In turn, Leahy made it clear that if war broke out in Europe, Roosevelt would send the US fleet to the American base at Pearl Harbor in Hawaii in order to act as a deterrent to the Japanese. In the event that both countries found themselves at war with Germany, Italy and Japan, he thought that the US fleet would concentrate on the Pacific. Since they could not hope to defend their forward base in the Philippines, the Americans might use Singapore to take on the Japanese – providing that the British could also send at least some capital ships to give the impression to the American public of a joint effort.[103]

In retrospect, the grand strategic division that Leahy suggested – created de facto by the vacuum left by the collapse of the Singapore strategy – looks a lot like the way that the Anglo-American alliance would organize the war that broke out in December 1941. At the time, however, the talks offered some reassurance but little certainty. Their extreme secrecy indicated just how isolationist public opinion in America still was: any suggestion that the two navies were talking would jeopardize plans for co-operation. There was no pledge to come to Britain's aid if America was still at peace. Crucially, despite repeated suggestions over the next two years from British admirals, the US navy had no intention of deploying its ships to Singapore before the outbreak of war.

Meanwhile, back in Tientsin, the British police had arrested four suspects in the murder of Cheng Lien-shih, and handed them over to the Japanese for interrogation. By spring 1939, this was a well-established procedure: provided they showed on their return no visible sign of having been tortured, the evidence thus gathered would be used to turn the suspects over for a trial in a Chinese court that was collaborating with the Japanese. This time, however, the men retracted their confessions, and Chiang Kai-shek intervened to say that the Chinese government wanted them released. This ruptured the pretext behind which the British had been hiding – that the collaborating court represented the legitimate government. Trapped, the British authorities interned the men.[104]

Back in London, Chamberlain was furious at the mess that had been allowed to develop at Tientsin. The British sought ways to hand back the Chinese suspects without losing face. Yet for the Japanese, the incident had become a means to demand much more, including complete recognition of their plans for a new order in Asia and an end to British support for Chiang. On 15 June 1939, the local army commander decided to impose a blockade on the British concession. Roadblocks were thrown up and traffic was halted. As they passed through Japanese checkpoints on their way in and out of the concession, the white inhabitants were subjected to humiliating searches and abuse. As officials in Tientsin complained, the Japanese seemed set on showing that, 'Orientals can insult Englishmen with impunity' because the 'British Empire is too enfeebled to react'.[105]

Indeed it was. Without abandoning the Eastern Mediterranean – which it now did not want to do – two capital ships were the most the Admiralty could spare to reinforce Britain's position in the Far East. That was far too small a force to raise the stakes in the negotiations over Tientsin. Nor – notwithstanding the discussions that were now taking place about future strategy – were the Americans about to come to Britain's aid in a crisis that preceded the start of a war – and which they thought that British incompetence had started in the first place. The chiefs of staff advised the Cabinet that without America's help, it 'would not be justifiable . . . to take any avoidable action which might lead to hostilities with Japan'.[106] The British government had no choice but to negotiate and submit as gracefully as it could.

Eager though they were to drive the British out of China, Japan's leaders did not want to push the Tientsin crisis to the point of war. Since the start of the year, the Japanese government had been debating whether to conclude a military alliance with Germany. Everyone wanted the security of a German alliance against the Soviet Union. No one except the army wanted to take the risk of committing Japan to a war against Britain, France and the United States while so much Japanese strength was being used up in China. Talks with Germany broke down, however, leaving Japan diplomatically isolated. The Japanese Foreign Ministry, navy and powerful business corporations all feared American economic sanctions, and were anxious to avoid creating a situation in which the British could successfully call on American help. Even the army, which was otherwise keen to force bigger concessions from the British and to assert its own right to make policy in China, had its attention occupied elsewhere. Since May 1939, clashes between Soviet and Japanese forces on the Mongolian border had escalated into major fighting. At the start of July, against orders from Tokyo, officers in Manchuria took the offensive, but were stopped in their tracks by a determined Red Army defence. With China still not pacified, Japan was in no position to win a northern war against the Soviet Union *and* pick a fight with the Western powers. Ironically, the British weren't the only ones who were worried about a conflict on three fronts.[107]

The problem was the intensity of the anger against Britain that had now been inspired among the Japanese population as the army sought to build support for a German alliance. During July 1939, more than a million people were estimated to have taken part in anti-British rallies and demonstrations in Japan.[108] The ferocity of the emotions thus aroused showed signs of getting out of hand: any Japanese politician who suggested compromise would be threatened with assassination by extremist groups.

On 22 July 1939, after a week of discussions in Tokyo, the British ambassador, Sir Robert Craigie, and the Japanese foreign minister, Arita Hachirō, agreed a set of accords that were meant to lay the grounds for further discussions on policing and economic relations and hence resolve the crisis. Without US help and with war drawing nearer in Europe, the British were forced to abandon their previous policy and to recognize the legitimacy of Japan's occupation of northern China. In London, the government hoped that it would be able to sell the accords as simply promising a friendlier attitude towards Japan. There was no possibility that Japanese ministers would publicize it as anything other than the humiliating climbdown it actually was.

Four days later, however, the US announced that it was abrogating its commercial treaty with Japan. This was not actually a sign of a hardening American mood. On the contrary, it reflected how much money American businesses were making out of Japan's rearmament boom as shipments of oil and scrap iron flowed across the Pacific. The impetus in Congress to abrogate the treaty came not from any desire to show displeasure at Japanese behaviour in East Asia, but instead from businessmen who hoped it could be renegotiated on better terms, although Roosevelt's administration gladly backed the move because it would mean that the White House could impose economic sanctions without reference back to Congress.

The British, however, took this as a sign that the Americans wanted to take a tougher stance in the Pacific. The best way to secure American support in the Far East would be to back them up and defy the Japanese in the economic discussions that were now taking place. With anti-British feeling still running high, the Japanese were unwilling to accept any compromise. The talks continued through August with both sides expecting that they were going to fail. This raised the dangerous possibility of a further breakdown in Anglo-Japanese relations, driven on by the strength of popular animosity in Japan, in which Britain would find itself having moved towards a Far Eastern conflict far in advance of any possible assistance from the United States. In addition, from mid-August, German pressure on Poland was backed up with increasingly violent threats of military action. Might war break out in the west and the east at the same time?

Inadvertently, the Soviet Union now saved the British Empire. First, on 20 August 1939, the Red Army launched a major counter-offensive against the Japanese on the Mongolian border. By the end of the month, they had driven back the Japanese army. Two days later, it was announced that the USSR and Germany were about to sign a non-aggression pact. Its public clauses declared that the Soviet Union and Germany would remain at peace for the next ten years and give no assistance to the other's enemies in the event of a war. Secret addenda, which became apparent the following month, laid out how Poland would be divided between the two, and awarded the Soviets a sphere of interest through a wide swathe of Eastern Europe. Ribbentrop, Hitler's foreign minister, had been able to give his Soviet counterpart Molotov what the Western democracies had not: a free hand to dismember other states to address the security concerns of the Soviet Union.

No one had expected this. In Japan, the news of the defeat in Mongolia had been kept from the public, but the Nazi-Soviet pact could not be concealed. Suddenly, the Soviets were freed of the threat of a war in the west, and all Japan's diplomacy and strategy was called into question. The government fell, and the anti-British movement collapsed. With the attention off Tientsin, local concessions to the Japanese – including the handing over of the four murder suspects – allowed the crisis to be resolved, and the blockade was finally lifted in March 1940.

'WE MUST FINISH THE NAZI REGIME THIS TIME'

In Europe, the strategic implications of the Nazi-Soviet pact were just as dramatic. Germany's eastern front was now secure. It could attack Poland not just without fear of Russian intervention but in cahoots with the Red Army. Access to Soviet raw materials and a porous eastern border would help to protect Germany against the effects of an Anglo-French blockade. On the other hand, this alignment with the Bolsheviks gave Mussolini the excuse he was looking for to avoid any immediate military commitment to Germany under the Pact of Steel.

In London, news of the pact came as a shock, but though it made it all but certain that Germany would invade Poland, it had little effect on the British and French governments' determination to respond with a declaration of war. The loss of such a powerful potential ally in the east did not change the argument that now was the moment when the western democracies must enter a trial of strength. As General Pownall, vice chief of Britain's imperial general staff, explained to his diary at the end of August:

> We must finish the Nazi regime this time. To compromise and discuss is useless, it will all happen again. If the Nazi regime can be so discredited that it disappears from Germany by German action, i.e. without a war, so much the better. If that doesn't happen we must have a war. We can't lose it. Last September we might have lost a *short* war. Now we shouldn't, nor a long war either. But that the regime must go I am convinced.[109]

Even Sir Horace Wilson had decided that the time had come to deal firmly with the Nazis. On 31 August Birger Dahlerus, the Swedish businessman who acted as Göring's go-between with the British, rang Wilson to propose a peaceful settlement based on the Poles giving the Germans everything they wanted. When Dahlerus tried to blame the whole crisis on the Poles, Wilson put the phone down on him.[110]

PREPARING FOR BATTLE

Well before August 1939, the physical preparations for war became much more apparent in the UK. A huge programme of government construction was under way. In total, the estimated cost to completion of all the defence-related works being built by autumn 1939 was £284 million – about seven times the government's annual expenditure on social services in 1938.[111] The Admiralty was building a large new underground armament depot at Dean Hill in Hampshire, mine depots and reinforced oil-storage tanks in Pembrokeshire, and a new munitions factory at Caerwent in Monmouthshire, as well as £3 million-worth of new protective measures at the naval bases at Rosyth, Scapa Flow and Invergordon. The War Office was building training depots and stores at Longtown in Cumberland, Chilwell in Nottingham and Donnington in Shropshire. It was also engaged on a rushed new programme of camps for the recently conscripted militiamen.

By 1939, the RAF had 158 airfields in the UK, three times more than in 1934.[112] Each was a major building project, requiring the levelling, drainage and sewing of long grass runways (easier to camouflage and more forgiving to land on than concrete) and the erection of accommodation for aircraft, equipment and personnel, usually in that order. Each cost, on average, about the same as a naval cruiser.[113] Behind them lay a rapidly expanding network of stores (including major sites in Cheshire, Shropshire and Gloucestershire), repair depots (at Warrington, Hartlebury, Abbotsinch and Stafford) and a massive new training base at St Athan. A quarter of the Air Ministry's construction budget was allocated to building new factories, such as the massive new Spitfire works then under way at Castle Bromwich, near Birmingham.

Meanwhile, the Ministry of Supply had taken over the building of Royal Ordnance factories. Before rearmament began, state munitions' production had been concentrated in three factories. By September 1939, six more had opened and another twelve had been approved, including works at Bridgend, Bishopton and Chorley. Most were positioned as far away as possible from German airfields and British cities, in Wales, north-west England and Scotland. They were immense sites, with their own power and water plants and rail lines, laid out over hundreds of acres of flat land to minimize the hazards of explosives' production and dotted with bunkers to store their dangerous output.

Alongside this expanding structural presence, the armed forces also sucked in more men. For most of the inter-war period, the Territorial Army had struggled to recruit. After Munich and *Kristallnacht*, however, its ranks filled with new volunteers. In Warwickshire, for example, enlistment between May and October 1938 was twice what it had been the year before, and between August and October ten times higher. The expansion of the Territorials' anti-aircraft role saw the formation of new workplace units from organizations as diverse as London Transport, Lloyd's of London and the Frigidaire factory in Wembley. Nationally, the result was that by the end of the year, the Territorial Army had over 200,000 members and was within a few hundred men of its peacetime recruitment target. When the number of Territorial infantry battalions was doubled in spring 1939, new recruits poured in: 88,000 in April alone. The introduction of conscription served a strategic and diplomatic purpose for the government, but it did not reflect a shortage of volunteers.[114]

Efforts to improve air-raid precautions were the most visible part of the preparations for war. Despite the German bombing raids on London during the last war, this was still a very new way to think about fighting. For all the discussion of air attack since 1918, no one really had any experience – beyond reports from China and Spain – of what a modern air war between two major European powers would be like. The year after Munich saw extensive debate over shelter provision, with the Labour and Liberal parties demanding more state action and the construction of deep underground shelters. Official policy, however, was that, since there was no guaranteed protection against a direct hit, the dispersion of the population in small shelters would better minimize casualties than their concentration in larger bunkers. Building deep shelters for all of Britain's city-dwellers would have been extremely expensive, and would have restricted the forces' expansion programmes. Government policy was also conditioned by the fear that deep subterranean bunkers would encourage a 'shelter mentality', from which the huddled masses would never emerge to continue the war effort.[115]

Instead, there was the Anderson shelter: a small, mass-produced steel structure for erection in individual gardens or backyards. It was distributed free to those who lived in vulnerable areas and earned less than £250 a year or who were compulsorily covered by the National Health Insurance Act. Everyone else had to pay £5. One-and-a-half million Andersons were provided between February and September 1939. For those inner-city households without sufficient backyard space to erect an Anderson, local authorities and landlords were meant to provide shelters in basements, streets and public spaces. As with the rest of the ARP system, official shelter provision was based on the presumption that air attacks would be brief but devastating, take place in daylight and involve prolific use of poison gas. Both Andersons and public shelters were meant to offer a short-term, quickly accessible form of protection.[116]

In the year after Munich, the structure of civil defence developed significantly at national and local levels. The spring of 1939 saw the appointment of regional commissioners who would take charge of each of the thirteen Civil Defence regions into which the country was divided. Most local authorities now had in place an ARP controller – normally the town clerk, a professional local civil servant – to direct emergency preparations, and to report to committees of councillors and municipal officials. The first half of 1939 saw a stepping up of efforts to survey shelter needs and in the conduct of ARP exercises of varying levels of elaborateness. Nevertheless, ARP remained as much a matter of discussion as practice, and where local authorities were late starting, they found themselves involved in a desperate competition for available supplies of equipment and materials. Even within the same cities, boroughs varied significantly in their level of planning and provision. An independent report into local authority ARP in June 1939 suggested that 'in many areas' there was 'still no decision as to methods'.[117]

A network of ARP workers was meant to provide the human counterpart of air-raid shelters. Some of them were in full-time paid posts, but the majority were part-time volunteers. At the lowest level, air-raid wardens were meant to be the equivalent of Anderson shelters – local volunteers who would make sure that their neighbours abided by the blackout regulations and provide the first line of reporting and response in the case of raids. Behind them were teams of decontamination, rescue and first-aid workers as well as firefighters and policemen. The whole system of emergency response for raids was to be directed by control centres mostly located in, or close to, council offices.

The first appeal for ARP workers in March 1938 had met a less than overwhelming response. By that June, only 200,000 potential wardens had come forward towards a total target of a million, and only a quarter of them had received any training. As with the Territorial Army, recruitment accelerated rapidly between 1938 and 1939. An auxiliary fire service, to provide paid part-time support to local fire brigades, was instituted in 1938: over the next year, the number of firemen nationally increased from 5,000 to 75,000, 85 per cent of whom were auxiliaries. When Mass-Observation questioned ARP workers in Fulham, the three most-frequently given reasons for joining were 'A Desire to Help', 'Sense of Duty' and 'Patriotism'. Two respondents explained their range of motivations:

> Man, upper working class, aged 45: 'Well I suppose more or less it's in the blood, isn't it? I done four and a half years in the Great War, so it comes natural really.'
>
> Woman, upper working class, aged 28: 'Everybody else seemed to be doing it. I just wanted to do something . . . It seemed to be the right thing to do.'[118]

By July 1939, the national total of ARP staff was close to a revised target of 1.6 million, but whereas some areas had over-recruited, many of the most vulnerable urban boroughs were still struggling to fill their ranks.[119] Left to themselves, most people were not getting ready for war. Despite the huge increase in voluntary participation in Britain's defences between 1938 and 1939, the total numbers involved were at most only about a tenth of the adult population.[120]

It had been intended that a third of those recruited for ARP work would be women, who expected to work as nurses, drivers and wardens but not on the 'heavy rescue' work parties that would undertake the exploration of bombed buildings. By 1939, the Women's Voluntary Service – a body originally founded the previous year at the instigation of the home secretary to lobby local authorities to accelerate their precautionary measures against air attack – was also taking a significant role in planning evacuation and post-raid welfare. Recruited under the leadership of the formidable philanthropist Lady Stella Reading, by the outbreak of war the WVS had a centre in most counties of England and about 165,000 members. Almost entirely they were middle-aged, middle-class housewives. The unpaid organizers of the inter-war world of Women's Institutes and whist drives for the local Conservative Association were now preparing themselves to withstand the impact of enemy air attack.[121]

ARP remained the subject of political controversy. At a national level, both Labour and Liberals criticized the government's unwillingness to provide deep shelters as a further instance of its inadequate preparation and its lack of care for the people. For the government's opponents, a foreign policy that had missed the opportunity to avoid a war was matched by an ARP policy built on blatantly class lines. Even after 1938, some more left-wing councils dragged their feet on their ARP schemes.[122]

More frequently, however, local politicians of every political stripe worked up plans while blaming the failures of central government for their shortfalls. Civil defence was a civic responsibility. In Glasgow, for example, the lord provost, Patrick Dollan, and his wife Agnes, major figures in Scottish socialism and anti-war resisters in the last great conflict, now became leading lights in drumming up support for the city's ARP services in what Dollan called 'the defence of civic and national freedom'. Fighting Fascism meant getting ready to resist the bombers too.[123]

Plans for evacuating the vulnerable similarly mixed controversy and compliance. On 5 January 1939, the Ministry of Health issued a circular laying out the *Government Evacuation Scheme* for England and Wales. At the same time a similar scheme was being worked out for Scotland. Given the aim of removing millions of children and adults from Britain's big cities, the only way to provide accommodation in the reception areas was to rely on billeting evacuees in private homes. Householders would be paid a billeting rate of 10s. 6d. per week for the first unaccompanied child, and 8s. 6d. for each thereafter. Those who were unwilling to take evacuees voluntarily would be compelled to do so by the local billeting officer.

Billeting rates were not exactly generous, but by the start of spring 1939 offers had been made to look after more than 2.5 million unaccompanied schoolchildren across England, Wales and Scotland. Yet the threat of the state invading the home to force housewives to take in other people's children aroused considerable anger among some potential billetors, particularly in those areas, such as rural Kent, where a rich mythology already existed around the excesses of visiting urban hordes. Accommodation that was privately reserved for family and friends making their own way out of the cities did not have to be offered for billeting. By February, this designation had been applied to more than a million rooms in the reception areas, a sixth of all their surplus accommodation.[124]

SPEAKING FOR BRITAIN

How did Britons react to the slide to war? One way to get a sense of that is by using the polls conducted by the British Institute of Public Opinion (BIPO). The Institute had been founded in 1936 when Henry Durant, a PhD student at the London School of Economics, was offered the chance to lead a British outpost of the opinion-polling business set up in the US by George Gallup. Gallup's aim was to let ordinary people influence government policy by assessing their attitudes, but he also recognized that there was money to be made in selling evidence of opinion to newspapers. Both aspects appealed to Durant – a working-class boy made good with a public-school scholarship and a City job as an insurance actuary, but also a member of the Labour Party. Rather like Mass-Observation, therefore, the BIPO was social research with political intent – and where Mass-Observation was just trying to keep the wolf from the door, Durant also wanted to run a profit-making business.[125]

The BIPO's most commonly employed technique relied on paid researchers living in different parts of the country conducting interviews with a sample group of about 1,500 adults. This sample was meant to replicate the nation as a whole in terms of age, class, gender and geographic distribution (although the BIPO did not cover Northern Ireland). Interviewers were not meant to ask the same person twice, or to ask more than three people in the same street or firm. Otherwise, they had free range about how diligently they sought out their interviewees, not least in judging the social class to which they thought they belonged. Respondents were asked questions with a relatively limited range of answers, and the results were presented in easily understood percentage form.

It was these headline figures that made the BIPO's findings newsworthy. From 1938, the sole right to publish the Institute's findings was purchased by the Liberal-supporting *News Chronicle*, and for the next year, the paper was the Institute's only paying customer. The *News Chronicle* had in theory no editorial control over the polls, although it hung its own news stories on their findings. In practice, Durant sometimes used questions passed on to him by the editor from the chairman of the paper's board, the Quaker chocolate magnate

Laurence Cadbury, and promoted opinion polling as a means to show how unpopular the National Government's foreign policy had become. Nonetheless, Durant's aims were idealistic, and he was more committed to the cause of voicing what the public were thinking than misrepresenting them for a political ideal.

During 1938, the BIPO surveys demonstrated the ways in which appeasement split opinion. Both before and after the *Anschluss*, only a quarter of respondents would admit that they were in favour of 'Mr Chamberlain's foreign policy', while almost three-quarters thought that Eden had been right to resign. Only a third, however, thought that the UK should definitely 'promise assistance to Czechoslovakia if Germany also acts toward her as she did toward Austria'. In the immediate aftermath of the Sudeten crisis, just over 50 per cent of those questioned agreed that they were satisfied with Chamberlain as prime minister, as against 40 per cent who disagreed. Although these approval figures fell in November, as disillusionment with the settlement grew, they were back up by the end of the year.[126]

By the start of 1939, Munich was clearly seen as a postponement, rather than as a deliverance. Asked to decide which of a number of statements came nearest to their own view of 'Mr Chamberlain's policy of appeasement', 28 per cent picked 'It is a policy which will ultimately lead to enduring peace in Europe'; 46 per cent 'It will keep us out of war until we have time to rearm'; and 24 per cent 'It is bringing war nearer by whetting the appetites of the dictators'.[127]

Well before Hitler demonstrated his contempt for the Munich settlement by crushing the rump Czech state in March, the BIPO's results suggested that opinion had shifted against extremisms of the right. At the end of 1938, asked whom they would like to win in a war between Russia and Germany, 61 per cent chose the former against only 9 per cent for the latter. In January 1939, asked whether, if they had to choose, they would rather live under Communism or Fascism, two-thirds chose the former, less than a quarter the latter.[128] By April, in a marked change from the views expressed after the *Anschluss*, 73 per cent of respondents favoured guaranteeing the borders of small nations. Notwithstanding evidence of support for Cripps and Churchill, Chamberlain's approval rating remained solid as his government took a tougher line with Germany. By August, as the situation in Eastern Europe deteriorated, 76 per cent of those surveyed by the BIPO agreed that if Germany and Poland went to war over Danzig, the UK ought to fulfil its 'pledge to fight on Poland's side'.[129]

These polls had no effect on government policy. There is no evidence that ministers thought of them as anything other than what they would have expected from the paper that published them. Their findings did, however, accord with a much broader sense in the British press that public opinion had shifted against appeasement in the spring of 1939. Even those papers that did not support the government's guarantee to Poland, such as the Beaverbrook-owned *Daily Express* and *Evening Standard*, highlighted that the move, as the latter put it, 'accords with the changing outlook of the British people'.[130]

The belief that another dose of Munich would be unpopular strengthened the hand of those within government who wanted Chamberlain to take a stronger stance against Germany. It also helped to underpin the Labour leadership's conviction that defying Hitler was not just ideologically necessary but politically advantageous. On 16 August, Labour's own *Daily Herald* explained clearly to the party's supporters that further appeasement could not be tolerated: 'Nothing is more desirable than the pacification of Europe. But it will not be obtained by such means. The lesson of Munich is decisive. There cannot be another.'[131] By the end of August, the *Daily Mail*, which had so assiduously supported the Munich agreement a year before, was editoralizing a public unwillingness to give in once more to Hitler's threats: 'our patience is becoming exhausted. We will not continue indefinitely under the shadow of war . . . If we have to fight we shall know that we have done all in honour possible to preserve peace.'[132]

Had public attitudes really changed? Arguably, a straight line led from the opinions expressed in the Peace Ballot of 1935 to public reactions to German aggression over 1939. Most Britons thought war was evil, and the majority thought that ultimately those who persisted in trying to wage it should be countered with military force.[133] That had always been the stance of leading figures in the League of Nations Union such as Lord Cecil and Gilbert Murray. What had altered was the extent to which Fascism in general, and Nazism in particular, was seen as the existential enemy in a battle for civilization in which the front line was edging closer to British doorsteps. This was the feeling that led many former advocates of pacifism – including the publisher Victor Gollancz, the novelist Storm Jameson and the scientist J. D.

Bernal – to change their minds over the course of 1939 and come round to the point of view that Hitler must be fought.[134]

The concern with trying to understand the implications of Nazi ideology was apparent in the success of Penguin Specials such as *What Hitler Wants*, which sold 150,000 copies after its publication in 1939. Such books never reached more than a small fraction of the reading public, but by the autumn of 1939, there was no need to have grappled with *Mein Kampf* to recognize the Führer as a rather more traditional sort of enemy: the villainous, jumped-up foreign autocrat who was breaking promises, acting unfairly, laughing at Britain and trying to take over the world.

Chamberlain's foreign policy had never been based on building a consensus at home, but one consequence of his pursuit of peace was that by summer 1939, any failure to compromise had to be laid at the German dictator's door. The personal antipathy expressed against him by ordinary Britons during the Sudeten crisis only became more marked over the subsequent year. Hitler's evident determination to have a war aroused a deep anger that came from the same place as popular royalism. If this was not the bombastic nationalism of the early twentieth century, it was an emotion often expressed in essentially patriotic terms. Right up until the last moment, however, wanting to stand up to Hitler did not mean accepting that war was inevitable. On the contrary, the hope was widely expressed that he would back down in the face of firmer action.

As August ended, Britons readied themselves for war without quite yet being convinced that it was going to come. Mass-Observation (M-O) now sent out a request to its national panel of respondents to start filling in a crisis diary. A twenty-eight-year-old medical student in Edinburgh, having spent the 28th playing golf and reading, reported 'plenty of chatter': 'NR (man, 65) very petulant with Hitler, but he is having business worries and in addition is "socketing" his mashie shots. Very dramatic manner of condemning Hitler, with a wonderful air of personal indignation.' Later on, he had an argument with two older women about the 'advisability' of war: 'They held that loss of "honour" was worse than war but that war was terrible – all the poor dead children etc.'[135]

The next day, a young male bank clerk in Kent recorded what his customers were saying. The international crisis was 'almost universally topic of conversation, ousting subject of holidays'. But they were:

almost entirely optimistic about situation. 'There will be no war' and such remarks very prevalent. Only one person contrary: he hopes for war or else 'British Empire' will lose prestige . . . One person possessed a fatalistic view: 'If it comes, it comes, that's all we can say.' One woman most indignant with Nazi-Russian non-aggression pact: 'They are both a lot of scurrilous rogues. Neither of them will keep his word. Two such opposite things – Fascism and Communism – cannot be united.'[136]

On the same day, another M-O diarist, a thirty-seven-year-old middle-class housewife in Blackheath, 'determined to have one more decent cut and set', made her way into central London to get her hair done. On the way, she bought more nails to fix up the inside of her family's air-raid shelter, and looked out for places where she could hide if the bombing began. 'How soon', she mused, 'one becomes war minded':

> In the train I looked for shelters in the little back gardens of the houses between New Cross & London Bridge. How many of them had no room at all for an Anderson. Tried not to picture the havoc a medium sized bomb would create in one of those narrow streets.[137]

Two days later, Walter Musto, a sixty-year-old government cloth inspector who was keeping a diary for himself, wrote about the prospect of conflict for almost the first time that year. Unconsciously, he echoed Chamberlain's words to Halifax after Munich:

> A gigantic tidal wave of political, financial and personal complexities surrounds almost to extinction the essential factors of dispute, which appear to me to be elementary and turn on the abandonment of a powerful few of those principles of sound ethics generally accepted, at least by the more entrusted races, the world over. But so it is and the 'man in the street' can do little to dissect the course of events except prepare for the worst whilst hoping for the best.[138]

'THERE ARE SO FEW PACIFISTS'

Alongside this mix of patriotism, fatalism, anger and optimism must be set continuing opposition to the idea of war. The British were much less divided about whether to go to war in 1939 than they had been before the fighting broke out in 1914, but even so, one in four of those questioned by the BIPO in August did not support the UK standing by its territorial guarantee to Poland. A substantial proportion of the population did not want to fight on this issue, including British Fascists and Communists, the Beaverbrook press and a persistent body of absolute pacifists. Yet they felt themselves increasingly on the outside as the majority swung behind standing up to Hitler, even with all the risks that entailed.

Since 1938, Oswald Mosley had set the British Union of Fascists to campaign for peace, an approach that may have helped to restore partially BUF membership from the trough of 1936–37. On 1 September, he issued a message to party members encouraging them not to fight in 'a quarrel of Jewish finance' – although, because Mosley knew that it would be scrutinized by the security services, he was careful to say that Fascists in the armed forces should obey orders. Over the following months, the BUF instructed its members in how to register as conscientious objectors – not because they thought that they would secure exemption from service, since they had no objection to violence in itself, but in order to publicize their opposition to the 'Jewish War'.[139]

The Communist Party of Great Britain found itself in a profoundly difficult position after the Nazi-Soviet pact. Having campaigned for a unified anti-Fascist front, it was now ordered into a volte-face by Moscow, promoting the pact as a brilliant piece of diplomacy that would avert war and denouncing any co-operation with the imperialist powers in their confrontation with Germany. Even the CPGB's own party secretary, Harry Pollitt, found this impossible to stomach and lost his post as a result. Both the resultant confusion and the disjuncture with popular opinion set back recruitment to the party.[140]

Beaverbrook was convinced that rising Anglo-German antagonism was principally the fault of Jewish sympathies in rival newspapers and mistaken entanglements in Europe. He believed that Britain's security lay in imperial isolationism. Reassured by improvements in rearmament, and certain above all of his own power to influence events, he set his papers to try to secure a breathing space for negotiation. Between January and mid-August 1939, the *Daily Express* insisted eight times that 'Britain will not be involved in a European war'.[141]

The pacifism that had proved so popular in the UK at the start of the 1930s was not totally extinguished. Pacifism remained deeply ingrained at a local level within the Labour movement, parts of which continued to press against any involvement in war. The Peace Pledge Union, which had responded to the government's national service campaign with its own 'peace service' handbooks, advising work that could be undertaken to stop a conflict, claimed an increase in membership after the introduction of conscription, but overall it was rendered increasingly irrelevant by the passage of events. Leading pacifists' continued enthusiasm for appeasing Germany laid them open to the charge of sympathy with Fascism.[142]

Across the country, pacifists struggled with the moral quandaries posed by their faith. Two of them were Arnold Monk-Jones and Eileen Bellerby, teachers living in London and Cheltenham respectively, who met and fell in love during the last months of peace, and became engaged in June. Part of their long-distance courtship – alongside comparing notes on patent eye-strengthening exercises – was a discussion of peaceful principles. Eileen's pacifism was more absolute than Arnold's, but over the summer, she argued him round. At the start of September, he told Eileen that he would refuse military service if he were required to undertake it:

> I am fully convinced that universal pacifism, say, in this country, would have prevented war; because the more pacifists there are, the better the future state of the world. The counter consideration that troubles me is this: once we are at war, avoidable though it may have been in the past, ought we not to work for the victory of our side, as being slightly the less bad of the two? If my pacifism now increases the chance of a German victory, is it sound?[143]

Eileen comforted him: 'I don't think you need worry that your pacifism will increase the chance of a German victory. There are so few pacifists even now that the number can't make much difference to the fighting.'[144]

'CONSTRUCTIVE OPPOSITION'

Even after the Nazi-Soviet pact, Chamberlain was determined not to give up on peace. Hoping that signs of British seriousness would make Germany step back from the brink, he tried to keep open lines of communication with the Nazi leadership. His apparent prevarication encouraged his opponents' fears that he would find a way to leave Poland in the lurch.[145]

On 24 August Parliament, rapidly recalled, passed in a single day the Emergency Powers (Defence) Act, which handed over to the authorities, in the cause of national security, all but complete control over the lives of British citizens for the duration of the coming conflict. The next day, the commitment to Poland's independence was reiterated with the formal signing of the Anglo-Polish alliance. In the last days of August, the Fleet, reservists and Territorials were mobilized. During the early hours of 1 September, German troops invaded Poland. This meant war.

Chamberlain now sought to broaden his government by bringing his opponents into office. Significantly, it was Churchill to whom he turned first, offering him both a ministerial appointment as first lord of the admiralty and a place within the smaller War Cabinet that would be set up to streamline decision-making during the conflict. Churchill had experience of war management, of course, and now that war had come his restless aggression might be turned to advantage rather than pose a threat to peace. Chamberlain's approach also indicated the extent to which Churchill had, in the last months of peace, replaced Eden as the foremost Conservative dissident. Churchill gladly accepted the chance to serve the nation once more. At his instigation, Chamberlain also found space for Eden, albeit at the Dominions Office and outside the War Cabinet.[146]

Labour's leaders trod a careful path. They wanted simultaneously to ensure Chamberlain stood up to Hitler and doom him politically while avoiding the charge that they were undermining the war effort. Attlee had spent the summer of 1939 recovering from surgery on his prostate. While he offered commentary from his convalescent bed in Wales, day-to-day leadership devolved to his deputy, Arthur Greenwood, who in late August and early September put in the performance of a political life otherwise drowned in drink. In the Commons, Greenwood attacked the prime minister's policies while emphasizing that Labour would back the government if it confronted Hitler.

Behind the scenes, the senior leaders of the Labour movement had already decided that they would not allow themselves to be co-opted by Chamberlain. On 1 September, the prime minister tried to give Labour a junior place in a reformed coalition. The offer was rejected. Instead,

Labour adopted a position of 'constructive opposition'. That meant in practice supporting the fight against Nazism, denying Chamberlain the chance ever to claim that he was genuinely a national leader, but leaving open the possibility that it might serve in another coalition under a different prime minister.[147]

Chamberlain aided Labour's cause by botching the political theatre of the declaration of hostilities. Assured of the Dominions' support, and angered by Hitler's apparent determination to plunge the world into conflict, by 1 September Chamberlain had decided that Britain would have to fight. Co-ordinating an ultimatum to that effect with the French would be an important signifier of allied unity. Daladier, however, asked for more time, partly because he still needed to bring round his foreign minister, Bonnet, who was arguing for peace, partly so that the French army could get further with its mobilization. The British government accepted this delay on the basis that it would allow the evacuation of vulnerable civilians from London and other cities.

On 2 September, the suggestion came through that the Germans might be willing to consider a peace conference under Italian auspices. That afternoon, Halifax and Chamberlain argued to the Cabinet that, since Britain was waiting for France anyway, it was worth waiting another day to see whether Hitler would take up this opportunity. Both made it clear that negotiations could only take place once German troops had been withdrawn to their own territory. They were argued down by a group of ministers, including Hoare, Wood and Hore-Belisha, who thought that this would give the wrong impression about British resolution. At their insistence, it was agreed that war must be declared at midnight, but Chamberlain told his colleagues that he must consult with the French on this basis. When he and Halifax did so, they were told that Paris still wanted more time: they decided that French requirements should take precedence over the decision of the Cabinet.[148]

That evening, Chamberlain gave a brief statement to the Commons about the European situation. Although many MPs were aware of the difficulties in negotiation with the French, he was concerned not to reveal the divisions across the Channel. But the result was that he gave the impression of having decided to keep his options open. Rather than giving a timescale for the opening of hostilities, he explained that if Hitler pulled back, Britain would still be willing to oversee German-Polish negotiations.

It was a complete misjudgement of the mood of the House. MPs had been waiting for their prime minister to lead them into battle, and Chamberlain's apparent prevarication gave a remarkable opportunity to his opponents. As Greenwood stood up to reply, Leo Amery, incandescent with fury, squeaked across the Chamber: 'Speak for England, Arthur!' From the opposition benches, other MPs followed up with 'Speak for Britain' and 'Speak for the Workers'. It was of vital importance for Labour's political future that Greenwood was seen to do the former, not the latter. The Labour deputy leader recognized what he had to do, and gave the most important speech of his career. This was his finest hour.[149]

Whatever the reasons for delay, Greenwood asked: 'how long are we prepared to vacillate at a time when Britain and all that Britain stands for, and human civilisation, are in peril?' However 'hard it may be to the right hon. Gentleman – and no one would care to be in his shoes tonight', there must be 'no more devices for dragging out what has been dragged out too long. The moment we look like weakening, at that moment dictatorship knows we are beaten. We are not beaten. We shall not be beaten. We cannot be beaten; but delay is dangerous.'[150] His victim, still waiting on word from Paris, could only promise that he would try to give the Commons a more definitive statement the next day.

French tardiness was not Chamberlain's fault, but he had put in a disastrous political performance. Being forced to war by a malevolent dictator was one thing; having to be forced into it by your own opposition quite another. Severely shaken, the prime minister was then faced with a rebellion from within the Cabinet. Ministers who had thought they had already decided on war were furious at his apparent betrayal. Now, they were even joined by Sir John Simon, who also insisted on a speedy declaration of hostilities.[151] At 11.30 that evening, the Cabinet reconvened, and it was settled that, no matter what the French did, an ultimatum would be issued to Berlin at nine the next morning. Two hours after that, when Hitler failed to withdraw his forces from Poland, Britain declared war on Germany.

'I AM CERTAIN THAT THE RIGHT WILL PREVAIL'

For most Britons, the last hopes of peace had already been blown away on 1 September by the news that German forces were bombing Warsaw, the announcement that schoolchildren and vulnerable adults would be evacuated from major cities the following day, and the implementation, that evening, of a full blackout. In Bristol, a junior law librarian noted the immediate effects for Mass-Observation:

> 'BRITAIN MOBILISES' yell the posters. Already a few men are to be seen outside the post office, with their kit bags. And a young solicitor I know is patrolling the street in a special constable's uniform. To quote headlines 'Britain is ready'. Mr B, 41-yr old clerk, ARP warden, comes in, shakes his head over Hitler 'The only thing to do now is to smash him' he says, like everyone else.

There were minor compensations: 'Dad didn't take the usual explosive tonight. I suppose worry is a cure for constipation.'[152]

In Cambridge, a twenty-five-year-old secretary felt her world fall apart when her father interrupted her lunch with an announcement of the attack on Warsaw.

> All our plans for the future were shattered, everything in ruins. My fiancé knew that his new job, which he had not yet started on, the job he had always set his heart on, would have to be abandoned. His academic career would be at an end. And our married life might be at an end too. However, we decided to marry the next day if possible instead of waiting till next week. We went down to the Registry office and found they could just fit us in, although they were working overtime with marriages. We went back home, and spent the evening helping to darken the windows with old curtains. Went to bed exhausted and slept soundly.[153]

At his Territorial Army post in Yorkshire, Gunner Ewart Clay recorded a similar sense of dislocation. He was not keeping a diary, but he knew he was living through a historic moment and so wrote an account at the time of his own experience of going to war. A sub-editor on the *Yorkshire Evening Post*, the son of pacifist parents and himself a former member of the PPU, Clay had forsworn his earlier refusal to fight after Hitler marched into Prague, and joined the Territorials in March 1939. Already on duty during August, he recalled shortly afterwards that 1 September had been the day when the mood on his station changed:

> It took an hour to force my mind from its accustomed groove . . . and to realise that henceforth, for weeks or for years, and perhaps forever, the old ways were closed to me, that my family were to be left to plough their own furrow in a world out of its sense, and that my wife was now facing, without what support my presence might have given, the prospect both she and many other women feared and abominated more than anything else in the world.[154]

Not everyone was so downcast. When Clay's brother-in-law wrote to him to describe the atmosphere at home, he noted that: 'A peculiar excitement pervades the atmosphere. Quite a few people, mostly men, seem glad that the hour to "get Hitler" has arrived. Complete lack of imagination in most cases as to the real consequences of war.'[155]

On Sunday 3 September, church attendances were smaller than expected as people stayed in to listen to the prime minister's explanation that Germany had ignored Britain's final ultimatum and that consequently the two countries were at war.[156] Chamberlain laid out a moral cause for the nation: 'Now may God bless you all. May He defend the right. It is the evil things that we shall be fighting against – brute force, bad faith, injustice, oppression and persecution – and against them I am certain that the right will prevail.'[157]

Across London and much of the south-east, the announcement was followed by the first false alarm of the war, as an unexpected French plane triggered an air-raid warning. For Private G. E. Tapp, a Territorial soldier, the siren announced

> to England that once again we were the opponents of Germany in the fight for . . . what? On our side – the settlement of the European problem – to be brought about only by the complete destruction of Hitler's regime. To crush Nazism and all it stands for, and to bring peace to Europe. Hitler's motive can only be guessed at. His real aim, even if clear to himself, must be forever a secret of that warped brain. We are now soldiers on active service – with a Cause.[158]

There were less idealistic reactions. The Bristol law librarian recorded his response to Chamberlain's speech:

> He claims to have done everything possible for peace, and I suppose he has, within his limits. He's not evil, just incapable of any large imagination or foresight. He's not directing events, he's just being shoved protestingly about. After the speech come announcements of the closing of places of entertainment, about shelters and gas masks. And then, to leave no doubt in any one's minds, to prove that we are fighting for the old loyalties and not for a new world, the National Anthem was played. To hell with the anthem, and the silly old Empire. My sister, in accordance with instructions, goes at once to report to the hospital. Father, jittery, goes upstairs with sheets of paper to black out, permanently, every window in sight.[159]

Pride, cynicism, duty, survival: all four would characterize Britain's experience of its second great war.

PART THREE

Being at War

II

Limited War

As it turned out, the outbreak of war was the greatest anti-climax in modern British history.

The first Britons killed by enemy action died on 3 September, when the German submarine U-30 torpedoed the liner SS *Athenia*. Of the 1,418 passengers and crew aboard, 112 were killed, including 68 Britons and 30 Americans.[1] The next day, British aircraft unsuccessfully attacked German warships in Wilhelmshaven and Brunsbüttel. There was, however, no sign of the much-anticipated air assault on British cities. It took until 16 October for the first British civilian to be hurt in an air raid, when a machine-gun bullet fired as British fighters pursued German bombers after an attack on naval vessels in the Firth of Forth wounded a housepainter in Leith. Otherwise, despite frequent false alarms in the first weeks of the war, the aerial apocalypse was markedly absent. On the European mainland, the Germans advanced rapidly through Poland, aided by the invasion of Soviet forces from the east on 16 September. By 6 October, the Poles had been completely defeated and their country divided between the conquerors. Meanwhile on the Western Front, the French and British armies remained on the defensive, waiting for the Germans to make the first move.

This was not what the all-devouring contest for the future of civilization was meant to be like. Before long, Britons were calling it the 'Bore War'. Later, they would come to use the Americanism 'Phoney War'. For the French, it was the *drôle de guerre*. In many ways, this 'funny sort of war' was just a continuation of the colder conflict that had been under way since the previous autumn, except that now the Allies attempted to deter Germany not with the threat of conflict, but with the certainty of defeat in a drawn-out war. Yet for all the lack of action, the 'Bore War' was a crucial period in determining military and economic mobilization, political destiny, and whether the war would be fought to a finish at all.

RUNNING THE WAR

The onset of hostilities resulted in a new structure of government. New ministries – Home Security, Information, Food, Economic Warfare and Shipping – were brought into being alongside the new-born Ministry of Supply. At the top, Chamberlain formed a War Cabinet with nine members. It combined the core of the National Government – Chamberlain, Halifax, Simon and Hoare (now lord privy seal) – the four forces ministers – Chatfield, Churchill, Wood and Hore-Belisha – and the strategic experience of Lord Hankey, who returned from retirement as minister without portfolio.

The War Cabinet was the ultimate arbiter of British strategic policy. It was often attended by the chiefs of staff – Admiral Sir Dudley Pound, General Sir Edmund Ironside and Marshal of the Royal Air Force Sir Cyril Newall – but preliminary discussion of military matters was soon hived off into a Sub-Committee for Military Co-Ordination, where they met with the service ministers under Chatfield. Other Cabinet commit-tees directed the mobilization of the economy. The Ministerial Priority Committee, also chaired by Chatfield and set up just before the out-break of war, oversaw issues of labour, transport, production and construction. After hostilities began, it was partially superseded by a Ministerial Committee on Economic Policy, chaired by Simon, which took charge of broader questions of economic priorities and organiza-tion. On domestic issues, there was similar overlap between Committees on Home Policy, Civil Defence and Food. This sedimentary layering of committees maximized co-operation between different departments, but it also left the government open to charges of over-discussion and delay. Chamberlain was still reluctant to appoint individual supremos to take charge of defence and the war economy. Or rather, he saw no reason to dilute the existing power of the prime minister and the Treas-ury to try to balance competing strategic demands.[2]

Britain's new alliance with France also required a structure of co-ordination and control. The Allies set up the Supreme War Council, a forum attended by the most senior ministers and military officers from both countries. The general staffs from both sides of the Channel liaised through the Allied Military Committee. On the civil side, Anglo-French committees for purchasing and economic co-ordination were formed to arrange for the mutual production of raw materials and munitions and the buying of supplies and equipment from the USA.

Compared with the last war, these structures were put in place remarkably swiftly. While detailed arrangements were already agreed to ensure that Britain would provide the coal needed by French industry, however, there was little progress in co-ordinating military production. It took until the end of 1939 to reach agreement on how the cost of the war would be split (60:40 between the UK and France, in line with their respective national wealth). The Supreme War Council provided the means to iron out differences in private and demonstrate mutual commitment in public, but it did not mean that the Allies shared a genuinely joint approach to the waging of the war. When push came to shove, it was the differences between them that would prove decisive.[3]

'HOLD ON TIGHT'

The Allies entered the war with a strategy of long-term military mobilization combined with economic disruption.[4] Since the start of 1939, they had planned together on the basis that Germany would start 'more fully prepared than ourselves for war on a national scale', with 'superiority in air and land forces, but ... inferior at sea and in general economic strength'.[5] The pressure would be on the Germans to win a short war. It was expected that they would follow up their attack on Poland with an offensive in the west, probably through neutral Belgium and Holland because of the strength of the French border defences along the Maginot Line. The Allies must absorb and repel this assault while they built up their strength. Their financial reserves and control of the seas would allow them to accelerate their own industrial mobilization. The Royal Navy would cut off Germany's seaborne trade, while diplomatic action and pre-emptive purchasing would restrict the flow of raw materials from neutral Europe. If economic strangulation did not spark a revolt against Hitler, it would create the military conditions for a battlefield victory within three years.

This was a very sensible strategy. It played to the Allies' strengths, and it was based on an understanding that, in the age of total war, military power existed well beyond the battlefield. Yet in an era of ideological battles, leaders in France and Britain would find this cautious, measured strategy difficult to sustain.

Bearing in mind the anxieties of the 1930s, British ministers could consider themselves fortunate that the UK was fighting Germany alone. They presumed that the Nazi economy was already operating close to its limits and that Germany would rapidly be affected by an economic blockade. They also thought that Hitler's decision to carry his country into war had left him politically vulnerable at home. They therefore believed that the war would end not with the Allied armies utterly crushing German resistance in the ruins of the Reich – an outcome that had not been achieved in the last war even after all the bloodshed of the Western Front – but rather via negotiation with a successor regime after the Germans had themselves got rid of Hitler. Here was one of the most important but least appreciated consequences of the last war: when they visualized victory, none of the men who led Britain into war imagined the campaigns of 1945.

The war they thought they had in front of them looked bad enough. Depressed at the failure of his efforts to preserve the peace, Chamberlain briefly contemplated resignation. He soon rallied, however, bolstered by the conviction that however little he enjoyed war, no one could do a better job of being prime minister. Before long, he had convinced himself that a long and bloody war might not actually be necessary. As he explained to his sister in early September:

> There is such a wide spread desire to avoid war & it is so deeply rooted that it surely must find expression somehow. Of course the difficulty is with Hitler himself. Until he disappears and his system collapses there can be no peace. But what I hope for is not a military victory – I very much doubt the possibility of that – but a collapse of the German home front. For that it is necessary to convince the Germans that they cannot win.[6]

Still furious at the betrayal of the Munich agreement, Chamberlain had no intention of compromising with Hitler again. Once more reasonable Germans grasped his attitude, he thought they would depose the Führer and come to the negotiating table rather than continue with a war they did not want and could not win. After Poland had been defeated, Chamberlain discounted reports that Hitler was preparing an early offensive in the west. He did not think the Germans would risk getting stuck in another bloody, trench-bound stalemate like that of 1914–18. Chamberlain still believed that Britain should get ready for a long total war, partly as an insurance policy, and partly because evidence of its commitment to the fight was vital to convincing the Germans they were bound to lose. While he wanted to push on the war effort, however, he did not want to go so hard in the present that he broke British power in the future. Nor could Chamberlain see the point of escalating the intensity of military operations: that might make it harder for peace sentiment to gain ground in Germany. If the Allies held firm and looked determined, he was sure, enemy resistance would crumble from within.[7]

This was a typically rational Chamberlain prognosis. Having perceived the logic of German defeat, Chamberlain presumed the Germans would see it too, and that he could therefore fine-tune Britain's effort to secure a quick victory at minimum effort. The price to be paid if the Allies had to fight a drawn-out total war, however, was equally inescapable, and it is hard not to see Chamberlain's optimism as a bulwark against despair. After the War Cabinet decided to announce to the public that it was planning for a three-year war, Ironside noticed that the prime minister had 'put his forehead on the table and kept it there for nearly ten minutes. When he eventually looked up he looked more than ghastly.'[8]

Chamberlain's belief that Hitler would not attack in the west distinguished him from his colleagues, but they didn't disagree about the overall direction of the war.[9] Simon feared the onset of 'intense warfare' in the spring but still wanted to restrain expenditure in the hope of preserving Britain's purchasing power in the long term.[10] Like Chamberlain, Halifax was against precipitate military action, but recognized the diplomatic necessity of demonstrating British determination to the French. The foreign secretary was particularly keen to preserve neutral opinion, restrict any expansion of the war and to keep Italy and Japan from joining Germany's assault on the democracies.[11]

Churchill's impulses were more combative. From the start, the new first lord of the admiralty was a disruptive element in the War Cabinet: always harking back to his experience of the last war and commenting on the minutiae of other ministers' business.[12] His colleagues also suspected that the constant stream of minutes and letters from Churchill's office were intended to create his own archive 'for the purpose of quotation in the Book that he will write hereafter'.[13] Having offered his opinion on everything, Churchill would be able to pick selectively to prove he was right when he produced his own account of how he had won the war.

Unlike Chamberlain, Churchill's instinct was to try to seize the military initiative. No sooner was he in office than he ordered plans drawn up to send battleships into the Baltic to cut the flow of raw materials to Germany from neutral Scandinavia. He also wanted to drive on industrial mobilization on the home front. While Churchill wanted the war fought harder and more quickly, however, he did not differ in his fundamental analysis of how Britain would win. Rather, his interventions fitted within the broader scope of British strategy: attacking the German economy while building up the army on the Western Front.[14] He talked of the war as a fight 'to save the whole world from the pestilence of Nazi tyranny',[15] but, like everyone else, he presumed that the end of the conflict would come through negotiations with a new German government after it had overthrown Hitler.

Discussions in September about how to adapt rearmament plans demonstrated the differences between senior ministers about how to approach the war. One of the consequences of Churchill's wide-ranging engagement with strategy was that he was an unusually unselfish first lord. Rather than fight for more resources for the navy, he wanted to shift its construction plans to provide the multitude of smaller vessels that would be required for escort duty and minesweeping. Although work continued on the five battleships already due for delivery between 1940 and 1941, plans to lay down new battleships were put on hold until the emergency programme of smaller escort ships was completed. In the air, unlike at sea, planned expansion increased still further. Reports of the Luftwaffe's role in defeating the Poles re-emphasized for Chamberlain the importance of building up British airpower, and the Air Ministry was allowed to up its production target from 2,000 to 2,550 aircraft a month by 1942 in the so-called 'Harrogate Programme' (named after the town to which the Ministry had been evacuated).

The army's future occasioned more disagreement. Under the plans laid down in spring 1939, it was meant to grow to thirty-two divisions over the next two years. Now, Hore-Belisha proposed to build a fifty-five-division army over the same period: thirty-two from the UK, fourteen from the Dominions, four from India, plus another five divisions' worth of equipment for Britain's allies. This would mean an army rather smaller – although much more mechanized – than that Britain had deployed at the end of the last war. It would be about half the size of the French army on the Western Front in 1940. Churchill and Halifax supported the plan, with the former arguing that forty divisions should be ready for battle by the end of the first year of war. An army this big would be necessary to convince the French that the British did not mean to leave them, as Churchill put it, paying 'almost the whole blood tax on land'.[16] Yet as he later admitted, neither he nor any of the other ministers involved actually had any idea what a modern division really meant in terms of manpower. The British wanted an army with lots of machines, but that meant they would need lots of soldiers behind the lines maintaining tanks and trucks or bringing up supplies of petrol and spare parts. The total number of men needed to support each division was much higher than in the last war. Churchill, like the rest of his colleagues, had picked a number based on what they wanted rather than what they knew the country could achieve.

At the time, Hore-Belisha's call for a fifty-five-division army aroused serious objections on other grounds. Chamberlain was anxious not to impinge on air force expansion. The Ministry of Supply objected that it was struggling hard enough trying to meet the thirty-two-division target: there was not the industrial capacity within the UK to equip more than twenty divisions over the next twelve months. Even General Ironside – an early proponent of a larger army – made it clear that he only really wanted troops who were properly equipped.

Looking over the forces' programmes as a whole, the chancellor, Sir John Simon, was appalled. Together, if they went ahead as planned, they would require such heavy purchasing in the United States that the UK's dollar reserves would be exhausted by the middle of 1941 – well before the end of a three-year war.[17] When the War Cabinet discussed the matter at the end of September, however, ministers were unwilling to resolve that the war effort would have to be restricted because of a lack of funds. Simon recorded their verdict in his diary: 'The only thing that matters is to win the war, even though we go bankrupt in the process. There would be no comfort if we lost the war in the reflection that we still possessed a credit balance of dollars.'[18] The War Cabinet therefore approved the fifty-five-division target as the ultimate goal of British war production for the army. In so doing, however, Chamberlain demonstrated his reluctance to go too far too fast.

> It was certain that we must plan for expansion now, and by planning he meant not only the preparation of schemes, but the siting, erection and equipment of factories and the provision of materials and labour. This would cost a certain amount of money and effort, but would not commit us to carry out the programme to its full extent at any particular time, or, indeed, at all. On the other hand, unless the plans were initiated now, it might prove to be too late.[19]

As this suggested, fifty-five divisions remained a vague aspiration rather than a concrete goal. In fact, the Ministry of Supply and the War Office continued to plan on what they thought they could actually equip – which was the thirty-two divisions already agreed on, albeit prepared for very heavy levels of wartime wastage – and the Treasury refused to pay for the increases in capacity necessary to reach the higher figure.[20] This fitted well with the prime minister's actual approach to the war: keeping the effort commensurate with Britain's means, limiting dollar expenditure to make sure it lasted out the war, and trying to maintain a healthy export trade at the same time as developing military production. So far as he could, Chamberlain intended to keep the dogs of war on a tight leash.[21]

The first great challenge to British strategy came from across the Channel. For years, it had been an article of faith with France's soldiers that in any conflict with Germany, they must face their opponents with a war on two fronts. The abandonment of Czechoslovakia, the Nazi-Soviet pact and the rapid collapse of Poland removed any hope that the Germans would be forced to split their armies between east and west. When the war began, the French therefore thought about opening a new theatre of operations, in the Balkans. They hoped that an expeditionary force landed in Greece would rally the countries of Southern and Central Europe against the Nazis, pre-empt any German drive for the region's raw materials and force Hitler to face a new threat from the south. This was the start of a long-running theme: the idea of a Southern Front would entice desperate Allied strategists throughout the war. The French commander-in-chief, Maurice Gamelin, was reluctant to divert any forces from the Western Front, but the

Balkan plan received extensive support from Daladier and from General Maxime Weygand, the French commander in the Middle East, who would get to run any such expedition.[22]

When Daladier broached the idea at the Supreme War Council meeting on 22 September, however, the British refused to play ball. They questioned the military and logistical feasibility of a Balkan intervention, and feared that it would provoke Italy to declare war. Sir Alexander Cadogan, the top civil servant at the Foreign Office, recorded Chamberlain's bomb disposal effort: 'PM threw gentle showers of cold water on it, and the French didn't seem entirely convinced by their own argument. It's moonshine to me.'[23] Moonshine or not, Daladier continued to press the project as the autumn went on. This persistence demonstrated both the gaping hole left in French strategy by the absence of an Eastern Front and a loss of faith in the outcome of a long war. As the French worried more and more about whether time was really on their side, so they would press more and more urgently for immediate military action.

For the moment, British optimism trumped French gloom. The government stayed carefully clear, however, of laying out what a successful end to the war would actually look like. Ministers and officials recognized the advantages of setting out clear objectives as a means of establishing the Allies' moral supremacy, but they didn't want them to get in the way of winning the war. Chamberlain told the War Cabinet in early September that he 'was unwilling to attempt to define our war aims as this might have the effect of tying us down too rigidly and might prejudice an eventual settlement'.[24] The Soviet assault on Poland made it even less likely that the British government would lay out a vision for post-war Eastern Europe. As Cadogan noted: 'We can no longer say "evacuate Poland" without going to war with Russia, which we don't want to do!'[25]

In practice, the one aim on which the prime minister was wholly set was the 'destruction of Hitlerism'.[26] By this he meant simply that the German dictator would have to go: after Prague, there was no way that Hitler's word could be trusted. As he put it privately in mid-October: 'that accursed madman. I wish he could burn in Hell for as many years as he is costing lives.'[27] Halifax, although keener on a statement of war aims, shared the same perspective. Both men accepted that a peace settlement might be possible with a successor government that still contained leading Nazis. The idea that Hitler's German opponents might be persuaded into launching a coup, if they thought that they could thereby stop the war, was very tempting, and the Foreign Office spent a lot of time exploring every potential avenue for negotiation.[28] Meanwhile, the mistaken belief that they were in communication with German army plotters led MI6 into its greatest disaster of the early war, when two British agents turned up in the Dutch border town of Venlo, at what they thought was a meeting with the officers involved, only to be kidnapped by the German intelligence services. They had been stringing the British along from the start.[29]

The poverty of intelligence about German capabilities and intentions was one of the distinctive features of British decision-making at this stage of the war. Like the rest of the British war effort, the intelligence organizations were undergoing a period of rapid expansion, a growth in personnel that itself complicated the analysis of information about the enemy. Yet there were important developments for the future. During the last months of peace, the British were informed that Polish intelligence had established methods to crack the encryption of the Enigma machine, which was used by the German armed forces to encipher their communications. Improvements in the Enigma technology had blinded the Poles since 1938, but from the summer of 1939 British resources were applied to the techniques they had developed.

Only at the start of 1940, however, were the Polish code-breakers – now evacuated to a post outside Paris – and the Government Code and Cipher School in the UK, able to make the first wartime decrypt, which allowed them to read communications from the last quarter of 1939. And only in the spring of 1940 would the British start to regularly and with little delay decipher the Luftwaffe Enigma. The different settings used by the German army and navy remained for the moment largely secure (in contrast, the Germans soon re-broke the Royal Navy's main cipher, which they had already been reading before the war). Even the data from the Luftwaffe was for the moment more useful in building a picture of the enemy's command structure than in providing any evidence of their intentions. Other intelligence sources allowed the British to establish a reasonably good picture of the size and deployment of the German army, but they gave little reliable indication of the ways in which German planning was developing during the first months of the war.[30] Industrial intelligence was similarly limited. Economic warfare was central to British strategy, but it relied on having a very precise picture of what was happening in Germany, and reliable statistics on German production of and access to key raw materials proved very hard to establish. By January 1940, for example, the Ministry of Economic Warfare had received 'almost a dozen' estimates of German oil consumption. Each of them was completely different from the others.[31]

While British strategists were overly pessimistic in their estimates of German economic and air power, they underestimated Hitler's willingness to take military risks. No one was more guilty of this than Chamberlain, but he was far from alone. The prime minister's great fear, once it was clear that a knock-out blow would not immediately be unleashed on the British home front, was not a German military offensive, but rather that Hitler would use a peace deal of his own to attack Allied morale – that having seized what he wanted from Poland, the Führer would offer to stop the fighting. For the British and French people, devoid of 'the strong centripetal force of mortal danger', such an offer might be very tempting, and it would get Hitler what Chamberlain thought he wanted: an eastwards expansion of territory without a major war. Given his antipathy to the Nazi leader, the prime minister was determined to resist this 'peace offensive', while still leaving open the way for a genuine peace move from a different German government.[32]

From the end of September, the 'peace offensive' duly got under way, first with a further round of covert visits by Göring's Swedish friend Birger Dahlerus to explore a possible settlement, then, on 6 October, in a broadcast speech by Hitler to the Reichstag. Poland had ceased to exist, he told his listeners, but on everything else he was sure he could reach an agreement with his opponents. The Allies immediately rejected this gambit in private, but the difficulty of finding a form of words that would not solidify German sentiment behind Hitler meant that it took longer for them to make a statement in public. It was not until 12 October – after senior ministers had spent days discussing what to say – that Chamberlain formally responded in the House of Commons. There, he insisted that Britain was fighting for 'freedom' and 'progress', and that the Germans would have to make a concrete demonstration of their commitment to peace before negotiations could begin. What exactly they should do was left deliberately vague. The Germans had got themselves into this mess – now they must work out how to get themselves out of it.[33]

Hitler's peace offer had already bolstered Chamberlain's confidence that he had the right strategy to win a waiting war:

> Hold on tight. Keep up the economic pressure, push on with munitions production and military preparations with the utmost energy, take no offensive unless Hitler begins it. I reckon that if we are allowed to carry on this policy we shall have won the war by the Spring.[34]

The Führer took a different perspective. He was indeed worried about Germany's prospects in a long-term conflict. That, however, drove him not towards peace but rather towards more desperate action. Even as the Allies were considering his peace offer, he instructed his generals to plan an immediate attack into the Low Countries and northern France. From bases there, Germany would have a better position from which to launch air and sea raids on the UK. As senior German officers recognized, such an offensive carried no prospect of escape from a new variant on the same slogging battle of attrition that they had undergone in the last war. They were rescued by the weather. As Europe entered one of the coldest winters for a generation, poor conditions meant that plans for a Western Front offensive were repeatedly postponed, then put off until the following spring.[35] One of the consequences of these delays was that over the winter of 1939, the Allies received repeated rumours that a major German offensive was imminent. When these failed to be substantiated, they strengthened Chamberlain's conviction that Hitler couldn't risk a military offensive at all.[36]

'AT THE MOMENT, THE SEA EMPIRE IS AT A DISADVANTAGE'

As it was, 'holding on tight' was pretty much all that Britain could do. The military choices made during the years of rearmament had left it with armed forces that were well equipped to conduct a long-term maritime war and to defend the UK from aerial attack, but which could do very little to affect the course of the war on the European mainland. Eleven days into the war, Ironside recorded that since Gamelin had no desire for offensive action, the balance of the contest would be decided by the differences between Britain and Germany: 'It is a war of a Sea Empire against a Land Empire and at the moment the Sea Empire is at a disadvantage ... The more I look into our strategical position the more serious does it seem.'[37]

At sea, the war, though often boring, was very far from phoney. While a convoy system for Allied and neutral merchant vessels was put into place, German U-boats, mines and surface raiders exacted a steady toll of ships during the first months. The Royal Navy itself suffered high-profile losses during the early weeks, including the aged aircraft carrier *Courageous*, sunk by a submarine in the Western Approaches on 17 September, and the battleship *Royal Oak*, torpedoed on 14 October during a daring U-boat raid on the fleet anchorage at Scapa Flow. The decision, taken relatively late in the 1930s, to return to the base at Scapa meant that there had been little time to repair its defences, and the British fleet was now forced to change location between Scottish harbours while its deficiencies were made good. This complicated the Admiralty's efforts to stop German capital ships reaching the high seas.

Meanwhile, Churchill despatched Britain's aircraft carriers to join the hunt for the U-boats. This not only exposed them to disproportionate risks – as the loss of *Courageous* indicated – but it also showed a very poor understanding of how to catch submarines. Air power would prove crucial to the war against the U-boats, but the ocean wastes hid the submarines just as well as the convoys. Sending out hunting groups with valuable capital ships without good intelligence was just a waste of resources.[38]

A new German weapon caught the British by surprise. Laid by planes or submarines and sitting on the sea floor, magnetic mines were detonated by the influence of a ship's electro-magnetic field as it passed overhead. The heavy underwater blast wrecked delicate electronic equipment and broke the victim vessel's hull. The British had experimented with their own magnetic mine before the war, but had not developed any counter-measures. The Germans laid 470 of these mines in the first months of the war. Because they were extremely difficult to detect, and the British did not know how many they needed to find, they caused disruption out of all proportion to their actual number. At one point in November, all but one deep-water channel into the Port of London was closed by reports of mining, and the most important docks in the country were almost shut down. By the end of the year, magnetic mines had also severely damaged the battleship HMS *Nelson* and the brand-new cruiser HMS *Belfast*.

By then, however, the Germans, who had not prepared for an all-out attack on British shipping, had run short of mines. In the meantime the British had swiftly devised a solution: a programme of 'degaussing' ships by fitting loops of electric cable around their hulls to neutralize their magnetic field, coupled with the 'LL-sweep', in which small boats drew long cables through the water, pulsing a current to create a field that would set off the mines behind them. There was an extraordinary run on cable manufacturers throughout the world, but the threat of the magnetic mine was quickly countered.[39] It was the first instance of the technological back and forth that would continue for the rest of the war. In this struggle between rival industrial economies, there were almost no super-weapons – only innovations that might secure a temporary advantage before being factored out when they forced an enemy response. The appearance of a new threat, however, could force an opponent into a desperate reaction that would soak up resources that could have been used on something else.

These early setbacks had little effect on the colossal preponderance of maritime strength with which Britain entered the war. Even without counting in the French Marine Nationale, the Royal Navy dwarfed the Kriegsmarine, not only in its current strength but also in its programme for refitting and construction. The bulk of German vessels were more modern than their British counterparts, but the performance gap was not significant enough to make up for their enormous numerical deficit. In 1939, unlike in 1914–18, there was no prospect of the Germans even attempting a major fleet action to challenge British naval supremacy. Instead, the Germans adopted a strategy of sneaking capital vessels out into the Atlantic to conduct prolonged raids on merchant shipping. This not only indicated their overall weakness, but also combined high risks and diminishing returns. The longer such raids went on, the more likely the British were to be able to concentrate strength against them, and any loss to the Germans was proportionately much greater than that to their opponents.[40]

In this light, the period of the Bore War was actually one of unsurprising British naval success. The British presumed that the rapid introduction of a convoy system and improved underwater sonar detection by escort

Table 1. British and German comparative fleet strengths,
September 1939

	British Commonwealth	Germany
Post 1906 Battleships	8 (7)	0 (2)
Aircraft carriers	7 (5)	0 (1)
Battlecruisers and pocket battleships	2 (1)	5
Cruisers	66 (23)	6 (5)
Fleet destroyers	100 (32)	17
Escort destroyers, sloops, corvettes	101 (78)	0
Post 1927 Submarines	60 (9)	57 (29)
Registered merchant fleet (gwt, vessels over 1,600 gwt only)	17,524	3,762

Numbers in brackets = ships under construction or being refitted. Source: S. Roskill, *The War at Sea, 1939–1945*, I (London, 1954), pp. 577–92, 614; naval-history.net; C. Behrens, *Merchant Shipping and the Demands of War* (London, 1955), p. 23.

vessels would stop any offensive by German submarines, and by the end of 1939 the expectation seemed to have been fulfilled. Once the convoy system was in place, merchant-ship losses to U-boats declined rapidly, and nine German submarines had been sunk by British forces since the start of the war. That was a fifth of their operational strength. Another nine U-boats were sunk before the end of March 1940.[41] On 13 December 1939, the most successful German commerce raider of the early war, the pocket battleship *Admiral Graf Spee*, was tracked down after a long hunt across the Atlantic by three cruisers – two British and one from the New Zealand navy – and fought to a standstill off Uruguay at the Battle of the River Plate. Forced into the neutral harbour of Montevideo, threatened with internment, short of fuel and fearing that British reinforcements were on their way, the German commander, Hans Langsdorff, scuttled his ship, then shot himself.

Meanwhile, the Royal Navy had continued the long, boring work of winning the maritime trade war. During the first six weeks of the war, the British seized 338,000 tons of contraband goods on their way to Germany. By the start of January 1940, the Northern Patrol – which covered the vast swathe of ocean north-west from the Shetlands, via the Faroes and Iceland to Greenland, making use of armed merchant cruisers, civilian liners requisitioned at the start of the war and fitted with naval guns to allow them to undertake routine escort and patrol work – had sent 248 neutral ships for inspection at the contraband control base at Kirkwall, on Orkney, and intercepted 17 German merchant vessels, most of which were scuttled by their crews to avoid capture.[42]

By April 1940, the Germans had lost about 300,000 gross weight tons of merchant shipping (proportionately more of their merchant fleet than the 800,000 tons the British had lost over the same period, almost all of which had been replaced either by new ships or by the re-employment of captured German vessels). A million tons of German shipping was stuck in overseas ports for fear of capture, and of the eighty-six German merchantmen that had evaded the blockade and got home, only four would even attempt a voyage beyond European waters over the coming year. German merchant ships had effectively disappeared from the high seas.[43]

Yet the Royal Navy's colossal maritime preponderance did not easily translate into rapid offensive success. The search for the decisive attack was the dominant note of Churchill's whole time at the Admiralty, not just because he was naturally belligerent, but also because he recognized how important it was to seize the initiative in an area where Britain was so strong. His wide-ranging strategic enthusiasm meant he was keener on accelerating the whole British war effort than fighting his departmental corner. Churchill's decision that the navy should be relatively parsimonious in its demand for resources put him at loggerheads with admirals who wanted to build up a fleet big enough to see off the Italians in the Mediterranean and the Japanese in the Pacific, as well as the Germans in the North Sea. While the first lord was all for sending aged battleships charging into the Baltic, the chief of the naval staff, Admiral Pound, wanted to preserve his forces for future conflicts. Pound supported the idea of an early naval offensive against Italy in the event of a three-front war. After the conflict with Germany broke out, the admiral persuaded his fellow chiefs of staff to raise the 'period before relief' for Singapore to six months.[44]

'THE BEST HOPE OF OBTAINING DECISIVE RESULTS'?

In comparison with the Royal Navy, the RAF proved ineffectual. Since 1936, the RAF in the UK had been organized by function into separate Fighter, Bomber and Coastal Commands. The last was by far the smallest: it had not been given priority during the years of rearmament. Coastal Command's main job at the start of the war was reconnaissance over the North Sea, primarily to provide warning of any breakout of German surface ships. It lacked the aircraft, munitions and tactics to tackle enemy submarines, which it had been presumed would be dealt with by the Royal Navy.[45]

Fighter Command had been much better favoured during the 1930s, especially after the shift to domestic defence in 1938. Following the despatch of fighters to France to provide air cover for the British Expeditionary Force, the Command had thirty-five squadrons, twenty-two of which were equipped with modern Hurricanes and Spitfires. This left its total strength well short of the fifty-three squadrons that were then thought necessary to defend the UK, the shipping routes along the east coast and the fleet base at Scapa Flow. During the first months of fighting, there were few actual German incursions to fight off: Fighter Command's heaviest losses came on 6 September when a mistaken warning of a German attack resulted in a mass scramble, during which British forces shot down three of their own aircraft.[46]

The war revealed a striking disjunction between Bomber Command's presumed purpose, its scope for action and its actual capabilities. Since 1918, the RAF had emphasized the power of bombing as a strategically decisive weapon, and Bomber Command was conceived as an independent force. The air staff had worked up sixteen Western Air Plans for the employment of Bomber Command in the event of a war with Germany. These included a plan for a 'counter-force' attack on the German air force and air industry (WA1); plans to attack the German navy and protect British trade (WA2, WA3, WA7, WA12 and WA15); and proposals to set light to German forests, bomb Nazi party headquarters and drop propaganda leaflets on Germany (WA11, WA13 and WA14 respectively). Most time was spent on WA5, the plan for a massed bombing attack on German industry. Variants of this plan called for attacks on German oil supplies, and on the heavily industrialized area of the Ruhr. Like many of the RAF's other proposals, these were based on the assumption that accurate bombing of key targets could quickly cripple Germany's ability to prosecute the war.

Once the British started formal discussions with the French in early 1939, however, it soon became apparent that Bomber Command would not be allowed to attack the German home front. The French, much weaker in the air than the British, did not want to provoke German raids on their own cities. As importantly, the British government feared the consequences for neutral opinion if they were seen to have opened such a bombing war. Although rules for the conduct of air warfare laid out at The Hague in 1923 had never been ratified, the international law relating to the bombardment of civilians was very clear: it was illegal not only deliberately to target non-military objectives, but also to undertake operations that would carelessly place a civilian population at risk.[47]

When the war began, therefore, Bomber Command was restricted to attacking enemy forces and military installations and the dropping of propaganda leaflets over Germany. It was assumed that Britain would at some point in the future 'take the gloves off' and begin a wider bombing campaign, but only after the Germans had justified it by initiating their own aerial atrocities. In fact, at the outset of war both sides at least attempted to abide by international law. In Poland, German air operations in support of ground troops killed a lot of civilians, but while the British publicized these casualties, they were not seen to justify retaliation against German cities. Despite continuing opposition from the French, the air staff promoted an attack on the Ruhr as a potential response to a German offensive in the west. In that case, they argued to the War Cabinet, 'the best hope of obtaining decisive results' from bombing would be an assault on a dense industrial region with a population 'which might be expected to crack under intensive air attack'.[48]

Yet such an attack was actually completely beyond Bomber Command's capabilities. As had become increasingly obvious to its commander, Air Chief Marshal Sir Edgar Ludlow-Hewitt, during the final years of peace, the British didn't have the planes or the crews to conduct a successful bombing offensive. On the outbreak of war, about half of Bomber Command's aircraft were Battles and Blenheims, light

bombers with small bombloads and limited range. These were despatched to France as the 'Advanced Air Striking Force' in order to bring
them within range of Germany. Its longer-range aircraft were all
twin-engine models, two of which – the Hampden and Whitley
bombers – dated from the first half of the 1930s. Together with their
more modern counterpart, the Wellington, they were relatively slow
and lightly armed. Although categorized as 'heavy' bombers, they
could not carry the sort of payloads necessary to inflict major damage
in a single trip.[49] Following a rapid expansion in numbers during the
late 1930s, British bomber crews were also short on training and
experience. Unlike the Luftwaffe, which had devised a means of using
intersecting radio beams to help its crews find their objectives, the British had no electronic navigation aids at the start of the war. As late as
August 1939, 40 per cent of Bomber Command's crews were unable to
locate a target within a British city during daylight exercises. By night,
when they had to navigate by the stars, things were even more
difficult.[50]

By 1939, plans were in place to improve Bomber Command's striking power, both through additional training of its aircrews and through
the arrival of much larger, longer-ranged, four-engined bombers –
genuine 'heavies' – which had been ordered back in 1936 and were
expected for delivery in 1941. Ludlow-Hewitt proved an extremely
cautious commander. He feared that if Bomber Command had to
launch an attack against German industry in its current state, it would
suffer such heavy losses that it would never complete these expansion
plans.

The policy restrictions of the early war were therefore something of
a lucky escape for Bomber Command. The limited operations it did
undertake served only to emphasize its inadequacies. Of the twenty-nine
aircraft that flew off to launch the first British air attack of the war,
against German ships off Wilhelmshaven on 4 September 1939, only
sixteen found the target, seven of which were shot down. Most of the
losses were to anti-aircraft fire. One crew managed to bomb the Danish
town of Esbjerg, 110 miles from their target. The damage to German
vessels was minimal. Three months later, the British tried to attack the
German fleet again. Three raids in December concluded with catastrophic losses to a force of Wellingtons that attempted a daytime raid
on German vessels in the Heligoland Bight. Of twenty-two aircraft that

reached the area, only ten returned. This time, most of the losses were to German fighter aircraft. The disaster led Ludlow-Hewitt to demand the indefinite postponement of plans for a daylight attack on the Ruhr.[51]

Meanwhile, Bomber Command's heavier aircraft had also been sent on night-time missions to drop propaganda leaflets over Germany. These were difficult and hazardous because of the perils of long flights in winter conditions, but the rate of loss to the German defences was low. Here at least was a means to keep the Command in being and in training until new equipment arrived, but it was a sorry position for what was meant to have been Britain's strike arm. In the spring of 1940, the chiefs of staff accepted that, for the moment, Bomber Command was in no position to contribute to the winning of the war.

'UNFIT FOR WAR, PRACTICALLY IN EVERY ASPECT'

At the start of September, five divisions of regular British troops moved to France where they made up the first tranche of the British Expeditionary Force (BEF). This was a significant achievement given that, when the first formal commitment of their presence was made at the start of 1939, the War Office had lacked not only any transport plans, but even the maps of France necessary to create them. By mid-October, 160,000 British troops had arrived, and that number doubled over the winter of 1939–40 as a further eight divisions, composed of Territorial Army units, moved across the Channel. This military contribution was still, however, extremely small relative to that of France, which by 1940 had deployed 104 divisions along the Western Front. Although the BEF's commander had a right of appeal to London, he was formally placed under French command.[52]

The British army in 1939 was a curious mix of innovation and conservatism, hindered by recent changes in strategic policy and unable to live up to its dreams of modernity. For most of the inter-war period, its senior officers presumed that it would have to send some form of force to mainland Europe in a future conflict. Drawing on the lessons of the last war, they developed a doctrine on paper that would allow the army to fight a modern all-arms battle. This was not, however, what it actually got to practise in peace. Scattered in imperial garrisons and short of training areas at home, the army undertook large-scale manoeuvres only once every ten years. Budget restrictions undermined the early British lead in armoured warfare. The slow pace of inter-war promotion and a tradition of unquestioning obedience inhibited the intellectual development of the officer corps, and the army struggled to fill its annual quota of recruits. During the years of rearmament, equipping a field force had come a distant fourth behind the needs of the RAF, anti-aircraft defence at home and the Royal Navy. The sudden acceptance of a continental commitment in the last months of peace had brought rapid expansion, but only at the cost of disruption and confusion.[53]

The aspirations for the new fifty-five-division army were Herculean. Never to be realized production plans called for it to be supplied with 66,000 artillery pieces, 192 million rounds of artillery ammunition and 31,000 tanks in the first two years of the war – per annum figures much higher than those achieved in 1918, and for weapons that had in the meantime become more complicated.[54] As these numbers indicated, the army aspired to fight a land war of massive technological intensity. Machines were meant to provide the means to mitigate the heavy casualties of 1914–18.

When the fighting actually began, however, few British units were fully equipped. Some had no experience with the new weapons they were expected to use. The BEF was the only one of the armies on the Western Front that could claim to be fully motorized. It had only been able to make up the number of trucks it needed, however, by extensive requisitioning of civilian vehicles. Many of them quickly broke down for lack of servicing and spares.

The British planned to put proportionately many more tanks into the field than any other combatant, but for the moment, their armoured units were still afflicted by the relatively low priority they had received during the years of rearmament. The Vickers Light Tank Mark VI made up the majority of armoured vehicles available to the BEF in September 1939. It was the one really successful design of the mid-1930s but, designed primarily for reconnaissance, it was better suited to imperial policing duties than to going head-to-head with enemy tanks in the north-west European countryside. In 1932, the British had abandoned attempts to build a multi-purpose medium tank on grounds of cost. Since then, heavier tank designs had bifurcated between 'cruisers' – faster, lighter-armoured vehicles intended for rapid advances – and 'infantry' tanks – whose thick armour allowed them to provide close support for the slow-moving infantry during an assault. Cruiser tank designs were still being introduced when the war broke out. None deployed with the BEF until the arrival in France of Britain's 1st Armoured Division in April 1940. Instead, the BEF's heavier armoured component was made up of a single brigade of fifty infantry tanks. These were well protected, and some of them were equipped with a 2-pounder anti-tank gun that could knock out any of their German opponents, but like their cruiser counterparts, their mechanical reliability was poor.[55]

Unlike the Germans, who had chosen to integrate their air forces closely with their army, the British did not have the aircraft, the experience or the communications to co-ordinate air support for their ground troops. The Advanced Air Striking Force had gone to France to put it in range of Germany, not to provide assistance on the battlefield to the BEF. The RAF thought that tying its planes to the army would represent a waste of valuable air resources.

The Expeditionary Force that spent the winter of 1939–40 digging fortifications in northern France was not, therefore, the mechanized elite favoured by British military theorists between the wars. With lots of infantrymen, it was closer to the army of civilian volunteers that had fought on the Somme in 1916 than to the high-tech, well-coordinated behemoth that had advanced to victory in 1918.

As secretary of state for war, Leslie Hore-Belisha had proved an eager and publicity-hungry reformer. Visibly influenced by his civilian advisor, the military 'expert' Basil Liddell Hart, Hore-Belisha had overhauled the upper ranks of the army in 1938. This brought to the fore two younger generals, Edmund 'Tiny' Ironside (who was a hulking six-foot four), and John 'Tiger' Gort (one of the most decorated soldiers in the army, having won the VC, DSO and MC with three bars). In summer 1939 Gort was chief of the imperial general staff, the professional head of the war, and everyone presumed that Ironside would command the BEF. Hore-Belisha, however, dissatisfied with Gort's performance at the War Office, appointed them the other way around. Neither was temperamentally well suited for his job. Ironside lacked the political nous to function well at the interface between ministers and generals; Gort enjoyed the day-to-day detail of soldiering too much to revel in the diplomatic drudgery of Allied command. He often gave the impression that he would rather have been running the regimental sports day, or storming a pillbox single-handed, than attending another staff conference.[56]

Below Ironside and Gort was an army struggling to manage its new scale of operations. The number of qualified staff officers was too few to run the BEF, oversee the expansion of the army and man the War Office in London. British regular troops were relatively well trained and some had extensive experience in small unit actions on the edge of Empire, but many of the men in the army were military novices: at least half of the Territorials called to the colours in summer 1939 had been recruited since the start of the year and both regular and TA units had to be made up to full strength with new conscripts, none of whom had served before July. There was no problem with the flow of men, but turning them into effective soldiers would take time. As a frustrated Ironside explained to his diary, 'You can only make war with actual trained divisions.'[57] Out in France, the commander of the BEF's II Corps, General Sir Alan Brooke, thought that this was exactly what he didn't have. At the end of November, he confided to his diary:

> On arrival in this country and for the first two months the Corps was quite unfit for war, practically in every aspect. Even now our anti-tank gunners are untrained and a large proportion of our artillery have never fired either their equipment or type of smoke shell they are armed with. To send untrained troops into modern war is courting disaster such as befell the Poles.[58]

Gort, a naturally more obedient soldier, thought Brooke was being too negative.[59] The need to reassure the French meant that troops had to be sent across the Channel whether they were ready or not, and even poorly trained Territorial divisions could be employed on the construction of defences on the Franco-Belgian border. By the spring of 1940, however, three of these formations were still classified as fit only for labouring duties.

In practice, therefore, after eight months of war, the BEF had just ten divisions that were really capable of front-line service. As 1939 turned into 1940, most British troops were shivering in freezing billets or finding solace in the cafés of northern France. Chilblains, venereal disease and hangovers inflicted many more casualties than the enemy. When the German spring offensive came, British generals agreed, everything would depend on how well the French army fought.[60]

'NOW YOU KNOW THERE'S A WAR ON!'

The tightly controlled war that Chamberlain wanted to fight therefore actually fitted well with the capabilities of Britain's armed forces. For the moment, Germany's maritime trade was pretty much the only thing that could be attacked with a reasonable possibility of success. This was less a failure of strategy than the outcome of specific decisions about how to balance resources between the wars. If, however, Britain was to shift from the defensive to the offensive as the war went on, its economy would have to be harnessed to the necessities of battle.

The first months of the conflict saw a significant shift in the mobilization of manpower. New legislation extended the extent of male military conscription, although there was as yet no move to compel civilian war work as well as service in the forces, or to conscript women. The call-up of reservists and auxiliaries, the extension of conscription and a healthy flow of volunteer recruits swelled the armed forces by about a million men between August and December.[61]

Over the same period, munitions production also increased. The time lag between decisions being made by ministers, instructions being written by civil servants and orders going out to manufacturers meant that until the end of 1939, British factories were still working on pre-war expansion plans. Overall output therefore continued to reflect the defence priorities set during the final months of peace. The emphasis was on making aircraft and anti-aircraft guns, not tanks and howitzers. It took until November for the requirements for the thirty-two-division army announced in April 1939 to be issued to industry. By that point, the politicians had decided that they needed to equip another twenty-three formations.[62] There were substantial relative increases on peacetime output, but the absolute quantity of material produced for the army remained unsurprisingly small. In the first quarter of 1939, for example, British industry had made a grand total of two 25-pounder field guns. Between September and December, it made 111 of these guns, although none of the wheel assemblies on which they were mounted.[63] More significantly, however, there was substantial investment in capacity for the future. Between the outbreak of war and February 1940, work began on another eleven new Royal Ordnance factories, all intended to begin production by the spring of 1941.[64]

The outbreak of hostilities brought industrial disruption. Reservists were called up. The imposition of blackout regulations and the commandeering of rail and road transport for military use and civilian evacuation interfered with industrial logistics. Imports were initially disrupted by the temporary closure of the east coast ports (as a precaution against air attack), the marshalling of ships into convoys and the reluctance of neutral shipping to sail into a war zone. New government contracts brought their own delays while shifts in production took place. Competition for limited stocks of raw materials, components, machine tools and skilled workers continued. The onset of an unusually severe winter led to increased absenteeism and transport delays. Despite increases in production, deliveries to the armed forces fell behind schedule. So too did plans to expand war industry.[65]

Meanwhile, the British state brought into action a wide range of regulations designed to direct resources towards the war effort. Raw materials such as timber and steel became subject to Control Boards, run by the Ministry of Supply, which issued licences for importation and usage. A system of export licensing was put into place to ensure that essential items did not reach the enemy. Conglomerates formed under the auspices of the Ministry of Supply and the Ministry of Food became the sole purchasers of commodities such as wheat and oil. The railways – previously run by four major private companies – were taken into national ownership for the duration. Some commodity prices and all rents were regulated. Agricultural subsidies, ministerial exhortations and, ultimately, compulsory dispossession were used to increase domestic arable production, and reduce reliance on imported foodstuffs. As a result, between 1939 and 1940, the area of land under the plough in the UK increased by 1.5 million acres.

Financial restrictions included a requirement for the Treasury to approve all external transactions. Currency exchange was tightly restricted to maintain foreign reserves and shore up the value of sterling. Banks were instructed to limit lending to prevent speculation and to encourage investment in government bonds. The state also took to itself the right to sell off gold and foreign assets belonging to British citizens in order to fund its own spending overseas.[66]

Three-and-a-half weeks into the war, Sir John Simon announced his first wartime budget. This raised the standard rate of income tax from 27.5 to 37.5 per cent, lowered tax thresholds and increased the rates of surtax and estate duty. Duty on beer went up 1d. a pint, on tobacco by 1½d. an ounce and on sugar by 1d. a pound. Businesses that made more money than they had before the war now became liable to a 60 per cent Excess Profits Tax. All together, increased taxation was expected to raise £995 million by the end of March 1940, to cover government expenditure that was anticipated to rise to £1,933 million. The difference between the two was to be found from additional borrowing, with the first war bonds to be issued in the spring of 1940 after the markets had recovered from the disturbance of the outbreak of hostilities.[67]

Simon's forecast increase in defence spending – up from £382 million in 1938–39 to £1,000 million in 1939–40 – was relatively modest given the immense task that lay before the Allies. It reflected in part how high expenditure had already risen during the last full year of peace, but also how long it would still take to crank military production up to full speed. Press reactions to the budget, however, demonstrated how dramatic the fiscal burden felt at the time. The *Daily Mail* criticized Simon's 'method' as 'far too precipitate . . . the large all round increases in taxation, inflicted without warning, will mean a severe dislocation of trade and industry'. The *Daily Express* accused him of 'going to work with a meat axe' on the pockets of the public, while the *Daily Mirror* put its case with the headline 'NOW YOU KNOW THERE'S A WAR ON!'[68] Nonetheless, their resigned conclusion was that the cost of the war must be borne somehow, and that it would be better to pay more in the present than to store up still larger debts for the future.

Taken all together, the measures imposed at the start of the war were a remarkable extension of official intervention that would have been unthinkable in a time of peace. They laid the groundwork for the much further-reaching controls that would be introduced as the conflict went on. They also indicated, however, the expectation that time was on Britain's side, the government's hope that victory might be achieved without too much impact on the civilian economy, and the reality that controlling such a complex organism took time.

Shifting from peace to war was not simply a matter of flicking a switch. It was a couple of months, for instance, before most of the

Ministry of Supply's Control Boards even began to operate. To start with, controls were often inconsistent and incomplete. Deciding on controls meant working out which parts of the economy ought to have priority. There was no central direction about how to do this, and so individual boards worked on an ad hoc basis. Substantial sectors remained for the moment untouched by official restrictions. While the war remained phoney, private, pre-war stockpiles endured, the munitions industries were still working up to full pace and there was only limited pressure for the government to get involved in order to maximize economic efficiency. Motivation was limited too: ministers had gone to war to preserve national security, not to extend the reach of the state.[69]

The war did not end unemployment. In fact, the jobless totals increased, from 1.23 million in September 1939 to 1.5 million in February 1940. In the midst of a total war, Britain seemed unable to shake off the enforced idleness of the 1930s: at the time and after, no statistic served better to damn the National Government's gradualist approach to economic mobilization. Yet the unemployment figure was itself in part a result of the conflict. The number of long-term unemployed actually fell during this period by 86,000, a decrease thanks largely to the revival of heavy industry in the distressed areas as rearmament progressed. Other parts of the economy were, however, badly hit by the onset of hostilities, including the entertainment sector and private house building; 1939 was a better year to be a shipyard riveter than a Butlin's redcoat. With war industry still accelerating, those who lost their jobs when the conflict started were not immediately sucked into munitions factories. The government remained reluctant to control civilian workers in the same way as military conscripts.[70]

The problems of industrial mobilization persisted into 1940. During the first quarter of the year, another 350,000 men were called up into the armed forces. By June, three-quarters of the country's engineering workforce were working on government contracts. Output continued to increase: the index of aircraft production was 38 per cent higher in April 1940 than it had been in September 1939. Artillery, tank and ammunition production also all rose. Although unemployment reached a wartime peak of just over a million and a half in January and February, thereafter it fell rapidly. By April, the jobless total was under a million.[71]

Progress in increasing production, however, was well behind the targets set at the start of the war. In the aircraft industry, for example, the impressive growth in production during 1939 proved hard to sustain. In the first months of 1940, a bottleneck in the supply of aluminium extrusions held up the entire sector, with some machines standing idle for want of components. Meanwhile, under the pressure of operations, the RAF found that it needed more spare parts for its existing planes. Instructions to the aircraft industry to produce more spares restricted increases in the number of finished aircraft. Under the Harrogate Programme, British factories were meant to deliver 1,001 planes in January. In fact they delivered 719. By April, actual deliveries had risen to 1,081, but this was still 175 aircraft behind the target figure for that month. Delays imposed by production bottlenecks meant that the intake of new workers to the aircraft industry slowed almost to a standstill during the first quarter of 1940. These industrial shortfalls rang alarm bells in Whitehall about the organization of the war economy and offered ammunition to the government's critics in Parliament.[72]

Every combatant country struggled with the transition to war. For all that it had spent years under totalitarian control, Germany came close to economic meltdown in the last part of 1939. A combination of Allied blockade and lack of foreign reserves meant that German import volumes collapsed to about 20 per cent of their pre-war levels, forcing dramatic measures from the Nazi state. Determined on early offensive action, Hitler completely re-prioritized the allocation of industrial effort, abandoning plans to build a large surface navy and concentrating resources on the production of artillery ammunition and aircraft. German munitions output stagnated – partly because it took time to restructure production to meet Hitler's new plans, partly because 4 million reservists had been called up into the armed forces, disrupting the wider economy, and partly because the rail movements required to move troops between the Eastern and Western Fronts wrecked the distribution of coal. It was not until the start of 1940, as the new schedules of raw materials kicked through, that the German war economy recovered sufficiently to deliver the weaponry necessary for a major offensive on the Western Front.[73]

Like Germany, France suffered economic consequences as it mobilized its huge military reserves. The departure into the ranks of skilled workers from tank and aircraft factories meant that output slumped during the first months of the war, dispelling the optimism that had developed since Munich. Despite the best efforts of the new French Armaments Ministry to restore the situation, it was never able to meet targets set by soldiers who vastly overestimated the strength of the German forces ranged against them. Despair about the state of munitions production increased the French sense of strategic crisis, but it also opened up political rifts about the way the war was to be run. For many French conservatives, fighting Communism at home was at least as important as fighting Nazism abroad. That left little room to forge a compromise in which the state, big business and trade unions would collaborate to mobilize the economy.[74]

In the UK too, the direction of the war economy became the subject of fierce political debate. The underlying framework of co-operation established before the war, however, persisted despite the outbreak of hostilities. British business leaders generally accepted that state intervention in the wartime economy was not some sort of capitalist end-of-days. If it was to happen, they thought it was better they were involved. During the first months of war, industrialists flocked into government service to run the new Control Boards. British trade unionists despised Chamberlain, but they also wanted to defeat Fascism. Opposing the war effort might see them sidelined as unpatriotic: they hoped that they would be able to extract a better deal for their people by working with the government to handle the provision of industrial manpower.[75]

The National Government was by nature better attuned to the interests of business than those of organized labour, but having invited the unions to assist in rearmament after the *Anschluss*, it was now unable to exclude them. Chamberlain knew that he needed trade union co-operation, and at the start of the war he asked the TUC to participate in the committees that would manage mobilization. Sir Walter Citrine readily accepted, ensuring union involvement was enshrined throughout the bureaucratic machine, from the Food Control Committees that determined prices and supplies at a local level, via the Tribunals that decided on applications for exemption from conscription, to the Supply Council of the Ministry of Supply, which took decisions about munitions production, and the National Joint Advisory Council, set up by the Ministry of Labour as a forum for senior business and union leaders to discuss industrial issues.

Trade union agreement was particularly important to plans for industrial dilution – the key means of expanding the workforce as the momentum of war production developed – the control of skilled labour and the limitation of wartime inflation. Union leaders were willing to barter these against the introduction of greater economic planning – not just as a means to win the war but as an absolute good. At the same time, the organizations representing big business also came round to more central planning as a prerequisite for increased munitions production. On both sides, the extension of state power came to be seen as a logical response to the exigencies of war.

'WHERE SHE STANDS, WE STAND'

Britain's declaration of war brought in the Commonwealth by choice and the Empire by definition. Just over an hour after Chamberlain announced the outbreak of hostilities, the Australian prime minister, Robert Menzies, also took to the radio to tell his compatriots that 'in consequence of a persistence by Germany in her invasion of Poland, Great Britain has declared war upon her and that, as a result, Australia is also at war'. For Menzies, it was an inevitable development: as a lawyer he took it as constitutionally self-evident that once George VI was at war with Germany, so were all his Dominions. As he told his radio audience: 'one King, one flag, one cause'.[76]

In Wellington, the New Zealand government exercised its ability to declare war in its own right. As a result of the time difference and the decision to wait for confirmation from London that Germany had not complied with the British ultimatum, this did not happen until 11.30 on the evening of 3 September, although the proclamation of war was backdated so that it coincided exactly with that of the UK. Two days later, the Labour prime minister, Michael Joseph Savage, then gravely ill, broadcast to New Zealand. He told listeners that: 'Both with gratitude for the past and confidence in the future, we range ourselves without fear beside Britain. Where she goes, we go. Where she stands, we stand.'[77]

Canada took slightly longer to join the war. On 3 September, the Canadian prime minister, Mackenzie King, also went on air to promise that his country would take part. Canadian politics, however, made it more important for him than for his antipodean counterparts to give the impression that Canada was acting independently of the UK. King explained that 'it would be up to Parliament to decide the form and scope of Canadian participation', and it took until 9 September for a resolution approving the country's full involvement to be passed through the legislature. Canada formally declared war the following day.[78]

In South Africa, the outbreak of war was more divisive. Prime Minister J. B. M. Hertzog, an Afrikaner nationalist, saw no reason for fighting on Britain's side in what he regarded as a purely European conflict. He wanted the country to remain neutral. The South African parliament rejected neutrality by eighty votes to sixty-five, and Hertzog was deposed by his own party in favour of his pro-war deputy, Jan Smuts. When Hertzog went to the governor-general, Sir Patrick Duncan, to ask for a general election, Duncan exercised the royal prerogative to refuse his request.[79]

Ireland stayed out of the war. For the taoiseach, Éamon de Valera, neutrality was the only option for a small nation, still striving to achieve its independence, to escape the global Armageddon. Since neutrality demonstrated Irish freedom and defied British power, it received widespread public support. Ireland's refusal to join in Britain's war had significant military consequences. Much to Churchill's fury, the Royal Navy was not allowed to make use of the former treaty ports, much reducing the reach of its escorts into the Atlantic. The British also worried that Ireland would function as a conduit for German spies or a re-provisioning base for their submarines, or even fall prey to an invasion.

Inevitably, however, given the country's economic dependence on the UK, Irish neutrality had what de Valera called 'a certain consideration for Britain'. The Irish government shared vital meteorological data, provided extensive co-operation on matters of intelligence and security (including eventually joint military exercises) and gave preferential treatment to British servicemen who strayed over the border. Perhaps as importantly, de Valera's stance neutered more extreme nationalists and ensured that Britain did not have to deal with a hostile neighbour on its western shore. In practice, British naval dominance made a German invasion of Ireland unlikely, but an aggressively antipathetic neighbour could have made Britain's life much harder rather than covertly aiding its cause.

With the exception of some skilled agricultural workers, the Irish government did not stand in the way of those of its inhabitants who wished to travel to Britain to work or serve. The first days of the war saw Irish ports overflowing as emigrants returned home and private evacuees and potential conscripts sought safety. Over the following months, however, the flow returned to usual, as thousands of Irishmen and women travelled to Britain, some seeking employment, others, unlike the taoiseach, eager to join the fight against Hitler.[80]

In the Middle East, the governments of Egypt and Iraq resisted British pressure to make a declaration of war. The British, represented in Cairo by the forceful ambassador, Sir Miles Lampson, had long accepted the Egyptian monarchs' habit of forcing out governments formed by the electorally successful nationalist party, the Wafd, in favour of their court favourites. They thought they had a better chance of influencing arbitrarily appointed ministers than those holding a genuine popular mandate. Lampson had known the young Egyptian king, Farouk, since he was a child, and liked to believe he could control him.[81]

When the Egyptian premier, Muhammad Mahmud, resigned in August 1939, Farouk selected a palace official, Ali Maher, to replace him. He was efficient and competent, but he was also strongly anti-British. Ali Maher dismissed ministers who supported the UK, and refused to declare war, but he did declare martial law and break off diplomatic and trade relations with Germany. The British pondered whether they should use the threat of military force to make Farouk dismiss Maher. They decided, however, that it was better not to run the risk of destabilizing Egyptian politics still further by intervening against the prime minister.

The Iraqi army, unlike its Egyptian equivalent, played a major role in politics. At the end of 1938, in the latest of a series of coups, it had installed a new government under Nuri as-Said. Nuri wanted to work with the British, but there was a strong strand of anti-imperial feeling among the Iraqi military and political elite, in whom a rising Arab nationalism had been stoked by anger at British policy in Palestine. It was no accident that when the mufti of Jerusalem, Amin al-Husayni, escaped from Lebanon in October 1939, he went to Baghdad, where he received a warm welcome from those who opposed Britain's continued presence in the Middle East.

In April 1939, the young Iraqi monarch, King Ghazi, had died after crashing his sports car into a lamppost. In a sign of hostility to the British, rumours ran wild that they had been responsible: in Mosul, the mourning for the king turned into a riot, during which the British consul was battered to death with a pickaxe. Ghazi's son was still a child, and under the regency of his uncle, Emir Abdul Illah, the Hashemite royal family became even more dependent on British support for its survival.

In September 1939, Nuri as-Said wanted to declare war alongside the British, but the army officers who had put him in power did not. Nuri did, however, declare a state of emergency, intern German nationals and break off diplomatic relations with Berlin. The British shied away from trying to force Iraq into a declaration of hostilities because they feared that Nuri – a weakened presence, but still on their side – would be displaced as a result. Here, as in Egypt, their goal was stability in the Middle East so that Britain could concentrate on the war against Germany.

'THE BULWARK OF BRITISH RULE IN INDIA'

There was no choice about whether India would go to war. If, by September 1939, the constitution devised in 1935 had come fully into effect, then the viceroy, Lord Linlithgow, would have had a federal assembly with which to consult about a declaration of hostilities. Despite his best efforts, however, it had not: the requisite number of princes had not signed up to the plan for an Indian federation by 1 September 1939, the date the British had set for their accession. Britain's declaration of war therefore committed India to hostilities too. Linlithgow's announcement of this fact on 3 September, without any apparent discussion with the major political parties, antagonized nationalist opinion.[82]

In fact, Linlithgow had been keeping Gandhi up-to-date with the progress of events. The two men met on 4 September. Gandhi viewed the war as both a human catastrophe and even further evidence of the redundancy of Western materialism. Yet he told the viceroy that he could not help but regard the conflict 'with an English heart', and wept at the idea of London's great buildings being pounded into dust by

German bombs. He said that he would back the British and encourage Congress supporters to lend their non-violent soul-force in support of the war effort. Yet he was no longer in charge of the Congress. Instead, the decision about what the party should do lay with Jawaharlal Nehru.[83]

Nehru saw the conflict as an inevitable consequence not just of Fascism but also of British imperialism. Though he wanted to see the former defeated, he was by no means bound to support the latter. On the contrary, he viewed the outbreak of war as an opportunity both to put the British on the spot about India's future and to assert his own power within the Congress. He composed a demand for a clarification of war aims that was put to the British on 14 September. If they were truly committed to democracy, Nehru told them, they should commit to granting India full independence. In that case, the Congress would co-operate fully in the war effort. If they would not, it would withdraw its support from the war. When Linlithgow, with the approval of the Cabinet, responded simply by repeating Britain's commitment to allowing India to achieve Dominion status after the war, Nehru instructed the Congress ministries that now governed eight out of the eleven Indian provinces to resign. He thus broke the very effective relationship that had been building up between provincial Congress politicians and British officials as they got used to governing in harness together. Instead, he was able to drive the Congress towards a confrontation with the Raj.

Linlithgow remained one of the great supporters of the 1935 constitution, which he had done a lot to draft, but he now saw his job as making sure that India was mobilized as effectively as possible for Britain's war. To that end, he was willing to explore the possibility of bringing Indian politicians into his Executive Council, which was the closest thing the Raj had to a central government. He still believed that the best route would be to build an Indian federation. He did not think that constitutional concessions to the Congress were in Britain's interest, not least because of the consequences they would have on communal relations.

When he heard the news that the Indian National Congress was withdrawing from provincial government, Mohammad Ali Jinnah, the leader of the Muslim League, was overjoyed. He recognized this as an overplaying of the Congress's hand, which would reduce its influence on the government of India and advance the claims of the Muslim League. He ratcheted up communal tensions, declaring 22 December 1939 a 'day of deliverance', on which Muslims should celebrate their liberation from the tyranny of Congress provincial rule, and became even firmer in his position that he could not accept any settlement of constitutional questions on the Congress's terms.

In Britain, the moderate Conservatives of the Chamberlain government believed that something had to be done to address the Indian impasse. It was not just that without Congress's co-operation it would be difficult fully to mobilize India for the war, but also that the party's withdrawal from government raised the prospect of another civil disobedience campaign and resultant crackdown from the authorities. At the very least, that would absorb valuable resources and damage Britain's claims to be fighting for freedom. At worst, it might endanger its control of the situation in India altogether. There was also a feeling that the exigencies of war ought to provide a moment for a dramatic appeal to Indian opinion. The problem was how this was to be done, given Indian suspicions of British intentions and Linlithgow's rather plodding approach. The marquess of Zetland, the secretary of state for India; Halifax and Butler, at the Foreign Office; and Sir Samuel Hoare, therefore all welcomed an offer of intercession from Sir Stafford Cripps.[84]

Like other members of the British intelligentsia, Cripps had been energized by the outbreak of war. He expected to be called upon to fulfil some great public service – as he had done in the last conflict – and prepared himself for action by resigning his lucrative practice at the Bar, only to find himself at a loose end as the call to office failed to arrive. Cripps was not the sort of man to take this opportunity to withdraw from public life. Instead, he sought to establish himself as an unofficial envoy who could address the great international problems brought into sharp relief by the war.[85]

The issues on which Cripps wanted to work showed both his ideological commitments – he welcomed the Red Army's invasion of Poland as a saving force in the class struggle that would liberate the Polish people – but also his understanding of geo-politics – he saw the Molotov-Ribbentrop pact as evidence of the essential pragmatism of Soviet foreign policy rather than an inevitable alignment of totalitarianisms. Since Soviet co-operation was probably a precondition of defeating Hitler, he thought, Britain should find out what it could do to trump the Nazis' offer. This was also the view to which both Lord Halifax and Rab Butler in the Foreign Office now increasingly inclined, and they supported Cripps' idea of travelling to Moscow as a route to improving Anglo-Soviet relations. Cripps also recognized the importance of Nationalist China as the front line of a struggle to contain Japanese aggression. Here too, and again with the backing of the Foreign Office, he wanted to go to see conditions in Chongqing for himself. Given the importance of America in the conflict on which Britain had now embarked, a visit to Washington would also be most useful. In the course of the world tour – and quest for employment – that was now shaping in Cripps' mind, he decided that he should also call in on India, where he already had an idea about how to smooth the path to independence from the Raj.

Cripps had been building an interest in India since the mid-1930s. The principal vector through which this developed was his friendship with Nehru – established by letter and constructed in person when Nehru visited Britain in 1938. The two men shared an interpretation of the world built on class struggle, and that made Cripps a receptive audience for the education that Nehru gave him in Indian politics: a righteous Congress, representing a truly united India, struggling for a democratic future against the divide-and-rule imperialism of the British, the despotism of the Indian princes and the self-interest of the landowners who made up the Muslim League. This perspective – and Cripps' own aspirations for the war – underpinned the plan that he had drawn up to solve the stalemate in India, and which he tried out on Whitehall in the autumn of 1939.

In order to demonstrate its commitment to freedom and democracy, Cripps suggested Britain should offer India full Dominion status, including the right to secede from the Commonwealth. As soon as the war was finished, a representative assembly should be formed to settle the terms of a new Indian constitution by majority vote. Britain and India would guarantee its implementation – and the protection of communal rights – by a fifteen-year treaty. This was effectively the scheme preferred by the Congress leadership. These proposals were met with some approval from Zetland, Halifax and Butler, all of whom facilitated the round-the-world trip on which Cripps now embarked. As Zetland told Chamberlain, Cripps' visit might provide a way to break the constitutional logjam: at the very least, the attraction of his plan was that handing over the constitutional problem to Indians would mean that any subsequent inability to agree a satisfactory solution would not be Britain's fault.[86] Cripps went as an entirely unofficial envoy, but with the good wishes of those who believed that building a more progressive Empire was a crucial part of winning the war.

During December 1939, Cripps toured around India, meeting politicians and officials to discuss the future. He was clearly and publicly Nehru's guest, and he was predisposed to be impressed by his meetings with the Congress leadership and dismissive of Jinnah's argument that the problem of minority rights could not be settled by a majority decision in a democracy. Since he saw the question in terms of class rather than community, Cripps was optimistic about the ease with which a political solution could be found. The sticking point was how a constitutional assembly should work – so the British should seize the initiative by bringing the party leaders together and presenting them with a plan that would address their anxieties on that score. That put a lot of emphasis on Linlithgow's ability to do the dirty work of inspiring, cajoling and coercing. Cripps suspected that Linlithgow – 'by nature', as he put it, not 'a negotiator at all but rather a judge' – was not up to the job, a belief confirmed by a meeting with the 'rather sphinx-like' viceroy at which he did all the talking and Linlithgow sat quietly, taking notes.[87]

Back in London, meanwhile, Zetland had been promoting something very like the Cripps plan to Linlithgow and the Cabinet. Chamberlain – while not committing himself – accepted Zetland's argument that something needed to be done. From New Delhi, Linlithgow responded much more frostily. Having spent the previous three years trying to get agreement on the 1935 constitution, the viceroy had a more accurate sense that the sort of settlement Cripps wanted could not just be magicked up out of thin air. He saw no reason simply to submit to demands from the Congress, and in the process give away Britain's negotiating position and antagonize the Muslims, who were at least supporting the war effort. He framed his response in terms that made very clear what, in his view, the changes of the 1930s had been all about:

After all we framed the Constitution as it stands in the Act of 1935, because we thought that way the best way ... of maintaining British influence in India. It is no part of our policy, I take it, to expedite in India constitutional changes for their own sake, or gratuitously to hurry the handing over of the controls to Indian hands at any pace faster than that which we regard as best calculated, on a long view, to hold India to the Empire.[88]

Zetland disagreed. On 2 February 1940, he asked the Cabinet to approve the idea of India being offered the right to make its own post-war Dominion constitution, subject to a treaty with Britain and agreement between the parties on how to construct the representative assembly.

This proposal was firmly blocked by Winston Churchill. He could not, he told his colleagues, share the general enthusiasm for resolving the tensions between Muslims and Hindus:

> Such unity was, in fact, almost out of the realm of practical politics, while, if it were to be brought about, the immediate result would be that the united communities would join in showing us the door. He regarded the Hindu-Muslim feud as the bulwark of British rule in India.

Sir John Simon backed him up, explaining that 'there was every reason for not going any faster than we were obliged to' (perhaps the most characteristic statement of his long fence-sitting career).[89] Sir John Anderson – a former Indian civil servant – who had previously agreed with Cripps that the British could not rule India indefinitely by force, shared the view that Linlithgow, as the man on the spot, ought to be the one who determined policy. As Zetland pondered a renewed appeal to the Cabinet, Churchill and Simon wrote to Chamberlain to make clear that they would oppose any further concessions to the Congress. By the start of 1940, with much else on his plate, the prime minister had little incentive to open up a row with senior ministers about an initiative that still looked like it could be put off to a later date.

Meanwhile in India, Jinnah had taken advantage of the Congress's withdrawal from government to up the ante. On 23 March 1940, at a huge meeting in Lahore, the Muslim League passed a resolution calling for those provinces where Muslims were in the majority to be allowed to form their own 'independent states'. Jinnah's eyes were not on the war but on the end of British rule. The League had now staked out its position if the British tried to give a single, united India its independence.[90]

To the Indian National Congress, both Jinnah's claim to represent all of India's Muslims and his call for the country to be partitioned were unacceptable. Yet as so often, the Congress was divided. Discontented and out of office, party members wanted to stage another civil disobedience campaign. Congress leaders doubted that, in the circumstances of the war, such a campaign would receive mass support. In the aftermath of the Lahore resolution, it would look even more like an offensive to achieve a Hindu India: it might even lead to a civil war. With the British apparently undisposed to negotiate, any resort to civil disobedience could only be a stopgap to keep the party together, rather than a positive step towards gaining India its freedom. Moderate Congressmen, such as Chakravarti Rajagopalachari, argued that it was time to reverse their policy and work with the British to support the war effort. During the spring of 1940, the Congress Working Committee sat through a long series of meetings at Wardha debating what to do next.

In London, those who had opposed any concession to the Congress celebrated. On 12 April 1940, Chamberlain's assistant private secretary, John Colville, recorded in his diary a conversation at Number 10 between Sir John Simon and P. J. Grigg, another former Indian civil servant who was now the permanent under-secretary at the War Office.

> Simon was quite amusing in describing what he called 'the masculine and simple view' adopted by Winston in the Cabinet. Winston rejoiced in the quarrel which had broken out afresh between Hindus and Moslems, said he hoped it would remain bitter and bloody and was glad that we had made the suggestion of Dominion status which was acting as a cat among the pigeons. Both Simon and Grigg agreed that this was not the moment to give anything away in India: we must remain firm as a rock, because British rule was today essential in India.[91]

'OUR ABILITY TO PROVIDE EQUIPMENT IS THE LIMITING FACTOR IN OUR WAR EFFORT'

Meanwhile, the Commonwealth and Empire had been moving to war. At the outset of hostilities, it was not fully clear what the military contribution of the Dominions would be. Of their small armed forces, the navies were the most involved in imperial defence planning, and at the start of the war they essentially acted as part of the Royal Navy. When it came to armies, the Dominions' experience of the First World War simultaneously raised the expectation that they would send expeditionary forces to fight alongside the British in Europe and made any such mission politically controversial. In Australia, where fears of the Japanese threat to the north ran high, the despatch of troops overseas was particularly difficult. Nonetheless, during the first three months of the war, all the Dominions committed to sending land forces outside their borders. A Canadian division began to arrive in the UK from December 1939. When New Zealand announced that it would send a division too, that forced the Australians to follow suit. South African troops, recruited on the basis that they would serve only in Africa, began to be deployed outside the country in the summer of 1940. All these forces initially relied on voluntary recruitment, although Australia introduced conscription for its home defence militia in October.[92] Dominion divisions would serve under British command for the rest of the war, but the final decision about their employment always rested with their government back home. In this, as in other areas, the wartime Commonwealth functioned more like an alliance than an empire.

When it came to the air, the British hoped that the Dominions would provide trained aircrew rather than aircraft. Drawing on pre-war connections between the Commonwealth air forces, at the start of hostilities the British proposed that the Dominions, and particularly Canada, should host the training facilities necessary to produce the large numbers of aircrew necessary for an air war over Europe. As well as providing safe training areas for British personnel, this would also involve the raising of significant contingents of Dominion aircrew. The proposal was championed by Vincent Massey and Stanley Bruce, the Canadian and Australian high commissioners in London, and negotiations over the scheme began in Ottawa in October.

The British suggested an immense programme, requiring 54,000 staff and 5,000 aircraft, that at its peak would turn out 2,200 trained aircrew a month, at a cost of about a billion Canadian dollars over three years. When the Canadians baulked at the scheme, a smaller one was developed, requiring a mere 3,500 training aircraft to produce 1,900 aircrew a month by early 1942. This was still a colossal undertaking, which demonstrated the incredible ambition of Britain's airpower advocates. As a point of comparison, the Luftwaffe, which stuck with its pre-war system of flying training during the first half of the war, would turn out only 1,662 new fighter pilots during the *whole* of 1942.[93]

In 1939, however, the process of agreeing the air training plan also demonstrated how far the requirements of national politics now impinged on imperial co-operation. Negotiations took place around the proportion to be paid by the UK (which provided aircraft and equipment), Canada (which bore the brunt of the expense and ran the whole operation) and the other Dominions, as well the number of airmen who would take part. Mackenzie King pushed discussions to the brink of collapse by insisting on further conditions: a commitment that the UK would buy Canada's wheat harvest (it had already committed to purchase large quantities of Australian and New Zealand commodities in order to keep their economies afloat), a public statement that this could be Canada's main contribution to the war, which he would present to the isolationist lobby at home in the forthcoming election, and an agreement that Canadian personnel would serve primarily in squadrons designated as distinctly part of the Royal Canadian Air Force. This helped to drag the negotiations out until mid-December, at which point the British conceded all his demands. The first schools of what would be known as the British and Commonwealth Air Training Plan opened at the end of April 1940, with the first graduates emerging the following September.[94]

The contribution of the Dominions to war production was similarly slow to get started. Despite attempts to develop munitions and aircraft industries in the antipodean Dominions in the 1930s, it was clear that Australian, New Zealand and South African troops would all be dependent on British-made equipment. Canada expected to make more of an industrial contribution – not least in the production of motor vehicles – but it too had done little to build up arms manufacture before the outbreak of war. Moreover, British orders were inhibited by the fact that Canadian purchases had to be paid for out of a dwindling stock of dollars.[95]

India was traditionally the manpower reserve of the Empire. Indian troops were meant to reinforce the Middle East or to relieve British soldiers of garrison duties so they could be redeployed to Europe. In

November 1939 the Westminster government agreed to pay and maintain all Indian forces stationed outside the Raj for the duration of the war. At first, the Indian army grew only slowly, from 160,000 to 170,000 Indian officers and other ranks between 1 October 1939 and 1 January 1940.[96] Although Indian arsenals made some small arms, artillery pieces and ammunition, most of their heavier equipment requirements would have to be met from the UK.[97]

At the start of the war, the British did not plan to use the manpower of the African colonies to expand the Empire's military effort. As the colonial secretary, Malcolm MacDonald, explained to ministerial colleagues at the start of 1940, existing units of African troops might be expanded to undertake additional garrison duties, but

> our ability to provide equipment is the limiting factor in our war effort, not our ability to provide manpower. For at least the next two years the raising of new combatant units in the Colonial Dependencies will not on strict military merits be practicable, because all the available supplies of equipment will be required for units considered to be of superior fighting quality, raised in this country or the Dominions.[98]

Financially, however, the whole Commonwealth and Empire was immediately drawn into the war. The pre-war sterling bloc now became a wartime Sterling Area. Within its boundaries, British expenditure was funded by local governments, and the payments credited to blocked accounts in London, the so-called 'sterling balances'. The British controlled the repayment of these balances. They were to prove a crucial mechanism in financing the war, allowing Britain to acquire crucial commodities and pay and provision servicemen overseas while building up sterling liabilities for the future. For the British, the fact that they were going to repay the sterling balances was both a marker of their imperial good intentions, and a crucial element in maintaining international confidence. In practice, however, the sterling balances provided Britain with interest-free loans, the repayment value of which would be steadily eroded by inflation. As the war spread around the globe in the years after 1939, and the largest balances were built up by India and Egypt, some of the poorest people in the world would be paying the immediate costs of Britain's war.

Most members of the Sterling Area also pooled their reserves of foreign currency and precious metals under London's control. British spending from these reserves was also credited to the blocked balances. The UK therefore benefitted from the overseas earning power of colonial exports, above all Malayan tin and rubber and South African and Australian gold. Over the first sixteen months of the war, British contributions to the dollar earnings of the Sterling Area were only just over half those provided by imperial commodities, and only a third of those that came from the sale of Dominion-mined gold. To save dollars, countries within the Sterling Area also agreed to implement controls on currency conversion and restrict imports from the US. As well as lending money to the UK through the sterling balances, therefore, they also forwent the American manufactured goods that they would otherwise have been able to buy. Membership of the Sterling Area stopped countries spending the money they had earned. This sacrifice was a cause of considerable resentment, and during the early period of the war, import and currency controls were not as stringent as they would subsequently become. South Africa, with its mineral reserves and where involvement in the war remained politically controversial, was notably lax in implementing the restrictions.[99]

The international effects of the Allied war effort extended well beyond the British and French empires. Using its control of the seas and the Allies' economic and financial power, the UK attempted to persuade neutral countries to accept the terms of the Allied blockade. Such suasion was harder than it had been a generation before because of Britain's relative economic decline, but the Allies could still offer huge markets and financial security, as well as threatening to cut off supplies that might be re-exported to Germany.

Countries in Central Europe, their economies closely aligned with the Reich, proved all but immune to Allied influence. Others were more vulnerable. As the Spanish foreign minister put it to a British negotiator, his country would accept Allied economic restrictions 'not because we love you, but because the British Empire is our best market'. Like Spain, Argentina, Brazil and Portugal all allowed UK purchases to be credited to sterling balances held in London. Again, this was a marker of British economic power: the scale of existing UK capital assets in these countries operated as a guarantee against default. By the spring, the threat of the blockade had even persuaded Denmark to enter into an agreement to cut its agricultural exports to Germany. This was a policy the Danes would have found it very hard to follow without provoking their neighbour had the Nazis not invaded in any case in April 1940.[100]

In the Mediterranean, Britain tried to use its economic influence to achieve diplomatic objectives. In an attempt to keep Mussolini sweet and Italy out of the conflict, the British committed to purchasing large quantities of Italian vegetables. In the hope of promoting a pro-Allied bloc in the Balkans, they also purchased the bulk of the Greek and Turkish tobacco crop.[101] From flying schools in Alberta to farms on the Black Sea, Britain was building a global war.

CASH AND CARRY

The most crucial aspect of that worldwide conflict lay in the Allies' developing relationship with America. Since November 1938, Roosevelt had tried to shield the US from the twin evils of totalitarianism and war with his own programme of rearmament. He hoped that the prospect of American factories turning out huge numbers of warplanes for despatch to the democracies would deter Germany from opening hostilities. If that didn't work, the groundwork would at least have been laid to prevent a Nazi victory. Notwithstanding the strength of isolationist feeling in the States, Roosevelt wanted to find a way to help Britain and France against Hitler. He was determined that this could happen without America being dragged into the war, but if the worst came to the worst and the democracies crumbled in the face of German aggression, US rearmament would at least have readied his country for battle.[102]

When the war broke out, Roosevelt duly sought to avoid American involvement while enhancing the likelihood of Allied victory. America's pre-war neutrality legislation automatically imposed an arms embargo on both sides, prevented them raising loans for the purchase of munitions, and prohibited US citizens, ships and aircraft from venturing into the combat zone. The president, however, privately reassured Britain and France that they would have his support.

In early October, Roosevelt arranged the setting up of a Western Hemisphere Neutrality Zone: an area patrolled by the US navy, within a line drawn 300 miles from the coast of all non-belligerents in the Americas, out of which the combatants were instructed to keep their armed forces. The British government was rightly sceptical of America's ability to enforce the Zone, but accepted the argument that it would operate in the Allies' favour, since US forces would take on the responsibility of policing these waters against raids on merchant shipping. To allow the Americans to implement these patrols, the British secretly agreed to lease them land to build bases in Trinidad, Bermuda and St Lucia. This was the start of a long shift of Atlantic power away from the UK to the US during the war. In 1939, however, Hitler was just as wary as Roosevelt of drawing America into the war. To begin with, the operations of German naval vessels in the western Atlantic were tightly restricted, in order to avoid any incidents of the sort that had provoked US belligerence in 1917.

By 4 November, Roosevelt had steered through amendments to the Neutrality Acts. These allowed both sides to make purchases in America providing that they paid up front in dollars and transported them in their own ships. Given their much larger reserves of foreign currency and their control of the sea lanes, this 'Cash and Carry' system could only benefit the Allies. The new legislation confirmed to Hitler that, having won the war in Europe, Germany would ultimately have to confront America too.

Roosevelt's policy was welcome news in Paris, where the French looked to American industry as a source of aircraft to make up their own production shortfalls. At the start of 1939, they had placed an order for 550 American aircraft. This was followed up with an order for another 4,500 planes after the war began. These aircraft, scheduled for delivery in October 1940, were meant to lay the path for an Allied offensive by bridging the air gap with Germany.[103]

London's approach was rather different. Although the Foreign Office and the service ministries regarded America as a potentially useful source of military supplies, the Treasury was much more sceptical. For the moment, US munitions output was tiny relative to that of Britain and France. By the time the Americans had geared up production enough to make a difference, the Treasury argued, Britain would either have won the war or run out of dollars. Chamberlain thought US support would be useful because it would help to convince the Germans they could not win, rather than because it would have any practical impact before the war was decided. The need not to strengthen isolationist feeling by bombing German civilians or harsh enforcement of the economic blockade reinforced Chamberlain's own preference for a limited war, but while he was happy to co-operate with the Americans, he was not about to depend on them. As during the years of appeasement, the British prime minister worried that American meddling would upset his carefully laid plans. When the US despatched a mission to Europe at the start of 1940 to investigate the possibilities of a negotiated peace, he thought it would only encourage the Germans to hold out for better terms.[104]

British spending in the States initially concentrated on buying self-reliance rather than finished weapons. America's arms industry might be tiny, but its engineers made the sophisticated machine tools that British factories needed to convert to war production. The USA was also a vital source of raw materials, including rare metals such as molybdenum that were essential in the manufacturing of the best armour plate, airframes and ammunition. The British hoped that American arms factories would be used only to top up what they themselves could not produce. Of the $720 million which the UK planned, in January 1940, to spend in the US during the first year of the war, 27 per cent was meant to go on raw materials, 17 per cent on machine tools, and 11, 7 and 2 per cent on supplies for the air force, army and navy respectively.[105]

Managing this flow of supplies required the creation of a British administrative body on the far side of the Atlantic, and once the Neutrality Acts had been modified, the British Purchasing Commission, under the directorship of the Canadian industrialist Arthur Purvis, came into being on 7 November 1939. As Purvis worked through the problems of securing and co-ordinating orders with US industry, he worked closely with the US Treasury secretary, Henry Morgenthau. They built a friendship that would be very important for the future.[106]

Nonetheless, Anglo-American relations remained hedged around with misunderstanding and suspicion. Since the British were prohibited from raising public or private loans in America, UK purchases had to be funded either by selling British investments in the States or by earning dollars with exports to America, and the British briefly attempted an export drive to the US. When the British restricted non-essential US imports, in order to preserve their dollars for as long as possible, they breached the terms of the 1938 Trade Agreement. Overseas purchasing in the cause of diplomatic influence also affected dollar imports, with

Greek and Turkish tobacco imports partially replacing those from the US, much to the fury of the American agricultural lobby. During the 1930s, long-running American concerns about British protectionism had been stoked by the introduction of imperial preference. Now, the Americans feared that the British were taking advantage of the war to enlarge and reinforce their economic bloc. Roosevelt was keen to contain Fascism, but he had no more interest than any other American politician in fighting to preserve the British Empire.[107]

THE *DRÔLE DE GUERRE*?

The National Government's approach to the first months of the war was soon cast as foolish or inadequate, but the tightly controlled version of the conflict preferred by Chamberlain was over-optimistic rather than irrational. If anything, the problem for the prime minister was that it had too much logic and not enough passion. Despite Chamberlain's desire to restrict the war, the National Government also managed to lay down the foundations for a much more total prosecution of the conflict in years to come.

It's hard to say whether the choices made about how to fight in the early autumn of 1939 were the 'right' ones strategically. Britain's options were so restricted that it is difficult to see what other decisions were available. Certainly the attempt to fight a limited war while preparing for a more total conflict was not stupid or cowardly. If Hitler's generals had had the sense to turn against him, or if a rash German offensive on the Western Front in November 1939 had led to a trench-bound stalemate, swiftly broken by the implosion of the German economy, Chamberlain's strategy might have been celebrated subsequently as a wily husbanding of national resources rather than a rush into the abyss. In that counterfactual case of an early Allied victory, Labour's decision to stay out of the wartime government would have seen it castigated yet again as irresponsible and unpatriotic. It is interesting to speculate what the effect of this might have been at a post-war general election.

The domestic implications of the Bore War are easier to ascertain. For Britons, a second great war was initially dominated not by the impact of enemy action, but instead by state attempts to protect the population and to mobilize military power. Without the unifying power of imminent peril, there was no pressure to resolve the political antagonisms of peace. These were not deep enough to doom the war effort, but they were sufficient to condemn the prime minister as the conflict span out of his control.

12

Boredom

On 1 October 1939, Winston Churchill gave a radio talk on the war situation for the BBC. In the second half, he turned from international affairs to matters on the home front:

> When a peaceful democracy is suddenly made to fight for its life, there must be a lot of trouble and hardship in the process of turning over from peace to war ... Meanwhile, patriotic men and women ... must not only rise above fear; they must also rise above inconvenience and, per-haps, most difficult of all, above boredom. Parliament will be kept in session, and all grievances or muddles or scandals, if such there be, can be freely ventilated or exposed there.[1]

It was an acute summary not just of the domestic difficulties of the Bore War, but also of the perils it held for Chamberlain's premiership.

'HOME IS NOT WHERE ONE LIVES ...'

Fear and inconvenience had started just before war was declared as, in the early hours of 1 September, the great evacuation got under way from British cities. Across the country, hundreds of thousands of evacuees – schoolchildren, mothers, pregnant women, the disabled – gathered at official departure points, where trains, buses and boats carried them off as quickly as possible to the reception areas.

It was an immense exodus. In total, with teachers and helpers, almost a million-and-a-half children and adults were moved as part of the official evacuation. In London, 241,000 children were collected from 1,600 assembly points.[2] More child evacuees came from the capital than anywhere else, but more children in total came from other urban areas: 84,343 from Greater Manchester; 79,930 from Merseyside; 71,393 from Glasgow; and 44,205 from the sides of the Tyne. Most of their journeys were, by modern standards, relatively short – perhaps 40 miles – although some of them took hours on packed trains. More than a quarter of a million went to the Home Counties, 73,000 to East Anglia, almost 57,000 to Wales.[3]

These official evacuation schemes were just part of an even larger movement of population away from British cities. Wealthier individuals and institutions arranged their own departure and accommodation. Businesses decamped to emergency premises in rural towns. The BBC despatched performers and technicians to Bristol and Evesham. The machinery of key government departments was also moved away from London: the Admiralty to Bath, the Air Ministry to Harrogate and the Ministry of Food to Colwyn Bay.

As a tidal wave of children, mothers and civil servants headed for the country, a ripple of the miscreant and the infirm were pushed back to their homes. More than 5,000 prisoners and Borstal inmates were released early; 140,000 hospital patients were turned out of their beds to make way for expected air-raid victims, including many awaiting treatment for tuberculosis.

Between late August and early September 1939, therefore, well over 3.5 million Britons were on the move.[4] At the time and thereafter, it was the government evacuation of the vulnerable that attracted the most attention. As an exercise in emergency logistics, the official scheme was a remarkable success. The planning skills of local government officials, the hard work of 40,000 teachers and helpers who accompanied the evacuation parties and 127,000 WVS members who helped with their arrival, and the marvels of the public transport network together managed to convey a million-and-a-half people in short order without a single casualty.[5]

Their work was much eased by the fact that, nationally, only about 40 per cent of the evacuees expected under the government programme actually turned up. Rates of evacuation varied across the country. Salford and Newcastle evacuated more than 70 per cent of their child populations, Glasgow 42 per cent, but Edinburgh and Sheffield only 28 and 15 per cent respectively. About half of London schoolchildren were evacuated. The reasons for these shortfalls also varied. Some families had already moved their children. Others were unable to organize themselves to the official timetable. For many parents, getting the children away had seemed like a good idea in theory, but in practice their fear of disaster encouraged them to keep their families together. One of the consequences of the lower than anticipated turnout of evacuees was to allow the government scheme to be compressed into fewer days, with the result that it was completed before the outbreak of war.[6]

As an exercise in child welfare or the preservation of human dignity, official evacuation was rather less successful. The embarkation and transport of evacuees was fraught with problems. In London, the fear of catastrophe if air raids hit mainline stations overcrowded with waiting children meant that trains were filled with evacuees as they arrived and sent off again as quickly as possible. That broke up school parties and disrupted the programme of arrivals in reception areas. Elsewhere, transport provision differed according to the quality of local authority planning, and stories of confusion were legion. Rail delays turned some journeys into drawn-out nightmares, both for children – for whom the adventure of a school trip had turned into an epic of separation, boredom and despair – and for their accompanying helpers, their patience and ability to comfort their charges decreasing by the hour.

The luckier evacuees arrived where they were expected and were quickly made welcome in a willing billet. The less fortunate were unexpected and unwanted: unloaded in an area that had prepared for someone else, conveyed to a church hall where potential hosts picked and chose according to who looked least dirty or most useful round the house, then carted off to a hazardous, or abusive, home away from their friends and siblings. Given the scale of the operation and the confusion involved, it sometimes took weeks for accompanying teachers and billeting officers to sort out the mess and restore a semblance of normality – tracking down children, sharing classrooms with local schools and attempting to resolve the worst conflicts that had arisen between evacuees and hosts.[7]

The newspapers, keen to reassure parents and keep up morale, emphasized that the nation was coming together to offer safe refuge. The *News Chronicle* headlined its report on 1 September: 'CASTLE AND COTTAGE WILL GIVE GUESTS WARM WELCOME'.[8] The *Daily Express* had a report from 'somewhere in Buckinghamshire', where 'Lights were burning in cottages and big houses as women prepared spare rooms and put hot water bottles in the beds in which London children would sleep.'[9]

Even where it went according to plan, evacuation was a tearing process. In Preston, a diarist for Mass-Observation recorded the arrival of evacuees in his street:

> what 'things' they were! Dressed in 'old clo' man [second hand] coats, dirty, common – . . . The official in charge disposed of them in a business like way . . . in spite of the shock the evacuees gave me I'm afraid a lump rose in my throat when one girl asked nervously, 'Can't I stay with my sister', she was told 'No, you go there and she will be across the road. You will be able to see her every day.' I was sorry for the girls because they were so forlorn.[10]

By its nature, evacuation brought Britons into contact with the unfamiliar. For individual households, even accommodating members of the same extended family meant a sharing of space that exposed the intimate variety of day-to-day routine. In terms of religion, reception areas that knew only church or chapel were unready to meet the needs of Jewish or Catholic evacuees. In more rural settings, evacuation highlighted the gaps between country and city life – the supposed pleasures of fresh air, nature walks and birdsong offset for evacuees by the scarcity of shops and cinemas, restricted hours of pub opening and the daily hardship of agricultural life.[11]

The gap between urban and rural was compounded by the separations of class. At the time, much media attention was devoted to the transformative effect of evacuation on Britain's stately homes, but the majority of hosts were actually middle- and working-class families who were not able to insulate themselves from their guests. The evacuees on the government scheme, meanwhile, came disproportionately from the least well off families in the inner cities who had no other option for escape. The official programme of evacuation, therefore, supervised by the upper- and upper-middle-class doyennes of the WVS, took children and mothers from the poorest urban areas and sent them to live with better-off, but not necessarily wealthy, householders in the reception areas.[12]

What resulted was a profound clash of cultures that was intensified by the stress and uncertainty of evacuation.[13] As soon as the evacuees arrived, a flood of stories from the reception areas described dirty children and slatternly mothers wreaking havoc on accustomed domesticity. On 4 September, for instance, the Mass-Observer in Preston, out on his rounds as a printer's agent, reported tales that were being repeated across the country:

> much talk about evacuees. I heard that the children were filthy, bug-ridden – wore dirty clothes, would not eat proper food for they wanted toast and fish & chips. Some of the kids had to wear fresh clothes. Many housewives buying their guest a complete rig-out from pyjamas to coats.[14]

His neighbour had taken in

> a mother and baby but was deeply thankful to get rid three days later. The mother was filthy, she switched on the lights in the middle of the night, ate food with her hands, and let the baby tension on the carpet! My neighbour is a house proud woman; she was in tears most of the time.[15]

The same tone was reflected in more formal reports. The clerk of one Welsh rural district council wrote that the majority of the evacuees who arrived in early September 'were not in a fit state of cleanliness to be received in any clean home', 'In some cases, as a result of their filthy habits, every scrap of bedding, clothing, and even blinds and curtains had to be destroyed.'[16] The WVS's Lincolnshire county organizer recorded householders' shock at 'the disgraceful and disgusting conditions in which a certain portion of the population lives' and reserved particular condemnation for the behaviour of evacuated mothers, mostly 'the low slum type . . . some of them out for what they can get, most of them dirty, many of them idle and unwilling to work or pull their weight'.[17] In mid-September, a bitter debate took place in the Commons in which rural MPs aired complaints from their constituents about, as one put it, 'the dreadful scourge . . . placed upon the homes of Britain'.[18]

How fair were these stories? In reaction against attacks on evacuated mothers, one billeting officer countered that her experience was of 'nice, decent women who fitted in to the best of their power and tried to bear with country conditions'.[19] Labour MPs representing urban constituencies angrily defended their people against charges of deliberate fouling of billets while highlighting the very poor living standards that persisted in the slums. Meanwhile, the Ministries of Health and Education sought to defend themselves against the charge that their pre-war activities had been found wanting.[20]

At least some of the instances of lousiness and bedwetting were worsened by the circumstances of evacuation: the close-packed trains, the upset of separation and the difficulties of locating distant toilets in strange houses. Disastrous though children's incontinence could be to the domestic economy of poorer hosts, its reporting rate was not unaffected by the chance to claim an additional laundry allowance from the government.

A significant portion of evacuees were visibly the products of childhood poverty. Evacuation came early on a Friday, when the weekly wages of the working class were most tightly stretched, and at the end of summer, before families had invested in new shoes for the winter. A subsequent study of more than half a million child evacuees found that, of those from London, 27 per cent had parents who were either dependent on out-of-work benefits or on very low incomes. In Liverpool and Sunderland, the equivalent figure was 40 per cent.[21]

Many therefore simply could not meet the official guidance about what clothes and boots to take with them. Of the 31,000 Newcastle children registered for evacuation, for example, about one in eight were judged to have inadequate footwear and one in five insufficient clothing. The same sort of thing was true for headlice: an investigation spurred by reports of this apparent plague found not only that city children were more likely to be infested than those in the country, but also that rates of lousiness were much higher in urban schools than had been made apparent by the well-advertised but perfunctory peacetime inspections.[22]

The scale of the government scheme meant that it inevitably included evacuees who were chaotic and unpleasant, just as it also involved hosts and officials in the reception areas who were unsympathetic snobs. Probably neither should be taken as typical relative to the stoic endurance that was actually evident on both sides. Stories of unruly evacuees also revealed how different the lives of the urban working class were from those of middle-class families in the reception areas. Asked later in the war what they thought of Oxford, evacuees from the East End of London explained: 'If we play ball in the streets a window opens and an old lady puts her head out and starts telling us off.' Months of nagging can be heard in an evacuated girl's account of what was different in her new home: 'I cannot do as I like in the house. I must also come in when I am told and sit down and eat my meals properly and not run out into the street with a slice of bread in my hand.' Explaining what she had learned from evacuation, one girl commented sagely that: 'Home is not where one lives, but where one has all the people one loves and knows.'[23]

Cultural clashes could be played for laughs. In mid-October, the Hampstead writer Gwladys Cox enjoyed 'an amusing wireless sketch' in which:

> An aristocratic couple were heard entertaining their slum evacuees, whose manners and behaviour were execrable. The master of the house, however, assures his perturbed wife that, in a very short time, a refined environment will refine the children. In the end, the squire and the lady, by trying to ingratiate themselves with their guests, fall to the children's level, and develop shocking speech and manners themselves.[24]

Most people, however, didn't find evacuation a funny experience. In the words of an M-O diarist from Chelmsford (who emphasized 'This is not a personal bias as an evacuee lives with us and is harmless'), 'I think the evacuation idea must have been evolved by an unimaginative unpsychological Robot. One cannot put up with another type of life with one for years or vice versa.'[25] As she appreciated, alienation cut both ways: the strain quite as grim for the evacuated as for the billetor.

The criticisms levelled at the parents of working-class evacuees usually underestimated the difficulties they faced. Although some schools and local authorities in the danger areas appealed for donations of boots and clothes, little public money was available to kit out evacuees. Rumours from the reception areas that children had been sent away in their worst clothes to elicit charitable donations misinterpreted evacuees' reluctance to admit that their scarcely packed bags contained the best they had. For parents who remained at home and in work, tight household budgets posed awful questions: should they meet hosts' demands for more money for clothes, send sweets to remind their children of home, or buy a rail ticket so that they could visit in person and see conditions for themselves?[26]

For mothers who had accompanied children in the evacuation, the situation was even worse. There had been no official preparation for what they were to do after their arrival. They were separated from much of the support network of family and friends that had sustained them at home, they worried about husbands and parents left behind in the cities, and were forced to fit around someone else's household routine. When they stayed inside, their domestic habits were criticized; when they walked the streets they were seen as lazy or negligent; and if they complained they were seen as ungrateful. Devon's inspector of education explained that the restrictions of life in billets

> create a very bad psychological disturbance for both mothers and children. They become difficult, the children cry and are irritable, and the nervous energy of the mother is sapped. Sometimes she punishes them for nothing at all and at others she is over indulgent and sentimental.

There was an understandable desire 'to escape from the billet' but the evacuated mother had 'nowhere to go. She does her shopping but lingers over it, shop-gazing and gossiping . . . I have seldom, if ever, since the war, been in the busy, crowded Exeter High Street without seeing these mothers and children wandering about looking miserable.' God forbid that they should seek distraction or entertainment, let alone a drink:

> I am told that the audience of the afternoon performances at the local picture houses contains a considerable number of mothers and young children, and they are also seen outside the local public houses in the evenings, the toddlers waiting for their mothers who are inside.[27]

The situation of the billetors was not really any easier. Most had volunteered, rather than been compelled, to take evacuees into their homes for a period of uncertain duration. Aside from the disruption to their own family life, accepting evacuees could also mean considerable expense. The allowance paid by the government was steadily eroded by rises in the cost of living during the first months of the war, at the same time that the incidental expenses of billeting – laundry, medicine, bus tickets – began to accumulate for hosts.

As well as the immediate confusion, the scale of relocation created its own problems. A large chunk of the population had moved suddenly away from the educational, medical and welfare services that had grown up to support them, at the same moment that local authority staff and doctors were mobilized into civil defence and the armed forces. By itself, this meant a decrease in the quality of provision; a trend perpetuated by disagreements between district councils in the target and reception areas about who should bear the costs. As before the war, local councils attempted to recoup the costs of medical and social services expenditure from patients and recipients whose earnings fell above a variety of means tests. From October 1939, central government also tried to recover some of the money it was spending on billeting allowances from parents, 'in accordance with their ability to pay'. The scheme had widespread public approval, but the work required to track down families who were in motion between addresses and across local government boundaries meant that the cost of recovery probably outweighed the sums returned to the Exchequer.

These efforts reflected a wider stringency in the provision of assistance that was based on both finance and morality. Official funding was made available relatively quickly to ease the worst cases of hardship among evacuees. It was not, however, well publicized, and it was provided only after thorough investigations into family circumstances. Worried about the implications of inflation, the government wanted to avoid pumping too much money into the economy by taking on the maintenance of every child in the country. Ministers and civil servants phrased their caution over expenditure in terms of their fear that poorer parents would 'forget' children who had been evacuated and abdicate their family responsibilities to the state.[28] This got things almost entirely the wrong way round.

'SO IGNORANT OF MY NEIGHBOURS . . .'

In fact, the greatest obstacle to the long-term success of the official evacuation scheme was that family ties were too strong. When the bombs did not begin to fall on British cities, evacuees returned home in droves. The rate accelerated as autumn turned to winter. Despite an official campaign to 'Leave the children where they are!', by the start of December about a third of schoolchildren, and two-thirds of mothers with young children, had gone back. In January 1940, a nationwide count revealed that almost half of all the children evacuated the previous September, and about nine out of ten mothers, had travelled back to where they had come from.[29]

Some were responding to a hostile reception from hosts. For others, the practical difficulties had become too much to bear. Only in the face of imminent death and destruction was evacuation an attractive option; now, parents wanted children home and adults were sick of living in other people's houses. Given the opprobrium levelled at them in the reception areas, it was unsurprising that evacuated mothers left first and in higher proportions. They were then condemned for irresponsibly exposing themselves to danger. Rates of return were also higher among poorer families – perhaps spurred on by the government's attempts to recoup costs, although the least well off were exempt – and those who remained were disproportionately older male children from households with higher incomes. In total, about half of London's schoolchildren stayed away, but elsewhere the tide of evacuation ebbed more completely. Clydebank in Scotland, for example, had a reasonably good take-up of its initial evacuation, with 3,400 out of 7,500 children departing at the start of September and another 600 by the end of the year. Within two months, however, half of those evacuated had returned, and by the end of 1940, fewer than 5 per cent of Clydebank's children were still away from home.[30]

In the expectation of air attack, at the outset of the war urban councils had shut schools and shifted staff to the emergency services. Two thousand schools across England and Wales, including two-thirds of all those in London, had been requisitioned for use by the military or ARP. As a result, those children who either stayed at home or returned from evacuation were left without education or the public health services that went along with it. Similarly, urban hospitals, which were being paid a premium to keep their beds clear for air-raid victims, transferred staff from maternity care to casualty clearing sections. Amid fears of an epidemic of delinquency or disease, by November 1939 plans were in place to re-open emergency schools in cities (although it was not until the spring of 1940 that, under-resourced and overcrowded, they began to open in the capital), and the Ministry of Health pressed hospitals to re-open wards for the sick.[31]

The first months of the evacuation scheme therefore saw a struggle between the presumptions of official planning and the realities of the Bore War. In retrospect, it says much for the fear of bombing and the expectations of a dutiful populace that evacuation was contemplated at all. It would only ever have been judged a success if a rain of bombs and gas had actually followed the onset of hostilities. As Whitehall tried to ameliorate the situation in the evacuated and reception areas by encouraging local authorities to spend more on medical services and school meals, it also drew the lessons that any future programme could only work if it was on a smaller scale, came after air raids had actually begun and left out mothers completely. Even so, there were few takers when families were offered the chance to sign up for a new scheme of child evacuation in the spring of 1940.

For experts, evacuation offered a remarkable professional opportunity. Once under way, it engaged a wide range of child psychologists, welfare workers, medical investigators and social science researchers. At least 240 studies of evacuation were published during the 1940s: it was an unprecedented phenomenon, examined to an unprecedented degree. For British child development experts, their work with evacuees strongly confirmed a pre-existing belief in the crucial importance of the family – and mothers in particular – in building psychologically healthy and socially well-adjusted young people. These findings would play an important part in shaping the provision of child welfare services for a generation to come.[32]

Evacuation was also a political event. The state in which evacuees arrived in the reception areas fed directly into the debates about nutrition, health and government welfare policies that had characterized the late 1930s. For some, the evacuation served to reveal the poverty of which they had previously been ignorant. Neville Chamberlain's daughter reported to him the shocked response of one society hostess: 'I never knew such conditions existed, and I feel ashamed of having been so ignorant of my neighbours. For the rest of my life I mean to try & make amends by helping such people to live cleaner & healthier lives.' The prime minister took a rather different view. Although disappointed 'that all the care & money spent in the schools has not produced a better result', he was still convinced that 'however bad conditions are ... they are infinitely better than they were 20 years ago'.[33]

Evacuation was used to support the arguments of those who wanted to see a more dramatic improvement in the lives of the poor. In a radio broadcast in December 1939, for example, Margaret Bondfield, a former Labour Cabinet minister, and now the chair of the Women's Group on Public Welfare, a non-partisan body set up to investigate the social problems revealed by evacuation, explained that the behaviour of 'a small minority of dirty, ill-mannered and destructive elements' was the result of the poor conditions in which they had grown up. 'Let us now face the fruits of our neglect with courage and determination to end poverty, ignorance and slums,' she declared. 'Unless we can win *this* fight on the home front, the end of the War may find us defeated indeed.'[34]

The main effect of evacuation, however, was to confirm a well-established view of the very poor as immoral, irresponsible and dangerous. This happened even among those who were keenest to improve Britain's inner cities, most of whom stuck to the script of progressive politics in the previous decade: the state should do more to help, but its role must be to re-educate the 'slum mind' of problem families who were incapable of rescuing themselves.[35]

'THE BLACKOUT DEPRESSES ME FRIGHTFULLY'

For all the scale and drama of evacuation, the majority of Britons were not involved either as refugees or as billetors. Other air-raid precautions had much more widespread effects. The shift to war was obvious in the transformation of British cities. Key buildings and monuments were hidden behind walls of sandbags. Tumescent barrage balloons floated overhead to ward off low-flying enemy bombers. Everyone was meant to carry a gas mask. The warbling note of mistaken air-raid sirens drifted intermittently through the early autumn air. In case the bombers arrived after nightfall, come dusk the entire country was blacked out. All street illuminations were extinguished and householders and business owners had to ensure that their buildings did not emit even the slightest chink of light.

For the first eight days of the war, all places where large crowds might be at risk of bombing were closed, including dance halls, theatres, cinemas and many sports venues. Newspapers, newsreels and the BBC were required to submit to a system of voluntary censorship, run out of the new Ministry of Information, designed to ensure that nothing useful leaked out to Germany. Lest their transmissions aided enemy navigation, the BBC shut down its regional broadcasts and its nascent television service in favour of a single national radio pro-gramme. This bore a steady stream of bulletins without much news, official exhortations to good wartime behaviour, and light music, much of it instrumental versions of popular tunes played by the apparently tireless BBC organist Sandy MacPherson, who appeared fifty-five times in the first two weeks of the war.[36]

A Lancashire schoolteacher told Mass-Observation: 'The blackout depresses me frightfully. I was alone the other night in a strange town and I felt like sitting down in the middle of the road and weeping.'[37] In the countryside of 1930s Britain, the unlit night was still familiar, but for the city-dwelling majority, the blackout meant a sudden plunge into Stygian darkness. Those who ventured outside entered a world of near misses and collisions, as road signs, lamp-posts, kerbs, sandbags, pedestrians, cyclists and cars turned into invisible hazards. After four months of war, 17 per cent of those questioned by the BIPO in January 1940 claimed to have suffered a physical injury as a result of the black-out.[38] Petrol was the only commodity rationed from the outbreak of hostilities, which reduced the number of vehicles out and about, but road deaths rose from 6,648 in 1938 to 8,272 in 1939.[39] In this war, the first casualties came from the very measures designed to protect the population from the enemy.

During those early jumpy days, the blackout offered a constant reminder of the threat of air attack. On 18 September, Mass-Observation's Bris-tol law librarian diarist recorded:

> My uncle visited us today. He has a black out complex. Whenever I switched a light on, he started jumping about, crying passionately 'Put that damn thing out'. It was all quite unnecessary as we are well blacked out. Aunt got a bit narked. When uncle said, in extenuation, 'Well, I was in the last war', she said 'So was I'.[40]

Since the bombers failed to come, a host of ARP wardens kept them-selves busy by searching out the slightest infringements of the blackout. By the end of 1939, in the UK outside Scotland, 64,918 people had been found guilty at magistrates' courts of breaches of the regulations re-lating to lights and sounds. Among them was a police inspector from

Nottingham, who on being told by a passer-by that he was showing a light from his police station bedroom, promptly summonsed himself and was fined ten shillings.[41]

Offences against the blackout constituted more than 99.9 per cent of all the convictions under the Defence Regulations in the first months of the war. The remainder was made up almost entirely of those found guilty of minor security incursions. Sixteen unfortunates were convicted after they made the mistake of keeping pigeons in a prohibited area. At the same time, however, fewer vehicles on the road thanks to petrol rationing meant a quarter fewer motoring convictions in England and Wales in 1939 compared to 1938. The number of those found guilty of being drunk or disorderly also fell, though not as dramatically. In an era when killing yourself was still against the law, so did the total of successful and attempted suicides.[42] Boring though the war was for the moment, it seemed temporarily to have made life more worth living.

Some people positively welcomed the darkness. An eighteen-year-old student opined to Mass-Observation that: 'Personally I like the Blackout; to walk in the dark exercises the mind, star-gazing is easier, and sex more sexy.'[43] Whether this reflected actual experience or merely aspiration, for those whose private lives depended on illicit encounters in public spaces – young men and women too closely chaperoned at home for anything but a 'knee-trembler' against a wall, or men used to seeking each other out in the parks and toilets of big cities – the new obscurity, and the availability of air-raid shelters, certainly widened the scope of opportunity.[44]

For others, however, the first months of the war occasioned more frustration. The rates of marriage jumped by about a fifth in 1939 compared to 1938, the approach and outbreak of war encouraging a rash of weddings before it was too late. Fears of war also dissuaded couples from bringing children into an uncertain and increasingly expensive world. Once the conflict began, evacuation and enlistment separated husbands and wives. During the first two years of the war, the pre-war decline in the birth rate accelerated. Whether from separation or anxiety, in an era when the overwhelming majority of children were born in wedlock and abstinence remained a major form of contraception, there was less married heterosexual sex than before.[45]

Newer forms of entertainment were also badly hit, as wartime measures suffocated the leisure culture of pre-war urban life. With buses, trucks and trains requisitioned by the military, it was harder to move around. Those who could get out found little to do. The closure of cinemas – for a brief moment, thanks to the local council's presumption of its safe location, Aberystwyth was the only place where films were being shown anywhere in the UK – meant the removal of the most popular form of public entertainment. Stadia were also requisitioned by the services and crowds limited to the capacity of air-raid shelters, and so many football matches were cancelled that the leagues effectively shut down. The football pools would have been hard hit, but they closed in any case in order to ease the load on the Post Office. Constrained by the Ministry of Information, the BBC offered no explanation to listeners of its newly reduced service. The Corporation's efforts to provide 'background listening that didn't require too much concentration between News Bulletins' were constrained by the small staff of actors and musicians who were initially evacuated to Bristol and the Ministry's insistence on approving everyone who might appear on air. As the BBC's own analysis explained, the result was that every live show 'from the *White Coons* to *Gentlemen You May Smoke* – had a tendency to sound the same, because the same people were in it'.[46]

The Ministry of Information faced a difficult situation.[47] Official conviction that communicating with the public would be important in time of war had not been matched with much clarity about its remit and role. From an early stage, the Ministry did grasp the crucial point that it needed to manage the news, but there was little competence in its performance during the early months of the war. Although it was nominally in charge of censorship, decisions about what could be published were actually in the hands of the service departments, which proved reluctant to release any information at all. Once French radio had announced the arrival of the BEF on 11 September, the British press were allowed to report the same news, only for the War Office to rescind permission late on the same day. Only after police had swooped to confiscate newspapers that had already gone to print did the War Office decide that the ban could actually be lifted after all. The Ministry of Information took much of the blame for the resultant confusion and its reputation with the press never really recovered.

The middle-class dons and civil servants who had been brought in to staff the new ministry thought that the people needed to be exhorted to

play their part in the war. From an early stage, they sought to emphasize that this was a conflict in which everyone would have to play their
part. Yet finding the right words to convey this sentiment proved difficult. An early government poster infamously declared '*Your* courage,
your cheerfulness, *your* resolution will bring *us* victory'. Given the
political divisions of the 1930s, the choice of pronouns was probably
unwise, and Fascist graffiti artists changed the 'us' to 'Jews' with
alarming frequency.[48] With the high diction typical of the Ministry of
Information at this point, another poster asserted 'Freedom is in peril:
Defend it with all your might'.

Unsurprisingly, with little military progress for the newspapers
to report, during September the inefficiency of wartime restrictions
became a central topic of press discussion. The papers complained
about large numbers of full-time ARP staff who now sat idle, the worst
absurdities of blackout enforcement and the inadequacies of the BBC's
wartime service. Even more ire was directed against the Ministry of
Information, which was portrayed as an over-stuffed nest of bureaucrats that was trying incompetently to keep everything secret. The case
for the defence was not assisted when the minister of information, the
elderly lawyer Lord Macmillan, admitted to Parliament that he had not
been able to find out what his department was meant to be doing.

Once the bombs failed to arrive, the first flush of emergency measures were actually adapted fairly quickly. Before September was out,
cinemas and dance halls had been allowed to re-open, albeit with
limited hours. ARP staff levels were hastily reduced. The blackout
too was eased, to allow pedestrians to carry torches and better lighting
for cars. In December, shops were permitted to illuminate their windows very softly in the evening. A new system of regional leagues,
which required less transport, even allowed competitive football to
resume.

The BBC also responded quickly. By late September, some of the
most successful pre-war shows, including the immensely popular *Band-
wagon*, were back on the air. During the late autumn, it pushed
back against government controls by developing its own programme of
talks by independent commentators as 'postscripts' to the nine o'clock
news. In early 1940, it started up a new Forces Service aimed at meeting the BEF's desire for lighter music and variety. Having bounced
back from the opening of hostilities, the Corporation was already on

its way towards its wartime apotheosis as a source of news and entertainment.[49]

The Ministry of Information fared less well. It briefly lost control of censorship – ironically to the very armed forces who had actually got it into so much trouble with the press – and its staff numbers were slashed. Chamberlain considered getting rid of it completely before handing it over to a new minister, the former BBC director-general Sir John Reith, in the following spring. He proved no more able to rescue its reputation than his predecessor.[50]

None of these measures could make the Bore War exciting. Mass-Observation used a bank manager's account of his evening to illustrate what life in Britain was like as autumn turned to winter in 1939:

> Had a nice night last night. Tommy bloody Handley on the wireless again; read every book in the house. Too dark to walk to the library, bus every 45 minutes, next one too late for the pictures. 'Freedom is in peril', – they're telling me![51]

'I'M WONDERING WHAT IS GOING TO HAPPEN WHEN I'M CALLED UP'

Between August and December 1939 about a million men joined the armed forces. They came from four main sources: men who had recently served in the military and remained liable to call-up in the event of war; part-time Territorial soldiers and RAF and Royal Navy Auxiliaries who were mobilized to full-time service on the outbreak of hostilities; men conscripted under the Military Training and National Service Acts; and volunteers who joined without being compelled.

Not everybody who was liable for national service was conscripted. By the end of 1939, all men in England, Wales and Scotland between the ages of twenty and twenty-three had been required to register at the local offices of the Ministry of Labour. Fear of inflaming Irish national-ism meant that conscription was never introduced in Northern Ireland. Potential conscripts were medically assessed, and could be exempted from service on the basis of physical disability, conscientious objection, employment in essential industries (not only directly war-related work, but also other trades judged critical to the functioning of national life), or family circumstances. Those selected for the armed forces might have their service deferred until there was training space available to accommodate them. So although 486,309 men presented themselves for registration between September and December 1939, only 122,200 conscripts entered the armed forces over the same period. In this phase of the war, more men – 192,500 in total – joined as volunteers than as conscripts. As before the war, some were motivated by patriotism, a sense of duty and the desire for adventure. Others had in their minds the prospect that they might be conscripted in future: in one survey of 200 men who had volunteered in 1939, 62 per cent noted that they had expected to be called up anyway.[52]

One powerful reason for volunteering was the chance that it gave a serviceman to influence his subsequent military career. All recruits could express a preference about which armed service they went into, but volunteers were more likely to get their first choice.[53] The preferences men expressed revealed a great deal about the esteem in which the different armed forces were held. Twenty-nine per cent of all those registered under the National Service Act between September and December 1939 said that they wanted to join the RAF. It was perceived as the most modern and glamorous of the services. All its aircrew were volunteers, but most of its personnel were groundcrew who kept airfields working and aircraft flying. The RAF was therefore attractive both to those young men who wanted to soar above the clouds and to those who wanted to keep their feet on the ground but well away from the quagmire of infantry combat. The RAF took in 33,700 men in the first four months of the war, only 2,000 of whom were conscripts.[54]

If the Royal Navy was not seen as so progressive, it retained an immense amount of traditional popular respect. Fifteen per cent of those registering for service in the first four months of the war expressed a preference for the navy and only a third of its intake in this period were conscripts. In comparison, although some regiments retained a good deal of local affection, the army as a whole was regarded as the most old-fashioned, undemocratic and potentially horrendous of the services. Conscripts who wanted to end up in its ranks had simply not to express a preference. Even the army managed to take more volunteers than conscripts in 1939, by a ratio of 3:2, but for the rest of the war it would struggle with the quality of its pool of recruits.[55]

This hierarchy of military esteem was echoed in attitudes to the three women's 'auxiliary services': the Women's Auxiliary Air Force (WAAF), the Women's Royal Naval Service (WRNS) and the Auxiliary Territorial Service (ATS). As their titles suggested, these bodies were meant to provide support to the fighting forces, rather than to serve in the front line, and there was a strict prohibition on women bearing arms. To begin with, the auxiliary services were not expected to play an important military role, and for the first two years of the war there was little official effort to recruit women. Nonetheless, by December 1939, 43,000 women had volunteered to join the three services – almost twice the number that the government had thought it would need before the war began. By the middle of 1940, there would be 20,500 WAAFs, 10,000 WRNS and 36,400 members of the ATS. Like its male counterpart, the WAAF was regarded as modern and exciting. WAAFs had important jobs in the RAF's communications network and had some of the associated glamour of aircrew. The smaller WRNS was seen as more socially exclusive. The ATS managed to appear simultaneously old-fashioned and disreputable: officered by horsey aristocrats, clothed in unflattering uniforms, and expected to wash, cook and type for soldiers with whom they were widely presumed to be sleeping. Since they were enrolled, rather than enlisted like male servicemen, at the start of the war female recruits could leave whenever they chose. More than 13,000 ATS members left the service in the first fifteen months of the war.[56]

About 2 per cent of the men registering for national service during 1939 requested that they be placed on the register of conscientious objectors. These men then went before local tribunals tasked solely with judging whether their objection was genuinely held. 'Genuine' objectors could be granted total exemption from any service, directed to undertake civilian work of national importance, or be registered for military service on a solely non-combatant basis. Given the difficult job of judging the extent of other people's beliefs, tribunals tended to accept clearly articulated explanations of long-held religious or moral conviction and to suspect that more confused, or more recently converted, objectors were trying to shirk their duties to their fellow citizens. They were generally unwilling to accept political objections as 'genuine' unless they could be seen in moral terms. The atheist Communist who objected to service in this war because it was imperialist was less likely to be exempted than the Christian socialist who refused because all wars were wrong.[57]

The total rate of objection among this first tranche of conscripts was lower than might have been anticipated, given the strength of popular pacifism in the early 1930s, but it was enough to lead to a significant backlog of cases during the Bore War. By the end of 1939, 14,995 men had provisionally registered themselves as conscientious objectors, but local tribunals had heard only 4,812 cases, of which 849 were rejected. Of the rest, more than half were required to do non-military work of national importance. Tribunals often directed men to work in agriculture or forestry on the basis that they could thereby help the country without injuring their principles, but the need for rural labour varied sharply across the country, so that objectors who had been told to get a farm job were soon complaining that they were unable to do so.

For those who volunteered for service or accepted their call-up, the shift from civilian to military life began in much the same way no matter which armed service they had entered. New recruits reported to unfamiliar barracks where they were issued uniforms and subjected to hours of close-order drill ('square-bashing'). The exposure to military discipline, dress, diet and accommodation could all come as something of a shock. One of the militiamen registered under the Military Training Act in summer 1939 and called up at the outbreak of war recalled his first day in the army:

> We had khaki clothes thrown at us, boots that you were lucky if you got a proper left and right that fitted more or less, and you hoped for the best, a kit bag, I won't describe the underwear and vest, they were so coarse as to be un-wearable, shirts, khaki shirts, again, they were so coarse that to those of us that had known better things it was like wearing sackcloth and a complete range of torture . . .
>
> We slept that first night, or rather we lay on the bare floor. I don't think anyone slept, there were moans and groans and sounds of 'Oh Mother' all night long. After two or three nights of very little sleep, you slept from sheer exhaustion. After two or three weeks, of course, things got a little bit better.[58]

Like evacuation, enlistment meant exposure to difference: not only between civil and military life, but also between men who now had to live in close proximity. Here too, close encounters of the class kind could both reinforce existing prejudices and bridge social divides. In the barracks of the Royal West Kent regiment in Canterbury, Ben Hooper, who had been a student at Durham University, then a science teacher, found that he was the only 'educated bloke' in a hut full of men 'of the labourer type'. As he confided to his girlfriend,

> I've been very tactful and only spoken when asked. Actually they're quite decent working lads from either the East End of London or Canterbury. Funnily enough, barring the sergeant I'm the only one who puts pyjamas on (we're allowed to wear our own). The thought of wearing the same woolen long pants and thick shirt day and night for a week does not strike me as being too good. Of course the first night I heard quiet asides, but last night the inoculation made most of them sweat, especially as we have plenty of blankets over us, and I think my hygienic ways struck them all more favourably.[59]

Ewart Clay, the Yorkshire journalist turned Territorial gunner, noted in a letter to his wife the strange alliance formed between his sergeant, 'Blackie', a man with a 'prize fighting face' and a manner to match, and his commanding officer: 'a tall, lean young man with ability, dry humour and money'. Together, they staged

> strange drunken frolics. They have entered the mess in the small hours aglow ... picked smaller sergeants from their beds, lifted them above their heads, and dropped them onto the bare wooden floors in their nightshirts, then kept them awake for a couple of hours while they sang and laughed. The two men differ in upbringing, education, social status and worldly possessions. They don't even share the same language. Yet they are kindred spirits – they are revelers with strong heads and tough bellies.[60]

Clay's account also showed, however, the extent to which service remained defined by class. Officers and men were expected to lead different lifestyles. Officer selection was a matter of meeting upper-middle-class social mores as well as displaying military aptitude. For many servicemen, the frustration of being made subordinate to men of lesser talents served to reinforce a sense of resentment at the established order.[61]

The volunteer who enjoyed the sort of hearty rough-and-tumble in which Blackie and his officer were engaged could find much to enjoy in

these first months of military service: physical fitness and male cama-
raderie with little actual physical danger. For the conscript who wanted
peace, privacy and contemplation, there was little choice but to endure.
For both, enlistment also meant separation from family and friends. By
March 1940, 27 per cent of those surveyed by the BIPO said that military service had been responsible for parting them from someone 'who
was dear to you, such as a member of your family, your fiancé(e) or
sweetheart'. Only 4 per cent said the same thing of evacuation.[62]

In Bolton, Mass-Observation's fieldworkers often overheard people
worrying about how those left behind would cope. A reservist with a
wife and two children, on his way to the barracks at Bury, explained:
'The Army's all right when you're young, but it's no good when you're
settled down and married. It's got nothing for you.' In a chip shop, a
man tried to reassure Mrs Lyall, a 'fat woman of fifty or so', who had
just realized that her son would shortly be conscripted: 'He'll be all
right. You've nothing to worry about.' 'Yes, but I won't be all right,' she
said, 'I had enough last war, they took my husband then, now they
want my two lads.' A twenty-seven-year-old man, 'upper wc', set out
his own situation:

> All these things you hear, like what the Germans are doing in Poland,
> make you want to go and join up, I should like to, but I'm wondering
> what is going to happen when I'm called up. There are only my father
> and mother, both invalids, and Eric (brother) will go first, so they'll have
> no one to look after them. It worries me a lot.[63]

'PRICES ARE SLOWLY GOING UP'

Military pay and allowances were not exactly generous. A private's
basic pay was fourteen shillings a week. If he was married, a portion of
this was compulsorily allotted to his wife, together with a fixed allowance that increased if they had children: all together, a mother of two
with a husband in the ranks got thirty-eight shillings a week at the start
of the war. This was just over half the average weekly take-home pay of
an adult male worker in manufacturing industry in late 1938. Military
service did not, however, necessarily mean an immediate reduction
in household income. All government departments, and some private

businesses, agreed to make up the pay of enlisted employees. Service-men's living expenses – accommodation, food, medical and dental care, clothing, laundry – were all paid for by the state. For the middle-class recruit bedded down in his scratchy vest and drawers on a hard floor with a single blanket, struggling to digest the products of an overworked cookhouse, these might not have felt like much of a boon. Many young servicemen spent whatever spare money they had on buying additional food from the canteen. Nonetheless, entry into the armed forces cocooned men to some extent from the war's impact on the civilian economy.[64]

A whole range of goods soon got more expensive. In the short term, this had much more to do with transport difficulties than government controls. The expense of wartime insurance and the decrease in the availability of neutral merchant shipping meant that import costs rose. Supplies of food remained sufficient at a national level, but distribution difficulties (thanks to military requisitioning of transport and ARP restrictions), panic buying and stockpiling all led to some local short-ages. Prices went up, and increased rates of duty after the war budget pushed them higher still. The working-class Cost of Living Index – a rather outdated measure, based on what had been thought necessary items of expenditure in 1914, but still a significant one because it was the measure against which wage agreements were made – rose by 12 per cent between September and December 1939. The cost of food items within the Index increased by nine points between September and October alone.[65]

For some, increased earnings took some of the edge off price increases. Although short-term unemployment increased as workers were laid off from house-building and the leisure industries, the depart-ure of men into the armed forces and the continuing stimulus of defence spending meant that those with jobs were often working longer hours. With controls on employment all but non-existent, it was not uncom-mon for employers working to fulfil government contracts to poach skilled workers from their competitors by offering higher wages. For some people, therefore, the start of the war meant more money.[66] The worst hit were those dependent on a fixed income: landlords (since rents had been controlled at the war's outbreak), servicemen's wives, old age pensioners and the unemployed (increases in allowances were put through only several months into the war).

In October 1939, the BIPO asked respondents whether, apart from the budget, they had experienced 'any change in employment or income as a direct result of the war'. Only 7 per cent said they were better off, against 32 per cent who said their situation had become worse, and 61 per cent who said that they had as yet not been affected. The gradual drain was recorded in late October in the diary kept by George Beardmore, a jobbing clerk-cum-novelist who had already lost his job as a result of the war:

> Prices are slowly going up. The twopenny bars of chocolate are to be smaller and restricted to standard lines, i.e. milk, plain, and with or without nuts. Gone are multitudinous varieties such as the egg-flips, almond, grapefruit, and sandwiches. Sausages are now 7d a pound – beef that is. The makers say that skins now cost them more. 1d is charged for delivering papers. Bread is up ½d a quarter. Lyle's Golden Syrup unobtainable, presumably because it stores well.[67]

In a useful instance of the opportunities as well as the problems created by the war, Beardmore quickly found a new job, tracking down rate-payers who were in arrears to Wembley Council after evacuating to the countryside. 'The technique', he soon learned, was 'simple. You have to get in touch with the missing household's milkman, who apparently knows everything about everyone, including the infidelities, and if he doesn't know, ask the postman.'[68]

Uncertainties about the food situation delayed the introduction of rationing. Pre-war planning for food rationing had drawn directly on the experience of the last conflict. The ration was meant to solve the problem of rising prices and growing queues by assuring everyone equal access to a fixed quantity of the foodstuffs that were expected to become scarce: meat, fats and sugar. The government anticipated that rationing would only be publicly acceptable if it were seen as a response to shortage and because it would be limited to a few items. Differences in individual need would be made up from a wide range of unrationed goods, including bread and potatoes.[69]

By September 1939, the framework for food rationing was well developed. The country had been arranged into nineteen divisions, within which 1,400 local food control committees would oversee registration, regulation and distribution. Fifty million ration books had been printed ready for issue to householders, who would be required to

1. A street party celebrates the coronation of George VI, 12 May 1937.

2. (*top*) British troops search Arab men in Palestine, December 1937.

3. (*bottom*) Dressed in their protective gear, members of the Esher Air-Raid Precautions Decontamination Squad appeal for new volunteers outside the offices of the local council, February 1938.

4. 'We Are Proud of You: God Bless You'. A London florist sets out her tribute to Neville Chamberlain's achievements at Munich, October 1938.

5. Minister of Air Sir Kingsley Wood (*centre*, peering into fuselage in glasses), at the opening of a new aircraft factory in Reading, January 1939. Pre-war rearmament accelerated after the Sudeten crisis.

6. (*top*) A carefully staged (and strikingly middle class) Ministry of Information photograph shows a smiling hostess welcoming a mother who has come to see her two evacuee children. In reality, relations on both sides were not always so cheerful.

7. (*bottom*) The Bore War. British soldiers, wearing labels to indicate the extent of their 'injuries', play at being dead and injured during an air-raid exercise on the south coast, 25 February 1940.

8. (*above*) Ernest Bevin enjoys the support of British workers.

9. (*left*) Clement Attlee and Arthur Greenwood (*right*), leader and deputy leader of the Labour Party, contemplate their entry into office, 1940.

10. Winston Churchill checks on the attitude of the press, St Andrews station, October 1940.

11. (*above, left*) Lord Beaverbrook in characteristic listening pose: a picture taken as he travelled with Churchill to America in December 1941.

12. (*above, right*) Anthony Eden (in trademark Homburg hat) meets British troops in the Western Desert, February 1941.

13. (*below*) Herbert Morrison demonstrates his pride in London's fire services, 1942.

14. Merchant ship number 449 slides down the slipway into the Clyde, 19 November 1941. Shipworkers at the bottom of the photograph are already preparing to lay down the next hull.

register with a retailer. The retailer would take coupons from the books alongside payment for the allocated ration, then pass the coupons on to the Ministry of Food in order to secure further supplies. Yet the introduction of rationing was delayed by ministers' uncertainty about public reaction. They feared that restrictions would suggest that Britain didn't have enough food to go round, damaging morale and handing a propaganda victory to the Germans.

Soundings of public opinion for the War Cabinet at the end of October suggested that there was broad approval for rationing, although Churchill worried that the press would complain at further 'interference with the liberty of the individual'. Chamberlain quoted with approval a report from a social worker in the East End: 'In his view, if the working classes were persuaded that everybody was equally restricted and that wealth could not obtain concessions, and that supplies could be obtained in an orderly manner without inconvenience, rationing would be easily accepted.'[70] The appearance of fair shares for all was to remain the basic tenet of wartime rationing policy. That made the case for bacon and butter, both of which were already in relatively short supply, and which the War Cabinet decided would be rationed from January. Meat and sugar were for the moment left unrationed, but by the start of December, problems with supply and high levels of purchasing (as those who could do so stocked up on sugar in anticipation of restrictions), forced the decision that these too should be rationed – sugar from January, meat from March 1940. The initial ration was four ounces of bacon and butter and twelve ounces of sugar per person per week. Meat was rationed by value, with each person entitled to buy 1s. 10d. worth a week.[71]

Public responses to the announcement of rationing were generally favourable. The *Daily Express* launched a campaign in early November to 'Stop Rationing!' – 'It is absolute nonsense. It gives the people a sense of insecurity. It makes them feel that their supplies are unreliable'[72] – but this set it firmly against the tide of popular opinion. A BIPO poll in the same month indicated that 60 per cent of those questioned thought food rationing was necessary, against 28 per cent who thought it was not required.[73] Although M-O recorded a range of grumbles about the specific nature of rationing – in the words of one working-class man 'quarter of a pound of f— bacon a week. Not a bloody square meal in it'[74] – it also found general approval of the idea of fair shares for all. For some, the minor personal sacrifice of consumption in pursuit of victory was positively enticing. Having listened to a broadcast by W. S. Morrison, the minister of food, Richard Brown – a designer at an engineering firm in Ipswich, an eager wartime volunteer and, incidentally, an enthusiastic reader of the *Express* – totalled up his family's rations in his diary and concluded that:

> We shall have to cut down a little more on sugar, but not much. We ought to manage on 3¾ lb a week and as for butter, I like margarine just as well. Morrison explained it was to conserve cargo space for munitions and to save foreign currency.[75]

'BUGGER OWD HITLER'

As 1939 drew to a close, however, food rationing still lay in the future. A more immediate problem was what to do about a blacked-out Christmas with money getting shorter. Some were cutting back:

> heaven knows, we can't afford it these days. I've told the kiddies some story or other about Father Christmas being a German, so he can't come over this year. We won't be able to afford all those little things – what with butter going up and one thing and another, we've got to save a bit.[76]

Others had decided on a blow-out:

> 'Well,' I says to him, 'well, we ain't got much money, but what we <u>have</u> got will go a longer way now than it will next year,' I says. 'Particularly,' I says, 'if we're all dead. So we might as well have a proper do for Christmas and spend the money while we've got it, and while we're here to have it.'[77]

For Tom Harrisson and Charles Madge, surveying the first months of the conflict for Mass-Observation's book *War Begins at Home*, there was an obvious explanation: 'The need for a very merry Christmas has been very real this year, because people have felt so low and dull about the course of the war. If there had been energetic and encouraging leadership all the way along, this condition would not have developed.'[78] In a book that went on to influence many subsequent interpretations of the Bore War, Harrisson and Madge examined government poster campaigns, evacuation, the fate of the Ministry of Information and the introduction of rationing, and concluded that complacent officials had failed to communicate the real purpose of the war to the people.[79] Instead, the 'masses' had been left to make up their own minds, with the result that they simultaneously lacked a purpose (apparently, 32 per cent of those questioned by M-O 'could give no positive war aim'[80]) and had fallen back on 'wishful thinking' about the likelihood of victory. Leaving people to their own devices was 'a weakness on the home front'.[81] Instead, domestic morale needed 'constant attention and supervision by skilled and trained technicians'. Not coincidentally, this was exactly the sort of monitoring that Mass-Observation itself might be able to provide.[82]

To begin with, it had seemed likely that the war would provide a host of opportunities for social research, as the Ministry of Information sought both to assess the impact of official policies and to keep an eye on popular morale. Government contracts would provide the regular income to allow Mass-Observation to fulfil a higher purpose; in Harrisson's words 'producing a unique documentary account of a civilisation at war'.[83] They would also help to keep Mass-Observation's male staff out of the clutches of conscription. A trial commission was swiftly secured through the Ministry's Home Publicity department, exploring reactions to its leaflets and posters. This quickly fell victim to the press outcry against the Ministry of Information. Wary of accusations that his department was spying on British civilians, the minister of information, Lord Macmillan, severed links with outside researchers. Mass-Observation was left high and dry. As Harrisson and Madge put together *War Begins at Home*, they were still scrabbling around for work. The book was not only a report on findings: it was also a job application.[84]

In fact, pretty special pleading was needed to make domestic morale appear fragile. Contrary to Harrisson and Madge's argument, evidence gathered by the BIPO in the early days of the war suggested the strength of popular support for Britain's participation. A September survey, after war had broken out, found 89 per cent of those asked answering 'yes' to the question 'Should we continue to fight until Hitlerism goes?' This was even higher than the 77 per cent who said that they would disapprove of the government discussing peace proposals with Germany – suggesting that the desire for peace and the desire to get rid of Hitler could go hand in hand. Thirty-one per cent thought that the war would be over within one year, but 33 per cent thought it would last longer than two. Eighty-four per cent of those questioned thought that the Allies would beat the Germans, 12 per cent that there would be a stalemate, and only 1 per cent that Britain would lose.[85] This might have reflected the patriotism of pre-war national life, but it wasn't really wishful thinking. Germany was in a very poor position to take on the UK.

Opposition to the war remained very much in the minority. A small but vocal group of Conservative peers campaigned against the war and had to be squashed by Halifax in the House of Lords. On 4 October the Conservative backbench 1922 Committee debated whether to ask for a negotiated peace. The outcome was a resounding defeat for the pacifists. On the left, Lansbury, Lloyd George and George Bernard Shaw all spoke out against the war, and in early November the twenty backbench Labour MPs of the Parliamentary Peace Group signed a memorandum demanding immediate peace talks. They were carefully corralled by the party leadership.[86]

Elsewhere, the first weeks of the war saw the Communist Party of Great Britain undergo a tortuous process of realignment to get itself behind Moscow. By the end of September, the Communists were advocating revolutionary defeatism to end the war and bring down the National Government. At the start of October, a new CPGB manifesto declared that the war was not 'for democracy against Fascism. It is not a war for the liberty of small nations. It is not a war for the defence of peace against aggression. This war is a fight between imperialist powers over profits, colonies and world domination' – a stance that at least made sense of Soviet actions as defensive counter-measures against imperialism and Fascism.[87]

BIPO surveys in November 1939 and February 1940 picked up a significant undercurrent of anti-war feeling, with about one in ten of those asked about the conduct of the conflict responding with statements classified by the pollsters as 'Stop the War'.[88] Police reports submitted to the Home Office in November, however, suggested that the minority who were against the war were not swaying public opinion. 'Subversive and pacifist propaganda' was 'widespread but its scale is nowhere great, and its reception is generally hostile'. This hostility was manifested in such extreme forms as 'heckling, the breaking of a window at a Fascist headquarters, and the marked fall in the attendances at a cinema in which a Fascist meeting had been held'.[89] By the first months of 1940, the percentage of those willing to say that they would approve of peace discussions with Germany had risen from 25 to 29 per cent: but given the expectation of an eventual negotiation after an Allied victory, this did not necessarily reflect rising opposition to the war.[90]

Whatever its moral, political and strategic consequences, the course of foreign affairs during the last year of peace had given Britons a pretty clear idea about what they were fighting against. The BIPO's September survey found that 92 per cent of respondents believed that the enemy was the Hitler government rather than the German people.[91] Despite official anxieties about whether 'getting rid of Hitler' was enough of a goal, when the BIPO asked in October whether the Allies should 'draw up and publish their war aims', 44 per cent of those questioned said yes, but 30 per cent said no and another 12.5 per cent stated that the aims were 'already explicit enough'.[92] In November, Mass-Observation conducted a 'Working Class War Questionnaire' in Bolton that included a question about what the country was fighting for. The sample was small, but answers included:

W40: 'To do away with Hitlerism of course.'

W42: 'We're fighting to save these little countries being oppressed and we must stop him while we can.'

W55: 'I don't know, they tell us what their [sic] fighting for don't they, it seems all right to me.'

W25, munitions worker: 'Well, we're fighting for our country I suppose.'

W55: 'They're supposed to be oppressed in Germany and we're supposed to be free; still, that's a question isn't it?'

W40: 'When one man wants too much we've got to stop it that's all. But I don't like the idea of war.'

W32: 'Don't know.'[93]

None of these might have counted as a 'positive' war aim by Harrisson's lights, but a more 'negative' war aim – stopping Hitler – obviously had resonance even among those who were pessimistic about what would happen next. As an 'unemployed 40 year old woman' explained: 'It's always us working and poor people that suffer you know. Course it would be better than having a dictator over here wouldn't it? That would be terrible.'[94]

The first months of the war contained much that was disruptive, difficult or plain annoying, but there was very little to turn more Britons against a government that had already divided opinion before the conflict began. The BIPO's November and February surveys indicated that around 60 per cent of those asked were 'satisfied' with the government's 'conduct of the war', against just under 20 per cent 'dissatisfied' (a group distinct from those who wanted to stop the war).[95] Chamberlain's approval figures actually went up after the outbreak of war, with around 64 per cent of the BIPO's respondents declaring themselves satisfied with or approving of him as prime minister in October, November and December. In the final survey of 1939, interviewees were given the choice between Chamberlain and Churchill as prime minister: they chose the incumbent by 52 to 30 per cent.[96] Mass-Observation's 'Working Class War Questionnaire' suggested why Chamberlain's popularity had improved:

> W55: 'First I thought Mr Chamberlain was rather a slowcoach: he should
>   have up and at 'em. Since then I think he's done a very good thing.' . . .
> M36: 'He's different from what he was two years since; he's a proper
>   fighting man now.'[97]

The Home Office reported at the end of October that, 'The general public appear to have settled down to the inconveniences and restrictions due to the war; their reaction to war conditions might be described as one of resigned approval.'[98] Blackout, evacuation and conscription notwithstanding, this was still Chamberlain's preferred version of the war: controlled, restrained, its impact as limited as possible. Compared to what they had been expecting, very few Britons had a problem with that. The war might be boring but at least it was bearable. In the words of a forty-year-old miner in Bolton: 'I'm not botherin' about the bloody war, let me have the old cowheel pie and a pint now again, then I'm satisfied. Bugger owd Hitler.'[99]

While the Bore War continued, there was little to undermine the faith that Britain would eventually win, like it had always done before. Given the country's economic strength, this 'assurance of victory' – in the title of an early pamphlet from the Ministry of Information – was not necessarily misguided.[100] Whether or not it was correct, this conviction was not a weakness that would crack unless people were better educated by self-appointed experts – but rather a strength that would allow morale to bounce back from the shocks still to come.

THE POLITICS OF BOREDOM

Having condemned him for not going to war quickly enough, Chamberlain's domestic opponents now attacked him for fighting with insufficient urgency. The desire for a more active war effort encouraged the formation in early September of the All-Party Parliamentary Action Group, chaired by the Liberal National MP Clement Davies. This tail-end of the Popular Front ultimately grew to a membership of about sixty MPs. Davies' increasingly dissident stance was demonstrated when, at the end of the year, he resigned the whip to campaign against the government as an independent. He was to play an influential role in bringing together Chamberlain's enemies from across the political sphere.[101]

Meanwhile, the group of backbench government MPs that had formed behind Anthony Eden in the later 1930s – the so-called 'Glamour Boys' – continued to meet after the outbreak of war.[102] They too presumed that the government needed to be pressed into action. One of their number, the National Labour MP Harold Nicolson, summed up their conversations at the start of the war:

> one comes back to the point that Chamberlain did not want this war, and is continually thinking of getting out of it. He may be right. But he has not behaved with sufficient honesty and moral courage to carry the country with him.[103]

With Eden having become a government minister again, Leo Amery took a leading role in the group's activities. Amery spent the early days of the war fuming at government inactivity. He wanted more military aid to the Poles, a larger army to support the French and more controls on the economy, as well as the bombing of Germany. On 5 September he recorded in his diary:

> our Air Force are still not allowed to bomb Essen or even set fire to German forests. In the coffee room I tackled Kingsley Wood on this. He was

very stuffy and evidently has been responsible for all this, on some mistaken notion that we are winning American sympathy, and forgetting that we are doing nothing really to help the Poles . . . Went away very angry.[104]

On Amery's later account, Wood responded to his question about why the Black Forest wasn't being bombed with the words: 'Are you aware that it is private property?'[105] The words might have been apocryphal, but the anecdote stuck, although given the inaccuracy of British bombing in autumn 1939, if the RAF had tried to hit the Black Forest, they would probably have missed.

As they swapped stories of official incompetence, the Eden Group pondered how they would do better and tried to work out who would replace Chamberlain when 'the real war' started. Churchill was a popular candidate: his talent for self-publicity well served in his radio broadcasts, and his years out of office saving him from the ignominy of involvement with appeasement.

This turn against Chamberlain marked the 'Glamour Boys' out from other Conservative critics of the prime minister who, if no more pleased with his leadership, were less certain that he had to go. Another node of Conservative criticism formed around members of the Cecil family – Lord Salisbury, Viscount Cecil, Viscount Cranborne and Viscount Wolmer. The Cecils were mainstays of the political establishment whose forefathers had been involved in the running of the country for the best part of four centuries.[106] They also had a track record of attacking Chamberlain's foreign policy – Viscount Cecil had headed the League of Nations Union and Cranborne had been Eden's parliamentary under-secretary and had resigned alongside his boss in 1938. To the Cecils, appeasement smacked of 'truckling to dictators': a fundamentally un-British policy, unsuitable for a great nation.[107]

Now that war had been declared, Salisbury worried that Chamberlain was leaving space open for another bout of negotiated concessions to Hitler, and doubted that any of his ministers had the strength of character to defy him. Like other Tory critics, Salisbury seized on the idea of appointing an economic supremo to direct domestic mobilization, and was keen on escalating the air offensive against Germany. Above all, he saw it as a matter of national duty to keep a watchful eye on Chamberlain, channelling the voices of traditional

Conservatism to pressure the prime minister to fight the war as if he wanted to win.

Plenty of people at Westminster suspected that the prime minister's position was vulnerable because of the position that Labour had taken. As Baldwin had recognized years before, mobilizing the country for a total war would require an administration that could represent itself as embodying the entire nation. At a practical level, the government must have the active support of the trade unions if it were to undertake the industrial effort necessary for victory. It was already plain that this would not be given while Chamberlain remained in office. Once the conflict escalated, the political consequences seemed inevitable. After a meeting of the Eden Group on 3 October, Nicolson recorded the argument that:

> when the war really begins, there will be such an outburst of public indignation that a Coalition Government will have to be formed. It is evident that none of the Opposition leaders will enter a Cabinet which contains Chamberlain, Simon and Hoare, and that therefore the removal of these three will take place almost automatically.[108]

Such predictions were frequent among informed political opinion during the first months of the war. At the start of 1940, having dined with Amery the week before, General Ironside explained to his diary that any War Cabinet simply had to include 'the Labour people': 'You cannot run a war so largely a matter of material, without the active and willing cooperation of the men who make the material. Apparently Labour will not work with Chamberlain and are remaining out of office till he goes.' Ironside did not think that it would be an easy departure: 'The people have great confidence in the PM and it will take a great revulsion of feeling to get him out.'[109]

If the war had dealt a political trump card to the Labour Party, then it was part of a hand that still needed to be played with caution. By itself, Labour had nowhere near enough MPs to challenge the government's parliamentary majority. Many Labour activists were either unconvinced of the war's merits or frustrated that their party was not taking more direct action in pursuit of socialism. Notwithstanding their personal loathing for the prime minister, Labour's leaders had to phrase their attacks on Chamberlain carefully, criticizing the running of the war without appearing partisan. During the first months of the conflict, they achieved a remarkable but often-underappreciated success, simultaneously controlling their supporters and condemning Chamberlain without squandering the party's political capital.[110]

Immediately after the outbreak of war, Labour and the Liberals negotiated an electoral truce with the government. While the war lasted, it was expected that there would be no general election. If parliamentary seats fell vacant in the meantime, the last incumbent's party would be allowed to put up a candidate for the subsequent by-election without opposition from its main opponents. Minor parties and fringe groups continued to contest by-elections, but the effect was to preserve the parliamentary status quo of 1939 for the duration. From the start, the truce proved unpopular with local Labour activists, but for their leaders it meant that they could demonstrably put country before party while simultaneously closing down internal demands for a more aggressive assault on the government.[111]

Within strict limits, Labour was in fact collaborating closely with the wartime administration. Although Labour had refused Chamberlain's attempt to bring it into coalition, it liaised closely with government departments. And at the same time as violently criticizing the government to their members, trade union leaders readily accepted the prime minister's request to involve themselves in the mechanics of mobilization. In so doing, however, they emphasized that Labour's acquiescence was crucial to the war economy and that this would be limited while Chamberlain remained in power.

Instead, Labour stuck with 'constructive opposition'. As Arthur Greenwood made clear to the Commons in responding to Chamberlain's pledge on 3 September to continue the fight until Nazism was overthrown:

> as long as that relentless purpose is pursued with vigour, with foresight and with determination by the Government, so long will there be a united nation. But should there be confused councils, inefficient and wavering, then other men must be called upon to take their places. We share no responsibilities in the tremendous tasks which confront the Government, but we have responsibilities of our own, which we shall not shirk.[112]

Given the spectre of 1931, some Labour activists were wary that their leaders would choose power over party. Harold Laski – a professor at the London School of Economics and a leading light of the Labour intelligentsia – demanded that Labour should lay down a specific shopping list of requirements that would have to be met before they joined the government. Although they issued regular statements on party policy, however, Labour's top men fought shy of defining exactly what they wanted from the war. They preferred to maintain their freedom of manoeuvre while absorbing internal frustrations into the labyrinthine processes by which the party deliberated policy.[113]

Labour had spent much of the middle part of 1939 in the throes of a leadership battle as Hugh Dalton and Herbert Morrison again attempted to depose Attlee. They criticized his apparent timidity, but although the Labour leader might have lacked charisma, he now began to display a steely acumen. Having returned from his sick bed at the end of September, in mid-November he despatched his challengers. Over the months that followed, he took an increasingly important role in Labour's campaign against Chamberlain. Attlee's carefully moderated criticisms bolstered his party's credentials as a necessary component of any wartime government.

In Parliament, in pamphlets, in public meetings and in radio broadcasts, Labour attacked inefficiency in everything from the management of conscription to the composition of the War Cabinet. The evidence was plain: unemployment remained too high and munitions output too low. Labour's solution was simple: more central planning, not only as a means to achieve its political objectives, but also as a rational response to the exigencies of war. As Greenwood put it in the Commons on 5 December 1939: 'time will show that the greater the urgency of the national situation the more the public interest must dominate, and the more the community must take charge of the general direction of its affairs'.[114]

HOW TO PAY FOR THE WAR

Everyone who had been involved with the war economy last time round knew that there were going to be two big problems. The first was the supply of labour – how could unskilled workers be brought in to expand the workforce without disrupting industrial relations, and how could skilled workers be made to stay in the same place rather than moving from company to company in pursuit of higher wages? The second problem was inflation. The Treasury's great fear was that as the state invested massively in fighting the war and squeezed civilian consumption, more money would chase fewer goods in a wage-price spiral, driving up inflation, adding further to the cost of the conflict and dividing society.

In both areas, the government initially preferred to rely on voluntarism rather than compulsion. The Control of Employment Act passed in September 1939 was severely limited in scope to avoid antagonizing the unions. Only one order was issued under its terms during the first nine months of the conflict. Instead, the government hoped that the attraction of employment and the desire to serve would bring workers into the munitions industries, while the education of the public in the need for mutual sacrifice would encourage acceptance of job dilution and of calls for restraint. This was the political script underlying Sir John Simon's budget, with the breadth of tax increases intended to persuade Britons that everybody would have to do their bit, but the expectation that individual self-denial and saving would also serve to hold back inflation.[115]

The problems with this approach were quickly apparent. The government's desire to see wages restrained was at odds with its expectation that the labour market, operating freely, would fulfil the demands of war industry. The increase in the Cost of Living Index occasioned by the outbreak of war automatically triggered demands for wage increases. The government's economic advisor, Lord Stamp, responded in November with a call to compulsorily restrict wage increases well below equivalent rises in the CLI.

Stamp was the archetype of the National Government's commitment to British business expertise. Born to modest middle-class parents, and a committed Methodist, he was a self-made man who had risen spectacularly through the ranks of the Inland Revenue before the First World War. Between the wars, he sat on the Board of Directors of the Bank of England, and was president of the London, Midland and Scottish Railway. During the 1930s, Stamp undertook a huge range of public work, including national inquiries into debt, taxation and the coal industry. In 1939, he was seconded from the LMS to become the government's chief advisor on economic mobilization. Stamp headed a small staff of senior economists who attempted to co-ordinate wartime economic policy. The fact that he kept up his railway directorship at the same time as trying to oversee the war effort was the subject of much negative comment from the government's critics.[116]

Like Chamberlain, Stamp believed that the development of purely military power needed to be balanced against other priorities: defending the strength of sterling, maintaining British exports and restraining inflation. Since wage earners accounted for about two-thirds of consumer spending, Stamp thought that holding down workers' pay was the best way to avoid an inflationary spiral. He put much less emphasis on limiting business profits, on the basis that they would leak out more slowly into the economy and have less immediate effect on inflation. Stamp also had an old-fashioned sense of social responsibility. Pay increases should not cushion British workers from the inflationary consequences of the conflict. On the contrary, only by being exposed to the ravages of price rises would they realize the gravity of the national endeavour. Fighting the war would be costly, and it was everyone's duty to bear the price.

Rather than resort to compulsion, however, the government tried to persuade trade union leaders to hold back wage claims in the national interest. In November, faced with the revelation from the Ministry of Food that prices were about to rise by another 8 per cent – which would make large pay awards inevitable – the government began a programme of food subsidies. These were initially intended only to ease negotiations with the unions for the next six weeks, but over the winter of 1939–40, they were announced to the public and extended for another six months. By the start of 1940, they were costing the government about a million pounds a week.[117]

The trade union leaders could see no reason why their people should bear the cost for the war, when what was needed was restrictions on prices and profits. To their members, Citrine and Bevin promised that involvement in the war meant continuing the fight of labour against capital. As Bevin told readers of the *Transport and General Workers' Record* in February 1940: 'The working classes are faced with two offensives, one by Hitler which we must defeat, and one by the bankers which, if the Government does not stop, will lead to the defeat of our nation.'[118] To the government, meanwhile, they explained that while they understood its problems, they were sadly in no position to help:

The leaders of the workpeople have a real appreciation of the many difficulties that are not at present in the minds of the rank and file, but they are in no doubt that, if they are to maintain their authority they must be able to carry their people with them and that they cannot ignore the psychological factor. The process of education in the problems of war economy can only proceed gradually and must be accompanied by a sense of real equality of sacrifice. There must be no justification for doubts whether reference to the dangers of a wage-costs spiral ignores the possibility of a prices-profits spiral.[119]

In the spring of 1940, the government had to continue with its existing strategy – food subsidies to limit wage demands, plus a publicity drive to encourage restraint in expenditure from every sector of the population.

John Maynard Keynes believed that there was another way of doing things. During the last years of peace, Keynes' ideas about economic management had begun to chime with the Treasury's desire to mitigate the consequences of borrowing to fund defence. Yet for the moment there was no job for him in Whitehall. When the war broke out, Keynes was still recovering from a severe heart illness that had almost killed him eighteen months before. He was both too senior and too disruptive a figure to be reincorporated easily into the civil service machine. Instead, he joined other leading lights from the last war, including Sir William Beveridge and Sir Walter Layton, in a group of self-proclaimed 'Old Dogs' who now serenaded their successors by howling about how badly the new conflict was being run.[120]

During the autumn of 1939, Keynes tried to make a major intervention on economic policy: first in a lecture at Cambridge, then in a memo sent, among others, to Simon and Attlee, then in articles in *The Times* on 14 and 15 November. All developed the same point: the need to manage the colossal increase in domestic spending that would accompany a total war. There would, Keynes was sure, be no problem in getting the money. With the government controlling foreign exchange and interest rates, it could easily borrow sterling at low interest for long-term repayment. Indeed, the Treasury was already realizing that, bearing in mind the low returns available while loans had been cheap in the 1930s, it would have no problem selling war bonds to British investors so that it could fight a 'three per cent war'.[121]

Keynes was more concerned about inflation as the state poured money into the war economy. The ideas developed out of the *General Theory* gave him a distinct insight into the problem. For Keynes, inflation was not something that could be limited by appeals to individual responsibility. Rather, it was an inevitability unless the state could extract from the economy the same amount of money it was putting in. Keynes too focused on wage-earning households because they made up so much of the national income. Yet these same households would have to spend proportionately more of their income on rising prices. Whether it came as a result of wage controls or wage rises, an 'inflation tax' that effectively forced them to bear the cost of the war would not be a fair reward for their endeavours.

Keynes initially fought shy of using rationing to counter inflation. Partial rationing, he argued, would simply force demand onto whatever was left out. Full rationing was inefficient and anti-democratic – it was wrong to pretend that everyone had the same preferences when they plainly did not. Keynes deprecated both the tax rises announced in Simon's budget and his appeals for voluntary investment in National Savings. Neither would be sufficiently large to meet the inflationary pressures created as munitions production took off.

Instead, Keynes proposed a new scheme of 'compulsory saving', severely graduated by income, which would cover the great majority of wage earners as well as existing taxpayers. Part of these savings would be taken to finance government expenditure. The rest would be credited to individual locked accounts at the Post Office Savings Bank, which would be released to savers at the end of the war. This phased release would produce a counter-cyclical pressure to relieve what Keynes believed would be an inevitable post-war slump.

Keynes' proposals attracted a lot of publicity over the winter of 1939 – he reckoned more than had been generated by *The Economic Consequences of the Peace* – and a reworked version was published as *How to Pay for the War* in February 1940. Keynes knew that if his scheme were to be implemented, it would have to have Labour's support. His belief that wage earners should enjoy the fruits of their labours (albeit in delayed form) meant that his plan had always had a progressive edge. Now, in an effort to attract Labour, he honed this still further by adding family allowances and a tax on capital into his plans. Hidden though this was by his talk of compulsory saving, however, Keynes' fundamental aim was economically liberal. He saw the limitation of consumer expenditure as a means to avoid totalitarian controls. Measures directed, as he put it, at the 'pocket' rather than the 'pantry' would allow the preservation of individual choice within a managed market economy.[122]

In the political circumstances of the Bore War, this made Keynes' plans impracticable. On their first publication, they received widespread approval from his fellow economists, leading City figures and most of the press. Predictably, the *Express* condemned them as another restriction on liberty. Any attempt to address working-class incomes, however, required the co-operation of the trade unions, and despite Keynes' best efforts, this was unforthcoming. Keynes retitled 'compulsory saving' as 'deferred pay', but however he dressed it up, the immediate consequence of his proposals would be a restriction of working-class incomes at a point when unemployment was still high and the cost of living was increasing. There was a well-founded suspicion that money handed over to the government was not going to come back. More importantly, Keynes and the Labour Party were aiming for something fundamentally different. Labour wanted economic controls not as a stopgap to win the war, but because they were a step on the way to a centrally planned economy, in which consumer choice would be replaced by the determining power of the state. It was always unlikely that they would partake in Keynes' plan to preserve market capitalism. Moreover, Labour still hoped to win a far higher price for their co-operation than the implementation of 'deferred pay' for the working classes.

Treasury civil servants thought *How to Pay for the War* was another instance of Keynes being too clever for his own good. Like the chancellor, they shared Keynes' belief in the need to hold back working-class spending as the war economy took off, but they did not think that there was much alternative to voluntarism until the war itself had educated the public in the need for controls. They also lacked faith in Keynes' back-of-an-envelope estimates about how much money would need to come out of consumers' pockets in order to restrain inflation. No one at this point, including the Treasury, had the calculations of national income necessary to determine the precise figures it wanted to underpin its policy. *How to Pay for the War*, however, drove on the invention of the methods necessary to determine these numbers. Meanwhile the government continued with its piecemeal approach: not hamstrung by

Labour's 'patriotic opposition', but under permanent notice that an escalation of the war effort would require a change in political circumstances.

Stamp and Keynes' desire to create a war economy in which some market mechanisms survived was not outlandish. At the peak of mobilization in 1943, this was what Britain would actually have, albeit with the balance rather more towards the restriction of choice and away from the control of incomes than either of them would have liked. In the winter of 1939, however, it was not politically possible to implement policies that would affect wage earners without the active support of the trade unions. In practice, the leaders of organized labour did not require a fully socialist solution before they would co-operate with the government, but they did have to be included in any compromise. That put Chamberlain on borrowed time as prime minister.

'WE SHALL GET NO CREDIT FOR IT'

Since he had the support of the bulk of the Conservative Party in the Commons, however, it was far from clear that Chamberlain was going to be forced out. If he was right in his prognosis of the war – the armed stand-off lasting only a short while before the Germans cracked – then the peaks of national mobilization might never have to be scaled and the government's ad hoc solutions would endure. If he was wrong, and some great crisis occurred, then Labour might find it much harder to balance 'patriotism' and 'opposition'. By the start of 1940, Tory rebels and Labour leaders were in serious discussions about how they might topple the prime minister, but the consequences of failure were too high for any of them to take the risk of wielding the first blow.

Having fought off an attack of gout that left him almost crippled in November, Chamberlain's self-confidence was strengthened by the absence of any of the much-promised offensives on the Western Front. Obviously, as he had predicted, Hitler was too scared to chance an attack. With Churchill already in the Cabinet, he felt no need for any further great ministerial reshuffle that might have appeased discontented Tories or undercut wider concerns about the competence of his appointments. He did briefly consider getting rid of Sir John Simon, sounding out Lord Stamp about whether he might take up the post of chancellor, but Stamp prevaricated and Chamberlain decided to leave the National Liberal leader in place. The change would not have done much to persuade his opponents of his intention to escalate the war effort.[123]

Indeed, the only major shift in office came with the resignation of Leslie Hore-Belisha in January 1940. In November, the war minister had criticized the army's defensive preparations in France, giving the generals an opportunity to take umbrage. They had always thought Hore-Belisha was an untrustworthy Jewish glory hunter. Now they had their proof. In December, in one of the last great aristocratic intrigues of British politics, they complained to the king that they were being deliberately undermined. Chamberlain pondered moving Hore-Belisha to the Ministry of Information: a course from which he was diverted by Halifax's advice that a Jewish minister in charge of the news would be a gift to Nazi propaganda. On 4 January, Chamberlain offered Hore-Belisha the presidency of the Board of Trade, a demotion that he was unwilling to accept. Instead, he tendered his resignation and joined the ranks of the prime minister's enemies on the backbenches.[124]

The resignation caused a press storm. The *Daily Mail* announced 'Belisha resigns after clash with generals'. The *Sunday Graphic* promised 'Inside Story of why Belisha had to go: Challenged a Code, Defied a Caste'.[125] Hore-Belisha thought of himself as a potential prime minister, but though he toured round the offices of the *Daily Mirror*, the *Daily Express* and the *News Chronicle* discussing his political position, he backed down from confronting Chamberlain during his resignation speech in the Commons. *Truth*, the weekly newssheet run by Chamberlain's ally Sir Joseph Ball, launched a nasty anti-Semitic campaign against Hore-Belisha in an effort to neutralize any potential threat to the government.[126]

For the first time since the outbreak of war, approval of Chamberlain in the BIPO poll for January dropped below 60 per cent. Given the deficiencies being endured by the army, there might have been a serious warning note for the government in the newspapers' argument that an energetic democrat had been got rid of by the forces of tradition. Could an antiquated old guard really lead the new Britain to victory? For Chamberlain, however, such criticisms distracted from what the government had actually achieved:

The food situation has been improved out of all knowledge, the shipping problem has been firmly gripped, economic warfare is being waged with remarkable efficiency, the Dominions are being kept in line with us without friction (no easy or simple task) . . . We are already subsidising food to the tune of about £50 millions a year to keep down cost of living & shall have to do more, but we shall get no credit for it.[127]

The only thing he left out was the need to be seen to be winning the war.

13

Escalation

Within all the combatant countries, as the Bore War progressed, the pressure to escalate the conflict grew. In the UK, it made the National Government's attempts to control the war effort increasingly unsustainable. At the start of May 1940, it gave Chamberlain's opponents the opportunity they needed to unseat him. As the military situation moved to a crisis, Britain got a new prime minister and a new government. The politics of the 1930s were brought to an abrupt end.

'THUG AND VULTURE'

In the autumn of 1939 it had seemed that the forces of totalitarianism were on the march throughout Eastern Europe. Worried by the prospect of Nazi expansionism, the USSR sought to safeguard its security by seizing territory from neighbouring states. The news, on 16 September, that Moscow had followed up its non-aggression pact with Germany by sending troops into eastern Poland came as a shock to those Britons who had idolized the 'new civilization' being built in the Soviet Union. The Communist Naomi Mitchison recorded for her Mass-Observation diary that she felt 'like hell deep down because of the Russian news . . . it is knocking the bottom out of what one has been working for all these years'.[1] To more conservative minds, like that of the writer and critic Osbert Sitwell, Soviet behaviour just proved what they had long believed, that 'Moscow and Berlin' were 'two ugly masks to the same face. There is little to choose, except in daring, between thug and vulture, and we are fighting for a way of life in which thugs and vultures will no longer dare to attempt control of the fates of other beings.'[2]

As far as the British people were concerned, Poland's fate did not automatically turn the Soviets into the national enemy. BIPO polls in the early autumn of 1939 suggested that although opinion was divided on Soviet actions in Eastern Europe, a majority of respondents felt that the Russians did not intend to aid Germany in defeating Britain and France. When he broadcast on the war situation at the start of October, Churchill held back from an outright attack on Soviet behaviour:

> We could have wished that the Russian armies should be standing on their present line as the friends and allies of Poland, instead of as invaders. But that the Russian armies should stand on this line was clearly necessary for the safety of Russia against the Nazi menace.[3]

The Soviet quest for territorial security did not, however, stop with the dismemberment of Poland. By mid-October, Moscow had also pressurized the Baltic States into signing military pacts that left them nominally independent, but subject to occupation at Stalin's will. Soviet demands on Finland then became increasingly bellicose, culminating in a full-scale invasion on 30 November.

The Finns were not expected to hold out for long against the might of the Soviet Union, but with its best officers purged, the Red Army fought poorly and took huge casualties in the first battles. As the Finns appealed for international assistance, the Russian advance was temporarily halted on the Karelian Isthmus. It was plain to all sides that it would be only a matter of time before the sheer weight of the Red Army overcame the defenders.

In Britain, the spectacle of a gallant little nation under assault from the Communist colossus attracted widespread sympathy. Journalists initially focused on the horrors of the Russian attack, but as the Finns held out, they were increasingly impressed by their powers of resistance.[4] Politicians on all sides condemned Soviet aggression – Chamberlain told the Commons it had 'outraged the conscience of the whole world' – but reactions from the Labour movement were particularly fierce.

The strong emotions aroused by a distant conflict echoed responses to the civil war in Spain. Just as with Spain, Finland was the subject of voluntary fundraising campaigns and anxious visits from concerned politicians. Again, public opinion soon rallied behind the underdog, although the Finnish invasion did not totally eliminate friendly feelings for the Soviet Union on the British left. Asked in December whether Soviet Russia or Nazi Germany was more dangerous, 24 per cent of the BIPO's survey chose the former against 57 per cent who chose the latter. In March 1940, however, 47 per cent answered negatively when asked whether the British government should try to 'establish friendly relations with Russia' (compared to 7 per cent who had responded the same way to a similar question a year before). Forty-one per cent thought 'that one day we shall have to fight Russia'.[5] When Churchill gave another broadcast on the war situation in March, he reverted to the sort of language he had used to describe Russia in the aftermath of the Bolshevik revolution: 'Everyone can see how Communism rots the soul of a nation, how it makes it hungry and abject in peace, and proves it base and abominable in war.'[6]

As with Spain, there were urgent demands for the government to do something about Finland. Unlike the Iberian tragedy, however, this was a clear case of international aggression – formally condemned by the League of Nations – in which there was from the start much greater domestic agreement about who was in the wrong. There was neither time nor spare munitions to meet Finland's requests, but the British government allowed the despatch of a significant quantity of anti-quated kit: by the spring of 1940, the UK had supplied Finland with 100 planes, 114 artillery pieces, 185,000 shells, 100 machine guns, 50,000 hand grenades and 10,000 anti-tank mines.[7] The War Cabinet also sanctioned the raising of a small body of 'volunteers' to serve alongside the Finns – a rag-tag assembly of just over 200 men who arrived in Finland too late to add their questionable military value to the defences.[8]

Critically, for all the antagonism aroused by the Soviet invasion, in Britain it did not lead to a war against Germany being turned into a military crusade against all forms of totalitarianism. From the outset, Britain's leaders maintained publicly that Russia's actions were symp-toms of an international malaise *caused* by Germany.[9] Defeating Hitler had to remain the first goal. In another repeat of what had hap-pened during the Spanish Civil War, public demands from the Labour movement for the government to do more were matched by private insistence that this must not endanger British security. In France, in contrast, the Russo-Finnish conflict helped to crystallize much more radical views of the war that threatened a fundamental change in Allied strategy.

'A PROFOUND EFFECT ON THE DURATION OF THE WAR'

French anxieties about whether they could actually win a long conflict had increased as the Phoney War went on. As French arms programmes faltered, ministers and officials became more and more concerned that their forces would be outmuscled by the German military. Chamberlain's restrained approach to strategy and the slow expansion of the BEF did little to reassure the French about British intentions. They feared that economic warfare was having little effect, not least because of German access to Russian raw materials. French suspicions about the Soviet regime were heightened by the Finnish invasion. In France, the pressure on the government to aid the Finns was much stronger than in the UK, with right-wing politicians arguing loudly for military action to counter Communist, as well as Nazi, aggression. By the start of 1940, the French were frantic for a speedy victory, and primed to look for a new front in Northern Europe.[10]

British strategists never suffered from quite the same sense of desperation, but in London too, questions were asked about whether more needed to be done to *win* the war. Short of information about what was actually happening in Germany, officials in the Ministry of Economic Warfare worried about the leakiness of the blockade. That encouraged calls to take more dramatic steps to knock out supplies of critical raw materials – iron ore and oil – in the hope of a quick fix to the problems of a long war.

Even before the USSR attacked Finland, that meant taking the conflict to Scandinavia. During the 1930s, economic warfare experts had identified the crucial importance of the high-phosphorous iron ore from the Gällivare mines in northern Sweden for German industry. Swedish ore was transported via two routes. During the summer, it went through the port of Luleå, at the top of the Gulf of Bothnia. During the winter, when Luleå was iced up, it passed over the Norwegian border to the port of Narvik, and thence through Norwegian coastal waters to the Baltic. Over the winter of 1939, ministers and senior officers spent a lot of time discussing how these routes might be cut.

At the Admiralty, Admiral Pound's refusal to risk his battleships had stymied Churchill's pursuit of naval operations in the Baltic.[11] In early November, Churchill's attention turned to Narvik. Britain was already planning to lay a 'northern barrage' of mines to control entry to the North Sea. If it were extended into neutral Norwegian waters, ore-carrying ships would be diverted into the open ocean, where they could be intercepted and impounded by the Royal Navy. Churchill's plans were backed up by reports from the Ministry of Economic Warfare (MEW). Just shutting off the Narvik route over the winter would have 'extremely serious' consequences for German industry. As November ended, Churchill's friend Desmond Morton, now director of intelligence at the MEW, asserted that 'A complete stoppage of Swedish exports of iron ore to Germany now would, barring unpredictable developments, end the war in a few months.'[12]

The Russo-Finnish War opened up new strategic questions about the future of the 'neutral north'. Would Sweden and Norway be dragged into an anti-Soviet conflict? Would Germany respond with a Scandinavian invasion designed to secure its essential supplies of ore? Could the Allies intervene in neutral countries while still claiming a moral ascendancy over the dictatorships? The need to pre-empt possible Soviet or German action – and to be seen to act in support of the Finns – increased the pressure to open a Northern Front.

On 16 December, Churchill presented his plans for a Narvik operation to the War Cabinet.[13] 'No other measure is open to us for many months to come', he explained, 'which gives so good a chance of abridging the waste and destruction of the conflict, or of perhaps preventing the vast slaughters which will attend the grapple of the main armies.' The violation of Norwegian neutrality was justified by the great rewards on offer. Norway's scope for retaliation would be limited by the threat of a British naval blockade that would inflict 'economic and industrial ruin'. Churchill insisted: 'We are fighting to re-establish the reign of law and to protect the liberties of small countries ... Small nations must not tie our hands when we are fighting for their rights and freedom.'[14]

This was precisely the point on which Halifax disagreed. The foreign secretary persistently resisted military action to cut off Swedish

ore. Blocking the Narvik winter route, he argued, would only antagonize the Scandinavians, driving them into the German camp, and upset
international opinion, particularly in the United States. Besides, it
would only work in the winter. He favoured diplomatic pressure to
persuade the Swedes to reduce their exports all year round.

Rather than come to an immediate decision, the War Cabinet
charged the chiefs of staff to investigate the military options more fully.
There, Churchill had an ally in General Ironside. During the first
months of the war, he had become convinced that the Allies 'must start
a vigorous policy of forcing the Germans to disperse. We must not sit
supine, hoping that something in our favour will come to pass.' To
Ironside, in plans for a Scandinavian expedition, the British had 'stumbled upon the one great stroke which is open to us to turn the tables
upon the Russians and Germans'.[15] Admiral Pound also gave his support to operations in Norway, not least because they seemed a better
option than letting Churchill pursue the same objective through the
Baltic.

On the last day of 1939, the chiefs suggested 'a fundamental change
in our policy'. They put forward plans for a full-scale military expedition that would land Allied troops and secure the ore field itself. Hitler
would have to respond, tying up his military resources in an offensive
campaign in difficult terrain and perhaps ruling out a German attack
that year on the Western Front.

If the Soviet invasion of Finland presaged territorial ambitions
further north, the ore-field expedition might lead to a military confrontation with the USSR. The chiefs were willing to accept this risk. They
were confident of their ability to take on Soviet forces, particularly if
the seizure of the ore mines knocked Germany out of the war. The
chiefs hoped that the Scandinavians would acquiesce to the Allies
occupying the mines because they wanted protection by them from the
dictators. Such co-operation, they emphasized, was a precondition for
the expedition to go ahead.[16]

Churchill suspected that the service chiefs had laid down this proviso in order to scotch his plan, but during January, he and Ironside
came round to each other's schemes. Opinion in the War Cabinet, however, turned against any Scandinavian operation at all. Halifax sounded
out the Norwegian and Swedish governments, but both opposed anything that might bring them into the war. The Dominions announced

themselves against the violation of neutrality. Rather than pursue a military option, the War Cabinet opted for discussions with the Swedes about potential reductions in ore exports. They also agreed to set up a Finnish Aid Bureau to organize the provision of arms and volunteers. As a concession to Churchill, however, the chiefs of staff were allowed to consider plans for seizing the Swedish ore fields even against Scandinavian opposition. They increasingly came to favour this option as the only way to steal a march on Germany before it began an offensive in the west.[17]

The French were similarly keen for action. In January, their navy came up with a plan to send troops to retake the Finnish Petsamo peninsula from the Soviets. The aim was to provoke a German response that would allow the Allies to intervene in Scandinavia, but the operation would also appease right-wing French politicians who were clamouring for a fight with Bolshevism. Daladier, desperate to try to keep his government together, promised planes and weapons to the Finns and pressurized the British to do the same.[18] For the British, however, the Petsamo project was a distraction. Ironside concluded that it was 'directed against Russia and not against Germany'. The British War Cabinet rejected it, but still felt that they 'ought to do something, even if it were to divert from ourselves the odium of having allowed Finland to be crushed'.[19]

When the Supreme War Council met in Paris on 5 February, the British and French agreed to use Finland as a cover to get what they wanted in Sweden. The Finns, now desperate for military assistance in the face of looming defeat, would be prevailed upon to make an appeal for Allied aid and to request publicly that the Swedes and Norwegians let Allied troops pass through their countries. The Allies, in turn, would promise to protect the Scandinavians if the Germans attacked. A large expeditionary force would then be despatched to safeguard key Norwegian ports and occupy the ore fields. This objective, rather than getting troops to Finland, was the point of the operation, but that meant accepting the risk of being dragged into a war with the USSR.

While the Allies waited for the Finnish appeal, Churchill worried that the Germans would strike first. When a German supply ship, the *Altmark*, carrying British prisoners taken by the *Graf Spee*, took shelter in Norwegian waters, he successfully demanded that British ships be allowed to violate Norwegian neutrality and capture the vessel.[20]

Although Halifax once more blocked naval attacks on the northern shipping route, Churchill also pressed for speedy action against Narvik, arguing that the Allies should prepare to occupy the port even if the Scandinavians rejected Finnish pleas for assistance. Chamberlain agreed that the Allies must not allow their offer of help to appear 'a mere sham'. When it came to issuing orders to commanders who might have to open fire on the Norwegians, however, the War Cabinet prevaricated. Ironside described ministers as 'a bewildered flock of sheep faced by a problem they have consistently refused to consider. Their favourite formula is that the case is hypothetical and then they shy off a decision.'[21] Eventually, however, Chamberlain accepted that the decision would have to be delegated to the commander on the ground. Despite his distaste for war, this prime minister knew when to stand back and leave things to the military.

The next day, Finland surrendered. Churchill attempted unsuccessfully to convince his colleagues to launch the Narvik operation anyway, but Chamberlain now joined Halifax in preferring diplomatic efforts to win over the Swedes. Much to Churchill's frustration, after months of discussion, British strategy appeared to be back at square one.[22]

On the far side of the Channel, however, the signing of the Finnish-Soviet armistice occasioned a political crisis. During a dramatic debate in the French parliament, an emotional Daladier was attacked both by anti-war politicians and by those who accused him of not fighting hard enough. On 20 March, he won a motion of confidence by 239 votes to 2, but there were 300 abstentions. Daladier resigned and was replaced by his minister of finance, Paul Reynaud. The French parliament remained furiously divided, however, and Reynaud feuded with his embittered predecessor, who remained in office as minister of defence. Reynaud proved even keener than Daladier on opening up new military fronts in the hope of winning the war before France went under. By the end of March, he was pressing the British not just to reconsider a Scandinavian expedition, but also to undertake operations even further afield.[23]

From the start of 1940, French military planners, convinced that Soviet supplies were helping the Nazis, had pondered direct action to shut down the supply of oil from the Caucasus. They favoured bombing raids to set light to the oilfields round Baku. During the spring, the French sought ways to turn what had been vague plans into practical

ICELAND

NORTH
ATLANTIC
OCEAN

② Winter route

Narvik

Iro
m

NORWAY

SWEDEN

Summer ro

UNITED
KINGDOM

①

North
Sea

IRELAND

Bal

HOLLAND

③

BELGIUM

GERMANY

G

④

Bohemia
& Moravia

SLO

FRANCE

HUN

YUGOSL

PORTUGAL

SPAIN

ITALY

Mediterranean Sea

Allied strategic options, winter 1939–spring 1940

Petsamo

Soviet invasion

White
Sea

FINLAND

ESTONIA   Soviet
                blockade
                and
LATVIA   invasion

LITHUANIA

U S S R

Soviet
occupied

Soviet
occupied

OLAND

ROMANIA

Caspian Sea

Black Sea

Baku

BULGARIA

⑤

⑥

TURKEY

① potential Allied naval
   intervention in the Baltic to cut
   trade and provide aid to Finland

② mining of Norwegian coastal
   waters and/or intervention at
   Narvik to occupy town and
   take over Swedish iron ore mines

③ bombing of the Ruhr

④ Operation Royal Marine –
   floating mines down the Rhine

⑤ intervention in the Black Sea
   to interdict flow of Soviet
   oil from Baku

⑥ airstrikes against Baku

0   400 miles
0   500 km

action. This went beyond the risks of intervention in Finland to encompass a direct attack on the Soviet Union.[24]

Some senior British officials found the 'Baku project' attractive. For the MEW, it was an opportunity to bring down Germany by knocking out a key raw material. For the RAF, it offered a chance to show that air power really could be decisive. They dreamed of long-distance squadrons wreaking havoc on oil production with precision bombing.[25] Yet these plans never made much progress at the highest level in London.

In practice, no British leader was sufficiently desperate to think that attacking the Soviet Union was a good idea. Where the French looked to spark a new front in Southern Europe, the British preferred to keep the Eastern Mediterranean quiet while they concentrated on beating Germany. Chamberlain and Halifax were both certain that Nazi and Soviet ideologies pointed Germany and the USSR in different directions. When Chamberlain read Reynaud's proposals, 'he went through the ceiling'.[26]

Halifax and Rab Butler together discounted the idea that Britain had a responsibility to fight the Soviet Union on moral grounds. To counter suggestions for an anti-Soviet offensive, the foreign secretary highlighted the dangers. Not only would a war with the USSR antagonize the British left, but the Soviets might respond by attacking India. During the spring of 1940, Halifax attempted unsuccessfully to secure a rapprochement with the USSR, even sending Stafford Cripps on a mission to Moscow to try to get the Soviets to sever their trade with Germany. Growing demands for action against the Soviet Union, however, made it harder for British leaders to oppose other proposals to escalate the war.

When the Supreme War Council met again at the end of March, Chamberlain calmly talked out most of Reynaud's plans. He insisted that the Allies were still well able to fight a long war. The pressure to help the new French government was nonetheless very strong. So the conference agreed to British plans for offensive operations: Churchill's long-standing project to float mines down the River Rhine ('Operation Royal Marine') and the mining of Norwegian waters.

No sooner had the decision been taken than the French hesitated. Anxious about German retaliation, the Reynaud government demanded a three-month delay before the Rhine was mined. The British decided to go ahead in any case with their Norwegian plan. A warning note to inform Norway and Sweden of British intentions was despatched on 5 April. The next day, Royal Navy ships set out, ready to start minelaying two days later. In case the Germans reacted with their own invasion of Norway, the British also readied ground troops for pre-emptive landings at Narvik.

After four months of prevarication, the British had therefore settled on the plan that Churchill had originally put forward. The ice in the northern Baltic was just about to melt. Had the Narvik operation been launched when it was first suggested, it might well have imposed a significant burden on the German war economy. It would probably not have brought the decisive rewards that the MEW promised, but it would certainly have contributed to the long-term attrition of German resources. The diplomatic cost of violating Scandinavian neutrality might well have been high, but domestically, a Norwegian mining mission in late 1939 would have offered much-needed evidence of the government's decisiveness and commitment to victory.

The more elaborate schemes for Scandinavia and Baku indicated the consequences for Allied strategy once confidence in a long war started to diminish. Whatever his other flaws, Chamberlain at least applied a rational brake to the recklessness. What he could not fully resist was the resultant pressure to escalate the Allies' military endeavours. The plans that were actually put into action still fitted Britain's initial strategy of limited attacks on the enemy economy. Had it not been for other events, however, the summer of 1940 might have seen the 'Baku project' carried through to its logical conclusion: a great war against Communism and Nazism. That might have been morally sound, but it would also have been strategically disastrous.

'THE LIMITS OF TIME'

At the end of January, Lord Stamp presented ministers with the results of his investigation into national resources. Stamp argued that the military programmes settled on at the start of the war were not only out of sync with each other, but also fundamentally mismatched with what the country could actually do.[27] The shift to war production and the increase in shipping prices had hit the value of Britain's exports, which were six points lower in 1939 than in 1938. Meanwhile the UK was also having to spend more overseas – not only for imported materials, which had themselves gone up in price, but also to hire additional shipping. Consequently, the balance of payments had worsened. The deficit for the first year of the war was already shaping up to be £400 million. Stamp reiterated that the UK could not safely cover more than £150 million of this from its currency reserves if it wanted to fight a long war. Another £100 million might be borrowed from the Empire or raised by the sale of overseas assets, and a new export drive (which would compete with military production) might at the most optimistic earn £50 million. That would still mean a hole of £100 million in the first year alone, which would have to be covered either by selling assets and reserves more quickly or by scaling back on imports.

The figures on manpower made even worse reading. To meet the forces' programmes, Britain would have to increase greatly the engineering workforce, from 1.86 million at the start of the war to 4 million by late summer 1941. Stamp pointed out that this would involve 'an occupational and geographical re-distribution of the population in a limited time for which there is no precedent, either in the last war or in totalitarian Germany'.

Little progress had been made by the end of 1939. Prolonged, regionally concentrated unemployment had left deep pools of jobless workers who could not immediately make the transition into the munitions industry. Civilian consumption was still high, so skilled labour was occupied on non-military production, and the government was unwilling to allow wage hikes in the defence industry in case it drove up inflation. Despite national agreement on the relaxation of union practices, job dilution was proceeding very slowly. For the moment, labour shortages were not holding back production, but within the next six to nine months, they would become so acute as to force a reduction in military output.

Stamp concluded that 'the programme of war effort is not capable of achievement *within the limits of time* specified, though we have no reason to suppose that it is not within our national capacity, given time enough and an adequate dynamic for the transfer of labour'. Continuing with current plans would only worsen the problems. Instead, Stamp wanted production targets scaled back, then reworked with better co-ordination. He insisted that he wanted to fight more sensibly, not less hard, but his proposed solution would mean accepting that there were economic limitations on an all-out pursuit of victory.[28]

Stamp's criticisms were fundamentally correct, but they had very little effect on plans for war production. Having considered his survey, the War Cabinet decided to put off the achievement of the fifty-five-division target for the army until some vague point in the future and to aim instead for the equipment of thirty-two divisions by the end of the second year of the war – which was what the Ministry of Supply and the Treasury were already doing in any case. For all the faults that existed in the administration of war industry, there was no overwhelming sense that mobilization had been so badly bodged that Britain needed to start again. Nor was there much demand in Whitehall or Westminster for a de-escalation of the war effort. On the contrary, the pressure on the government was to intervene more actively in order to solve the problems of production and provide the mass of munitions that would be necessary for the intense combat to come.[29]

The visions of total conflict that had loomed throughout the 1920s and 1930s were now to be fulfilled. Only the state could solve the problems of a crisis so huge, so complex, and so fundamental for national security. Even Stamp, scarcely a cheerleader for central planning, emphasized the need for increased official co-ordination if economic mobilization was to be carried through effectively.

Incrementally and individually, government departments were already taking a greater role in organizing the war economy. From the start of the year, the Ministry of Labour increased the work of government training centres and set up a scheme of area boards and production officers to co-ordinate the employment of skilled workers at a local level. Following the launch of an export drive in February, on 16 April the Board of Trade issued a statutory order cutting supplies of cotton and linen goods to British domestic wholesalers by 25 per cent.[30] At the National Joint Advisory Council, trade unionists and business leaders negotiated about the best ways to control wages, profits and inflation. Both groups wanted more central planning. By the start of May the Ministry of Labour had agreed to impose stricter controls on employment in order to minimize shortages and avoid the poaching of skilled workers.[31]

Even Sir John Simon's second war budget, presented on 23 April 1940, showed signs of this escalatory pressure. The chancellor kept the

basic rate of income tax at 7s. 6d., the level announced the previous
September, but put up the top rate of income tax to seventeen shillings
in the pound and lowered the threshold at which it was charged from
£2,000 to £1,500 of income a year. Duties on beer, whisky and tobacco
also went up, as did postal charges. Simon introduced a new purchase
tax, levied on wholesalers of non-essential consumer goods, which
would eventually be levied in October 1940 at a rate of 25 per cent. The
budget also included new legislation limiting company dividends as
a means to encourage investment in government bonds, but Simon
rejected Keynes' suggestion of compulsory saving. Instead, he espoused
the virtue of increased voluntary investment in the National Savings
scheme. All this was meant to enable an increase in government expenditure from £1,817 million in 1939/40 to at least £2,000 million in
1940/41.[32]

Privately, Simon had confessed to his Treasury advisors that when it
came to tackling inflation, he found himself 'in a bog'. He did not feel
for the moment that he could ask basic-rate income tax payers to bear
any more of the burden than they already were, nor that he could
impose income tax, compulsory saving or wage restrictions on the bulk
of the working class. It was, he acknowledged in private, 'absurdly
optimistic' to believe that National Savings (which had raised only
£132 million since September 1939) could assuage the inflationary
dragons let loose by the war. Hence the introduction of purchase tax –
the precursor to VAT – which as well as raising revenue was also
intended to soak up consumer expenditure without increasing the Cost
of Living Index. If neither of these measures fully answered the question of 'how to pay for the war', Simon's announcement that voluntary
restrictions on personal expenditure were now 'on trial' might have
cleared the way for more compulsion in the future.

Elsewhere, too, the waters of war lapped over the banks of limitation. Despite the initial focus on raw materials and machine tools, the
Air Ministry had always wanted to buy more aircraft from the US as a
way to accelerate the expansion of the RAF. With all British and French
production capacity taken up by government orders, buying from
America was the only way to get more planes. By early 1940, the British
had ordered 1,320 aircraft and 1,200 engines in America. In contrast,
the French had already placed orders for 2,000 aircraft and over
6,000 engines. When the French announced that they were sending a

mission to the US to buy still more planes, Chamberlain was reluctant to follow suit. Whatever America's long-term potential, in the short term US air production was well behind that of Britain. A sudden growth of America's aircraft industry might interfere with its supply of machine tools for British factories. The British, however, could not ignore French insistence on the importance of spending now in order to build up US capacity for the future, or American official enthusiasm for Allied investment.[33]

During March, the Allies agreed to order another 4,600 aircraft and 8,000 engines, for delivery by September 1941. They would cost $614 million, spread 60:40 between France and the UK. The effect of the finance on the US aircraft industry was absolutely crucial. In the eighteen months from the start of 1939, France and Britain spent about twice as many dollars on aircraft orders as the US military. They thereby began to provide the funding that would kick-start American war production.

The numbers of aircraft ordered from America were still relatively small relative to the output of British factories, but the implications for Britain's finances were significant. With the total for all dollar imports running at $199 million since September 1939, exports struggling and the need to restrain foreign expenditure recently re-emphasized, the decision to purchase US aircraft added in one swoop another $210 million (about £50 million) to what Britain would have to pay out in the second year of the war.

During the spring of 1940, the UK began gradually to head away from limitation and laissez-faire, and towards a war in which short-term strategic security trumped long-term financial caution and the state directed the economy for military and civilian ends. The apogee of these trends could not be reached under the National Government, but its inability to match escalation with action would play a key part in its replacement by a new administration.

'MISSED THE BUS'

While ministers struggled with how to scale up the war effort, the opposition had no such difficulties in intensifying their criticisms of the government. In Parliament, during the first months of 1940, Labour and Liberal attacks became more acute. The focus was 'patriotic' criticism of the government's lack of economic planning and co-operation.[34] Speaking in support of a Labour motion demanding the appointment of an economic supremo to oversee 'the successful prosecution of the war' at the start of February, for example, Herbert Morrison espoused the need for 'a general power of direction, of decision, and finally, of drive'. The Liberal Sir Archibald Sinclair complained: 'nobody feels the throb and rhythm of a powerful driving force operating from Whitehall or Downing Street in the economic field'.[35] It didn't matter that Labour and Liberals disagreed about exactly what 'planning' meant: both could agree that government inefficiency was endangering the nation. Given the difficulties of securing the blockade, equipping the armed services and shifting to military production, there were plenty of examples to demonstrate that, as Dalton put it, the government was being 'much too gentlemanly, too slow-witted and too traditional in the conduct of this war.'[36]

Labour's leaders remained more or less allied in their attitude to Chamberlain, despite a temporary wobble in March and April when it appeared that the prime minister might offer some of them office in return for entering into a new coalition.[37] They had to keep their nerve: if the cold war turned hot before they had deposed Chamberlain, then opposing him would become much more difficult. Yet as Ernest Bevin's increasingly antagonistic public statements made clear, there was little chance that a more intense war would secure Chamberlain's future. Speaking to the Transport and General Workers' Union festival in Bristol on 3 February 1940, he insisted that:

> If the Government is going to take the occasion of this war to invade the liberties of my people, I will lead the movement to resist this Government – or any other Government. This is not the only Government that can win the war: there is an alternative Government. The appetite for compulsion is growing and there is no ground for it.[38]

These were words for the brothers, since union bosses had already made it clear to the government and to employers that they were quite happy to see workers compelled, provided that they were brought in on the deal. Such interventions were also, however, shots across the government's bows. Only an administration that took account of trade-union opinion would be able successfully to mobilize the war economy.

During the first months of 1940, concerns that the UK was losing the initiative to Germany became more widespread among the political elite as a whole. The trend was most obvious in the editorials of *The Times*, which shifted from support for the government to criticisms of its organizational deficiencies. At the start of January, the paper declared that: 'Time is only on our side, our superiority in resources will only prove decisive, if we employ the time to mobilize our resources as efficiently as the enemy has mobilized his.'[39] *The Economist* and the *Manchester Guardian*, as well as *The Times*, criticized Simon's budget on the grounds that, as the latter headlined its leader, 'Too Little Courage' had been shown in driving on war on the home front.[40]

Among Conservatives too there was evidence of rising concern as the months of apparent inactivity wore on. Tory MPs who had left Westminster to serve with the colours experienced the problems in equipping the army at first hand. There was much regret at the failure to sustain the Finns. The group of dissident MPs around Leo Amery remained convinced that Chamberlain had to go. Amery and Macmillan were both asked to involve themselves in the Finnish Aid Bureau. This was meant to distract them, but instead it simply created further opportunities to attack the government. From the start of the year, the Cecils began putting together a 'Watching Committee' of MPs and peers who wanted to press for more determined action at home and abroad. By March, the Committee had twenty-eight members. Some of them also belonged to the Amery group, but others, such as Sir Patrick Spens, the chairman of the 1922 Committee, were normally outright supporters of Chamberlain.[41]

Frustration with the course of the war did not necessarily mean a desire to get rid of the party leader. In his diary for the first months of 1940, Cuthbert Headlam, a Tory politician who was setting himself up for selection as a candidate in a safe seat in Newcastle, expressed repeated concern about the Allies' readiness to withstand a German assault on the Western Front. He also recorded his support for the prime minister:

> I wonder how long Neville will last? The longer the better in my opinion both because he seems to me to be the right sort of war PM and also because I don't want Winston – and if anything happens to Neville, I can see no other choice at the moment but Winston – the country wants him.[42]

Among those who wanted Churchill rather than Chamberlain was the newspaper executive Cecil King. The nephew of the press baron Lord Rothermere, King was a director on the boards of two of the most remarkable newspapers of the late 1930s, the *Daily Mirror* and the *Sunday Pictorial*. King was a quiet Wykehamist with a progressive political outlook, a wide streak of rebellious arrogance and an almost pathological inability to deal with other people. At the *Daily Mirror* he had the good fortune to work with the editorial director Guy Bartholomew, a brilliant journalist who had helped to turn the *Daily Mirror* into a very successful newspaper during the First World War, and who now took the chance offered by falling circulations to reinvent it as a much more modern product. Using new techniques of market research, King and Bartholomew aimed to pitch the *Mirror* at the cohort of young, working-class consumers with disposable incomes who were emerging as a result of changes in Britain's economy. Gradually, during the second half of the 1930s, a paper that had come to look very old-fashioned turned into something that felt much more exciting: a jaunty blend of banner headlines and big pictures, with more human interest and sports stories than 'serious' news, but always keen to acknowledge the intelligence of its readers, and with a page of much-loved American-style cartoon strips. The changes were cautious and slow, and although the *Mirror* moved away from supporting the Conservatives after the 1935 election, it did not transfer its allegiance to Labour.[43]

In 1937, much to Bartholomew's annoyance, King poached a visionary young Welsh journalist from the offices of the *Daily Mirror*, Hugh Cudlipp, to be editor of the *Sunday Pictorial*. There, Cudlipp carried through with much greater speed many of the changes that King and Bartholomew were introducing at the *Mirror*, creating a strand of tabloid journalism that would play a proud role in British public life for the rest of the century. With King's support, Cudlipp also took a strong stance against appeasement, penning a series of powerful attacks on the government's pre-war foreign policy.

By 1939 the *Mirror* and the *Pictorial* were both selling about 1.4 million copies a week. That put them just behind the *Daily Mail*, and almost a million behind the *Daily Express*. Their circulation continued to rise after the outbreak of hostilities, and their tone became increasingly radical. Patriotic, entertaining and suspicious of the political establishment – they were to prove well suited to the mood of the country at war.[44]

Given his newspapers' rising sales, King thought he had good claim to know what the public wanted. For all that he thought of himself as a democrat, however, like more old-fashioned pressmen he also liked the idea of wielding influence in political intrigues behind the scenes. He loathed Chamberlain, and for the previous few months, both papers had been boosting Churchill for the premiership. Not for the last time, King hoped to play a part in toppling a prime minister. On 8 February, he had lunch with the first lord of the admiralty and his family, an occasion he recorded in his diary. Churchill, he noted, drank glasses of beer and port alternately during the meal, but claimed to have given up brandy for the duration.

King derided Chamberlain as 'too old, of dreary appearance, with a sorry record of appeasement' and lacking 'all the qualities of leadership in anxious times'.[45] Telling Churchill that 'the country' regarded him as a real leader, King described a survey by Mass-Observation (a body of which Churchill had never heard), which had found that he was the popular choice to take over the reins at Number 10.

Well aware that he was speaking to a pressman, Churchill's response was simultaneously guarded, misleading and revealing. He professed his loyalty to Chamberlain – a 'tough buccaneer', 'a hundred per cent for vigorous prosecution of the war' and much better than Anthony Eden: he preferred Chamberlain over Eden as prime minister 'by eight to one'.[46] Anyway, 'the premiership was not much of a catch these days'. Not, of course, that he would refuse his country's call, but:

> he would only take it if offered him by common consent; that he would not take the job as a prize in a fight, as then he would have two fights on his hands – with his opponents in the Party and with the Germans. His attitude was that Chamberlain had the entire support of the Conservative Party; therefore he was quite safe. And public opinion? To hell with public opinion . . . in time of war the machinery of Government is so strong it can afford largely to ignore popular feeling.[47]

King thought Churchill an antiquated figure – 'Of the current trends of political thought . . . he knows little and cares less' – but got the impression that 'he likes being at the Admiralty, and has no particular reason to change the current arrangement. He thinks we are going to win – he doesn't know how, or why, or when – so why worry?'[48] Since he had little time for Attlee ('very limited intelligence and no personality', he wrote of him at a later meeting: 'If one heard he was getting £6 a week in the service of the East Ham Corporation, one would be surprised he was earning so much'[49]), King was baffled at Churchill's complaint that Labour was pressing the government 'very hard'. Churchill, he recorded, 'fatuously seemed to think' that Labour 'could at a pinch turn the Government out'.[50] King might have had more of a grasp of the new politics, but Churchill had a better understanding of the old.

At the end of March, the death of Sir John Gilmour, the minister of shipping, gave Chamberlain the chance to stage a reshuffle that might have appeased his opponents. There were rumours that he intended to offer Cabinet seats to Labour. Churchill advised Chamberlain to put Kingsley Wood in charge of the war economy in order to answer some of his enemies' criticisms. When the reshuffle came, however, the only major change was that Churchill took over the chairmanship of the Military Co-ordination Sub-Committee.[51]

Chamberlain argued that he had reallocated the Cabinet posts to get a better fit with his ministers' personalities, but the reshuffle that wasn't infuriated his Conservative critics. Not only had their complaints been ignored, but none of them had been given a place in the government. The day after the reshuffle was announced, the Watching Committee held its first formal meeting. Lord Salisbury then visited the prime minister to suggest he form a smaller War Cabinet, relieved of departmental responsibilities and therefore free to concentrate on strategy. Chamberlain was polite but dismissive. From mid-April, the Watching Committee became increasingly convinced of the need for a more fundamental reworking, up to and including a change of prime minister. Salisbury tried out the idea on Churchill and Halifax, but with little success.[52]

Despite these signs of dissidence, Chamberlain remained confident. On 4 April, in a widely reported speech to the Conservative Central Council, he claimed to feel 'ten times as confident of victory' as he had at the start of the war. For all the rumours and bluster of the last seven months, Hitler had not launched his much-promised offensive when he'd had the chance. Now the Allies were much stronger than they had been at the war's beginning. Their military and economic might would now allow them to set the tempo. Chamberlain put things simply.

Hitler had 'missed the bus'.[53] Five days later, as British ships began laying mines off Narvik, German forces invaded Denmark and Norway.

'TO TURN IN A MOMENT OF
DIFFICULTY'

The Germans had been planning an operation to secure the iron ore
supply from Scandinavia since December 1939. Wary of Allied
counter-action, they prioritized speed of action. German airborne
forces seized key airfields, and warships landed troops at ports along
the Danish and Norwegian coasts, including Oslo, Trondheim and
Narvik. Denmark fell swiftly. Norwegian resistance was more prolonged, although much disadvantaged by the surprise of the initial
attack and German command of the air.

The invasion took the Allies by surprise. The British had assumed
that the enemy would respond to their minelaying, not that they would
pre-empt it. They took it for granted that British naval superiority in
the North Sea would deter Germany from landing troops from the sea.
Intelligence information that, when put together, provided strong evidence of what the Germans actually intended was assessed piecemeal,
and discounted by the armed services and Foreign Office.[54] When the
first reports were received that the German fleet had left port, the
Admiralty thought that the Kriegsmarine was trying to break its commerce raiders out into the Atlantic. The British had already loaded
troops aboard Royal Navy cruisers to act as a rapid reaction force in
case their minelaying sparked a German invasion of Norway. Now
these units were rapidly disembarked, and the ships raced off in misplaced expectation of a naval battle on the route to the open ocean.

As the scale of the German invasion became clear, requests for help
from the embattled Norwegians competed with the original aim of
interrupting the flow of Swedish iron ore. Churchill tried to keep the
focus on Narvik. The northern port needed to be secured before Allied
forces were sent further south. Now that he was chair of the Military
Co-ordination Sub-Committee, Churchill had more influence on strategy
than before, but he still had to secure the approval of the War Cabinet.
There, Halifax and Chamberlain were strongly influenced by the need
to be seen to be helping the Norwegians. They thought Allied forces

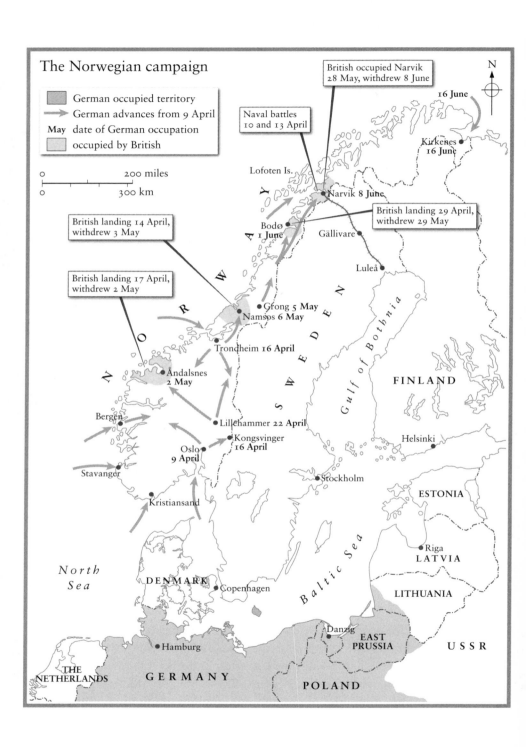

The Norwegian campaign

German occupied territory
German advances from 9 April
May date of German occupation
occupied by British

0   200 miles
0   300 km

British occupied Narvik
28 May, withdrew 8 June

Naval battles
10 and 13 April

16 June

Kirkenes
16 June

Lofoten Is.

Narvik 8 June

British landing 14 April,
withdrew 3 May

British landing 29 April,
withdrew 29 May

Bodø
1 June

Gällivare

British landing 17 April,
withdrew 2 May

Luleå

Grong 5 May
Namsos 6 May

Trondheim 16 April

Gulf of Bothnia

FINLAND

Åndalsnes
2 May

Bergen

Lillehammer 22 April

Helsinki

Kongsvinger
16 April

Oslo
9 April

Stavanger

Stockholm

ESTONIA

Kristiansand

Riga
LATVIA

*North
Sea*

DENMARK Copenhagen

LITHUANIA

Baltic Sea

Danzig EAST
PRUSSIA

USSR

Hamburg

THE
NETHERLANDS   GERMANY

POLAND

N

should aid in the attempted recapture of Trondheim. Between 10 and
13 April, the Royal Navy trapped the German ships that had carried
troops to Narvik in the surrounding fjords. All were either sunk or
scuttled. In London, this raised expectations that the port itself would
be rapidly retaken. Attention shifted to planning an assault on Trondheim, with landings at Åndalsnes and Namsos between 14 and 19 April,
designed to envelop the defenders from both sides.

In fact, Narvik proved a tough nut to crack. With only a small force
available to him, the British military commander on the scene, General
Macksey, proved unwilling to launch an amphibious assault. Instead,
he insisted on landing outside the town and advancing against it overland with the Norwegians. That would all take time. Further south, the
attempt to launch a pincer movement against Trondheim rapidly turned
into a debacle.

Ill-prepared British units suffered from frequent changes of plan.
Crucially, they lacked protection against the German air force. The
Luftwaffe laid waste to the ports at which the British had landed and
provided effective support to German troops on the ground. After
heavy losses and little progress, it was decided on 26 April that the
Allies should evacuate central Norway and concentrate solely on Narvik. There, much to London's frustration, an assault was repeatedly
delayed by concerns about the strength of the German defences. Not
until the very end of May did Allied troops finally take the city, only to
be evacuated shortly afterwards anyway as the position on the Western
Front deteriorated. On 8 June, that evacuation cost the Royal Navy the
aircraft carrier HMS *Glorious* (together with two destroyers), sunk by
the German battlecruisers *Gneisenau* and *Scharnhorst* with the loss of
almost all hands.[55]

As April turned to May, it was clear that something had gone very
wrong in Norway. Despite the reassertion of British naval dominance –
the fighting around Narvik cost the Germans half their entire destroyer
strength – the land campaign revealed significant deficiencies. The
tactical difficulties faced by British troops were compounded by British
strategists' uncertainty about what they were trying to achieve and the
disastrous assumption that they could improvise an amphibious operation in inhospitable terrain without adequate air support. This was a
really critical point for naval warfare for the rest of the war. Shore-based
aircraft were a major threat to navies at sea, and they were even more

dangerous if ships had to come close to shore to support a landing or evacuation. Neither the equipment nor the doctrine of the Royal Navy between the wars had prepared it to fight the sort of battle it had to undertake in Norway. Its aircraft carriers were well armoured, but the planes that flew off them couldn't compete with modern fighters. In the Norwegian campaign, there were simply too few of them to challenge German dominance of the skies.

Churchill was as guilty as anyone of underestimating the challenges, and he and Admiral Pound compounded the problems by trying to interfere in operations from the Admiralty War Room. Unlike other ministers, however, Churchill had at least remembered the point of intervening in Norway and tried to prioritize Narvik – an objective that would have fallen more quickly if forces had not been diverted towards Trondheim.[56]

News of the reverse in Norway at the end of April angered the government's opponents in London. Confusion, delay and disappointment: the campaign seemed to have borne out all their criticisms of the way the war was being run. Wary that Churchill was being talked of as a possible successor, Chamberlain covered his flank by giving him the right personally to direct and guide the chiefs of staff without prior consultation with the Military Co-ordination Sub-Committee. This was a step closer to his becoming an over-arching defence supremo. Some Chamberlain loyalists were disgusted by the fact that Churchill had profited personally from the disaster, and the Tory whips spread the story that the Norwegian debacle had been his fault in the first place. This only served to further enrage Churchill's supporters on the backbenches.[57]

Leo Amery now functioned as a crucial link between the All Party Action Group, the 'Glamour Boys', formerly associated with Eden, and the Watching Committee. It was decided that the debate on 7 May on whether to adjourn Parliament for the Whit recess – normally a formality – would be used to show the scale of opposition to the government's conduct of the war. Through Clement Davies and Harold Macmillan, these dissident groups were in contact with the Labour leadership. Davies tried to get Attlee and Greenwood to force the Commons to divide on the adjournment debate – effectively turning it into a vote of confidence in the government. Labour had stepped up its attacks still further during April, but Attlee refused to act as a battering ram for the rebels. Labour might come to the nation's aid if sufficient cracks had already opened up on the government benches, but he would not run the risk of reuniting the Conservative Party – and appearing unpatriotic – by leading the charge.[58]

As the debate neared, both the government's supporters and its opponents knew they were in for a fight. David Margesson, the government chief whip, told the Conservative MP 'Chips' Channon: 'we are on the eve of the greatest political crisis since August 1931'.[59] No one, however, was certain what the outcome would be.

In the autumn of 1938, the government had had a majority of 222 MPs. Since then, that had been whittled away by wartime absences, disagreements over strategy and by-elections. In the summer of 1939, however, similar votes of confidence had been won by margins of 164 and 169 votes. In May 1940, as he set the government's formidable whipping operation under way, Margesson was aiming for a majority of a hundred.[60] Chamberlain, surveying his prospects, thought he would once more be able to win over wavering Conservatives. The worst scenario he envisioned was that the government's majority would be reduced to just over sixty votes. If so, he planned to carry on in office but make another appeal to Labour to enter the government.[61]

What would subsequently be called the 'Norway Debate' began on 7 May 1940. It would be remembered as an occasion of remarkable parliamentary theatre. Attlee began the attack on the government: 'The Prime Minister talked about missing buses. What about all the buses which he and his associates have missed since 1931?'[62] Sir Roger Keyes, the Conservative MP for Portsmouth and hero of the First World War, arrived in the full uniform of an admiral of the fleet to attack the management of the naval war. Amery addressed to the government the words Oliver Cromwell had supposedly used to the Long Parliament: 'You have sat here too long for any good you have been doing. Depart, I say, and let us have done with you. In the name of God, go!'[63]

Like pretty much all the critical speeches, Keyes' and Amery's attacks were strategically misconceived. They lamented the lack of British intervention in Finland – which might have dragged Britain into a catastrophic war with the Soviet Union – and asked why more attention had not been paid to recapturing Trondheim – which would have done nothing to cut Germany's iron ore supplies. No one involved later reflected that they had been demanding action that would have made things even worse. What mattered – at the time and afterwards – was that they were condemning indecision and delay. Both of those certainly had characterized the government's tortuous discussions over Scandinavia.

The next morning, the Parliamentary Labour Party agreed to press for the debate to be carried to a division. Forewarned, Chamberlain sent his parliamentary private secretary, Lord Dunglass (later Sir Alec Douglas-Home), to offer the Tory rebels another reshuffle if they backed him in the lobbies. The offer was rejected.[64] That afternoon, Morrison announced that Labour would move for a vote: 'The issues of the war are too great for us to risk losing it by keeping in office men who have been there for a long time and have not shown themselves too well fitted for the task.'[65] Chamberlain reacted angrily:

> I say this to my friends in the House – and I have friends in the House. No Government can prosecute a war effectively unless it has public and Parliamentary support. I accept the challenge. I welcome it indeed. At least we shall see who is with us and who is against us, and I call on my friends to support us in the Lobby tonight.[66]

This was a direct challenge to Conservative rebels and an appeal to his majority. If it wielded the threat that his opponents would be made to seem unpatriotic, these scarcely seemed like the words of a national, non-partisan leader. They infuriated Chamberlain's opponents, who continued their attacks.

David Lloyd George spoke, putting the blame on inadequate pre-war preparations and telling Churchill not to turn himself into 'an air raid shelter to keep the splinters from hitting his comrades'.[67] Duff Cooper stood up to remind members that they had been here before: 'Again and again we have met in this House, sometimes summoned suddenly in an emergency, always to record a setback, a disaster, always to listen to the disappointment, the astonishment and the surprise of the Prime Minister.'[68] He too demanded a restructuring of the Cabinet. Closing the debate for the government, Churchill protested:

> Exception has been taken because the Prime Minister said he appealed to his friends. He thought he had some friends, and I hope he has some friends. He certainly had a good many when things were going well. I

think it would be most ungenerous and unworthy of the British character, and the Conservative party, to turn in a moment of difficulty . . .[69]

The House then divided. Two hundred and eighty-one MPs voted for the government, two hundred against it.

It was not immediately clear what this meant. Although well short of the whips' target, the government majority was certainly not obliterated. Only thirty-eight government MPs had chosen to vote with the 'noes'. The list of those voting against was predictably full of anti-government rebels. All the sound and fury of the previous two days had actually done very little to change how MPs voted in the lobbies. This was a significant revolt, but it was far from decisive. What mattered was how it was interpreted. Even those who had supported the government saw it as evidence that Chamberlain would have to engage in a major reconstruction and bring Labour into office.[70]

Notwithstanding the battering he had received, Chamberlain had not given up on the premiership. Getting rid of those of his ministers most associated with appeasement would answer his critics and make room for Labour. Simon and Hoare offered themselves up as sacrificial lambs. Despite Chamberlain's mutual antipathy with the Labour leaders, he hoped they might accept a patriotic appeal to enter office under him. If they would not, plans needed to be put in place for an alternative administration. Bearing in mind the party's majority in the Commons and the difficulties of a wartime general election, a new government would still have to be led by a senior Conservative. On the afternoon of 9 May, Chamberlain, accompanied by Margesson, held a meeting with Churchill and Halifax and asked which of them would put themselves forward to replace him.[71]

Many people, including the king, the Labour leaders and much of the Tory party, presumed that Halifax's blend of moral probity and level-headedness meant that he ought to succeed Chamberlain. Halifax, however, immediately announced that he was unwilling to become premier. The problem was not constitutional – a means could have been found for a peer to lead the government despite not having a seat in the Commons – but rather political. Halifax knew that if he took the job, he would have to establish his prime ministerial authority with Churchill squatting like some ominous bullfrog on the lily-pad of military strategy. As a major figure in a Churchill-led Cabinet, on the other hand, he might be able to serve the nation by directing his rival's enthusiasm onto the paths of righteousness. If Churchill made such a bad job of the premiership that he had to be replaced, then perhaps a regretful Halifax would have to do his duty to country, God and king, wield the axe and take up the reins.

Churchill was affected by no such considerations. Kingsley Wood, who had now abandoned his former loyalty to Chamberlain on the basis that he could never form a national government, had already advised the first lord of the admiralty to face down any attempt to install Halifax as prime minister. If Chamberlain could not continue, Churchill said, he was very ready to take his place.[72]

It was still far from certain, however, that Chamberlain would actually have to depart. When he met with Halifax, Churchill, Attlee and Greenwood that evening, indeed, he acted as if he expected to be able to carry on. Chamberlain asked the Labour leaders whether they were willing to serve under him, and if not, whether they would serve under someone else. For years, Labour had suffered under the lash of Chamberlain's scorn. Now Attlee and Greenwood were being asked to decide his future. They were already resolved that they would not join a government of which he remained head. The earlier discussion about who else might become prime minister was not disclosed to them, but such was their animosity to Chamberlain that they were in fact willing to accept either Halifax or Churchill as an alternative. They made clear that the answer to Chamberlain's first question would probably be 'no', but they also insisted that they would have to take both issues to the National Executive of the Labour Party, which was meeting the next day in Bournemouth in preparation for the party's annual conference.

This was the most important moment in the whole process. Attlee and Greenwood were not actually under any obligation to talk to their party. Had they put aside their hatred of the prime minister and accepted Chamberlain's offer of places in a new government, they might have met the demands of national unity, but they would also probably have split their party. Had they just refused outright, Chamberlain might have reached out to alternative collaborators, including Herbert Morrison, who was waiting eagerly in the wings. As it was, the self-imposed requirement to seek the opinion of the Executive enabled Attlee and Greenwood to preserve the integrity of the Labour movement without appearing unpatriotic.[73]

It was as well for them that this preliminary meeting happened when it did. On the early morning of 10 May, German forces attacked Holland, Belgium and France. The opening of the major Nazi offensive in the west seemed to offer a lifeline to Chamberlain's premiership. Who could refuse his appeals to enter a new, more widely 'national' ministry in their country's hour of need?

The answer was the Labour leaders, now in Bournemouth and therefore at one remove from the military news flowing into London.[74] Labour's NEC duly passed a resolution that, while the party would not serve under Chamberlain, it would take 'its share of responsibility, as a full partner, in a new Government which, under a new Prime Minister, commands the confidence of the nation'.[75] In response to a phone call from Downing Street, Attlee dictated the decision down the phone, then returned to London. Chamberlain now recognized that he could not continue as prime minister. He went to Buckingham Palace to offer the king his resignation. Churchill was immediately called to take his place.

From late that evening and over the following weekend, Churchill and Attlee hammered out the membership of a new government. It was more genuinely 'national' than its predecessor, with Liberal as well as Labour members. There would be a five-man War Cabinet: Churchill, as prime minister and minister of defence, Chamberlain as lord president, Halifax as foreign secretary, Attlee as lord privy seal and Greenwood as minister without portfolio. Simon was booted upstairs, with a viscountcy, to become lord chancellor. Hoare, whom Churchill had never forgiven for the Government of India Act, was despatched as ambassador to Madrid. Kingsley Wood was rewarded for his disloyalty to Chamberlain by being made chancellor, Ernest Bevin joined the government as minister of labour, and Herbert Morrison came in as minister of supply. Churchill remained minister of defence, but the service ministries were divided up between the three parties, with Archibald Sinclair becoming air minister, Anthony Eden moving into the War Office and the Labour politician A. V. Alexander becoming first lord of the admiralty. Lord Beaverbrook was appointed to lead the Ministry of Aircraft Production, a new department created by Churchill in an effort to increase the supply of planes to the RAF.

These were all significant changes in leadership that marked a clear distance from the former administration, but two-thirds of Chamberlain's ministers continued to hold office under his successor. This reflected one of the key political realities of May 1940. The Conservatives retained a dominant majority in the Commons. Most of them still supported Chamberlain. When Churchill entered the Commons as prime minister for the first time, to promise that he had nothing to offer but blood, toil, tears and sweat, the Conservative benches remained stonily silent. When Chamberlain arrived, they stood up and cheered. The greatest winner from the political upheaval was the Labour Party. With less than a third of the Commons, it got sixteen places in the new Cabinet and two-fifths of the War Cabinet. Despite signs of restlessness when the Bournemouth conference finally discussed the NEC's decision on 13 May, the Labour movement entered office more or less united and in control of its own destiny. It was the greatest success thus far of Attlee's time as leader, and it gave him and his party a position on which they could capitalize in years to come. With German troops advancing rapidly through the Low Countries and Conservative backbenchers infuriated by the overturning of the political tables, however, both the war against Nazism and the war for socialism still had to be won.[76]

'HE'S NEVER DONE ANYTHING, HOWEVER HARD HE'S TRIED'

It was politicians, not public opinion, who despatched Chamberlain. By the time he left office, however, he was not a popular prime minister. The decisive change in mood happened very quickly. As the situation in Scandinavia grew worse in April, Mass-Observation was surprised to note the 'comparative absence of any inclination to attach blame to the Government for incompetency, half-heartedness or tardiness'. Instead, people were angry with the newspapers and the BBC, which had overstated British successes at the start of the campaign and were now having to backtrack on their earlier enthusiasm.[77] Even on 26 April, the *News Chronicle* reported a BIPO survey which found that 57 per cent of respondents approved of Chamberlain as prime minister. This was a figure higher than he had enjoyed in the aftermath of Hore-Belisha's resignation at the start of the year.[78]

That all changed at the start of May. When Chamberlain took to the airwaves on 2 May to explain British failures in Norway, a twenty-year-old woman in Great Baddow, Essex, recorded her reaction for M-O:

> Effect of Chamberlain's speech negative, disappointing, however much I try to look on the bright side (When my sister told me about the evacuation of southern Norway yesterday I did not believe her). Chamberlain seemed all the time to be trying to make excuses for a weak policy. Effect on my family the same, only more so. It's a loss of prestige for us, says my father and my sister's young man.[79]

Reports of Chamberlain's opening statement in the Commons on 7 May occasioned strong responses:

> 'Bastard Chamberlain.'
>   'Well I don't really know who's to blame for the whole thing, but from Chamberlain's speech I would say that he's got the wind up this time.'
>   'He's grown stale, and he's got a nasty habit of saying "my efforts" and "what I've tried to do"; that I don't like at all. He's never done anything however hard he's tried.'[80]

The BIPO's poll in early May indeed revealed that only 33 per cent of those asked approved of Chamberlain as prime minister, whereas 60 per cent disapproved. Even some of those who supported Chamberlain now doubted he was up to running the war. 'I think Chamberlain is our proper leader', ran one of the responses collected by Mass-Observation in the middle of the Norway debate in the Commons. 'Personally I wouldn't like to see him go. But I'd like to see him more ruthless. He's too much of a gentleman for the man we're fighting against.'[81] Of course, people had been saying this sort of thing for years, and it was hard to believe that the prime minister would actually be displaced: 'It reminds me of the other "Chamberlain must go" outcries . . . he weathered the others all right. He's there for the duration.'[82] On the final day of the Norway debate, the young law librarian in Bristol who was keeping a diary for M-O stayed up to hear the result. Presuming that Chamberlain had won through yet again, he

> left a bulletin for father to read six hours later, when he left for work. In tabloid style, I headlined:
> GOVERNMENT WINS 281–200
> CHURCHILL'S APPEAL SWAYS HOUSE

WE ARE IN GREATER PERIL THAN LAST WAR – FORGET PARTY –
SAYS FIRST LORD.

Father wrote on my bulletin, 'Thanks old man, best result, I think'.[83]

When the news finally broke that Chamberlain might have to resign, people wondered who would replace him. In Caister army camp, near Great Yarmouth in Norfolk, Denis Argent, a pacifist who had been conscripted to serve on labouring duties in the Non-Combatant Corps, recorded the reaction of his colleagues on 10 May. 'Several blokes . . . had got hold of papers' and were disappointed that all the news was about Chamberlain rather than the opening of the German attack in the west.

> The result was that lunchtime talk was chiefly of necessary government changes, with suggestions for Prime Minister chiefly favouring Church-ill. No one had a good word for Chamberlain at our table, and Halifax wasn't even mentioned. Eden seemed to hold high favour amongst us pacifists . . . Rather amazing, and two people mentioned this to me – was the fact that the *Mail* found itself forced at long last to attack Chamberlain.[84]

When Mass-Observation collected reactions to the restructured gov-ernment three days later, they found cautious but worried approval for the new prime minister. As one man put it: 'I think it's grand for the country, but hard on the individual. Churchill will slaughter the lot of us, but win the war.'[85]

14

The Battle of France

Everyone knew that there might be a major campaign on the Western Front in the early summer of 1940. Even the enthusiasm for economic warfare and new theatres of operation, so evident in Allied strategy since the start of the war, came in reaction to the presumed alternative: a climactic struggle in the cockpit of Europe between the German and Allied armies. It was widely anticipated that such a confrontation would be bloody, terrible and decide the outcome of the war. What came as a surprise was how quickly it was all over. Within weeks of its formation, Churchill's new government was faced with a dramatically altered strategic situation: France defeated, Germany triumphant and British forces sent scurrying back across the Channel. France's rapid fall, and the expulsion of British forces from mainland Europe, shaped the rest of Britain's war in the west.

THE SHOCK OF BATTLE

The initial German blow landed in the north-west on 10 May.[1] Spear-headed by airborne assaults on key locations, German Army Group B rapidly cracked open the Dutch and Belgian border defences and pushed towards Amsterdam and Brussels. In response, General Gamelin ordered French and British troops to move forward from the defences they had prepared, to link up with the Belgians and halt the German advance. By 14 May, they had taken up positions on the River Dyle, just as Dutch forces surrendered after the bombing of Rotterdam. The next day, French, British and Belgian units managed to repel German attacks along the river line.

Had the Germans been following the plans they had initially drawn up for their attack in the west, this defence of the Dyle might have represented a reasonable success. The German high command had originally aimed not at an outright military victory over France, but rather the capture of air and sea bases in Belgium from which the UK could more easily be attacked. This limited operation was militarily practicable, but offered the Germans little hope of the decisive victory they needed if they were to avoid a repeat of the last war. On 10 January, a German aeroplane carrying an officer with secret documents relating to the plan crashed in Mechelen in Belgium. Their loss stimulated the introduction of a new scheme, in which the main German effort would be undertaken by Army Group A, further south, through the forests of the Ardennes. It would then curve to the north-west, cutting off and destroying the Allied forces trapped to the north.

In practice, therefore, the Franco-British advance into Belgium had all the success of a hedgehog sticking its head into a food can. Even as Allied troops moved towards the Dyle on 13 May, the leading units of Army Group A had already traversed the Ardennes and fought their way across the River Meuse, defeating the poorly prepared French reserve divisions that opposed them. Mal-coordinated French counter-attacks failed to recapture these bridgeheads. On 15 and 16 May, German armoured units broke out. Over the following days, as French and British troops in Belgium withdrew to avoid encirclement, the Allies only managed to inflict local injuries on the dangerously over-extended German advance. On 20 May, Gamelin was relieved of his post and replaced by General Weygand. That same evening, the first German tanks reached the Channel at the mouth of the Somme. German Army Group A now formed a block across the rear of the Allied armies trapped to the north, while Army Group B pressed against their front, seeking to cut them off from the sea.

Detached from the reality of the confused forces in the northern pocket, Weygand attempted to organize a Franco-British break out towards the south. This resulted in a small attack by British tanks and infantry south of Arras on 21 May, but plans for a larger operation never got off the ground. In fact, it became increasingly obvious to those caught inside the trap that the only viable option – particularly as the Belgian army disintegrated in the north – was to hold a collapsing perimeter for as long as possible while the troops within were evacuated by sea. Worried by the pace of the advance and eager to assert his supremacy over his generals, on 24 May Hitler told them to halt, slowing the pace of German ground assaults on the pocket and thereby aiding the evacuation. From 26 May, under heavy air attack from the Luftwaffe, British ships began to take off soldiers from the port of Dunkirk and the surrounding beaches. Over the next week, 198,315 British and 139,111 Allied personnel were rescued. Most of the latter were French troops, who received orders to evacuate only on 29 May. On 4 June, with all the British capable of escape gone, the last French troops manning the defences surrendered.

The Germans now turned south. On 6 June, they breached the new line the French had set up on the River Somme. On 10 June, after a lengthy period of vacillation, Italy joined the war on Germany's side, attacking southern France in an effort to grab her own share of the spoils from her defeated neighbour and opening new theatres of operations against the British in the Mediterranean and Africa. On 14 June, the Germans reached Paris. The French government had left the capital, moving along roads crowded with refugees, four days earlier. While isolated units continued to fight against the Germans, and forces in the south successfully held off the Italians, organized French military resistance was effectively at an end. The French high command was already demanding an armistice. On 16 June, Marshal Philippe Pétain, the hero of the First World War, replaced Reynaud as prime minister. The next day, the new French government opened negotiations with the Germans and Pétain told French forces that they would have to stop fighting. On 22 June, France signed an armistice with Germany.

The durability of the French army had been a cornerstone of British strategic planning since the war began. Its large size, modern armaments and massive fortifications were all expected to forestall German attacks until Allied economic power could be brought to bear. All this made the sudden collapse of May–June 1940 all the more shocking. What had happened?

STRANGE DEFEAT

The popular iconography of the Fall of France was quickly established: German tanks crushing all before them, dive bombers screaming down

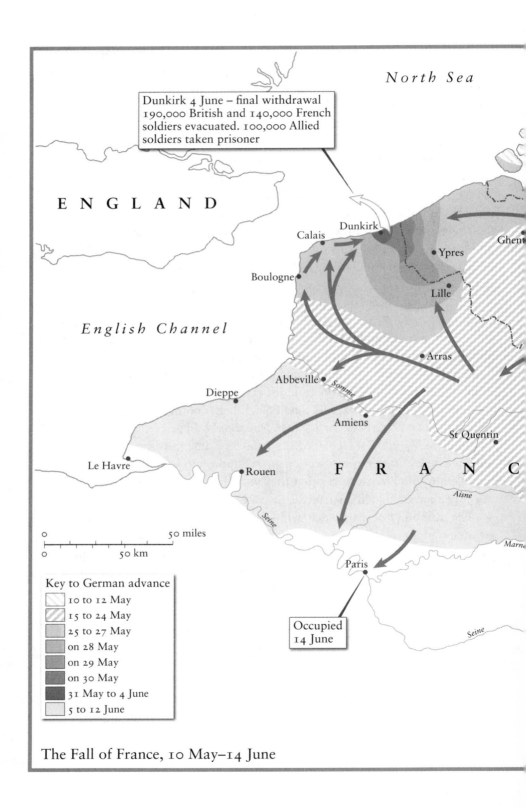

North Sea

Dunkirk 4 June – final withdrawal
190,000 British and 140,000 French
soldiers evacuated. 100,000 Allied
soldiers taken prisoner

ENGLAND

Calais • Dunkirk • Ghent
• Ypres
Boulogne •
• Lille
English Channel

• Arras

Abbeville • Somme
Dieppe •
Amiens • St Quentin

Le Havre • FRANC
• Rouen
Aisne
Seine
50 miles
50 km Marne

Paris •

Key to German advance
10 to 12 May
15 to 24 May Occupied Seine
25 to 27 May 14 June
on 28 May
on 29 May
on 30 May
31 May to 4 June
5 to 12 June

The Fall of France, 10 May–14 June

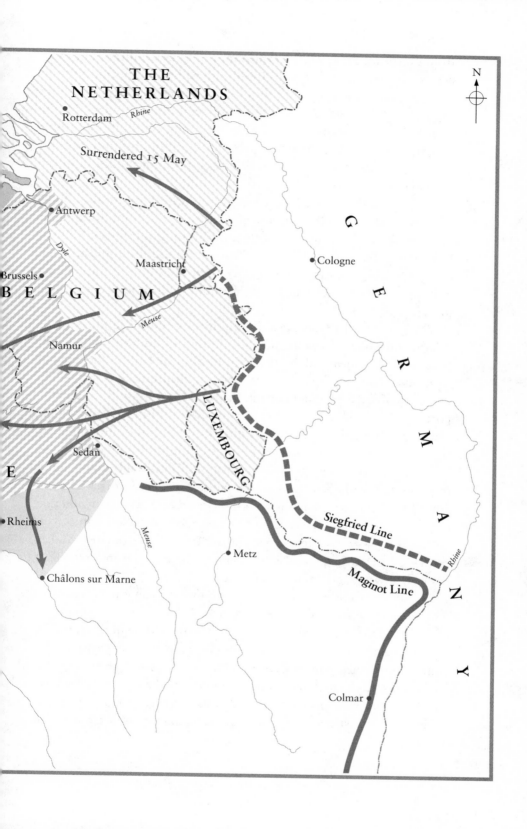

from overhead, French infantrymen quivering in the dirt below. To a degree this reflected reality. The speed with which German mechanized units exploited their victories was crucial to their success. Close air support certainly assisted the Meuse crossings around Sedan, driving French artillerymen away from their guns and stunning those who remained. These visions of a high-tech Blitzkrieg enacted by a mechanical master race, however, concealed more traditional aspects of the campaign.

Aside from the nine armoured divisions into which German tanks were concentrated, the majority of German formations were much more traditionally equipped. Much of their mobility depended on boot leather and literal horse power. Most of the German soldiers who entered Belgium and Holland in May 1940 did so not via aeroplane, motorbike or half-track truck, but the same way their fathers had done in 1914 – on foot.

The key actions that enabled the Germans to cross the Meuse – the fulcrum on which the whole campaign hinged – were won not by tanks but by infantrymen and combat engineers, who had to traverse the river under fire and fight their way into fortified French positions. To the north of Sedan, around Dinant, they did so almost without air support. The tactics used by German troops at the lowest level – infiltrating enemy positions, leaving strongpoints to be dealt with by follow-up troops, allowing junior officers to control the fire of automatic and heavy weapons – were not new inventions. They had grown up in response to the challenges of trench warfare between 1915 and 1917, and by 1918 had been employed to some degree by every army on that earlier Western Front. Having had a chance to make a lot of mistakes, and gain a lot of experience, against the Poles, German commanders proved particularly good at implementing these tactics in 1940. That did not, however, guarantee them success.[2]

The Allies were not exactly underequipped with the weapons of modern war. In total, the defenders in 1940 had more tanks, combat aircraft and artillery pieces than the attackers. Although the variables of armament, armour and reliability make a precise comparison difficult, many Allied tanks were at least a match for their German equivalents. In the first major tank encounter of the war, at Hannut on 14 May, German tank losses exceeded the French by a factor of 3:2. When the heaviest British and French tanks counter-attacked German columns in late May, they proved impervious to most anti-tank weapons, and were only halted by mechanical breakdown, lack of fuel or heavy artillery fire.[3]

What the Germans did have were better communications and organization. A greater proportion of their tanks were equipped with radios, so they were easier to co-ordinate, and their divisional commanders operated close to the front line in specially equipped vehicles that allowed them close control of their troops.[4] German armoured divisions contained a mix of tanks, infantry and artillery that made up a mutually supporting force. The Allies dispersed many of their tanks in smaller units across the front, but given their overall superiority in numbers this was less dangerous than might be supposed. More serious was the fact that the armoured formations they did possess were less well balanced, very much less well practised and less logistically resilient than their opponent's. But if these factors contributed to tactical success, they are not sufficient to explain the crushing nature of the strategic victory.

Some Allied troops performed poorly during the battle. The French 55th Infantry Division disintegrated at Sedan, the poor training of some British Territorial units was all too apparent, and once the retreat had started, there were frequent instances of panic, mass flight and confusion. Nonetheless it is far from clear that Allied troops in general were less well motivated than the Germans. French troops in particular kept fighting long after the initial debacle in the north: the German casualty rate in the second part of the campaign, from 4 June onwards, was almost twice that sustained from 10 May until the evacuation of Dunkirk.[5]

At the core of German success lay the simple fact that they were willing to take risks to concentrate strength against weakness. The outcome of the most important battles of the campaign, around the Meuse crossings, depended on the ability of second-line French divisions to withstand the best that the German army and air force could throw at them. At each end of their line, the German forces operated at a numerical disadvantage. In the crucial Ardennes sector, forty-five divisions, including seven of the nine panzer divisions, faced eighteen French divisions. But achieving this concentration meant deploying nearly all of Germany's military strength in the front line, as well as committing a disproportionate amount of its limited fuel stocks. Had the gamble not paid off, the Germans would have been left without a strategic reserve and unable to pursue mobile operations.[6]

Three key Allied shortcomings exacerbated the effects of the German victory on the Meuse. First, Gamelin's decision to commit the best French troops in an effort to link up with the Dutch in the first days of the campaign was a gamble of his own – but not one justified by the potential rewards. Having the extra Dutch divisions might have been useful to the French, but not so much that it outweighed the resultant loss of the Allied reserve, marooned in the north while events unfolded further south. British concerns about the Germans gaining air and naval bases in the Low Countries meant that they went along too easily with a plan that put the Allies on the back foot from the start. Meanwhile, the rigorous maintenance of Belgian and Dutch neutrality meant that the French and British were unsure what they would find as they moved forward on 10 May.[7]

Second, the failure of Allied intelligence to identify the main point of the German effort meant that there was no attempt to counter the move through the Ardennes until it was too late. Had the Allied air forces that spent the second week of May covering the advance towards Holland instead been bombing the German columns packed tightly on the forest roads, the result might have been a colossal traffic jam that would have prevented any rapid exploitation of the bridgeheads on the Meuse.[8]

Third, the speed of that exploitation revealed the failings in French military doctrine and Allied co-ordination. The Germans emphasized the need to embrace the inevitable chaos of battle by decentralizing decision-making to the commander on the spot. In contrast, French commanders were taught to construct their battles methodically, slowing down enemy penetrations before repelling them with carefully organized counter-attacks. This approach, though well suited to the slower-tempo battles of the last war, left the French off the pace in this new conflict. By the time attacks were put together, their targets had moved on, spreading confusion and disruption as they went. The result was a progressively worsening loss of control within the French army.[9] That breakdown exacerbated the problems of maintaining Allied unity. Notwithstanding the systems of command set up during the Bore War, the French and British remained deeply distrustful of each other's intentions. As their front collapsed, not only their communications but also their faith in each other completely disintegrated.[10]

Initial German success was therefore the result of specific military contingencies: a concentration of strength that reflected their need for a quick victory; good fortune in the play of chance in the battles for the Meuse crossings; and the particular inadequacies of their opponents in the fast-moving campaign that unfolded. The speed and scale of the German victory were bound to be demoralizing. That it resulted in French surrender also reflected the path that politics had taken in 1930s France. Faced with military disaster, and presuming that Britain would be unable to fight alone, France's senior generals told its politicians there was no choice but to seek an armistice. Their eagerness to end hostilities was based less on a calculation of strategic possibilities than on a determination to preserve the army as a traditional institution around which France could be rebuilt. They were not about to retreat to France's overseas colonies and leave the home front to the Communists who they thought had undermined the war effort. Having lost faith in the Third Republic and the battle against the invader, they preferred to abandon both, seek peace and construct a new nation that could return to traditional French values.[11]

Though humiliating and terrifying, the defeat of summer 1940 was much less conclusive for Britain than it was for France. Small as it was, there was little that the BEF could have done by itself to alter the course of the campaign. It had scarcely made contact with the advancing Germans in Belgium before it was on the retreat back into France. Its hardest fighting came at the end of May and the start of June, as it retreated into the Dunkirk pocket and tried to get as many of its soldiers away as possible. Nonetheless, the strategic defeat in which it was caught up highlighted many of the British army's shortcomings.

The commander of the BEF, General Gort, actually had two jobs to do. As head of a national contingent, he had to interact with politicians and with the senior officers of the Allied high command. As army commander, he had to direct the operations of the Expeditionary Force. He was better at the latter than the former. When the fighting commenced, he moved to a forward command post, separated from his bulky headquarters, from which he journeyed out to visit his corps commanders as the battle developed. On the road, he was out of touch with the broader picture and out of easy contact with his allies. As he concentrated on his army, Gort did not question why he was getting no instructions from the French generals of whose forces the BEF was meant to be part.[12]

Gort's absences from GHQ would have mattered less if the BEF's communications had been better. With insufficient and unreliable radios, however, British forces depended on the French telephone system (which proved all too vulnerable to German bombing and the intransigence of local exchange operators) and despatch riders (who struggled to negotiate roads crammed with refugees). Gort's communications network held up well enough for him to co-ordinate the BEF's retreat, but not to allow the rapid flow of information that might have allowed the British to catch up with German operations. That adaptation was not aided by the lack of signals intelligence on the enemy. On the battlefield, the British did not listen in to German communications or attempt to secure their own transmissions. At a strategic level, the German change of cipher keys on 1 May imposed a temporary blackout on the Government Code and Cipher School's ability to read Enigma traffic. Even when the new Luftwaffe key was broken in mid-May, the systems were not yet in place to cope with the mass of material thus produced, to turn it into operationally useful material, and to get it securely to commanders on the ground.[13]

When it came to combat, the British army was placed under enormous stress in its first campaign. Having abandoned the fortifications it had spent the winter building and forced to cover large areas of ground as the front fell apart, British units were unable to create the thick defensive belts necessary to withstand the German thrusts. On 25 May, at the most extreme example, the BEF's divisions were being asked to hold fronts about three times longer than the maximum foreseen as practicable before the fighting began. Whereas the most important German attacks received close help from the Luftwaffe, the BEF got little direct support from the RAF until it was on the beaches at Dunkirk. Thrown into the desperate battles to bomb the Meuse bridges, the light bombers of the Advanced Air Striking Force suffered horrendous losses entirely out of sight of British ground troops. Struggling under a rain of German bombs, British soldiers felt abandoned by their pilots. Bombed, outflanked, isolated and retreating, some of Gort's subordinates broke under the strain.[14]

The 21 May counter-attack by British forces south of Arras was subsequently highlighted as an example of how easily the campaign might have turned. When British 'I' tanks from the 1st Army Tank Brigade hit the German 7th Panzer and SS Totenkopf Infantry divisions in the flank, they caused panic out of all proportion to their number. The standard German anti-tank gun was unable to penetrate the British tanks' armour. Yet this minor advance also revealed the difficulties afflicting the Allies. Confusion over when the attack was going to take place and what it was supposed to achieve meant that it was poorly set up. The hastily thrown-together British force of two tank and three Territorial infantry battalions was meant to work with the 3rd French Light Mechanized Division, but there was actually little co-operation. With scant artillery support, the British tanks and infantry rapidly became separated as the latter went to ground under German fire. When the tanks pressed on, they fell victim to a defence line hastily constructed by 7th Panzer Division's commander, Erwin Rommel, who had scraped together heavier artillery and anti-aircraft guns that could destroy the rampaging British vehicles.

Not for the last time, in the midst of a freewheeling battle, the Germans improvised better than the British. Ironically, Rommel's reaction did more than the British tanks to slow the pace of the panzers' advance. When he reported back to headquarters, he claimed that he had fought off an attack by five enemy divisions. Rommel blew his own trumpet so hard that he frightened a German high command already worried about the vulnerability of their advance, and thus contributed to the decision to rein in the panzer divisions before they were cut up by Allied counter-attacks.[15]

Notwithstanding his failings, Gort got the key decisions from a British perspective right. On 20 May, he stood up to the chief of the imperial general staff and the War Cabinet and refused to retreat south-west towards Amiens as ordered, a move that would have exposed the BEF's flank to the advancing Germans. On 25 May, realizing that Weygand's plans for another, full counter-attack were illusory, Gort chose to concentrate on a defensive battle to make sure of an evacuation from Dunkirk, a decision reinforced when a British patrol surprised a German staff car carrying plans to strike through the Belgians in the north and cut the BEF off from the sea. Much to the French general's disgust, and to the discomfiture of the War Cabinet in London, Gort withdrew two divisions from Weygand's proposed attack and used them to help form a secure left shoulder on which his army could withdraw. It was this manoeuvre, much assisted by Hitler's 'halt order', that allowed a coherent perimeter to be held while so many British soldiers escaped. Gort displayed a realistic appreciation of the dire circumstances without giving in to despair like his French counterparts. For all his failings as an inter-allied commander, his determined bravery actually fitted him well for a desperate battle to preserve his army against the odds.[16]

Short though the campaign was, there were a few signs that the army was not entirely a hopeless case. Between 26 and 29 May, General Brooke's II Corps fought a complex defensive battle between Ypres and Wytschaete, withdrawing at night to new positions and holding off German attempts to overwhelm its flanks. II Corps' units impressed their opponents with their fire discipline and tenacity: significantly, they were supported by the greatest weight of artillery fire deployed by the British army in the whole first three years of the war.[17]

More significantly, the eventual evacuation also demonstrated the UK's continuing aerial and naval strength. From the outset of the campaign, the French had pressed the British to send more RAF fighter squadrons to help fight off the Luftwaffe's assault on their ground forces. Although the need to bolster their ally and to make up for rising losses forced the British to reinforce their fighters in France, they fought shy of eroding any further their own air defences and refused to send as many aircraft as the French wanted. As the northern pocket shrank, RAF units were withdrawn to the UK. When it came to extricating the BEF from Dunkirk, however, the British were able and willing to commit every RAF fighter squadron. Flying now from British bases, RAF aircraft crossed the Channel to try to protect the waiting troops. Much of the resulting air combat took place out of view of the beaches, but it undoubtedly helped to lessen the pressure on the encircled soldiers below.[18]

Meanwhile, the Royal Navy organized at short notice the extraction of a huge number of servicemen, albeit without most of their heavy equipment. The flag officer at Dover, Vice-Admiral Bertram Ramsay, put together a flotilla of 900 ships, more than 200 of which were private motor craft, most of them manned by naval personnel. For all the credit subsequently given to these 'little ships', however, more than two-thirds of those evacuated were taken off by British and French naval vessels or by large passenger ferries. Despite the RAF's endeavours, the work was carried out under regular air attack: twenty-eight British destroyers were lost or severely damaged while helping to get the army out of France. The whole operation, however, demonstrated Britain's continued maritime predominance. German submarines and motor torpedo boats sank ships on the evacuation run, but with the Kriegsmarine still licking its wounds from the Norway campaign, there was no prospect of a German surface fleet cutting off the BEF from the sea.[19]

'WHEN WE GOT TO DUNKIRK IT WAS WORSE . . .'[20]

All battles are confusing for those who fight them, but for the soldiers of the BEF, the campaign of 1940 was more baffling than most. Information was in short supply. Having advanced into Belgium in response to the German offensive, British troops were quickly ordered into a retreat without having actually lost a battle. Hastening from one point to another in a foreign land, for some it was days before they realized that they had been heading backwards, let alone that they were about to be evacuated.

Despite the influx of conscripts since the summer of 1939, this was still a heavily volunteer army, with a relatively high proportion of pre-war regulars and Territorial soldiers. Many of its units retained the communal identity and loyalty built up during the years of peace. It was also, however, an army comparatively untested in the fire of battle. Commanded by men who had been tried in the furnace of the First World War – at times, over the very same ground on which they were fighting this second time around – its younger soldiers had not previously undergone the strains of combat against well-led opponents from a modern industrial state.

As the BEF struggled to catch up with an enemy who always seemed one step ahead, perhaps their most universal experience was physical exhaustion, compounded by hunger and thirst as the supply system fractured under the weight of the German advance.

From 3 am Sunday to 3 am Monday I had a bare two hours' sleep in the garden and during this period two meals consisting of two slices of bread and a slice of meat roll. The other meal was two slices of bread and cheese with the addition of some chocolate and jam. I slept from 3 am to 4 am and then had a meal of scrounged and looted food – jam, bread, cakes and biscuits – not at all adequate. On Monday we rested until 1.30 pm and had bully beef and a slice of bread at 6 pm and a mouthful of tea at 11 pm. Again no sleep until 5 am having some bacon, beans and tea before sleep ... There was a shortage of liquids – no water, half a pint of tea and mouthful of wine in thirty-six hours.[21]

Little wonder that in these circumstances, British troops enthusiastically made off with whatever they could find from the houses and shops they passed, or that the army's cohesion broke down as men lost contact with their units and fended for themselves. Ironically, the same problems were afflicting German soldiers, driven on to exhaustion and at the far end of their supply lines. In the final battles around Dunkirk, all the combatants were running on empty.

Much of the fighting around the Channel ports was small-scale, improvised stuff between infantry units operating at close quarters. Neither side had many chances to fight well-organized, carefully planned battles in which massed artillery pieces unleashed the full concussive potential of modern war. For the inexperienced Territorials and conscripts of the BEF, this was a terrifying introduction to the physical consequences of combat. Fighting as an infantryman in Calais on 25 May, gunner William Harding watched as

some riflemen with bayonets ran across our front. A tail end chap was hit by a mortar bomb, which resulted in a low wall looking as if buckets of red paint had been thrown over it. The man completely disintegrated, with his head resting on his neck, his arms and legs close by. His face had a slight smile on it.[22]

Fighting meant killing as well as being killed. Holding the Escaut Canal, 2nd Lieutenant Jimmy Langley of the 2nd Coldstream Guards shot a German who had picked off two of his comrades:

It was my lucky day and I can only assume that having had two 'kills' at the same spot the sniper did not think anyone would be fool enough to offer him a third. I had thought he would be some way back ... and had he not moved I doubt if I would ever have spotted him ... he was lying on the top of the bank in a clump of nettles not 50 yards away, with his field glasses slowly sweeping our lines ... Once I had seen him the rest was comparatively easy, but nonetheless I was violently sick when it was over.[23]

Whether under fire in defensive positions or being strafed from the sky as they retreated, the BEF's soldiers had to endure bombardment. The resultant feeling of vulnerability was perhaps worst on the 'antheap upturned'[24] of the evacuation beaches. They offered so little natural cover as the troops awaited escape, so close yet so far. Alan Macdonald, a captain in the Royal Artillery, recalled:

lying flat on the sand listening to the shriek of the bombers and the crack of explosions. I can still see the hand of the person next to me one time. It was only a few inches from my face as we two lay prone. It twitched with nerves, the knuckles gleaming white as his hand clenched and unclenched, the fingers biting into his thigh.[25]

In an account published the year after Dunkirk, another officer remembered the 'stench of blood and mutilated flesh' on the beaches. 'Not a breath of air was blowing to dissipate the appalling odour that arose from the dead bodies that had been lying on the sand, in some cases for several days. We might have been walking through a slaughter house on a hot day.'[26]

The bodies lay amid a wasteland of abandoned equipment, for as the army withdrew it left behind it a huge quantity of destroyed and abandoned kit. The desolate wreckage of trucks, tanks, motorbikes and guns made a telling impression on the Germans. General von Bock, the commander of Army Group B, wrote in his diary:

The scene on the roads used by the English retreat was indescribable. Huge quantities of motor vehicles, guns, combat vehicles, and army equipment were crammed into a very small area and driven together ... There lies the materiel of an army whose completeness of equipment we poor wretches can only gaze at with envy.[27]

Lionel Tucker was a twenty-one-year-old private with the Royal Army Ordnance Corps. Like many soldiers, for him the retreat consisted of a step-by-step shedding of the material manifestations of military service. Just outside Cassel, as the full scale of the defeat became obvious, he was instructed to disable his charges:

> We drained the sumps and drained the water and bayonetted the tyres
> and smashed the carburettors and done all sorts of damage that was
> heart-breaking really when you'd been looking after them so well, and
> then . . . we were on the march into Dunkirk . . . and believe you me that
> twenty-one miles was the worst twenty-one miles I'd ever done in my
> life: we were strafed, we were bombed, we dived into ditches and all the
> rest of it . . . I thought to myself on the way, I shall be glad when we get
> to Dunkirk, but when we got to Dunkirk it was worse . . .

On 1 June, having spent a day on the beach waiting for evacuation with
nothing to eat or drink, he was ordered into the town to await rescue
from the crowded mole in the harbour.

> I thought to myself, right, if I've got to swim for it, I don't want all this
> on, so I slung me tin helmet over, I slung me rifle in the water, I slung all
> me pack, Bren gun pouches, everything I had, gas mask, everything, I
> was just in my clothes.

When he finally got aboard the passenger ferry *Maid of Orleans*,
Tucker 'flopped right down on the deck and went asleep, and I didn't
know anything more until someone come along and kicked me in the
backside and said . . . "C'mon mate, we're in Dover".'[28]

Men as well as equipment had been left behind. Of the 66,246 casualties suffered by the BEF since September 1939, 41,567 were prisoners
of war. In practice, officers were often reluctant to try to make their
men fight genuinely 'to the last man'. Where escape was cut off and
further resistance seemed futile, they usually told their men to surrender rather than suffer 'useless' losses. Others, however, particularly
where they were convinced they were helping the army get away, staged
desperate last stands against the odds.[29]

The shock of battle, the need for escape and the slow grind of hunger
and tiredness all put morale under threat. Some units were able to
maintain their discipline and cohesion all the way back to the beaches
and onto the boats. Others were deliberately broken up to evade the
encircling Germans, or crumbled as shattered men staggered away
from the line of march, woke up to find their comrades had gone, or
took their chance in the confusion to head for home.

In the circumstances, it was perhaps surprising that the BEF did not
dissolve more completely. But the mixture of defeat and disintegration

certainly called the military hierarchy into question. Private Joe Catt of the 5th Royal Sussex described the moment when he and his comrades were told to fend for themselves:

> When you realize the people you are supposed to obey don't know what they're doing, that's when you begin to get a bit worried. When one has been trained to jump at the sound of the sergeant's voice, can you begin to imagine the feeling of panic when officers ordered us to make our own way to Dunkirk? Most of us had no idea where it was, or even what it was.[30]

The sense of betrayal after capture could be equally corrosive. Having already been badly mauled in their first contact with the Germans on 20 May, the 2nd Battalion of the Royal East Kent Regiment was forced to surrender when it found itself surrounded eight days later. One of its officers later remembered scenes that were

> pretty nasty . . . scenes of bad behaviour by British soldiers . . . blaming the officers, effing and blinding and being absolutely bloody. And I remember . . . trying to pull them together . . . and I found someone behind me and it was my CO with a bottle he'd picked up and he was just about to hit anybody who'd dare touch me. But that was [the] sort of thing that can happen in abject defeat when there's no water to drink and . . . all discipline gone. They weren't our soldiers.[31]

Humiliation, dejection and despair were common currency among soldiers who knew they had been forced to run away. Those lucky enough to be extricated from Dunkirk travelled back in trepidation, expecting jeers rather than cheers from the home front on their return.

The pattern of losses as a result of the battle for France was far from evenly spread. The army's logistic and support troops, further removed from the front line and closer to the ports, made up the bulk of soldiers evacuated at the start of the Dunkirk operation. Fighting units, particularly infantry units that had borne the brunt of the combat, had suffered higher casualties, but were also often so disrupted by the process of evacuation that their soldiers were initially scattered across the south of England. Most of these battalions took weeks to reassemble. The 51st Highland Division, captured essentially complete at St-Valéry, had to be rebuilt from scratch. For all the severity of the materiel destruction, however, most of the army's personnel survived and returned. The shock of defeat was not compounded by the even higher losses that would have been sustained if the Germans had actually cut the British off from the coast.

'NOW THE "TOTAL WAR" BEGINS'

The battle for France was just as confusing for those charged with directing Britain's war as it was to those doing the fighting on the ground. From the outset, British strategists focused on the dangers to the security of the UK. Rather than part of a plan to win a quick and decisive victory over France, they presumed that Germany's thrust into the Low Countries was an attempt to improve its position for a long war. Having pushed their way to the Channel coast, the Germans would hold a new line in France while opening an attack on the UK from their new air and sea bases in Holland and Belgium. In reaction against their failure to predict the assault on Scandinavia, the chiefs of staff and their intelligence advisors now not only presumed that the Germans were already well prepared to invade the UK, but also lost confidence that they would be able to spot such an attack coming. For most of May and June, Britain's military and political leaders were struggling not only with an incomplete picture of the unfolding campaign across the Channel, but also with the panicked sense that their own islands might be subject to unexpected attack.[32]

For all the confidence that Britain had placed in the durability of the French army, the risk that France was headed for a total collapse was recognized in London at a very early stage. On 15 May, five days into the campaign, Reynaud phoned Churchill to tell him, 'We are beaten, we have lost the battle.' By 17 May, a Cabinet committee had already begun to consider the consequences if the French were forced to abandon Paris and the BEF had to be totally evacuated. It took much longer, however, for the British to become certain that their ally was beyond rescue.

The German offensive spurred on the escalation of Britain's war effort. In response to the movement of German troops, on the night of 11 May the RAF bombed Mönchen-Gladbach, its first night bombing raid against a German target in an urban area. From 12 May, the War

Cabinet considered whether the moment had come to 'take the gloves off' and begin 'unrestricted air warfare', bombing targets in Germany without regard for whether this might lead to civilian casualties. On 15 May, it gave approval for such bombing, provided that it aimed to fulfil military objectives. That night, Bomber Command despatched ninety-nine medium bombers against the Ruhr.[33] As Alexander Cadogan in the Foreign Office put it in his diary: 'Now the "Total War" begins!'[34]

This step was not surprising. Since the previous September, Chamberlain's Conservative opponents had made the unleashing of the air war a key demand in their campaign against him. When it came to bombing, Churchill had none of his predecessor's moral and legal qualms. Attlee was also an enthusiastic supporter. Even though German air attacks had not, as yet, been directed at British cities, they argued that the Luftwaffe had deliberately targeted civilians in Poland and Holland. The fightback against such an evil enemy must not be disabled by misplaced scruples.

In fact, when it came to the air war, the argument that the Germans had started it was open to debate. Luftwaffe attacks on Warsaw had killed large numbers of civilians, but they did so in the course of supporting ground operations against the Polish army and thus were legal within the bounds of contemporary international law. On 14 May, the Germans bombed Rotterdam, killing hundreds of civilians (an event not referred to in the British Cabinet discussions), but again in the context of a ground assault.[35] The broader brutality of the Nazi regime was evident enough, but nonetheless, what Britain was now undertaking – bombing raids as the sole form of attack against distant targets without regard for civilian losses – was unprecedented. At the time, what weighed heavily on the War Cabinet was the damage that unrestricted bombing would do to Britain's reputation in neutral America. The deteriorating situation on the Western Front overcame this anxiety: Allied military survival meant more than preserving Britain's good name across the Atlantic.[36]

The opening of the German campaign in the west had already led the new British government to abandon previous restrictions on overseas spending, and from mid-May, Britain bought in America on the basis of military need rather than financial prudence. It was clear that this meant that Britain would run out of dollars even sooner than had been anticipated. On 15 May Churchill, in his first personal note to President Roosevelt after he became prime minister, had indicated that, 'We shall go on paying dollars for as long as we can, but I should like to feel reasonably sure that when we can pay no more you will give us the stuff all the same.'[37] The president felt no need to reassure him about anything of the sort. In a major change from the days when the Treasury had control of the purse strings, however, Churchill and the Foreign Office were optimistic that America would provide some means of economic aid when British reserves were exhausted.

Meanwhile, the news from France deteriorated. For the embattled French even more than the British, the immediate fear was that the Italians would now abide by their pact with Germany and enter the war, attacking France's southern border and opening hostilities in the Mediterranean. The French were keen for the Allies to make concessions now to keep Italy peaceful. They persuaded the British to join them in a covert request to President Roosevelt, asking him to issue an apparently independent proposal for Italy to make clear its territorial claims as a prelude to full participation in an eventual peace settlement. On 25 May, the Italian ambassador in London asked for an interview with Halifax and broached the idea of an Italian-organized conference at which Mussolini would play European arbiter in return for a recognition of Italian interests. Halifax played for time, but was attracted by the notion that the Italian dictator, scared by the scale of Hitler's successes, might act as a restraining influence on his ally if it came to arranging a compromise peace.

On 26 May, Reynaud came to London for meetings with Churchill and Halifax. Before he arrived, the prime minister told his colleagues to prepare themselves for the fact that the French premier might say that his country 'could not carry on the fight'. Halifax told the War Cabinet 'to face the fact that it was not so much now a question of imposing a complete defeat on Germany but of safeguarding the independence of our own Empire and if possible that of France'.[38] To that end, he raised the question of his interview with the Italian ambassador. Halifax had concluded that meeting by emphasizing that everyone wanted peace and security. Churchill retorted that he had no intention of seeing those aims achieved because the Germans had achieved a total domination of Europe.

The prime minister and foreign secretary then had their interviews with Reynaud, who gave a gloomy picture of the military situation. He raised the question of making concessions to Italy in an effort to keep that country out of the war. The problem for the French was that, apart from some sort of shared rule of Tunisia, they did not have that much that Mussolini wanted. Reynaud appealed to the British to offer up some of their Mediterranean possessions – he talked of declaring Gibraltar, the Suez Canal and Malta neutral territories – in return for an improvement in France's position. Halifax was keen at least to approach Mussolini: less in order to keep Italy out of the war than because he hoped to find a route to a general settlement in which the Italians would pressure Hitler 'to take a more reasonable attitude'.

That evening, the War Cabinet met again at Admiralty House. Once more, discussion quickly moved from concessions to Italy to the broader issue of a European peace deal. Churchill argued that the British still had 'powers of resistance and attack' which the French did not, and that the French desire to 'get out of the war' would 'drag' Britain 'into a settlement which involved intolerable terms'.

In his circumlocutory way, Halifax took issue with Churchill:

> he attached perhaps rather more importance than the Prime Minister to the desirability of allowing France to try out the possibilities of European equilibrium. He was not quite convinced that the Prime Minister's diagnosis was correct and that it was in Herr Hitler's interest to insist on outrageous terms. After all, he knew his own internal weaknesses. On this lay out, it might be possible to save France from the wreck.

Churchill, although insistent that it would be impossible to get a peace that Britain could accept, finally agreed that an approach could be made to Mussolini. As the meeting closed, Halifax reminded his colleagues that 'if we got to the point of discussing the terms of a general settlement and found that we could obtain terms which did not postulate the destruction of our independence, we should be foolish if we did not accept them'.[39]

In the meantime, the chiefs of staff had produced a paper on British chances if the French capitulated. This recognized that air superiority would be crucial to any successful attack on the UK. Providing it could fight off the German air force, they argued, the UK would be able to hold out while it mobilized international and imperial resources to build up its military power. That would depend on the USA giving 'full economic and financial support, *without which'*, they emphasized, *'we do not think we could continue the war with any chance of success'.* The chiefs asserted that, with the UK secure, there was still a hope that Germany might yet be defeated 'by economic pressure, by a combination of air attack on economic objectives in Germany and on German morale and the creation of widespread revolt in her conquered territory'.[40]

This bolstered the prime minister's case, but not as much as Churchill might have wished. On 27 May, the War Cabinet reconvened, joined by Sinclair as leader of the Liberals, but without any other ministers or senior military officers, to consider matters again. Two gambits were now in play – Roosevelt's approach to Mussolini, which had been made the day before, and further pressure from the French for the Allies to make a direct appeal to Italy, laying out precisely what territory was up for grabs if it stayed out of the war. As before, this quickly led to the consideration of a broader settlement with Germany.

Sinclair, Attlee and Greenwood all pronounced themselves opposed to any further approach to the Italians. The Labour leader pointed out that it would have 'no practical effect and would be very damaging to us'. Churchill agreed that it 'would ruin the integrity of our fighting position in this country'.

> At the moment our prestige in Europe was very low. The only way we could get it back was by showing the world that Germany had not beaten us. If, after two or three months, we could show that we were still unbeaten, our prestige would return. Even if we were beaten, we should be no worse off than we should be if we were now to abandon the struggle.

Chamberlain also believed that negotiations with the Italians were probably pointless, but thought them worth pursuing for a little longer: first to keep the French in the fight, and secondly to avoid giving them the excuse of British intransigence if they decided to make a separate peace.

Halifax had listened to Churchill work himself into a rhetorical lather (as he put it in his record of the meeting, 'Winston talked the most frightful rot'[41]). Now, he decided it was time to make clear 'certain rather profound differences' with his colleagues. First, he 'could not recognise any semblance between the action which he proposed, and the suggestion that we were suing for terms and following a line which would lead us to disaster.' Only the previous day, he reminded the prime minister, Churchill had said that he would consider terms that allowed the UK to retain its 'vital strength' in order to 'get out of our present difficulties'. Now he was saying that Britain had to fight to a finish no matter what. If the Germans were willing to offer an acceptable way out, Halifax thought that would be better than staking the country's future on whether or not the Luftwaffe could knock out Britain's aircraft factories.

> The issue was probably academic, since we were unlikely to receive any offer which would not come up against the fundamental conditions which were essential to us. If, however, it was possible to obtain a settlement which did not impair those conditions he, for his part, doubted if he would be able to accept the view now put forward by the Prime Minister.

Or as he put it in his own account, if Churchill and the Labour leaders really believed what they were saying 'and if it came to the point, our ways must separate'.

As far as the foreign secretary was concerned, his threats of resignation left Churchill full of 'apologies and affection' – as indeed it had to, given the political dangers of a Halifax walk-out. The prime minister did not think that Halifax was making the War Cabinet's job easier by insisting on 'academic' arguments, but he at least considered the hypothetical: if Hitler 'was prepared to make peace on the terms of the restoration of the German colonies and the overlordship of Central Europe, that was one thing. But it was quite unlikely that he would make any such offer.'[42] What the War Cabinet actually settled on was Chamberlain's solution: stringing out discussions with the French by insisting that Roosevelt's initiative must be allowed to run its course before any other approach was made to Mussolini.

By the time the War Cabinet met the following afternoon, Roosevelt's appeal had been rejected and the French had once more demanded that the Allies stage their own explicit approach to Rome. Halifax again used this to open the possibility that Mussolini might act as a mediator in a wider peace settlement. He reminded his colleagues: 'we might get better terms before France went out of the war and our aircraft factories were bombed, than we might get in three months' time'. This time, every other member of the War Cabinet was against him. Churchill proclaimed that 'nations which went down fighting rose again, but those which surrendered tamely were finished'. This was just what had driven Halifax to distraction the previous day: Churchill working 'himself up into a passion of emotion when he ought to make his brain think and reason'.[43]

During a brief adjournment, Churchill took the chance to speak to an assembly of ministers from outside the War Cabinet, to whom he preached a rousing sermon on the subject 'we shall fight on'. Whereas, at its most 'academic', the discussion in the War Cabinet had been about whether negotiating now would get Britain a better deal, to this audience he cast the choice in stark terms: defiance and victory or surrender and a probable Fascist takeover. In Amery's account:

> One thing he was clear about was that there could be no greater folly than to try at this moment to offer concessions to either Italy or Germany, the powers which were out to destroy us. There was nothing to be done at any rate until we have turned the tide, except fight all out.[44]

Put in those terms there was no choice: when the War Cabinet reconvened, Churchill was able to recount that their fellow ministers 'had expressed the greatest satisfaction when he had told them that there was no chance of our giving up the struggle. He did not remember having ever before heard a gathering of persons occupying high places in political life express themselves so emphatically.'[45]

In the meantime, Chamberlain had managed to construct with Halifax a message to Reynaud that followed Churchill's line – there was no point in making a potentially disastrous appeal to Mussolini – but left open the possibility of a future approach to Italy if circumstances changed, which both provided a diplomatic escape route and spared the feelings of the foreign secretary.

These discussions have received a huge amount of attention from historians, but perhaps the most striking aspect of them is the fog of uncertainty in which all the participants struggled. The Dunkirk evacuation was only just getting under way, and no one knew how many troops would be saved. France's fate was not yet sealed. The expectation was that Germany had prepared to invade the UK – which it had not – assuming that it could gain the upper hand in the air. Everyone involved was massively over-optimistic about the damage British

bombers would do now the gloves were off, as well as about the underlying weaknesses of the Nazi regime. To the wider Cabinet, if not to his
senior colleagues, Churchill inflated the prospects of imminent American involvement in the conflict.[46]

Neither Halifax nor Churchill knew the future course of the war. As
it turned out, the Luftwaffe would not prove capable of fulfilling the foreign secretary's fears of German air superiority. Churchill's mercurial
personality and the importance he gave to performing the role of heroic
leader make it difficult to gauge his assessment of British prospects
exactly, but it is clear that, compared to Halifax, he still believed that
the UK could win the war – not just as an article of faith, but as a
matter of judgement on international and economic strength and the
relative strategic situation. In so far as he envisioned victory, however,
it seems to have looked more like what the British government had
aimed for in 1939 than what it would end up pursuing from 1943: a
decisive bargaining position, not grinding the Third Reich into dust. As
a response to Halifax's pedantry, in late May 1940 the prime minister
was at least willing to consider a settlement in which Germany got
back its former colonies and was allowed control of Central Europe,
but he correctly judged that this was not what was on offer in the long
term.

Churchill was wrong about the possibilities of a peace deal with
Hitler, who would happily have left Britain its empire for the moment,
providing that Germany could dominate the European mainland. Halifax, however, was the more mistaken: wrong if he thought that Britain
could just dip its toes in the water of a peace conference without serious
consequences, and wrong to think that some sort of enduring settlement would be obtainable for a country defeated by the Nazi regime.
Seeking peace in 1940 would have confirmed Hitler's perception of the
UK as a declining, decadent empire – the successor to the Ottomans or
Habsburgs – the pieces of which would be swallowed up by the rising
powers of the new global struggle. Even leaving aside the moral and
political implications of negotiating with Nazism, talking with Hitler
from a position of weakness was not a route to lasting security.[47]

It would also have represented a very poor return on Britain's
strategic investment. The UK had spent very heavily on long-term
programmes of rearmament designed to allow it to prevail over Germany in 1942. By May 1940 it was clear that these would be dependent

on massive financial and economic support from America, but if Churchill was too positive about the prospects of securing that aid in the near future, it was reasonable, given the course of Anglo-American relations since 1937, to presume that it *could* be secured, and that the price to be paid would be better than that demanded by a victorious Germany. Whether the UK could convert its defensive strength into offensive power remained to be seen, but again, it was not misguided to presume that this would be the outcome if the rearmament programmes were allowed to fulfil their potential.[48] What was very unlikely, as Churchill pointed out, was that this potential would be reached if Britain backed out of the war. Leaving aside possible German demands to restrict the British armed forces, making peace in the summer of 1940 would have antagonized the Labour movement and the Americans, thus exacerbating problems of industrial relations and dollar supply that had previously hampered rearmament. Having jumped out of a confrontation with Germany when the going got tough, the UK would not have been able to jump back in again with better prospects further down the line.

Presented in these terms, and shorn of the rhetorical flourishes, it was Churchill's case that was more rational and reasoned, and Halifax's that suffered from an excess of emotion – above all a profound irritation with Churchill, the man whom he had allowed to seize the premiership just two weeks before. In the end it was that frustration, not arguments over the continuation of the conflict, which brought the foreign secretary close to resignation. Halifax, the intellectual fencer, was personally annoyed by the mode of argument of Churchill, the emotional all-in wrestler, but they were also fighting over a bigger issue: could the foreign secretary, as he intended when he renounced the premiership, compel his errant colleague to see sense? For the moment, by threatening resignation, he could; but Churchill's appeal to the wider Cabinet – which effectively prevented any further discussion of negotiations – demonstrated that this would not necessarily be the case in the future.[49]

Halifax never thought that he had been suggesting 'ultimate capitulation'. Critically, the discussions of late May were not the start of a war/peace split within the British government. And as that suggested, however important Churchill's rallying of faint hearts felt at the time, he was not the sole reason that the UK did not sue for peace. On the contrary, the balance of argument in any case lay with carrying on the fight.

The logic of that case was apparent in the way that Chamberlain altered course to give more support to Churchill's position than to that of Halifax. It was Chamberlain who – whatever his personal feelings about his recent usurpation – consistently put forward the common ground on which the War Cabinet found agreement. His ruthless willingness to string the French along about an approach to the Italians showed off his bureaucratic acumen and echoed the ways in which he had tried to talk out demands for military adventures during the Phoney War.[50] That move suggests deeper continuities too. During his time as premier, Chamberlain had sought to balance negotiation and deterrence in his dealings with Germany, but since war broke out he had been very clear that agreement was impossible while Hitler remained in power. The events of May 1940 did not change his mind. The War Cabinet discussions about possible negotiations might look like a decisive moment,[51] but this was a turning point at which there was no turn. The collapse of France profoundly affected the course of the war, but it did not break the British government, nor change the fundamental direction of its strategy.

'TWO NATIONS AT WAR WITH EACH OTHER'

It was by no means certain in late May that France would actually drop out of the war. Until the middle of June, British hopes that France might somehow be persuaded to stay the course persisted, alongside a growing reluctance to commit too much to the ailing alliance. As the French attempted to build a new defensive line along the Somme and Aisne rivers, they repeatedly demanded that the British send fresh troops and aircraft to reinforce the two BEF divisions that remained in France and help them hold the line. Now severely outnumbered and trying to withstand a decisive assault, the French understandably felt abandoned. In London, the chiefs of staff and the War Cabinet weighed up the advantages of supporting their ally against the risks of invasion and the fear that forces sent to France would be caught up in an unavoidable defeat.[52] Having been sent back to France to report on the

attitude of its senior officers, General Henry Pownall, the former chief
of the general staff of the BEF, summarized the position neatly in his
diary in the first days of June:

> There is a very difficult balance to be held. If the French are going to
> crack and we have got to fight it out for ourselves (as is extremely prob-
> able) we do not want to waste our resources (especially air resources) in
> a fruitless way to sustain them. On the other hand there is always the
> chance that the French, or part of them, will hold out sufficiently long,
> *if we help them*, to enable us to come to their aid and stop the rot –
> remembering too that the Germans are far from fresh and must be
> having great administrative difficulties . . . Winston said in this connec-
> tion, 'I *wonder* if we can hold them?' An insight into his real thoughts.
> Great morale raising speeches, necessary as they are, do not necessarily,
> or even often reflect the inward appearance of those who make them.[53]

In fact, Churchill proved far keener on reinforcing France than his
War Cabinet colleagues or his military advisors. By the start of June,
most ministers and officials in Whitehall were convinced that nothing
more could be done to help a nation that would not save itself. Increasingly querulous demands for assistance were seen as preliminaries
for blaming British intransigence for a French defeat. As Cadogan put
it, however, 'sentimental Winston' was easier to convince that something might be saved.[54] Between 2 and 4 June he dragged out the War
Cabinet discussions in an effort to persuade his colleagues, arguing
that: 'We could never keep all that we wanted for our own defence
while the French were fighting for their lives.'[55] In practice, there
was little enough that the British could offer: since most of the troops
evacuated from Dunkirk had come away without their equipment, they
were in no position to be immediately sent back into the fight. Nonetheless, the British did eventually despatch several additional air
squadrons, the fresh 52nd Infantry Division and part of the 1st Canadian
Division, which began landing at Cherbourg during the second week
of June.

By this point, the French position on the Somme and Aisne had collapsed (engulfing the two British divisions, the 51st Highland and 1st
Armoured, that had remained after Dunkirk), and Italy had entered the
war. With a catastrophic military defeat now inevitable, the voices
within the French government demanding an armistice grew stronger,

although a minority of ministers, including Reynaud, argued instead that the war could be continued from colonial North Africa. On the evening of 12 June, Weygand told the French Cabinet that they needed to seek an armistice. The next day, Reynaud asked Churchill whether Britain would release France from the alliance agreement that it would make no separate peace.

Although the end was now clearly in sight, the prime minister continued to explore ways to avoid a total French surrender: first by demanding that Reynaud send telegrams to Roosevelt appealing for American assistance; secondly by insisting that the British troops recently arrived in France should keep fighting on the Atlantic coast as part of the so-called 'Breton redoubt'. Both endeavours were in vain. Roosevelt promised supplies but could not offer military aid. General Brooke, who had been sent out to command the 'second BEF', reported that there was no hope of holding out in Brittany. When Churchill told him that he had been sent to France 'to make the French feel that we were supporting them', Brooke responded that 'it was impossible to make a corpse feel' and that he must withdraw.[56] In a second evacuation, less well known than Dunkirk, another 140,000 British troops escaped from the west coast of France.

All of this might seem a good example of Churchill's heart ruling his head. He plainly was deeply affected by the extent of French sacrifice, and endangered British forces by sending them to France when it was apparent to those around him that they could make no difference to the immediate outcome of the campaign. When Churchill proposed sending more fighter squadrons across the Channel, Halifax told him to inform the French that they would do more good defending British factories.

Churchill invested too much in the hope that the French armed forces might be able to salvage something from the wreckage, but the advantages of keeping France in the fight were so considerable that some risks were warranted. If a collapse was inevitable, there was a strong case for trying to influence which way France fell. In any case, it was in Britain's interests to secure as much as possible of France's war-making potential, and above all the French navy, from German clutches. If French battleships were handed over to the enemy as part of a peace deal, then British maritime superiority might be threatened just at the moment when the sea was keeping the UK safe from a German invasion and the opening of a new front in the Mediterranean was stretching the Royal Navy's resources to the limit.[57]

The question of what would happen to French ships was crucial in determining the British response on 16 June, when Reynaud once more requested that France be released from its alliance agreement so that it could seek a separate armistice. He made it clear that his government would not surrender the fleet, but that if the British refused his request, he would resign, and his replacement might not follow suit. In London, the War Cabinet consented, providing that the French navy set sail immediately for British ports. In a bizarre and dramatic attempt to keep their ally in the fight, the British offered the French, on the same day, an 'indissoluble union' of the two countries, including common citizenship. The roots of this proposal lay with future architects of the European Community, including Jean Monnet, but the fact it was put forward said more about London's desperation than its federalist enthusiasm. In Bordeaux, the opportunity to subsume themselves in a new cross-Channel endeavour appealed neither to those French ministers who wanted to fight on to save their nation nor to those who now regarded peace as their patriotic duty.[58]

It was the latter who dominated the new government formed under Pétain after Reynaud resigned on the evening of 16 June. The next day, Pétain's government asked the Germans for armistice terms, which were received on 21 June. The British initially found cause for optimism in signs that the French were also preparing to fight on from their African empire. Although the condition that the fleet sail to the UK had never actually reached the previous French Cabinet, the British were reassured by Admiral Darlan, the head of the French navy and Pétain's minister for the admiralty, that he would never surrender his ships, and by the despatch of additional vessels to North African ports. Briefly, the British thought about buying the whole French navy, or asking the Americans to purchase it, rather than have it fall into Axis hands. The French, however, were not about to give up what was in fact a key bargaining chip as they sought to secure a decent settlement from Germany.[59]

Since hopes remained that the Pétain government was one with which the British could work, when General Charles de Gaulle, a French soldier and former junior minister under Reynaud, asked to be allowed to use the BBC to make a radio broadcast against the armistice, the War Cabinet turned him down. Subsequent representations to senior ministers, however, led to this decision being reversed, and on 18 June de Gaulle made what would subsequently be a famous appeal to Frenchmen at home and abroad to keep fighting. Shocked that this might subvert a French government they still wanted to influence, over the next few days the Foreign Office sat hard on de Gaulle's attempts to declare that he had formed a new government-in-exile in London.[60]

British uncertainties rapidly resolved between 22 and 24 June as the terms of the Franco-German armistice became clear. In some ways, the Germans exacted a harsh price. The whole of northern France, including Paris and most of the country's heavy industry, was occupied, with the costs borne by the rump French state. Somewhere between 50,000 and 90,000 French soldiers had been killed during the campaign.[61] Even at the lower estimate, that meant a rate of combat fatalities per week about 60 per cent higher than the French had suffered during the Great War, which disproves any suggestion that the French army didn't fight hard. About 1.5 million French service personnel had also been taken prisoner by the Germans, many in the period between Pétain's announcement of the armistice and the moment when it came into effect.[62] Most of these prisoners of war were retained in German hands as hostages to their country's good behaviour.

In other ways, however, the French got off lightly. Southern France was left unoccupied and the Pétain administration was allowed to form a new seat of government. At the start of July it took up residence in the spa town of Vichy. The French empire was left untouched. Crucially, the French did not have to surrender their navy, but their warships were to return to their home ports, then be demobilized and disarmed under Axis direction. The armistice with Italy, which was agreed between 23 and 24 June, followed roughly the same lines, with France's Mediterranean ports demilitarized, but no wholesale annexation of French colonial possessions in Africa. With the signatures on both complete, the two armistices came into effect together on 25 June.

The conclusion of the armistice negotiations meant the final rupture of the Anglo-French alliance. The speed of the French acceptance of German terms convinced the British that the Pétain government had acted in bad faith and should be treated as effectively under enemy control. What remained of France would shortly be made subject to

Britain's economic blockade. On 23 June, the British government recognized de Gaulle's formation of a French National Committee as a potential part of a new French administration-in-exile, although it was still not clear whether anyone would rally to his flag. On 24 June, Churchill told the War Cabinet to expect that Pétain's government 'would inevitably be drawn more and more into making common cause with Germany'. The French fleet 'must at all costs' be put either under British control or 'out of the way for good'. In future, relations between the UK and the France that had accepted the armistice 'might well approach closely to those of two nations at war with each other'.[63] The cross-Channel partnership was no more, and now the former allies were sailing into dangerous waters.

'THE FLEET WILL REMAIN FRENCH OR WILL NOT EXIST'

British strategists had long judged that Italy would be a good enemy to fight. Highly dependent on imports, Italy would be hard hit by the blockade and would act as a drain on German raw materials, while its African colonies would be easily cut off from reinforcements and supplies. What concerned them most was the Italian navy's ability to dominate the Mediterranean, resupplying Libya, blocking the shipping route to the Suez Canal and outflanking ground defences in the Middle East. In mid-May, faced with the growing likelihood of Italian belligerence, Britain had reinforced its fleet at Alexandria, under Admiral Andrew Cunningham, with four battleships, an aircraft carrier, six cruisers and sixteen destroyers. With the help of a French cruiser squadron, Cunningham was meant to control the Eastern Mediterranean. On the other side of Italy, the British relied on the French navy to dominate the Western Mediterranean and stop the Italians from interdicting the vital convoy route up from Africa's Atlantic coast. The French navy also played a key role in British contingency planning in the event of a Japanese attack in the Far East. Although British naval planners had toyed in the 1930s with the idea of knocking out the Italian fleet as the opening gambit in a three-front maritime war, they had settled on a more defensive plan in which the French would hold the line in the Mediterranean, while British ships from Alexandria would be sent out to relieve Hong Kong and Singapore.[64]

The probability of French surrender therefore posed significant problems for British naval strategy. In mid-June, Admiral Pound, the first sea lord, briefly considered withdrawing the fleet from Alexandria and concentrating it at Gibraltar to try to guarantee control of the Atlantic. Cunningham and Churchill successfully opposed the idea on the basis that it would ensure the loss of Britain's entire position in North Africa and the Middle East.[65] Instead, the Royal Navy despatched further reinforcements – two battleships, a battle cruiser and an aircraft carrier – to Gibraltar to form a new squadron, 'Force H', under Admiral James Somerville. This would take the place of the French fleet in contesting control of the Western Mediterranean and protecting the East Atlantic convoy route.

France's empire in the Middle East and Africa ran from Syria and the Lebanon, via Algeria, Tunisia and Morocco to Senegal, Guinea, Gabon and the French Congo. During the second half of June 1940, the British hoped that colonial France might be rallied to the Allied cause, or at least persuaded to deny its resources and bases to the enemy. With their forces already overstretched, the British had to rely on the power of negotiation to bring the French around. These efforts failed, partly because French colonial governors followed the lead coming out of Bordeaux, and partly because British offers of assistance looked to French eyes worryingly like a grab for territory. When the British took decisive action to control the future of the French navy, they guaranteed that imperial France would not be fighting alongside the British Empire.[66]

As Britain's decision to hold the Mediterranean in June 1940 demonstrated, the Royal Navy was still remarkably strong compared with its European rivals.[67] Despite the fears of invasion, Britain could redeploy its warships in an effort to maintain control of its global supply lines and the security of its empire. Such naval superiority was crucial for British survival and the War Cabinet was not willing to see it undermined. As soon as France began to totter, the British had considered the prospect of naval intervention to keep French capital ships out of enemy hands. When the armistice was signed, the British moved from thought to action.

As France's European war ended, its major vessels were scattered in different locations. Some had crossed to Plymouth and Portsmouth. The battleship *Richelieu* had gone to the big French naval base at Dakar and its unfinished sister ship, *Jean Bart*, used its engines for the first time to reach Casablanca. Powerful French squadrons remained at Toulon, Alexandria and the naval base at Mers-el-Kébir, near Oran in Algeria. The French Admiral Darlan was determined to keep control of all these vessels, but he was also uncertain about how his officers would react to the armistice.

On 25 June, worried that the Royal Navy would trap him in port, the captain of the *Richelieu* sailed his ship out of Dakar. The French Admiralty, anxious that he was about to defect, swiftly ordered him back. The British, however, thought that this was the first step in the French bringing their fleet home to hand it over to the Germans.[68] On 27 June, Darlan sought to reassure the British: 'I repeat that the fleet will remain French or will not exist.'[69] The War Cabinet decided on the same day that force could be used to ensure that French ships did not end up in Axis hands.

Just before dawn on 3 July, Royal Navy boarding parties rushed aboard French vessels in British ports. Most gained control without a fight, but on the giant French submarine *Surcouf*, a gun battle broke out that left three Britons and a French sailor dead. In Alexandria, with both sides fearing a bloody battle at close quarters, Cunningham eventually persuaded the French to keep their ships where they were and render them incapable of immediate action.

Meanwhile, Force H arrived off Mers-el-Kébir to demand a decision: the French ships must either be handed over or disarmed. When the French refused to do either, the British warships opened fire. One French battleship was blown up. Another, and a battlecruiser, were damaged and beached. One battlecruiser escaped unharmed with four destroyers to Toulon. On 6 and 8 July, the British followed up with carrier-launched air attacks on Mers-el-Kébir and Dakar, the second of which disabled the *Richelieu*.[70]

In total, the operations resulted in the deaths of almost 1,300 Frenchmen and 5 British servicemen. Briefly, it seemed as if a full-blown war might erupt. On 5 July, French aircraft dropped bombs into the bay off Gibraltar, and diplomatic relations between France and Britain were broken off three days later. For the moment, however, an all-out confrontation was avoided, and on 12 July, the British announced that for the moment they would take no further action against the French navy providing it did not head for enemy-controlled ports.[71]

In retrospect, the War Cabinet's fears for Britain's maritime security were not well founded. The French would probably not have allowed their capital ships to fall under German control – when the Germans tried, in 1942, the French scuttled the vessels rather than hand them over. In 1940, even if the Germans could have secured the French battleships, making use of them would have been much more difficult than simply putting on board a different crew. At the time, Hitler was actually far more concerned about French destroyers reinforcing the British than getting warships for the Kriegsmarine, which helps to explain why the French navy got away so lightly in the armistice negotiations.

By the start of July 1940, the British presumed that Vichy French hostility was certain in any case, and the drastic steps taken against the French fleet did eliminate a risk that, however small, was unacceptable to Britain's global strategy. Of the nine French battleships and battle-cruisers afloat in late June 1940, only one was now in any condition to fight. In the longer term, a blockaded France would not be able to restore its fleet to a position where it could affect the outcome of the conflict. While public relations was not the point of the operation, the brutal attack on a former ally made an important statement, at home and in America, about Britain's determination to carry on the fight.[72]

Yet the attack on Mers-el-Kébir had a heavy and lasting cost. The antipathy created by Britain's actions – particularly in the French navy – would make it even more difficult to win France's colonies back to the Allied side. Over the coming years, as Britain struggled to defend its empire, it would repeatedly be brought into confrontation with its former ally. The sailors killed at Mers-el-Kébir would not be the final casualties of this Anglo-French conflict.

PART FOUR

Battles of Britain

On 13 July 1940, George King, a legal clerk living in Sanderstead in Surrey, composed another entry in the diary he was keeping for his son, Cyril. He and his wife had had no news of their boy for weeks now, since the War Office had told them that he was missing, presumed captured, at Dunkirk. They struggled on, checking the casualty lists in the paper, hoping that they would get a telegram or a letter to tell them where he was. George was an old soldier of the last war, who had seen action at Gallipoli, and he had an idea of the things that could happen to a man in battle. The best thing, he found, was to keep his wife talking to other people. That way they could both stop thinking for a bit.

In the evenings, in the scant time he got between turning out for the Home Guard, George tried to set down some of his thoughts. What had started as a letter had soon turned into a journal. George wanted to make sure that when Cyril was found, he'd be able to catch up with everything that had happened in the meantime. Tonight, like a lot of nights, George was angry. Who had let things come to this?

> Heavens! Summing this mess up, I daily think that all our rulers of the past few years should be shot at once. They <u>must</u> have known the position yet did absolutely nothing but smoke a pipe, do nothing and talk about 'tranquillity' and 'Hitler missing the bus'. The one man who kept on storming (Winston Churchill) is now Premier, and has the terrible task of getting us out of the hole, which we shall do somehow, if we can blast a way through or round the damned Civil Service.[1]

In comparison to the glacial pace of the Bore War, May 1940 marked the start of a period of extraordinary drama. For the next year, the UK was the target for major German air and sea offensives, while the

Italians, belatedly joined by the Germans, threatened the Empire in the Middle East. The result was not just one, but rather a series of battles of Britain that lasted until the summer of 1941: campaigns in the skies, the seas and on land in which the central issue was whether Germany could force the UK out of the war.

Britain's position was not as perilous as it at first appeared. Despite its stunning success over France, Germany could not complete its unexpected victory. Yet the threat of invasion, the fear of fifth columnists and the opening of an air campaign against the UK all transformed the home front into a theatre of war and produced a sense of profound crisis. Anger, disappointment and patriotism combined in a potent brew. With a new regime in Downing Street, and Labour back sharing power, the politics of the 1930s were thrown sharply off course.[2] This was a moment of great uncertainty and great opportunity, in which reputations were broken and made. The repercussions would be felt for decades to come.

The battles were fought in the skies overhead, in the waters of the Atlantic and the sands of the Western Desert, but also in the docks and the factories. As the restraints under which the war had previously been fought were thrown off, this was a period of tremendous military and industrial mobilization. The rapid escalation of the country's economic war effort had more significant consequences for everyday British life than any direct action by the enemy.

Simultaneously, British resistance accelerated a remarkable shift in international relations. The only way to overcome the new strategic situation created by the Fall of France was for the UK to become more dependent on America, ceding money and power in return for economic support. For the British, this was a story of frustration, disappointment and decline, but for Hitler, it was proof that he was facing an Anglo-American bloc against which he would eventually have to fight a transatlantic war. The only way to be sure of having the resources for that struggle, and to complete Germany's destiny, was to complete the drive to the east and open a new conflict against the Soviet Union. Meanwhile, the continuing European crisis offered opportunities for expansion to an increasingly desperate Japan. The Battles of Britain would lay the path to a bigger, more terrible, war.[3]

15

Finest Hour

Long before he got to work, Sir Horace Wilson must have known that 11 May 1940 was going to be a difficult day. The previous evening it had been announced that Neville Chamberlain had resigned and was going to be replaced by Winston Churchill. As Wilson, the permanent secretary of the Treasury and the head of the Civil Service, walked through 10 Downing Street on the way to the office he had occupied since 1935, the junior officials were all aflutter. Who was going to go and who would be kept on by the new prime minister? As soon as Wilson opened the door to his room, he got part of the answer.[1]

Sitting in his chair was Churchill's henchman, Brendan Bracken. As usual, his shock of red hair was askew and there was a malicious glint in his eye. Bracken was the new prime minister's most loyal follower, and he had spent the last nine months intriguing shamelessly on Churchill's behalf against Chamberlain. Many people claimed to see a physical resemblance between the Irish-Australian newspaper owner and his hero, and scurrilous (and false) rumour had it that Bracken was Churchill's illegitimate son. Next to him lounged Churchill's actual offspring, Randolph. There was no mistaking whose child he was, although despite his best efforts to emulate his father, Randolph only outdid him in pugnacity and love for the bottle. They had come to tell Wilson to clear out.

Churchill and Attlee were negotiating over the new government, and the Labour leader needed another scalp to take back to his party. Labour blamed Wilson for the severity of the anti-union legislation that had been introduced after the General Strike of 1926, as well as his hard work for Chamberlain since 1937. Attlee insisted he had to go.

Churchill was more than happy to comply. Now Bracken told Wilson that if the prime minister ever caught sight of him again, he would be sent into exile as 'governor of Greenland'.

Wilson duly vacated the building. He was only saved from being sacked when the new chancellor, Kingsley Wood, in an unusual display of loyalty, reminded his colleagues that getting rid of a civil servant for implementing the policies laid down to him by ministers would wreck the whole system of British government. Instead of Greenland, Wilson was exiled to his office in the Treasury until he reached the minimum age for retirement in 1942. He was swiftly shuffled out of public life and never held a major post again.

It was an extraordinary defenestration. Under Chamberlain, Wilson had been one of the most powerful men in the country. Now his influence vanished overnight. Chamberlain had hardly been averse to getting rid of inconvenient opponents and inconvenient advisors, or the use of political dirty tricks – as Sir Robert Vansittart, Anthony Eden and Leslie Hore-Belisha could all attest – but this was something else. Wilson might completely have misjudged Hitler and perpetuated appeasement, but he was a legitimately appointed civil servant, who had risen to the top of his profession by dint of ability and application. Now he was despatched in brutal fashion by two men who were only in Downing Street because they belonged to the coterie of hangers-on around the new prime minister. Under Winston Churchill, the style of government was plainly going to be very different.

'WINSTON'S PROBING AND RESTLESS MIND'

This was exactly what Chamberlain's supporters had been afraid of. At the Foreign Office the evening before, the former prime minister's private secretaries, Lord Dunglass and Jock Colville, had cracked open a bottle of champagne with Rab Butler and Chips Channon, and toasted Chamberlain as the 'King over the Water'. Butler, recorded Channon, 'believed this sudden coup of Winston and his rabble was a serious disaster'. The 'good clean tradition of English politics', he lamented 'had been sold to the greatest adventurer in modern political history'. Referring to Churchill's American mother, Butler called the new prime minister a 'half-breed . . . whose main support was that of inefficient but talkative people of a similar type'.[2]

Butler's habit of speaking his mind would shortly get him into serious trouble, but looking at the associates that Churchill brought with him into office, it was easy to see what he meant. Bracken had made a place in London society by revelling in the reputation of a sharp-mouthed, quick-witted charlatan. Having accompanied his idol from the Admiralty to Downing Street, he now became the new prime minister's personal private secretary and was elevated – despite the protests of the king – to the Privy Council. Bracken controlled who got to see Churchill and had a major say in all forms of prime ministerial patronage, including church appointments, which fascinated him but bored his master. He liked to act as Churchill's political fixer, keeping him in touch with what was being said in the bars and on the backbenches at Westminster and doling out preferments to keep potential critics happy.[3]

Lord Beaverbrook, who accepted Churchill's request to become minister of aircraft production, fitted a similar mould. Beaverbrook and Churchill's long friendship was reinvigorated by the emotional support that the press lord provided for Churchill during a period of great strain. 'The Beaver' inspired profound loathing among more conventional members of the British establishment (including Churchill's wife, Clementine, who hated the 'bottle imp', and the king, who tried, again unsuccessfully, to block his appointment as well). Many observers failed to appreciate the strength of Churchill and Beaverbrook's intellectual bond. Both were highly reactive men who relied on their instincts in ways that more considered colleagues considered naive. Their shared history meant that Beaverbrook knew how to listen to Churchill's stories, and say the right thing to the prime minister when he was feeling down.[4]

Beaverbrook and Bracken brought out the Tory side of Churchill: Tory not just in terms of nationalism, imperialism and anti-socialism, but also in its original, anti-puritan sense of an exuberant dislike of convention and a louche enjoyment of personal indulgence.[5] This was the Churchill of boozy dinners, smoky late-night arguments, jobs for his in-laws and cronies, spending the day in garish dressing-gowns and ploughing through ministerial boxes in bed.

It is impossible to imagine Neville Chamberlain conducting business in this way, but for Churchill, it was part of a political life. Decades before, he and Lloyd George had employed a strand of Edwardian sociability – all-male dinners with good food and drink – to advance their political careers: forging bonds with wealthy businessmen and press barons such as Beaverbrook, building links with clubbable colleagues, all of them doing favours for each other behind the scenes. By 1940, Churchill had developed this tradition into the lifestyle of the court with which he surrounded himself. It prized the wit of the powerful, and disdained serious men like Chamberlain or Attlee because they were boring. It was all very corrupt and nepotistic, and in the eyes of many more democratic politicians it was deeply unsound.

Ironically, this may also have been one of the reasons that Butler was kept in his post at the Foreign Office. On reappointing him, Churchill remarked on not only Butler's knack of answering parliamentary questions 'without giving too much away', but also the fact that after the tumult of the India Act, Butler had invited him to a reconciliatory party at his house. To the new prime minister, this was the sort of thing that mattered.[6]

For those who could fit into Churchill's world, induction into his inner circle could be a lot of fun. Jock Colville, for example, who had been surprised by the attachment he had developed for Chamberlain and went back to work at Number 10 wearing a 'cheap and sensational-looking' suit that he thought would match the new government, soon found himself being drawn in, like the rest of the secretariat around the prime minister, as he danced attendance on Churchill.[7] Colville was young, handsome, upper class and arrogant (one of his colleagues compared him to Mr Darcy): a combination that Churchill liked.[8] The nature of his job meant that he spent a lot of time with the prime minister and his family, including Churchill's youngest daughter, Mary, to whom he became devoted.[9] Like many of the people around the prime minister, Colville was keeping a diary, which made very clear how quickly he was enchanted by his new boss.[10] Having initially doubted the wisdom of Churchill's appointment, on 19 May 1940 Colville wrote that 'Whatever Winston's shortcomings', he seemed

to be the man for the occasion. His spirit is indomitable and even if France and England should be lost, I feel he would carry on the crusade himself with a band of privateers. Perhaps my judgements of him have been harsh, but the situation was very different a few weeks ago.[11]

By the time he had been working for Churchill for a month, Colville had decided that:

> Chamberlain had drive, but he had not Winston's probing and restless mind: he expected his subordinates to work with the same tirelessness and efficiency that he did himself, but he never questioned their ability to do so. Winston, on the other hand, is always looking for shortcomings and inspires others to be as zealous ferrets as himself.

It was 'Winston and Beaverbrook', Colville declared, 'who have really galvanised the country and the Government departments'.[12]

Whether or not this was an accurate interpretation of how the country was mobilized, it was certainly how Churchill liked to see himself: the dynamo driving on the war effort. That was reflected in the way he organized his administration. Churchill's new place as prime minister and minister of defence positioned him at the hub of political and military decision-making. Through his military adjunct, General Ismay (another member of his inner circle, a loyal attendant but a strategic non-entity), Churchill was in constant touch with the chiefs of staff. Ismay acted as military secretary to the chiefs of staff, and Churchill sometimes sat in on their discussions. Churchill also chaired the Defence Committees of the Cabinet (one on operations, one on supply), to which went strategic issues that raised wider questions of policy before they were taken to the War Cabinet for approval. (From here on, references to the Defence Committee indicate the Defence Committee (Operations).)

Churchill was no dictator, but his domination of the structures of strategy gave him an influence over military matters that Chamberlain had never wanted, let alone possessed. He was absolutely convinced that this was an essential part of leading the country in war, and he would have left office if it had been taken away from him. Under Churchill, strategic debates spilled out of the committee room and into a never-ending discussion between the prime minister, favoured advisors and experts and the chiefs of staff. Unlike Chamberlain, Churchill enjoyed the excitement of being at war. He was fascinated by the minutiae of uniforms and weapons and loved the idea of returning to the front line himself. Senior officers found it hard not to be won over – at least for a while – by his boyish enthusiasm for the fight. Yet they also struggled to cope with Churchill's approach to military strategy.

The new prime minister had a strong and creative imagination, and a lot of experience drawn from his long political career. Sometimes this afforded him deep strategic insights, but it also meant that he was prey to peculiar obsessions that drove his colleagues to despair. As the campaign in Norway had shown, he was particularly keen to find a way to use Britain's command of the seas to gain an offensive advantage against its enemies. In the first months of his premiership, he was also in much need of some quick military victories to secure his political position. General Dill, the new chief of the imperial general staff, summed up the problem with Churchill as strategist in a letter to Lord Gort: 'I'm not sure that Winston isn't the greatest menace. No-one seems to be able to control him. He is full of ideas, many brilliant, but most of them impracticable. He has such drive and personality that no-one seems able to stand up to him.'[13] Of the three chiefs of staff in place in May 1940 – John Dill, Dudley Pound and Cyril Newall – Dill stood up to him most and consequently took the main force of the prime minister's disdain.[14] Churchill believed that strategy needed to be tested by argument, and when the chiefs opposed him he tried to batter them into submission on his home turf – late night meetings with everyone else's eyelids drooping – or to circumvent them by coming up with his own schemes and communicating direct with commanders in the field. To his enemies, this was just further evidence of his irresponsibility.[15]

Churchill liked to paint himself as a decisive leader. In war, as in politics, his first, impetuous instincts were almost always aggressive, but given time to reflect on the verdict of history, hesitations crept in more than he would subsequently like to admit. Churchill was not a great believer in making long-term strategic plans, let alone sticking to them. Things changed too quickly in a war, he believed, to be tied down. He normally assumed they were going to get better – because he was an eternal optimist with a strong belief that his country was destined for glory. This, combined with a habit of getting involved in the matter at hand to the exclusion of more distant contingencies, would contribute to some colossal British disasters over the next five years.

Churchill's involvement in the design of operations was matched by a remarkable interest in the material side of the war. He proved no keener than his predecessor to appoint a single production supremo who might have the status to challenge for his job. Yet Churchill himself was intensely interested in weaponry, production statistics and supplies. Since he dominated both the Defence Committees, which approved the equipment plans of the armed forces, turned them into broad objectives for the supply departments to follow, and took the final decisions in contests of priority between them, he effectively operated as his own minister of production.[16]

This was one of the areas where Churchill relied on the help of another crony, Professor Frederick Lindemann, the Oxford physicist who acted as his scientific advisor. Lindemann was a teetotal, non-smoking vegetarian, but he and Churchill shared similarly reactionary views on race and democracy, and Lindemann, like Bracken and Beaverbrook, provided that combination of adulation and argument that Churchill needed from his confidants. 'The Prof' was given a remit to roam at will over the science and statistics of government. Among other things, Churchill got him to produce his own analyses of departmental data so that the prime minister did not have to rely on what he was being told by his subordinates. By boiling down the numbers of the war effort into a digestible form, Lindemann helped Churchill feel that he was on top of the whole machine. Not coincidentally, Lindemann's statistical analyses often backed up the arguments that the prime minister wanted to make at the time. Another Churchillian crony, Major Desmond Morton, fulfilled a similar role to Lindemann's when it came to matters of espionage and intelligence.[17]

Having finally achieved the premiership, Churchill was desperate to hold on to it, but he was no better a political strategist than a military one. To an extent unusual in a politician who had made it to Number 10, Churchill's belligerent nature, addiction to cliques and frequent giving of hostages to fortune often threatened to undermine his own position. The turmoil of Chamberlain's fall had left Westminster a seething mass of ambition and anger. With no solid bloc of party support behind him, to begin with Churchill appeared politically vulnerable. Perhaps Chamberlain would not be the last prime minister to be toppled before the end of the war?

As his predecessor's fate had shown, Churchill was dependent on Labour's participation in the government. Initially, the party seemed to struggle to acclimatize itself to power. Inside the War Cabinet, neither Attlee nor Greenwood had Churchill's charismatic force. Having done so well for Labour since the start of the war, during the second half of 1940 Greenwood underwent an alcoholic decline, while Attlee busily used his influence behind the scenes rather than leading from the front.

Two Labour ministers outside the War Cabinet were much more publicly visible than either Attlee or Greenwood. At the Ministry of Supply, Herbert Morrison employed all the skills of organization and publicity he had learned at the London County Council. As minister of labour, Ernest Bevin was at the forefront of the government's mobilization of manpower. Over the next year, they would become extremely powerful figures on the home front. Yet the formation of the new coalition had also tied up the Labour leaders with Churchill's fate. Having struggled so carefully to rework the political landscape, it was now extremely difficult for them to leave office without sacrificing their hard-won reputation for responsibility.[18]

Though Labour's involvement was vital to the government's legitimacy, the balance of parliamentary power still lay firmly with the Conservatives. That helps to explain why, for all the drama of Sir Horace Wilson's removal from Downing Street, the changeover in ministerial personnel in May 1940 was actually much more limited than talk of a revolution might suggest. Churchill's capture of the premiership left many Conservative MPs fuming. Most continued to give their loyalty not to the new prime minister, but to Chamberlain, who remained leader of the party. It was not surprising, therefore, that David Margesson remained as Conservative chief whip. Not only had he helped to ease the transition of power, but the prime minister also needed Margesson to maintain discipline on the backbenches. Churchill and his cronies fully expected that he might shortly face a counter-coup from his own side.

In the War Cabinet, Halifax and Chamberlain hoped to hold back Churchill's impetuous nature – acting, in Lord Hankey's simile, like two wise old elephants standing each side of his untrained bull – but they also remained Churchill's biggest rivals for the premiership: the men who were expected to step in when he slipped up. Perhaps the most dangerous figure from Churchill's point of view, however, was Anthony Eden. Like Churchill, Eden was marked by his opposition to appeasement, but he was also youthful, progressive and already nominated by Baldwin as the Conservative Party's heir apparent. Churchill appointed him secretary of state for war. Eden liked being in charge of the army: it brought him close to the war and allowed him to keep a prominent place in the public eye. Though Churchill could not for the moment bring him into the War Cabinet, Eden was able to involve himself more closely than any other service minister in the rolling, informal argument over strategy. Eden was often irritated by Churchill's insistence on interfering in military affairs, but he too found it easy to be swept up by the prime minister when he turned on the charm. Over the summer of 1940, Eden came to believe that Churchill was the best war leader the country could have – at least for the moment. Churchill and his entourage, however, never forgot the danger that Eden might like to hurry on the succession.[19] Like Chamberlain and Halifax, the threat that Eden posed was of a resurgence of that moderate Conservatism that had kept Churchill out of office for almost the whole of the 1930s. One of the great stories of the period 1940–41 was the way in which a mixture of ill-fortune, misjudgement and intrigue despatched each of these rivals, while Churchill, with some assistance from Adolf Hitler and the Luftwaffe, established his reputation as a national saviour.

'A KIND OF FUEHRER'

The start of the German offensive in the west sparked an immediate response on the home front. Chamberlain and Bevin both now drew up plans for the government to take more compulsory powers. Indicatively, Chamberlain's were the furthest reaching:

> The control over persons would be such as to enable the competent authority to require and direct the services or labour of every individual over 16 years of age. The control over property would be such as to enable complete command to be obtained of all means of production and means of defence.[20]

As Chamberlain explained to the War Cabinet on 22 May, 'He did not think that the public would take this amiss. Indeed, he thought that at this, the gravest moment in our history, they would regard anything less as insufficient.'[21] That afternoon, Parliament passed in a single sitting the Emergency Powers (Defence) Act 1940, which confirmed ministers' right to put through any regulations judged necessary for the defence of the country without further legislation.

Formally, this was just a renewal of the powers conferred on the government at the start of the war, but with an invasion apparently looming, the new administration made clear that it would use them differently. Presenting the Bill to the Commons, Attlee explained that:

'we are taking control, in a time of emergency, so that in the national interest we may utilise all our resources for the common weal'.[22] Industrial production, profits and wages could all now be made subject to government control, with the supply ministries empowered to intervene in private enterprises; Excess Profits Tax would be raised to 100 per cent; and the minister of labour would have the power to direct anyone to any work.

As Bevin himself later put it, on 22 May he 'suddenly found myself a kind of Fuehrer with powers to order anybody anywhere'.[23] It was widely presumed that this was the precursor to the immediate introduction of industrial, as well as military, conscription. Bevin, however, was a fan of what he called 'voluntary-ism'. For the moment, he held back on conscripting civilian workers. Nor did he use his powers of direction to remedy shortages of skilled labour, instead telling factories to implement greater dilution with more unskilled recruits. He did, however, subject workers in essential industries to new controls, introducing regulations on the re-employment of miners, dockers, agricultural labourers and munitions workers in an effort to ensure that they were not attracted elsewhere by higher wages.[24]

He also staged a crucial intervention in industrial relations. On the same day that the government's emergency legislation was announced, Bevin reformed the National Joint Advisory Committee into a new, smaller, Joint Consultative Committee, where employers and union leaders would meet as equals to help him establish labour policy. At the start of June, in line with Bevin's wishes, the JCC decided that the government should not try to control wages, but that it should ban strikes and lockouts for the rest of the war, an instruction shortly given legal force in the Ministry of Labour's Order No. 1305. Weeks before, Bevin had been telling the previous government that he would resist compulsion at all costs. Now he was enacting compulsory measures that would have been unthinkable to his predecessors.[25]

These measures were just part of a noticeable acceleration of domestic mobilization. By the end of June, the supply ministries had issued control orders covering 1,500 firms and the Board of Trade had cut supplies for the production of civilian consumer goods by a third, to maximize military output and release labour for munitions.[26] Between April and June, 426,000 recruits joined the armed forces, an increase of more than a third on the figure for January to March.[27] Unemployment fell to

645,000 people.[28] Morrison called for workers to 'Go To It', moving to seven-day-a-week working and giving up their Whit holidays in order to

> work our fingers to the bone for our sons and their future. We are going to do whatever lies in our power to match, and to be worthy of, the sacrifices that are being made for us. We are going to cut down our leisure, cut down our comfort, blot out of our thought every private and sectional aim.[29]

The transformation to total war was very far from complete, but the change of gear was obvious.

During June, the system of Cabinet committees that dealt with the home front was overhauled. Typically, it was Attlee who played a leading role in pruning back the structures that had become overgrown during the previous administration. The Ministerial Priority Committee was replaced with a Production Council. A revamped Economic Policy Committee was supposed to consider the broader arrangement of the civil economy. Together with the Civil Defence, Food Policy and Home Policy committees, the Production Council and Economic Policy Committee were overseen by a new Lord President's Committee that would tie together their work.[30] Four out of five of the home front committees were chaired by Attlee or Greenwood. Just at the moment when 'socialist' policies had become unavoidable as a means to accelerate the war effort, Attlee secured Labour's influence across the home front.[31]

As lord president, however, it was Chamberlain who co-ordinated all these committees. Although he was devastated by the loss of the premiership, and in worsening pain from an undiagnosed cancer, he now became a driving force in mobilizing the whole country. Since, with some significant exceptions – munitions production and food imports – Churchill was not interested in the organization and management of civilian life in the same way that he was in military affairs, he liked the fact that he could leave such matters in the safe hands of his predecessor, while he got on with fighting the war.

'SATELLITES OF THE MONSTER'

One immediate use to which the Defence Regulations were put was to guard against the menace of subversion. By the time the Germans attacked France and the Low Countries, the British were already very worried that they faced an enemy within. At the end of the 1930s, reports of Germany's seizure of Austria and Czechoslovakia had emphasized the role of a 'fifth column' of agents provocateurs and domestic Fascists. After the war began, German radio propaganda emphasized the help that the Nazis were already getting from British dissidents: most famously in the English-language broadcasts of William Joyce, 'Lord Haw-Haw', from Hamburg.[32] In the spring of 1940, the speed of German victories encouraged the belief that Denmark and Norway must also have been undermined from within. By mid-April, the *Daily Express*, *Daily Mail*, *Sunday Dispatch* and *Yorkshire Post* had all taken up the idea that Britain was riddled with fifth columnists.[33] Inside government, the Home Office held out against any precipitate action, but public concerns strengthened demands from the military and the Security Service that all potential subversives must be detained.

Suspicions fell on German and Austrian expatriates, their numbers swollen in the late 1930s by Jewish refugees from Nazism. At the start of the war, largely because it lacked the resources to do anything else, the Home Office had classified these 'enemy aliens' according to the degree of risk they seemed to pose. It interned only the thousand or so in Category A, the most supposedly dangerous. On 12 May, however, internment was extended to all German and Austrian males between sixteen and sixty living within a widely defined coastal strip from southern England to north-east Scotland. The round-up brought in about another 2,000 internees, including large numbers of anti-Nazi German merchant seamen, and academic refugees who had found shelter at the University of Cambridge.[34]

The German capture of Scandinavia and the opening of the campaign in the west also strengthened official anxieties about an invasion. British strategists had long presumed that the Germans would push forward into Holland, Belgium and northern France to establish bases from which they could launch air and sea attacks on the UK, but that they would get sufficient warning to fight off any attempted invasion before it reached the shore. The failure to spot the invasions of Denmark and Norway, however, led to a profound crisis of confidence in the capacity of British intelligence to predict where the enemy would strike next.[35] During May and June, no one was willing to rule out the possibility of a surprise attack, and as the Germans swept through Holland and Belgium, the British accepted that they would, in their efficient, Teutonic way, have prepared to launch themselves across the North Sea against an under-protected United Kingdom. On 21 May, Ismay told Churchill that the chiefs of staff feared that the Germans had 'the plan for the invasion of this country worked out to the last detail', and that the government should prepare itself.[36]

A key presumption about any such invasion was that it would be headed by German parachutists. During the Phoney War, the commander of Home Forces, General Walter Kirke, had worked on the basis that any invasion would start with an airborne *coup de main* to seize a port at which more troops could be landed. With the bulk of the army's fighting units in France, Kirke's forces were small and underequipped. He hoped that local garrisons would hold out against the airborne attackers while he rushed mobile reserves to their aid. In April, news reports about the successes of German paratroopers in Norway caught the popular imagination. With military patrols few and far between in large parts of the country, concerned citizens who were worried about the enemy descending undetected started to form their own groups to guard against an invasion.[37]

During the first days of the attack on Holland, fears about paratroopers and fifth columnists combined. On 11 May, even *The Times*, which had condemned the 'hysterics' of the press in late April, argued that the public must be prepared to fight invading parachutists who would land in civilian garb and be fluent English speakers.[38] On 13 May, the Sunday papers were plastered with images of parachute-filled skies and warnings of how an invasion might strike the UK.[39] Harried by MPs and worried by the prospect of vigilantism, the War Office hastily put in place its own scheme for 'Local Defence Volunteers'. On the evening of 14 May, Eden, newly appointed as war secretary, broadcast an appeal on the BBC asking men between the ages of sixteen and sixty-five who were willing to serve in these local units to register at their nearest police station. The response was as remarkable as the rush to the colours at the start of the First World War. Within six days, 250,000 men had come forward to join the 'parashots'.[40]

On the same day as Eden's speech, Sir Nevile Bland, the British ambassador to the Netherlands, arrived back in the UK. Still stunned by his experiences, Bland wrote a report on the Dutch disintegration that was widely circulated in Whitehall. In the event of a German attack on the UK, Bland warned, fanatical Nazi youths would be parachuted in to 'cause as much death and destruction as they could before being killed themselves'. They would be helped by foreign women who had come into the country disguised as maidservants. Bland insisted that he had

> not the least doubt that, when the signal is given, as it will scarcely fail to be when Hitler so decides, there will be satellites of the monster <u>all over the country</u> who will at once embark on widespread sabotage and attacks on civilians and the military indiscriminately.[41]

After Bland's paper was considered at the War Cabinet on 15 May, Sir John Anderson, the home secretary, issued the order that all male enemy aliens classified as 'Category B' were to be interned on the following day. Anderson was fighting a rearguard action against mass internment, but he highlighted to the Cabinet the range of groups against whom action might now need to be considered, including British Fascists and Communists.[42]

The authorities had initially been cautious about detaining home-grown dissidents. The Security Service had both Communists and Fascists under surveillance, but it was the latter who became the focus of the crackdown on fifth columnists. MI5 now revealed links between an American, Tyler Kent, a fiercely isolationist cypher clerk at the US embassy who had collected secret cables demonstrating Roosevelt's support for the Allies, and the 'Right Group', an extreme far-right organization headed by the anti-Semitic Conservative MP Archibald Maule Ramsay. Some of Kent's stash of telegrams had been passed through the Right Group to the Italian embassy, and thence back to Rome and Berlin.[43]

Ramsay had also held secret meetings with representatives of other Fascist groups, including Oswald Mosley's British Union. During May and June 1940, Mosley maintained the British Union's policy of no co-operation in the 'Jewish War' and immediate peace negotiations. As the crisis in France deepened, he further limited the circumstances in which his patriotic followers ought to fight for their country – now they should wait not just until Britain was in danger, but until it was actually invaded.[44] In the circumstances, Mosley's opposition to the war aroused great popular anger. When he appeared at the Middleton and Prestwich by-election in May 1940, he was nearly lynched.

When MI5 officials met with the home secretary after Tyler Kent had been arrested, they insisted that his involvement with the Right Group was part of a much wider Fascist network of subversion. On 22 May, the War Cabinet agreed to extend the Defence Regulations to allow the internment of anyone believed to possess 'hostile associations', or to have the potential to engage in 'acts prejudicial' to the prosecution of the war. Later that day, Mosley and other BUF leaders were detained, followed by another 747 British Fascists over the next month. News of Mosley's detention met with widespread public approval, but it also fed a wildfire of suspicion and rumour as every busybody and fantasist in the country went on the lookout for fifth columnists.[45]

On 11 June, after Italy entered hostilities, all adult Italian men in the UK were detained without trial. On 24 June, following the French armistice, the internment of all Germans and Italians who had been classified as Category C – posing no threat – began, and continued for the next two weeks. In total, between May and July, well over 26,000 Germans and Italians were deprived of their liberty.[46] Some of them were indeed Nazis or Fascists – although many British Italians had joined the party as a matter of course rather than of ideological attachment. The overwhelming majority were not.

The huge numbers being processed during the early summer totally overwhelmed any system for accommodating or screening internees, and many were subject to deprivation, theft and verbal abuse. Eventually, most 'alien' internees ended up in camps on the Isle of Man, but the British tried to foist the most supposedly dangerous on the Dominions. The resulting deportations in fact swept up many who had been classified as posing no threat, dividing families and contributing to a tragedy when the liner *Arandora Star*, carrying 1,190 internees to Canada, was torpedoed by a U-boat on 2 July. Fewer than 600 of them survived.[47]

In fact, there was no fifth column. MI5 had, through a mix of luck and judgement, rounded up almost every German agent in place in the UK in the early days of the war, and had just begun to turn them back on their former masters in the double-agent deceptions that were to yield significant fruit later in the war. One of their early successes was to pass on the identity cards with which German intelligence equipped the next round of agents it attempted to insert into the UK, with the result that they, too, were swiftly apprehended.[48] Yet it was precisely because these bogeymen weren't there that they got such a grip on the imagination. As a pamphlet issued by the Ministry of Information explained: 'Anyone who thinks ... that it "can't happen here", has simply fallen into the trap laid by the fifth column itself. For *the first job of the fifth column is to make people think that it does not exist.*'[49]

'A DIRECT, CHILDISH TIME'

Meanwhile, recruitment to the Local Defence Volunteers rolled on. By the end of June, 1.4 million men had put their names down. The War Office's plans for these volunteers fitted them into existing Army Command areas and Territorial Associations, but made it very clear that they were not to count themselves as proper soldiers. LDV units were built around geographic locations (for example, 'A' (Winchester City) Company, 5th Hampshire Battalion), or places of employment. Glasgow, for instance, raised two railway battalions of Local Defence Volunteers, three from the Post Office and four other 'works' units, including one recruited almost entirely from the different departments of the city council. These were the closest this conflict would come to the 'Pals' battalions of the last war.

Service in the LDV was unpaid, and originally there was no formal rank structure. The local police were required to screen applications and disbarred men suspected of Communist associations. In Northern Ireland, fears that weapons might be handed over to the IRA were circumvented by making the LDV an offshoot of the mainly Protestant Royal Ulster Constabulary. This essentially excluded Catholics from its ranks. As far as the War Office was concerned, women were not meant to bear arms and should stick to supporting the LDV, if at all, with cups of tea and first aid, but in this first flush of voluntary enthusiasm, some local groups also involved women who wanted to defend themselves.[50]

In practice, there were few weapons to go round. The army released some rifles, but the regular forces were short of weapons themselves. Instead the LDV had to rely on sporting and hunting guns (the War Office made a nationwide appeal for private owners to hand them over on 23 May), on petrol bombs (of which a million and a half were under manufacture in the south of England by 10 June) and even on swords and cudgels. By mid-May the more active groups were already assembling caches of weapons, organizing patrols and prevailing on their wives to sew the brassard arm bands that every volunteer was meant to wear. Until uniforms arrived, these were their only protection, if they were captured by the Germans, against being shot as guerrilla fighters rather than treated as prisoners of war.[51]

Since the volunteers had been warned that neither uniform nor identification was necessarily evidence of bona fides, they felt fully entitled to stop and question anyone they came across after dark, including courting couples, delivery drivers, the emergency services and members of the armed forces. They were encouraged by local organizers eager to foster aggression as a replacement for proper weapons. Occasionally, farce descended into tragedy. On at least sixteen occasions during June 1940, innocent travellers were killed or wounded when they failed to stop at LDV roadblocks.[52]

These roadblocks were just part of the physical preparation against the prospect of invasion. Although anti-invasion planning had previously centred on an attack over the North Sea, German successes across the Channel now put more or less the whole southern and eastern coastline under threat. First independently, then at official suggestion, women, children and the elderly began to be evacuated from this vulnerable area. By mid-July, approximately 127,000 people had left the seaward edge of East Anglia. Another 80,000 had gone from Kent.[53] Behind them, beach defences of barbed wire, trenches, mines and scaffolding-pole obstacles began hastily to be erected. The Royal Navy rushed 600 spare big guns out of storage to cover possible landing beaches and ports. By late May, open rural spaces were being covered with poles, wires and, over roadways, giant steel hoops to prevent a landing by German gliders. At the start of June, it was announced that church bells were only to be rung as a warning sign in the event of invasion, and orders went out to remove or cover up signposts so that newly dropped enemy paratroopers would not know their location.[54]

On 27 May, General Ironside replaced Kirke as commander of Home Forces. This was meant to be a job that suited the bluff soldier better than dealing with politicians as chief of the imperial general staff. Like Kirke, however, he faced a shortage of troops and equipment. When he began, it was far from clear how much of the BEF would escape from

Dunkirk. The rescue of hundreds of thousands more soldiers than expected brought up the army's strength, but most units arrived back in the UK in a state of disorganization and without their heavy equipment and transport. Briefly, there were not even enough rifles for all the regular soldiers, let alone the LDV. There were still more than 200 infantry and cruiser tanks in the UK on 10 June, but for the first two weeks of his appointment, Ironside did not have a single 2-pounder-armed tank under his direct command. His sole mobile reserve for East Anglia, the 2nd London Division, had only two anti-tank guns.[55]

To try to get round these shortages, Ironside adopted a very static defensive approach. Every village would be turned into a strongpoint by the LDV, backed up by 'stop lines' of fixed fortifications that would seal off any bridgehead. By the last weeks of June, an enormous construction effort was under way across eastern and south-eastern England to dig anti-tank ditches, build pillboxes and lay minefields. Although overseen by the Royal Engineers, much of this work was undertaken by civilian contractors. By 25 June, they were building 900 pillboxes in Kent alone. Put up at speed by firms without experience of military construction, many of the defences were sited incompetently and poorly built, and would have acted as death-traps for anyone who had to defend them.[56]

Even at the time, it was hard to take some of the defensive preparations wholly seriously. One Essex clergyman pointed out the flaw in his churchwarden's suggestion that the church noticeboard with the village name on it ought to be taken down:

> I wonder if you have considered the possibility of removing the name Wanstead from all the tombstones in the Churchyard on which it occurs. That of course would be quite as much a guide to a parachutist as a notice board outside the Church . . . If you are thinking of taking this action, which seems to me as necessary as the other, it will be a very considerable task, and I presume that the owners of the graves will probably require compensation for the damage.[57]

Yet many more Britons did now regard themselves as being in the front line, and were swept up by both suspicion and excitement. In a lightly fictionalized account published the following year, the writer Margery Allingham confessed that an account of her village's preparations to fight off parachutists looked childish written down but it was a direct, childish time, quite different but more entirely satisfying than any other piece of life which I at least have ever experienced. It was big enough and sound enough to fill you, and if it went to your head a bit the luckier you.[58]

In fact, Hitler was only just about to ask his armed forces to *start* planning for a *possible* invasion of the UK. Always better at starting wars than finishing them, the Germans had attacked in May without any scheme for what they would do next. The Wehrmacht's senior generals, who had not believed they could win such a stunningly swift victory, expected to be bogged down in the trenches of Flanders. Hitler knew that destiny was on his side, but presumed that once the French had surrendered, the British would see sense and follow suit. Throughout the period in which the British were most worried about an attack catching them unprepared, the country was under no danger of invasion whatsoever.[59]

'THE ATTRIBUTES OF A VICTORY'

As official worries and public fears fed off each other, the idea that the UK might be invaded at any moment had important consequences for reactions to the military catastrophe that unfolded in France. One way to get a sense of what it was like to live through those tumultuous days is to examine the reports on civilian morale prepared by the Home Intelligence Department of the Ministry of Information. After nearly being shut down due to the press kerfuffle over the Ministry in autumn 1939, Home Intelligence had been revived under a new director, Mary Adams. A politically progressive former research biologist and BBC television producer, Adams was married to an anti-appeasement Conservative MP.[60] Her department's job was to analyse attitudes on the home front, mainly to improve the design of government publicity. She had known Tom Harrisson, one of the directors of Mass-Observation, since 1933 and their friendship led to M-O securing a new three-month research contract with the Ministry, starting in April 1940.

The deal allowed M-O to continue its long-term mission of recording everyday life, but it also meant a final break between Charles

Madge and Tom Harrisson. Madge had grown weary of their disagreements and didn't want to spy for the government, but he had also managed to secure his own research grant. He now parted ways with Mass-Observation to conduct an investigation into working-class attitudes to saving and spending for John Maynard Keynes, who wanted data to support his campaign for compulsory saving. By the time Madge presented his findings, Keynes had an office in the Treasury. There really was no escape from the war effort.[61]

Home Intelligence was about to start producing a weekly report on domestic morale when the German offensive began in the west. From mid-May, it produced a daily report on public opinion.[62] Each consisted of a short overall summary followed by points from the thirteen Civil Defence regions of the UK. At this stage, the reports were based heavily on two sources. The first was phone conversations from London with the Ministry's regional intelligence officers about the mood in their surrounding area, as understood through their contacts with pillars of local society, including doctors, businessmen, WVS organizers and trade union officials. The second were reports from Mass-Observation. M-O's paid investigators based in London, Bolton, Worcester and rural Suffolk conducted a twice-weekly 'News Quota', in which they asked about sixty people in the street what they thought about recent events, and Harrisson provided regular updates on a variety of topics, some of which went into the Home Intelligence summaries almost verbatim.

The reports therefore relied a lot on personal impressions, but they were a genuine attempt to gauge what was being talked about across the country, and they at least offer insights into what the people involved in compiling them thought was happening around them over time. The pressure to produce more quantified results led Adams to agree that summer to the setting up of the Wartime Social Survey, initially under the direction of academics at the LSE, which was intended to sample attitudes more scientifically and on a larger scale.

The existence and fate of the reports were themselves significant. Some senior officers within the Ministry of Information were very worried in late May about the 'danger of a break in morale'.[63] Most of the time, Adams offered a more positive reading that was in line with what Harrisson had been saying since Munich. Public opinion was mostly sound for the moment, but it was also highly volatile, and therefore in need of leadership. Despite a widespread circulation within Whitehall

British Civil Defence Regions, 1940

in the summer of 1940, however, the morale reports had little influence outside the Ministry of Information. At the end of July, when the press revealed the existence of the Wartime Social Survey and christened them 'Cooper's Snoopers', the minister of information, Duff Cooper, had to defend Home Intelligence against the charge that they were 'spying round the homes of ordinary citizens, who are already sufficiently harassed and perturbed'.[64] The outcry ensured that the WSS was limited to practical issues of domestic policy rather than questions of morale. Ironically, given that its activities had come closer to domestic espionage than anything planned by the WSS, Mass-Observation escaped from the debacle unscathed.[65]

The early daily reports make it clear just how hard it was to work out what was happening in the Battle of France while it was being fought. On 18 May, Home Intelligence noted widespread gloom at the news from France and the Low Countries. A few days later, things seemed to be looking up – in London on 21 May morale was 'considerably improved. A general feeling that "we are holding them", particularly finding expression among the working classes' – only to be cast down again on 22 May when Reynaud's remark that 'only a miracle can save France' was reported on the BBC six o'clock news.[66] By 24 May, however, the morale summary argued that: 'The acute tension of a week ago has been relieved and there is a tendency for people to believe that they now know the worst.'[67]

In fact, the collapse of news from the battlefront had helped to conceal how bad things actually were. With reporters caught up in the retreat, newspapers relied on official announcements that matters were serious but not catastrophic: isolated German units had broken through, but the Allied front line would soon be restored.[68] Only over the next week did the full extent of the military disaster in northern France become clear.

On 28 May, the BEF's director of military intelligence, Major General Noel Mason-Macfarlane, who had returned to London, briefed reporters that the army had been let down by their allies and by a lack of pre-war military spending. Over the following days, the papers duly laid responsibility for betraying 'Gort's Unbreakables' at the door of the Dutch, the Belgian king Leopold, and the failures of British rearmament.[69] On 29 May, Home Intelligence reported widespread public anger at Belgium. In the North Midlands, for example, 'Defection of

Leopold' was being 'suggested as sign of Fifth Column activities in upper strata of society.' In comparison, however, only the Southern England region recorded an 'Undertone of criticism of late Government for having underestimated Germans.'[70] That evening, identified as a 'senior British commander', Mason-Macfarlane broadcast in the BBC's 'Postscript' series, which followed the nine o'clock news. 'Your BEF', he told listeners, 'virtually encircled through no fault of its own', had 'displayed a level of leadership, efficiency and gallantry rarely equalled in the history of the British Army.'[71] Whether to bolster public morale or to protect the army's reputation, Mason-Macfarlane was laying a thick propaganda smokescreen. Whoever was to blame for the defeat, it was not the soldiers.

Now all eyes focused on Dunkirk. On 30 May, with the evacuation officially announced, Home Intelligence suggested that: 'Many people think the Army will succeed in fighting its way out with heavy losses. Few appear to believe the situation is hopeless. The net feeling is one of suspense.'[72] As news of the number of men who had been got away began to filter through, the tension eased. As one of M-O's diarists, an eighteen-year-old female art student in London, put it: 'I feel much better today. Must be because the BEF are safer. News this evening very reassuring. I haven't met anyone these past few days who now thinks we'll lose. They <u>were</u> thinking that a few days ago.'[73]

The evacuation from Dunkirk was immediately portrayed in terms of heroism and national pride. The Pathé Gazette newsreel released on 3 June, for example, declared, over shots of returning servicemen:

> For weeks they have been shelled and bombed from three sides. They had to stagger back into the sea to survive. They were betrayed, but never defeated or dispirited. Round these men there hangs an atmosphere of glory. They're still in formation. They're still grinning, past the mud and oil on their faces.[74]

In a cinema in London, a Mass-Observer noted that this sequence 'gained a higher response of applause' than anything he'd ever seen. 'The whole item lasted about four minutes; for nearly a quarter of that time, that is, a full minute, there was applause. Hitherto the loudest applause has been 10 seconds for the survivors of the Altmark'.[75] The next day, just as Churchill was insisting to the Commons that 'We must be very careful not to assign to this deliverance the attributes of a victory',[76] the daily morale report began by arguing that this was exactly what was taking place: 'in general terms ... the retreat is accepted as a "victory", as a "lasting achievement", as a sign that "we cannot ultimately be beaten", that "we shall always turn a tight corner to our advantage".'[77]

The following evening, J. B. Priestley spoke in the 'Postscript' slot: the first in a series of talks that he had lined up after being badgered by his wife to do more for the war effort.[78] Priestley told listeners that, like them, he had been following the news from Dunkirk: 'now that it's over ... doesn't it seem to you to have an inevitable air about it – as if we had turned a page in the history of Britain and seen a chapter headed "Dunkirk"?' He celebrated 'the little pleasure steamers' that had rescued troops from the beaches, and concluded by reinstalling Dunkirk within a story of national salvation: 'our great grand-children, when they learn how we began this War by snatching glory out of defeat, and then swept on to victory, may also learn how the little holiday steamers made an excursion to hell and came back glorious.'[79]

The counterpart to the passions engendered by the epic of Dunkirk, however, was the question of who was to blame. With the BEF rescued, the hunt for scapegoats ramped up. At the end of May, the *Daily Mirror* and the *Daily Herald* had led the way in blaming the last government for underequipping the BEF. Now they were joined not only by the *News Chronicle*, but also by the *Observer* and *Daily Mail*.[80] On 6 June, the *Mirror* upped the ante with an aggressively worded editorial, demanding

> the instant dismissal from the Government of the few (yet too many) survivors from the old loitering gang ... The habit of muddle and misjudgement cannot be corrected, as the crisis intensifies, in men who did not even realise that a crisis was approaching. We hope that the Prime Minister's courage may be equal to the task of dismissing exalted muddlers.[81]

'WE WERE ALL SUPPOSED TO BE WORKING HARMONIOUSLY TO WIN THE WAR'

Despite their anger with Churchill, Conservative MPs did not want immediately to overthrow another prime minister in the midst of a national crisis. They still had, however, the controlling majority in the Commons, and many hoped he would shortly be replaced by someone who suited them better: perhaps even a resurgent Chamberlain. Meanwhile, the Conservatives made clear their displeasure by remaining silent for Churchill's appearances in the Commons. They would tolerate his presence, but only because Chamberlain and Halifax were there to keep him on the straight and narrow. Faced with their hostility, and conscious of the voting arithmetic left over from the 1935 election, Churchill knew that he needed to get the Conservatives onside.

Meanwhile, Labour had not let the formation of the Coalition Government stop its campaign against the former prime minister. Labour's *Daily Herald* was one of the first to take up the cry for the expulsion of the 'old gang', and Labour ministers were not shy about explaining the faults of their predecessors to the public.[82] The anger that Chamberlain had long aroused among his opponents meant that plenty of other people were also happy to administer a kicking while he was down.

Chamberlain was sure that the newspaper 'hate' that blew up against him from late May was being organized by his political enemies.[83] That infuriated his supporters, and he and they both expected Labour MPs to attack the former prime minister in the Commons.[84] On 5 June, Chamberlain visited Churchill and offered to resign. The prime minister was having none of that. He did, however, take the opportunity to convince Chamberlain that Lloyd George – Churchill's old friend, Chamberlain's old enemy and the last figure of political significance not in the government – ought to be given a ministerial appointment, a chance that Lloyd George subsequently turned down. After the War Cabinet met on 6 June, Chamberlain asked Attlee, Greenwood and Sinclair 'what they were doing to allow these venomous attacks by members of their parties to go on while we were all supposed to be working harmoniously to win the war'.[85] The following day, after Churchill warned newspaper editors that they risked breaking the government, the press 'hate' ceased. Chamberlain thought it 'like turning off a tap', which just showed 'how completely artificial the whole thing was'.[86] The relief would not last long.

'I THINK WE HAVE REACHED WHAT
THEY CALL A CRISIS'

At the start of June, most people still expected that France would fight on no matter what. Over the next few days, while the German offensive on the Somme got under way, a trace of optimism remained. Confidence in the eventual outcome remained strong. A countrywide effort to increase National Savings in the week 9–15 June saw the formation of 18,000 new savers' groups and doubled the average weekly rate of investment to £20 million. Notwithstanding the worsening news from France, people were willing to put money on Britain winning the war. In the run-up to the Bromley and Bow by-election, Mass-Observers noted that, although people were more confused about how the war would end, 'Expressed hostility to Hitler' was 'especially strong'. The comments they collected included 'Kill Hitler and all the Germans, we should do to their women and children what they do to ours' and 'I'd get hold of Hitler and cut him under the throat.'[87]

The newspapers might have let up somewhat on Chamberlain, but the public had not. Between 12 and 19 June, ten out of thirteen Civil Defence regions reported criticism against the previous government on at least one occasion. On 12 June, for example, 'Returning BEF without equipment' was said to have 'produced anti-Chamberlain feeling in Somerset'.[88] The next day in the North-East there was 'Strong anti-Chamberlain feeling on account of our apparent inability to help France.'[89] The day after, Wales reported: 'Continued resentment against last Government and growing outcry that we should make more use of our manpower.'[90] As this suggested, criticism of the past became bound up with concerns about the running of the war in the present.

Despite all the signs, when the French capitulation came it caused consternation. In Ipswich, Richard Brown recorded how people learned of the armistice on 17 June:

> The news was just mentioned at 1 o'clock and there was lots of uncertainty. Some people who listened didn't hear it, others did, and at 6 o'clock, everyone was at home to hear for himself. Then came confirmation and the awful gnawing fear – what will become of their fleet and air force?[91]

Mass-Observation's immediate report suggested that: 'People are so thunderstruck by the magnitude of the catastrophe that they are as yet unable to express any coherent attitude to it.' It too summed up the chief reaction as 'What will happen now?'[92] From the streets of Bolton, M-O's investigators reported a wide range of reactions:

> M45C*: 'I think we have reached what they call a crisis. Now they will have to prove that "Britons never shall be slaves". There is no doubt that we shall be exterminated.'[93]
>
> M45C: 'We fight alone now. They've all deserted us. But they haven't won yet. We shall all have to put our shoulder to the wheel. We can't give up now. Life wouldn't be worth living under the terms they would give us. It will be a different kind of warfare now.'
>
> F45C: 'It's going to be pretty bad for us. If France and England can't do it together I don't see what we can do alone. It's going to be a tough fight. It looks as though all we can do is give up. It's no use throwing away a lot of lives when there is no hope. We have a good navy and a good air force but they can't last out against him.'[94]
>
> F40C: 'I bet the King and Queen are packing to go – if they've not gone already. I bet the damn government's getting ready to fly too. They'll all leave us – as usual. We shall probably be on the trek by the end of the week. Nowhere to fly to. This country should have kept out of it from the start.'[95]
>
> Soldier, 25D to M55D: 'I tell you it's all right. They're shitting themselves for nothing. We shall hold him.'[96]

The Home Intelligence summary on 17 June argued that: 'The public are ready and determined to follow the Prime Minister if he gives the word, but if that word is not given there are signs that morale may change rapidly for the worst.'[97] The following evening, Churchill was persuaded to deliver his 'Finest Hour' speech, earlier given that day to the Commons, for a BBC broadcast. Sixty per cent of the adult population were listening in as he laid out the course of the campaign in

---

* Mass-Observation interviewers used a simple code to identify the social class of the people with whom they spoke or whose conversations they overheard. This was based on what they looked and sounded like: A – rich people; B – the middle classes; C – artisans and skilled workers; D – unskilled workers 'and the least economically or educationally trained of our people'.

France and ended by declaring that the 'Battle of Britain' was about to begin.

> The whole fury and might of the enemy must very soon be turned on us. Hitler knows that he will have to break us in this Island or lose the war. If we can stand up to him, all Europe may be free and the life of the world may move forward into broad, sunlit uplands . . . Let us therefore brace ourselves to our duties, and so bear ourselves that, if the British Empire and its Commonwealth last for a thousand years, men will still say, 'this was their finest hour'.[98]

The effect was not quite the one intended. Unseen by listeners, an unwilling prime minister had delivered the whole of this stirring speech with his cigar in his mouth. This affected his diction. Home Intelligence noted 'widespread comment on his delivery'. Mass-Observation's report was franker: Churchill was 'widely suspected of being drunk'.[99]

The prime minister's talk certainly did not rally everyone to the cause. Over the following few days, Home Intelligence kept reporting evidence of 'defeatist' talk, including 'working class women', 'lower-middle-class women' and 'small "white collar" men', asking 'suppose we do lose the war, what difference will it make to us; we could not be any worse off under Hitler; it's the bosses he's after'.[100] Some of the bosses were just as defeatist: the index of thirty leading shares, which had stood slightly above its pre-war level at 70.6 before the Germans invaded Scandinavia, fell to 50.4 on 24 June after the announcement of the French armistice terms. Two days later, it fell below fifty points for the only time in its existence, before patriotic City boys, and investors with a good eye for a killing, quickly rushed in and pushed values back up.[101] Within Whitehall, there were signs of official concern that public pessimism might spread: Churchill demanded a publicity campaign to discourage rumour-mongering, the Home Office arranged for several well-publicized prosecutions for spreading defeatist stories, and the Ministry of Information contemplated stricter press censorship, a campaign of public lectures about what Britain was fighting against, and a positive statement of war aims to counter the appeal of Hitler's new order.[102]

As Home Intelligence always emphasized, however, 'pockets of defeatism' represented a minority view compared to the 'prevailing determination to "fight to a finish"'.[103] Sober or otherwise, Churchill clearly articulated that determination (if not, on this occasion, much else), and that obviously struck a chord. In July's BIPO poll, 88 per cent of respondents said that they approved of him as prime minister. Whether it was his leadership, or an underlying faith in victory, or the fear of being thought a fifth columnist, or just the fact that, unlike the French, the British hadn't been invaded – or even bombed much yet – and were still in the war, public expressions of confidence soon returned. As the action got closer to home, talk of defeat did not totally disappear, but it did diminish.[104] Now the wait was on for what most people presumed was an imminent invasion.

'WE HAVE GOT TO SEE THE JOB THROUGH ON OUR OWN, AND WE CAN DO IT'

It was a very difficult time to oppose the war. The Peace Pledge Union's leaders were threatened with prosecution when anti-war posters were put up in May, and four activists who persisted in pasting them up were subsequently jailed.[105] The government preferred to use the threat of the Defence Regulations to limit CPGB activity rather than launch a wholesale attack on British Communists, but it did threaten to ban the *Daily Worker* for encouraging defeatism, and later in the summer, one Communist shop steward was interned for allegedly obstructing production.[106]

The weight of popular disapproval and internal dissent, however, were bigger problems than official repression. As the threat of German victory drew nearer, PPU membership fell, and the movement was publicly abandoned by many of its most high-profile supporters. As the Union's national group secretary, John Barclay, explained: 'Pacifism faced by military dictatorship and no longer sheltering behind it – this is something that may cause complete renunciation of previously held convictions.'[107] The rate of conscientious objection among men registered for national service fell from 1.8 per cent of those registered from April 1939 to April 1940, to 0.6 per cent of those registered between May and July 1940.[108]

For the CPGB, things were no easier. The party's response to the Fall of France was to call for the removal of the 'Men of Munich' and the installation of a 'People's Government' that would make 'a complete break with the interests of the ruling class', but it continued to oppose the conflict itself as an imperialist war. Now, the party's recruiters found that they lost their audience on the factory floor if they strayed from labour relations to international affairs. As branch members became caught up in the patriotic mood, the CPGB had to send out circulars warning Communists against any 'tendencies to national defencism'.[109] Any other tendency, however, meant alienation. As the security officer at Woolwich Arsenal reported in the course of an investigation into alleged Communist subversion, his suspects were 'hanging themselves by pursuing a policy that the bulk of the working people abominate'. As the works' shop stewards told him: 'If they are not removed it may well be that their colleagues will take the law into their own hands.'[110]

As the CPGB's struggles suggested, the crisis of May and June aroused strong patriotic feelings. Yet this patriotism took many forms. At its most conventional, the drama reaffirmed that old Protestant sense of the British as God's chosen people, being tested in the fire on the route to redemption. Sunday 26 May was appointed a National Day of Prayer, on which the king asked his people to 'with one heart and soul humbly but confidently commit our cause to God and ask His aid that we may valiantly defend the right as it is given to us to see it'.[111] The response to the king's call was remarkable. Westminster Abbey was packed out. Churchill insisted that senior ministers and civil servants should attend despite the risk of air attack, members of the public queued around the building to get in, and the BBC relayed the service live as part of a day of religious programming. The Leicester diocese reported that the size of congregations had been 'beyond anything experienced in the last quarter of a century. In many churches large queues waited to get in, and in some places it was impossible to find accommodation for everyone.'[112] Cyril Garbett, the bishop of Winchester, recorded an extraordinarily busy day in his diary:

> Preached at 11.0 in the Cathedral to an enormous congregation . . . At 3.0 addressed a huge crowd in the Guildhall, Southampton: 2000 unable to gain admission stood outside while the service was relayed to them by loud speakers. Tea with Gordon Hooper at Milford and preached in his church: a packed congregation. On the way home stopped at the Sports

Centre at Southampton to give the blessing at an open-air service: I was told there were about 4000 present.[113]

In Surrey, Walter Musto and his wife 'attended divine service, there to add our prayers to the national cry to high heaven for strength and endurance and courage in this time of trial and testing, and to crave a word with God on our own account'.[114] These prayers, of course, were duly rewarded with the army's deliverance from Dunkirk.

The patriotism of the summer could also take on a harsher edge. Britons blamed their former allies for defeat. At the Kodak factory in Harrow, for example, it was reported that 'Anti-French feeling' had grown 'very strong since the capitulation. People remember at end of last war our soldiers said they would rather fight with the Germans than with the French.'[115] In Surrey, on 23 June, George King wrote in the diary he was keeping for his son that the French seemed

> to have given in completely to all that the Boche has demanded. To me, it is almost unbelievable, but then I start to think of the France of the last war, and then it isn't . . . However, it is no good saying any more about it; we have got to see the job through on our own, and we can do it.[116]

For a young Belgian refugee arriving in the UK that May, the sense of a national superiority that had been confirmed by the war was what struck him most forcefully about his new home:

> The Englishman is a rabid nationalist. They are perhaps the most nationalist people in the world. When you hear the English talk of this war you sometimes almost want them to lose it to show them how things are. They have the greatest contempt for the continent in general and the French in particular.[117]

Yet the French collapse could also be used to attack British failures. In an atmosphere still rife with suspicion of the fifth column, the belief that the French people had been betrayed by their leaders sparked invidious comparisons.[118] On 2 July, the annual conference of the National Union of Railwaymen passed a unanimous resolution demanding the removal of all those 'associated with the previous Government's policy of appeasement'. A spokesman explained: 'I do not want to mention names and I do not want this gang to be subjected to any torture. I want to see them put in a position where they cannot possibly betray this country in the way in which Marshal Petain betrayed France.'[119] Criticisms of the 'old gang' now showed signs of metastasizing into a much wider discontent, with criticisms taking in 'those at the top', 'cumbersome old machinery' and 'the Civil Service'.[120] Contrary to the fears of the Ministry of Information, these were not signs of a split that would endanger the war effort, but they did show the way in which military peril could be used as a way to talk about what was wrong with the country as a whole.

A PEOPLE'S WAR?

One of the groups that Home Intelligence noted were being publicly criticized was 'those in charge of the LDV'. The most widespread complaint among volunteers was the lack of equipment. Boyish enthusiasm only took them so far: if the Germans were coming they wanted to be properly armed. Throughout the summer, small arms remained in short supply and it was not until August that rifles were available in adequate numbers even for regular army units. The lack of equipment was held up as evidence of official incompetence.

The War Office had originally decided that the LDV should have no formal rank structure so that professional officers never found themselves under the command of amateurs. In practice, local LDV units were often set up by the sort of people who took charge of much of civic life: middle-class businessmen in the cities, landowners in the countryside. Before long, charges were being levelled that LDV groups were being run like golf clubs, with the wrong sort – Jews, Labour Party members, trade unionists – not allowed to join.[121] When it came to picking area organizers, the War Office usually selected retired senior officers. Whatever their military views, they were easily caricatured as out-of-touch 'Colonel Blimps', demanding discipline, unquestioning obedience and eager to refight the last war.

For some commentators on the left, the flood of recruits to the LDV looked gratifyingly like the people rushing to the fight against Fascism. It also summoned memories of the militias of the Spanish Civil War. Foremost among them was Tom Wintringham. An RFC despatch rider in the last war, and a Communist since the 1920s, Wintringham had established himself as the radical left's leading military expert in the 1930s. He had led the British battalion of the International Brigade in Spain, before being expelled from the CPGB. By mid-May 1940, Wintringham was a well-known and widely read writer – the military correspondent of the *Daily Mirror* and a contributor to the popular periodical *Picture Post*. A collection of his articles, rushed out in July as a Penguin Special, *New Ways of War*, sold 75,000 copies.[122]

Wintringham set out for readers the tactics for guerrilla fighting he had learned in Spain (including instructions on how to build a do-it-yourself grenade), demanded the democratization of the army and called for the fighting of a 'people's war'.[123] This was not a comforting, all-in-it-together version of the conflict, but one run by 'committees of public safety or councils of action' formed out of an armed citizenry:

> There are those who say that the idea of arming the people is a revolutionary idea. It certainly is . . . after what we have seen of the efficiency and patriotism of those who ruled us until recently, most of us can find plenty of room in this country for some sort of revolution, for a change that will sweep away the muck of the past.[124]

Unlike the CPGB, however, Wintringham wanted to get rid of capitalism in order to fight the war better and harder.

With the help of Edward Hulton, *Picture Post*'s publisher, Wintringham set up his own school to train LDV members in the grounds of Osterley Park, a stately home just outside London. There he and other Republican veterans of the Spanish Civil War taught volunteers in the tactics of irregular warfare. Whereas the regular army looked on the LDV as essentially a static guard force, and more traditional LDV leaders focused on close order drill as the starting point for training, Wintringham's lessons were about how to kill people and blow things up. Three thousand pupils attended the school over the summer of 1940. Whatever they made of the politics, they loved the explosions. Worried though they were by the staff's ideological inclinations, War Office officials also valued the aggression it imparted. On 30 September they closed down Osterley Park, and absorbed the staff and curriculum into their own training system. Wintringham resigned nine months later.[125]

Radical though it was politically, Wintringham's vision of a grenade-wielding nation-in-arms was militarily archaic. The whole trend of British defence policy was in the other direction: high technology weapons wielded by a skilled elite, with most people making or servicing machines rather than fighting in the front line. Thankfully, Britons never had to fight a 'people's war' of the sort Wintringham envisaged. If they thus missed out on the chance for a radical reordering of democracy, they did at least escape the slaughter experienced in Spain and China, Eastern and Southern Europe, the USSR and Germany. Britain's war would do a lot of damage to other people: its own escaped remarkably unscathed.[126]

'LOYALTY, UNION AMONG MEN WHO HAVE JOINED HANDS'

At Westminster, the news of defeat released the scent of political opportunity. As the French surrendered, Amery, Macmillan, Boothby and Clement Davies, acting in consort with Lloyd George, launched the so-called 'Under-Secretaries Plot'. Writing to Churchill, Boothby claimed there was a 'revolutionary spirit in the country which ought to be turned to advantage'. It was a 'young man's war', and the old guard – with the exception of Lloyd George – were too old to prosecute it successfully.[127] Instead, the plotters would help to form a new all-powerful Committee of Public Safety that would sweep away bureaucratic slowness and really get things done. Churchill told the plotters that any minister who had a problem could resign his post and give his criticisms full voice without the burdens of office. That ended this episode, but not the need for Churchill to defend his predecessor from parliamentary attack.[128]

Speaking to the Commons on the 'War Situation' on 18 June, the prime minister publicly rejected any parliamentary inquest into pre-war policy as 'a foolish and pernicious process' from which no one would emerge unscathed. Two days later, in a 'secret session' of the Commons (meaning that the proceedings were not recorded and reported, which was meant to allow a fuller discussion of war topics without revealing information to the enemy), he once again spoke up for Chamberlain. As his notes set out:

Tell the story Chamberlain's actions.
Imperative there should be loyalty, union
    among men who have joined hands.
Otherwise no means of standing
    the shocks and strains which are coming.[129]

By this point, Labour's leaders too had decided to call off the 'hate'. They worried that if Chamberlain was pushed out of government, he might become 'a centre of disaffection and a rallying point for a real opposition' from discontented Conservatives.[130]

Attlee too faced potential threats to his leadership. Herbert Morrison was still eager to usurp him. He was angry that he had been sent to the Ministry of Supply when he had expected to be chancellor, a better reflection, he thought, of his status and abilities. Ironically Morrison was wrong – his talent as an organizer and a politician would have been wasted at the Treasury – but his frustration was a problem for the Labour leader. Fortunately for Attlee, Bevin cordially hated Morrison ('Don't trust a word the little bastard says,' he stage-whispered to other ministers), and he and Attlee now formed a powerful anti-Morrison axis at the top of the Labour movement.

After some confusion over who now counted as the 'opposition', Labour MPs had continued to position themselves opposite the Treasury bench on which Labour ministers, as members of the coalition, now sat. Since Attlee could no longer act as leader of the opposition, whoever took his place might use the opportunity to challenge his authority. Acting unilaterally, Attlee chose the uninspiring Hastings Lees-Smith as his replacement. He could be relied upon not to rock the boat too much while Labour's leaders were in office.[131]

This mattered because, for Labour, joining a coalition government in the midst of a national crisis brought some uncomfortable feelings of déjà vu. The left wing of the party was particularly worried that ministers would once more be tempted by the rhetoric of responsible national unity and step off the path to socialism. In fact, Attlee remained convinced that 'practical socialism' was not only an absolute good but also essential to win the war. The policies adopted by the new government – increased conscription, the elimination of wartime profit, extended rationing, greater economic controls – were practically social-ist (not least to Conservative eyes) in that they were statist, collectivist and egalitarian. Labour ministers also promoted 'practical' measures that would improve the lot of the working class, claiming responsibility for the provision of subsidized milk to mothers and schoolchildren (in fact put in place by Lord Woolton, the minister of food, but approved by the Food Committee that Attlee chaired), and, later in the summer, pursuing increases in unemployment and service allowances and the abolition of the Household Means Test. By early July, Attlee was also pressing his colleagues to provide

> a definite pronouncement on . . . policy for the future. The Germans are fighting a revolutionary war for very definite objectives. We are fighting a conservative war and our objects are purely negative. We must put forward a positive and revolutionary aim admitting that the old order has collapsed and asking people to fight for the new order.[132]

Committed though he was to such reforms for their own sake, he also needed something to throw to his critics within the Labour Party, none of whom were convinced that the window-dressing of practical socialism came close to the far-reaching social and economic change that Labour ought really to be implementing.[133]

Complaints from the left that Labour was passing up its chance were to be a standard feature for the rest of the war. In the summer of 1940, they missed the point. Labour's demolition of the Chamberlain government was a remarkable political achievement, but its power within the Coalition had still to be established. Public anger at the last government was undeniable, but it was rooted in Chamberlain's failure to achieve unity and protect national security. A Labour Party that prioritized a domestic revolution would have imperilled both these things. The Labour ministers' approach – using the war to promote socialist solutions but not, in the final reckoning, putting them ahead of a national effort to defeat Hitler – was politically smart as well as strategically astute.

'WE ARE A SOLID NATION'

MPs and peers were no more immune than their constituents to feelings of confusion and gloom as France fell. On the Conservative benches, there was plenty of depression about Britain's prospects, anxiety about air bombardment and concern about the implications of Churchill's determination to fight an all-out war, but there was no great desire to surrender to Germany. The majority of Labour MPs were determined to defeat Fascism, but the twenty or so Labour members who made up the Parliamentary Peace Group continued to demand 'a just peace with disarmament'. This disparate assembly, including pacifists and left-wingers opposed to an 'imperialist war', was led by Richard Stokes, a Catholic and a convinced anti-Communist, who feared that the Anglo-German struggle would only benefit the Soviet Union. In a bid to bring Lloyd George on board, Stokes assured him that he could get thirty MPs and ten peers of all parties to back a call for peace. Understandably, given that this meant the support of less than 5 per cent of the Commons, Lloyd George said that he would rather wait until another military defeat had turned the country against the prime minister.[134]

Although Churchill did not have to face down a powerful peace lobby in the Commons, he was very sensitive to the strategic and political dangers posed by discussions of a negotiated peace. One way to deal with these threats was to talk up the government's determination to fight on, the strength of Britain's defences and the imminence of America's entry into the war – as Churchill did during the secret session in the Commons on 20 June. Another way was to prohibit any talk of a peace deal with the Germans. At the end of May, Churchill had issued an edict to ministers and senior civil servants, instructing them, while not 'minimising the gravity of events', to show 'confidence' in their circle 'in our ability and inflexible resolve to continue the war until we have broken the will of the enemy'.[135]

It must have been with interest, therefore, that he read the telegraphic traffic occasioned by a chance meeting between Rab Butler, the parliamentary under-secretary at the Foreign Office, and Björn Prytz, the Swedish ambassador, on 17 June 1940.[136] Prytz and Butler met each other by accident while they were both taking a post-lunch walk. Part of Butler's job was to maintain good relations with all the ambassadors in London: they fell to talking and Prytz accompanied him back to his room at the Foreign Office. Paul Reynaud had just broadcast on the radio to announce that France was requesting an armistice. Things looked very bleak, and Prytz asked Butler what Britain planned to do next. Depressed at the French surrender, and still bitter about

Churchill's assumption of the premiership, Butler made the mistake of speaking his mind. According to the telegram Prytz sent back to Stockholm later that day:

> Britain's official attitude will for the present continue to be that the war must go on, but he assured me that no opportunity for reaching a compromise peace would be neglected if the possibility were offered on reasonable conditions and that no 'diehards' would be allowed to stand in the way in this connection. He thought that Britain had greater possibilities of negotiation than she might have later on.[137]

At that point, Butler was called in to see Halifax. When he returned, he told Prytz that the foreign secretary had a message for him: 'Common sense not bravado would dictate the British Government's policy', but this did not mean a desire for 'peace at any price'.[138]

Anxious about the twin threat from the Soviet Union and the Nazis, Swedish ministers were eager to see an end to the war. They were also under a lot of pressure to allow the Germans transport rights across their territory to newly occupied Norway. If the British were putting out peace feelers, that would give the Swedes a good excuse for giving way. When Prytz's account of his conversation with Butler arrived, the Swedish foreign minister, Christian Günther, promptly asked the British ambassador, Victor Mallet, whether it meant that London wanted the Swedes to act as intermediaries with Berlin.

When Mallet put this query to the Foreign Office, an embarrassed Butler insisted that Prytz (a fluent English speaker) had misunderstood what he meant. Meanwhile, Prytz's account was shown to Swedish politicians who were discussing whether to give in to German demands, then leaked to the press; Mallet then intervened to try to suppress the story.[139] That occasioned another flurry of telegrams. Churchill saw all of them, as well as Prytz's original message, which had been decrypted by British intelligence as it left the Swedish embassy. On 26 June, the prime minister sent a chiding note to Halifax:

> Butler held odd language to the Swedish Minister and certainly the Swede derived a strong impression of defeatism ... I was strongly pressed in the House of Commons in the Secret Session to give assurances that the present Government and all its Members were resolved to fight on to the death, and I did so, taking personal responsibility for the

resolve of all . . . any suspicion of lukewarmness in Butler will certainly subject us all to further annoyance of this kind.[140]

Halifax and Butler stuck to the story that Prytz had got the wrong end of the stick. There the prime minister let matters lie.[141]

Contrary to the accusations sometimes levelled subsequently, the Prytz correspondence did not provide evidence that either Butler or Halifax was secretly seeking to make peace with Hitler. Churchill was absolutely right, however, to say that Butler had given an impression of British policy that was very different from that which the prime minister had put forward in public. Halifax had, by this point, accepted the arguments that Churchill had put forward to the War Cabinet at the end of May – better to fight on for the next few months at least, on the basis that Britain's negotiating position was bound to improve – and his message to Prytz – if it was his, rather than Butler putting words in his mouth – specifically rejected 'peace at any price'. He too, however, had been implicated in an event that had allowed a foreign ambassador to persuade himself that Britain wanted a compromise peace, and in terms that were derogatory of Churchill's 'bravado'.[142]

Everyone involved knew how the words spoken at the Butler–Prytz meeting would look if they came out. Yet while Churchill had suddenly benefitted from a remarkable gift from his political opponent, it was not one that could be easily used. Halifax stuck by Butler and protected him, and Churchill needed Halifax's support. Halifax may have protected Butler simply out of loyalty to a younger colleague, but he may also have calculated that providing he stood firm, there was little that Churchill could do.

The problem was that the Swedes didn't keep the story to themselves. On the contrary, rumours about peace moves from members of the former British government now spread like wildfire among the embassies of Europe. They soon came full circle back to the UK. By the end of June, isolationist US newspapers were reporting a story that Chamberlain and Halifax, backed by a section of the Conservative Party, were scheming to get rid of Churchill and hold peace talks with Hitler. It was totally untrue. In turn, the tale was gleefully retold by the anti-Chamberlain press back in the UK. To scotch the rumour, Chamberlain, by now a very sick man, had to take to the airwaves on 30 June. He struck a familiar note:

We are a solid nation, which would rather go down to ruin than admit the domination of the Nazis ... If the enemy does try to invade this country, we shall fight him in the air and on the sea; we will fight him on the beaches with every weapon we have.[143]

Again, however, a big radio speech did not quite come off. Towards the end of the broadcast, Chamberlain's throat suddenly dried. Embarrassed listeners thought he had broken down in tears.[144]

The continuing clamour for Chamberlain's dismissal only bolstered Tory determination to support their party leader. On 3 July, when Clement Davies staged a meeting for MPs to try to form another anti-Chamberlain front, Conservative loyalists found out about it, packed the room and shouted the plotters down. The next day, Churchill was rewarded for his efforts to defend his predecessor when he announced the action against the French warships at Mers-el-Kébir to the Commons. Warned that stories about Conservative defeatism might put off the Americans, Chamberlain passed the word for the Tory whips to orchestrate a display of support for the prime minister. Having sorrowfully explained the attacks on the French, the prime minister closed with a word to those who were questioning the commitment of his government at home:

The action we have already taken should be, in itself, sufficient to dispose once and for all of the lies and rumours that have been so industriously spread by German propaganda and Fifth Column activities that we have the slightest intention of entering into negotiations in any form and through any channel with the German and Italian governments. We shall ... prosecute the war with the utmost vigour by all the means that are open to us until the righteous purposes for which we entered upon it have been fulfilled.[145]

Initially, the Conservative benches remained as quiet as ever. Then, at a signal from David Margesson, Tory MPs rose as a man and cheered Churchill to the rafters. It reminded Chips Channon of the way that they had once applauded Chamberlain: 'Only it was not little Neville's turn now. Winston suddenly wept.'[146]

'THIS STRONG CITY OF REFUGE'

During July, British confidence gradually returned. In Whitehall, the intelligence services continued to warn about a surprise invasion, and the armed forces remained jumpy during the first half of the month. Nonetheless, the Chiefs of Staff Committee now began to work on the basis that the country would not be taken completely unawares. The UK was sufficiently well defended to force the Germans to stage a major invasion, and the preparations would be apparent both from photo-reconnaissance flights of the Channel ports and from Luftwaffe attacks to attempt to gain air superiority. Increases in armaments production, and particularly in the output of aircraft, bolstered official confidence in the UK's ability to hold out against invasion. In comparison with the levels that would be reached later in the war, British war production was still very low: in the third quarter of 1940, for example, British factories made 498 anti-tank guns, less than a twentieth of the number they would turn out in the same period of 1942. In comparison with the levels of early 1940, however, the expansion was dramatic. It owed a lot to the extraordinary efforts of British workers and managers as they slaved round the clock to make more weapons, but it also paid testament to the successes of British rearmament before and after the outbreak of war. By the summer, the British were catching up with and overtaking the Germans in the production of aircraft and of tanks.

Table 2: Selected British munitions production, 1940

	Jan–Mar	Apr–Jun	Jul–Sept
Fighters	703	1,409	1,901
Medium bombers	253	552	619
Tanks	218 (2.65)	340 (5.5)	392 (7.17)
(000 tons total)			
Field guns	20	196	525
Anti-tank guns			
(towed and	297	395	498
tank-mounted)			

Source: CSO, *Fighting with Figures: A Statistical Digest of the Second World War* (London, 1995), pp. 158–71.

The British did not know exactly how well they were doing in production terms relative to their opponents, but new, lower estimates of German aircraft strength derived from Enigma decrypts did encourage the belief that the country would be able to withstand the enemy's initial onslaught. By mid-July, the Security Service was more or less convinced that there was no British fifth column worth worrying about, and as the Home Office regained control of internment policy, those who had been locked up over the previous months began to be screened and released. Complaints about the government's lax approach to searching out fifth columnists began to be replaced with criticisms of its overly authoritarian approach to civil liberties.[147]

Looking forward to the future of the war after dinner on 12 July, according to John Colville, Churchill foresaw three months of fighting to make sure an invasion couldn't happen, but doubted whether it was 'a serious menace'. He intended nonetheless 'to give that impression' when he next broadcast on the war, because 'the great invasion scare' was 'well on the way to providing us with the finest offensive army we have ever possessed and it is keeping every man and women tuned to a high state of readiness'.[148] When he spoke two nights later, the prime minister offered a crusader's call:

> We are fighting by ourselves alone; but we are not fighting for ourselves alone. Here in this strong City of Refuge which enshrines the title-deeds of human progress and is of deep consequence to Christian civilization . . . we await undismayed the impending assault. Perhaps it will come tonight. Perhaps it will come next week. Perhaps it will never come . . . But be the ordeal sharp or long, or both, we shall seek no terms, we shall tolerate no parley; we may show mercy – we shall ask for none.[149]

He also announced that he had a much better name for the LDV: the 'Home Guard', which was what they now became, at the cost of much time spent re-sewing those crucial identifying arm brassards.

During July, the country's ground defences visibly improved. Construction was well under way of the 'GHQ line', a mix of anti-tank obstacles, pillboxes and trenches stretching in a semi-circle from inner East Anglia across the southern edge of Greater London. Across the country, further 'stop lines' were also being planned: thirty-three were meant to snake across Scotland, twenty-one through Wales – principally to protect Liverpool and the Midlands against a German attack from the west – and eight across Northern Ireland.[150] By the end of 1940, 28,000 pillboxes and gun emplacements had been built in the UK.[151]

Most of the great defensive lines, however, were never completed, let alone manned. General Ironside's static plans were now subject to criticism from his own subordinates and from the prime minister. The fortifications were good for morale, but they would tie down military resources while yielding the initiative to the invader. On 17 July, General Brooke, who had been put in charge of Southern Command following his return from France, took the chance of an inspection by Churchill to voice his concerns. Two days later, he replaced Ironside in command of Home Forces. Reflecting later, Brooke remembered how limited the forces at his command had seemed, and the crushing burden of maintaining everyone else's confidence: 'to come into continuous contact with all the weakness of the defensive material at your disposal . . . and with it all to maintain a calm and confident exterior is a test of one's character, the bitterness of which must be experienced to be believed'.[152]

Nonetheless, the steady flow of new equipment meant that Brooke could aspire to a more agile defence. Where Ironside had locked field artillery and anti-tank guns up in fixed fortifications, during the summer Brooke pulled them back to support his more mobile divisions, which would rush to concentrate their strength against any invasion, while more recently formed, less well-equipped 'County' divisions formed the outer crust of defences along the beaches. By the end of the summer, Brooke's plans focused on a very rapid counter-attack that would drive any German landing straight back into the sea.

Before any invasion could be launched, however, the Germans would have to gain control of the skies. The Luftwaffe's move up to bases in northern France and Scandinavia now exposed the UK to more frequent air attack. From 10 July the Germans probed British air defences and attacked the shipping route along the eastern English coast. German air incursions by day and by night caused significant disruption to civilian life and industrial production, more so because air-raid sirens were initially sounded over a very wide area.

All this looked very much like the preparatory work for an invasion, and on 19 July the British received confirmation from an Enigma decrypt that Hitler had indeed ordered his forces to begin planning for an attack. On the same day, Hitler gave a speech to the Reichstag in which he anointed himself victor and offered a negotiated peace to save the world from further war. Halifax, who this time had needed no persuading of the pointlessness of talking to Hitler, used the opportunity of a regular radio broadcast on 22 July publicly to turn Hitler's offer down flat. As usual, the foreign secretary talked of Britain's as a Christian cause, mentioning God twice a minute during his short broadcast.[153]

During July, public morale recovered. According to Home Intelligence, the action at Mers-el-Kébir was 'generally welcomed and even the fact that many French sailors lost their lives has been allowed to pass with little comment'.[154] The announcement that tea, cooking fats and margarine would be rationed, and the disruption being caused by the sounding of air-raid sirens, caused much more extensive complaint.

Meanwhile, official attempts to counter public defeatism got off the ground. The Ministry of Information organized meetings and lectures – more than 5,000 of them across the country by the end of July – with titles such as 'The Civilian's Part in Defence' and 'What German Occupation Means'.[155] The BBC put on an array of programmes celebrating British national character, as exemplified in the deep tradition of the English countryside, in the voices of working people (in programmes with titles like 'Everyman and the War' and 'We Speak for Ourselves') and in a shared heritage of liberties and freedom.[156] These went down rather better with the public than some of the prosecutions for rumour-mongering and a new Ministry of Information publicity campaign urging Britons to 'join the Silent Column'.

Following widespread complaints that the government did not trust the people and was trying to ban grumbling, both the prosecutions and the 'Silent Column' had to be abandoned. Attempts to control morale lagged behind a recovery that had already taken place. When Mass-Observation interviewed working-class men and women on the streets of London about Hitler's peace offer in mid-July, they were in optimistic and angry mood:

> F55D: 'We've got him where we want him now – no jokes. He's ours for the asking.'
>
> F45C: 'I heard he was asking for terms. Let's give them to him – our terms.'
>
> M40C: 'Cor, don't take no notice of <u>him</u>. Peace? Not at <u>his</u> price. We're going to win, lady, – and at <u>our</u> price.'
>
> F40D: 'It was his usual lot of yollop – Peace! Friends with Britain!'

The investigator in Mill Hill concluded that:

> The opinion is that Hitler has 'cold feet'; that he does not want to go on with the war; that we should take advantage of his attitude to make a bid for victory. From these people one gains the impression that invasion, even if it is a possibility, is something that may be dismissed with a flick of the fingers.[157]

Until September, there was a continual public expectation that a German invasion was imminent. Each day that it did not arrive could therefore be taken as proof that the British were beating Hitler. Whether or not the Germans were ever actually coming mattered much less than the feeling that each of their repeated non-arrivals represented another British victory.

GUILTY MEN

Despite the clamour of public criticism after the Fall of France, at the start of July Chamberlain's position at Westminster still seemed assured. Churchill needed him, the Conservative Party would fight to protect him and even Labour's leaders had decided they'd prefer it if he didn't oppose them. Outside Parliament, however, the attacks on the 'old gang' continued.

On 5 July, Victor Gollancz published the short book *Guilty Men*, written by the pseudonymous 'Cato'.[158] *Guilty Men* bundled all the criticisms of the previous government into a wider critique of defence and economic policies between the wars. It staged very personal attacks on the characters of Ramsay MacDonald and Stanley Baldwin, as well as on Chamberlain, Inskip, Halifax, Wilson and Margesson. They were blamed for the sufferings of soldiers at Dunkirk, 'the finest army which Britain had ever put into the field', but 'an Army doomed *before* they took the field'.[159] *Guilty Men* ended with a capitalized plea:

> THE MEN WHO ARE NOW REPAIRING THE BREACHES IN OUR WALLS SHOULD NOT CARRY ALONG WITH THEM THOSE WHO LET THE WALLS FALL INTO RUIN ... LET THE GUILTY MEN RETIRE, THEN, OF THEIR OWN

VOLITION, AND SO MAKE AN ESSENTIAL CONTRIBU-
TION TO THE VICTORY UPON WHICH ALL ARE
IMPLACABLY RESOLVED.[160]

Guilty Men was one of the greatest, most influential political polemics in modern British history. The term itself, a brilliant encapsulation of
the thesis, damned the inter-war Conservative Party at a stroke. Like all
polemics, *Guilty Men* contained some notable distortions. Churchill was
portrayed throughout as a far-sighted genius and Labour's opposition to
rearmament was glossed over. The most remarkable, however, was that
Lord Beaverbrook was listed as one of the supermen trying to save Britain, without any mention of his support for appeasement or his efforts to
obstruct the escalation of the domestic effort during the Phoney War.

There was a good reason for this omission. In fact, 'Cato' was a
cabal of three men – Michael Foot, Frank Owen and Peter Howard –
all of whom were employed as editors or columnists at Beaverbrook's
newspapers. He might not have told them to write *Guilty Men*, but he
certainly knew who they were, and the book did a very good job of
settling the scores Beaverbrook had with the respectable Conservatives
of the 1920s and 1930s.[161]

Whether it was accurate or not, in the circumstances of 1940 *Guilty
Men* explained an awful lot. The book's sharp tone, easy explanations
and anti-establishment associations – it was banned by both WH
Smith's and Ryman's and Gollancz sold it from barrows in Fleet Street –
all contributed to making it a runaway success. More than 200,000
copies were eventually printed.[162]

'Cato', however, was certainly not a lone voice. The National Government had never really restored its relations with the popular British
press after Baldwin's attack on the newspaper barons as 'harlots' in
1931. Faced with the threat to peace and national security at the end of
the 1930s, the press proprietors had been willing to back Chamberlain,
but most of them had never liked him, and many journalists had
become disillusioned with the government's efforts to control reporting
even before the outbreak of war. Now, the way was open – under the
grounds of patriotism – for the former prime minister's opponents to
extract their revenge.

The day before *Guilty Men* came out, 'Cassandra' – the *Daily Mirror* columnist William Connor, a vicious-tongued Ulsterman and a

long-term critic of Chamberlain – launched a broadside that showed how far all the elements of the national crisis could become bound up together in a mixture of nationalism and radicalism:

> The moral bankruptcy of this country has been unmasked in the last few months – a degrading and terrible spectacle. It ranges from selfish money-scavengers to the disreputable remnants of the worst gang of political pests who ever sabotaged the future of a great and honourable nation. To fight for the rehabilitation of this same guilty crew would be a tragic farce. Fortunately, the temper of our people and their determination to forge a new order, is a guiding light that will not fail. They are not sacrificing all for the resurrection of the evils that led us to the edge of the abyss. It is unlikely in the future that we will create homes fit for heroes. BUT IT IS CERTAIN THAT WE WILL NOT ERECT PALACES FOR THE POLITICAL AND FINANCIAL TRAITORS OF THE PAST![163]

In the last war, this had been the language with which the extreme right had condemned Jews, Bolsheviks and other enemies within during the dark days of 1917–18. Now it sat comfortably with the populist left.

In the month after the Norway debate, these sorts of attacks turned more and more people against Chamberlain. By mid-June, Home Intelligence's reports had pointed out that 'staunchest Tories', 'business men' and 'people of all classes' were displaying 'anti-Chamberlain feeling'. A BIPO survey published in the *News Chronicle* on 8 July indicated that 77 per cent of respondents thought that Chamberlain should be removed from the government: given that number, many of those calling for his removal must have been the working-class voters who had backed the Conservatives during the 1930s.[164]

Shortly after *Guilty Men* came out, J. B. Priestley started to make the same case about the bad old days between the wars in his radio 'Postscripts'. Like 'Cato', Priestley cast the 1920s and 1930s as wasted years of economic suffering, but as he explained to listeners on 21 July, now things were changing. The 'huge collective effort' demanded by the war meant that:

> We're actually changing over from the property view to the sense of community, which simply means that we're all in the same boat. But,

and this is the point, that boat can serve not only as our defence against Nazi aggression, but as an ark in which we can all finally land in a better world.

There was nothing new in Priestley calling in vaguely leftist terms for the building of a new Britain. Now, however, outraged Conservatives complained that he was proselytizing for socialism. For the moment, Priestley's calls for reconstruction were just a minor note in his paeans of praise to ordinary heroism, but he knew the appeal of being the outspoken underdog. In his next broadcast, he discussed the criticisms that had been levelled at him and explained that they were not going to get him off the air. Soon, one in three of the listening population was tuning in to the programme – a higher proportion than for any other non-ministerial speaker.[165]

'EVERYTHING WE OUGHT TO STAND FOR WILL GO BY DEFAULT'

In the short term, all this had absolutely no effect on Chamberlain's position at Westminster. No matter what the public thought, the most powerful men in the land preferred to keep him inside the government. The short term, however, was all he had left. For some time he had been afflicted by problems with his digestion. By mid-June, he was in severe pain. At the end of July, he was forced to go into hospital for an operation that failed to relieve him of what turned out to be terminal bowel cancer. For the next six weeks, while he convalesced, he was unable to play any part in political life. It would be cancer, rather than the condemnation of 'Cato', which ended his political career.[166]

Even before the severity of Chamberlain's illness was revealed, this was a depressing time for Conservative MPs. As the defeat of the move against the 'Men of Munich' in the Commons demonstrated, the Conservative Party was still a powerful political force. For all his discontent with the job, Herbert Morrison had made a powerful job of tackling the Ministry of Supply, but when Churchill pondered promoting him to take Chamberlain's place on the War Cabinet, Wood and Margesson vetoed the move on the basis that it would unacceptably alter the party balance. Churchill promoted Beaverbrook to the War Cabinet instead, an elevation that left the press lord chuckling that he was 'not nearly such a Conservative as Herbert Morrison!'.[167]

That summed things up for more traditional Tories: most of the 'Conservatives' in office weren't really Conservative at all; their younger colleagues were heading off for the armed forces; Chamberlain was dying; and the socialists were making party political capital out of the war. At the end of July, the Conservative Cuthbert Headlam, newly returned to the Commons as the MP for Newcastle North, noted in his diary attending a debate which

> was mainly conducted (as all debates now are) by the Labour Party – it is odd how the Conservatives, even the stock bores who usually keep talking, have passed out of the picture . . . those who might intervene in debate more often feel, as I do, that there is no object in making speeches nowadays – all the same, I feel that we are mistaken and ought not to allow the Socialists such a free run . . . It is altogether a bad out look for the future and it looks as if everything we ought to stand for will go by default.[168]

A few days earlier, Kingsley Wood's emergency budget had demonstrated just how bad things were from the point of view of the Conservative squirearchy. Wood's stated aim was to meet the gap between revenue and war expenditure, the rate of which had risen since the spring from £2,000 million to £2,800 million a year, or £57 million a week. Income tax went up to 8s. 6d. in the pound, and Pay-As-You-Earn taxation was introduced for the first time. Dramatic increases in the top rates of surtax and estate duty exacted an unprecedented levy on the wealthy, while beer duty went up by 6d. a pint and tobacco duty by 1½d. an ounce. Two rates were announced for purchase tax, one of a third on luxury items and another of a sixth on more necessary goods such as furniture.[169] Crucially, Wood did not extend the bottom bracket of income tax liability to include those earning under £250 a year.[170] The press criticized him for not being socialist enough. *The Times*, under the headline 'SHIRKING THE ISSUE', lambasted Wood for being 'afraid to trust the nation's capacity for self-sacrifice'.[171]

'ACTIVE AND PAINFUL EVOLUTION'

The sense that a fundamental political change had taken place was embodied in the leaders that were now written for *The Times* by the paper's assistant editor, Robert Barrington-Ward, and E. H. Carr, a former Foreign Office official turned professor of international politics. Having survived the trenches of the last war, Barrington-Ward saw it as his life's duty 'to strive for the creation and organisation of peace, above all things, and for the liberating truths at home at whatever cost to conventional opinion. Revolution cannot do it . . . but evolution, active and painful evolution must.'[172] Now he believed it was *The Times'* job to prepare its readers for an accommodation with the wartime advance of socialism.

Carr had been an ardent enthusiast for Lloyd George's promises of social reform in the 1920s and had become fascinated in the 1930s by economic planning. He had also supported appeasement as the only realistic option. Now recruited by Barrington-Ward to spice up the paper's editorials, he was determined to promote a planned future. Over the next year, as Barrington-Ward slowly replaced *The Times'* ageing editor, Geoffrey Dawson, he and Carr took the paper's leader tone sharply to the left, where it remained for the rest of the war. The eclipse of Dawson, an important supporter of the Chamberlain government, was another example of the revolution sweeping the British elite in the summer of 1940.[173]

On 1 July, *The Times* published Carr's leader on 'The New Europe'. Faced with Nazi domination, he argued, Britain must counter-attack with a positive alternative to Hitler's new global order: a European federation rooted in the 'common values' now current in Western European democracy.

If we speak of democracy, we do not mean a democracy which maintains the right to vote but forgets the right to work and the right to live. If we speak of freedom, we do not mean a rugged individualism which excludes social organization and economic planning. If we speak of equality, we do not mean a political equality nullified by social and economic privilege. If we speak of economic reconstruction we think less of maximum production (though this too will be required) than of equitable distribution.[174]

This was a provocative intervention designed to influence opinion. The exigencies of war were making an unanswerable case for increased state involvement in the economic life of the country, but whether that should endure into the peace remained very much a matter of debate. For most Conservatives, socialism remained a political anathema: the very opposite of the freedom for which they were fighting.

When the Ministry of Information tried to put together a positive statement of war aims, it was clear that a post-war Britain was still too controversial a topic for the embattled Coalition to discuss. Harold Nicolson, the National Labour MP and parliamentary secretary to the Ministry, drew up the first draft in July. A failed diplomat but successful writer and broadcaster, Nicolson never let his complete incomprehension of the working class get in the way of a belief that something needed to be done to improve the lives of the people. He too wanted to avoid the horrors of class conflict, and had 'always been on the side of the underdog'.[175] Now he came up with the same war aims that Carr had put forward. As Nicolson summed it up, only a 'pledge of federalism abroad and socialism at home' would offer an 'alternative to Hitler's total programme'.[176]

When he presented these ideas to Duff Cooper, the minister agreed on what a big alternative to Nazism would have to look like, but doubted whether he could present such 'an apple of discord' to the Cabinet. Socialism was the sticking point. In the rewritten version that Duff Cooper took to his colleagues for discussion on 26 July, the s-word had been carefully removed. Instead, domestic war aims were to be a commitment that 'the abuses of the past shall not be allowed to reappear. Unemployment, education, housing and the abolition of privilege should form the main planks of such a platform.'

This was the sort of thing that the cleverer sort of moderate Conservative – men like Halifax and Eden – could get behind. Weasel words about the 'abolition of privilege' aside, it was more or less what they thought they had been working for in any case. Churchill, however, was far too busy with the war to think about subsequent reforms.

The prime minister was a man who was moved by grand visions – and those visions could include projects of social progress – but in practice his idea of domestic reforms tended more towards Edwardian electioneering stunts than the construction of a social democracy. Allergic as usual to planning for the future, he was reluctant to over-promise on what would happen next. Given his simultaneous dependence on Labour co-operation in government and on the gloomy and angry Conservative majority in the Commons, he had little reason to open up issues that would lead to party political dissent.

Attlee, on the other hand, did want progress on war aims, not least to placate the left of his party with a firm commitment to future change. Thanks to his pressure, as well as that from Duff Cooper, on 23 August the War Cabinet agreed to set up a War Aims Committee to 'consider means of perpetuating the national unity achieved . . . during the war through a social and economic structure designed to secure equality of opportunity and service among all classes of the community'.[177] The new committee, however, did not actually meet until October. When it despatched its recommendations to Number 10, they disappeared without trace. This was a topic that Churchill's 'restless and probing mind' preferred for the moment to leave undisturbed.[178]

16

'What will happen now?'

Like some strategic Krakatoa, the French surrender spread an ash cloud of shock and uncertainty across the world. On the far side of the Atlantic, through North Africa and the Mediterranean, and in the Far East, Britain's leaders, and its friends and enemies, had to work out their next steps. As it turned out, the British Empire's position was not nearly as critical as it had at first appeared. Nineteen forty opened up the final cracks in the façade of British imperial power, but it also demonstrated a colossal, if finite, global strength. It was this that allowed the UK to continue to shape the course of the war.[1]

'THE VOICE AND FORCE OF THE UNITED STATES'

On 16 May 1940, Roosevelt had reacted to Germany's French offensive by laying before Congress a massive rearmament programme that would see American forces supplied with 50,000 aircraft a year. This was five times the number of planes that Britain and Germany would make between them in 1940. With Germany apparently set on overturning the global balance of power, Congress approved Roosevelt's plans. Shortly afterwards, it also backed the 'Two Oceans Navy Expansion Act': a proposal to expand the US fleet by 70 per cent over the next five years, including the construction of eighteen aircraft carriers and seven battleships, so that it was big enough to fight in both hemispheres at once. For the moment, with American industry not mobilized for war, these plans were still a very long way from achievement, but the president's ambition was clear. He wanted to turn American economic might into military power.[2]

In comparison to Chamberlain's gloom about British reliance on the United States, Churchill gazed much more hopefully across the Atlantic. In part this was a necessary performance: the prime minister's frequent, confident references to US aid were a means to reassure anxious colleagues in Westminster and Whitehall. It also reflected a genuine belief in the historical power of a shared Anglo-Saxon heritage and an acute perception of the two nations' strategic interests. Churchill was tone deaf when it came to American culture, and he consistently overestimated the extent of American fellow feeling with the UK.[3] In the new circumstances created by the Fall of France, however, he knew that greater American assistance was vital, and hoped that US concerns about the security of the Atlantic would make this lifeline easier to secure.

Most British ministers and senior officials believed that the Americans, if they offered any help at all, would extract a heavy price. As Britain's gold and dollar reserves dwindled, the country would be forced to give up assets that could not be restored – at the very least, by selling off valuable UK investments in America to pay for the products of US industry. The question of whether it was worth accepting a permanent reduction in British power in order to fight Hitler now that he dominated the European continent was what underpinned Halifax's interest in exploring German peace terms at the end of May. Committed as he was to fighting an all-out war against Germany, Churchill hoped that Britain would not have to make this choice. He believed that a mixture of sentiment and scare tactics would secure American support sooner rather than later.

At the start of his premiership, on 15 May 1940, Churchill warned Roosevelt that 'the voice and force of the United States may count for nothing if they are withheld too long', but much to his frustration, American help did not come easily.[4] Personally, Roosevelt believed that the best way to safeguard his country's security was to supply the Allied war effort. Isolationism, however, remained politically powerful in America, and Roosevelt was pondering whether to run for re-election for a third term in November 1940. His defence programmes were not therefore presented as preparation for intervention in the European war. During June, nonetheless, the president provided as much aid as he could to the democracies. While it still looked as if France would stand, Roosevelt and his Treasury secretary, Henry Morgenthau, pushed through the sale to the Allies of half a million rifles, 900 field guns and 130 million rounds of ammunition, left over from America's involvement in the last war. After the French collapse, Britain took on the whole of this contract, using the rifles to equip the Home Guard. On 17 June, to maintain US business confidence and guarantee the continued operation of the industrial plant it had already helped set up, Britain also took financial responsibility for all the orders for new munitions that the French had placed in America over the previous year.[5]

This expenditure raised Britain's dollar commitments in America over the next twelve months to $1,640 million, at a point when the British estimated they had only $2,000 million in the 'war chest' of currency reserves. Still more dollars had to be spent, however, in order to accelerate the war economy. Cut off from its usual ore supplies on the continent by the German advance, the Ministry of Supply bought steel and aluminium from America, as well as precision machine tools to equip British factories. Prodigious overseas spending would help to slingshot British munitions production past its German equivalent, but it also led to an even more rapid erosion of the dollar reserves.[6]

The French collapse made the Americans worry that Britain might also make peace. From the middle of May, Roosevelt repeatedly sought assurances from Lord Lothian, the British ambassador in Washington, and from Churchill, that if Britain gave in, the Royal Navy would not be allowed to fall into German hands. In his 4 June speech declaring British defiance in the aftermath of Dunkirk – best known for the insistence that 'we shall fight on the beaches' – Churchill slipped in the declaration that even if Britain itself was 'subjugated and starving', the Empire would continue the fight 'armed and guarded by the British navy'.[7] He was reluctant to make any clearer public statement for fear of the effect on confidence at home, although he happily played on Roosevelt's anxieties by making clear that while he would not surrender the fleet, if he didn't receive the support he was asking for, he might be replaced by someone who would. Since they depended, for the moment, on the British fleet to stop any German encroachment into the Atlantic, the Americans were in no position to put matters beyond doubt with a Mers-el-Kébir-style strike on Scapa Flow.

Many Americans presumed that the UK would follow France into surrender. The US military, desperately in need of weapons as they began an unprecedented programme of peacetime expansion, opposed the sale or transfer of any further armaments, on the basis that they would be lost when Britain gave up the fight. Following the transfer of French contracts to the UK on 17 June, progress in discussions of further American support ground to a halt as Washington waited to see what would happen on the far side of the Atlantic.[8]

Britain's defiance during July laid the groundwork for renewed talks about American aid. The announcement of Roosevelt's massive rearmament programme had opened the danger that existing British orders in the States would have to compete with the demands of the American armed forces. As the head of the British Purchasing Commission, Sir Arthur Purvis, reluctantly accepted, there could be only one winner: the Americans would inevitably prioritize their own security. The more hawkish elements within the Roosevelt administration, however, were frustrated by the continuing limits on US military spending. In a secret meeting on 24 July, Treasury Secretary Morgenthau suggested to Purvis that rather than the British accepting a steadily eroding portion of US arms production, they should instead greatly increase their order for future deliveries. By expanding the total requirements on US factories, they could help to build the capacity that would assure their share of output. At Morgenthau's prompting, Purvis immediately asked to step up Britain's order for aircraft by 3,000 planes a month from January 1941. In addition to Britain's existing order for 1,000 aircraft a month, and the 2,000 a month allocated to the American forces, this expansion meant that the US was now working towards building 72,000 aircraft every year.[9]

These aircraft orders were the first dose in a regime of financial steroids that would produce an air force of unmatched size and strength. Whether America entered the war and supplied the pilots as well, or just sent over the planes for the aircrew turned out by the British Commonwealth Air Training Programme, this aerial armada would eventually result in immense offensive power.[10] Simultaneously, similar but smaller efforts were under way to fill the gaps in British munitions production and merchant shipbuilding with orders that would also energize American industry.

Together, such plans represented a very substantial investment in a transatlantic war machine. From the Fall of France to the end of 1940, as it attempted to push the US arms industry into battle, Britain spent about as much in America as it had done on its own rearmament during the whole of 1938.[11] That was the problem. By the end of July, Britain's 'war chest' of currency reserves was down to $1,280 million, with more than $200 million flying out of it each month. Meanwhile, British exports slumped as the country's engineering effort was ploughed into military production. During August, the Treasury warned that by the end of the year, British reserves of gold and dollars would be exhausted. The War Cabinet decided that, notwithstanding the risks of financial dependence on America, there was no choice but to continue spending in order to overcome the strategic advantage the enemy had now accrued. As Beaverbrook summed it up: 'We cannot match the Germans in manpower and must, therefore, overcome our deficiency by machines.'[12]

North of the American border, Canadian leaders too were concerned by the possibility of British defeat. Back in 1937, Mackenzie King, the Canadian prime minister, had promised that in the event of a German attack on the UK, Canadians would 'swim the Atlantic' to come to the UK's aid. Now, Canada abandoned its previously limited approach to the war for a full-out effort within the Commonwealth. Like every other Dominion, in May 1940 Canada experienced a great upsurge of patriotic feeling among the British-identifying parts of its population. The country immediately despatched its few destroyers to help defend the mother-island, accelerated the departure of Canadian troops across the Atlantic and passed the National Resources Mobilization Act, which extended government controls to cover everything apart from conscription for military service overseas. Unlike the rest of the Commonwealth, Canada had significant industrial potential, and although its munitions sector remained tiny for the moment, it could plan to make a meaningful technological contribution to the imperial war effort. From June 1940, British orders poured in to Canadian industrialists. By the end of the year, contracts were being placed for Canada to deliver 72,400 motor vehicles, 100,000 rifles and 42,600 light machine guns.[13] The Canadian government was also forced to think about what it would do in the event of a British collapse. In August 1940, it signed the Oldenburg Agreement with the United States, which arranged military planning for the mutual defence of the

North American continent. The old patterns of imperial reliance might not have broken, but the balance of global power was shifting.

THE WESTERN FLANK

With German power reaching from Norway to the Breton coast, the Atlantic assumed much greater significance as a battleground in the struggle to mobilize warring economies. Cut off from its usual European sources of supply, Britain would have to rely much more on the flow of resources from west to east, while Germany's naval reach was now extended much further into the Atlantic. Even in early May, Britain acted to secure that supply line by occupying Iceland, then a province of Denmark, although the Americans insisted that Greenland, also a Danish possession, should remain neutral.

As things went from bad to worse in France, it seemed possible that Fascist Spain would either enter the war, or allow Axis troops passage through its territory to attack the British naval base at Gibraltar. Britain attempted to meet this risk by buying Spain off. In March, it had already offered Spain a £2 million trade credit to spend on purchases from the Sterling Area, and when Sir Samuel Hoare arrived as the new ambassador in Spain on 1 June, he offered economic concessions, including licences to import goods through the blockade. Meanwhile, the British also arranged for the payment of immense bribes to senior Spanish generals (about £2.5 million that autumn alone) on the condition that their country kept out of the war.[14] As France crumbled, Franco showed signs of favouring the Axis, moving Spain on 12 June from a state of neutrality to one of 'non-belligerency', allowing German U-boats to resupply in Spanish ports and raising the possibility of entering the war with Berlin.[15] In case they lost Gibraltar, and to forestall Axis attempts to establish a presence in the central Atlantic, the British prepared plans from June to seize the Azores and the Canary and Cape Verde islands from Spain and Portugal. Notwithstanding the threat of invasion at home, two brigades of Royal Marines were kept on readiness to make sure Britain could control the Atlantic islands.[16]

There were limits to the projection of naval power. Further south, the possibility that the French port at Dakar in West Africa would be

opened to the enemy posed a potential threat to the north–south shipping route in the eastern South Atlantic. After the actions against the
French navy in early July, the chiefs of staff briefly favoured another
attack to destroy Dakar entirely. Yet there were not enough ships and
troops spare to undertake such an operation, which would in any case
heighten the risk of dragging Vichy France into outright war with the
UK. At the start of August, de Gaulle and Churchill cooked up plans
for a British fleet to carry Free French troops to seize Dakar and rally
French West Africa to the Allied cause. Despite Churchill's enthusiasm
for the project, the chiefs approved it only providing that it involved no
major military commitment and that there was proof that de Gaulle's
troops would be welcomed in without a fight.[17]

To the north, as fears of invasion grew, British ministers had grown
increasingly worried about neutral Eire being used as a back door for
an attack on the UK. The treaty ports given up by the National Government in 1938 were now critical assets, not only to protect the whole
island of Ireland, but also to base convoy escorts. In the second half of
June, Churchill sent Malcolm MacDonald (the new minister of health,
who as Dominions secretary had originally negotiated the handing
over of the ports) to Dublin to offer de Valera a reunited Ireland if
he agreed to allow British forces back into his country. Viscount
Craigavon, the prime minister of Northern Ireland, violently rejected
such plans, but Chamberlain, who took charge of the negotiations in
London as lord president of the council, was ready to overrule him.
Given the urgency of the situation, Ulster would have to demonstrate
its commitment to the British cause by sacrificing its existence for the
sake of national defence. Churchill, although less worried about the
invasion of Eire, saw a wonderful chance to reincorporate a united
Ireland into the Commonwealth. De Valera, however, was not to be
persuaded. Irish reunification was not worth the cost of British reoccupation, nor the loss of neutrality that must surely follow, particularly
since he was convinced that the British were about to lose the war and
would have to sue for peace. Much to Craigavon's satisfaction, London
gave up in the face of de Valera's intransigence, although detailed plans
were prepared to move troops south to fight alongside the Irish army in
the event that the Germans did invade. Nineteen forty generated some
powerful forces, but not powerful enough to reunite the island of
Ireland.[18]

'DICTATORS FADE AWAY — THE BRITISH EMPIRE NEVER DIES'

Meanwhile, the ripples caused by Italy's entry into the war spread out through Britain's African empire. In the Sudan, Kenya, Uganda and Nyasaland, more African men were recruited into the imperial armed forces as Britain sought to shore up its defences. In South Africa, where the invasion of Holland temporarily united Boer and British opinion against the Axis, General Smuts successfully pushed to lift restrictions on where South African troops could serve. Only whites were allowed to serve in combat units, but Smuts would be able to offer three brigades of them to the campaign in East Africa. The demand for military labour, however, led to the inauguration of the Non-European Army Services, which began recruiting in June 1940.[19] At the same time, the closure of the Mediterranean made Freetown, Simonstown and Aden into much more important ports and naval bases. From September, Takoradi in West Africa would also become a key departure point for aircraft which, to avoid the long voyage round the Cape, were delivered boxed up from the UK, assembled, then flown across the continent to the Middle East.

There, Lieutenant General Sir Archibald Wavell, Britain's commander-in-chief of the Middle East, and his fellow sea and air commanders, Admiral Cunningham and Air Chief Marshal Sir Arthur Longmore, faced a formidable task. The area for which Wavell was responsible was 4.5 million square miles, stretching from Egypt, through Cyprus, Palestine, Transjordan and Iraq, round the shores of the Persian Gulf and southwards into the Sudan and Somaliland. Initially, the whole theatre looked highly vulnerable. The Italian army in Libya had about four times as many troops as the British forces defending Egypt, and it was assumed that it would immediately attempt to seize the Suez Canal. In East Africa, the Italians had nearly 300,000 men under arms, compared to 10,000 British and Commonwealth troops.[20] The Italian navy was larger than the forces available to Cunningham at Alexandria, and from its Abyssinian bases it could be expected to interfere with British shipping moving through the Red Sea.

On the day France surrendered, Wavell issued a stirring order to his troops: 'The British Empire will, of course, continue the struggle until victory has been won ... Dictators fade away – the British Empire never dies.'[21] It seemed a bold assertion. As well as the Italians, the Vichy French colonies in Lebanon and Syria were now also potentially hostile, and German success in France had encouraged Arab opponents of British imperialism.

The Egyptian government of Prime Minister Ali Maher rejected British calls to declare war on Italy. The Egyptians promised to cut ties with Rome and intern Italian citizens, but dragged their feet on both. What really convinced the British to move against Ali Maher, however, was not his reluctance to enter the war but rather the fact that he had steadily been losing popularity. On 23 June 1940, the British ambassador, Sir Miles Lampson, went to see King Farouk and told him that the British would impose martial law unless he got rid of Ali Maher. Lampson hoped that Farouk would now turn to the Wafd Party – which, though nationalist, had made it clear that it would co-operate with the British during the war in return for a troop withdrawal after it. Instead, Farouk made another palace appointment, choosing a politician called Hassan Sabry, who was more pro-British but had no more of a popular mandate than his predecessor. He proved just as unwilling to declare war. The British pondered taking military control, but as the Italian threat gathered pace in Africa, they decided they lacked the troops. Although fighting would rage over its soil, Egypt remained technically neutral until almost the end of the war.[22]

In Iraq, the government of Nuri as-Said had fallen in March 1940, and he was replaced by Rashid Ali al-Gailani, a strong nationalist who was hostile to British influence. Rashid Ali refused to break off relations with Italy in summer 1940, and insisted that the price of Iraqi belligerence would be a solution to the problem of Palestine and the independence of Syria and Lebanon. The Allied defeats encouraged pro-German feeling among those of Iraq's army officers who were eager to see an end to British rule. Anti-British feeling was particularly pronounced among four senior army officers, the so-called 'Golden Square'.

At the start of July, concern for the security of Britain's position in the Middle East was such that London proposed sending an Indian division to garrison Iraq, but this deployment was abandoned in favour of meeting the more immediate threat from Italy in East Africa.[23] While the British did not have the military strength to challenge Rashid Ali, however, they could exert economic pressure to get him removed. In January 1941, Nuri as-Said and the regent of Iraq managed to force Rashid Ali out, but the Iraqi government's stance on joining the war remained unchanged.[24]

'A BIG BUTCHER'S BILL WAS NOT NECESSARILY EVIDENCE OF GOOD TACTICS'

As well as his military role, therefore, Wavell also had to deal with complex issues of international diplomacy and imperial politics. At his suggestion, a Cabinet Sub-Committee on the Middle East, comprising the secretaries of state for war (Eden), India (Leo Amery) and the Colonies (Lord Lloyd) was formed in London to provide him with policy guidance. What Wavell did not get was a minister permanently resident in the Middle East who could actually undertake some of the work involved in running what was rapidly becoming a crucial part of the British war effort.

Fortunately, Italy's military commanders proved unwilling to take full advantage of their position. Mussolini had hurled his country into war so as not to lose out on the spoils of German successes in France, but his generals had been planning on another two years of preparations before their forces were ready for battle. They were very conscious of how vulnerable their country, and Italy's African colonies, would be to blockade. Despite Mussolini's urging, his generals in Libya and Abyssinia sat tight, preferring to husband their resources rather than to start the fight.

Churchill also felt the need to inject some vigour into his commanders. He thought his admirals paid too much attention to the dangers of Italian air attack, and chivvied Cunningham to strike out against Italian communications in the central Mediterranean. In fact, 'ABC' (as Cunningham was known by his initials) was a very aggressive naval commander who was determined to get to grips with the Italians. The first encounters between the two navies over the summer demonstrated that the Italian capital ships were quicker than the British, but since they largely displayed this capacity in heading away from their opponents, it was clear that Cunningham was already on his way to dominating the enemy. The Italian air force meanwhile also proved much less effective than had been expected. This only increased Churchill's belief that more could be done, particularly if Malta, the tiny crown colony island south of Sicily, could be brought into play.[25]

In the 1930s, Malta had been seen as so vulnerable to Italian air attack that it would be impossible to defend. Now, however, it offered a vital staging point between Gibraltar and Alexandria, particularly because of its deep water harbour at Valetta. Malta was, however, woefully short of defenders. On 11 June, Italian bombers attacked for the first time, causing some panic but little damage. Again, the British were fortunate that the Italians had not at this point planned an invasion. By the end of the summer, Churchill was pressing for Malta to be reinforced and turned into a sally-port from which British forces could interrupt Italian supplies to their African colonies.[26]

Wavell insisted that he needed reinforcements, particularly of tanks and aircraft, if he was successfully to confront the Italians. If anything, however, Churchill wanted to bring troops home from the Middle East. He proposed raising a Jewish army to hold Palestine so that British battalions could be brought back to the UK. Concerned that this would turn Arab opinion definitively against the British, the army and the Colonial Office blocked his plans.[27] Instead of reinforcements for the Western Desert, the prime minister sent Wavell detailed suggestions about how better to use the troops he already had. Since Wavell believed, with some justification, that Churchill didn't have much grasp of what it takes to run a modern army, their correspondence became increasingly tetchy.

Eden tried to help by bringing Wavell to London at the start of August. It was a disaster. By the standards of the British army, Wavell was an intellectual – a linguist, poet and scholar. When Churchill aggressively questioned his judgement, however, he became tongue-tied. For the prime minister, this was evidence of his incapability, and although General Dill, the chief of the imperial general staff, and Eden backed Wavell up and made sure that, for the moment, he kept his job, Churchill never really regained confidence in him.[28]

Eden and Dill formed a powerful partnership at the War Office. They agreed with Wavell that reinforcements had to be sent to the Middle East.[29] Dill infuriated Churchill, not only because he stood up to him and told him what he couldn't do, but also because he responded to Churchill's goading with carefully argued written papers rather than

by shouting back in the prime minister's face. Churchill liked to position himself as a spurrer-on of overly cautious generals, and he soon
cast the CIGS as 'Dilly-Dally'. Now, however, it was Dill who demonstrated an impressive willingness to accept calculated risk in the pursuit
of strategic goals.[30] During August, he decided that tanks and anti-tank
guns should be withdrawn from the UK and sent to reinforce Wavell's
troops in Egypt. Given that British production was booming and that
Enigma decrypts had made clear that no cross-Channel offensive would
be launched for another six weeks, it was not quite as dangerous a gamble as it might appear. In his history of the war, Churchill carefully cut
Dill out of the credit for the decision, while his cheerleaders celebrated
it as an example of the prime minister's daring spirit.[31]

When the Italian generals finally moved into action, they didn't get
very far. In East Africa, they captured the Kenyan outpost of Moyale in
July and in August pushed the garrison out of British Somaliland. Seeing that British losses had been few, Churchill demanded an inquiry
into whether the colony had been prematurely abandoned. Wavell (who
could give as good as he got by cable at least) told him that 'a big
butcher's bill was not necessarily evidence of good tactics'.[32] This
put-down did not improve his relationship with the prime minister.

In the Western Desert, British troops awaited the Italian attack from
Libya. Across the border, the Italians too were waiting – a quick
advance into Egypt, planned to coincide with the Germans landing in
England, and when London surrendered they would be able to claim
their prize at minimal cost.

'THE PROSPECT OF GERMANY ESTABLISHING A HEGEMONY OVER THE CONTINENT'

While world attention was focused on the Fall of France, the USSR completed the territorial seizures that had begun after the Nazi-Soviet pact.
In mid-June the Baltic States were compelled to change their governments and allow in Soviet troops, and then were incorporated into the
USSR. Romania was forced to cede territory in Bukovina and Bessara-
bia. The recognition of these border changes would subsequently form
an important bone of contention in Anglo-Soviet relations.

The British and Soviet governments had been talking about a trade agreement since March with little progress. In May, the British despatched Sir Stafford Cripps to Moscow – initially as an exploratory negotiator, then as a replacement for the British ambassador – in the hope that he could speed things up. Halifax and Butler fought for Cripps' appointment because they believed he might find a way to bring the Soviets onside. When Cripps arrived in mid-June, however, he was stonewalled by his hosts. Molotov simply ignored his requests for discussions on trade until early August, and then stated that until the British recognized the Soviet takeover of the Baltic States as legitimate (and handed over the gold the Baltic governments had stored in London), there could be no progress in their negotiations. In fact, in the summer of 1940, Britain had very little to offer to attract the Soviets away from their non-aggression pact with Hitler except the threat of an eventual German victory. After the French armistice, Churchill gave Cripps a personal letter for Stalin in which he raised the issue of 'how the States and peoples of Europe are going to react towards the prospect of Germany establishing a hegemony over the Continent'.[33] When Cripps delivered the letter on 1 July, Stalin reacted derisively. The Germans might well be trying to dominate Europe, he said, but they lacked sufficient seapower to do it. It was an acute judgement, but one that held out little hope for any Anglo-Soviet rapprochement.

In reality, Stalin *was* worried by Germany's rapid victories in the west, and expected Britain either to follow France into defeat or join Hitler in an anti-Soviet alliance. Over the summer, the USSR drastically accelerated its own rearmament programme. Convinced that the German military were well ahead, Stalin hoped to preserve the Nazi-Soviet pact for as long as possible so that his forces would have a chance to catch up. For that reason, he was eager to provide the raw materials and grain that Germany needed to keep the European economy going in the second half of 1940.[34]

'BIG ELEMENT OF BLUFF'

The Japanese used the crisis in Europe to try to cut off Nationalist China's external sources of supply. In the middle of June, they insisted that the French shut the railway line running north from Indochina, and the British close the Burma Road. On 5 July, the War Cabinet discussed whether Britain would have to acquiesce. Appeals for American support had been rebuffed. Churchill, 'dwelling on all the inconveniences of a war with Japan', argued that 'In the present state of affairs, he did not think that we ought to incur Japanese hostility for reasons mainly of prestige.' He suggested that by shutting the road, the British could show the Americans why they ought to be taking the lead in the Far East.

Sir Alexander Cadogan, the permanent under-secretary at the Foreign Office, thought there was little chance of that. '[I]t is hopeless to put the US on the spot,' he noted in his diary. 'They simply won't stand there.' He and Lord Halifax both feared that giving in to the Japanese in Burma would lead the Americans to believe that the British were beaten in the war against Germany. In the War Cabinet, Halifax was hawkish, insisting that there was a 'big element of bluff' in Japanese attitudes. He argued that the British would lose less 'by standing up to Japanese blackmail than by relinquishing our principles'.[35] Churchill's caution won out, however. The British agreed to close the Burma Road, but only until the middle of October. This coincided with the period of the monsoon, when the Road's capacity was at its lowest in any case.

For more aggressive officers within the Japanese military, meanwhile, the collapse of France and Holland – soon, it was presumed, to be followed by the UK – opened the chance to grab a resource-rich South-East Asian empire and escape the threat of American economic strangulation. On 16 July 1940, they brought to power a new government, headed by Prince Konoe, which announced its intention to build a new, self-sufficient economic bloc in China and South-East Asia: the 'Greater East Asia Co-Prosperity Sphere'. The new Japanese foreign minister, Matsuoka Yō suke, told the British ambassador in Tokyo that given that Britain opposed the creation of this new order, it was 'difficult to see how [a] fundamental clash of interests and purposes could be avoided'.[36]

For the moment, more cautious Japanese naval officers used the threat of American intervention to warn against a headlong rush into war. The risk of Japanese expansionism, however, was an important influence on reactions from the eastern Dominions. In Australia and New Zealand, as in Canada, Germany's advance to the Channel coast encouraged a powerful popular feeling of Britannic co-community, but it also stimulated official anxieties about strategic security. In a radio address of 16 June, Prime Minister Menzies told Australians, 'We are an integral, proud and British community, and to preserve those attributes must practise a community of sacrifice . . . at this fateful hour, the watchword is "All In".'[37] One in six Australian men of military age had already volunteered for the armed forces by March 1940, but the response to the summer's military crisis was another surge of volunteers: 102,000 men between July and August. Australians could enlist either for service at home or in the Australian Imperial Force, which would serve overseas. On 11 July, recruitment for the latter was closed because it was feared that it would harm enlistment for domestic defence. The Australian government also planned a dramatic expansion of the war economy, spending £14 million on new factories and expanding the munitions workforce from 15,000 to 150,000 by June 1941.[38]

New Zealand too saw a surge of fellow feeling for Britain's plight. The country's Labour government responded to the crisis in Europe, and to patriotic public pressure, by introducing military conscription for the first time. In the opening nine months of the war, 38,000 New Zealanders had joined up, but in the two months between conscription being announced in May and voluntary enlistment ending in July, another 27,000 entered the armed forces. New Zealand had no war industry to speak of, but its farmers campaigned to send vast surpluses of eggs and butter as free gifts to the people of the UK.[39]

The opening of the war in the Mediterranean, however, finally led the British to tell the Australians and New Zealanders definitively that there was 'no hope' of despatching a fleet to Singapore in the 'foreseeable future'. Though the British continued to assert that the Royal Navy would sail out to eastern waters if Australia or New Zealand were actually threatened with invasion, the Singapore strategy was in abeyance. The Australians were furious.[40]

For Churchill, concentrating all Britain's available strength on the European war was not a difficult decision. As his nervousness over the Burma Road suggested, he recognized that this would have implications for the Far East. Nonetheless, he argued that the risk of a conflict with Japan was relatively low. Australia and New Zealand were simply too far away for the Japanese to undertake an invasion. Singapore was a well-defended fortress: capturing it would be a lengthy and complex operation. As he explained to the Australian and New Zealand premiers in August 1940, the greatest danger would come from an even worse upheaval in Europe, if 'Germany can make a successful invasion of Britain'. All the more reason for putting everything into the fight in the West.

Bogged down as they were in China, and cautious by inclination, the Japanese were unlikely, Churchill argued, to start a difficult war against the European empires that would inevitably lead to a conflict with the United States. A war with America was one Japan was bound to lose. Even though there was as yet no grand Anglo-American alliance, let alone a joint strategy, Britain should therefore act as if there was and rely even more than before on the deterrent value of the US navy in the Pacific.

In August 1940, the chiefs of staff reviewed the situation in the Far East. They described a situation of great vulnerability:

> In the absence of a fleet, we cannot prevent damage to our interests in the Far East. Our object must, therefore, be to limit the extent of the damage and in the last resort to retain a footing from which we could eventually retrieve the position when stronger forces become available.[41]

The second sentence was key, because despite their weakness, the British could not bring themselves to countenance losing Singapore. In the event that the Japanese attacked, the territory was not going to be relieved, but to act as if it was likely to fall would stop it working as a deterrent to Japanese ambitions, discourage the Pacific Dominions from playing their full part in the European war and make the Americans less likely to accept the responsibility of protecting British possessions in the Far East. The chiefs therefore endorsed the pre-war scheme for the defence of Malaya – with the air force taking the lead and the army guarding the airfields – even though its principal purpose – holding the enemy at a distance from Singapore until the fleet arrived – now no longer applied.

British Commonwealth forces in Malaya were very weak. The chiefs of staff estimated that the RAF needed 336 aircraft to carry out its mission of protecting the peninsula. At the moment, there were eighty-eight, none of which were fighters. To guard the naval and air bases, they thought the army needed twenty-seven infantry battalions – the equivalent of three divisions. There were currently nine battalions in the Malaya garrison. The chiefs therefore proposed gradually to reinforce Malaya with what planes and troops could be spared from the European war until, hopefully by the end of 1941, they were strong enough to put the existing plans into operation.

With Britain heavily committed to an air war over Europe and an escalating campaign in the Mediterranean, it took a remarkable optimism – and an under-assessment of Japanese combat strength – to presume that enough air power would be allocated to the Far East to allow it to form a secure basis for the defence of Malaya. Significantly, however, this was *not* the gap that would open up between Churchill and the chiefs of staff about the Far East from the autumn of 1940 on. Rather, the prime minister opposed plans to reinforce Malaya at all. He couldn't see why overcautious commanders wanted to lock up the Empire's strength guarding against a distant contingency, when every effort needed to be ploughed into the fight against Germany. Nor could he see the point in planning to defend the whole peninsula, when so long as the 'fortress' of Singapore and its approaches were strongly held, the Japanese would be deterred from even trying an attack.

When Churchill used the word 'fortress', he saw in his mind's eye something like Verdun in the Great War: an array of concrete forts, ditches and barbed wire from which could be mounted a prolonged defence. Yet the military applied 'fortress' to Singapore purely as an administrative term, to denote the position of the garrison commander. Northern defences for the island had not been built, because the point of fighting for Singapore was meant to be to keep the naval base in use, and that could only be done – as the military appreciations of the 1930s had made clear – by holding the enemy much further up the peninsula. None of the senior officers around Churchill corrected his misapprehension. Either they put it down to his natural floridity of expression, or they shied away from having yet another fight with a prime minister whose pugnaciousness outweighed his skill as a military commander. Even if they had managed to rectify his understanding of the situation, it would have made very little difference to his attitude. The European crisis meant that Churchill was willing to run a strategic risk in Asia. It was not enough, however, to make him change his mind about India.[42]

'A REVOLUTION WHICH MEANT THE END OF THE IMPERIAL CROWN IN INDIA'

For the Indian government, the immediate focus in summer 1940 was on the consequences of the new conflict around the Mediterranean and Middle East. This was where the Indian army was meant to play its part in winning the war. In May 1940, New Delhi drew up fresh military plans involving the setting up of six new divisions and their equipment with 3,000 vehicles. Military recruitment rocketed, with the Indian army doubling in size, from 170,000 at the start of 1940 to 340,300 at the start of 1941.[43] The elongation of the shipping route from the UK by the closure of the Mediterranean placed a new pressure on supplies to the eastern Empire. Starting in September, an investigatory mission led by Sir Alexander Roger explored ways to expand Indian industry and use it for war production, including plans for a major state-funded growth in munitions manufacturing that would have allowed India to equip all its own forces. In a sign of the drive towards a new mobilization, in June 1940 the Indian viceroy, Lord Linlithgow, suggested plans for a new Eastern Group Supply Council that would get every Commonwealth country east and south of Suez to co-ordinate resources and production, in a quest to become more self-sufficient and to aid the British war economy.

Since the spring of 1940, the leaders of the Indian National Congress had been arguing about its strategy. At an open meeting at Ramgarh in March, Jawaharlal Nehru had pushed through resolutions reiterating the demand for full independence, and calling for a constituent assembly to decide India's future based on universal suffrage, rejection of any co-operation with the British war effort, and the start of a campaign of civil disobedience. In the months of discussion that followed, however, he was outmanoeuvred by his more moderate opponents. Following the Muslim League's resolution demanding an independent Pakistan, on 21 June, the Congress Working Committee accepted the argument of the Madras politician Rajagopalachari that the 'problem of the achievement of national freedom has now to be considered along with the one of its maintenance and the defence of the country against the possible external and internal disorder'.[44] On 7 July, the Congress issued a fresh demand for post-war independence, but accompanied it with a proposal that in the interim, a new Indian 'National Government' should be formed, with would be composed in such a way as to secure the confidence of the Indian politicians elected in 1937. The door was open, just a crack, for the British to make the Congress a new offer of participation in the wartime government in return for post-war reforms.

In London, a new secretary of state had arrived at the India Office. Leo Amery and Churchill had known each other since their schooldays at Harrow, where Churchill, mistaking Amery for a younger boy because he was so short, had pushed him into the swimming pool. Amery – a prize gymnast who was obsessed throughout his life with maintaining a high state of physical fitness – duly responded by throwing the much larger Churchill into the deep end. This was pretty much the basis for their relationship for the rest of their lives: although as Amery would sadly reflect on seeing the prime minister later in the war, Churchill had clearly let himself go since then.

Amery was a passionate believer in a modernized British Empire, a global network in which notions of separate national or racial identities were replaced by a devotion to a Commonwealth ideal. He and Churchill had clashed bitterly over the Government of India Act, but they had been on the same side over appeasement. Having played such a pivotal role in the fall of the Chamberlain government, Amery was disappointed not to get a seat on the War Cabinet when Churchill formed his coalition. With the war spreading to the Mediterranean and the Middle East, however, he knew that the India Office would be an important position – though one that would inevitably lead to clashes with the prime minister. As the war went on, Amery would grow increasingly impatient with the antics of a man whom he never considered his intellectual equal. In summer 1940, though, he was impressed, like many others, by the sheer force of Churchill's personality as he grappled with the big issues of the war.[45]

When it came to India, Amery wanted to launch a new policy. His predecessor, the marquess of Zetland, knowing what fate awaited someone who had campaigned for concessions to the Congress, had resigned when he heard that Churchill had become prime minister. Like Zetland, Amery was soon visited by Stafford Cripps, with his bright ideas for a constituent assembly, and, again like his predecessor, he was impressed by the idea of breaking the Indian deadlock. In the circumstances of summer 1940, Amery understood that Britain needed a bigger contribution from India and that a government with greater Indian involvement would be better placed to get it. He pushed Lord Linlithgow to try out the same policy that Zetland had advocated earlier in 1940 – India given the right to frame its own constitution, British responsibilities guaranteed by treaty, and a promise of a united India becoming 'a partner-member in the British Commonwealth on the same footing of Independence as the United Kingdom and the Dominions'.[46]

The viceroy initially demurred, but after France fell, he was convinced enough of the need for a new departure to seek a meeting with Gandhi on 1 July, where he sought to establish how Congress would react to a new declaration from the British, committing themselves to a constitutional assembly and the achievement of Dominion status within a year after the end of the war. Gandhi – concerned as ever to maintain a solid front to the British – reiterated the importance of full independence. Nonetheless, Linlithgow now told Amery that he was willing to ask the leaders of the major parties whether they would be willing to join an expanded version of the viceroy's Executive Council. If enough of them were in favour, and if the British Cabinet agreed, he would circulate an invitation to join the war effort and issue the promises he had tried out on Gandhi. The Indian National Congress would have been made a generous offer that conceded much of what it had demanded: at worst it would be embarrassed, at best divided between extremists and moderates.

Perhaps there was an opportunity here for the sort of compromise that Cripps had been so eager to promote, with the British trusting the Indians to come up with their own constitution, Congress trusting in British good intentions and willingness to fulfil their promises, and the independence of a united India eventually managed in terms that left fewer people dead. It seems unlikely. Too much bad blood had already flowed under too many bridges, and there was still a great deal between what most Congressmen wanted and what Amery and Linlithgow wanted and were willing to give. What certainly shut this avenue, however, was Churchill's reaction as Amery proposed the idea of a specific promise on Dominion-hood to the Cabinet.

Amery knew that it would be difficult to get any change on India past the prime minister, and he spent a lot of time in trying to make sure that he would have the backing of other ministers. When the topic came up for discussion at the Cabinet on 12 July, however, and he found himself under attack from Churchill and his diehard colonial secretary, Lord Lloyd, Amery found that he was alone – Halifax was absent, Attlee and Greenwood were feeble, Simon (having promised Amery his backing) 'ran out', and only Chamberlain offered any support.[47] Worse, Churchill was inspired to write directly to Linlithgow to find out why he and Amery were proposing such a radical departure when everyone's attention ought to be on the peril of invasion facing the United Kingdom. Linlithgow too now backed away, complaining that Amery had not told him that he hadn't secured the Cabinet's approval beforehand and redrafting the proposed declaration to remove much of its force.

On 25 July, when the matter came up before the Cabinet again, Churchill launched a 'tremendous onslaught' on Amery, whom he accused of misleading his colleagues.[48] He insisted that all the correspondence between Amery and Linlithgow should be shared with ministers (a particularly humiliating demand, not only because it was perfectly normal for secretaries of state and viceroys to correspond privately, but because Amery and Linlithgow had shared their free and frank reflections on Churchill's prejudices over India). He himself would take charge of redrafting the viceroy's proposed declaration and, as he told Amery the next day: 'he would sooner give up political life at once, or rather go out into the wilderness and fight, than to admit a revolution which meant the end of the Imperial Crown in India'.[49] As Amery, who would have resigned if there hadn't been a war on, reflected somewhat disingenuously:

> he just cannot get away from certain phrases and certain instincts, and it was hopeless to try and point out to him that what I was suggesting was well within the four corners of pledges and statements made again and again, and could hardly be so revolutionary if Zetland . . . had proposed it months ago and Linlithgow and all his governors assented.[50]

As rewritten by Churchill, the statement Linlithgow actually put forward on 8 August 1940 was much weaker and more clearly a repetition of what had been offered before: transition to Dominion status at some unspecified point after the war, places for 'representative Indians' on the Executive Council, but no free hand for Indians to choose the manner in which they might become independent. It also included a commitment that the British government would not accept any proposed system of government 'whose authority is directly denied by large and powerful elements in Indian national life'. Since Muslim-majority provinces were a key part of India's industrial and military contribution to the war effort, Muslim co-operation had become even more important to the British. The Muslim League hailed the 'August offer' as a victory, because it enshrined its say in future deliberations.[51] The Indian National Congress, however, had already decided that what was on offer from the British was unacceptable: Nehru declared that Dominion status was 'dead as a doornail'.[52] At the start of September, Congress authorized Gandhi to start a new civil disobedience campaign.

'RUSSIA'S DESTRUCTION MUST THEREFORE BE MADE A PART OF THIS STRUGGLE'

After France fell, Hitler and the German high command weighed up what to do if the British did not, as they hoped, see sense and negotiate. In July, Hitler ordered his armed forces to begin detailed planning for an invasion of the UK. The Luftwaffe prepared a full-scale offensive to gain air superiority over southern England, which would get under way from mid-August. Assuming that could be achieved, the army and navy would launch a seaborne invasion no earlier than the start of September.

The Luftwaffe had suffered heavy losses in the French campaign, but Göring was bombastic about its chances of defeating the RAF. For the German army and navy, however, there was always a degree of unrealism about the invasion planning. German generals proposed to land much larger numbers of troops than could be transported or supplied. The Kriegsmarine was all too well aware of its weakness relative to the Royal Navy, but did not want to be blamed for scotching the invasion. It therefore began to assemble shipping in the Channel ports. The only way to get enough boats was to requisition the huge river barges from the Danube and the Rhine. No matter the outcome in the air, had the Germans ever decided to load their army into these crucial components of their industrial transport network and sail them slowly into range of the Royal Navy, the result would have been a very rapid end to the war. Hitler was well aware of the risks involved and remained lukewarm about the project. An invasion might be attempted if an unambiguous victory could be achieved in the skies, but throughout the summer the Germans were also exploring other options.[53]

One, much favoured by the German navy, was to strike at the global, seaborne roots of British power. Germany should build up a big U-boat fleet to blockade the UK. Meanwhile, it would strike towards North Africa and the Middle East, working with Italy, Spain and Vichy France to seize Gibraltar and the Azores at one end of the Mediterranean, and Alexandria and Suez at the other. With its imperial back broken and its maritime supply lines cut off, Britain would be forced to sue for peace while the Germans established their own African empire. Some of Hitler's generals were also keen on a Mediterranean campaign that would secure the flank of their new possessions in Western Europe and leave Germany safe to concentrate on a siege of Britain. Briefly, Hitler seemed enthusiastic, awarding top production priority to U-boats and aircraft and allowing planning to begin for the capture of Gibraltar. He doubted, however, that victories in the Mediterranean would knock Britain out of the war. He now took it for granted that the British were being aided by America, and provided that link held, British resistance would continue.[54]

The German Foreign Ministry, in contrast, looked to a different way of taking on the British. Ribbentrop was already seeking to knit Germany, Italy and Japan together in a new pact. He looked forward to bringing in the USSR as well. With the Soviets threatening India, Japan East Asia and Italy the Middle East, Britain would simply be overwhelmed. Here too, Hitler was doubtful. In Stalin's position, he would use his control of essential resources to coerce German policy. He couldn't believe the Soviet dictator wouldn't want to do the same. He knew an eventual confrontation between Nazism and Bolshevism was inevitable, but what mattered was timing. If Germany just sat tight in its new Western European empire, it would be crushed between the Americans and British on one side, and the Russians on the other.

During June and July, therefore, while his troops were preparing possibly to attack the UK, Hitler also began to talk about eliminating the USSR. This would not mean abandoning the war in the west, but rather finding a solution to the problem of continued British resistance. At the end of July, General Franz Halder, the head of the Germany army's general staff, summarized Hitler's thinking:

> Britain's hope lies in Russia and the United States. If Russia drops out of the picture, America, too, is lost for Britain, because elimination of Russia would tremendously increase Japan's power in the Far East. Russia's destruction must therefore be made a part of this struggle, Spring 1941.[55]

17

The Battle of Britain

A German invasion of the UK was therefore highly unlikely unless air superiority could be rapidly established over southern England. It was this that the Luftwaffe sought to achieve between July and October 1940. The resultant campaign is usually thought of in terms of air-to-air combat, but from the start it involved large numbers of people on the ground as well: as participants, as spectators and as victims, both of airborne violence as the Luftwaffe unleashed its bombs, and of boredom, as frequent, widespread air-raid warnings disrupted work and forced people into the shelters. After they failed to overcome the RAF's defences, the Germans had eventually to postpone their invasion plans, but there was no let-up in the aerial attack. Rather than a clear dividing line, the daytime Battle of Britain melded fuzzily into the night-time Blitz on British cities.

WORKERS IN THE FRONT LINE

The British encounter with life under assault from the air began in the middle of July, as the Luftwaffe started the preliminary attacks that were meant to pave the way for its more serious offensive later in the summer. These included reconnaissance flights, attacks on shipping lanes and nuisance raids designed to test out British defences. In this initial phase, the Germans had marginally the upper hand: German planes sank 30,000 tons of British ships from the coastal convoys, forced the destroyers of the Channel Patrol to leave Dover because of threat of bombing, and downed 150 British aircraft for the loss of only 105 of their own.[1]

The beginning of the air battle overhead had immediate consequences for those on the ground. The point of German attacks was not to kill civilians, but given the vagaries of bomb aiming and the proximity of civilian housing to military targets, civilian losses mounted. During July, 299 civilians were killed and 355 wounded by German aircraft.[2] Although German aircraft now became a much more common sight, particularly to those on the eastern and southern coast, the most frequent experience was of hearing the siren without seeing any plane. Each German attack sparked a warning that covered a very wide area, sending people rushing to the shelters in places that were never bombed. Other places were attacked without warning. Public bafflement persisted about which siren notes signalled a raid was imminent and which the all-clear. A system of gradated warnings that was meant to clarify the likelihood of an attack initially only heightened the confusion.

The battle involved people in other ways. Round the southern English coast, spectators watched the fighting over the Channel, although what they saw – fast, distant, over very quickly – was much easier observed than understood. Radio and newspaper reporting, and the public relations campaigns waged by the Ministry of Aircraft Production, carried the battles to a wide audience.

In Britain's factories, the summer of 1940 was a period of remarkable expansion and extraordinary effort. About half a million people joined the workforce in the war-related industries during 1940. By the end of the year, almost a million Britons were working on engineering and explosives contracts for the Ministry of Aircraft Production, more than for either of the other armed forces.[3] The big increases in new employees and the resultant re-grading of jobs led to labour disputes, and despite Bevin's Order 1305, there were actually more strikes in the metals and engineering sector in 1940 than in 1939, although the average duration of stoppages was much shorter.[4] Those annual figures, however, concealed a significant drop in strike action between June and September 1940, as workers heeded the call to arms.[5] By July 1940, day shifts in the main aircraft factories were averaging 63.6 hours a week, and night shifts 64.9 hours. Since industrial accidents increased alongside exhaustion, there were casualties in the factories as well as in the skies.[6] Between July and August, the Ministry of Aircraft Production's average output was 56 per cent higher than it had been over the previous three months.[7]

Nonetheless, this increase was held back by the interruptions caused by air-raid warnings. The practice of halting work and taking cover when they were sounded meant that the German air offensive caused extensive disruption well before it really got under way. Beaverbrook highlighted the problem to the War Cabinet at the end of June. He believed that aircraft workers ought to be subjected to military-style discipline, but the government rejected compulsion and instead negotiated with employers and unions about the best way to maintain output. 'Roof spotters' were immediately suggested as a solution: factory workers stationed on the roof of their plant who would provide early warning of an actual attack, while their colleagues kept on working after the siren sounded.

While national negotiations about roof spotting went on, individual factories were also grappling with the question of what to do after the sirens sounded. Some managers thought that workers rushed too readily to the shelters to escape their labours, but dawdled on the way back. Some shop stewards were reluctant to endanger their comrades' lives to maintain profits for bosses who had spent too little money on ARP.[8] Male workers insisted that they would stay at their posts only if adequate shelters were provided for their families. It took until the start of September for a national scheme to be agreed in which the RAF trained a core of spotters who, in turn, instructed others, in order to provide cover for essential industries.

Whereas earlier ARP propaganda had told people to protect themselves, now they needed to be convinced to put themselves at risk. From July, as ministers encouraged workers to stay at their posts, the government promoted the idea that everyone was now in the front line and had to play their part. Here was another version of the people at war, one rapidly taken up by the national and local press, the BBC and the newsreels. Civilians were told that they too were now soldiers in the front line, and bearing up under bombardment was one of the things they had to do.[9]

'THE ANTEROOM FOR A BLOODY CREMATORIUM'

The major air offensive that was meant to prepare the way for the invasion opened on 14 August and continued for the next month and a half. Most of the Luftwaffe's effort went initially into daylight attacks on RAF bases and other military infrastructure, particularly in south-east England, while Fighter Command sought to prevent German planes reaching their targets. In practice, the Germans attacked lots of other things as well – factories and ports, shipping lanes with mines, and night-time nuisance bombing in an effort to exhaust the defenders and keep civilians awake. During late August, the Germans undertook an escalating series of attacks on London, which culminated in a series of massive day and night raids between 7 and 15 September. The RAF's continuing ability to fight off these raids contributed to the realization in the German high command that daytime air superiority could not be achieved in time to launch a cross-Channel invasion.

Of the two air forces, the Luftwaffe had the more difficult task. As long as the RAF's air defences remained in existence, the British had won. Throughout the battle, Air Chief Marshal Hugh Dowding, at the head of Fighter Command, sought to balance the destruction of German attackers, the protection of targets on the ground and the preservation of his squadrons.[10]

The Germans had two significant advantages. Their bases along the north European seaboard allowed them to choose the location and moment of attack and potentially to divide or surprise the defenders. German aircrews were initially more practised than their opponents and their tactics were better tested. Yet the Luftwaffe also faced the severe difficulty of trying to improvise a decisive campaign almost from scratch. Since the start of May, 28 per cent of the German air force's strength had been destroyed and another 36 per cent damaged in the battle for France. It was operating from new bases with elongated logistics. Badly damaged aircraft had to go all the way back to Germany for repair. The Luftwaffe's expansion had focused on the provision of battlefield support to the German army. Now it was being asked to lay the groundwork for an invasion. The German air industry produced fewer planes than its British opponent, while the Luftwaffe's training system did not

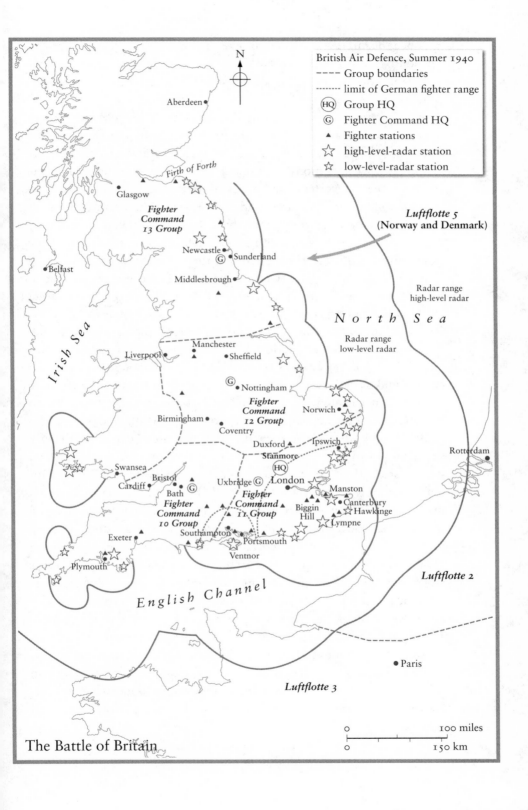

British Air Defence, Summer 1940
- - - - Group boundaries
········· limit of German fighter range
(HQ) Group HQ
(G) Fighter Command HQ
▲ Fighter stations
☆ high-level-radar station
☆ low-level-radar station

N

Aberdeen

Firth of Forth

Glasgow

Fighter Command 13 Group

Newcastle
(G) •Sunderland

•Belfast

Middlesbrough

Irish Sea

North Sea

Radar range
high-level radar

Radar range
low-level radar

Manchester

Liverpool• •Sheffield

(G) •Nottingham

Fighter Command 12 Group

Birmingham• Norwich

Coventry

Duxford ▲ Ipswich

Stanmore

Rotterdam

Swansea

Bristol•

Cardiff•

Bath

Uxbridge (G) London

Manston

Fighter Command 10 Group

Southampton

Fighter Command 11 Group

Biggin Hill

Canterbury
Hawkinge
Lympne

Exeter•

Portsmouth

Ventnor

Plymouth

English Channel

Luftflotte 5
(Norway and Denmark)

Luftflotte 2

•Paris

Luftflotte 3

The Battle of Britain

0   100 miles
0   150 km

produce the aircrew it needed to take the fight to the enemy.[11] The dispersion of German effort between air bases, industrial sites, nuisance raids and mining operations demonstrated the strategic naivety of its senior officers.[12]

At the start of August, the Germans had a bomber force of 1,438 planes (of which 949 were fit for action), and 414 twin-engined and 1,065 single-engined fighters, of which 320 and 878 respectively were ready for operations.[13] Thanks partly to the faltering armaments drive and partly to the complexities of its procurement process, Germany's bomber fleet was made up of relatively light aircraft. Even the best German bomber, the Junkers Ju88, for example, could carry only a third of the bomb-weight of the Avro Manchester, the worst of the heavy aircraft ordered for the RAF in the late 1930s and just coming into service in late 1940.[14] German bombers could not protect themselves from enemy interceptors, and had to be escorted to their target by German fighter aircraft. The German single-engine fighter, the Messerschmitt Bf109, was at that point probably the best in the world, but its performance was reduced when it flew at the bombers' lower altitude. Worse, the Bf109's tanks only just held enough fuel for it to reach London with cautious flying. Its range now became the effective limit of concentrated German daylight attacks: they were unable to reach the heart of the British air industry in the Midlands.[15]

By the time August began, Fighter Command had expanded to sixty squadrons, forty-eight of which flew Spitfire or Hurricane fighters. From a strength of 1,112 aircraft, 715 were serviceable.[16] Fighter Command not only had the advantage of fighting over home turf, which meant that pilots who survived the destruction of their aircraft could quickly return to duty. More importantly, it benefitted from a fully-functioning warning and control system, in which information about incoming attacks from coastline radar stations and Observer Corps posts inland was filtered through Fighter Command's headquarters, then back out to the several sector control rooms based at major airfields in each of the Command's four Groups – 10 (west of England), 11 (south-east England), 12 (Midlands and East Anglia) and 13 (the north). Sector commanders guided the scrambled fighters into combat, and then back to the safety of base. This system meant that the British could respond flexibly to German incursions, without exhausting its aircrew and aircraft by keeping constant standing patrols of aircraft aloft. The channelling of information and control increased the chance of the British matching their defensive efforts to the scale of German attacks and reduced the risk of being divided and defeated in detail. The Germans enjoyed no such centralized system: once German planes were airborne, they could not be directed en masse to overwhelm the already committed defenders.[17]

The British defences therefore depended on the acquisition, analysis and transmission of information. At the start of the main battle, German bombing of radar and sector control stations caused the British severe anxiety. Attacks on airfields in the south between the middle of August and the start of September put the system under severe strain. To the south of the capital, raids on 30 and 31 August destroyed the operations room at Biggin Hill. Despite the best efforts of a dogged team of civilian Post Office engineers, the communications network threatened to break down. When the Germans switched away from bombing airfields, they gave an important respite that allowed repairs to be put in place.

Between the wars, air combat had often been envisioned as a cleaner, more gallant alternative to the muddy wasteland of ground warfare. In fact, this was as grimly an attritional battle as any fought on the Western Front.[18] Aerial dogfighting was a bitterly confused, rapidly disordered business in which hunter could rapidly become prey. In the determinedly non-heroic tone often affected by fighter aircrew, 73 Squadron's unofficial war diary caught the risks involved in its account of one pilot, H. W. 'Tubby' Eliot, who had been lucky to escape after he

> apparently got mixed up with some He113s, and was busy writing his initials on the Hun's backside so that he could convince the I[ntelligence] O[fficer] that it was his, when he was set on [by] some of the aforementioned Hun's boyfriends. He baled out and did a delayed drop of 15,000 [feet] before pulling 'the string'.[19]

Having been burned about the eyes and leg ('slightly crisped' as the diarist put it), Eliot had nonetheless escaped from hospital and returned to his unit. He would be killed five years later, at the age of twenty-three, as a Wing Commander with a DSO and DFC.

In fact, when it came to killing the enemy, pilots were relatively inefficient. Between July and November 1940, about 2,300 pilots served with Fighter Command, but only just over a third even claimed to have shot down an enemy plane, and the proportion actually doing so was even lower.[20] In the air combat arena, new gladiators were highly vulnerable and might have little chance to improve their skills. One unit, 222 Squadron, for example, arrived at Hornchurch on 30 August still using flying formations that had been abandoned by other units. By the end of the same day, it had lost half its planes and a quarter of its pilots.[21] In both air forces, a hard-core of more experienced men did the bulk of the execution, marrying excellent reactions with the ruthless despatch of weaker opponents, which was one reason why the RAF benefitted from an influx of veteran airmen from Poland and Czechoslovakia. Even experienced pilots, however, were vulnerable to lapses of concentration under the strain of unrelieved operational flying, and squadron casualties mounted rapidly. When the station chaplain at RAF Duxford remarked to the adjutant that summer that the frequent changes of personnel had given the mess the air of a railway station waiting room, he got the bitter reply, 'Not a railway station. This is the anteroom for a bloody crematorium.'[22]

An army of ground crew had to maintain the precisely repeated rounds of maintenance and replenishment necessary to keep the planes in the sky. In a fighter squadron they outnumbered the pilots by at least five to one, but were now themselves often under air attack as the Germans targeted British bases. Ronald Pountain, an armourer with 64 Squadron, left a detailed description of the inspection routine with which he began every day.

> For me, that meant, first of all, taking off the 14 access panels . . . Next, unload the guns and clean them using a cleaning rod and 4 by 2 . . . Having cleaned the guns, check that the trolley acc[umulator] was plugged in and switched on, and then go under the starboard wheelbay and set the safe and fire switch from safe to fire . . . Having set the switch to fire, up into the cockpit and sit in the pilot's seat. Switch on the gunsight and test all functions including the dimmer switch. Clean the lens and reflector glass. Very important. No armourer wanted his pilot to go chasing a speck of dirt on the reflector glass halfway to the Pas de Calais. Switch off the gunsight. Turn the safety ring on the pilot's firing button from Safe to Fire and press the button while listening for the breech blocks to clang forward. Set the safety ring back to safe. Remove the filament from the gunsight . . . Replace it with the spare filament in

the filament holder next to the gunsight and fit the original filament in the holder. Test the gunsight again. Down to ground again. Set the safe/ fire switch back to safe. Check that all the breech blocks are forward and, using a special feeler gauge, check that the firing pins have all released. Re-load the guns and replace all the access panels.[23]

That was before testing the engine, then getting the pilot's equipment prepared ready for the aircraft to go.

Servicewomen were also involved in the battle. By September 1940, there were about 17,000 women in the Women's Auxiliary Air Force, just over a quarter of them in Fighter Command. Although, like all women in the armed forces throughout the war, they were not permitted to bear arms, the jobs they were given within the information network meant that they played key roles in the defensive system: reporting radar results, operating telephone exchanges and collating and plotting information about each raid on the 'plot tables' at Fighter Command headquarters and the sector operations rooms.

In retrospect the British never looked like losing the battle of attrition. Thanks to the systems of training, production and recovery established before the fighting began, the supply of pilots, new and repaired aircraft by and large kept pace with the losses in combat. Between June and October 1940, the RAF lost 915 fighters around the UK, but in the same period, British industry produced 2,091 Spitfires and Hurricanes.[24] Even the damage done to the airfields was either quickly fixed or worked around with the establishment of emergency facilities. Nonetheless, there were moments of great anxiety for the British as the battle developed. Fighter Command began the main phase of the battle about 130 pilots below its established strength. By the end of August, the deficit had grown to about 180 pilots, and aircraft losses temporarily exceeded the number of replacements held in store. Dowding had rotated units in and out of the front line in an effort to maintain their fighting power. By the start of September, he had run out of fresh squadrons and had to take pilots and planes away from areas outside the south-east in order to keep 11 Group close to full strength.[25]

Fighter Command knew that it was inflicting damage on the Luftwaffe. In fact, it overestimated the number of enemy planes that had been shot down by at least a third. Yet even though the picture was being clarified by Enigma decrypts, the British still thought the Luft-waffe was much larger than it actually was. Concerned that this was a battle the RAF might be losing, Dowding maintained a relatively conservative strategy, designed to keep his Command in being.[26] By mid-September, he could count on more than 650 serviceable fighters, with another 428 in reserve or in transit, while the number of available pilots had risen to 1,500.[27]

German losses too were severe. In the period from 13 to 19 August alone, about 10 per cent of the aircraft initially deployed against Britain were destroyed.[28] In total, between early July and the end of October, the Luftwaffe lost 1,733 aircraft. During September, German fighter strength was down to about 500 planes. The German air industry did not outpace these shortfalls in the same way as its British equivalent: between June and October it produced only 988 single-engine fighters. The range of activities that the Germans had attempted to undertake played an important role in wearing down their strength through acci-dents and mechanical and physical exhaustion. Aircrew losses had been high, and it was here that the German lack of preparation told most strongly against them. Most of the German casualties came from the bomber crews, but the damage to the experienced corps of fighter pilots had the greatest effect. During September the Luftwaffe had only half or less the number of fighter pilots who were available to the RAF: it was the men in the Messerschmitts, not the Spitfires, who were by this point the real 'few' of the Battle of Britain.[29]

The Luftwaffe was even more optimistic than the RAF about its enemy's losses, overestimating its success by a factor of three or four. Since they had started the campaign by underestimating their oppo-nent's numbers, this encouraged a belief that Fighter Command must be close to defeat.[30] The sense that it was now time to achieve a decisive result led the Luftwaffe to shift the focus of attack all out against Lon-don. The Port of London was a major economic objective, but the capital was also a symbolic objective. Faced with an assault on the imperial capital, the RAF would have to take to the skies, where the Luftwaffe's fighters would complete its destruction.[31]

'KEEPING EVERYBODY AWAKE
AND TIRED'

The intensification of the air battles had a big effect on people on the ground. As the fighting escalated in August, so the civilian death toll grew. On 19 August, for example, the Germans attacked eleven aerodromes, but also hit houses in Chelmsford, Colchester, Dover and Chatham. On the same day, a raid set light to the massive naval oil tanks at Llanreath, near Pembroke Dock in West Wales. This sparked the largest conflagration since the Great Fire of London, which burned for the next two-and-a-half weeks, killed five of the firemen who tried to contain it, and raised a cloud of smoke that could be seen across the country. That night, raiders were reported over Derby, Middle Wallop, Portsmouth, Bristol, Liverpool, Hull, Newcastle, Edinburgh and Glasgow. By midnight, twenty-three civilians had been killed and seventy-four injured.[32] In the course of August as a whole, more than 1,100 civilians were killed and over 1,500 seriously wounded in air attacks. Casualties were reported in every Civil Defence region except Northern Ireland, and were more evenly distributed across the country in August than at any subsequent point in the war.[33]

If the battle's reach was broad, its touch remained relatively light. During August and early September the majority of bombing raids were carried out by sorties of between one to six planes. The destruction was widely dispersed, but did not threaten to expunge entire cities. At the time, however, people felt that some of these raids were extremely heavy. Large numbers of British civilians suddenly felt overwhelmingly exposed to the possibility of violence from the skies.

Reactions to these summer air raids varied widely. Although night bombing is normally seen as something that happened after the Battle of Britain had finished, in fact it was probably the sort of air attack whose impacts were most widely felt from the start. The feeling of helplessness could induce panic. In Bristol, the law librarian diarist for Mass-Observation had heard plenty of aircraft overhead since the war began, so the noise of engines in the early hours of 11 August did not overly disturb him:

There was a burst of gunfire, but I couldn't see any flashes. It was just another friendly raid. But when, for the first time in my life, I heard the screech of falling bombs, I wasn't so sure. It was a most unpleasant sound. I got back from the window and nipped across the room. The squeal seemed to prolong itself indefinitely. For several hours, while I tried to find the door in the dark, it continued. At last came the explosions – about five – loud, but apparently reasonably distant . . .

I was really windy, I hadn't expected anyone to go so far as to actually drop bombs within a few miles of me.[34]

Others remarked on the excitement of feeling themselves in the front line. A well-off solicitor's wife, living in Sevenoaks and volunteering as an ambulance driver, watched an air battle over the town that culminated in the bombing of its gasworks, and recorded that her

own feeling was one, I am rather ashamed to say, of exhilaration, and heightened sensibility. I was glad not to be frightened, but I was like a mongoose, frankly curious to see what would happen next. Nobody showed any fear, I noticed people were a bit white as the planes went over us, and I expect I was too.[35]

A few days before, she had noted with disapproval the way a young working-class woman evacuated from Broadstairs after bombing had become 'ungummed and so fussed with tears and gulps' when German aircraft again appeared in the skies:

Heaven knows one can get panicky, but that class is somehow trained to show fear and be 'highly strung' while a more educated class, and all men such as the service men are expected to be steady and that must help enormously.[36]

When air combat took place in daylight, people on the ground were often to be seen standing outside and watching dogfights overhead. The prime minister himself was captured by the newsreel cameras enjoying the spectacle of air combat during a visit to the south coast. On the other hand, during the second half of August there was a rising tide of complaints about the *lack* of warnings from some of those in areas that had been raided: 'that sirens are not sounded, and that they are sounded after planes are heard and the "All Clear" given before the raiders had left'.[37] In places that had been attacked, even these lighter raids had begun to reveal some of the problems with Civil Defence preparations, including the lack of help for those who had been bombed out of their houses and now had no idea what to do next. Sometimes air-raid warnings were in place for a whole night. Those who used the shelters now had to try to sleep in structures that had been designed to protect them during brief but intense daylight attacks. Some tried to make their Anderson shelters more homely with decorations and furniture, but it was a difficult task for what was basically a cramped, corrugated iron-lined hole in the ground. As Mass-Observation reported at the end of August, in those streets, predominantly working class, where residents had to rely on public shelters, there were

> many complaints . . . that they are cold, draughty and smelly (some have no doors, so that cats have free access), there are no seats for children and old people, and seldom lavatory accommodation . . . Public shelters at present hold a mixed bag of children and old people who want to go to sleep, people who want to sing and talk, crying babies, people who want to smoke. This leads to much extra strain and considerable trouble.[38]

The discomfort, distress and derangement to everyday life contributed to demands for reprisals. Mass-Observation collected some extreme comments from Londoners – 'They ought to have a taste of their own medicine. Their women don't mind about our women. We ought to go over and bomb their women and kids. They want Lebensraum. That's the way to give it them'[39] – but M-O's investigators argued that these were uncharacteristic. Although 'recent all night raids' had led to strong demands 'for retaliation on Berlin . . . this desired retaliation is not in bombing civilians on [sic] masse so much as in keeping everybody awake and tired'.[40]

This seems to be borne out in the account of a German plane coming down off Herne Bay on 24 August. The crowd was angry, but it didn't turn into a lynch mob. As a local schoolboy recorded:

> the front was packed with people. Soon the motorboat was within a few hundred yards of the shore. The crowd increased (if that was possible) and the road was full of vehicles of every description, ambulances, trailers, even military lorries. Tin hats were to be seen in great abundance . . . Luckily I was near the front and saw him well . . . The whisper spread

through the crowd 'Jerry, German' etc. He had on a dingy blue-grey uniform, with wings sewn on and an iron cross . . . His hair was dishevelled and his face streaked with yellow grease. He appeared quite unhurt but extremely sullen for he wouldn't take his eyes off the ground. He didn't speak a word.

The crowd was silent except for a few remarks. The man next to me growled his disapproval and other remarks Mum, Dodie and Peter heard were 'Now he'll taste some butter', and a policeman said 'Treat him rough!'. He was bundled into an ambulance and that was the last we saw of him.[41]

For both sides, the reporting of the battle was itself an important part of the struggle. In the three months from 23 July, the Air Ministry issued 859 bulletins to the BBC and the press that detailed how the battle was progressing.[42] Official British and German statements about their own aircraft losses and the number of enemy planes that they had shot down became a key way in which the attritional struggle in the skies was understood. They provided the basis for the scoresheet headlines that rapidly became standard: '144 DOWN OUT OF 1000', for example, or 'ROUND 2: THE COUNT IS 69'.[43] In contrast, the effects of the German attack on the ground were reported in much vaguer terms, as the censors sought to restrict the passage of any information that might be useful to the enemy. Much to the annoyance of locals who wanted their part in the war to be recorded, air raids were described in regional terms ('a city in the north-east', for example, rather than 'Hull'), and specific incidents were reported only after a lengthy time lag.

There was also some public concern about whether the figures for shot down planes were accurate, not least because listeners to German propaganda broadcasts heard very different numbers. The Air Ministry responded by explaining in detail how it ensured its figures were accurate. In fact, fighter pilots' claims were very difficult to check, a problem that was never explained to the public, and the scoresheets reflected the mistakes that both sides were making in their assessment of the damage being done to the enemy. While the Air Ministry was remarkably honest in the circumstances about the scale of British losses – over the course of the battle it understated them by only 18 per cent – it overstated the number of German planes that were shot down by 76 per cent. Relatively speaking, these were more accurate numbers than those put out by the Germans, who claimed to have shot down three-and-a-half times more British aircraft than was actually the case.[44]

From a very early stage in the battle, therefore, the impression given in the British media was that the RAF had the upper hand. Critically, its successes were understood not simply in terms of the air campaign, but as repulses of an invasion that would otherwise inevitably have taken place. A rumour that Hitler had intended to invade on 15 August had been widely publicized. The next day, the papers proclaimed that British defiance had, for the first time, forced him to change his plans. Ten days later, Home Guardsman George King set out his impressions of how things were going in the diary he was keeping for his missing son, Cyril:

> our defences (thanks to the handful of gallant lads in the Air Force) are holding and I am getting much more bucked about things. I freely confess that for weeks after Dunkirk I thought we were in Queer Street, but thanks to the German passion for thorough organisation, he did not invade us. It could have been done then with success, but there would be an entirely different story to tell now![45]

King still did not know if his son was alive. It was not until the start of October 1940 that he and his wife found out that Cyril was indeed a prisoner in Germany, and started to receive letters from him. He survived the war and was liberated in April 1945.[46]

As the intensity of air attacks increased, stress was once more placed on the role that ordinary civilians must play in resisting the onslaught. As the *Daily Express* instructed readers on 17 August:

> The misery and destruction brought to the homes of the lowly mean only one thing now – we are all front line householders. We must all behave like good soldiers and realise that we are fighting for the right to live in peace, for the right to live without a tyrannous master.[47]

When Churchill addressed the Commons on 20 August, he started with the people: 'The fronts are everywhere. The trenches are dug in the towns and streets. Every village is fortified. Every road is barred. The front line runs through the factories. The workmen are soldiers with different weapons but the same courage.'[48] He then praised the airmen: 'Never in the field of human conflict was so much owed by so many to so few.' In an often-forgotten part of Churchill's speech, he made very sure to include with the 'few' the bomber crews who:

night after night, month after month ... travel far into Germany, find their targets in the darkness by the highest navigational skill, aim their attacks ... with deliberate careful discrimination, and inflict shattering blows upon the whole of the technical and war-making structure of the Nazi power.

The belief that their country was hitting back, as well as taking it, was a crucial part of how the war was presented to the British people during that 'Spitfire Summer'. As Home Intelligence reported, the speech was well received: 'From Northern Ireland comes the comment that it is the most forceful and heartening he has yet made. Newcastle reports that it has created a strong feeling of confidence.' The report from Bristol quoted the words of a resident: 'Everyone feels now that, come what will, we are top dogs; the past week has shown that we shall win no matter what slight doubts there were before.'[49]

Churchill's description of British bombers' activity accurately reflected what he thought they were doing. When his Cabinet had unleashed the night-time offensive against German industrial targets that May, the intention was to strike precisely at the German military machine and war economy. Over the summer, aircrew had been returning with news of their success.[50] In fact, these reports were wildly over-optimistic about the accuracy of their navigation and bomb-aiming. Even where they found the right city, as they managed with Berlin at the end of August, British bombers were distributing their payloads so widely that the Germans presumed that they could only be trying to damage morale. Ironically, the British thereby contributed to the escalating abandonment of any restrictions on suitable targets for air attack. When the Germans turned their attention to the bombardment of London, it was with the certainty that any civilian casualties would be just retribution for the indiscriminate air war that the British had already begun.

'CROMWELL'

London had in fact been bombed several times in the last week of August, but the raids that hit on 7 September were something different. During the day, 350 German planes launched a concentrated raid on the docklands to the east of the city that started huge fires in the wharf-side warehouses; 11 Group was unable to re-deploy its squadrons quickly enough to stop them. That evening, a second wave of attackers swept in to hit the fires then burning around the London docks. Over the next week, another three similar attacks all saw the bombers continuing to get through and the RAF suffer heavy losses.

The change in the point of attack also handed advantages to the defenders. The extra time it took the bombers to reach London gave the operations room controllers more chance to organize the RAF fighters, but it also enabled controversial 'Big Wing' formations, sent down from 12 Group in East Anglia, to swoop on German bombers that were short on fuel and separated from their fighter escorts. On 15 September, the next big German raid on London was fought off with heavy losses: thirty bombers and twenty-six fighters shot down, against twenty-nine RAF fighters.[51] Both sides again got the number of aircraft they had destroyed wrong, and the Luftwaffe continued to think that air superiority over southern England was within its grasp.

The ferocity of battle, and seemingly unrelenting German intent, signalled to the British that an invasion loomed. At the start of September, the assembly of boats in French harbours and Enigma decrypts about German units practising embarkation had both seemed to indicate that preparations were now in place for an assault. On 7 September, the code word 'Cromwell' was issued by Home Forces, indicating that anti-invasion units should take up battle stations, and for the next fortnight there was a state of high alert in the expectation of an attack. Even Churchill, so confident earlier in the summer, was anxious that the Germans might gamble on landings before the autumn weather set in. On 21 September, he repeatedly rang up the Admiralty to inquire about the weather in the Channel, and at the start of October reminded the Defence Committee that the risk of invasion persisted.

Hitler, however, had already concluded that an invasion was impossible. On 19 September he ordered that plans for amphibious landings in the UK should be postponed. On 12 October an invasion in 1940 was called off for good, although the Germans tried to maintain the impression that an attack might be imminent in order to keep up the pressure on the UK.[52] The air campaign, however, continued. Hitler doubted that bombing alone would force the British to sue for peace, but he could not order the Luftwaffe to cease its attacks without granting his opponents a victory.

While the German high command turned its attention to the possibilities of a campaign against British interests around the Mediterranean, the Luftwaffe was therefore left to try to knock the UK out of the war by itself. Despite the heavy losses of 15 September, daylight raids continued. There were huge daytime dogfights on 27 and 30 September, and smaller daylight combats took place on every day of October. From mid-September, however, the main effort of the bomber offensive shifted towards a night-time assault on Britain's trading economy, aimed principally on the docks of London.[53]

Only at the very end of October did the British government formally decide that the immediate threat of invasion had diminished, although it was expected that it would return with full force the following spring. Long before this, however, the public had come to the conclusion that the invasion had been defeated. The stand-to on 7 September had encouraged a widespread belief that an attack was imminent. The RAF's successes on 15 September were enthusiastically reported, and people developed their own ideas about what had happened to the much expected German landings. On 16 September, the Home Intelligence summary stated that:

> Most people anticipate an invasion within a few days, and are very confident that it will be a failure. Rumours that it has already been attempted and has failed are reported from many quarters ... From Nottingham comes the rumour that hundreds of German bodies have been floating in the Channel ... In Northampton it is said that the attack was launched on the West Coast. Invasion rumours are also reported in the South-Western Region and in Scotland.[54]

By the end of September, the press were already declaring that a decisive victory in the air battle had been achieved. Fears of invasion and fifth columnists would not disappear while the war lasted, but they would never burn with as much intensity as they had done in the critical months of May and June. As Britons entered the prolonged endurance test of the night-time Blitz, they believed that their country, by its uniquely stubborn resistance, had already managed to thwart Hitler's plans.

18

The Means of Victory

While the drama of the Battle of Britain unfolded, events elsewhere determined the course of the war. At the start of September, fresh evidence of American support for the UK confirmed Hitler's view of the conflict in the west as a transatlantic struggle. The recasting of global trade in response to the Fall of France allowed the UK to survive – albeit at the cost of heightening its dependence on the US – while at the same time preventing the Germans from reaping the full benefits of their new hegemony in Europe. Germany had not won quite the decisive victory that had been imagined: the only solution was further to expand the war.

'AN UNNEUTRAL ACT'

As the summer went on, the British continued their diplomatic campaign to secure more significant support from America. There was disagreement in London about how this should be done. For all his public optimism, in private Churchill was in favour of playing tough with the US. He hoped that American fears about what would happen to the Royal Navy if Britain surrendered would allow him to lever further aid from Roosevelt – in particular the transfer of American destroyers for which he had been asking since May. The Foreign Office pressed for Britain to take a friendlier line, offering up bases in the western Atlantic and military secrets in an effort to win American favour. Churchill hoped to appeal to American sentiment; the Foreign Office appreciated that trading off Britain's position was a more realistic stance.

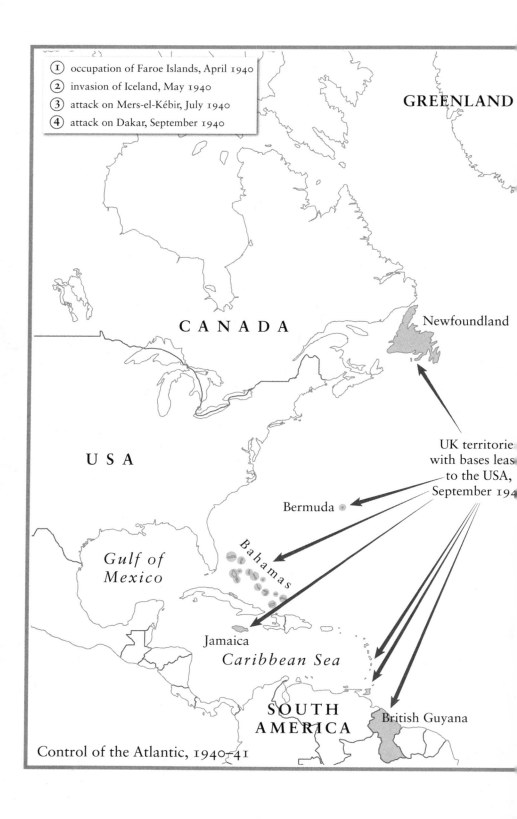

1. occupation of Faroe Islands, April 1940
2. invasion of Iceland, May 1940
3. attack on Mers-el-Kébir, July 1940
4. attack on Dakar, September 1940

GREENLAND

CANADA

Newfoundland

UK territorie
with bases leas
to the USA,
September 194

USA

Bermuda

Gulf of
Mexico

Bahamas

Jamaica
Caribbean Sea

SOUTH
AMERICA

British Guyana

Control of the Atlantic, 1940–41

N

② ICELAND

① ᛰ Faroe Is.

Former
Irish Treaty
Ports

German Blockade

BRITAIN

A T L A N T I C
O C E A N

E U R O P E

Azores

Gibraltar
• Mers-el-Kébir
③

German, US and
British all have
plans to defend
or invade 1940–41

Cape Verde Is.

④
Dakar

AFRICA

1000 miles
1000 km

During August, Roosevelt allowed discussions to open about a deal that linked the destroyers, the bases and a guarantee from the prime minister that the British fleet would not be handed over to the Germans. Churchill was unhappy, not least because the offer of British territory opened him up to attack from die-hard Tories, including the colonial secretary, Lord Lloyd. In the end, however, he had little choice but to acquiesce. The Destroyers-for-Bases deal was agreed between the UK and the US on 2 September 1940. Two weeks later, British scientists arrived in America to hand over top-secret weapons technology, including development plans for the atomic bomb and a working cavity magnetron, the key component for microwave radar sets that were crucial for night-fighter interceptions, bomber navigation and submarine hunting. In the long term, the transfer of military-scientific information welded British intellectual capital to American industrial capacity, laying the path for the production of weapons that would be crucial to the ways the Allies would fight in the latter half of the war. In the short term, British scientists in the US reported back that the Americans had no idea of the colossal efforts that were going to be required to achieve victory.[1]

The most important aspect of the Destroyers-for-Bases deal was not the ships' naval contribution but rather the fact that their transfer was, as Churchill called it in his history of the war, 'an unneutral act'.[2] It confirmed Hitler in his belief that he was facing an Anglo-American bloc that could only be defeated if he knocked out Russia and thereby released Japan to distract the United States. In South-East Asia, meanwhile, Japan had taken advantage of the European collapse to extract trade concessions from the Dutch East Indies and to base troops in French-controlled Indochina. Roosevelt responded by slapping an embargo on iron and steel exports to Japan and moving the US fleet from California to Pearl Harbor in Hawaii. More aggressive Japanese officers and politicians argued that an alliance with Germany was the only way to deter America, frighten the Chinese into surrender and secure the resources they might need if war came. On 27 September, Germany, Italy and Japan signed the Tripartite Pact, an agreement to come to each other's aid in the event of an attack by a currently neutral power. Since the Pact explicitly excluded the USSR, it could only be aimed at America. The effort at intimidation failed. As popular opinion in the United States swelled against the idea that the Axis powers were ranging themselves against America, Roosevelt told the fleet to stay at Pearl Harbor and offered further loans to China to keep it in the fight.[3] The three-month closure of the Burma Road ended in October: the British responded to the Tripartite Pact by now keeping the Road open. The Japanese were furious.

In the West, the tangling up of US and UK defence interests was crucial to the eventual outcome of the war, but in the short term, the return from British entreaties had been pretty poor. The value of the long-term leases on the bases vastly outweighed that of the destroyers, which had been poorly designed in the first place and arrived in a disastrous state of disrepair. As the British placed larger orders with American suppliers – above all to meet the huge aircraft construction plans – they came into conflict with the American armed forces, who worried that their own expansion plans would be ruined by the diversion of resources to the UK. As their own rearmament programmes got under way, the Americans pressed the British to accept reductions in deliveries for which they had already paid. In October, Roosevelt made a public commitment to provide 'all aid short of war', and members of his administration promised that some financial solution would be found to Britain's dwindling gold and dollar reserves. All that a frustrated Churchill could do was to submit to the American electoral cycle, and hope that things would get better once the president had won re-election in November.

SHIPPING

The role of destroyers and bases within Anglo-American discussions highlights the importance of protecting the Atlantic shipping lanes and maintaining the flow of seaborne supplies. This was the other great Battle of Britain that got under way during the summer of 1940: the struggle to ensure the arrival of the imports necessary to sustain the growing war machine while also fighting a burgeoning international war. It was an immense campaign, fought not only in desperate encounters on the high seas, but in distant purchasing offices and shipyards on both sides of the Atlantic and in British ports, marshalling yards and fields.

The seizure of French ports greatly extended the German navy and air force's reach into the Atlantic. As the British moved convoy routes north of Ireland to avoid attacks across the Bay of Biscay, the result was a choke point in which German submarines could find rich pickings. The U-boat fleet was smaller than at the outbreak of war, and it now lost the ability to break the Admiralty's convoy code for the first time since the start of the war. Karl Dönitz, its commander, struggled and failed to keep the Führer's attention on the drawn-out campaign to starve Britain into submission. In August, however, Hitler permitted a move to unrestricted submarine warfare, which allowed the U-boats to attack submerged and without warning. Most attacks were still launched by single U-boats, but from September, German submariners also pioneered new 'wolf pack' tactics, in which large groups of U-boats were concentrated against convoys, striking en masse to overwhelm any escort and run riot through the herded merchantmen.

The Royal Navy was not able to provide much protection. The new escort vessels rushed into construction after the outbreak of war were only just starting to arrive. The navy's destroyers were concentrated on the southern and eastern coasts against the threat of invasion. So too were the aircraft of RAF Coastal Command. What escorts there were struggled to protect their charges: their crews were inexperienced in anti-submarine work; ships seldom served together long enough to establish a common understanding over tactics; and detecting the enemy was very difficult, both during the day, when the escorts' sonar sets struggled to pick up signs of submerged U-boats, and at night, when surfaced submarines attacked. With no access for the moment to the version of the Enigma machine used by the German navy, the Admiralty in London could pinpoint U-boats only when they broke radio silence to report a convoy, were spotted by a patrolling ship or aircraft, or attacked a ship that got off a distress signal. All this only allowed informed guesswork about what they might do next.[4]

Most convoys escaped un-attacked, but the rates of sinkings now began to increase ominously. In the first eight months of the war, the Germans had sunk 1.2 million gross tons of British and Allied shipping, about a third of it through U-boat attack. Between July and September, U-boats sank 153 merchant vessels, totalling 759,000 gross tons.[5] This was only slightly less than the entire tonnage of shipping launched from British yards during the whole of 1940.[6]

Serious though these losses were for the British-*owned* merchant fleet, the British-*controlled* fleet actually expanded from the summer, thanks to the sudden availability of ships from previously neutral countries in Europe. Until now, the substantial Norwegian and Dutch fleets had been reluctant to sail into combat zones. Now their governments-in-exile made them available – albeit at great expense – for British charter. The British also requisitioned French and Danish merchant vessels. Between the end of March and the end of September, the gross tonnage of foreign vessels in use by the UK grew from 267,000 tons to more than 2.9 million tons. Over the following year, as foreign ships completed contracts and became available for re-hire, they too were taken under UK control.[7] Meanwhile, although US output of merchant ships was for the moment small, the British hoped that the orders they had placed in the US would be enough to start the expansion of American shipbuilding. US yards had much more room for expansion than their British equivalents – only they could hold the solution in the long term to the depredations of the German assault.

In the short term, German sinkings mattered much less to Britain's import capacity than the immense disruptions of the global war. One problem was that convoys of ships provided protection but slowed down voyage times, because convoys had to travel at the pace of the slowest vessel. Longer voyages meant fewer trips for the quicker ships. Another difficulty was that Britain was now cut off from its traditional – and nearby – sources of food and raw materials on the European mainland, just at the same time that the closure of the Mediterranean added greatly to the length of a ship's journey to the Middle East, India, Malaya, Australia or New Zealand. Now that ships had to round the Cape rather than pass through the Mediterranean, a voyage to Egypt was 10,000 miles longer than it had been before. Notwithstanding Britain's dollar difficulties, the increased journey times, with all their consequences for shipping space, pushed purchasing departments towards greater reliance on the United States rather than the eastern Empire. The huge reworking of the pattern of global shipping movements meant that the average round voyage for ships importing into the UK increased by at least 30 per cent after the Fall of France.[8]

At the same time, the opening of the war in North Africa and the Middle East meant a new shipping burden. Most of the supplies with which this conflict was fought would come from India and Egypt, paid for by the accumulation of huge sterling balances in London, but the military equipment and reinforcements necessary for offensive action against Italy all had to be shipped around southern Africa, often at short notice and maximum priority, and with no plan for a return voyage with a full hold. Contingency planning absorbed still more ships that could have been used to carry imports. The schemes to capture the Azores, for example – variations of which would be kept on hand for the next three years – locked up twelve large ships that had to be set aside as potential transports.[9]

There were further delays once ships reached UK waters. Those bound for the east coast could not travel through the Channel, but had to sail to Scotland, then pass in slow convoys southwards. The risk of air and sea attack reduced the quantity of goods that could be moved around Britain by sea. It also resulted in restrictions on the number and size of ships that could unload in the east coast ports, particularly in London – an enormous shipping terminus in times of peace.

As a result, the ports on the west coast – primarily those on the Clyde, the Mersey and in the Bristol Channel – were required to take in a much greater proportion of the nation's imports. The total volume of arrivals through these ports was not much different from during peacetime, but what was landed was often of a very different nature. The western ports lacked the wharf space, specialized unloading facilities, refrigerated storage and transport links to get everything quickly off the boats and away to its destination. Since British mined coal could no longer be carried in the same quantities along the coast, much more of it had to go by rail. During the summer, that overwhelmed the railways and made it still harder to move other cargoes on from the docks. The unloading of ships was slowed further by the darkness of the blackout and the frequency of air-raid warnings. From the summer of 1940, the situation in the western ports appeared increasingly chaotic.[10]

'FROM THE SEAS TO THE QUAYS'

Britain's supply situation was greatly complicated by the European cataclysm, but not, for the moment, insurmountably so. Indeed, the remarkable thing about the UK in 1940 was that its remaining global wealth and continuing control of the seas meant that it could adapt to the loss of Europe and kick-start American munitions production before the arrival of US economic aid. In contrast, Nazi-dominated Europe would find it much more difficult to overcome the economic shifts that resulted from Hitler's dramatic military success.

Germany's new hegemony in Europe greatly improved its access to strategic resources. Before May 1940, 40 per cent of Romania's oil production had been bought by the UK. On 27 May, the Romanians signed a new pact agreeing that all their oil should go to Germany. The Swiss and Swedes eagerly sold the Germans precision machine tools, weapons and iron. In the 1930s, they had been two of the poorest countries in Europe. By the 1950s, they would be two of the richest. Meanwhile, from its newly conquered territories, Germany acquired huge stocks of weapons, some raw materials and oil, and the use of some of Europe's most industrialized economies.

On the other hand, the UK's refusal to yield cut this new European bloc off in large part from the network of global trade. At the end of July, the British announced an escalation of the blockade, based on 'the notion that the whole of Europe must now be regarded as being actually or potentially under enemy control and all goods imported into it as being actually or potentially at enemy disposal'.[11] All cargos now had to be covered by a 'navicert' – a certificate of permission from the Ministry of Economic Warfare – or else be presumed to be on their way to the enemy. Any shipping company that wanted to make use of British controlled water, fuel, repair or insurance facilities had to agree to submit to these regulations: all access would be denied if they carried goods without a navicert. Navicerts would be issued for imports to European neutrals only on the basis of what the British thought they needed for domestic consumption.[12]

Germany's successes made the task of blockade conceptually simpler. The complex network of treaties and voluntary agreements negotiated during the Phoney War was replaced with compulsory limitations on supply. Europe would be allowed enough to survive, but not enough to support the Nazi war machine. The emphasis on administrative certification rather than physical interception, however – the move of the blockade 'from the seas to the quays' as newspapers at the time put it – indicated how much harder the blockade weapon had become to wield. The Royal Navy was busy with many more urgent tasks in summer 1940, and its patrols against blockade runners essentially stopped. This was a paper-based blockade, and that meant that it was, for the moment, full of holes.

Compulsory certification and the control of shipping facilities depended on US co-operation to be really effective. The State Department in Washington worked with the British to restrict some imports, but that co-operation was not wholly forthcoming until the spring of 1941.[13] The Ministry of Economic Warfare had to tread carefully in compelling American shipowners for fear of increasing isolationism. Vichy France continued to import a lot of goods through the Straits of Gibraltar and across the Mediterranean, most of which the British suspected were going to Germany and Italy. Attempts to restrict food deliveries to France raised significant humanitarian concerns in America.[14]

As importantly, the British could do nothing to control overland European trade, and there was now little reason for any of the countries with which they had negotiated restrictions on exports to Germany to abide by those agreements. Portugal, for example, more than doubled its exports of tungsten to Germany between 1939 and 1941.[15] The biggest gap in the blockade was to the east. Since Stalin wanted to keep Hitler on side for as long as possible, the USSR continued deliveries to Germany: a million tons of cereal and animal feed, 700,000 tons of oil and nearly a million tons of timber in 1940.[16]

Notwithstanding these breaches, however, the blockade mattered. For one thing, it cut off Europe from overseas supplies of fertilizers. Nineteen forty was a poor harvest year across much of continent in any case, thanks to heavy rain at the end of 1939. Grain production slumped and livestock were slaughtered for want of feed. Germans did not go hungry – the Reich drew on its big stockpiles and dragged in grain supplies from Romania – but Nazi officials gazed enviously at the wheatfields of the Ukraine. In the big industrial centres of Occupied Europe, rations were soon low and the black market flourished. Food shortages restricted the productivity of manual workers – notably in coal mining – and contributed to the economic stagnation of Germany's new domains.[17]

Even more striking were the limitations on Germany's oil supplies. Counting in the Dutch and Norwegian ships that were now available to charter, Britain and America between them controlled 95 per cent of the world's tanker fleet. Oil was one of the few areas in which the Americans co-operated fully from July 1940 in enforcing a stricter blockade.

Deliveries from Romania and Russia, plus its own – immensely costly – synthetic oil production, gave Germany about 5.5 million tons of oil in 1940. This was half what the British imported into the UK alone during the same year. Germany captured just under another million tons of oil during its conquest of Western Europe. Altogether, it had just enough to supply its own needs, but not to support the other countries that were now encompassed by the blockade. Italy was wholly dependent on imported oil: as soon as its pre-war stocks were used up it began to act as a drain on German supplies. France was effectively de-motorized by the occupation – it was reduced to just 8 per cent of its pre-war consumption of motor fuel from the summer of 1940 onwards. Before long, fuel shortages would also affect the German armed forces' ability to train their servicemen and German industry's ability to test new engines.[18] Such shortages would not, as the British hoped, bring about an internal German collapse, or limit the operational freedom of the Wehrmacht, but they did ensure that the Germans could never fully employ the industrial potential of the huge area they now dominated. Strategically, as well as ideologically, the conquest of Western Europe would not be enough.

'THE NAVY CAN LOSE US THE WAR, BUT ONLY THE AIR FORCE CAN WIN IT'

Over the summer, Churchill, the Defence Committee and the chiefs of staff hammered out a strategy for victory. There was one key difference from the Phoney War: with the French gone, it was taken as given that the British would not be able to fight their way back onto the European mainland while the German army remained unbeaten. Instead, they looked to ways of wearing down the Germans so that their soldiers could return across the Channel to polish off an already beaten enemy. This would take time, but so would the completion of the rearmament programmes that were already under way. At the start of September, the chiefs of staff emphasized that their forces would not be ready to move to a general offensive until the start of 1942. Between now and then, they would begin the process of grinding away at German military power, so that when they shifted to the attack, the war would be completed as quickly as possible.[19]

The tightening blockade played an important part in their calculations. Using figures provided by the Ministry of Economic Warfare, the chiefs predicted that Germany would be facing an oil crisis by the summer of 1941. If it did not act to improve its supply situation, this would eventually degrade its military capabilities. Churchill was more doubtful than the economic warfare experts that a lack of resources would bring Germany to its knees. As he explained to the War Cabinet: 'The weapon of blockade has become blunted and rendered, as far as Germany is concerned, less effectual on account of their land conquests.' He preferred to put more emphasis on bombing:

> The Navy can lose us the war, but only the Air Force can win it. Therefore our supreme effort must be to gain overwhelming mastery in the Air. The Fighters are our salvation, but the Bombers alone provide the means of victory. We must therefore develop the power to carry an ever-increasing volume of explosives to Germany, so as to pulverise the entire industry and scientific structure on which the war effort and economic life of the enemy depends, while holding him at arm's length in our Island.[20]

This was expressed in typically extreme terms, but the prime minister never placed all his eggs in one aerial basket. On the contrary, even with bombers taking the lead as the only weapon actually able to carry the war to the heartland of Germany, Churchill expected that economic warfare would have a part to play. So too would the British army – but not in the same prolonged slaughter that had been endured during the last war. Only once victory had been assured by bombing and blockade would a 'striking force' of fast-moving, tank-heavy armoured formations cross the Channel to conduct a final, swift and decisive campaign that would mop up the remnants of the Wehrmacht. All of this – but particularly the bombing – would be dependent on enormous industrial help from America. Churchill hoped that before too long, the Americans would join the war. He did not spend time pondering whether, in that eventuality, they would be willing to accommodate themselves to British strategy.

Other methods of wearing Germany down were also available. In July 1940, following a good deal of political wrangling, the Special Operations Executive had been set up – significantly, under the control of Hugh Dalton as minister for economic warfare – to carry out sabotage in Europe and to provide assistance for resistance movements in the occupied territories. Churchill also created a new Combined Operations Headquarters to carry out raids on the enemy coast. The long-term argument for raiding was that it would force the Germans to expend troops and resources garrisoning the furthest reaches of their new empire. A few small 'butcher and bolt' attacks were carried out – without much success – early in the summer, but Churchill's ambition went well beyond a few toughs knifing some German sentries. He dreamed of bigger operations in which he could use Britain's maritime manoeuvrability to seize back the initiative. Eventually, he hoped that major British forces landing from the sea would 'ignite' rebellions in Occupied Europe against a German army worn down by bombing and blockade.

In retrospect, the idea that a popular uprising in Europe would overcome the might of the German army and air force seems far-fetched. Yet here too, the belief in a 'people's war' aroused considerable enthusiasm on the British left. Dalton's fight for control of SOE was not just a battle of Whitehall demarcation: it also showed the same romantic belief in improvised citizen warriors that the British intelligentsia had displayed during the Spanish Civil War. Churchill too had a soft spot for guerrilla fighters – provided they were on Britain's side – but even more than that, he was an incurable optimist. Even more than most British people, Churchill was imbued with a patriotic providentialism born of a deep belief in national supremacy. Even in the tightest corner, something would turn up to deliver Britons in their hour of need. That meant that he was willing to foster all sorts of improbable ideas about how to win the war, but it would also encourage him to avoid taking decisions he found unpalatable. In the end, hoping for the best without preparing for the worst did not prove to be a successful strategy for preserving the British Empire.

Meanwhile, as the chiefs of staff made clear, there were good strategic reasons for defending the Middle East: 'not only as a base from which to exercise and intensify economic pressure, but as a barrier to prevent our enemies from breaking the blockade'.[21] Persian and Iraqi oil must be kept out of Axis hands. The Italian empire also offered tempting offensive opportunities. At the very least, the British could launch a spoiling attack that would set back an assault on Egypt. Meanwhile, British and Commonwealth land forces in the region would be built up to as many as thirty divisions by the end of 1941. Here was the place where ground troops could make a difference before the balance of the war turned decisively in Britain's favour. Assuming that the Axis powers could be held in the Mediterranean, during 1941 the British would begin 'medium operations of an amphibious nature' in preparation for the 'very heavy overseas attacks' that they would launch the year after.[22]

While there was general agreement among British strategists about the overall form that the war should take, that was overlaid on significant differences about how aggressive the British could be before they moved to the general offensive in 1942. Did the hope that Bomber Command would become a war-winning weapon mean that the RAF should take precedence over the army and navy? What was the relationship between defending the UK, taking offensive opportunities in the Middle East and providing some reinforcement to the eastern Empire? Were 'medium operations of an amphibious nature' vital efforts to seize the initiative, or dead-ends that would absorb much-needed resources? All of these would be important areas for debate over the coming year: none of them precluded the general agreement that Britain was fighting a long war, and that it could not return to Western Europe until the strategic balance had swung in its favour.

During September and October, the Defence Committee approved plans for continued rearmament in line with this overall strategy. The Ministry of Supply believed that it could complete its target of equipping fifty-five divisions by the end of 1941, but scaled back its ammunition production on the basis that, separated from the Wehrmacht by the Channel, the army would not be shooting as much as it would have been if it had been locked in a grim slogging match on the Western Front.[23] By the start of October, the Ministry of Aircraft Production was planning to produce 38,000 aircraft by December 1941, with monthly output rising from 1,620 aircraft in September 1940 to 2,762 by the end of the following year. Together with rising American production, this would sustain a Metropolitan Air Force of 270 squadrons, with a front-line strength of 4,295 aircraft, 1,600 of which would be the new heavy bombers. Another ninety squadrons would be available for service overseas – notably in South-East Asia, where Malaya's defence was now dependent on airpower in the absence of a strong Eastern Fleet – but their equipment would take second place to the establishment of a powerful bombing force at home.[24] With the Destroyers-for-Bases deal agreed, Churchill was argued round to the case that more capital ships would be needed eventually to deter the Japanese. In late October, the War Cabinet agreed to let the Admiralty start building new capital ships, subject to more urgent demands for other vessels.[25]

Whitehall continued to talk about American supplies in terms of 'topping up' British production, but the realization of these plans in fact placed substantial reliance on future American industrial output, as well as raw materials. Yet Britain's access to these supplies was dependent not only on some resolution being found to the issues of dollar finance, but also on whether America could make the goods – and whether it was willing to share them. Despite Churchill's assumption that the Americans would accept the moral duty of aiding Britain, in the autumn of 1940, these imperative strategic issues still had to be resolved.

'NEW ADVENTURES WITH INADEQUATE PREPARATIONS'

Churchill was always suspicious of grand strategic surveys. Things changed so rapidly in war: what was the point of tying oneself down? The early autumn of 1940 was no exception. In September, there were plenty of battles raging in the here and now. At home, the outcome of the battle for air superiority still seemed uncertain and an attempt at invasion seemed very likely. On 13 September, the Italian army in Libya finally launched its much-delayed attack, crossing the border to establish a foothold on Egyptian soil in the anticipation that the Germans would shortly knock the British out of the war. They advanced only 60 miles, well short of Wavell's main defences, before setting up camp and erecting a monument to their conquests.

Wavell promptly requested further reinforcements. Given the renewed invasion scare at home, Churchill was reluctant to send anything more. He had already issued very detailed instructions to Wavell about how to run his defence. Now he thought he ought to be looking to his existing resources to fight back. Eden, the war secretary, went out to Egypt in October to discuss plans for a counter-attack. Wavell was already contemplating an offensive, but the last thing he wanted was Churchill interfering. When Eden arrived, he and Wavell began a tour of the region. For the moment, Wavell kept his plans to himself.[26]

Meanwhile, British and Free French forces had embarked on their attempt to seize Dakar. To senior officers in London, it had never looked like a terribly practical affair. Dakar's defences were strong, suitable landing sites sparse and a lot of faith was placed in the likelihood that the garrison would welcome Free French troops coming ashore from a British fleet. Churchill, however, drove the plan through, inspired by the prize of stealing a march on the enemy and securing a powerful naval base that dominated the eastern side of the South Atlantic. In the meantime, further south, almost the whole of French Equatorial Africa had come over to de Gaulle's cause during the second half of August. Briefly, it seemed as if the operation against Dakar might secure the rest of France's West African empire; instead, it rapidly turned into a debacle.

The plans for 'Operation Menace', as it was codenamed, were frequently changed, even after the ships involved had put to sea at the end of August. While they were in transit, the Vichy French government sent a naval squadron from Toulon to reinforce its West African territories. The British failed to prevent it leaving the Mediterranean, and the ships' arrival in Dakar bolstered the French navy's control of the shore defences. After Mers-el-Kébir, French sailors had no intention of helping the UK. Churchill and the War Cabinet now wanted to cancel Menace, but de Gaulle and the British commanders of the expedition were keen to press ahead. They were allowed to proceed on 23 September, but the initial landings met with much heavier resistance than expected. Escalating threats of bombardment from the British ships merely wrecked any advantage of surprise. When they did open up, their shelling was much less effective than the return of fire from the defenders. The battleship *Resolution* was severely damaged by a torpedo from a Vichy submarine, and on 25 September the operation was abandoned.[27]

The physical costs of failure at Dakar were small, and the rewards on offer had been substantial. To his colleagues on the War Cabinet, Churchill was unrepentant: the operation had shown that 'we should be careful of embarking upon new adventures with inadequate preparations', he said, but 'nothing was easier or more fatal than to relapse into a policy of mere negation'.[28] On the home front, however, there was widespread adverse comment ('general disgust over the failure' and 'the biggest blow since the fall of France' were two reactions reported by Home Intelligence).[29] Much of the failure at Dakar itself was blamed on the French, but the Royal Navy's inability to stop the base being reinforced was also the subject of extensive criticism. At Westminster, the episode summoned up memories of Gallipoli and Norway, and encouraged those Conservative backbenchers who had always doubted Churchill's fits of strategic overenthusiasm.[30] Chips Channon thought it had shown 'the PM to be as incautious as ever. It is a deplorable affair and feeling in the Carlton Club is running very high against him.'[31] Something would have to be done.

19

The Beginning of the Blitz

During September and October, London became the focus of a prolonged and intense air campaign that aimed to force the UK out of the war. The Ministry of Home Security later estimated that about 20,000 bombs were dropped in the London region in these two months. In the first raids, most of the bombs hit the east of the City, north and south of the Thames, where the curve of the river made it easy to identify the key target of the docks. Here, the bombing sparked large fires in wharf-side warehouses and factories and wreaked havoc on the close-packed houses nearby. The vagaries of bomb aiming, and specific attacks on other targets, meant that the destruction crept westwards into Holborn and the City, and around the Thames to Fulham and Chelsea. Throughout September and October, however, it was the East End that received the heaviest bombing, and on whose population a huge amount of attention was now focused.[1]

This was bombing at a different intensity to that which had been experienced before. In Stepney, Nina Masel noted down reactions to the 7 September attack for Mass-Observation:

Warning went at 5pm. Almost immediately afterwards terrific crashes, bombs falling all round. Women in shelter stood up, holding each other. Some screamed ... All clear. Everyone groaned relief, went out and screamed with horror at the sight of the damage. Every street was damaged, bombs everywhere. Smoke and flames streaming from the docks. Shouting, finding relatives, chaos.

Unexploded bomb. Building fell on a group of men and women. Screams, groans, sudden rush back of the people followed immediately by a rush forward. Women fainted, mass hysteria, man threw a fit. Men, women and children crying and sobbing. Frantic parents searching for their young. Pub near by full of casualties. Dead and dying on the pavements. Someone sick.[2]

The scale and intensity of the first raids caught Londoners by surprise. That helped to make September the worst month of the entire war in terms of British civilian casualties: 6,968 men, women and children were killed and another 9,488 seriously injured; 5,730 of the dead and 9,003 of the wounded were in the London Civil Defence Region. During October, another 6,313 were killed and 7,949 wounded, of whom 5,090 and 7,268 respectively came from London.[3] Although the bombs themselves killed more victims than anything else, it was falling debris or collapsing buildings that caused the most casualties.[4] As the cityscape crumbled, it crushed hearts, broke flesh and bone and entombed its former inhabitants.

'THE PEOPLE OF THIS COUNTRY MUST STICK IT OUT'

The shift of the main German air effort towards the hours of darkness nullified the advantages the RAF had gained during the day. Fighter Command's defensive system could not function at night: it was too difficult to track the raiders once they crossed the coast, and the few available night-fighters struggled to intercept, let alone shoot down, the enemy. Dowding accurately predicted that only when dual-seater night-fighters were equipped with airborne radar would they be able to counter the bombers, but as yet such sets were unavailable. In the meantime, he was forced against his wishes to redeploy single-seater fighters to night-time duties, where they were useless. His reluctance to comply confirmed his reputation within the Air Ministry for 'stuffiness', and contributed to his removal from command of Britain's fighter defences on 24 November.

Anti-Aircraft Command, meanwhile, was short of guns and had for the moment no accurate way to direct searchlights or gunfire. All the gunners could do was to shoot immense quantities of ammunition – more than a quarter of a million rounds in September – into the night sky in the hope of hitting something, or at least spoiling the Germans' aim.[5] A huge redeployment of guns into the capital after the first big London raids bolstered morale with their noise (albeit at the cost of their own dangerous rain of shrapnel), but did next to nothing to ward off the attacks. Anti-Aircraft Command too needed more and better radar sets to direct its fire. Again these were in prospect but not currently available.

By the autumn of 1940, the British were working on a wide range of additional defences and counter-measures to night bombing. These included decoy lights and fires to divert the bombers, and ways of blocking or bending the radio beams that helped direct the Germans onto their targets. There were also schemes to attack the bombers with aerial minefields and rockets. Attempts to rush these into production, driven heavily by the enthusiasm of Churchill and his scientific advisor Lindemann, absorbed huge quantities of money and industrial effort. They ultimately proved completely useless.[6] In any case, in September, these technologies were either unavailable or unsuitable for protecting such an enormous and easily distinguishable target as London. Nor were Britain's own bombers able to inflict the damage that might have stopped the German attacks. As Churchill told the Cabinet on 15 October: 'There were good prospects that our defensive measures would be greatly improved within the next two or three months . . . Meanwhile the people of this country must stick it out.'[7]

'AN ISLAND SURROUNDED BY FIRE'

As bad as the casualties in the first heavy raids were, they were still much lighter than expected. The hospitals and the morgues were not overwhelmed. Nor was there the expected epidemic of psychological breakdown. In the first three months of the Blitz, the London Emergency Region as a whole recorded an average of only just over two cases of 'bomb neuroses' a week.[8] The problem was not the dead or the wounded, but the living, and the provision that had been made for them both while the bombers were overhead and after they had departed.

The onset of heavy bombing drove larger numbers of people than ever before to seek protection in the air-raid shelters. For those that did not have access to their own Anderson, that meant using some form of public shelter. The trench shelters that had been dug in parks were dank and dark, the street shelters stinking and apparently vulnerable – some had been mistakenly built with lime mortar, which then had to be replaced, and they acquired a deserved reputation for being liable to collapse if bombs went off nearby.

There were significant local variations even within the East End in the amount of shelter available. Stepney, which was bombed more heavily than any other borough in September, was particularly badly served. In part this was because its dense areas of working-class housing were not well-suited for putting up Andersons, but the very poor state of ARP preparations in the borough were also a consequence of local politics. Stepney's Labour-run council had protested strongly against the legislation of the late 1930s that required local authorities to put in place their own air-raid precautions. Most London boroughs appointed experienced local bureaucrats to implement their ARP schemes. Stepney Council appointed a politician, Councillor M. H. 'Morry' Davis, instead. Davis, the leader of Stepney's Labour group, was a party machine politician who was both inefficient and corrupt. During the last years of peace, the borough consistently lagged behind the rest of London when it came to air-raid planning.[9]

Further east, the borough of West Ham also had a very secure Labour council that had opposed government ARP policy before the war. It too appointed local politicians as its ARP controllers. The southern part of the borough, low-lying and close to the docks, was unsuitable for the construction of below-surface shelters, and West Ham too lacked enough shelter space for everyone who wanted it. Yet there was nothing inevitable about this shortage. Between Stepney and West Ham was Poplar, also Labour controlled and predominantly working class, and which had also initially protested against the shelter policy at the end of the 1930s. There, however, the council decided to implement official instructions as fully as possible. By autumn 1940, it had managed to provide Anderson shelters for 95 per cent of its population, and street shelters for another 20,000 people.[10] The differences between the protection available to Londoners in these neighbouring boroughs was a vivid illustration of the fragmented nature of the British state, and of the fact that incompetence and unwillingness to prepare for the future were not the reserve of any one political party.

Substantial deficits both in shelter provision, and in public trust in the shelters that were available, meant that when the heavy raids began, many East Enders were left without cover. Some responded by heading west, into the reinforced basements of the great department stores around Oxford Street. Others gathered in covered places that offered the illusion of safety: church crypts, factory cellars and railway arches. Stepney's 'Tilbury' shelter became particularly infamous. This vast network of underground stores and loading bays close to Liverpool Street station was soon holding up to 14,000 people a night, in appalling conditions.[11]

The other obvious place to take shelter – and the nearest approximation to the 'deep shelters' that anti-government ARP campaigners had wanted before the war – was the London Underground. Official policy was to deny access to shelterers, lest they block the transport network and refuse to come out. In the first days of the German bombing offensive, large crowds nonetheless gathered outside the entrances. Others simply bought tickets, went down into the stations and refused to leave. During the second week of attacks, the government surrendered and opened the stations. By the middle of September about 150,000 people a night were sheltering in the Underground.[12]

The public shelters, the unofficial refuges and the newly opened Tube stations now suffered from the same problems of mass occupation. Even structures designed as air-raid shelters were meant to provide protection from short but intense daylight attacks, and were not equipped to provide food, sleeping accommodation and toilet facilities for raids that lasted an entire night. Shelterers slept on the floors, crammed together in a fug of unwashed, frightened bodies. Tensions arose over preferred spots, or as sleepers were disturbed, as well as between Tube shelterers and commuters. In the unused Underground lines that had been opened to the shelterers, a minority took up permanent residence among the detritus: a testimony to the terror and destruction from which they had escaped above.[13]

A lot of people did not use the shelters at all. The first survey of night-time sheltering in metropolitan London, in early November, suggested that 27 per cent of the population were in household shelters, 9 per cent in public shelters and only 4 per cent in the Tubes.[14] The majority were somewhere else, some at work, most simply at home, perhaps under the stairs, many just staying in bed. A couple of months earlier, in the first days of the bombing, and in the areas that were most heavily attacked, the proportion of people who tried out some form of shelter was probably higher than this suggests, but the evidence of the dead – 54 per cent of those killed in London in this period died inside a building, only 32 per cent in a shelter – bears out the same point.[15] As well as practical obstacles to sheltering – the flooded Anderson, the over-full public shelter, the discomfort of the Tube – there were also powerful emotional factors at play: the sense of security of home, the fatalism encouraged by the randomness of the destruction, the excitement of danger and, perhaps above all, a pressing desire for sleep that grew over the nights of disruption until the prospect of a familiar bed overcame everything else.[16]

The problems did not cease with the all-clear. Pre-war predictions had overestimated the loss of life from bombing, but underestimated the damage to buildings and infrastructure that would result. The violent transformation of the built environment was one of the most striking things for observers at the time. Alan Seymour, driving a mortuary van to pick up the victims of the Blitz, found the overnight obliteration of once familiar buildings difficult to comprehend:

> It seemed impossible that so much damage could be done in so little time. It is this terrible abruptness which impresses me more than anything, and is, in my opinion, the chief morale effect of bombing. To see the result of years of work swept away in a second leaves one with an awful feeling of instability.[17]

At the start of December 1940, 32,160 houses in the London region had been demolished or were so badly damaged as to be beyond repair. Even where bombing didn't collapse or burn buildings, it blew off roofs, caved in walls and smashed windows, leaving houses temporarily uninhabitable. By the same point, another 466,765 houses had been damaged to the point that they required extensive repair.[18] By the middle of October, as many as quarter of a million Londoners had already been rendered homeless by enemy air attack.[19]

The communications and utility networks were also badly affected. In the first three weeks of bombing, 104 railway bridges in London were put out of operation. About one bomb in every eighteen that fell on London severed a water, gas or electricity main. Between September and November, 4,124 water mains were broken. Rubble and craters blocked roads, further disrupting transport.[20] Unexploded bombs added to the confusion. Of every hundred high explosive bombs that landed, about ten did not go off immediately – eight because they were duds, two because they were on delayed action timers. Every unexploded bomb resulted in a wide surrounding area being evacuated until it could be dealt with by military bomb disposal teams. At the peak, in late October and November, more than 3,000 unexploded bombs were awaiting disposal.[21]

Nowhere in London was adequately prepared to deal with the aftermath of the raids. In the most heavily bombed boroughs, there were immediate problems in providing food and water, both to the emergency services and to surviving residents. The large numbers of homeless posed a particular problem. ARP 'rest centres' had been established in London County Council schools and church halls. These had been envisioned as brief stopover points at which people would recover from a spell in the shelters before returning home. They were administered under the old Poor Law, which meant that care provided for local people would be paid for by local rates, while refugees from other areas would be paid for by the Treasury.[22]

Now, faced with a flood of those who had been bombed out, the rest centres lacked anything like enough beds, toilets, blankets, teacups and bandages to cope. Few had the kitchen facilities to provide anything more than sandwiches and tea. Nor were the rest centres ready to function as an onward point in a chain that led towards greater safety. They rapidly filled to bursting with the homeless who had nowhere else to go. As the bombing spread across London, the capital's rest centres continued to fill. Between 11 and 25 September, their population increased from 16,000 to 25,590, many of whom needed to be re-accommodated more permanently in requisitioned billets.[23]

Most of those 'bombed out', however, did not pass through the local authority rest centres. Some went and, finding a centre full, were thrust back on their own resources. Others did not know where the nearest rest centre was. Many went straight to friends or relatives. People who had lost everything to the bombs had to deal with numerous different administrative departments in different offices over the days that followed if they wanted to get help: the borough council for rehoming, the Unemployment Assistance Board for compensation for lost goods, the Labour Exchange for those out of work (a huge problem in the East

End after the first raids), the Ministry of Pensions for allowances for the wounded, the Ministry of Health for evacuation, the Ministry of Food for ration books. Information about where to go and what to do was usually scant, and Stepney Council was bombed out of its offices.[24]

A lot of people had responded to the first attacks by deciding to get out of East London as quickly as possible, a movement confirmed when the raiders returned on the following days. On 10 September, Home Intelligence's London bulletin stated:

> Exodus from East End growing rapidly. Taxi drivers report taking party after party to Euston and Paddington with belongings. Hundreds of people leaving Deptford for Kent. Increased tension everywhere and when siren goes people run madly for shelter with white faces. Contact spending night in West Ham reports loyalty and confidence unquenched but nerves worn down to fine point. Conditions of living now almost impossible and great feeling in Dockside area of living on island surrounded by fire and destruction.[25]

In West Ham, where local administration had broken down under the bombs, councillors demanded that the Ministry of Health evacuate the entire southern half of the borough. By the time transport was laid on, many of those who wanted to leave the borough had already gone. In Stepney, Nina Masel wrote down her conversations with people on the way out. A fifty-year-old man explained that his house was undamaged but his 'wife's nerves are to pieces. Every time we look out we see that big tenement building, all cut open by the bomb. She just cries all day. It's no good – she can't go on like this.' Asked why she was moving, a sixty-year-old working-class woman replied: 'I can't stand it. It's killing me. This ain't war, this is murder.' Like many others, she was going to relatives in a borough further away from the bombing.[26] Others went out to Epping Forest or the hopfields of Kent. Large numbers went by rail to towns to the north and west, including Reading, Stevenage and Oxford, where, without any official status as evacuees and unable to find billets, they ended up in another set of overcrowded, under-resourced ARP rest centres.

There were some signs at the time that the strain of the bombing had increased social tensions. Arguments over evacuation and shelter space led to heightened expression of anti-Semitism against the East End's large Jewish population. Expressions of prejudice were even more prevalent when Jewish and Irish refugees passed through the suburbs as they tried to escape the bombs. Anger and frustration at the poor state of public shelters and post-raid services was sometimes expressed in class terms. On 15 September, the Stepney Communist leader, Phil Piratin, led a sit-in demonstration at the well-appointed underground shelter of the Savoy Hotel. Meanwhile, the appearance of the urban working class, both as shelterers on the Tube, and as refugees in the Home Counties, elicited the same sort of middle-class disgust that had been apparent during the first great evacuation a year before. Not least because it was worried about possible social divisions, after Buckingham Palace was bombed on 13 September, the Ministry of Information put a huge amount of effort into publicizing the fact that the king and queen were as badly exposed as any of their subjects to the German onslaught. Nonetheless, a few days later, Harold Nicolson heard from the senior regional commissioner for London that their Majesties had been booed when they visited bombsites in the East End.[27]

'HITLER, YOU HAVE CAUSED ME A LOT OF TROUBLE'

None of this, however, portended a mass breakdown in Londoners' morale. Ethnic and religious tensions did not dissolve into communal violence. Piratin's demonstration ended with the all-clear and a whip-round for the Savoy's staff (and was all the better a publicity stunt as a result), but the enraged masses in the Tilbury shelter did not then storm the West End to turf the wealthy out of their well-protected beds. Notwithstanding the shock of the first attacks and the horrors of the continuing bombardment, the bombing showed no sign of turning popular opinion against the war.

The explosive epicentre of the bombing was a terrifying, confusing place, and the immediate results were often stunned despair and panic. For most people, these emotions were not permanent, although they were for many deeply shocking and for some unendurable. The raids also posed a set of challenges, relating to sleep, employment, transport, food, water, light, heat and accommodation, which were simultaneously prosaic and all-consuming. At the time, nobody knew when the bombing would stop. Perhaps they would have to live like this for years.

The questions bombing raised were less about the war in abstract and more about surviving its reality – could Londoners cope with the disruption and destruction of air attack and carry on their lives despite it?[28]

To a very great extent they could. Although it did not feel like it to anyone in the East End at the time, the quantity of bombs the Luftwaffe was able to drop in autumn 1940 was nothing like enough to stop a major city working. The area under the most intense bombing was small compared to the colossal size of the metropolis. Bombs struck across the capital – on 9 September every metropolitan borough reported some damage from them – but they were neither numerous nor heavy enough to inflict the sort of systemic shock foreseen by inter-war prophets of the 'knock-out blow'. On the contrary, the networks of railways, roads, household utility mains and food production were sufficiently complex that some sort of service could be restored fairly quickly, even to most of the worst-hit areas. Those who left their homes under the early attacks could find accommodation close by without abandoning their families or their jobs. Most Londoners were not under the worst of the bombing: for them, the Blitz meant lack of sleep, fear and discomfort, but not the destruction of their entire neighbourhood.

Individuals and communities adapted remarkably quickly to a new life under the expectation of air attack. Even where the bombing was heaviest a substantial minority of the population remained as long as they were able. Some displayed a bloody-minded determination not to be beaten. As a sign chalked on a shop front in the Isle of Dogs after five days of bombing declared: 'HITLER, YOU HAVE CAUSED ME A LOT OF TROUBLE WITH NO GAS AND NO WATER BUT TO HELL WITH YOU AND YOUR CONFEDERATES.'[29] There were other reasons for staying put: a reluctance to leave friends and neighbours, a desire to protect homes and businesses from the depredations of looters, and the necessity, for male working-class breadwinners in particular, of remaining in work. There was an incremental acclimatization. No one who chose to stay put knew that they were in for months of bombing, but over the course of September, many got used to the new routines: the sounding of the sirens, the move to the shelters, even the noise of the bombs. The Luftwaffe's shift towards night-time bombing and the regularity of its attacks may even have helped this establishment of a 'new' wartime normality.

In the mass shelters in the warehouses, crypts and railway arches of the East End and on the Underground platforms, some of the shelterers started to organize themselves. Collections were held to pay for cleaning; rules – formal and informal – were established about behaviour; and leaders began to be recognized – sometimes from among the shelterers themselves, sometimes in the form of local clergymen or air-raid wardens. In at least thirty Underground stations, committees were set up to manage the shelters. Older forms of community were also important. An untold number of neighbours provided help and accommodation to those in need.[30] An immense amount of charitable endeavour, much of it run by dutiful middle-class social workers, helped to fill a welfare gap. A very wide range of voluntary bodies, including local church groups, the Salvation Army, the Red Cross and St John Ambulance, the YMCA and the London Council of Social Service, as well as the WVS, stepped in to try to improve conditions in the rest centres, distributing food, clothes and blankets. The Lord Mayor's National Air Raid Distress Fund, set up by a letter in *The Times* on 10 September, raised a million pounds for distribution by the start of October, which was spent on purchasing food and drink for Tube shelterers, buying replacement clothes and furniture, and paying the cost of funerals.[31]

Central government quickly identified and began to address the civilian problems created by bombing. Responsibility for ARP and post-raid services fell principally to Sir John Anderson, as home secretary and minister for home security, and Malcolm MacDonald, as minister of health. In the week after the first big raid of 7 September, Anderson removed the ban on Tube sheltering, set up and received reports from a committee under Lord Horder that suggested means of improving hygiene in mass shelters, and arranged for the distribution of more household shelters. Working with the London Civil Defence regional commissioners, he initiated moves to erect bunks, toilets and canteens in the larger shelters, and to impose ticketing systems to manage numbers.[32] At the same time, MacDonald gave the London County Council 'a free hand' to spend on increasing the capacity of and improving the facilities within its rest centres. The Treasury would provide the funds without regard to the restrictions of the Poor Law. A major reorganization and reinvigoration of rest centres in central London duly followed. On 11 September the Ministry of Food asked the LCC to set up communal feeding centres, for which it would bear the costs, to provide hot food in areas affected by bombing.[33]

Ten days later, Anderson appointed two new special commissioners for the London Civil Defence Region. The lawyer and Conservative MP Henry Willink took charge of efforts to help accommodate the homeless, and Sir Warren Fisher was given responsibility for street clearance and the restoration of essential services. In an attempt to deal with the specific problems in Stepney, Anderson also initiated moves to replace the ARP controller with an official appointed directly by the Ministry of Home Security – a startling use of the Defence Regulations to over-rule local democracy, and one that occasioned criticism from civil liberties campaigners at the time.[34]

By the start of October, therefore, measures were well in hand in the capital to manage bombing – at least in its current form – as a civil problem. Some of these were about giving the people what they wanted – above all, letting them shelter in the Underground stations. Others were about adapting a civil defence system designed to meet the way air raids had been imagined to the reality of how they actually were. Anderson and MacDonald reacted as quickly as they could to the critical situation following the first raids. Anderson, however, was already under fire for his handling of the internment of aliens and the implementation of the Defence Regulations. As the architect of the pre-war government's ARP policy, he could now also be blamed for its inadequacies. An austere civil servant rather than a populist politician, Anderson did not deal well with the press or with MPs. He would not be left in post to complete the job he had started.[35]

'THE CIVILIAN POPULATION IS TAKING ITS DUNKIRK'

London was certainly not the only place in the UK being attacked from the air as summer turned to autumn in 1940. Although the capital's casualties were much higher than those in any other Civil Defence region, air raids continued elsewhere, including repeated attacks on the port of Liverpool and on the Supermarine aircraft works at Southampton. Nonetheless, the experience of really intense bombardment was

Table 3. British civilian casualties by Civil Defence region,
July–October 1940

	July–August		September–October	
	Dead	Injured	Dead	Injured
Northern	91	563	33	282
North-Eastern	33	284	19	274
North-Midland	26	150	26	136
Eastern	155	429	262	1,323
London	228	1398	10,480	37,768
Southern	263	810	264	880
South-Western	88	315	244	765
Wales	82	262	69	335
Midland	129	440	540	1,740
North-Western	71	426	591	1,350
Scotland	79	298	21	186
South-Eastern	203	596	724	2,930
Northern Ireland	0	0	0	0

Source: TNA, HO 191/11, 'Statement of Civilian Casualties in the United Kingdom, 1939–1945'.

extremely geographically limited. In early September, the very heavy attacks on the capital, its suffering and resilience became the focus of national concern.

On 15 September, the grand dame of British Fabian socialism, Beatrice Webb, recorded in her diary at her house in Hampshire that, since 'the sustained attack on London opened, we here have had a relatively quiet time – air raid warnings and all-clear notices, happening during day and night; but few and distant bombs or gunfire.' Even so, she felt closely involved because:

Letters . . . and the BBC and the newspaper reports describing the noise and danger, destruction of homes, hospitals and churches, of deaths and woundings of men, women and children, illustrated by pictures, lend a background of continuous tragedy, which even the good tempered heroism of the cockney and his perpetual sense of humour does not cancel out.[36]

The image of Londoners standing up to bombardment and the shock at pictures of the devastation in the docks were the two most striking aspects of how Britons outside the capital experienced the start of the London Blitz. This was not the message conveyed by those who had been beneath the bombing. A Mass-Observer in an army camp full of London recruits described the shock of the return from leave of a soldier whose house had been bombed:

> O.B. did not return till Monday lunchtime, over twelve hours overdue. We had all fantasised his death, his injury; and when he came in, there was a cheer. He stood between the cots, for a second, his usually white slumface flushed and drawn. 'East End,' he said, 'they wiped it out!' And then he ran to his cot, and lay there, with helmet and gas mask still slung, head buried in pillow, weeping.[37]

Radio, newsreel and newspaper reports, on the other hand, did indeed sometimes repeat clichés about cheery cockneys and national fortitude – like the Gaumont British account of the king's visit to bombed areas in the East End, released on 12 September, which explained over pictures of bombed houses that:

> Each one of us has now either endured bombardment or has close friends and relatives who have. So we know that we can stand up to havoc as well as Abyssinians and Chinese and Spaniards. In fact, we can do it better. These days are vital to the cause in which we fight; the hope of victory depends now immediately on us.

Then, over footage of crowds greeting the king (no booing here): 'in this time of tragedy, these people are still the same – ready to wave and laugh and cheer. Oh yes – this is the spirit that wins a war.'[38]

Other reporters took a different line, acknowledging the suffering of the East End but concentrating on its determination to endure. Emrys Jones, giving an eye-witness report for the *Daily Mail*, for example, explained: 'let me say here and now that I saw in East London little of the humour for which those parts are noted. No, there was a certain grimness in the faces of the people and cold anger seemed to pervade the smoke-laden air.'[39] Hilda Marchant, in the *Daily Express*, described

the stream of refugees from the East End in the context of another
1940 event that was already well-mythologized: 'The civilian population is taking its Dunkirk.' Marchant was one of the great reporters of
the era, described by an American colleague as 'a sort of Spitfire
attached to the ground . . . passionate in her belief in the common
people'.[40] She deliberately subverted conventions of civilian fortitude to
re-emphasize the strength and determination of the working classes:

> It is useless for me to begin to say those people I saw yesterday, homeless
> and uprooted, were brave. They were not thinking of that. The one uni-
> versal thing was that they were going to make their home again . . . how
> typical it was that the first big raid should crack at the little houses and
> the labouring families, and how useless it is to try to break these people.[41]

J. B. Priestley took the same theme but struck a more upbeat note in his
15 September 'Postscript', describing

> the strangest army the world has ever seen, an army in drab civilian
> clothes, doing quite ordinary things, an army of all shapes and sizes and
> ages of folk, but nevertheless a real army, upon whose continuing high
> and defiant spirit the world's future depends.[42]

This emphasis on people carrying on their lives in the front line did
not describe the full horror of being bombed, but nor did it pretend that
everyone was a hero. Not everyone could keep going, but if they could,
that would be enough. Little wonder that by 20 September, the North
Midland regional intelligence officer was reporting 'a general feeling of
admiration for the way in which "the Cockneys are standing up to air
raids"' or that in Northern Ireland on the same date, 'The manner in
which Londoners are standing up to bombing' continued 'to be
praised'.[43]

Similar versions of ordinary Britons' stoicism were also being broadcast to the United States by reporters including Ed Murrow, Vincent
Sheean and Quentin Reynolds. As they explained the changes that had
taken place in Britain since May, they painted a picture of a country
becoming more democratic as it stood up to Nazi aggression. Reynolds
voiced the commentary for the short film *London Can Take It*, shot at
the end of September by the Crown Film Unit for the Ministry of Information. It was intended to convince American audiences that Londoners
had displayed 'a surging spirit of courage the like of which the world

has never seen'. Reynolds emphasized: 'I am a neutral reporter . . . I can assure you there is no panic, no fear, no despair in London town . . . London can take it.' Cut down and retitled as *Britain Can Take It*, the film was released by the Ministry to British cinemas shortly afterwards. If audiences were already certain of national resilience, they were even more convinced when an American confirmed it for them.[44]

Praise for the endurance of ordinary people was not, however, the only way in which the Blitz was reported. In the columns of the *Daily Herald* and the *New Statesman*, the journalist Ritchie Calder castigated the poor organization and inadequate preparations that had let down the people:

> In this 'Battle of London' I have seen ordinary people behaving with a coolness and resource in the face of danger which one would only have expected from veteran troops. But you do not expect front line troops to stand unarmed, without support, under bombardment.[45]

Calder was a Scottish socialist and pacifist who had made his name before the war as a popular writer on science and sociology. He was the only journalist to have stuck with the Jarrow marchers throughout their journey, and he had served on Labour's pre-war ARP committee. In his writing on the Blitz, Calder cast himself as both adventurer and activist: he explained to readers both what he had seen on his journeys through the East End, and his usually unavailing efforts to get government departments to solve the problems he had found.[46] Calder would go on to serve as Director of Plans and Campaigns for the Political Warfare Executive, charged with projecting propaganda into Occupied Europe. A quarter of a century after the war's end, his son, Angus Calder, would write a brilliant and pioneering history of the British home front, *The People's War*, which argued that the high hopes of wartime democracy had been betrayed. His father got a thank you in the acknowledgements.

During the first month of heavy bombing, Calder *père* led the way in criticizing official ARP provision. He reported on the tragedy at South Hallsville school, where a crowded rest centre was bombed, and the squalid conditions in the Tilbury shelter. Calder blamed 'sometimes inadequate local councils' for their incompetence in the face of bombing: he would later write that 'Giving the task of ARP to local authorities was like giving to the Mayor of Dunkirk the task of evacuating the BEF.'[47]

He also, however, attacked central government for failures of imagination and sympathy in its ARP policy. Inadequate pre-war spending was the reason for the poor provision and protection of rest centres. Too little attention had been paid to the wants and needs of ordinary people, who should have been given the deep shelters they wanted. If borough councillors were incapable of fulfilling their civil defence duties, that was the fault of pre-war policymakers for relying on them in the first place.

In the *Daily Herald*, Calder's reports were front-page news. Other papers placed less emphasis on official failings and more on Londoners' bravery and endurance. Nonetheless, during late September there was extensive reporting about the inadequacy of welfare provision for the bombed, leading to calls for the appointment of 'dictators' to oversee improvements.[48] Tom Harrisson joined in too, with an article in the *New Statesman* on 28 September that used Nina Masel's account to detail the awful conditions in the Tilbury shelter. Harrisson closed with a rhetorical question: 'Here, surely, is a new low for urban civilisation? Yet there is really nothing else that people in that area can do. It is not the civilisation they have made, it is the one that has been prepared for them these many years past.'[49] Like evacuation and the Fall of France, the Blitz had become another site for political debate and discussion about the nature of Britain.

In the areas most heavily affected by bombing, meanwhile, the confusion that followed the initial attacks and the paucity of official provision had caused a lot of anger. In Stepney, Mass-Observers argued that:

> The local council is blamed for the lack of adequate shelters, and certain other specific points in the muddle, but on the whole, among the women at any rate, the blame is laid on some abstract 'they'. If asked who was to blame 'Churchill? The Government? The King? The council? The mayor? The Warden? God?' they would say 'no' to all, but 'they' embraces the 'powers that be' and most East End women never think beyond that. As far as the trouble in general is concerned, there is no hesitation in laying the entire blame on Hitler.[50]

The Communist Party of Great Britain tried to reap the benefit of this anger with the system. Since August, it had sought to capitalize on dissatisfaction with air-raid shelters and the rising cost of living with calls for 'A People's Government and a People's Peace'. This, it was hoped, would allow the party to rebuild the support that it had lost because of its opposition to the war. Before the war, Communists had taken a leading role in campaigning for 'deep shelters'. Now, they campaigned to protect the people and to discredit the government's ARP policy. On 11 September, the *Daily Worker* declared that:

> The rich have provided themselves with luxury shelters. They have evacuated their children across the Atlantic. But they still refuse the shelters that can alone give protection to the people. They remain callously indifferent to the fate they have brought on the people.[51]

In Stepney, the Communists were already well established, thanks not least to the moribund state of the local Labour Party. As well as Piratin's raid on the Savoy, Communist activists also led attempts to gain entry to Tube stations and factory basements, and tried to get elected onto shelter committees, where they pressed for better conditions and confronted local officials about inadequate provisions. On 17 September, J. B. S. Haldane, the editor of the *Daily Worker* and chairman of the Communist-organized 'ARP Co-ordinating Committee', took a deputation to Anderson to demand the immediate provision of deep shelters. The home secretary ignored him, but the attitude of ministers towards a group generally regarded as potential fifth columnists was pronouncedly hostile. After the Savoy raid, the War Cabinet resolved that 'strong action' should be taken to avoid such an event happening again.[52]

The CPGB's stance on the war remained unpopular, but their call for deep shelters undoubtedly struck a nerve. As the rush to the Underground had demonstrated, the idea of being well below the surface appealed to people much more than individual household or the communal, above ground, street shelters. The argument that distributing the population kept casualties down and avoided unnecessary costs to the war effort demanded a lot of emotional forbearance from those in the shelters. The BIPO's October 1940 survey suggested that while only a minority had been affected by bombing, the majority thought that deep shelters were a good idea. Three per cent of respondents said they had been injured in some way as a result of an air raid; 14 per cent that their houses had been damaged; and 20 per cent that bombing had made it harder to get to work. Sixty per cent, however, thought that the government had been 'unwise in favouring the building of surface shelters rather than underground shelters'. What the people wanted in this regard was pretty clear.[53]

GO TO IT HERBERT!

The strain of the constant raids and sirens marked the end for Neville Chamberlain. He had returned from convalescence on 9 September, but though he did his best to get back to normal – chairing the War Cabinet and returning to the Commons – he was not the same man. Weakened by his illness and in need of constant medical care, ten days later Chamberlain left London at the point of collapse. He now recognized that there was no prospect of his returning to public life, and he therefore offered his resignation to Churchill on 22 September. Initially, the prime minister refused to accept it, more out of politeness than in expectation of Chamberlain's recovery. A week later, he changed his mind, not because of the developing civilian disaster of the Blitz, or the tide of negative commentary about Anderson, but rather because of the humiliation at Dakar. A military failure after an amphibious adventure had toppled his predecessor: now Churchill decided that a reconstruction of his government might divert the critics. Chamberlain put himself at the prime minister's disposal.[54]

Churchill had initially hoped to appoint Eden as lord president of the council, but that was vetoed by senior Conservatives. Halifax, to Churchill's disappointment, refused to be moved from the Foreign Office. Chamberlain's departure did, however, open a space into which Anderson could be slotted. As things turned out, the new job suited him perfectly. Herbert Morrison replaced Anderson, and was in turn replaced at the Ministry of Supply by the businessman Sir Andrew Duncan. In recognition of the importance of his role on the home front, Bevin was elevated to the War Cabinet. Kingsley Wood, the chancellor, was also brought in to provide a Conservative counterweight to the minister of labour.[55]

Churchill brought in another wealthy businessman, Oliver Lyttelton, to take Duncan's place at the Board of Trade. Churchill had known Lyttelton's family for years, and he had met the son again when he was serving as a young Guards officer in the trenches during the last war. In

the years since, he had built a very successful career in the city, directing the world metal trade, and when another war came, he had become
controller of non-ferrous metals for the Ministry of Supply. Lyttelton
was successful, glamorous and slightly disreputable: his buccaneering
approach to securing stocks of precious metals raised howls of protest
from the Treasury. He fitted very well into Churchill's circle. Having
appointed Lyttelton president of the Board of Trade, the prime minister
persuaded him to become a Conservative MP. Anthony Eden regarded
him with immense and ill-disguised jealousy.[56]

Bearing in mind the difficulties that Anderson had experienced at
the Home Office, Morrison had regarded his new job with some trepidation. In fact, he benefitted from the plans that his predecessor had
already put in place. Crucially, however, Morrison did a much better
job of seeming to engage with the public.[57] He also had a better relationship with the press. He was already friends with Ritchie Calder,
who greeted his appointment in the *Daily Herald* with the headline:
'GO TO IT HERBERT'.[58] Morrison appointed Ellen Wilkinson,
the MP for Jarrow, as his parliamentary under-secretary with a
special responsibility for shelters. Like Morrison, Wilkinson had
already demonstrated during the 1930s that she combined a passionate desire to improve the lot of working people with a facility for
engineering good publicity. She was also Morrison's mistress. She now
applied her immense energies to improving conditions in the worst
shelters.[59]

Under Morrison's watch, the official response to the London Blitz
began to improve. The two special commissioners already appointed
by Anderson did a lot to make things better. Willink pressed local
authorities across Greater London to improve rest centres and to requisition empty housing as a means to move people on more quickly. The
population of the rest centres fell back to 10,500 by 7 October; although
it would rise once more after heavy raids in the future, it never again
reached the level of late September.[60] By the middle of October, Fisher
had a force of 8,700 army pioneers and 10,000 civilian workers clearing roads and fixing utilities. While the bombing continued, they
recovered an average of 700,000 bricks a week from London's roads,
which were sent back to boroughs to strengthen the protective walls
around public shelters.[61] Working together, Morrison and MacDonald
implemented the changes that had been suggested for improving shelter

conditions in September. Rules were introduced to govern entry and behaviour. Bunks, sanitation, heating and lighting began to be fitted in the big public shelters. More Anderson shelters were delivered, and those that were already in place were reinstalled with more watertight floors. Facilities to feed, care for and direct the homeless also improved. The struggle against borough-council inefficiency continued. When West Ham Council decided to appoint its seventy-year-old mayor as ARP controller in October, Morrison intervened to persuade them that a younger man with some experience of air-raid precautions would be preferable instead.[62]

In addition, Morrison moved to provide at least some of the deep shelters that the public so badly wanted. As he explained to the War Cabinet at the end of October, shelter policy would have to be adapted to recognize popular responses to 'prolonged night bombing':

> Many people will travel long distances to reach shelters which they specially favour, sometimes without proper regard to the reality of the protection afforded. Some people prefer the Tube stations and other large shelters which are cheerfully crowded and free from the noise of the raids . . . As a result there has been considerable over-crowding in shelters notwithstanding the fact that the public has behaved extraordinarily well.[63]

Time and resources did not permit the digging of deep shelters for everyone, but to remedy that overcrowding, Morrison wanted to bore out additional shelter tunnels for London, connected to the Tube, with the aim of accommodating another 100,000 people underground. The War Cabinet approved the intention, but Anderson in particular was worried about the presentation: would this look like the whole of the pre-war policy was being torn up?[64] When Morrison announced the new measures on the radio – from a script carefully edited by the War Cabinet – he emphasized that deep shelters could not be provided for everyone, and cautioned listeners to:

> Be on your guard against all who seek to make this deep shelter cry a means of defeatist agitation. Political schemers . . . who seek to destroy our will to take risks in freedom's cause are playing Hitler's game . . . He knows that if our people could be stampeded into putting a narrow personal safety before success, he would win.[65]

The public crisis of overcrowded shelters would be addressed, but the people were still expected to put fighting the war above their own desire for protection. New deep shelters were not in fact a construction priority for the government – work on the new tunnels would not even break ground until the end of 1941. As the winter of 1940 began, and the bombing continued, the London Underground remained the only deep shelter available.

'HIS POPULARITY IS ASTOUNDING'

By autumn 1940, public support for Churchill was sky high. After visiting Dover and Ramsgate with the prime minister in September, for example, General Brooke recorded in his diary: 'His popularity is astounding, everywhere crowds rush up and cheer him wildly, encouraging him with shouts of "Stick it!" '[66] Even the bumbling of the Blitz and the debacle at Dakar couldn't dent his standing with the British people. In October's BIPO poll, 89 per cent of respondents said that they approved of Churchill as prime minister.[67]

Churchill, however, was still very conscious of his political vulnerability. The memory of the last war ran deep, and his worry was that he was not another Lloyd George but another Asquith: not the man who won the war but the one who was removed along the way. He was keen to shut down criticisms of the government. On 7 October, after a series of articles appeared in the *Sunday Pictorial* and *Daily Mirror* attacking Anderson, Wood, Gort and Ironside, and demanding a more substantial Cabinet reshuffle, he asked the War Cabinet to consider tougher newspaper censorship, on the grounds that there was a 'dangerous and sinister ... attempt to bring about a situation in which the country would be ready for surrender or peace'.[68]

Morrison, supported by Beaverbrook, resisted this call to interfere with the liberty of the press, but the newspaper owners were called in to meet Attlee, who insisted on the need to avoid 'irresponsible' criticisms. The *Mirror* Group executive, Cecil King, told Attlee that he 'thought Churchill had no objection to our kicking poor old Chamberlain, but didn't like being hurt himself'.[69] He had already decided that the real problem was an article by the *Sunday Pictorial* editor, Hugh

Cudlipp, which had argued that the recent changes in the government had

> shown the same dilatory, short-sighted, party-serving spirit as Chamberlain. And Cudlipp, who signed the article, wound up with a quotation from Churchill's book *World Crisis*, in which Winston says there are good grounds sometimes in peace for a vacillating or cautious policy, but in war decisions must be clear-cut and ruthless, no personal or party considerations must hamper the war effort, and so on. Cudlipp's concluding words were: 'Mr Churchill, you have warned yourself.'

'Obviously', King told his diary, 'the article was not likely to please Churchill, but I had no idea a storm was at all likely.'[70] For the moment, the home secretary had deflected Churchill's anger, but the prime minister had not given up on his belief that the *Pictorial* and the *Daily Mirror*'s criticisms were unpatriotic subversion, nor on his desire to see the radical papers suppressed.

While Churchill fretted about Fleet Street, his 'fixer' Brendan Bracken worried about the need to secure the prime minister's position at Westminster. The formation of the Coalition Government had created a curious situation in the Commons. All the leading figures from the major parties were in the government, and there was no immediate prospect of a general election. Under the threat of air raids and with less business than usual to transact, the House met much less frequently than before, and its working days were shorter than normal. An increasingly large proportion of MPs became involved in the war effort: by February 1941, just over half of them would be in official service of some sort. Of those who were left, the more dedicated were kept very busy with the mountains of constituency work created by the war. The rest, however, became bored and fractious.[71] A minority – including the former war secretary Leslie Hore-Belisha, the Irish peer Lord Winterton and the Labour enthusiast for a negotiated peace Richard Stokes – made it their job to act as an opposition, forming a parliamentary awkward squad who would criticize the government at every turn. Yet though they were often irritating, none of these dissidents posed a threat to the prime minister. The real danger, as always, lay in a potential rebellion by the Conservative Party.

As Churchill's parliamentary private secretary, Bracken made it his job to keep in touch with opinion on the backbenches, and he knew that many Conservatives in the Commons were still doubtful about a man they regarded as a turncoat and strategic lunatic. An opportunity to strengthen Churchill's grip on the premiership was about to open up, however, because Chamberlain's illness meant that he would have to resign the leadership of the Conservative Party.[72]

Until 1965, the Conservatives did not hold competitive leadership contests: rather, the name that had emerged from consultations between senior figures was proposed for formal election by a meeting of MPs and peers. There was never any doubt that if a sitting prime minister put his name forward, he would be elected leader, but Churchill was at first reluctant to take on the post. His wife Clementine, remaining loyal to the Liberalism that had proved a sanctuary for Churchill between 1903 and 1924, counselled him against it because it would make him less of a 'national' leader, and taint him with the mantle of a 'party' figure instead.

Bracken and Beaverbrook argued Churchill round. They understood that becoming party leader mattered, not only because it would secure more Conservative support, but because if Churchill didn't take the job, someone else would. Baldwin had been grooming Anthony Eden for the role since the early 1930s. With the Conservative Party behind him, Eden would have been a formidable challenger. Instead, Churchill allowed himself to be nominated. On 9 October 1940, at a meeting of the Conservative electoral college at Caxton Hall in London, Halifax thanked Chamberlain for his service and proposed Churchill as the next party leader. Churchill was duly elected, with no one voting against, and then gave a speech in which he promised to defend the Empire and oppose the socialists. He was going to fail on both counts.

Chamberlain died on 9 November. Looking through its diarists' accounts of the day, Mass-Observation found both vituperative comments from those who despised his memory – 'We've said a long time now "C. must go". Pity he couldn't have taken one or two with him'[73] – and sympathy from those who had not accepted that he was a guilty man: 'We happen to live in a Conservative stronghold . . . Charlie said: "He has been hounded to death by his enemies." I can't set down how deep is my respect for the late Prime Minister.'[74] In Huddersfield in Yorkshire, two workers at a power loom were overheard comparing Chamberlain and his successor:

(J) 'I think it's what folk have said about him that's killed Chamberlain.'

(H) 'I don't know – he hasn't been so well for a long time.'

(J) 'No – but this war seems to have worn him down.'

(H) 'It won't wear Churchill down – that B—— has got "some 'at on him to 'natter' at" ' ['a reference' the Observer listening in added helpfully 'to his fat'].[75]

For those in whom the high drama of the summer had moved great hopes of a bright progressive future, Churchill's assumption of the party leadership was a depressing watershed. By October, J. B. Priestley was ready to take a rest from his 'Postscript' broadcasts. In the last programme of his first 'Postscript' series, broadcast on 20 October, he began by explaining very carefully that he had not been ordered off the airwaves by the BBC (thus immediately sparking the rumour that he had and stoking demand for his return). Instead, he explained, he felt that a glorious national moment was passing: 'the high generous mood, so far as it affects our destinies here, is vanishing with the leaves. It is as if the poets had gone and the politicians were coming back.'[76] In fact, of course, they had never been away.

20

Taking It

Despite the postponement of the invasion, Germany's attempt to besiege Britain continued. During the autumn of 1940, as they lurked off the North-Western Approaches, Dönitz's small fleet of U-boats began to exact a deadly toll on the merchant traffic into the UK. In September, the submarines sank 59 merchant ships, displacing nearly 300,000 gross tons. In October, they sent another 63 ships, displacing more than 350,000 gross tons, to the bottom of the sea.[1] Submarines were not, however, the only threat. Merchant ships were also assailed by long-range Focke-Wulf Condor aircraft, and by German naval ships on the surface. During 1940, German commerce raiders – converted merchant vessels carrying concealed armaments – escaped into the open oceans, where they preyed on isolated and unsuspecting ships far away from the main battleground in the Atlantic. They took a steady toll of merchant ships while evading British efforts to track them down.[2] More significantly, German capital ships began to venture out once more against the shipping lanes. In late October, the pocket battleship *Admiral Scheer* began a five-month voyage that took it to the Atlantic and Indian Ocean, and the heavy cruiser *Admiral Hipper* broke into the North Atlantic in December.

Sinkings from surface attacks were a much less serious problem than those from submarines. Over the autumn and winter of 1940–41, warships and commerce raiders sank just under 580,000 gross tons of merchant shipping, about a quarter of what the U-boats despatched over the same period.[3] The potential damage that a German capital ship could do if it got among an unprotected convoy, however, was much greater than a single submarine. When they got loose, therefore, the British had to delay sailings and to provide additional escort protection from their own battleships for the largest convoys. That further disrupted the flow of merchant ships, lengthened voyage times and obstructed the flow of imports into the UK.

While the shipping campaigns were fought out in terms of tonnages, the human cost was severe. Between January 1940 and June 1941, about 11,000 seamen in British ships were killed by enemy action, and about another 6,000 died later of wounds or suffered severe disablement as a result of these attacks. As a percentage of overall strength, the merchant fleet's losses were worse than any of the armed services.[4]

What became commonly known during the war as the Merchant Navy – formerly it had been the Merchant Service or the Mercantile Marine – had always been an imperial and multinational entity. At the start of the war, 132,000 of its sailors were British (including British resident sailors of Indian, African and Caribbean origin), 10,000 were overseas nationals and 51,000 were 'Lascars' – non-white sailors, predominantly Indian, but including some from China and Africa, who were recruited overseas and paid at significantly lower rates than British seamen.[5] By the spring of 1941, the British-controlled fleet was an even more international body. About one in five of its ships were foreign-flagged and crewed, most of them from Scandinavia and the Low Countries.[6]

Merchant sailors were a group apart. Mostly, they came from seafaring communities in the dockland areas of the larger port cities. They were disproportionately young and male: a quarter of a 1941 sample of seamen were aged between fifteen and twenty-one. Being a merchant seaman came with its own traditions: hard-drinking, casual employment on a voyage-by-voyage basis, and a sort of insular internationalism in which men travelled all over the planet aboard ships that were their own little worlds, never moving far from the docks no matter what port they landed in. Although merchant sailors remained officially civilians, they were subject to an archaic set of disciplinary articles that bound them to a ship. What had been judged normal behaviour for seamen in peace – drunkenness, absenteeism, desertion from ships where food was bad or working conditions poor – became subject to much greater levels of punishment and prosecution during wartime.[7]

Yet for many, the new peril on the seas did little actually to alter their day-to-day routine. Shipboard life was highly stratified by rank and location: for a stoker in the engine room, sailing in a convoy just meant a change in the rhythm of piling on the coal. Outside the area of greatest danger in the Atlantic, ships generally travelled on their own rather than in convoy. Large numbers were employed on the 'cross trades' between South America, India and the southern Dominions. Apart from the depredations of the commerce raiders, these routes were much safer than those up and down the eastern Atlantic, and across the northern passage in and out of the UK. Ships on the most hazardous routes were fitted with armour and armaments, sometimes manned by military gunners, but few at this stage of the war had the means to fight off even enemy aircraft, let alone a submarine.

Convoys varied depending on their load. Those carrying military reinforcements might consist of several large passenger liners with a powerful naval escort. Those plying the regular transatlantic route contained fifty or more ships, varying in size from big cargo liners and tankers to smaller 'tramp' steamers, but broadly categorized into 'fast' and 'slow', all under the command of a Royal Navy officer, the convoy commodore, who sailed, with a party of signalmen, on one of the convoyed merchant vessels. Convoyed ships had to maintain pace and station with each other: an alien experience for merchant shipmasters used to sailing on their own.

Most convoys passed without incident, but when they were attacked, the results could be devastating. To give just one example, the SS *Dayrose*, a small (4,000 ton) tramp steamer owned by the Claymore Shipping Company of Cardiff, sailed in twenty-two convoys between June 1940 and the end of 1941. Only two of them suffered losses to the main body of the convoy from submarine attack. In the first instance, a single U-boat sank four out of forty vessels; in the second, a wolf-pack attack sank seven out of twenty-eight.[8] Where there were escorts, their main job was to ward off attack by spotting the submarines before they could make a kill. In the face of massed U-boat assaults in the early months of the Atlantic campaign however, even those escort ships that were available found themselves helpless. When Otto Kretschmer, the captain of U-99, took part in a six-submarine attack on convoy SC7 in mid-October 1940, for example, the escorts began to search for him after he torpedoed the first merchantmen:

> I make off at full speed to the south-west and again make contact with
> the convoy. Torpedoes from the other boats are constantly heard

exploding. The destroyers do not know how to help and occupy themselves by constantly firing star shells, which are of little effect in the bright moonlight. I now start to attack the convoy from astern.[9]

Some convoy battles raged for days. Other attacks were over in an instant. For ships laden with a hazardous cargo, such as fuel or explosives, or something non-buoyant like steel, the end could be very swift. A vessel loaded with wood, on the other hand, might take a long time to go down.[10]

A sinking ship was a place of chaos and confusion:

One minute we had been on watch on deck or in the engine-room, or sleeping snugly in our bunks; the next we were engaged in a frenzied scramble through the dense, shrieking blackness which assailed us with squalls of freezing spray, and slipped and fell on the wet iron decks which canted faster and faster into the hungry sea with every passing second, hurting ourselves cruelly on things which we could not see during our wild rush towards the boat . . . '*What's happening? What's happening?*'[11]

Escape was no guarantee of rescue. In the first years of the war, protective clothing and survival gear were minimal, and only about one in three of those who had to abandon ship survived.[12]

For all the sporadic drama of the oceanic battles, the loss of ships to enemy action was not actually the biggest problem facing Britain's maritime transport network. Crucially, the German offensive hit a shipping system that was already under severe strain. Sinkings by the enemy threatened the long-term attrition of the British merchant fleet, but in the short term, the increase in journey times because of the closure of the Mediterranean ate up more British import capacity than anything else. It was compounded by the persistent congestion that had built up in British ports over the summer of 1940. By the winter, the tonnage of ships immobile each month while they waited to unload was equal to that being sunk at sea.[13]

The loss of access to east coast shipyards and a concentration on new construction now also led to a major backlog of repair work. Large-scale contracting of European merchant shipping helped to restore British losses, but these vessels had to be fitted with degaussing gear to protect them from magnetic mines before they could be brought fully into service. That also took up a great deal of space in the dock-yards as well as the time of the shipworkers. Efforts to speed up the production of munitions made things worse. In the second half of 1940, the British imported large quantities of US steel. Tossed about in unsuitable ships in the weather of an Atlantic winter, the unwieldy cargo caused internal damage that added to the queues in the repair yards. By January 1941, ships displacing 2 million gross weight tons were out of commission while they waited for work to be done.[14] Ashore, steel could not be moved away from the docks quickly because it had to be carried on specialized railway wagons. Heavy deliveries sat waiting for transport and contributed to the congestion at the docks.[15]

Efforts to reinforce Britain's imperial defences placed still more load on its diminishing carrying capacity. The ships assigned to supplying the Middle East during the second year of the war could only have brought in another 1.5 million tons of imports to the UK, but both the sort of ships involved, and the suddenness of the reallocation to military needs, imposed further disruption on imports. The fastest merchant vessels that could be used to transport troops were the 'reef-ers' – refrigerated cargo liners that normally carried chilled and frozen food. During the final months of 1940, the use of these ships to reinforce the Middle East caused the UK's refrigerated imports to fall by almost a third. Supplies of frozen meat from Australia and New Zealand were particularly badly hit. Indeed, military demands were a much more important factor than German attack in interrupting meat deliveries: over the winter, only about 7 per cent of the meat that was actually despatched to the UK was sunk along the way.[16]

From the end of October, with the danger of invasion receding for the winter, the British reallocated naval forces to try to protect the con-voys. Destroyers and planes were released from anti-invasion duties and the navy abandoned attempts to conduct separate anti-submarine patrols in favour of escorting convoys. The total number of escort ves-sels also increased, as the corvettes ordered in the navy's wartime expansion programme came off the slipways. Fifty-two Flower class corvettes were commissioned in the second half of 1940.[17] None of this eliminated the submarine menace, but it did mark the start of a shift in where their attacks took place. The increase in escort and air strength made it harder for the submarines to operate in the crowded sea space immediately west of the UK. Just forcing the submarines further out into the Atlantic had important consequences for their productivity and the future course of the battle, but it didn't stop ships being sunk.

Churchill initially hoped that the redeployment of escorts would stabilize the situation in the Atlantic without affecting the rest of British strategy. In November, he rejected calls from the Admiralty to reinforce Coastal Command with large numbers of long-range aircraft. For the prime minister, diverting resources from the long-term development of the bombing offensive to an essentially defensive campaign in the Atlantic was no way to go about winning the war.

Since German attacks were not the primary cause of the shipping shortage, naval solutions would not by themselves improve the import situation. At the end of 1940, ministers began to address the problem of port congestion with new schemes for direct management and the reform of dock labour. In an effort to get more use from existing shipping capacity, in November the War Cabinet agreed to lower the minimum speed at which merchant ships were allowed to sail independently of a convoy from sixteen to thirteen knots. This was meant to release faster vessels from the need to keep pace with their slower brethren, allowing them to make more voyages overall. It was a serious miscalculation. In fact, any advantage to imports in sailing ships independently turned out to be more than outweighed by the fact that they suffered losses more than twice as heavy as those that sailed in convoy.[18] Another million tons of shipping was sunk between December 1940 and February 1941.[19]

In retrospect, the key thing about these losses was that they were simultaneously heavy and insufficient. Ships were the lifeblood of a global war effort, and the damage done by the German maritime offensive contributed to a shortage of shipping that afflicted the UK for the rest of the conflict. Before long, the prospect of worsening rates of sinkings would create a sense of crisis in London that forced the British into a major effort to secure their maritime supply lines. Yet severe though they were, the quantity of ships sunk over the winter of 1940–41 never came close to the 750,000 gwt that Dönitz had calculated he needed to starve the UK into submission. At the point when the British were most vulnerable, he simply lacked enough U-boats to sink more.

One of the more astonishing things about the early under-sea offensive is how many ships fell victim to a German submarine fleet that at this point averaged only about sixteen boats at sea at any one time. In the end, however, that also imposed a limit on the damage Dönitz could do. Rather than investing resources in capital ships that were never numerous enough to take on the Royal Navy, the Germans would have had a much more efficient, dangerous force if they'd confined themselves to building submarines.

The German blockade of Britain ended up being much less effective than the British blockade of Germany. The UK would have to deal with a sharp decline in the quantity of goods it was able to import, and that would have important consequences for the functioning of the wartime economy, for the day-to-day lives of the civilian population and for Britain's relationship with America. Yet at the moment of greatest British vulnerability, the Germans were not able to cut their opponents off from the rest of the world. That was crucial in allowing Britain to continue the fight.

'THE RUBBLE ROARED ON INTO THE ASHES'

Throughout the German bombing campaign, the target – British ports and industry – remained the same, but the focus of the attacks shifted over the winter. In mid-November, the nightly bombing of London was interrupted as the Luftwaffe turned its attention to the aircraft factories of the Midlands. This began six months in which heavy raids on the capital were interspersed with attacks on other cities, the so-called 'provincial blitz'. On the night of 14 November, Coventry was subjected to an attack that killed 568 people and injured another 865. German propagandists coined the verb *coventrieren* to describe the obliteration of a city. The next night, the bombers returned to London, then, on 19–20 November, subjected Birmingham to its heaviest raid so far, which killed 450. At the end of November and beginning of December, Merseyside and Southampton were attacked. On 29–30 December an incendiary attack on the capital sparked massive fires in the City of London.[20]

In early 1941, the focus of the bombing shifted to the western ports, with raids on Cardiff, Bristol and Swansea as well as the naval base at Portsmouth. As the weather improved in March, German attacks intensified, with more use made of incendiaries to spark fires. In the middle of March, two nights of bombing demolished Clydebank, killing 528, badly injuring 617 and destroying a third of the town's houses. During April, Belfast was heavily attacked for the first time, in a raid that killed 900 people and injured another 1,500. London was severely struck twice, first on 16–17 April, then again three nights later. Then came a sustained attack on Plymouth that all but broke the city, and a week-long blitz of Merseyside that killed nearly 2,000 people and wrecked 66,000 houses. On 10–11 May, the Luftwaffe launched a final massive raid on the capital, killing or severely wounding more than 3,000 people.

Of the 28,555 British civilians killed and 31,455 severely injured by air attacks between November 1940 and June 1941, about two-thirds were hit in attacks outside the London region.[21] This was a much more 'national' experience of bombing than the initial Blitz of September and October 1940, albeit one that remained very geographically specific in its focus on a few urban areas.

If London got some respite from the shift to other targets in mid-November, and even more from the poor weather of December to February, which severely hindered German operations, it nonetheless remained the target of the largest attacks. Despite their growing experience, London's civil defenders could still be caught out by changes of German tactics. The raid of 29–30 December, for example, sparked nearly 1,500 blazes across London and overwhelmed the fire service. In the City and on the southern bank of the Thames, six great conflagrations, accelerated by a fresh wind, burned out of control and destroyed large numbers of buildings,[22] as described by one auxiliary fireman at the scene:

> The heat blistered the car paint. It blistered the men's faces. It blistered the pumps ... It hurt your eyes, hurt your nose. My chin was quite badly burnt and it blistered. As the roofs went in, so the sparks belched from the windows, as if blown by giant bellows. Then the shells of the buildings made well-ventilated, giant chimneys, and the rubble roared on into the ashes.[23]

The areas hit by extensive bombing and fire now stretched well beyond the East End, but the metropolis was big enough to absorb the impact of the heaviest raids without breaking down.

In fact, the great human problems of the early Blitz were on their way to being solved. Shelter capacity was increased and shelter conditions got better. By mid-January 1941, there were 1,317,500 shelter spaces available within the London Civil Defence Region. Almost 400,000 bunks had been installed in which shelterers could sleep.[24] Regulations had been introduced to govern shelter behaviour, shelter wardens appointed to make sure the rules were kept, and the ad hoc organizing groups of the early days replaced by the setting up of official shelter committees. Most of the larger shelters now had first-aid posts, and programmes of talks and entertainment and libraries set up to entertain and educate the night-time crowds. As the end of 1940 approached, the Ministry of Health worried that press reports were making the big shelters look too much fun: they feared that those who had evacuated themselves from London might be tempted back by the entertainments on offer underground. In fact, the numbers using the Tube for shelter decreased dramatically after the end of the nightly bombing. By late December, they were down to about 65,000 a night.[25]

London's post-raid services had also improved. By the end of 1940, the improvised, voluntary effort that had saved bombed-out Londoners in the early autumn was being replaced by a more formal, better supplied structure. By the spring of 1941, this included rest centres that were properly stocked to feed and care for the displaced, and advice services, including those run by the Citizens' Advice Bureau, to help victims of bombing with the bureaucracy of assistance, as well as a Londoners' Meal Service that ran communal dining rooms, offering free and subsidized food for those unable to cook for themselves, and a fleet of mobile canteens that brought hot food and drink direct to rescuers and rescued at the bombsites. One of the things that made things easier was that so many people had already left the worst-affected boroughs. By spring 1941, the population of West Ham, for example, was only about a third of its pre-war level.[26]

The number of people using the rest centres fluctuated with the heaviness of the raids, but the flow through them got better. Although the worst attacks in spring 1941 caused about twice as much housing damage in one night as had been done in a week at the start of the Blitz, the system never clogged up again in the same way that it had in September. The rate of housing repairs initially lagged behind the rate of fresh damage, but the reduction in raids thanks to the winter weather and the release of builders from the army allowed work to catch up.[27] Between the start of the Blitz and the end of January 1941,

41,000 houses in the London Region were destroyed, but of the 680,000 that were damaged but saveable, 'first aid' repairs had been undertaken on 644,000.[28] These were very basic – cardboard over shattered windows, tarpaulins over broken roofs, perhaps only a single room usable in the whole house – but they did offer what many of the bombed-out wanted, which was to get back into their own home as quickly as possible.

'EVERYONE WHO CAN DO SO IS LEAVING THE TOWN'

The pattern of the Blitz in London – a long period of continuous bombing followed by repeated heavy attacks – was distinct. Most provincial cities were struck by one or two nights of very heavy bombing, which then shifted on to a different target. There were some exceptions – Merseyside and Plymouth in 1941, and Hull, which had thirty raids between 1940 and 1941, culminating in a heavy blitz at the start of May that resulted in major fires and killed 400 people – but in most places the sudden shock of a big attack punctuated lengthy periods when raids were light or non-existent.[29]

Smaller cities were not as well positioned as London to withstand the aerial onslaught. They were less well defended with anti-aircraft guns, searchlights and barrage balloons than the capital, their emergency services and ARP schemes were seldom as well developed, and their shelter provision was also often lacking. Although great conurbations like Merseyside or Birmingham could, like London, absorb the damage of a heavy raid without breaking down, smaller towns were affected by attacks in their entirety.[30]

Coventry's ARP command system was fractured by the 14 November attack – key officials could not be found, telephone lines were down and the ARP control room was put out of action. When the fire brigade's water supply failed, the blaze that took hold destroyed about a hundred acres of the centre of the city, including the medieval cathedral and other well-known landmarks, as well as three-quarters of the city's shops. According to a visitor who arrived shortly afterwards: 'the only building of any size standing was the police station. Street after street which only a few days earlier had been a busy town centre was

now piles of rubble.'[31] After the raid, few instructions were available
for a dazed population, and rest centres in the surrounding area were
rapidly overcrowded, both with the bombed-out and those taking
refuge from possible further attacks.

In Southampton, two heavy raids on 30 November and 1 December
caused similar devastation. The death toll was relatively light, although
bad enough in a city of only 180,000 people – 137 killed and 250 injured.
The physical destruction was worse. Again, the first raid wrecked the
telephone system and water supply, hampering subsequent civil defence.
Again, the city's ARP control centre was knocked out, with no replacement set up to take its place. Southampton's mayor evacuated himself
to the country each night, its chief constable was injured on the second
night of the bombing, and the town clerk, seemingly broken by the
shock, wandered around in a daze.[32] Bishop Garbett described the
effect of the second raid when he visited the next day:

> the centre of the town destroyed: the damage terrible … The people
> broken in spirit after the sleepless and awful nights. Everyone who can
> do so is leaving the town. On the previous night hundreds slept in the
> [New] Forest or in cars on the country roads. The neighbouring villages
> and towns crowded with evacuees. Everywhere I saw men and women
> carrying suitcases or bundles, the children clutching some precious doll
> or toy, struggling to get anywhere out of Southampton.[33]

Attempts were made to pass on the lessons from these cities to those
yet to be attacked. When Hull was heavily bombed the following May,
its ARP network proved much more resilient than Southampton's,
emergency food supplies were quickly laid on and the bombed-out
guided effectively through smoothly working welfare centres. Few
places, however, had Hull's experience of repeated bombing in which
to hone a response. Elsewhere, brief nuisance raids left councils complacent about the quality of their preparations. The blitzes that hit
Belfast and Clydebank in early 1941 replicated what had happened in
London the previous September: confusion, terror, a search for shelters, inadequate rest centres, wrecked utilities, badly damaged housing
and a flood of refugees to the surrounding area.

Local authorities came in for a good deal of criticism, both from
beleaguered citizens and from central government, while the Blitz was
on, but even where ARP leadership was sound, the challenges faced

during and after an attack were profound. Howell Lang Lang-Coath, the town clerk and ARP controller for Swansea, described his duties during the three-day blitz of 19–21 February 1941 to his borough council.

> You should sit in that Control Room – hear all those reports coming in – hear all the terrible things that are happening. I can assure you that it is not a sinecure – it is a very responsible position, and one which I would rather not go through again ... I am there in that room, Mr Mayor and Gentlemen, and I know what is going on. I can imagine part of Swansea falling down, I can't go out to see for myself ... and it is a very apprehensive position to be in, and one in which you feel your position very acutely.[34]

Things became no easier after the bombers had gone. At the end of its blitz, Swansea had suffered 230 people killed, but it had also lost its telephone system, its water and gas supply, its entire shopping centre and market – including 171 food shops and butchers serving more than 22,000 people – and the Food Office, with all its ration records. Six-and-a-half thousand people were homeless. The port and docks, the target of the raid, escaped all but unscathed. Lang-Coath coped pretty well, taking personal control amid the devastation to ensure that essential services were maintained. He then had to face criticism from his council that he had failed to call a committee meeting to discuss his actions. Whatever else had been damaged, the pettifogging self-importance of some local politicians had obviously managed to survive.

A common feature of these provincial blitzes was the mass departure of large numbers of people whose homes were still standing. In fact, the same phenomenon had taken place in London, but there many of the escapees had gone less visibly to the capital's suburbs. From smaller towns and cities, their 'trek' away was more noticeable. Trekking often persisted well after the bombing had stopped. Come daylight, most of these trekkers would return to their jobs, before departing once more as night-time approached. In Coventry, during the period of heavy bombing in 1940, about a third of the city's population left in the two hours before the blackout. By the following October, about 25,000 people a night were still leaving for villages in the surrounding area.[35] In the spring of 1941, about 10,000 people from Southampton, including the mayor, left the city every night.[36] Something similar happened in Clydebank, Plymouth and Hull. Wealthier trekkers got in their cars and took off for hotels; poorer ones hitched lifts, took the bus or walked, then bedded down in farm buildings, church halls or even in the open air. Whitehall initially frowned on trekking as a sign of poor morale and a threat to production, but eventually accepted it as inevitable and set up 'cushion zones', with rest centres and hostels to accommodate the travellers.

In fact, trekking was not so much a danger to the war industry as a way in which the labour force was sustained. Trekkers might have been unwilling or unable to spend the night in a blitzed city, but neither could they afford to abandon jobs, wages and homes. Instead, they commuted back to houses, factories and offices despite the horrors they had experienced on the same streets. By seeking safety at night, they had found a means, however uncomfortable, to carry on their lives in the aftermath of bombing.[37]

'AN INSTRUMENT OF JUSTICE AND ACT OF SOCIAL SOLIDARITY'

Military solutions to the problem of the night-time bomber took a long time. Experiments with aerial minelaying proved a total failure, and were dropped in the spring of 1941. Meanwhile, the number of squadrons in RAF Fighter Command steadily increased as insurance against the risk of renewed daytime attacks, but British night-fighters still lacked the ability to locate German aircraft until the arrival of accurate airborne interception radar sets in March 1941. Just as British fighters were about to pose a real threat to Luftwaffe aircraft, the largest German raids came to a halt. On the ground, Anti-Aircraft Command had 1,691 heavy and 940 light anti-aircraft guns by May 1941, less than half what it was meant to have under the schemes of air defence laid down the previous August. It also had 840 of the new rocket projectors, with a very limited supply of ten rockets each. For AA Command too, what really made a difference was radar, but by May, there were still too few gun-laying sets to equip all of its batteries. AA Command did have lots of searchlights, but not enough troops to put them all into operation.[38]

Morrison's response to the blitzes of late 1940 was to implement a series of changes to the system of Civil Defence, as ARP was now officially renamed. At the end of 1940, he sought approval from the Cabinet for the right to conscript men for Civil Defence work, a measure embodied in the National Service Act of April 1941. To meet the increasing German use of incendiary bombs, Morrison advocated the extension of the existing network of volunteer fire-watchers into a 'big new army', who would look out for the bombs and douse them before a fire could get hold. After the great London fire at the end of December, Morrison lectured radio listeners that 'some of you lately, in more cities than one, have failed your country . . . every group of houses and business premises must have its fire party'. From January, all adults not otherwise engaged in work of national importance had to do fire-watching duties every month in schemes organized by local authorities. Every business had to have fire-watching parties organized to protect its premises during the hours of darkness. This rapid extension of compulsion caused a major fight with the trade unions, whose members objected that they were effectively being forced to do unpaid overtime to protect their bosses' property. Negotiations over remuneration and conditions continued well into the summer. Eventually, 6 million people were registered for what was by then known as the 'Fire Guard'.[39]

In Ipswich, Richard Brown recorded how his neighbourhood had responded:

> We had a successful meeting last night . . . There were nearly 100 there, a good result. Mr Parker is leader of our block and seems keen. That missus of mine, too, is having some helpful thoughts and suggestions on the subject . . . everyone seemed keen and interested in the job of leader-choosing and duties. They are working in our block in pairs, there being seventeen volunteers in sixteen houses, and we are taking one night complete when the siren goes. There will probably be two white boards to be hung over the gate of those on duty so the wardens can contact the right people and wake them if they, possibly oversleep, and I'm putting my pump outside each night when going to bed. As a warden I'm taking no active part but I'm sure interested to see it go well.[40]

Not everyone was so enthusiastic. At the end of March 1941, Diana Watson, a publisher's daughter who lived in central London, described her attempts to recruit fellow fire-watchers in a letter to her soldier brother, Graham.

> I have never quite realised before the stubborn resistance of the great British Public of all classes. I became rather bad tempered after several unsuccessful efforts to enlist the interest of some of our new neighbours and my last attempt happened to be a one-armed woman who was most offensive. Obviously active in any aspect in which she was interested, she shook her stump and claimed immunity on those grounds. Rather savagely I replied that I thought we would be lucky if at the end of the war anyone was left with arms, legs or teeth. Since then the spirit of neighbourliness is a little dimmed.[41]

Compared to fire-watching, Morrison was a much less enthusiastic convert to the idea of reforming the fire service. Not only had city brigades often proved inadequate to the scale of the blazes raised by German incendiary bombing, but reinforcement from neighbouring authorities was hampered by the lack of standardized equipment. As a former London County Council leader, Morrison was hugely proud of the London Fire Brigade, and he was also extremely worried about coming into conflict with local councils if he tried to take their brigades away from them. Only the heavy raids of April 1941 finally convinced him, but then he moved quickly. Before the end of May, Morrison had pushed through legislation to create a National Fire Service (NFS) for the duration of the war. It too was brought into being over the summer. The NFS meant that there could be a nationally co-ordinated approach to the fighting of fires. At maximum strength, in 1943, it would employ 381,000 full- and part-time firemen and women, almost twice the number in local brigades in spring 1940.[42]

The NFS apart, Morrison largely left the administration of civil defence in the hands of local councils, despite evidence of their failures in the face of the raids. Over the winter of 1940–41, he warned ministers that taking central control of civil defence would reduce the sense of local responsibility. The spring attacks raised the same issues of local incompetence, but the government's position was that trying to reform the system would cause more problems than it solved.[43] This was borne out by attempts to intervene in the two most badly run London boroughs, Stepney and West Ham. In Stepney, the Ministries of Home

Security and Health removed responsibility for ARP from the borough council in late 1940, and appointed a fresh ARP controller from outside the borough. Council staff refused to co-operate with this outsider, slowing down any improvements in the provision of shelters and services. As a result, the ministries tried a different approach in West Ham, leaving control with the borough, but stepping in to appoint a local councillor and clergyman, the Reverend W. W. Paton, as a new ARP controller. Paton was another friend of Ritchie Calder, and he had become a neighbourhood hero because of his efforts to aid the bombed-out in the borough during the early days of the Blitz. Nevertheless, he too struggled to get a grip on a recalcitrant local authority, and disagreements between him and his fellow councillors prevented any progress. Stepney and West Ham were still both lagging behind the rest of London when the German bombing ended in May 1941. Even if ministers and officials had wanted to change the structure of local control, the level of root-and-branch reform required to make it work was impractical in the midst of an ongoing aerial bombardment.[44]

Outside London, despite requests from local authorities, deep shelters were not built. An alternative solution was the 'Morrison shelter'. Designed by the structural engineer John Baker, this was a steel-framed cuboid with wire mesh sides that sat indoors, where it could double as a table, and into which two adults and two children could cram. It would support the weight of a collapsed house, it was easy to make and put up, and it offered protection to the vast number of people who did not want to go to a dank Anderson or a crowded public shelter, but instead sit out the Blitz at home. Construction was authorized in January, the first Morrisons became available for Londoners in March, and they were then distributed to other areas at risk of bombing. During 1941, the Ministry of Home Security ordered more than a million of them and advertised them under Morrison's name – a publicity campaign so successful that the home secretary became convinced that he had come up with the design himself.[45]

While Morrison was dealing with issues of civil defence, the Treasury had grappled with the question of how the government would pay for all the damage that had been caused. Before the war, the government had announced that it would pay compensation for buildings, furniture and clothing. Although it took responsibility for paying for essential repairs, it refused to set the terms of compensation until the fighting was over and it knew how much money it had. In June 1940, the chancellor agreed to make advanced payments on that compensation to families with an income of up to £400 a year to pay for new clothes and furniture if they were bombed out. Since these payments were administered by officials who had been used to dealing with the unemployed under the stringent terms of the 1930s, the first months of the Blitz saw frequent complaints that they were being too parsimonious – particularly from those middle-class victims of bombing who had not previously encountered the rigours of the Assistance Board's assessments.[46]

In December 1940, Kingsley Wood announced a new War Damages Bill that provided a comprehensive scheme of household insurance for the entire country. The chancellor called it 'an instrument of justice and act of social solidarity' – everyone would bear the burden of paying for the sacrifices of those whose homes were wrecked by the war. As passed in March 1941, the War Damages Act required property owners to pay a compulsory premium, calculated as a percentage of total value, every year for the duration of the war, with the state guaranteeing to make up any shortfall between receipts and the burden of eventual payments. Every householder – whether or not they owned the property – was given up to £400 of free contents insurance against war damage. Again, small grants from this sum would be paid out prior to the assessment of any claim to allow the bombed-out to start to rebuild their lives. The scheme for households, which the Board of Trade handed over to Lloyd's of London to run, eventually paid out £117 million in compensation. For the property scheme, the Inland Revenue collected a total of £200 million from property owners over the next five years. The War Damage Commission, which was set up to administer the property clauses of the Act, ultimately dealt with 4 million claims and paid out more than £1,300 million. Twenty years after the war finished, it was still paying for repairs to be completed.[47]

'NO SIGN WHATEVER WAS FOUND OF ANTI-WAR FEELING'

Civilian morale beneath the bombing was a key concern within government. The state of morale was closely monitored by the armed forces, the Ministry of Home Security and Home Office (including MI5), and the Ministry of Food, as well as by the Home Intelligence division of the Ministry of Information, which continued to employ Mass-Observation to investigate the state of public feeling.[48] Almost without exception, these bodies reported the same thing: despite the suffering, mistakes and occasional catastrophe, morale held up well, particularly in inner-city working-class areas that bore the brunt of the bombing and whose capacity for endurance had been so doubted before the war.

The provincial blitz posed Mass-Observation practical challenges. Its research in Bolton and London had been based on investigators integrating themselves deeply into the life of a community, but now it needed to report on raided areas where it lacked this fine-grained connection. Instead, Harrisson 'blitz-chased'. Rushing to a newly bombed town, he and a couple of paid observers would record their immediate impressions. Over the next few days, Harrisson would try to speak to local officials and business people, while his investigators talked to people on the streets. As a method of research, this tended to capture a small range of immediate reactions without a baseline of local knowledge.[49]

M-O's reports from the blitzed cities were dramatic and increasingly critical of failures in local leadership. Presented to Home Intelligence, these observations became part of what were now weekly morale reports from the Ministry of Information. Arriving on the scene in the immediate aftermath of heavy raids in late 1940, the blitz-chasers found people shocked and struggling to piece together their lives, but far from ready to give up. In Coventry after the 14 November raid, for instance, M-O reported:

> An unprecedented dislocation and depression . . . more open signs of hysteria, terror, neurosis, observed in one evening than during the whole of the past two months together in all areas . . . Helplessness and impotence only accelerated depression . . . several signs of suppressed panic as darkness approached.

The team, however, also 'stressed that no sign whatever was found of anti-war feeling, that there were very few grumbles'.[50] In Plymouth, 'Though raids were the principal topic of conversation, an unusual proportion of the raid talk was cheerful or humorous. There was relatively much whistling and laughing, relatively little grumbling.' Nonetheless,

M-O's report asserted that: 'there is no doubt that there is considerable depression and much pessimism about the future underlying a determination to carry on'.[51] For Harrisson, that made it all the more important to have well-prepared welfare and information services available to give the bombed-out what they needed: shelter, food and clear instructions about what to do next.

Mass-Observation's critical commentary annoyed the Home Office and the Ministry of Home Security. However much Home Intelligence protested that it was just recording what the people were saying – not whether their comments were justified – the Home Office took its reports of popular dissatisfaction with ARP as a direct, and unfair, attack on its performance. In September, it pressed successfully to limit the distribution of Home Intelligence's reports so that they no longer reached the Cabinet. When M-O's blitz investigations reached the Home Office over the winter, they provoked a furious response. Home Office officials could see little use in another department broadcasting public unhappiness with these failures to the rest of Whitehall and accused M-O of finding discontent and defeatism where there was none. As one put it, Mass-Observation was obviously made up of 'what is known as the "intelligentsia" and I think they would be very much better employed in doing something useful for the community'. The Home Office firmly blocked any further dissemination of M-O's reports.[52]

Unsurprisingly, when the heavy raiding resumed in the spring, the blitz-chasers showed frustration at the fact that nobody seemed to be listening. Visiting Plymouth after its prolonged blitz, M-O complained: 'Over and over again these reports have pointed out . . . the weakness of information services after a blitz. Yet it is impossible to see that anything serious has been done to alter this situation.' Without adequate leadership or support, the people of Plymouth were 'not defeat*ist* – far from it. But they are defeat*ed*. Their town has suffered a major military defeat, and they, the untrained and undisciplined soldiers of the Home Front, can (at present) do nothing much about it.'[53]

By this point, Tom Harrisson was deeply worried that some sudden reverse would unleash all the underlying war weariness currently being hidden by public celebrations of civilian stoicism into an unstoppable desire for peace. These fears said more about how he thought popular opinion worked than they did about those he was observing. What

Mass-Observation had picked up was how difficult and painful life in the bombed cities could be, and how inconsistently people lived up to the expected standards of cheerful endurance. What Mass-Observation could not draw out, in the space of a brief visit, was what this indicated about people's private thoughts. In retrospect, however, it is clear that it did not portend a mass breakdown of morale.[54] In fact, those who insisted on the strength of popular morale in the face of the bombing were correct: not because the British people were any more determined or cheerful than anyone else, or because – outside London – the state managed to solve the problems of the blitzed while the raids were on, but rather because morale was a very difficult target to attack.

'WE HAVEN'T STARTED THE RUDDY WAR YET'

Morale was not, of course, what the Germans were actually trying to bomb, although Göring did order some 'vengeance raids' that aimed at destroying property in London as a retaliation for RAF bombing raids on Berlin. As the strain of prolonged night-time operations took its toll on German aircrew, and the British managed to divert the radio guidance beams that the bombers used to navigate to their targets, so the accuracy of German bombing decreased, with the result that the bombers increasingly aimed to hit cities rather than specific locations. Nonetheless, the main target for the bombing campaign was always the British war economy, not civilian morale.

Economically, however, bombing was strikingly ineffective. Locally, raids could cause severe disruption to production. In Coventry in particular, the November 1940 attack caused heavy damage to the city's factories. More than 70 per cent of Coventry's largest industrial units were destroyed or seriously damaged by fire or explosion, and damage to the city's gas mains restricted supplies to local industry for the next three months. Bomb damage led to works being shut and workers being temporarily laid off. Even when production was restored, night-time absenteeism increased – in part because still-damaged buildings were colder, wetter and darker. It was six weeks before Coventry was using the same amount of electrical power that it had before the raid.[55]

Coventry, however, had its factories relatively close together and had been particularly badly hit. Most blitzed cities were back to their usual rates of activity in about a week. Thanks to the difficulties of bomb-aiming, munitions plants often simply escaped unharmed. The two bombing raids that struck Barrow in April and May 1941, for example, between them destroyed 100 houses and damaged more than 11,000 homes, killed 83 people and injured another 330, but left the Vickers shipyard completely untouched.[56] Even where they were hit, factory buildings proved much more vulnerable than the crucial machinery within them – the raids on the Midlands in November and December 1940 destroyed less than 0.5 per cent of the region's aero-industry machine tools, and damaged only another 4 per cent.[57] From the summer of 1940 onwards, the Ministry of Aircraft Production sought to disperse aircraft plants across multiple locations, parcelling out production to small engineering firms and taking over premises to ensure that output would continue even if the main factory was bombed. By October, 364 new sites had been secured for the manufacture of airframes and engines alone.[58] Although the manufacture of specific aircraft was on occasion interrupted, for the most part this approach worked: indeed, dispersal significantly increased the amount of productive floorspace available to the aero-industry.[59]

At Beaverbrook's insistence, the Ministry also initiated the building of four great underground aircraft factories. These were meant to protect essential production in the event of continued bombing. By the time they were completed, in 1944, the total cost was £12 million, four times the original estimate. As things turned out, they were completely unnecessary.[60] As this suggested, what the Blitz did for the Germans was to force the British to pay a lot of attention to protecting their country from further aerial attack. The continuation of bombing even as the weight of Germany's military effort shifted towards the east encouraged the British and Soviet governments to believe that Hitler intended to finish his war with the UK before he did anything else. The military, civil and industrial resources that the British dedicated to meeting attack from the skies – more than 2 million full- and part-time civil defence workers by mid-1941, an increasingly strong and technologically sophisticated network of fighter and anti-aircraft defences, and improved shelters, rest centres and other post-raid services – could all have gone into something else. The crisis of bombing forced a colossal organizational and infrastructural response from the British state.

Significantly, that response did not halt in May 1941. On the contrary, since the possibility that the Blitz would resume could not be discounted, resources continued to be ploughed into civil and anti-aircraft defences as the war went forward. Their continued improvement left the UK much better protected – but it also meant that the threat of German air power continued to exercise an influence on British policy long after its first strategic offensive had stopped.[61]

In terms of its primary objectives, however, the Blitz failed, and it did so primarily because the German air force did not have anything like the strength, bomb load or accuracy of attack necessary to break an advanced industrial economy. Looking forward to their plans for a massively expanded air force, this was one lesson that the British bomber chiefs marked well. Meeting the vice chief of the air staff, Arthur Harris, at the height of the Blitz, the American airman General 'Hap' Arnold remarked that the British people didn't seem to know they'd lost the war. Harris replied: 'Good God no. We haven't started the ruddy war yet.'[62]

'BOMB BACK AND BOMB HARD'

The bombing of British cities increased public support for the RAF to do the same to Germany and united popular opinion behind the idea of retaliation. Official policy was always to emphasize that British bombing was targeted solely on military objectives and that it was highly accurate, but from the start of the Blitz, the Beaverbrook press in particular argued that the only appropriate response was escalating retaliation against the enemy civilian population. As it headlined its report on the Coventry raid in mid-November: 'It is time now for our deepest, most inspired anger. Coventry cries: bomb back and bomb hard.'[63] The idea that Britain might bomb German cities, however, was always the subject of controversy: it was publicly opposed by pre-war pacifists and internationalists such as the writers Vera Brittain and George Bernard Shaw, as well as the bishop of Chichester, George Bell.[64]

The shift in attitudes can be marked in three British Institute of Public Opinion surveys during the months of bombardment. In October 1940, asked whether, in 'view of the indiscriminate German bombing of this country', they would 'approve or disapprove if the RAF adopted a similar policy of bombing the civilian population of Germany?', respondents were evenly divided, with 46 per cent for and against.[65] In January 1941, the Institute asked: 'What are your thoughts when you hear that there has been a very heavy air raid?' Twenty-eight per cent chose 'Wonder how the bombed people are getting on'; 24 per cent chose 'Intensify our bombing of military targets in Germany'; 23 per cent 'Bomb German civilians in retaliation'; 15 per cent 'Get better protection for people in this country'; and 10 per cent 'Find some way to stop the war'.[66] Three months later, with heavier raids resumed, respondents were again asked whether they would 'approve or disapprove if the RAF adopted a policy of bombing the civilian population of Germany?' This time, 54 per cent approved against 36 per cent who did not.[67] Significantly, all these questions presupposed that the RAF could choose who or what it was going to hit in Germany, when in fact its efforts at precision bombing over the winter of 1940–41 were much less accurate even than those of the Luftwaffe.

Tom Harrisson, who claimed never to have encountered a demand for revenge attacks in any of the bombed towns he visited, analysed the BIPO's results geographically to see if being blitzed affected attitudes. He found that whereas the balance of opinion in London was marginally against bombing enemy civilians, in areas that had not been bombed, people were much more in favour of reprisals. As the comments made by respondents to the April survey suggested, the rationales involved were both moral and practical. As classified by the BIPO, 37 per cent had said something like 'Let the Germans have a taste of it. They deserve it. An eye for an eye'; 15 per cent, 'That's as bad as Hitler. Don't kill women and children. Let's keep our hands clean. The less of that the better'; and 8 per cent, 'We can't win the war that way. It'll only come back on us. It's so futile.'[68]

As the Blitz wore on, public frustration at the apparent lack of effect of British bombing became increasingly pronounced. Home Intelligence reported on the aftermath of the raids on Clydebank and Glasgow that

> demand for reprisals is now becoming stronger among civilians; service men, home on compassionate leave, are blazing angry and all out for the heaviest possible reprisals ... Our bombing policy is described as 'flabby'. More and more it is being suggested that we should 'lay off'

military objectives for a few nights and instead annihilate one or more German towns – preferably Berlin.[69]

'WHAT A TRIUMPH THE LIFE OF THESE BATTERED CITIES IS'

There was no great unified national experience of bombing, but the Blitz was an event to which national meanings were ascribed. At the time, undoubtedly the most important was that the home front could take it. So far from cracking under the German bombardment, Britons had joined together to resist the onslaught. Civilians were in the front line. Civil defence workers were heroes. Morale remained unbroken. This version of the Blitz was assiduously promoted by the government, the BBC, the newsreel companies and almost all newspapers. Speaking to the nation on 27 April, the prime minister portrayed it as a valida-tion of traditional British values:

> What a triumph the life of these battered cities is, over the worst that fire and bomb can do . . . What a test of the quality of our local authorities, and of institutions and customs and societies so steadily built . . . The sublime but also terrible and sombre experience and emotions of the battlefield which for centuries had been reserved for soldiers and sailors, are now shared, for good or ill, by the entire population. All are proud to be under the fire of the enemy.

This was plainly not everybody's experience of the Blitz, and assertions from ministers and journalists about universal cheerfulness and high morale aroused considerable antagonism at the time.[70]

Yet – particularly when told in less bombastic tones than Churchill's – there was enough in this account of home-front resilience to strike a chord in a country that was already busily mythologizing the deliver-ance of Dunkirk and the defiance of invasion. Civilians were indeed in the thick of the action: during the second year of the war, civilian deaths from enemy action were about twice those suffered by the army, navy and air force combined. Some people, particularly those involved in civil defence, had been forced to deal with situations utterly beyond their pre-war lives, and some of them had found within themselves remarkable reserves of courage and endurance.

The Blitz certainly hadn't blown away class distinctions: bombs hit hardest at working-class areas, wealthier Britons were better able to escape attack or to deal with the consequences of being bombed out, and reactions to refugees and trekkers often reflected existing perceptions of class. People of different classes had, however, worked together to withstand the enemy's attack, society had proved more resilient than some had feared before the war broke out, and public depictions of the very poorest members of the urban working class now celebrated their endurance under the bombs rather than condemning their fecklessness and filth. Even if the relentless emphasis on civilian stoicism did not match how people felt personally, the overwhelming majority do seem to have felt that it was stoicism to which they ought to aspire. That may in itself have bolstered morale by keeping the innumerable personal crises caused by the bombing more private than they might otherwise have been.

For more progressive commentators, the story of popular endurance could be developed into a tale of a country being, as J. B. Priestley put it, 'bombed into democracy'. Looking at the ways in which Londoners had stood up to be counted – organizing their own shelters, stepping in to solve the problems of the homeless and the hungry, volunteering to put out incendiaries and fight fires – Ritchie Calder thought he could see a new sort of citizen emerging from the rubble. At the end of his book *Carry on London*, published in May 1941, Calder wrote:

> In a thousand ways, for a thousand common objects, people have learned to work together, to appreciate each other's values . . . New democratic institutions have come into being. Men, and women, have discovered latent qualities of leadership. They have become articulate. They have become active instead of acquiescent.[71]

Under the impact of bombing and displays of popular radicalism, the intelligentsia discovered a faith in the abilities of the working class that had been lacking before the war. In fact, although the heavy raids forced a lot of people to get involved with defending their homes and gave them an experience of working for the common good, it never came close to including everybody. Yet it was this sense of popular involvement that led politicians and commentators to hope that the spirit of service could be preserved after the war, and encouraged fond references back to the 'Blitz spirit' over the decades to come.

That it was possible at the time to turn the Blitz into something positive, however, should not obscure the pain, suffering and disruption that it caused. So a chapter on the Blitz should end not with Churchill or Calder, but with Jim and Hilda Curran and their children, Pat and Bob. Early on in the Blitz, the Currans' house in the East End of London was wrecked by bombing and Hilda and the children were evacuated to Cambridge. Before long, Jim had to write to her with more bad news. There'd been another raid.

> The Warning went about 9 and it was one continuous noise of gunfire, bombs and planes and didn't stop at all till 4.30. It is our worst experience since the raids started. Well dear there're plenty of others got to stick it just the same, I'm glad you're out of it when I see the women fetching their scared kiddies out of the shelters of a morning . . . when I went to work Thursday morning I found my firm pretty nearly burnt out . . . But nobody was hurt. Our firewatchers went down the tube when they dropped the first near one, that's why our place caught fire . . .
>
> So my luck didn't change for long did it, our house first now my firm, well dear so long as we are all OK I shan't worry so keep your chin up and we never know, it might end very quick yet.[72]

Now unemployed, Jim stayed in London to look for another job. At some point, he managed to travel up to Cambridge. Hilda wrote to him sadly about the aftermath of his visit:

> Well dear I felt awful after you had gone home and to make things worse I had a scene with the kiddies when they went to bed. Poor Bobby he sobbed and sobbed because he wanted his Daddy it made your heart ache to hear him. Anyhow I managed to cuddle him off to sleep but all through the night I could hear him sob in his sleep. Patsy cried too she wanted you all, especially her Nannie and Grandad. I tell you we were a lot of weeping willies. It's lovely having you come but the going back is so awful. I could kick myself for breaking down like I do but for the life of me I can't control myself however hard I try to keep a stiff upper lip.[73]

Home destroyed, separated by evacuation, wage-earner put out of work, struggling to keep going by themselves without assistance from the state, and trying to put a brave face on things because other people had it worse: for those whose lives were caught up in the maelstrom of bombing, this was closer to the true texture of the Blitz.

21

The Battle of the British Empire

On 5 November 1940, Roosevelt was re-elected as president of the United States for an unprecedented third term. In London, the news was greeted with joy and excitement, as noted by those avid Westminster diarists, Chips Channon – 'A real landslide, and I have yet to see anyone who is not delighted' – and Harold Nicolson – 'the best thing that has happened to us since the outbreak of war. I thank God!'.[1] Despite all the disappointments of the summer, Roosevelt had delivered just enough on his promises to convince British ministers and officials that, once his hands were freed by his return to office, he would lead his country quickly into the war.[2]

Contemporaries often found Roosevelt's character and intentions elusive. His unusual aptitude for emotional concealment, developed early in life, had only been reinforced by his battle to overcome the disabling effects of polio, which had to be carefully hidden from an electorate who would never have voted for a wheelchair-bound president. In office, he governed by faction – giving his subordinates a lot of responsibility and letting them fight against each other, but seldom putting them fully in the picture. This was partly to stop anyone else gaining too much power, but mainly because, as leader of the world's greatest democracy, Roosevelt liked to be able to tack the ship of policy to the wind of popular approval in order to reach his goals.[3]

In autumn 1940, the British, not for the last time, saw in Roosevelt what they wanted to see, but their hopes of a rapid American entry into the war turned out to be misplaced. Roosevelt still believed that it might be possible for the United States to defeat Fascism without actually becoming a belligerent. Despite his victory, he still faced strong isolationist sentiment in the country and in Congress, and he was far from certain that he could carry the American people into battle. He returned to the Oval Office certain that this would be a term of mighty tasks and epoch-making decisions, but expecting that he could keep the British fighting without putting America in the front line.

'THE SILLY, FOOLISH OLD DOLLAR SIGN'

By the time Roosevelt was re-elected, the British, with their pre-war dollar reserves running out, were struggling to pay for new American supplies; but finance was not their only problem. As shipping losses continued into the winter, the British needed American ships to make sure that the transatlantic supply line would keep running. Access to American shipping would make an immediate difference to Britain's ability to fight a global war. At the same time, they needed to accelerate American arms production. As US rearmament got slowly under way in the second half of 1940, American and British orders began to compete with each other for still-scarce munitions capacity in the States. The British ambassador in Washington, Lord Lothian, and the head of the British Purchasing Commission, Arthur Purvis, both warned that unless Britain shocked America into accepting full industrial mobilization, its vast potential might not be realized until it was too late.

Roosevelt, however, thought that he could take his time. As far as the US Treasury was concerned, total British investments in the United States in late 1940 still amounted to $2.5 billion, or about £600 million. There were other British overseas investments – in South America, but also in Malaya – that could also be sold off or handed over to the US government in order to raise additional funds. The British might not, the president accepted, be able to pay for American production indefinitely, but if they liquidated these assets, they could certainly keep going in the short term. Looking at US calculations of British resources, Roosevelt declared: 'Well they aren't bust – there's lots of money there.'[4]

The British thought that their position was much more acute than the Americans realized. Most of the easily sold British investments in America had already gone, and what was left would realize much less than its value if, in a desperate 'fire sale', it was all put to the market at the same time. The British thought that the Americans had failed to grasp how the sterling system worked. Britain's overseas financial edifice was built on the idea that there were at least some reserves of gold and dollars in London to back the whole thing up. If the Americans required the British to empty their pockets completely, it might upset the whole structure by which they were financing the rest of the war. As the Americans rightly suspected, however, the British were also reluctant to give up every part of their global financial empire in order to defeat Nazism on America's behalf. While the Americans worried that the wily British imperialists were fooling them into footing the bill, the British despaired about what they saw as the naive idealism of a juvenile great power.[5]

Like most of his countrymen, Churchill believed that Britain's willingness to fight on against the evil of Nazism was establishing a moral obligation on the Americans. They ought to be redeeming British sacrifices, not taking advantage of them. To an extent that now seems remarkable, the British persisted in viewing America as a sort of particularly powerful but recalcitrant dominion that could be educated into accepting its responsibilities. Given the vigour of US colonialism in the Americas and the Pacific, the British saw American criticisms of their own empire as hypocritical. Yet the Americans weren't the only people who were guilty of double standards. Given their reliance on imperial economic sacrifices, via the financial mechanisms of the sterling area, it ill-behoved the British to complain that the Americans were unwilling to pay for the war.

When the hopes raised by the presidential election were dashed, and Roosevelt continued his cautious policy, there was profound disappointment in London. Churchill, however, did not want to force the issue with the president. Hopeful as ever that something would turn up, he preferred to rely on the course of events to drive the Americans into action. Lord Lothian suggested a different approach. The ambassador believed that the only way to get things moving was to make it clear that, without US help, the UK would be unable to continue the war. On a visit back to the UK in early November, he persuaded the prime minister to write to Roosevelt, laying out exactly how bad the financial, shipping and supply situations were and insisting that without massive and immediate US aid, the British would be defeated. After multiple redraftings, the letter was eventually despatched on

8 December. Churchill, who called it 'one of the most important I ever wrote', insisted on putting the emphasis not on issues of finance, but rather the need for US merchant ships and escort vessels to help Britain in the Atlantic.

In the meantime, however, Lothian had returned to the US. On his arrival, on 23 November, he told the crowd of waiting reporters about the severity of Britain's position. Unlike the prime minister, he laid heavy emphasis on the imminent shortage of dollars. His intention was to start a public debate that would provide the momentum necessary for Roosevelt to take action. By the time the president, who had departed on a Caribbean cruise to recover from the rigours of the election, received Churchill's letter, British finances had become a major topic of discussion in the American press.[6]

This revelation of the dire straits in which the UK now found itself coincided with a reconsideration of American strategy. By the start of Roosevelt's third term, America's senior military leaders had become convinced that the USA would eventually be dragged into the gathering global maelstrom. They too wanted clarity from the newly re-elected president. The chief of naval operations, Harold Stark, put forward a range of strategic options, lettered from A to D. He advocated the fourth, Plan Dog. This was based on the principle that the defence of the UK was vital to US interests. Assuming that a future war pitted Britain and America against Germany, Italy and Japan, the US should remain on the defensive in the Pacific while taking the offensive in Europe. Without direct American assistance, the British would not have sufficient strength to defeat the Germans, and if Britain fell, the US would find itself 'alone, and at war with the world'. On Stark's recommendation, the Americans agreed to extend hitherto limited staff discussions into full-blown, but intensely secret, discussions of future joint strategy, which got under way in Washington at the start of 1941.

As the British prepared the final brief for their envoys to this conference, Roosevelt returned from his holiday with his mind made up about how to address the intertwined problems of British supply and finance and American politics and rearmament. On 17 December 1940, the president announced at a press conference that he wanted to lend or lease raw materials, equipment and munitions to the UK, on the basis that they would be returned or paid for – in kind rather than with money – at the end of hostilities. He described 'Lend-Lease' as taking 'the silly, foolish old dollar sign' out of the equation. The British would have to pay something, but it wouldn't be money they didn't have.

By committing itself in the long term to supply Great Britain in its fight against totalitarianism, America would guarantee its own safety without actually having to enter the war. In fact, Roosevelt's scheme also had the advantage of guaranteeing the investment that would be needed to expand America's arms industries in line with the president's dramatic rearmament plans. If America did have to fight, it would do so with an industrial economy already being geared up for war.

In one of his radio 'fireside chats', on 29 December, the president explained to the American people that he wanted the USA to act as 'the arsenal of democracy'. He returned to the same theme in his State of the Union address on 6 January 1941, telling listeners:

> we are committed to full support of all those resolute peoples, every-where, who are resisting aggression and are thereby keeping war away from our Hemisphere. By this support, we express our determination that the democratic cause shall prevail; and we strengthen the defense and security of our own nation.[7]

Roosevelt sold his policy not just in terms of protecting America, but also as an ideological crusade. Linking together the New Deal at home with an internationalism rooted in human rights abroad, he closed by asking Americans to 'look forward to a world founded upon four essen-tial human freedoms': freedom of speech and of religion, and from want and fear. 'That kind of world', he concluded, 'is the very antith-esis of the so-called new order of tyranny which the dictators seek to create with the crash of a bomb.'[8]

'A THOROUGHLY INADEQUATE SERVICE IN RETURN'

For the British, Roosevelt's announcement of Lend-Lease made the turn of the year a moment of relief and anxiety. With the staff talks about to go ahead, and Roosevelt apparently determined to supply the UK without getting it to build up vast dollar debts, the future might be bright. As with all Roosevelt's big ideas, however, the plans he had set forth were light on detail. In particular, the price that Britain would eventually be expected to pay for this beneficence was not laid out. Of more immediate concern, however, was the gap between the president's generous announcement and his legislation actually getting through Congress. At the start of December, British dollar reserves had gone down to $574 million, less than the $600 million that London thought necessary to operate the Sterling Area and meet dollar expenditure out-side the US, but also less than the $580 million due to US manufacturers before the end of February. Roosevelt's intervention had not saved Brit-ain from effective dollar bankruptcy. In the meantime, progress on placing the giant orders needed to fulfil the summer armament plans ground to a halt.

As far as the president was concerned, however, Britain was still far from 'bust'. When it came to covering the next tranche of payments in the States, Roosevelt's Treasury secretary, Henry Morgenthau, sug-gested that the British might like to expropriate the £200 million of gold that the French government had sent for safekeeping in Canada. Anxious not to antagonize the French any more than they already had, the British demurred. Sir Frederick Phillips, the British Treasury official sent to Washington to negotiate the rapids of dollar diplomacy, instead raised the possibility of handing over £42 million of gold that the South Africans had set aside for British use. After news of this trove reached the president, he announced to London on 23 December that the Amer-icans were going to take the bullion, and that an American warship was already on its way to pick the gold up.

This was the first that British ministers had heard of the proposal. An infuriated Churchill composed, but was dissuaded from sending, a letter to the president complaining that America was acting like 'a sher-iff collecting the last assets of a helpless debtor' – bad enough in any case, but intolerable when Britain was giving its all to fight a common enemy. Beaverbrook went berserk. The Americans had 'exacted pay-ment to the uttermost for all they have done for us. They have taken our bases without adequate compensation. They have taken our gold. They have been given our secrets and offered us a thoroughly inad-equate service in return.'[9] He suggested that Churchill should resist further US demands.

Beaverbrook was often able to articulate Churchill's worst fears, but on this occasion the prime minister did not follow his friend's advice. As 1940 closed, the UK was massively more mobilized than the United

States. In terms of munitions, a meaningful American contribution to the British war effort was at least a year away. Yet Britain needed American raw materials, food and shipping now, as well as the continued investment in plant and production that would see US-made weapons in British hands in the future. The only way to get that was to find a means to keep spending in the United States. That meant not only accepting the divestment of UK assets, but also kowtowing to the Americans to make sure that the Lend-Lease Act passed. When Lord Lloyd, the colonial secretary, complained at the end of December that the American occupation of Atlantic bases threatened a takeover of the British Empire, Churchill told him that gaining American support 'was of overriding importance and other matters must give way before it'.[10] The War Cabinet agreed.

Churchill had no more intention than Lloyd of letting the Empire go by the board, but he retained a belief that the war was just a stage on a shared Anglo-American journey. Present sacrifices on that voyage might well be validated by the changes that would come once the United States was more closely embroiled in the conflict. The UK's temporary lack of dollars did not mean that it had exited the rank of great nations, but rather that he needed to bind the Americans into British strategy. If America could be brought into the war, then the fact that the British Empire was for the moment much more capable of doing the actual fighting would rectify the imbalance in financial power. Throughout 1941, turning America into a combatant became Churchill's main strategic priority.

It wasn't just high imperialists such as Beaverbrook and Lloyd who regarded US intentions with suspicion. Even as they retained their belief that the Americans *ought* to help them, most British ministers also remained more pessimistic than Churchill about the price that the United States was demanding for its aid. Their worries were well founded. No amount of reference to the shared heritage of the English-speaking peoples was going to remove the fact that Roosevelt wanted to defeat Fascism *and* imperialism, and to replace British with American power – which was exactly what he was doing as he manoeuvred to implement Lend-Lease. Yet though the more defiant stand advocated by Beaverbrook sometimes tempted Churchill, it seemed unlikely to yield any better results. Rather than confronting the president, the prime minister preferred to woo him, in the optimistic belief that Roosevelt wanted to carry the American people into the war.[11]

The conviction of a shared Anglo-American destiny was a vital part of Churchill's hopes of victory, but (ironically) he was to prove particularly ill-suited to the task of convincing the Americans that Britain was the sort of modern, democratic society for which they should fight. Under a different prime minister, the UK might have made a more dynamic attempt to seize the initiative in transatlantic relations in 1940 and 1941 by building on the real achievements of the 1930s, committing itself to a clear set of war aims, including domestic reforms and imperial democratization, and taking concrete steps towards them before the end of the war. Given the strength of American prejudices about British imperialism and the depth of the UK's financial dependence, whether such an approach would actually have won over public opinion in the United States must be open to doubt, but it was certainly attractive to more progressive ministers, including Eden and Attlee, who wanted to take the opportunity of building a new and better world.

It never appealed to Churchill. He was fighting to preserve an old and doomed version of the British Empire, and though he was right to prioritize the securing of assistance from the United States, he was wrong to hope that it could be won cheaply. The construction of a wartime Anglo-American 'special relationship' would be something for which Britain paid heavily, and for a long time.

'PARALLEL WARS'

A rapidly prepared Bill to permit Lend-Lease, tellingly entitled 'An Act to Promote the Defence of the United States', was placed before Congress on 10 January 1941. Having waited for Roosevelt to be re-elected, now the British had to attend on the decisions of the American legislature. President Roosevelt, however, was not the only one taking vital decisions during the winter of 1940. In Berlin, Adolf Hitler was also about to make a crucial choice that would also determine the outcome of Britain's war.

For a brief moment in the summer of 1940, the German dictator had contemplated attacking Britain's position around the shores of the Mediterranean, but the more he thought about the strategy, the less keen he became. Italy and Germany might have been allies, but their intentions in the region were very different. As Mussolini put it, they were fighting 'parallel wars'. Hitler knew the British Empire was doomed, but he was not going to smash it just so that Italy could pick up the pieces. In any case, even if the Germans seized Britain's possessions in the Middle East, he doubted whether that would actually knock Britain out the war. Mussolini, in contrast, wanted to expand the Italian empire. That meant taking advantage of German military successes elsewhere, not letting the Germans into Italy's backyard. He waved away German offers of assistance in North Africa.[12]

Desperate for a quick win, but stymied by his generals' reluctance to advance in Egypt, Mussolini toyed with the idea of attacking Greece. The Germans warned him off: they wanted the Balkans kept quiet, not opened up as a new zone of conflict. In October, however, the Germans sent troops to Romania to support the new regime of General Ion Antonescu and to secure their supplies of oil. That convinced Mussolini that Hitler wanted to dominate the entire region. At the end of October, without German authority, Italian forces invaded Greece from occupied Albania.

Their attack turned into a disaster. Ten days after it began, the Greeks had fought the offensive to a standstill. During the second half of November, the Italians were driven back into Albania. The British sent RAF squadrons from the Middle East to help, and garrisoned Crete to release Greek troops to fight the Italians on the mainland. On 11 November, Admiral Cunningham's fleet launched a daring raid on the Italian fleet, using carrier-launched aircraft to strike at Italian battleships in harbour in the port of Taranto. One was sunk, another two damaged and the Italian navy withdrew further up the coast, easing the path of British supply convoys to Greece and Malta.

Mussolini was downcast. Hitler was furious. His ally's incompetence was endangering German security: based in Greece, British aircraft would be within easy bombing range of the Romanian oilfields. Reluctantly, he was forced to intervene. In mid-November, he decided against a full-blown German pincer movement against the Suez Canal. Instead, he would send Luftwaffe planes to Italy to dominate the Mediterranean, while the Wehrmacht took control in the Balkans and defeated Greece, thus protecting the right flank of a future advance into the Soviet Union.[13]

Italy was not the only country with which Germany could not co-ordinate its strategy. In the summer, the Germans had planned 'Operation Felix', a combined air and ground attack on Gibraltar that would put them in control of the exit from the Mediterranean, and give the U-boats a base from which to attack the central Atlantic. It depended on Franco's co-operation – and for that he demanded the secession of French territory in Morocco and Algeria. This presented Hitler with an insoluble conundrum: Spain could only be brought into the war at the cost of alienating the Vichy government and throwing the French empire into the Allied camp. As the winter drew on, a very poor harvest in Spain made Franco even more hesitant about starting a war with the British Empire. As part of their global war on Fascism, the British bolstered Franco's regime with deliveries of food that saved it from popular unrest. This was not an offer that the Germans could match. On 8 December, Franco told Berlin that Spain's economic weakness meant that he would have to cancel Operation Felix. This was a significant diplomatic victory for Britain, and one that owed a lot to the work that Sir Samuel Hoare was doing as ambassador. Hoare might have been a too-clever, two-faced appeaser, but that made him extremely well suited to keeping Spain out of the fighting. Britain was lucky to have him in Madrid.[14]

In any case, Hitler was increasingly focused on operations against Russia. From the summer of 1940, it was clear that, thanks to the economic blockade, Germany would only be able to make full use of its newly occupied territories by depending on Stalin's continued deliveries of food and oil. In fact, the Soviet dictator was determined for the moment to keep these shipments up, lest the Germans be tempted into an attack on the USSR before his mighty programme of rearmament was completed. Hitler, however, did not believe that he could trust him to keep his word.

From August 1940, Germany's munitions plans reflected Hitler's expectation that he would have to fight on two fronts in quick succession: a lightning-fast ground war to knock out the USSR, which meant colossal production levels of tanks and explosives, and a future air war against the UK and United States, which required huge investment in long-term aircraft production. The great loser in all this was the German navy's U-boat programme. In July, Hitler had briefly given it priority. By the autumn, submarine construction had been relegated in favour of the army's preparations for a new campaign in the east. The U-boats were the best way to cut off American supplies to Britain, but they could promise only a very distant victory. In the meantime, attacks on the Atlantic shipping lanes might, just as in the last war, force America into battle. Hitler was convinced that a war with the US was coming, but he didn't want it to start before the Wehrmacht had demolished the Soviet Union.

On 18 December 1940, Hitler issued the directive formally ordering the attack on Russia to take place at the beginning of the following summer. The strategic rationale of a war for resources was intertwined with an ideology of annihilation: from the start, this campaign was meant to be fought as a merciless struggle against those whom Hitler regarded as the implacable enemies of Nazism: Bolsheviks and Jews. The global war would be escalated not only to a new vast geographical arena, but also to an unprecedented level of barbarity.[15]

The shift of German efforts to the opening of a new Eastern Front shaped not only the immediate course of the war, but also its ultimate outcome. It was a long time before British strategists recognized for certain that it had occurred. In a survey of the war situation at the end of October, Churchill, his instincts about European geo-politics always sounder than his skills as a battlefield commander, correctly speculated to senior officers that Germany would turn on the USSR during 1941 because Hitler needed oil. This was, however, just one of the scenarios that the prime minister conjured up for future enemy operations over the winter. In contrast, British military intelligence and the Foreign Office insisted that Hitler would finish off the UK before starting another war. Churchill worried that his advisors were correct. As the Blitz and the assault on shipping continued, the British planned on having to meet two potential threats in the spring: an attempted invasion of the UK and a German offensive around both sides of the Mediterranean.

Had the British known for certain at an earlier date what the Germans were planning to do, they might have been able to take more advantage of the concentration of German force in the east. British intelligence successes in the second half of the war have become the stuff of popular legend: the failure to spot what the Germans were going to do next in the spring of 1941 was arguably even more important.[16]

'REPERCUSSIONS ALL ROUND
THE MEDITERRANEAN'

While Roosevelt was pondering the plan that would become Lend-Lease, and Hitler was deciding to crush the Soviet Union, the British had shifted from defence to offence in the Mediterranean.[17] When the Italians attacked Greece in October 1940, British strategists initially saw it as a chance to protect the Middle East. Air Marshal Longmore independently decided to send an RAF squadron to help the Greeks, but the Defence Committee's concern was to secure the island of Crete as a sea and air base that would act as an outer bulwark for Egypt. Within a few days, however, Churchill began to advocate more significant help, including financial aid and the despatch of more units from the RAF. The chiefs of staff agreed with him that there were sound political and military reasons for supporting Greece. The UK had guaranteed the country's security in 1939; Greek resistance might encourage the Turks to resist a future Axis onslaught around the eastern Mediterranean; and, if Greece could be defended, it might – as the Germans also realized – provide a crucial base for British bombers.

In Cairo, where Eden was visiting General Wavell, it looked a lot like the prime minister was getting distracted by another expeditionary adventure. Wavell now disclosed to the war secretary that he had his own plans for an attack in the Western Desert, followed by a siege of Italian East Africa. He hoped that by juggling his forces in time and space, he'd be able to defeat the numerically superior Italians in both places. Eden told Churchill of Wavell's plans to argue him off sending too much support to Greece, but he, Wavell and Longmore all accepted that the British would have to do something to help. They agreed to despatch additional RAF squadrons, even though this delayed operations in Egypt, as well as an infantry brigade to garrison Crete. When Wavell's offensive finally got under way, however, it proved unexpectedly successful. That opened up new possibilities on both sides of the Mediterranean.

The attack was launched on 9 December by the two divisions that made up the Western Desert Force, under Lieutenant General Richard O'Connor. The 7th Armoured Division had trained extensively in desert conditions, and the 4th Indian Division was the first formation to be sent overseas from the Raj. Aggressive action from RAF fighters and the bombing of Italian airfields allowed the attackers to move forward undetected. They took the Italians completely by surprise. Indian infantry accompanied by heavy Matilda tanks attacked the fortified camps around Sidi Barrani, while the lighter tanks of the armoured division moved round to cut off the single coast road to the west. Unexpectedly involved in a fight for which few had any heart, 38,300 Italian and Libyan troops surrendered.[18]

A delighted Churchill told ministers, 'In Wavell we have got a winner' and declared that the battle would 'make repercussions all round the Mediterranean and through the whole Middle East and as far as Moscow'.[19] They certainly reached Berlin. In early January 1941, Hitler decided that he would have to send two German divisions to hold the line in Libya. He hadn't changed his mind about attacking Egypt, but he couldn't allow the British to run riot in North Africa.

With the Western Desert attack a success, Wavell continued with his existing plans to transfer the 4th Indian Division southwards to join the attack on Italian East Africa. O'Connor had to pause any follow-up pursuit, much to his frustration, while Australian troops took the Indians' place. As signs of a German advance through the Balkans grew, the chiefs of staff and the prime minister pressed Wavell to finish off the victory in the desert and to complete the conquest of East Africa as quickly as possible.

O'Connor now converted what had started as a raid in force into a major offensive into Libya. The Italians were pursued back to the more heavily fortified bases at Bardia (taken on 5 January 1941) and Tobruk (22 January). With the Italian army now in full retreat, O'Connor despatched his armoured division across the base of the Jebel Akhdar peninsula to cut off their escape. Its advance elements reached the coast at Beda Fomm just ahead of the Italians on 5 February. Over the next two days, as the Italians failed to break through to safety, a 15-mile traffic jam of guns and transport built up along the coast road, punctuated by billowing smoke as British tanks and armoured cars swept in from the desert and shot up the trapped vehicles. Benghazi was taken on 6 February. The next day, the surrounded Italian troops on the coast surrendered. Since the start of the campaign, at a cost of fewer than 2,000 casualties, the British had captured 130,000 prisoners, nearly 400 tanks and over 800 guns. Just up the coast, at El Agheila, the

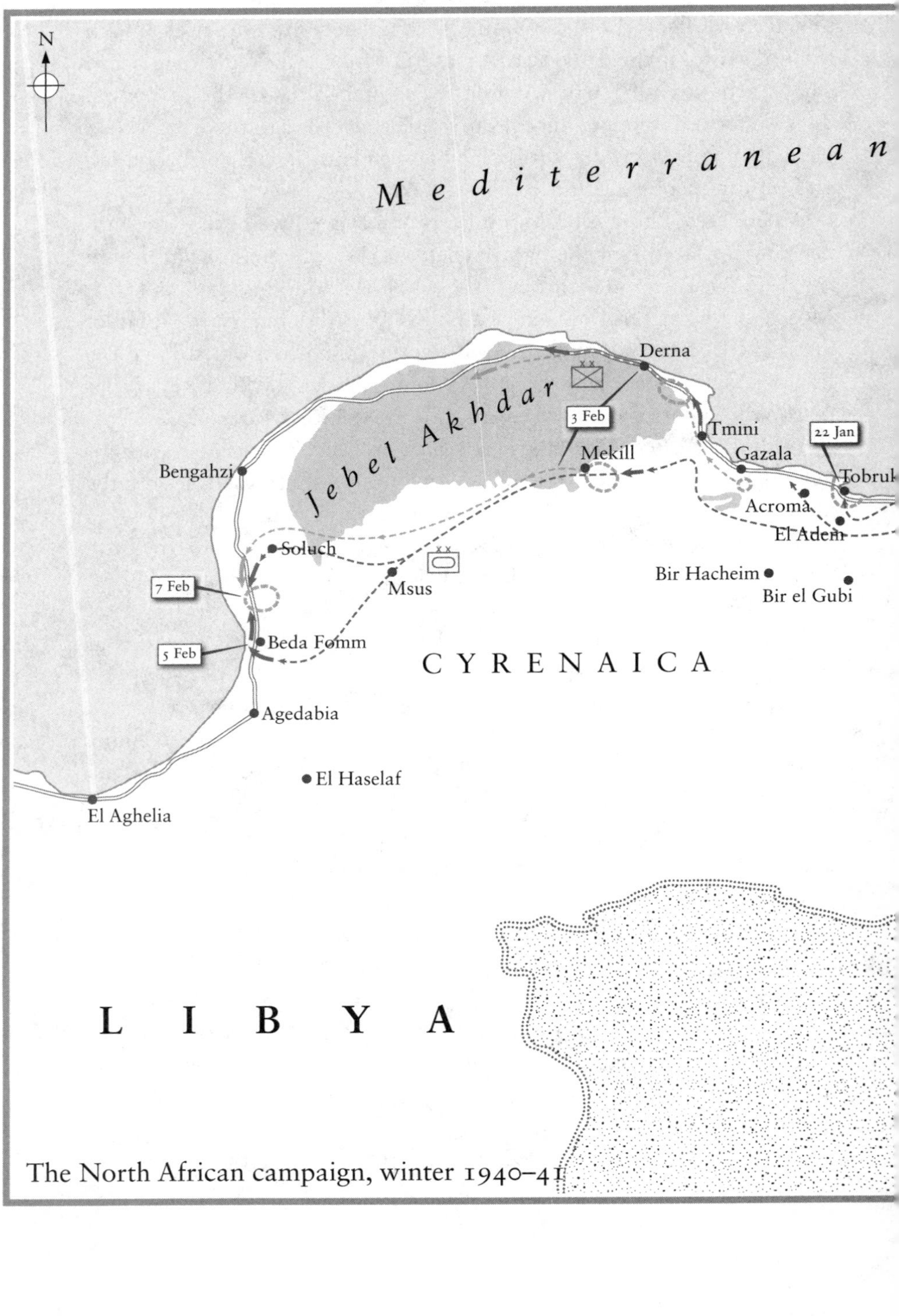

N

M e d i t e r r a n e a n

Derna

3 Feb

Tmini

22 Jan

Gazala

Mekill

Tobruk

Bengahzi

Jebel Akhdar

Acroma

El Adem

Soluch

Bir Hacheim

Msus

Bir el Gubi

7 Feb

CYRENAICA

5 Feb

Beda Fomm

Agedabia

El Haselaf

El Aghelia

LIBYA

The North African campaign, winter 1940–41

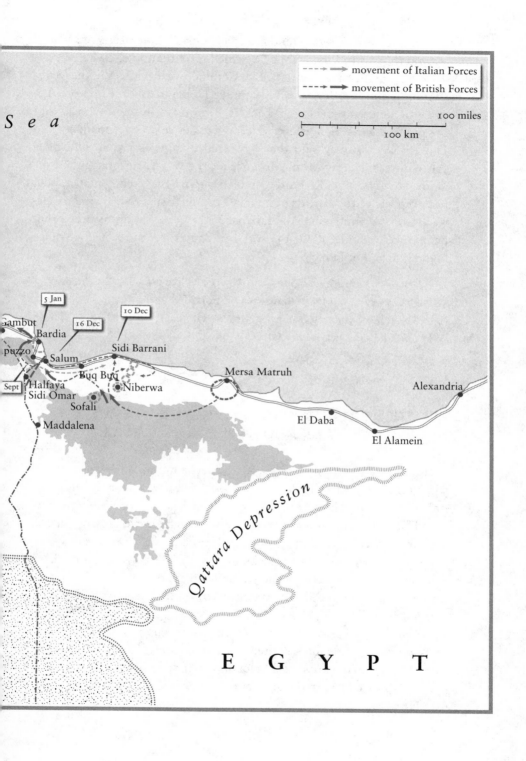

S e a

movement of Italian Forces
movement of British Forces

100 miles
100 km

5 Jan

ambut
Bardia

16 Dec

10 Dec

puzzo
Salum

Sidi Barrani

Mersa Matruh

Alexandria

Sept
Halfaya
Sidi Omar

Buq Buq
Niberwa

Sofali

El Daba

Maddalena

El Alamein

Qattara Depression

E G Y P T

pursuit was halted. O'Connor's troops were exhausted and their vehicles in dire need of repair, and the chiefs of staff had instructed Wavell to hold the line in Libya while he turned his attention elsewhere.

The dramatic successes of British Commonwealth forces in the Mediterranean and North Africa brought, as Home Intelligence reported, a sense of 'general satisfaction' back in Britain.[20] Churchill's stock with the public was as high as ever. Eighty-five per cent of respondents in a January 1941 survey said they approved of him as prime minister.[21] Journalists, including Alan Moorehead, the war correspondent of the *Daily Express*, and Richard Dimbleby, the BBC commentator, sent back reports of the crowds of hungry Italians desperately trying to surrender to the rampaging Australians. Mass-Observation recorded that people were joking about the war in a way they had not done since before the Fall of France:

> Every navy has its own drink. The Americans like rye whiskey, the British has its rum, but the Italians stick to port.
>
> Mussolini is having a bad Christmas. He can't even cook a turkey because he can't get hold of Greece.[22]

Perhaps you had to be there.

'THE TRUTH WAS HOWEVER, THAT WE HAD STARTED NO FIRES AT ALL'

Victory in the Western Desert stood out even more clearly in comparison with the failure of Britain's other offensive campaigns. After it was unleashed to attack targets in Germany in May 1940, Bomber Command had spent the summer and early autumn trying to destroy precise economic targets: oil plants, communications and aircraft factories. In comparison with German attacks during the Battle of Britain, these raids were small, inaccurate and – despite an almost total lack of opposition from the ground defences – inflicted no damage on the German war machine.[23]

Between mid-1940 and mid-1941, the consensus among the air staff and bomber commanders shifted, in fits and starts, away from precision attacks and towards the destruction of 'industrial areas' of German cities. This owed less to the growing awareness of how difficult precise targets were to hit, and more to British observations of German achievements during the Blitz. In its heaviest raids, with plenty of high explosive and incendiary bombs, the Luftwaffe had managed to cause a lot of damage to entire chunks of a city. Industrial plants were hard to hit and surprisingly resilient, but the homes, lives and will of those who laboured in them were much more vulnerable. Admittedly, the Germans had not managed to break British morale, but with enough planes and bombs, and against a population that lacked Britons' steely resolve, Bomber Command should be able to inflict major economic damage by killing and demoralizing German workers.[24]

By the end of 1940, Bomber Command was struggling to achieve any visible results. The arrival of the heavy aircraft that the RAF had ordered in 1936 – the Stirling, Manchester and Halifax – was delayed by the priority given to defensive fighters before the war and during the Battle of Britain. Instead, Bomber Command remained reliant on the Whitley, the Hampden and the Wellington: aircraft that were similar in performance terms to those now blitzing Britain. Like their German equivalents, the British aircraft carried a relatively small bomb load by the standards set later in the war, but they were even fewer in number and they had to travel much further. Between August 1940 and June 1941, the Luftwaffe dropped more than 31,000 tons of bombs on the UK. Between August 1940 and February 1941, the RAF managed only 9,000 tons in return. Proportionately, they had even less effect.[25] As with the Germans, bad weather reduced the number of sorties the British could fly and increased the rate of accidents among inexperienced crews. Unlike the Luftwaffe, British navigators lacked the assistance of radio direction technology to guide them to the place they were meant to be attacking.

Without such help, the difficulties of night-time navigation over a blacked-out Europe were immense. Precision bombing was basically impossible. When the RAF attacked the two oil plants at Gelsenkirchen in December 1940, for example, with nearly 300 aircraft, most of the bombs fell so far away that their craters could not even be seen on subsequent aerial photographs of the factories. No significant damage was done.[26] Area bombing was no easier, because British bombers still struggled to find whole cities. A Luftwaffe survey of south-west Germany for the year May 1940 to May 1941 found that 'just under 50% of bombs fell in open country, 20% in residential areas, 11.2% on communications, 8.2% on industrial objectives, 5.2% on military objectives, and 1.1% on inland harbours and waterways'. So dispersed was this effort that the Germans assumed that they were randomly aimed nuisance raids aimed at damaging morale.[27] When in December the British tried to launch a large-scale attack against the industrial centre of Mannheim, in response to the raids on Coventry and Bristol, only 101 aircraft of the 235 planned got airborne, thanks to bad weather. Their attack, scattered over the whole of Mannheim, killed 34 people and damaged 476 houses.[28]

For the crews involved, this second winter of bombing was a cold, lonely and terrifying business, but not one that was necessarily disheartening. The logbook of Flight Sergeant Guy Brisbane, then a navigator for Whitley bombers in 51 Squadron, for example, recorded a series of apparently successful missions against a wide variety of targets, including aerodromes in Norway, oil tanks at Hamburg, the oil refinery at Salzburgen and blast furnaces in Dusseldorf and Essen. In the period from April 1940 to July 1941, only twice did Brisbane's crew acknowledge having failed to locate their target, and only once did they bomb by 'dead reckoning' – releasing their bombs through thick cloud cover in the calculation that they were over the target. By October 1940, his accurate course finding and calm head had earned him a Distinguished Flying Medal.[29] When he reflected on his experiences later, however, Brisbane believed they had been deceiving themselves:

> I can remember hearing a new rear gunner in a crew of which I was a member, describing to the intelligence officer the numerous fires we had started at Oslo airfield during an attack in 1940. The truth was however, that we had started no fires at all. What the rear gunner had seen were incendiary bombs burning themselves out on the rocky surface of the airfield. He had not seen an incendiary burning before. I can also recall hearing tales of great fires in the target area which I am convinced were nothing more than a haystack burning in open fields.[30]

In October 1940, Sir Charles Portal moved from the head of Bomber Command to become chief of the air staff. He was replaced by Air Marshal Sir Richard Peirse. Peirse liked the idea of precision bombing but recognized some of the difficulties involved. Over the winter, Churchill complained to both Peirse and Portal about how little Bomber Command was achieving. Where was his decisive offensive? In

December, buoyed by a mistaken estimate that bombing had damaged German oil production, Portal seized the chance to prove the Command's usefulness by issuing a new directive that would concentrate its efforts entirely on knocking out the German oil industry. This was approved by the chiefs of staff and War Cabinet and given to Peirse in mid-January, with the proviso that when the weather was not good enough to hit the oil plants, he should go after industrial areas instead. In practice, Bomber Command had neither the equipment nor the skill to attack either of these targets in the midst of the grim winter weather. The oil plan didn't even get off the ground. As the spring of 1941 approached, Britain's main offensive weapon had thus far proved completely useless.[31]

SOE's attempts to set Europe ablaze were also sputtering out. The problem was the inverse relationship between Axis success and the willingness of the population of Occupied Europe to engage in acts of active resistance. German successes meant that co-operation and collaboration often seemed the most pragmatic choice for the inhabitants of the lands of the new Nazi *Grossraum*. Despite the problems caused by the economic blockade, sometimes they were actually better off under German occupation: in Holland, for example, levels of employment and wages were higher in 1941 than they had been the year before. Even where the will to resist remained, creating the clandestine organizations on which subversion would depend was, by its nature, a painstaking and time-consuming task. The speed of the Nazi success in 1939–40 had left little time to build the sort of 'stay behind' networks out of which successful subversive groups might quickly have grown. Those countries in which there had been most time to work – Czechoslovakia and Poland – were also the furthest away, and establishing effective resistance movements proved very difficult during 1940 and 1941.[32] It was February 1941 before the RAF parachuted the first three SOE agents into Poland. Three months later, the Executive put forward a plan to provide equipment for the underground movements in France, Poland and Czechoslovakia. It would have required the wholesale redirection of Bomber Command to the task of dropping supplies. This shift of strategic priorities was inconceivable and the scheme was rejected, but the idea of a European popular uprising would remain a central part of British strategy well into 1942.[33]

'GLAD FOR THE PROMISES AND PLEDGES FOR THE FUTURE'

Analysing domestic reactions to the announcement of Roosevelt's plans for Lend-Lease, Home Intelligence suggested that:

> On the one hand, people are glad for the promises and pledges for the future; on the other, they feel that achievement has not kept pace with the promises. This has tended to make a number 'curiously uninterested in American developments' while others draw cynical comparisons with the last war.[34]

For ministers and officials too, the question of whether promises could be turned into achievements would remain central to Anglo-American relations for the rest of the war.

For Churchill, a determination to get the Americans involved in the war had not precluded the seizure of political advantage at home. On 12 December, Lord Lothian died suddenly, a victim of acute kidney failure, for which, as a Christian Scientist, he had refused treatment. At this crucial moment in transatlantic history, Churchill had to choose a new ambassador for Washington. Whom would he pick to convince the Americans that the British were really a modern, egalitarian society that was fully committed to beating Nazism? The prime minister's first choice was the aged defeatist David Lloyd George. When he said he was too ill to go to Washington, Churchill's second choice was that stalwart man-of-the-people, Lord Halifax. Up until this point, Churchill and Bracken had shied away from pushing Halifax out, worried about the reaction from their fellow Conservatives. After the battlefield successes at Taranto and Sidi Barrani, the strength of public support for the government was enough for them to act. When an appalled Halifax tried to demure, Churchill told him not only that going to America was his national duty, but that he was politically doomed as a 'Guilty Man' if he stayed in the UK. Halifax had no choice. In mid-January, he duly set off across the Atlantic, carried in the newly launched battleship HMS *King George V* to make sure he arrived safely.

Once again, Churchill had used a foreign posting to dispose of a beaten enemy. Halifax's departure also allowed him to appoint Eden as foreign secretary and a member of the War Cabinet. To the prime minister's Tory critics, it was obvious that Churchill just wanted yes-men to nod through his strategic excesses.[35] Yet Halifax was also a high-profile figure who could be trusted to get on with Roosevelt and to run the crucial embassy in Washington, which he did faithfully and with some skill for the rest of the war.

To begin with, however, Halifax was something of a public relations disaster in the United States. Unlike Lothian, he had little feel for US politics. Aloof, aristocratic and effortlessly superior, he was easily caricatured by the isolationist press as the embodiment of everything Americans hated about the British Empire. Halifax returned the feeling with interest. Like many of the British ruling elite, he regarded America as a nation of adolescent barbarians. As he recorded in his diary, they were 'very crude and semi-educated ... national life has been pretty easy for them and they shrink from things that are hard'.[36] Like other British visitors, Halifax was initially baffled by his first encounters with the 'system' of government in Washington. It was all so different from the carefully ordered bureaucracy of Whitehall – so much jockeying for the attentions of a sickly president, so much obsession with public opinion, so little clarity from the top and so much apparently inconsequential talking on the telephone.

Churchill had no intention of Halifax taking the lead – as Lothian had done – in driving forward the connection with America. On the contrary, this was an area of the war in which both the prime minister and the president expected to take personal hold of the reins. Having committed himself to Lend-Lease, Roosevelt now despatched his own men to London to start to put the policy into action. Churchill dedicated himself to winning them over to Britain's cause.

The first to arrive, the president's friend and factotum Harry Hopkins, reached London just as Halifax was packing his bags on 8 January 1941. A self-made man and ardent New Dealer, who had initially wanted America to maintain its isolation from the European war, Hopkins called himself 'a catalytic agent between two prima donnas'.[37] Churchill saw him as his direct line to Roosevelt and, using the full force of his oratory and charm, laid out Britain's strategic situation, plans for the future and need for support, as well as his own desire for a personal meeting with the president. Hopkins was duly impressed, and became an advocate of immediate aid for Britain.[38]

Close on Hopkins' heels came other emissaries from Roosevelt. A

new ambassador, John Winant, arrived at the start of March to replace
Joseph Kennedy, whose anti-British reports had done much to sap official confidence in the UK's ability to hold out in 1940. Winant was a
rare thing, a Republican who did not despise Roosevelt. Worried that
he might run against him as a moderate opponent in the 1936 election,
the President had appointed Winant as the head of America's new
Social Security Administration, and from 1939 he had been director
of the International Labour Organization in Geneva, where he had
already met Britain's Labour leaders. Winant would remain American
ambassador in London for the rest of the war.

Shortly after Winant came Averell Harriman, a banker and businessman whom the president appointed as 'expeditor' of Lend-Lease.
Like Hopkins, Winant and Harriman also had to be impressed, not
only with Britain's determination to fight on, but also with the understanding that, as Churchill told Harriman, there was 'no prospect of
victory until the United States came into the war'.[39] Like Hopkins, they
were also brought into the louche, late-night world of Churchill's inner
circle. Both became intimately involved with Churchill's family: Winant
had an affair with the prime minister's daughter, Sarah; Harriman
with his daughter-in-law, Pamela.

With positive reports flowing in from his representatives in London,
Roosevelt was soon persuaded that Lend-Lease was a matter of urgency,
but it did not mean that the British were now given an easy ride. On the
contrary, as Kingsley Wood remarked at the time, America's intention
was 'to strip us of everything we possess in payment for what we are
about to receive'.[40] Morgenthau insisted that the British reveal the full
state of their finances for public discussion in Congress, and emphasized that while Lend-Lease was under consideration, the UK would
have to divest itself of further US assets to pay for current orders. In
January and February 1941, British payments were kept up on a
hand-to-mouth basis by Canadian purchases of sterling and $300 mil-
lion borrowed from the Belgian government-in-exile. The British were
also, however, encouraged to keep making contracts with American
manufacturers, with down-payments funded from small loans from the
US government, under the assurance that these would subsequently be
brought under the terms of Lend-Lease. With what now seems astonishing wishful thinking, the British trusted that this would be the case.
As the Bill approached final approval, it became clear that in fact

Lend-Lease would not be extended retrospectively to cover any of Britain's existing commitments in the United States. Instead, it would have to continue to find dollars from somewhere to pay what it already owed.[41]

All this was frustrating and humiliating for British ministers and officials, but as before, there was no choice but to acquiesce. Lend-Lease had to be passed, and that passage depended on demonstrating that the UK was willing to sacrifice its own prosperity in order to defeat Hitler. For all the disappointments thus far, the securing of American economic assistance in the future was the only way to secure the victory to which Churchill had committed the British in 1940. At the start of 1941, Sir Arthur Purvis totalled up what he thought the UK would need from America over the next three years: it came to $18.85 billion – about ten times what the British Commonwealth had spent on official orders from the USA since September 1939, and about eight times the value of the assets that the Americans thought the British still had in the States. When Purvis conveyed these figures to Roosevelt and Morgenthau on 10 February 1941, neither of them batted an eyelid. Indeed, Purvis was encouraged to scale up his estimates of British requirements. The larger they were, the more money the US government would secure through Lend-Lease to spend on expanding American arms production.[42]

The eventual passage of the Lend-Lease Act into law on 11 March did not mark an end to British financial travails. Congress still had to approve the appropriations of money that would allow the US government to put the new scheme into operation. To ensure that happened, Morgenthau demanded that the British prove their commitment to the cause by selling off the American Viscose Corporation, a huge synthetic materials manufacturer owned by the mighty Courtaulds textile empire. Sold at speed, AVC went for $54 million, a fraction of what it was worth. On 13 March, Sir Frederick Phillips was told that another US warship was on its way to South Africa to pick up still more of the Sterling Area's gold – in this case, millions of pounds that had already been allocated to cover British purchases from Canada. At the end of the month, negotiations of the leases for the island bases that had been swapped for destroyers in summer 1940 were also completed, entirely on American terms. In some ways, the British got off lightly. Roosevelt rejected suggestions from his administration that *all* British assets in North and South America ought to be liquidated before Lend-Lease went through. But the existing dollar commitments made sure that this was the path on which the Americans had put the British in any case.[43]

Lend-Lease was all about promises for the future. Congress initially authorised $7 billion of Lend-Lease appropriations. If all of this money had been spent on arms, it would have been the equivalent of about a quarter of British defence spending in 1941.[44] These were not financial grants to the British, but rather allocations of money to be spent by the US authorities to meet the needs of America's allies. In practice, the amount of aid that actually reached Britain in 1941 was worth just over $1 billion. Two-thirds of this went on food, raw materials and machinery. The munitions and military equipment that reached Britain via Lend-Lease in 1941 were worth only $17.6 million; they made up only 1 per cent of the arms used by British Empire forces that year, compared to 7 per cent from cash contracts placed in the US before the introduction of Lend-Lease.[45] Simply by removing Britain's major balance of payments problem for the duration of the war, however, Lend-Lease made the task of supplying the UK much easier. It also promised, over time, to provide the money to turn America into the sort of arsenal that the democracies really needed.

The British too had promises to make, but not yet. One of the many distinctively Rooseveltian features of the Lend-Lease Act was that while it made clear that payment would be expected for American largesse, it left the form and terms of reimbursement entirely in the hands of the president. The Act was passed without any exact specification from Roosevelt about what the 'consideration' that the British would have to offer up in return should be. It took some time for the US administration to work out exactly what it wanted, but by the summer it would follow the line set by the US State Department, for whom British dependence on American aid offered a unique opportunity to force the UK to give up imperial preference and financial controls at the end of the war. Britain would be made to fit in with an American vision of an economically liberal new world. The question of how exactly the Americans would make the British do this would drag on for the rest of the war.[46]

Economic discrimination was a divisive issue for the British government. A number of Conservative ministers, including Amery, Wood and Beaverbrook, were committed to imperial preference as the glue binding together the British Commonwealth – a grouping with just as much common interest and right to exist as the United States of

America. Within Labour ranks, there was a split between Hugh Dalton and Ernest Bevin, who thought that controls would be part of building a planned economy, and Arthur Greenwood, who was more willing to subscribe to America's liberalizing agenda. Most ministers and officials were not passionate believers in Empire or free trade, but they were extremely worried about a post-war future in which Britain, with its wealth and investments worn away and vast sterling debts incurred, would have to rebalance its trade in the face of an inevitable post-war slump. The only practical solution would be the permanent continuation of economic controls and the maintenance of the Sterling Area as an economic bloc.[47]

For most of 1940 and 1941, this was what John Maynard Keynes believed too. After the Germans announced the 'New Order' for how the economy of Europe would work after they won the war in summer 1940, Keynes was asked to prepare a response to it by the Ministry of Information. The 'New Order' was a plan for economic union, protected by currency controls and import tariffs, which promised to bring stability for the entire continent (provided its members agreed to subordinate their economies to Berlin). It was heavily influenced by German perceptions of the success of the wartime Sterling Area.

Keynes thought the Germans were right. British propaganda could question German motives but not the assumption that free trade was dead and that the future lay in heavily protected economic blocs. Britain would have to maintain the Sterling Area after the fighting finished, and it was already creating similar arrangements with European countries outside the Nazi orbit. Any counter-offer to that put forward by the Germans would have to be based on more of the same. What would make the British system better, in Keynes' view, was its international power and morality: unlike Germany, the British could offer a trading bloc that had much better access to global resources, intended to repay its wartime debts and aimed at better lives for everyone, not economic exploitation for the sake of destruction and pillage. To sum up Britain's fundamentally decent intentions, Keynes referred to a recent speech by Bevin in which he had argued that Britain's domestic war aim should be 'social security'.[48] This was what Keynes thought Britain could offer the world – but security would be based in economic protectionism.

Churchill, for all his devoted guardianship of the British Empire, was agnostic on the principle of imperial preference. He was still enough of an Edwardian Liberal to believe in free trade, and he was happy for the Americans to lead a multilateral bonfire of tariffs. He was not, however, willing to see Britain give up its advantages unilaterally, or to prioritize trade discussions over the unity of the Conservative Party. Like most of Whitehall, the prime minister's preferred approach was to drag out discussions over the 'consideration' for Lend-Lease for as long as possible in the hope that it would vanish if he could bring America into the war.

While the Lend-Lease Bill and its appropriations were making their way through Congress, the British and American military had been engaged on their secret strategic discussions in Washington. In preparing for the talks, the Americans expected that the British would try to turn the informal alliance that was developing between the two countries to their own imperial advantage. As a presidentially approved briefing note warned the staff officers taking part:

> we cannot afford, nor do we need, to entrust our national future to British direction. It is to be expected that proposals of the British representatives will have been drawn up with chief regard for the British Commonwealth. Never absent from British minds are their post-war interests, commercial or military. We should likewise safeguard our own eventual interests.[49]

When the discussions began, the gap in perspectives duly emerged. In line with Admiral Stark's 'Plan Dog', in the event of a world war against Germany, Italy and Japan, the Americans wanted to concentrate the first efforts of a future US-UK alliance on the war against Germany. That would mean adopting a defensive stance in the Pacific and sending the bulk of the US fleet to the Atlantic. Yet desperate as it was for more escort vessels, the British Admiralty didn't really need any more capital ships to help it in bottling up the German navy. Instead, it wanted the Americans to keep their fleet in the Pacific and to commit some units to Singapore to deter a Japanese advance on South-East Asia. This was just the sort of devious behaviour the US delegates had expected: the British were ignoring the fact that they couldn't win the war against Germany by themselves, and trying to get the gullible Americans to do the job of defending their empire.

Churchill, eager to get the Americans more involved in the war any

15. (*top*) The beach at La Panne, near Dunkirk, following the British retreat, June 1940. German soldiers were astonished at how many vehicles the highly motorized British army had.

16. (*bottom*) Armourers reload the ammunition in a Hawker Hurricane of 310 (Czechoslovak) Squadron, RAF Duxford, during the Battle of Britain.

17. (*above*) An ARP warden
and his dog survey bomb
damage in Poplar, East
London, 1941. Behind the
crater is a damaged, but
surviving, surface shelter.

18. (*right*) A woman sleeps
next to a broken latrine in
a north London gymnasium
converted into a temporary
air-raid shelter, 1940.

19. (*above*) A German Heinkel He-111 bomber, shot down by 92 Squadron RAF, lies by the side of the road in Somerset, 14 August 1940.

20. (*below*) Women war workers at a Royal Ordnance factory 'somewhere in Britain' stack shells, 1941.

21. (*above*) A crowd of
Italian soldiers taken prisoner
by Australian troops in Libya,
January 1941. The
destruction of an Italian army
in Libya was the first major
land victory for British
Commonwealth forces.

22. (*left*) British soldiers look
out from the rooftop of the
embassy in Baghdad, June
1941. After a coup in April,
the government of Rashid Ali
sought to drive out the
British, who responded by
reoccupying the country.

23. (*top*) Merchant ships being unloaded at a British port. Britain's access to supplies from around the world was crucial to its ability to fight the war.

24. (*bottom*) Valentine tanks of 17th/21st Lancers, 6th Armoured Division, prepare to be inspected by the king, September 1941. During 1941, Britain made more tanks than Germany, Italy and Japan combined.

25. An enormous poster in Canterbury advertises the city's War Weapons Week, part of the National Savings campaign. Here, as elsewhere, the war is depicted as a moral crusade in which everyone should take part.

26. (*above*) Workers at a tank factory in Smethwick, Staffordshire celebrate the despatch of military equipment to the Soviet Union. British tanks and aircraft made a real difference to the Red Army at the end of 1941.

27. (*left*) Winston Churchill watches from HMS *Prince of Wales* as President Roosevelt departs from their Atlantic meeting aboard the USS *Augusta*, August 1941. Churchill had agreed to a set of Allied war aims. Roosevelt had not agreed to join the war.

28. A Japanese aerial photograph of the first attack on HMS *Prince of Wales* and HMS *Repulse* (bottom), 11.13, 10 December 1941. *Repulse* has just been hit by a bomb. Two and a half hours later, both ships had been sunk.

way he could, hadn't even wanted the issue raised. He told the British mission to accept the American proposals and drop the discussion of Singapore. During March 1941, just as the Lend-Lease Bill was being passed, the British and Americans signed two 'ABC' agreements: ABC1, that if they were both involved in a global conflict, they would concentrate on defeating Germany before turning to Japan; and ABC2, that the British would have first charge on current American aircraft production until such point as the US was actually at war. For the time being, the US would keep its fleet in the Pacific, moving only a few ships to the Atlantic in order to release British vessels for despatch to Singapore. Both sides expected that this would be a big enough threat to dissuade the Japanese from starting a war.[50] These agreements indicated a further strengthening of the Anglo-American relationship, but they did nothing to lay out a path by which America might actually become a combatant. As the spring went on, and the British faced crises in the Mediterranean and the Atlantic, American involvement in the fighting looked as far off as ever.

'WE SHOULD GO FORWARD WITH A GOOD HEART'

During the first months of 1941, British policy towards Greece underwent a major change.[51] In early January, there were ominous signs of imminent German intervention in the Mediterranean. German troops were moving into Bulgaria, and German aircraft attacked a convoy sent through the Mediterranean, badly damaging the aircraft carrier HMS *Illustrious*. Churchill decided that the same reasons of strategy and politics that had made it necessary to help the Greeks in November now made it necessary to send much more extensive support – even though the Greeks did not actually want a British expeditionary force on their soil in case it precipitated a German invasion. Churchill told the Defence Committee that although 'the help which we could bring ... would not be enough to save them ... there was no other course open to us but to make certain that we had spared no effort to help the Greeks who had shown themselves so worthy'.[52] The smashing of Italian forces in Libya had protected Egypt's western flank; this would free up the resources for an expedition to Greece. That might have a big impact strategically if it stiffened up resistance to a German drive through the Balkans.

The prospect of halting the next German advance provided a welcome opportunity to Anthony Eden. In contrast to the War Office, where he had enjoyed being close to the fighting and been able to wield his influence in support of Wavell in the Middle East, Eden found being foreign secretary distinctly dull.[53] He was all too well aware that, just as the army had started to have some successes for the first time, Churchill had managed both to promote him and to move him further away from the war effort. With the prime minister keeping a close grip on Anglo-American relations, there wasn't much for Eden to do at the Foreign Office. Before long, he was complaining that 'There is no control here.'[54] Eden thought that he could construct a Balkan front in which Yugoslavia and Turkey would join Greece to oppose Hitler. At the War Office, he had opposed any distraction from the Middle East. Now, he too advocated greater support for Greece as a means of persuading her neighbours to join her in the fight. It was a very optimistic view, not least because the Turks and the Greeks hated each other. Had Halifax not been displaced, it seems very unlikely that he would have been drawn into such a fantastic scheme. Churchill egged Eden on.

Faced with the agreement of the foreign secretary and the prime minister, the chiefs of staff came round to the idea of intervening in Greece, even though General Dill and the War Office were convinced that there were no spare troops to send, that denuding the Western Desert would endanger Egypt, and that efforts invested in Greece would probably be wasted. On 10 February, Eden and Dill left London for a tour of the region in person to see what could be done. Britain's commanders in the Middle East had already accepted that they would have no choice but to send help to the Greeks. With a German invasion apparently imminent, the Greeks changed their mind about British aid. On 22 February, Eden agreed that the British would despatch troops to assist them, providing that the Greeks withdrew from their exposed positions in the north, which could easily be outflanked by a German move through Yugoslavia, to a defensive line further south. From Athens, Eden travelled on to Ankara, hoping that the promise to Greece could leverage a commitment from the Turks.

Most of the fighting troops that Eden was pledging would come from Australia and New Zealand rather than the United Kingdom. That made it all the more awkward that the Australian premier, Robert Menzies, had arrived in London on 20 February, eager to get reinforcements for the Far East and keen to establish himself at the centre of the imperial war effort. With the bulk of Australia's army deployed to the Mediterranean, he felt it was only fair that the Dominion should have more say in the construction of British strategy, and Menzies argued for the formation of an Imperial War Cabinet. He was impressed by Churchill's restless energy but worried by its implication for strategy, since he believed that the British prime minister had become so obsessed with defeating Germany that he had lost sight of his responsibilities to the Dominions. Menzies agreed with Lloyd George that Churchill was too busy enjoying the war to spend enough time running it.[55]

Eden's initial commitment to the Greeks was met in London with an air of grim resignation. As Sir Alexander Cadogan explained in his diary on 24 February:

> Read Chiefs of Staff report endorsing proposals for a Balkan expedition to help Greece. On all moral and sentimental (and consequently American) grounds, one is driven to the grim conclusion. But it *must*, in the end, be a failure. However, perhaps better to have failed in a decent project than never to have tried at all. A[nthony – Eden] has rather jumped us into this . . . Cabinet at 5. Menzies there. He evidently doubtful but the general sense was to go ahead with it. It's a nasty decision, but I *think* on balance, I agree with it. PM evidently made up his mind.[56]

When he reached Turkey, however, Eden found that while the Turks would quite happily take British money and weapons, they had no intention of supporting Greece if it were invaded. They were not in the front line of any German attack, and they had no immediate need or wish to antagonize Hitler. This wrecked any hope of creating a Balkan front, but Eden nonetheless reported back optimistically to the Cabinet on the positive attitude of the Turks. Back in London, Cadogan was astonished: 'what is he to say now to the Yugoslavs and the Greeks? The former will now of course curl up, and we shall be alone with the Greeks to share their inevitable disaster . . . But he seems quite happy. What's bitten him?'[57] 'This stunt trip', Cadogan concluded the next day, 'is a most disastrous one . . . It's a diplomatic and strategic blunder of the first order.'[58] Yet this was not the end to Eden's recklessness.

Churchill now turned against a Greek expedition. The military prospects looked poor, Eden had failed to deliver on Turkey and Yugoslavia, and with Menzies in London he worried about the imperial politics of the mission. The prime minister urged Eden to find a way out. The foreign secretary, however, having travelled back to Athens, had been met with a rapturous reception from a crowd terrified of an imminent German invasion. On 4 March, even though it was clear that the Greeks were not going to withdraw their forces to more defensible lines as agreed, he formally committed Britain to send an expeditionary force to Greece.

In his diary, Cadogan recorded that Eden's telegram announcing this commitment had occasioned an 'Awkward discussion' in the War Cabinet: 'PM evidently thinks we can't go back on A. and Dill, and I don't think we can – though I would if I could see any better alternative! K. Wood, Alexander and J. Anderson evidently out for A's blood.'[59] As Cadogan explained to Halifax in Washington, news of what Eden had done 'gave rise to mixed emotions in some of the members [of the War Cabinet] – annoyance that they should have been rushed in this way, secret satisfaction that if the thing went really wrong there was a good scapegoat handy!'[60] Churchill argued that they had no choice but to support Eden. Backing down would be a great blow to British prestige. Senior officers, including Dill, had all approved the operation (or at least swallowed their doubts in the belief that the politicians were going to go ahead anyway). On 7 March, he told the War Cabinet that there were good reasons to hope for success despite the odds and that 'we should go forward with a good heart'.[61]

At the same time that he was told to prepare his expedition to Greece, London pressed Wavell to accelerate his campaign against Italian East Africa. If the Italians could be cut off from the sea, their forces in Ethiopia could be starved into surrender, and Roosevelt would be able to declare the region free of hostilities. That would allow US ships to sail through the Red Sea and deliver supplies direct to the Middle East.[62] The initial plans for a long-term siege and Ethiopian uprising were soon superseded by a more conventional military pincer movement. In the north, the advance southwards from Sudan was blocked by Italian troops who fought much harder than their comrades in the Western Desert. It took until mid-March to build up an offensive strong enough to drive them out. The Indian army divisions involved were familiar with the tactics of mountain warfare from the Indian North-west Frontier: they were less used to fighting an opponent well-armed with artillery and automatic weapons. After two weeks of slogging forward from peak to peak, Indian and British troops finally broke through. On 8 April, the port of Massawa surrendered. The Red Sea coast was now clear, and Roosevelt indeed declared the whole of the Indian Ocean area a non-combat zone.[63]

Meanwhile, the advance northwards from Kenya had accelerated as the Italian defences crumbled. The force's commander, Lieutenant General Alan Cunningham (Admiral Cunningham's brother), had originally thought he would have to wait until his supplies were built up and the rains eased in May to launch his offensive. Instead, he managed to improvise a rapid advance through Somaliland, then up into Ethiopia. On 6 April, Cunningham's troops entered Addis Ababa. The offensive had had to struggle with climate and disease as much as Italian opposition: in the year from June 1940, the East African Force suffered only 1,154 dead and wounded in battle, but lost another 74,550 casualties to accidents and illness.[64] The remaining Italian troops were now surrounded in the north of Ethiopia. The last of them did not surrender until 19 May. By then, things had gone badly wrong further north.

'FOR THE MOMENT . . . OUR SUPREME EXERTION'

During the first months of 1941, both the import situation and the naval position in the Atlantic deteriorated. Over the first quarter of 1941, the total tonnage of imports was just over two-thirds what it had been in the equivalent period of the previous year. In February, the Ministry of Shipping announced that total imports in the second year of war would amount to only 31 million tons.

From the start of 1941 the Luftwaffe turned its attention to the west coast ports. The Foche Condors sank more ships in February than at any other point in the war. The *Hipper* set off on another hunting voyage from Brest at the end of January, and the following month, the pocket battleships *Gneisenau* and *Scharnhorst* also sailed into the North Atlantic. That (together with the *Scheer*) made four major

German warships at large in the shipping lanes, as well as the seven commerce raiders roaming further afield. The British could not catch any of them. As the spring approached, the British knew they must also look forward to a new German submarine offensive. Yet their additional military commitments in the Mediterranean imposed still further burdens on the available supply of shipping.

Churchill now sought urgent action to address both the German blockade and the shortage of merchant ships. On 27 February, he told the War Cabinet that the 'effort against this renewed danger' in the Atlantic 'must, for the moment, be our supreme exertion'.[65] Shortly afterwards, he insisted that Bomber Command should switch its attacks temporarily from German industry to ports and U-boat bases in France. Coastal Command was reinforced. On 6 March, in his role as minister of defence, Churchill issued a directive declaring that the 'Battle of the Atlantic' had begun. He sought to inspire a cross-government effort: a campaign against the U-boats and the Condors on the oceans and in their French bases, the development of new weapons to ward off air attack, but also renewed efforts to speed the unloading of ships and clear the backlog of repairs. He also established a new Battle of the Atlantic Committee, which he chaired himself, to oversee all aspects of the campaign.

In fact, the balance of the battle had already altered well before Churchill intervened. In February, Western Approaches Command, the naval headquarters in charge of the nearside of the Atlantic, had moved to a new, purpose-built bunker underneath Derby House in Liverpool, with a new commander, Admiral Sir Percy Noble. He took advantage of the growing number of ships under his command to form permanent escort groups, which trained up together in new tactics developed to counter the submarines. Escorts were increasingly fitted with radio-telephones, improving their ability to communicate with each other. High Frequency Direction Finder (HFDF) and shorter-wave radar sets were being introduced that allowed escorts to track their submerged opponents, as were more effective explosives, star shells and illuminating lights for attacking aircraft. Meanwhile, the Government Code and Cypher School was specifically targeting the German naval Enigma machine in an effort to improve British maritime intelligence.

As the number of ships per escort increased, and escort crews grew more experienced at their work, German submariners found

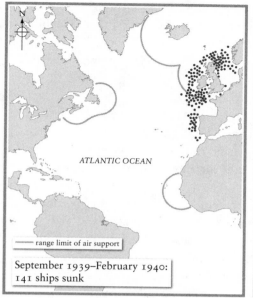

range limit of air support

September 1939–February 1940:
141 ships sunk

range limit of air support

March 1940–August 1940:
174 ships sunk

range limit of air support

September 1940–February 1941:
223 ships sunk

range limit of air support

First heavy attack on
unescorted shipping
at great distance from
U-boat bases

March 1941–August 1941:
225 ships sunk

The Battle of the Atlantic, 1939–41, showing how increased air cover and escorts
around the UK forced U-boats further into the Atlantic and made them less efficient

themselves involved in a serious battle for the first time. During March, U-boat as well as merchant ship losses went up. Five submarines were lost in total, including those captained by Günther Prien, Joachim Schepke and Otto Kretschmer – three of the great U-boat aces of the early war. This set the pattern for the rest of the long campaign in the Atlantic: escorts fighting against submarines as they sought to get among the convoyed merchantmen.

Even more so than for most combat servicemen during the Second World War, those defending the convoys had to cope with a mix of prolonged endurance against the elements interspersed with savage and terrifying combat. The great strain of their job was in constant waiting for an assault on the convoy that might never come. Unlike a bomber or a tank, an escort ship was a home as well as a fighting platform. Even in the best of weather and out of action, life aboard was cramped and uncomfortable. The new Flower corvettes, which did much of the donkey work of convoy protection during the first years of the war, were notoriously unstable in high seas. In the midst of an Atlantic winter, every space on the 200-by-30-ft boats would drip with water. Packed aboard were up to a hundred men, many of them wartime recruits with no naval experience, commanded by officers of the Royal Navy Volunteer Reserve: a mixture of pre-war amateur sailors and hard-bitten former merchantmen. Crewmen flung their grip from railing to railing, or tumbled flailing across the decks. Hot food and drink were essential to survival, but food storage and preparation were primitive and new arrivals would spend most of their time vomiting due to the corvette's violent motion.[66]

The drawn-out tension of awaiting U-boat attacks and the bitter awareness of the consequences for the merchant crews found a release in efforts to hunt down the enemy submarines. Most such searches ended in uncertain frustration, as contact was lost, or depth charges were fired to no discernible result. For embittered crews, there was a grim satisfaction in those rare occasions when they carried the hunt to a successful conclusion. Able Seaman J. E. Needham recalled the destruction of a tanker in a convoy his ship was protecting:

> The sea blazed with spilled fuel and survivors were picked up by the ship's whaler, smothered in diesel and many half dead, their skin burned like bacon. We packed 40 of them in the mess decks, gave them clothes,

many were in the sick bay and two died there. We made our first 'kill' the next day, the Asdic [sonar] picked up an echo and then lost it again ... We waited for hours circling the convoy then came another echo ... A pattern of depth charges was dropped and shortly afterwards the bows came up, grey-green and rusty, men in the water, waving arms. A lot of literature has been written about the 'killer' instinct. I think that day we all had it after seeing the pathetic burned crew of the tanker. There were no survivors picked up from the U-boat 'owing to enemy activity in the area'.[67]

Eventually, the destruction of the submarines was the only solution to the threat from the German blockade, but in the short term there was no relief from the losses being incurred by the merchant fleet. During March, it suffered the heaviest monthly losses of the war so far, with 136 vessels, totalling 517,000 gross weight tons, sunk in the North Atlantic and the waters around the UK.[68] At that rate, a quarter of the fleet currently under UK control would be sunk every year. In April, predictions of imports for the rest of 1941 came down to 28.5 million tons.

No other campaign linked the military and the civil so obviously as the Battle for the Atlantic. While the struggle between convoys and escorts continued, fears of an import crisis forced the government into action at home. A new Port Clearance Committee in Whitehall appointed officials with ministerial powers to cut their way through the chaos on the docks. Ernest Bevin took the opportunity to decasualize dock labour in the west coast ports in an effort to keep dockers on the job.[69] The administration of shipping arrivals with inland distribution was significantly improved after May 1941, when Churchill amalgamated the Ministries of Shipping and of Transport into a new Ministry of War Transport under his old friend Lord Leathers. Meanwhile, the Admiralty had agreed to open the eastern ports to smaller ships. This made organizing cargoes more difficult, but it reduced some of the load on the west coast ports.

At the same time, the rapid decline in the volume of imports forced Britain into stricter import programming. Despite warnings from the Ministry of Shipping, in autumn 1940, the Ministries of Food and Supply, who between them were responsible for almost all Britain's overseas orders, had laid out programmes for the second year of the war based on an annual total of 42 million tons of imports. As the winter wore on, and expectations of what could be brought in decreased, the Ministry of Shipping lacked instructions about what to prioritize, and food lost out. Food imports in the final months of 1940 equated to an annual rate of only 14 million tons.

With complaints about confusion growing, Churchill created a new Import Executive, chaired by the minister of supply, Andrew Duncan, to oversee and improve the flow through Britain's ports. The Executive accepted the Ministry of Food's right to 15.5 million tons of imports, and agreed that if total imports fell below 35 million tons, both ministries' allocations would be reduced in proportion. In the New Year, it became clear that total imports in the second year of the war would be more like 30 million tons. That would leave the Ministry of Food with only just over 13 million tons of imports. The minister of food, Lord Woolton, insisted that 15 million was the absolute minimum for national survival. In practice, the ministry's predictions of minimum possible levels always proved far too pessimistic, but Woolton held a trump card because he could argue that any further cutbacks would wreck morale. This was a case to which Churchill, a strong believer in the connection between belly and belligerence, never failed to listen.[70]

The combination of shipping shortfalls and the diversion of ships to carry emergency troop reinforcements to the Middle East struck particularly hard at British meat imports. To try to make maximum use of the 'reefers' that had been converted into troop transporters, they were put onto a triangular route, carrying soldiers from Britain to South Africa – from where they would continue their journey to the Middle East – then sailing across to Argentina to pick up meat for a return voyage to the UK. Nonetheless, the meat ration was cut back to 1s. 2d. a person a week in January. At the end of the month, Woolton told Churchill the meat ration would have to come down to 1s. per person.[71]

The next day, the prime minister intervened directly to set a new import programme. Assuming a total of 31 million tons during 1941, then both food and supply ministries should get 15 million each. Troopships should be taken out of service if necessary to make sure that meat supplies got through. The Ministry of Supply would have to scale down its plans to match. With Lend-Lease looming on the horizon, Churchill hoped that deliveries of processed raw materials from the States would allow a cut in industrial imports without harming military production. The prioritization of the Ministry of Food's demands at least imposed some sort of system, and it forced the Ministry of Supply to establish a more realistic matching of its requirements to the available shipping. The system of import programming that developed, as run by the new Ministry of War Transport, determined what arrived in the country for the rest of the war.

The British also hoped that the Americans would provide them with the ships to keep their global war going. As Churchill explained at the end of March: 'It is to the United States' building that we must look for relief in 1942.'[72] As soon as Lend-Lease was signed into law, Churchill sent Sir Arthur Salter, an academic and transport expert who had worked with the Americans on shipping in the last war, out to Washington as head of the British Shipping Mission. Salter sought two things: first, the allocation of existing US shipping to transport goods for the UK; and secondly, a huge expansion of American shipbuilding from which the UK would be given a slice. Salter soon grasped that to make things work, he needed to go direct to Roosevelt. The president promised, in typically vague terms, 'two million tons of aid for the democracies'.

Salter's second aim, a big increase in American shipbuilding from which it was hoped Britain would benefit, made a lot of sense in terms of production. Britain's shipbuilders were sometimes accused – at the time and afterwards – of being too outdated to manage the demands of wartime expansion, with owners' greed matched by workers' intransigence over arcane working practices. In fact, despite the poor state of industrial relations within the sector, British ship workers were relatively highly skilled and productive. In a small island with limited space around its port cities and multiple other demands on its resources, however, there was no way to expand output sufficiently to match the numbers of ships that were being sunk. In contrast, American shipbuilding had much more room to grow. By 1941, the US had already started to expand its merchant-ship construction as part of its rearmament programme – although it still built much less tonnage that year than did the United Kingdom – but Salter successfully lobbied for an even more dramatic increase – up to 5 million gross registered tons in 1942, about four times what British yards would manage. Salter recognized that he was in no position to demand a precise portion of this production. Instead, the British simply had to trust that, under Roosevelt's direction, the American administration would see the sense of allocating enough shipping to meet the UK's needs.[73]

'LITTLE ACCOUNT OF REALITIES'

While the shipping situation got worse, disasters struck in the Mediterranean. By March 1941, Malta was being heavily attacked by the Luftwaffe and Italian air force, and a German mechanized division had been successfully transported to Tripoli, where it formed the basis of the Deutsches Afrika Korps, under General Erwin Rommel. Rommel's daring exploits would make him a household name in Britain, but they would actually wreck Axis hopes of defending North Africa. His orders were to hold the line and wait for reinforcements. In the Western Desert, O'Connor and his veterans had been withdrawn to rest and refit, and to provide troops for the Greek expedition. Their place was taken by inexperienced and underequipped formations – one of which, 2nd Armoured Division, had to rely on captured Italian tanks to make up its numbers – under a new commander, Lieutenant General Philip Neame. This force was not ready to defend the gains of the previous winter. Enigma decrypts charted the build-up of Axis units in Tripoli, but they also reassured Wavell in his conviction that it would be a couple of months before his shaky defences had to face a counter-attack. To the south, the final breakthrough at Keren was about to release battle-hardened troops from Eritrea who could be brought north to hold off an offensive.

To the north, over three weeks, the Royal Navy managed to deliver almost 60,000 troops to Greece. There they formed 'W Force', under the command of General Maitland Wilson. Wilson's nickname was 'Jumbo'. Unusually for the British army, this was because he was actually very fat, rather than very small. As the officer commanding Egypt, Wilson had overseen the preparations for the successful offensive against the Italians. Now, with just two infantry divisions – one New Zealand, one Australian – and one armoured brigade, he faced a much more difficult task. The Greeks had none of the logistical or administrative network to support the newly arrived army, the British had to provide their own supplies, and fully equipped and logistically supported German troops were massing in Bulgaria to begin their assault. Wilson's forces were dependent on the vulnerable convoy route from Egypt.

At the end of March, however, this route provided one of the high points of the Royal Navy's Mediterranean war. Forewarned by signals intelligence that the Italian fleet was venturing out to attack the convoys, Admiral Cunningham headed out to meet them with the full strength of his fleet, including the aircraft carrier HMS *Formidable*, which had arrived to replace the damaged *Illustrious*. Torpedo attacks from *Formidable*'s aircraft crippled one Italian heavy cruiser, and after darkness fell, Cunningham used the advantage of having radar to detect the squadron that was coming to the damaged ship's aid. Taking the Italians by surprise, the British opened up with their heavy guns at close range. In total, three Italian heavy cruisers and two destroyers were sunk, and the battleship *Vittorio Veneto* damaged. Cunningham lost one Swordfish torpedo bomber. The victory asserted the Royal Navy's total dominance over the Italian fleet.

In Libya, however, Rommel was not content to sit and wait for reinforcements. Instead he decided to launch an immediate attack, which hit the British defences on the last day of March. German soldiers were only ever a minority of the forces available to Rommel. The great success story of 1941 in the Western Desert was the Italian army, which had managed to rebuild itself almost completely since its disastrous defeat at Beda Fomm. It provided most of the Axis troops and tanks. General Neame had planned a careful withdrawal by his advanced units. Instead, there was a rout. On top of their inadequate weapons and lack of desert experience, his units were badly deployed and were given conflicting orders. Half-way through the battle, Wavell, having lost confidence in Neame, tried to put O'Connor back in charge. The result was further confusion.

In contrast, Axis forces proved much better able to cope with the demands of the desert. Rommel spread his forces out in dispersed attacks. If the British had kept their nerve, that might have allowed them to defeat each isolated Axis sortie. Instead, the unexpected appearance of enemy troops caused panic. Neame and O'Connor were both captured, and their soldiers headed back pell-mell along the coast road. By 11 April, Libya had been completely evacuated, with the exception of the port of Tobruk, where the 9th Australian Division held out with their backs to the sea. All the territorial gains of the winter had been lost.[74] The speed of the disaster had a lasting impact. As Churchill complained to Eden, 'Far more important than the loss of ground is the idea that we cannot face the Germans and that their appearance is enough to drive us back many scores of miles.'[75]

As another German armoured division began to arrive in North Africa, Wavell and the War Office began to plan what to do if the Germans concentrated all their strength against the Middle East, and prepared for a withdrawal from Egypt. When a well-lubricated Churchill found out about these contingency plans, after dinner at Chequers on 27 April, he was incandescent with rage: 'Wavell has 400,000 men,' he shouted. 'If they lose Egypt, blood will flow. I will have firing parties to shoot the generals.'[76] In retrospect, what is more striking is that the War Office did not presume that Britain would lose even if the whole of the Middle East was captured. Providing the home islands were secure and the supply lines across the Atlantic were kept open, they believed, Britain could continue the war.

Now, threats multiplied across the Middle East and Mediterranean and out into the Atlantic. Vichy France seemed to be swinging increasingly into Germany's orbit. Fears revived of a German strike at Gibraltar or the Azores. At the start of April, with the support of the exiled mufti of Jerusalem, the group of pro-German military officers in Iraq known as the Golden Square launched a coup that put the anti-British politician Rashid Ali back into power. The regent of Iraq, Abdul Illah, fled to Basra, where he was taken aboard a British warship. The coup opened the possibility not just of Iraq turning against the British, but of an Arab nationalist uprising that would spread across to Palestine. As the British scraped around for reinforcements and argued about what to do next, Rashid Ali opened negotiations to secure military assistance from the Germans.

While the storm clouds gathered in Iraq, a German hurricane swept through the Balkans. On 6 April, after a British-inspired coup deposed the pro-Axis regent, the Germans crashed into Yugoslavia. That allowed them to outflank the Greek forces on the Bulgarian border and the Aliakmon Line, cutting off large numbers of Greek soldiers and breaking any attempt at an organized defence. General Wilson had the one great advantage of a stream of decrypted information from the Luftwaffe Enigma, which convinced him of the need to get out as quickly as possible and helped him to stay one step ahead of the pursuing Germans. As the RAF withdrew its meagre squadrons, W Force was left without air cover as it fled down the Corinth peninsula. Here, Dunkirk was replayed in miniature. From 23 to 30 April, 50,000 Commonwealth, Greek and Yugoslav soldiers were rescued by the Royal Navy, but they left behind mountains of wrecked equipment and 12,000 casualties. Twenty-six Allied ships were sunk in the course of the evacuation.[77]

In Britain, the defeats in North Africa and Greece, combined with the continuing Blitz and the news of worsening shipping losses, all contributed to anxiety and discontent about the direction of the war. 'Are the Germans always going to beat us whenever we meet them on land?', was a common question, according to Home Intelligence. 'How is it all going to end?'[78] In Parliament too, the failures encouraged serious criticism of the government's direction of the war. Eden was particularly blamed for committing British forces to Greece, but the gossip about the disasters around the Mediterranean also bore out what many of Churchill's enemies had been warning about him since the start of the war: that he was dominating discussion, refusing to listen to advice and interfering in matters that would be better left to commanders on the ground.

At the end of April, the Labour minister Hugh Dalton recorded his conversation over lunch with the Conservative MP Oliver Stanley. Stanley belonged to the same generation of back-from-the-trenches moderate Conservatives as Anthony Eden, and he had once been spoken of as a future party leader. He had been Chamberlain's president of the board of trade, and when Hore-Belisha was kicked out of the War Office in January 1940, Stanley had taken his place. Stanley was the only Conservative to refuse a place in Churchill's coalition in May 1940: he and Churchill loathed each other, and the prime minister managed to combine the offer of being Dominions secretary with a reminder that in his previous ministerial posts, Stanley had established a reputation for being indecisive and lacking drive. Though Stanley had returned to the army, he came back regularly to the Commons to criticize the government.[79]

On this occasion, no sooner had he sat down than Stanley began 'a long tirade against the Prime Minister and the Foreign Secretary'. Eden, he said, was not 'the sort of man who ought to be close to the Prime Minister . . . vain, weak and unreliable'. Although he blamed

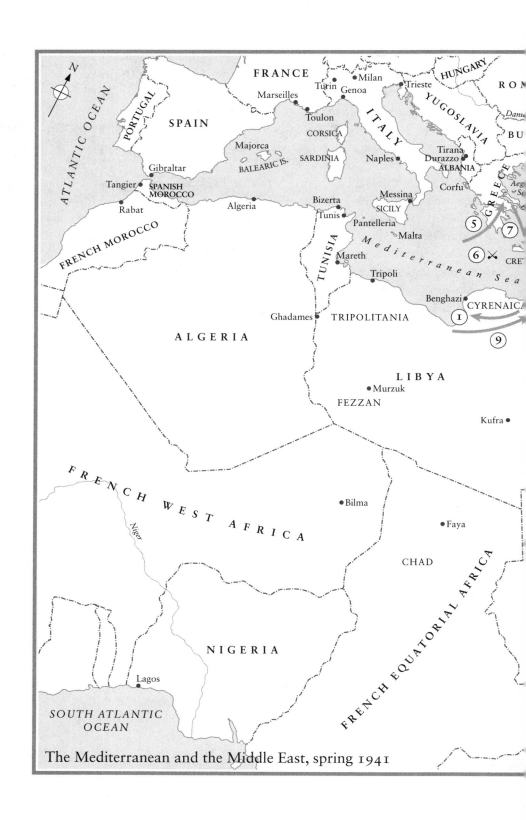

The Mediterranean and the Middle East, spring 1941

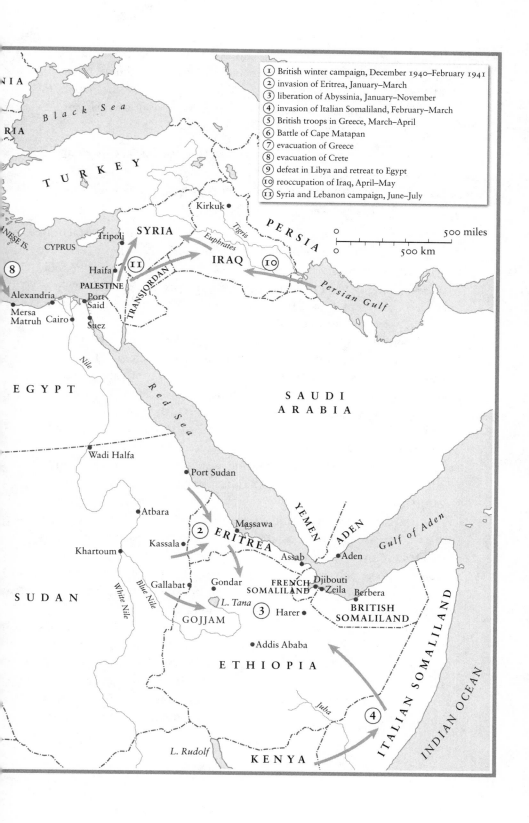

1 British winter campaign, December 1940–February 1941
2 invasion of Eritrea, January–March
3 liberation of Abyssinia, January–November
4 invasion of Italian Somaliland, February–March
5 British troops in Greece, March–April
6 Battle of Cape Matapan
7 evacuation of Greece
8 evacuation of Crete
9 defeat in Libya and retreat to Egypt
10 reoccupation of Iraq, April–May
11 Syria and Lebanon campaign, June–July

500 miles

500 km

Black Sea

TURKEY

NIA

RIA

DANESE IS.

CYPRUS

Tripoli

SYRIA

Kirkuk

PERSIA

Tigris

Euphrates

IRAQ

10

11

Haifa

PALESTINE

Port Said

TRANSJORDAN

Persian Gulf

8

Alexandria

Mersa Matruh

Cairo

Suez

Nile

EGYPT

Red Sea

SAUDI ARABIA

Wadi Halfa

Port Sudan

Atbara

Kassala

2

ERITREA

Massawa

YEMEN

ADEN

Gulf of Aden

Khartoum

Aden

Assab

Gallabat

White Nile

Blue Nile

Gondar

FRENCH SOMALILAND

Djibouti

Zeila

Berbera

SUDAN

L. Tana

3

Harer

BRITISH SOMALILAND

GOJJAM

Addis Ababa

ETHIOPIA

ITALIAN SOMALILAND

INDIAN OCEAN

Juba

4

L. Rudolf

KENYA

Churchill for the Greek disaster, he thought it was the combination of the two emotionally unstable men that was really to blame. Eden, he told Dalton, should never have gone to Athens, where 'he had been cheered in the streets and smothered in roses. How in such surroundings could he keep his judgement clear'?

> He then added, with a not unhappy smile, that many people were gunning after Eden now. He went on to criticise the Prime Minister, on the ground that he still imposed his strategic conceptions on the Chiefs of Staff, and was most impatient of any criticisms.[80]

Stanley told Dalton that he would definitely make a speech attacking the government in the forthcoming debate on intervention in Greece. Even Dalton, who loved to collect gossip of all sorts about his colleagues, thought he was being bizarrely indiscreet. Yet Stanley was plainly in ebullient mood. If Churchill and Eden went down together, who knew what possibilities might open up?

The debate was scheduled for 6 and 7 May 1941 – almost exactly a year to the day since the Norway debate that had resulted in Chamberlain being deposed, as Jock Colville, Churchill's private secretary, helpfully reminded him. The prime minister insisted on crushing the opposition by demanding that the debate be turned into a motion of confidence in the government. However bad things were, few MPs were so disgruntled that they were willing to run the risk of giving succour to the enemy while the fighting was still raging in the Middle East. The Conservative backbenches in particular were reluctant to go against their party leader now that he had lined himself up behind Eden. Instead, the attacks on the government would be led by two men who were easily dismissed as awkward has-beens, Leslie Hore-Belisha and David Lloyd George.

Opening the debate, Eden gave a very poor speech that was badly received by the House. At the end of the first day, Attlee came to his rescue with a speech that even Dalton thought was surprisingly effective. On the second day, Lloyd George rose to launch a rambling attack on the government and demand that Churchill form a War Cabinet of 'ordinary men', without departmental responsibilities, who could provide him with better strategic advice. Churchill closed the debate with a furious response, refusing to change the manner in which he ran the war, comparing Lloyd George to Pétain (a devastating label, because everyone knew the old man's preference for a negotiated peace), and telling the House that it should expect not just 'blood, toil, tears and sweat' but also 'mistakes, shortcomings and disappointments' before victory was achieved. The government won by 447 votes to 3. Stanley did not speak, and walked into the 'aye' lobbies with the rest of the government's supporters.[81]

The sledgehammer use of a vote of confidence did not halt the criticisms of Churchill. Many Conservative MPs still longed for a 'sound' leader, and the suggestion that the prime minister must somehow be separated from the conduct of the war remained a standard line for his opponents for many months to come. As the summer went on, and Churchill's promises that America would be lured into the war went unfulfilled, he was conscious of his political vulnerability. Yet a comparison with the Norway debate showed how strong his position actually was. The Labour leadership remained behind the government, and of the three men who had seemed the greatest threat to his premiership the year before, Chamberlain was dead, Halifax was in Washington and Eden was being blamed for the Greek debacle. So great was the slump in the foreign secretary's reputation that he was very grateful for Churchill's protection. Another twist had been added to a relationship that would have provided rich research material for a legion of Freudians. Frustrated though he often subsequently became with Churchill, Eden also knew the prime minister had saved him from disaster.

'THE SCREAMS OF THE SCORCHED MEN'

While the blame was allocated in London, the situation in the Middle East continued to deteriorate. When the Germans were slow to react to their entreaties for military help, the Iraqis forced their hand. On 30 April, the Iraqi army besieged the British airfield at Habbaniya, outside Baghdad. Now the Germans agreed to provide aircraft and pilots to support Iraqi ground forces, while the Vichy French bargained with the Germans to supply the Iraqis and to open Syrian airfields as staging posts for the Luftwaffe.

The chiefs of staff instructed Wavell to despatch a relief force from

Palestine to rescue the base. Wavell was very aware that the mufti of Jerusalem was doing his best to spark another Arab uprising in the Mandate: indeed, the mufti would shortly issue a *fatwa* calling for an Islamic holy war against the British Empire. The general believed that if he reduced the Palestine garrison by sending a relief column into Iraq, he would run the risk of facing another revolt. As far as he was concerned, protecting Egypt and Palestine was much more important than regaining Iraq.

Wavell underestimated the extent to which the years of conflict in Palestine from 1937 to 1939 had broken Palestinian Arab enthusiasm for an uprising against the British.[82] Downcast at being handed yet another burden, he told the chiefs of staff that their instructions took 'little account of realities' and advised the government to get the Turks to mediate with the Iraqis instead.[83] No one in London agreed with him. Churchill and the chiefs believed that a rapid military response was essential to stop the Axis gaining the initiative. Wavell was ordered to get a relief force on the road. An improvised column of armoured cars, lorries and requisitioned cars and buses, accompanied by the Bedouin scouts of the Transjordanian Arab Legion, rattled off across the desert at the end of the first week of May.[84]

By the time it got moving, the defenders at Habbaniya were already well on their way to fighting off the siege. The Iraqis were well equipped with artillery and machine guns, but in the absence of the Luftwaffe, they lacked effective air support. On 2 May the RAF opened hostilities. Wellingtons flying in from Basra, and training aircraft at Habbaniya converted to carry bombs, attacked the Iraqis non-stop for five days. When their artillery bombardment of the base failed to stop these attacks, the Iraqis withdrew, and the British quickly flew in more aircraft as reinforcements.

On 10 May meanwhile, Hitler's deputy, Rudolf Hess, suddenly appeared in the UK. Having decided that neither Britain nor Germany could win the war, Hess had stolen a plane and flown to the UK on a bizarre one-man mission to make peace in the west before Hitler launched his attack on Russia. With his plane running out of fuel, he parachuted to the ground in a field just south of Glasgow, where he was discovered, still entangled in his parachute, by a local farm worker. Hess was quickly bundled off into captivity, but no one in the British government quite knew what to do with him. They eventually decided he was probably mad. What the British definitely missed was the huge propaganda coup of announcing his flight before the Germans broadcast their own interpretation. The news of Hess's arrival in the UK sent rumours and conspiracy theories running around the world.

On 15 May, the attack that Wavell had been organizing on Rommel's positions on the Egyptian border, 'Operation Brevity', got under way. It was meant to bring succour to the besieged garrison at Tobruk. Although it achieved some initial success, Axis forces swiftly retook all the gains that the British forces had made.

By now, however, Churchill was hoping for a victory in the eastern Mediterranean that would turn the tables on the Germans. Since the British had taken over the island of Crete in November, work to fortify it had proceeded very slowly. In practice, it was a less than ideal outwork for the defences of Egypt – closer to Athens than to Alexandria, it was very vulnerable to air attack from the mainland. It was a strange place to pick to inflict a sudden reverse on an enemy who could be expected to dominate the skies. When the New Zealand divisional commander, Major General Bernard Freyberg, arrived to take charge of the island's defences at the start of May, he was not optimistic. The island's garrison was made up of a hodge-podge of troops evacuated from Greece, the RAF were quickly eliminated by Axis aircraft, and during daylight troop movements and naval supply runs became essentially impossible. To Churchill's excitement, however, an intelligence coup had given the defenders what seemed like an unbeatable advantage.

Well before the attack on Greece, German airborne forces had already worked up plans to take Crete with a massive invasion from the skies. In late April, Hitler's generals and admirals tried to persuade him to unleash these forces against Malta instead, freeing up the supply lines to Rommel's newly victorious troops in North Africa. Hitler, wary of being sidetracked into a Middle Eastern campaign, stuck with Crete instead. Since the operation had not been part of the original German invasion of Greece, the plans for it were now transmitted by radio in the Luftwaffe Enigma, which was fully readable to the British. For the first time, Enigma decrypts revealed a future operation in its entirety. Here, it seemed, was a chance to inflict a stunning defeat.

The information Freyberg got, however, encouraged him to believe that the main attack would come from the sea. His dispositions reflected that. On 20 May, when German airborne troops descended by parachute and glider, Freyberg's men inflicted devastating casualties. The Royal Navy smashed an attempted seaborne invasion, but fixed by their commander's fear of a further amphibious landing, Crete's garrison lacked the flexibility to finish the trapped paratroopers off. The island's rugged landscape and the Luftwaffe's domination of the sky made it very difficult to readjust the defence to meet the attack. As much by luck as by judgement, the Germans managed to seize an airfield through which to fly in reinforcements. By 27 May, it was clear that evacuation was once more the only option.[85]

Again, the navy came to the army's rescue, lifting off over 16,000 of the garrison over the next few days. Operating 400 miles from its base, under conditions of almost total German air superiority, the Mediterranean Fleet paid a terrible price. Troops had to be got off from the evacuation beaches at night, and any delay saw the Luftwaffe catch the ships as they made their way home. By the time the evacuation ended, almost half of Cunningham's fleet had been sunk or so badly damaged that it was put out of action. For ships crammed with rescued soldiers, the results were horrific.

On 29 May, for example, the cruiser HMS *Orion* was attacked repeatedly by German bombers as it returned from Crete. Her captain was killed, one of her gun turrets was put out of action, and then another bomb went through the bridge and every deck below, exploding in the stokers' mess at the bottom of the ship, which was full of evacuated soldiers. One officer went below to inspect the damage. All the lights were out and choking smoke had filled the decks. He tried to rig a hose to reach the fires that were now threatening the ship:

> As this mess deck appeared to have more wounded and shocked men in it, many of whom appeared to be off their heads, I found it difficult to get men to follow me . . .
>
> With one or two men I managed to get the fire out and opened some of the ports . . . and dumped some of the more beastly pieces of remains overboard . . . I then regarded it as safe enough to open the starboard ports and the draughts soon cleared the mess decks of fumes and smoke. We managed to get about thirty troops to assist but as the screams of the scorched men were still slightly demoralising the rescue party, I went

along to the sick bay and a sick berth rating arrived and crawled around and gave morphia injections . . .

Very few wounded were recovered from the stokers' mess decks and I regret that a number in both mess decks were either crushed or suffocated, as I did not feel justified in attempting rescue work or opening ports until I was sure that the fires were well under control.[86]

That night, the *Orion* limped into Alexandria. Shortly afterwards, she sank the short distance to the harbour floor. More than 260 men had been killed, and another 280 wounded, during the air attacks. It took two weeks for salvage crews to extract the dead. Together with severe losses being suffered in the Atlantic, the operations off Greece made May 1941 the bloodiest month of the Royal Navy's entire war.

'GENERAL DE GAULLE MIGHT HAVE DIFFERENT VIEWS'

In Iraq, at least, the situation had stabilized. The German attempt to provide air support was too little, too late. It was 11 May before German planes began to arrive to intervene in Iraq. Repainted in Iraqi colours, they went into action against the airfield at Habbaniya and the British relief columns, while the RAF fought back with raids on their bases in Mosul in northern Iraq, and at Palmyra in Syria. There were only twenty-one German combat planes in the Luftwaffe detachment. Most of its aircraft were transports that were meant to keep it supplied, but thanks to competition from the invasion of Crete and preparations for the attack on Russia, there were never enough. Short of fuel and supplies, the Germans also suffered heavy losses to RAF ground attacks. By the end of May, the remaining Luftwaffe crews were on their way back to Syria by road, and columns of British and Indian troops were approaching Baghdad.[87] Rashid Ali and the mufti of Jerusalem fled to Persia, then to Rome and Berlin. Back in Iraq the regent was restored to power, but the royal family's authority was ruined by their dependence on British support. The British decided that the only way to ensure imperial security was with a permanent garrison. Iraq would spend the rest of the war under British military occupation.

Since 1940, the British had wanted to get Syria and Lebanon, the

French-mandated territories in the Levant, under friendly control in order to protect their position in the Middle East. General de Gaulle was also set on securing the Levant for Free France, partly to provide his movement with a victory, a base, potential recruits and prestige, but mainly because he suspected that if the British had to intervene, they would keep the territories for themselves. In late 1940, however, the Vichy authorities had struck back hard at attempts to mount a Gaullist coup. There seemed no hope that the Levant could be brought over by political means alone. As the situation in the rest of the Middle East deteriorated in spring 1941, Wavell successfully insisted that the Levant had to be left alone, and the British even lifted the economic blockade.

De Gaulle, backed by General Spears, the prime minister's emissary to the Free French, wanted to abandon this quiescent stance. When the Vichy French allowed Axis forces to use Syrian airfields to support the rising in Iraq, Wavell found himself facing the danger of yet another front in his multi-faceted war in the Middle East. The Free French took the opportunity to demand permission to go ahead with the operations they had planned, but Wavell was having none of it. He insisted that the Vichy forces showed no sign of defecting, and that the Free French would require substantial British support. For Churchill, desperate for action as ever, this was just further evidence that Wavell was unfit for command. After another bitter exchange of telegrams between Cairo and London, he told Wavell to get on with it or resign. As it turned out, Wavell was right: no sooner had Churchill instructed him to help the Free French than they admitted that they were going to need British help to fight their way into the Levant.

Even as the last men were withdrawn from Crete and the fighting finished in Iraq, therefore, Wavell had to organize an invasion of Lebanon and Syria, which got under way, commanded by General Wilson, on 8 June 1941. Australian, Indian and British soldiers, including cavalrymen fighting on horseback for the last time, made up the bulk of the 35,000 attacking troops, fighting alongside battalions of Free French and a few platoons of the Palmach – the professional wing of the Haganah, the Jewish militia in Palestine, which had recently secured British permission to join the fight against Fascism. The majority of their 40,000 opponents were French colonial troops – Senegalese, North African Arabs and even a regiment of the French Foreign

Legion.[88] This was not what anyone had expected the war to look like back in September 1939.

Nationalists in Syria and Lebanon strongly resented French rule, and the Free French had originally planned to stir up trouble for the Vichy regime by declaring independence. Churchill, happy enough to sacrifice the French empire if it helped to preserve the British, enthusiastically endorsed the idea. De Gaulle, however, had no intention of handing over power to the nationalists: he told the British that if there was trouble with the locals, they should remember what had happened in Iraq, and step aside so that the Free French could put any nationalist rebellion down. Nonetheless, de Gaulle approved a proclamation of independence, which was broadcast on the radio by the Free French commander, General Catroux, as the Allied forces moved forward into battle.[89]

A tough fight awaited them. After some early reverses, the Vichy troops defended the Levant with professional pride and a bitter detestation of the Gaullist traitors. They had good knowledge of the difficult terrain and, unlike the attackers, possessed around eighty light tanks. Eventually, British naval, artillery and air superiority told, but it took five weeks to get the Vichy commander, General Dentz, to accept defeat. About 2,500 British, Australian, Indian and Free French servicemen became casualties, and about 3,500 of their opponents.[90] Much to the embarrassment of British commanders, the local population believed that they were being liberated. Advancing up the Euphrates with his 10th Indian Division, Major General William Slim found himself 'greeted by a distinguished-looking Syrian in European dress', who 'welcomed us ... as deliverers, and trusted the French would never return'. Slim could not bring himself to tell the excited man that he thought 'General de Gaulle might have different views'.[91]

'EVERY SINGLE ONE OF OUR PLANS HAS FAILED'

While Wilson's forces slogged their way through Syria, Wavell launched his main Libyan offensive of the summer, 'Operation Battleaxe'. This time, the auguries were better than in May. British armoured units had been reinforced by the arrival of new tanks, rushed post-haste through the Mediterranean in time for the attack. Rommel's obsessive attempts to capture Tobruk had been fought off by its Australian garrison. Now, as Enigma decrypts confirmed, his troops were struggling with the shortages imposed by their elongated supply lines. Air and sea attacks from Malta were wearing down the Italian merchant navy, and the Axis forces lacked enough motor transport to carry everything they needed so far from their supply ports. Intelligence about the poor state of Rommel's supplies only heightened Churchill's hopes of quickly reversing the Libyan defeat.

Yet Rommel had nonetheless managed to strengthen his defences in the aftermath of Operation Brevity. When British and Dominion troops attacked on 15 June, they not only failed to break through, but found themselves on the verge of being encircled. On 17 June, forewarned by the RAF, British commanders ordered a hasty withdrawal. The first full-blown tank battle with the Afrika Korps had proved a disaster – 91 of the 190 tanks with which the British had begun the battle had been knocked out or broken down. Rommel had lost only twelve. Only a lack of petrol and the canker of Tobruk held him back from a pursuit all the way into Egypt. A year after it began, Britain's North African campaign was back where it started.[92]

Churchill was furious. 'Every single one of our plans has failed,' he complained to the chiefs of staff.[93] His response was to blame the men in command. He had already replaced Air Marshal Longmore with his deputy, Air Vice Marshal Arthur Tedder. On 21 June, he decided to swap Wavell with Lieutenant General Claude Auchinleck, then commanding the army in India. Auchinleck had impressed the prime minister with a greater willingness to send troops to intervene in Iraq. Wavell had certainly been worn down by the weight of responsibilities he had to bear. Yet he was a victim rather than the cause of the crisis. As everyone involved had recognized, in the absence of a mythical Balkan bloc, it was always unlikely that the small forces Britain could send to Greece would actually turn back a full-blown assault by the Wehrmacht. What had not been foreseen was that this would in turn leave the Western Desert so vulnerable at the moment when trouble erupted in Iraq and Syria.

Wavell had had to throw largely inexperienced troops and commanders into battle. Unlike the Germans, they struggled to co-ordinate infantry, armour and artillery in order to get the best out of each. The invulnerability that British heavy tanks had enjoyed against the Italians disappeared in the face of the small number of 88mm anti-aircraft guns that the Germans deployed as tank killers during Battleaxe, but Italian anti-tank guns had also played a major role in stopping the British advance. The need to rush newly arrived tank reinforcements into battle after a long sea voyage increased problems of mechanical reliability. And when faced with the unexpected, British officers tended to wait for orders from above. Shortages of radios and the unreliability of communications meant that they were often slow to come into battle, and fought separately when they arrived. Ironically, bearing in mind how much Churchill's hopes were raised by the flow of Enigma decrypts, British officers on the battlefield discussed their movements openly over the radio, giving German intelligence units a steady flow of high quality tactical information. There was little sign, therefore, that the British were getting any better at taking on the Germans in open battle, but with American ships sailing supplies straight into the Middle East, Wavell's successor, Auchinleck, could be heavily reinforced. Perhaps he would prove better able to defeat Rommel.

The fighting in the Western Desert during the summer offensives was intense, and the surroundings grim, with the all-but unbearable heat, the shortage of water and the irrepressible flies. After his first period in the desert in July 1941, Gunner Graham Watson wrote back to his sister:

> The essence of everything is mobility so for days on end one only sees the people in neighbouring trucks which are parked at wide distances from each other to be safe from air attack. It is a dreary life ... In the afternoon one wants to sleep but the flies, which make life a purgatory, prevent this. The flies are hell. I have never seen anything like their persistency. They attack one in hordes. You brush them away and the same flies come straight back like an arrow. Life would be tolerable without them but they prevent all concentration.[94]

Yet in a funny way it was also a remarkably clean campaign, and not just because, compared to other battle fronts, few civilians were killed and neither side treated the other atrociously. Fighting against the Germans and Italians in the Western Desert didn't raise the same complex issues as combating Iraqi nationalism or struggling against French colonial troops in the Levant. Once they had beaten him, the British could romanticize Rommel as an honourable opponent who was doing his best for his country. They never said the same about Rashid Ali.

The fighting in the Middle East in 1940–41 was a milestone in the collapse of the European empires. Italy's imperial ambitions in Libya had almost been crushed: in East Africa, they were extinguished altogether. The proclamation of independence on 8 June 1941 marked the beginning of the end for the French empire in the Levant. For Britain too, the nationalist feelings that had broken forth in Iraq – and the response they aroused elsewhere in the Arab world – would not be long contained. In retrospect, the spectres of future humiliations could already be discerned.

Yet the important thing for the eventual defeat of the Axis powers was that, in the short term, the British Empire in the Middle East survived, and was in a stronger position than it had been a year before. The threats from East Africa, the Levant and Iraq had all been removed. The Red Sea supply line was secure. With Hitler unwilling to commit the German war effort to a campaign around the edges of the Mediterranean, the Axis had not been able to take advantage of the crisis the British had imposed on themselves, with their commitment to Greece and Crete, and to seize control of the Middle East. Whether that failure would prove important remained to be seen.

RELIEF IN THE ATLANTIC

In America, the spring crisis in the Mediterranean aroused all the fears of the previous year – that Britain would go under beneath the Nazi onslaught, or that appeasement would resurface, or that the Germans would run rampant through North Africa and the Atlantic islands and invade South America through Brazil. None of this pushed Roosevelt into the war. During April, he had moved cautiously to help with Britain's shipping problems. As well as removing the Red Sea from the combat zone as quickly as possible to increase the flow of supplies to the Middle East, he allowed British ships to be repaired in US ports. He also agreed that the Americans would use Lend-Lease money to build bases for Atlantic protection forces in Northern Ireland and Scotland.

Roosevelt held back, however, from transferring US navy ships from the Pacific to the Atlantic, or ordering American vessels to escort convoys through to the UK. Instead, he just extended the US navy's neutrality patrol zone to the twenty-sixth meridian, encompassing Greenland, where the United States had also got permission from the Danes to build a new base. These were important steps, but they were not enough to turn the tide in the Atlantic. The president was worried that he would be unable to get Congressional approval for escorting ships, but his attention had also been drawn to the Pacific. On 13 April the Japanese, unaware of the new war that the Germans were about to launch, signed a non-aggression pact with the Soviet Union. This concerned Roosevelt, because the Japanese were now free to turn their attention southwards, against European and American colonies in East Asia, without the threat of a war with the Red Army in Manchuria.

In London, the British government had hoped that, with Lend-Lease out of the way, Roosevelt's hands would be free to haul the United States into the war. Once again, they were disappointed. At the start of May, Churchill despatched an explicit appeal for America to enter the fray. The president ignored it. Ministers fretted about whether talking up the UK's successes or bemoaning its disasters would do more to bring the Americans in. Under pressure from his own Cabinet, Roosevelt took the opportunity of an easing of tensions in the Far East to reinforce the US fleet in the Atlantic. He reassured Halifax that he was only waiting for an 'incident' to open a shooting war in the Atlantic. At the end of May, he told the British that he would send troops to take over the garrisoning of Iceland. Once more, the British became optimistic, but when a US merchant ship was sunk by a U-boat in the South Atlantic, the president showed no sign of trying to catapult America into the war. Roosevelt was quite happy to accept a gradual escalation of undeclared hostilities with the Germans in the Atlantic, but he saw no need to risk a domestic political confrontation in order to overcome American isolationism.[95]

American naval help in the Atlantic took longer to arrive than the British had wanted, but by the summer of 1941, the balance was already moving against the Germans. From April 1941, Western Approaches Command produced a standard set of procedures for escort duties for the first time. The number of escorts kept increasing. By July, the British had twice as many escort vessels as they had at the start of the war.[96] Coastal Command was re-equipped with new, more modern aircraft, including longer-ranged US-built Catalinas and B24 Liberators.

In April, when Iceland became available as an airbase and refuelling point, escort and air protection could be extended still further out into the Atlantic. Coastal Command's aircraft were still not much use at destroying submarines – in the first two years of the war, in which they flew a total of more than 55 million air miles, only one U-boat been had sunk solely as a result of Coastal Command attack – but their mere presence deterred the Germans.[97] On 8 May, faced with these extensions of escort- and air-cover, Dönitz ordered his submarines further west and south, making it still harder for them to make contact with the convoys. During the second quarter of the year, although the fleet of operational U-boats grew, the tonnage they sank for each day they were at sea decreased. In this industrial campaign, such drops in submarine 'productivity' were critical.[98]

In the early summer, crucial intelligence breakthroughs began to give the British usable access to the Kriegsmarine's Enigma communications. The naval Enigma was more complex than that used by the Luftwaffe, and up until the spring of 1941 it had been decrypted only with a long delay, if at all. In the early summer, a mixture of deliberate targeting of German weather ships and the chance capture of a U-boat, U-110, with cryptographical material intact, allowed the British to read transmissions for May, with some delay, and for June and July almost concurrently with their intended recipients. For the first time since the war began, some of the intelligence gap with the German navy had been closed.[99]

Enigma decrypts helped to confirm that the newly completed German battleship *Bismarck* had put to sea with the cruiser *Prinz Eugen* on 19 May in order to stage another surface voyage against the convoy lanes. No further information was decrypted in time to help the hunt for them, but the early warning encouraged Admiral Tovey, the commander of the Home Fleet, to position his ships to catch the raiders as they steamed through the Denmark Strait. When the venerable British battlecruiser HMS *Hood* and the newly completed battleship HMS *Prince of Wales* confronted the German squadron, shells from the *Bismarck* blew *Hood* to pieces and forced the *Prince of Wales* to withdraw. The *Bismarck*, however, was also damaged; badly enough that it had to turn for home.

The *Prinz Eugen* managed to escape, but the *Bismarck* did not. With the German ship tracked sporadically from a mixture of shipboard radar, flying-boat sightings and radio intercepts, the Admiralty co-ordinated forces from across the world for its destruction. The scale of the forces that the British employed – in total, British operations against the *Prinz Eugen* and *Bismarck* involved eight battleships and battlecruisers, eight cruisers and two aircraft carriers – demonstrated the colossal imbalance of capital ship strength between the two sides. Crippled by a torpedo strike from an aircraft carrier based at Gibraltar, on 27 May *Bismarck* was bombarded into submission by battleships that had sailed from Scotland, and finally sunk by a cruiser that had been escorting convoys north from Sierra Leone.

The British didn't know it at the time, but it was the last time that a German surface raider would make it out into the Atlantic shipping lanes. Meanwhile, Enigma decrypts had also helped to reveal the position of the German supply ships that had been lined up to support the *Bismarck* on its intended voyage. Between May and July, the Royal Navy captured or sank fourteen of these ships – wrecking the infrastructure on which depended not only the disguised commerce raiders that were still abroad, but also any future voyage by a German capital ship.[100]

Bomber Command's senior officers thought that assisting the Royal Navy was just a distraction. They wanted to get back to what they thought was their real job: bombing Germany. British raids on the Baltic and Channel ports did not manage to destroy either the U-boat bases or surface warships. In April and May, Bomber Command dropped 829 tons of bombs on the French port of Brest, where the German cruisers *Gneisenau* and *Scharnhorst* were sheltering. These inflicted only minor damage on the ships, but they did force *Gneisenau* into the open harbour, where it was struck by a torpedo from a Coastal Command bomber. That put it out of action for eight months, ensuring that the cruisers did not break out into the Atlantic at the same time as the *Bismarck* in May.[101] Getting the *Gneisenau* to move was Bomber Command's only major contribution to victory since the start of the war.

From the start of June 1941, the Royal Canadian Navy, operating out of a new base at St John's in Newfoundland, began to escort convoys all the way to and from the middle of the Atlantic to Nova Scotia. The Canadians were initially less well equipped and trained than the British, but the fact that convoys now had protection across the entire Atlantic made things still more difficult for the attacking submarines.

In May, the Admiralty produced figures demonstrating that ships sailing independently were suffering losses at more than twice the rate of those forced to travel in convoy. Despite Churchill's reluctance, on 19 June the War Cabinet agreed to re-impose a minimum limit of 15 knots on ships that wanted to sail on their own. This was a crucial decision: it slashed the number of independent sailings on which the U-boats had continued to feast as the escort forces grew stronger. From June, the Admiralty started to use the information from the Kriegsmarine Enigma to route convoys around the U-boats, leaving the submarines waiting for targets that never came. This tactic only worked because the U-boat wolf packs had already been driven into the mid-Atlantic, where there was space for convoys to be moved around them. During June, there was little let up in the dismal figures of monthly tonnage sinkings. Yet during July, the quantity of tonnage being sunk plummeted, as the decision to make ships that sailed slower than 15 knots join convoys kicked in and those convoys were moved, as far as possible, out of harm's way. By the autumn, Dönitz was forced to send his U-boats elsewhere in search of prey. Churchill's sporadically intense approach to the Battle of the Atlantic appeared to have paid off. A temporary concentration of effort had been enough to win the fight against the submarines. Germany's attempt to blockade Britain into submission had failed just as completely as the Blitz.[102]

While the British and Canadians fought the submarines, American aid helped to ease their import problems. Since Lend-Lease reduced the need for British exports to the United States, ships on the transatlantic route did not have to load up fully before they departed British ports. That saved time and allowed them to make more journeys. Between April and October 1941, for the liners that carried most of the transatlantic cargo, the time saved in port by not reloading matched that won by quicker unloading thanks to the changes in working practices in the docks.[103]

As the situation in the ports eased, attempts were made to address the backlog of ship repairs. The Treasury agreed to fund repairs in overseas yards. Following Churchill's Battle of the Atlantic directive, a major effort was made to accelerate repairs in the UK, with the working day lengthened and special lighting used so that work could continue during the blackout. The Ministry of Labour tried to bring former ship workers back into the yards. Churchill scaled down the target for new merchant shipbuilding so that shipwrights could be transferred onto repair work. He also shut down the long-term naval programme of battleship and aircraft carrier construction that had been agreed the previous autumn. Work would continue on the capital vessels that could be completed by the end of 1942. Everything else would have to be forgone to deal with the immediate crisis.[104]

These efforts seemed successful. By July, the tonnage of ships awaiting repair in UK yards had fallen by 40 per cent, and the flow of vessels through the repair process was restored. Yet the problem had been displaced rather than resolved. Ships were now laid up in foreign yards instead (including in America, where repairs would eventually be carried out under Lend-Lease), and the total tonnage out of use because it was in need of repair remained about the same for the rest of the war. The changes of spring 1941 stopped the shipping system grinding to a halt, but they provided no way to restore the losses to the British merchant fleet, nor did they increase overall carrying capacity.

Even though they weren't sailing to the UK, American ships had started to play a major role in supplying the British war effort. Over the summer of 1941, when the British feared they were facing an oil crisis, the Americans organized a shuttle service of tankers to carry oil from the Caribbean to New York, greatly shortening voyage times for the British ships that carried it across the Atlantic. Indicatively, what the British meant by oil crisis was that they only had 4.5 million tons in their stockpiles. That meant that the British had in reserve almost as much oil as had been produced in the area of Europe under German control in the whole of 1940.[105] With the Red Sea declared free of combat, in June, nine US ships entered Middle Eastern harbours carrying cargoes of military importance. In July, thirty-two came with cargoes of munitions. Between then and the end of 1941, an average of sixteen American ships docked in the region every month. Alongside the military supplies came cargoes of consumer goods despatched by American companies keen to exploit the decline in British civilian exports to the Middle East. As goods and reinforcements poured into ports that were not equipped to handle the quantity of traffic, the Red Sea threatened to become choked with supplies.[106]

Lend-Lease also promised to help repair Britain's food position. America might not have been able to provide lots of munitions straight away, but it could provide large amounts of nutritionally dense tinned, dried and processed foods. During 1941, deliveries of canned meat and dried and condensed milk under Lend-Lease equated to about 60 and 70 per cent of British annual consumption respectively.[107] These ensured that the nutritional value of supplies for British civilians was kept up despite the fall in import volume.

What the US could not provide in 1941 was what the British most wanted, which was the fresh beef they had been denied by the use of 'reefers' to take troops to the Middle East. In America, the economic recovery produced by rearmament had sparked a livestock boom, but with the country still at peace, there was no food rationing. Newly employed Americans guzzled up all the beef they could get. In the end, the British had to increase orders from Argentina instead. The Ministry of Food was not, however, about to give up its hard won allocation of hold space just because America couldn't provide the meat it wanted. Instead, ships were filled up with wheat and sugar, which were available in large quantities. During the summer of 1941, the UK brought in about a million tons more grain and 700,000 tons more sugar from America than it could actually use. More grain was stockpiled than ever before in the history of the British Empire. None of it would ever be released for public consumption. The fears raised by the shipping crisis of 1940–41 meant that the Ministry of Food held it back against a future shortage. Eventually, it was stored so long that it had to be destroyed. Unsurprisingly, the Americans would in future find it difficult to take estimates of the UK's bare minimum needs for food imports seriously.[108]

'THE THREAT IN THIS AREA IS ONLY POTENTIAL'

The intensity of fighting in the Mediterranean and Middle East in the spring of 1941 made it even more difficult to reinforce Britain's imperial defences in the Far East. Since summer 1940, the chiefs of staff had tried to speed up the reinforcements that were necessary to their plans to use the RAF to defend the whole of the Malayan peninsula. Churchill opposed them. Faced with a worsening situation in the Atlantic, then with a crisis in the Middle East, he was not willing to send scarce planes to an inactive front. The prime minister remained convinced that the Japanese would not start a war that would inevitably bring in the Americans.[109]

As the situation in the Middle East got worse, Robert Menzies, still in London and sitting in on meetings of the War Cabinet and the Defence Committee, kept asking awkward questions. If disasters in the Middle East tempted Japan to attack, what help could Australia and New Zealand actually expect? Churchill restated his conviction that only the outright defeat of the United Kingdom would be enough to start a Japanese attack in the Far East. The Japanese, he argued, 'would not enter the war, unless a successful invasion of this country took place . . . they would be most unlikely to come in if they thought that by doing so they would bring in the United States of America'.[110]

Privately, British ministers had already agreed that Menzies' complaints could be put down to his political vulnerability to isolationist opponents at home. In Churchill's view, 'it would be wrong to give up sound strategical ideas in order to satisfy the ignorance of the Australian Opposition'.[111] Despite his best efforts, Menzies lacked the leverage to force any fundamental change of approach from London. The British belatedly consulted with the Australian and New Zealand governments about American plans to move warships from the Pacific to the Atlantic so that the Royal Navy could re-establish a presence at Singapore, but never gave them a permanent seat at the table when it came to deciding global strategy.[112]

Even as Menzies was being fobbed off, however, the concentration of effort on the Middle East became the focus of a row between Churchill and General Dill. On 28 April, still furious at his discovery of plans to evacuate Egypt, Churchill issued a directive asserting that the loss of Egypt and the Middle East would be a catastrophe second only to the fall of the United Kingdom. Led by Dill, the chiefs of staff responded by questioning his strategic priorities. They pointed out the continuing risk of an invasion of the home islands, emphasized that it would take three months for any reinforcements to reach Malaya and argued against any further commitment to the Middle East. For Dill, if scarce reinforcements should be sent anywhere, they should go to the Far East, where a small investment might bring greater rewards in terms of security. When Churchill insisted that it would be worse to lose Egypt than to lose Singapore, Dill reminded him that this was not the list of strategic priorities to which he had agreed at the start of the war. Being forced to abandon Egypt would be bad, but with the Mediterranean shut anyway, it would not spell catastrophe. It would be much harder to recover from losing Singapore. Laying all this out in writing, as Dill did, was not the best way to persuade the prime minister to change his mind. Churchill simply ignored him.[113]

This spat was significant more because of what it said about the deteriorating relationship between the two men than because it might have resulted in any meaningful alternative in the deployment of imperial strength. The security of the Far East had been relegated in British grand strategy – thanks not least to Adolf Hitler – well before Churchill became prime minister. The catastrophe of the Fall of France had determined Britain's course in way that neither Churchill nor Dill could alter. Despite Churchill's opposition, the chiefs of staff continued to reinforce Malaya, but they did so with the second-grade troops and equipment they had left after they had attended to the active fronts. Dill himself didn't really believe that it was possible to send meaningful reinforcements before the end of 1941: with good reason, because, as became apparent when a plan was considered to move battle-hardened Australian divisions from North Africa to the Far East, Britain simply lacked the ships to carry them.[114]

To try to make sure that the troops who were in Malaya were better prepared, Dill now appointed one of his protégés, Lieutenant General Arthur Percival, to take over Malaya Command. Percival had impressed Dill when he served under him as an instructor at the Staff College, and he was familiar with Malaya's defence problems, having served as the top staff officer there in 1936–38. Percival had shown himself a courageous leader during the last war, but he lacked experience commanding in combat. Since what was needed was someone to get formations on a quiet front trained and ready for battle, he seemed the ideal man for the job.

In June, when the joint planning staff drew up a wide-ranging appreciation of future strategy, they highlighted the continuing deficiencies in the defence of Malaya. The military garrison was being brought up to strength but lacked artillery. The air force had only 150 aircraft, less than half the minimum strength it needed. The planners warned that:

> The threat in this area is only potential; consequently it tends to become
> obscured by other threats which are more grimly real. But should it

develop, this threat may bring even greater dangers than those we now face . . . It is vital to take, as soon as possible, the necessary measures to secure the defence of Singapore.[115]

When the Defence Committee came to consider the paper on 25 June, Churchill put it aside. Such elaborate analyses were a waste of time: 'Much of the contents rapidly became out of date, and statements were often falsified before they were read.'[116] Three days earlier, Germany had invaded the Soviet Union.

22

Britain Beyond the Blitz

Before turning to the changes wrought by Hitler's attack on the USSR, it is important to consider the most significant phenomenon in shaping everyday British life between 1940 and 1941: not the Battle of Britain, nor the Blitz, but the dramatic mobilization of the economy for the purpose of fighting the war.

WAR MACHINE

Table 4: Selected British economic statistics, 1939–1941

	1939	1940	1941
GDP (% of 1938)	101	111	121
Working population (millions)	19.8	20.7	21.3
Armed forces (millions)	0.5	2.3	3.4
Workforce in engineering, shipbuilding and chemical industry (millions)	2.7	3.2	3.9
Unemployment (millions)	1.27	0.6	0.2
Industrial stoppages (working days lost, millions)	1.4	0.9	1.1
Aircraft production (total number)	7,940	15,049	20,094
Tank production (total number)	969	1,399	4,841
Defence expenditure (£ millions)	626	3,220	4,085

Table 4: Continued

	1939	1940	1941
Consumer expenditure as % GNP	76.2	60.4	54.6
Government expenditure as % GNP	19.6	39.9	47.2
Imports by 1938 volume index	97 (100)	82 (121)	
(munitions excluded, manufactured	94 (112)		
goods in brackets)			

Workforce figures for June each year. Sources: S. Broadberry and P. Howlett, 'The United Kingdom: Victory at All Costs', in M. Harrison (ed.), *The Economics of World War II: Six Great Powers in International Comparison* (Cambridge, 1998), pp. 44, 47; C. Feinstein, *Statistical Tables of National Income, Expenditure and Output of the UK, 1855–1965* (Cambridge, 1972), T19, T49; CSO, *Fighting with Figures: A Statistical Digest of the Second World War* (London, 1995), pp. 38–9, 47, 60–61, 166, 170, 207, 222; H. Parker, *Manpower: A Study of War-time Policy and Administration* (London, 1957), pp. 504–5.

This was the period of transition from armed peace to full-blown war. At its heart were the demands of military strategy, as set out by the chiefs of staff, modified by the Defence Committee and approved by the War Cabinet.[1] The manpower demands of the armed forces were met by the Ministry of Labour and the National Service Act, and their equipment needs by the supply ministries: the Admiralty (the only one of the service departments that retained responsibility for its own equipment), the Ministry of Supply and (after May 1940) the Ministry of Aircraft Production.

Between 1939 and 1941, the supply ministries became the dominant presence in the domestic economy. The Admiralty took charge of all UK shipbuilding, the Ministry of Aircraft Production also had responsibility for the radio and electronics industries, and the Ministry of Supply purchased nearly all non-food imports, administered controls on raw materials and ran the chemicals sector as well as providing equipment for the army. By mid-1941, four out of five workers in the engineering, shipbuilding and chemical industries were fulfilling government contracts. About a third of a million of them were employed directly by the Admiralty and the Ministry of Supply in the Royal Ordnance factories and the Admiralty dockyards.

The supply ministries also, however, continued to provide huge amounts of capital investment to create armaments capacity that was run by private industry. Contrary to pre-war predictions, much of this was managed by firms that already specialized in arms-making rather than by civilian manufacturers drafted in for their expertise in mass production. Aeroplane engines were one important exception, with car firms, including Rolls-Royce and Ford, taking a significant role in managing production. Tanks were another exception: the initial expansion of wartime production took place through companies that made railway locomotives and rolling stock, and the Nuffield Motor Corporation.

Across industry, the expansion of military production took place through a mixture of the provision of new plant, much of it state owned, and the conversion of existing capacity to government contracts. Between spring 1939 and spring 1942, the government provided £556 million for fixed capital for war production, £385 million of it for operations that were privately run.[2] As well as capital investment, the supply ministries could also offer tempting contracts – with fixed profits and access to raw materials, machine tools, factory floorspace and skilled labour that were otherwise unobtainable. The Ministry of Supply operated a strict range of controls over industrial materials and tools, while the use of factories and the construction of new buildings also became subject to government licence. As well as these controls on resources, during the second half of 1940, the Board of Trade – the key peacetime ministry for industry, but one relegated to the management of the civilian sector during the war – imposed drastic cuts on the output of civilian clothes and household goods.[3] Taken together, these measures were enough to push through the greatest part of the total wartime changeover towards government production, but they were not nearly enough to achieve the mighty programmes set out by the armed forces.[4] During 1941, civilian industry and labour became subject to much further reaching measures of direction, conscription and control.

The requirements of the forces stretched well beyond the engineering effort necessary to build modern weapons. The supply ministries purchased huge quantities of other equipment – uniforms, tents, barrack room furniture and paper, to name but a few – from commercial manufacturers. In 1941, more than a quarter of a million textile workers, about a third of the entire industry workforce, were engaged on contracts for the military, about 45,000 of them making boots and socks alone.[5] The construction requirements of the wartime state – from bomber stations, via ordnance factories, to refrigerated stores and silos for the Ministry of Food – were particularly large during the early years of the conflict. By 1941, half a million men, slightly over half the building labour in the UK, were employed on government construction projects. The service ministries engaged contractors for their own building programmes, but other departments' requirements was met by a new Ministry of Works and Buildings, set up in October 1940 under Lord Reith, the former BBC director-general and minister of information, which also ran the licensing system for civilian construction.[6]

Meanwhile, the UK was also forced to adapt to a rapid drop in its volume of imports. During the winter of 1940–41, plummeting predictions of future imports and rising shipping losses came to seem a much more dangerous threat than German bombing to the UK's ability to continue the war. This forced the government to seek emergency military, civil and diplomatic solutions to the shortage of shipping, but it only accelerated changes that were already under way in what Britain produced and imported.

In an effort to reduce the quantities that the UK needed to bring in, domestic output of bulky materials was increased. Four-and-a-half million tons more iron ore were mined in 1941 than in 1939. In agriculture, where arable and dairy farming took precedence over meat production, animal feed imports were slashed and government subsidies encouraged farmers to plough up pastureland for crops. Between 1939 and 1941, the area under arable cultivation in the UK increased by more than a quarter. The potato harvest increased by 2 million tons; the cereal harvest, including wheat and oats, by a similar amount.[7]

Those figures by themselves tell a lot about how the British diet changed during the war, but not everything, because none of this made the UK anywhere near self-sufficient. The nature of what was imported, however, underwent a fundamental change. Almost all imports were now brought in under the programmes developed by the Ministries of Supply and Food. During the first two years of the war, they imposed dramatic cuts on the imports of some goods, including textile fibres, clothing and newsprint. The German domination of Europe deprived Britain of its usual supplies of imported eggs, butter and vegetables, and these were not brought in from other sources. From the end of 1940, imports of fresh and tinned fruits, vegetables and nuts ceased, with the exception of a small quantity of oranges. In 1938, the UK had imported almost a third of a million tons of bananas. In 1941, it imported barely any, with catastrophic consequences for growers in the Caribbean.[8]

Imports of other goods, however – of lower volume but higher value – increased. Before the provision of economic aid from the US, the Ministry of Supply was allowed to use Britain's dwindling stock of dollars to purchase essential items in America. In 1940, it imported two and a half times more steel than it had done in 1939 (not necessarily with happy consequences, as we have seen). Machine tool imports between 1940 and 1941 were three times what they had been in 1938–39.[9] The Ministry of Food was not allowed to turn to the States while the UK was still dependent on its own dollars, but it too imported goods in more concentrated forms. From the start of the war, fresh meat had been imported frozen, rather than chilled, in order to save space. Flour imports (mainly from Canada) increased by 57 per cent between 1939 and 1940, and imports of tinned meat (from Argentina and Australia) rose by 20 per cent. After the provision of American finance the US also became a major source of food imports.[10]

Government controls over imported raw materials and manufactured goods reinforced the measures that were in place in any case to shift civilian production towards war work. Between 1940 and 1941, almost all raw materials came under the purview of the control boards operated by the Ministry of Supply (rubber, still in plentiful supply from Malaya and Ceylon (Sri Lanka), was a significant exception). Controls became increasingly strict. In 1941, only 25 per cent of the UK's steel supplies went to 'civilian' uses, a category that included the mining and power industries as well as civil defence. From the spring of 1941, the Ministry of Agriculture initiated a National Farm Survey that gathered information about every holding of five acres and above. Farmers called it 'a new Domesday book'.[11] By mid-1940, the Ministry of Food had already rationed all those foodstuffs that were in universal demand and for which it could guarantee a steady supply (the two criteria it applied before it would provide a fixed ration by quantity or price), and further price controls and rationing were introduced primarily to combat inflation rather than to ensure equal distribution.

Even though this wasn't how it felt at the time, in retrospect, British economic mobilization in this period was relatively smooth. The Churchill government inherited well-developed plans for the expansion of the munitions industry. The panic of summer 1940 imposed significant disruption, but Britain's fundamental strategic objectives remained broadly unchanged. There was no invasion, and neither the Blitz nor the German blockade seriously interfered with the growth of the war economy. Domestically, the new administration embodied a compromise between state, capital and labour that enabled the extensive exploitation of domestic resources without excessive social conflict. Internationally, the UK's wealth allowed it to survive the time between the great European realignment of summer 1940 and the arrival of financial aid from America, without any total interruption of supplies. Long-term programmes of rearmament could therefore continue.

The machinery that administered the war economy developed in fits and starts. The demands placed on industry by the armed forces and the restriction of overseas supplies drove on more extensive planning of production and tighter programming of imports, but there was no great national plan that matched together the different parts of the economy and laid out how they should work together. Rather, it was in response to the pressures of this period that the British state developed the structures, systems and overlapping economic controls that allowed more central planning and co-ordination, and still more extensive mobilization, in the future.

The coming into office of the Churchill government did not immediately solve the problems that had dogged its predecessor: the co-ordination of the competing needs of the supply departments, the control of manpower, and shortfalls in deliveries of weapons to the armed forces. Dramatic though the acceleration of 1940–41 was, the UK was a long way from peak mobilization or maximum war production, and it was already plain that the future demands of the military would require still greater efforts if they were to be achieved. From the summer of 1940, the government's direction of the war economy was subject both to disagreements within Whitehall and to growing criticism from the press and Parliament. As the clanking apparatus of an industrial total war picked up speed, it began to sweep up the entire population. Millions more people found themselves engaged directly in the war effort, whether in the ranks or at the workbench. The war machine involved everybody.

'THINGS THAT WE HAD TO GO WITHOUT BEFORE THE WAR WE GET NOW'

Coventry, early summer 1940. Charles Madge, having got a grant from the National Institute of Economic and Social Research, has gone to Coventry with a team of researchers to investigate saving and spending. They are struck by the signs of prosperity: 'Smart clothes in the streets . . . busy public-houses, crowded shops, long queues outside the cinemas.' The manager of one picture house tells them the sort of story with which they are going to become very familiar. He knows of an Irishman (or a young lad, or in some versions even a girl), formerly a cinema employee, who has just got a new job in an aircraft factory: 'He earned £10 9s in his first week, although he knew nothing about machinery. He told his former employer he only did 35 minutes work a night.'[12]

The sums involved were exaggerated, but the phenomenon was unmistakable. As the government poured money into fighting the war, this was a period of great economic growth, and one of the most striking results was a change in working-class income and employment. Firms with government contracts needed to replace men who had gone into the armed forces and to recruit new workers. Brand new ordnance factories started production and had to be staffed from scratch. Some people changed job, either by choice or because they were put out of work by further contraction in the consumer industries. Others were able to get work for the first time in years. Others still stayed in the same job while production shifted in front of them. In early 1940, there had still been more than a million unemployed. By mid-1941, the jobless figure was under 200,000 and falling. The working population had grown by a million-and-a-half people in the space of two years.[13]

The expansion of employment went hand-in-hand with the persistence of inflation. The rate of increase in the cost of food – so sharp in the first months of the war – slowed after the introduction of government subsidies at the end of 1939. Nonetheless, the price of food within the working-class Cost of Living Index was about 25 per cent higher in autumn 1940 than it had been at the start of the conflict. Clothes' prices rose much more rapidly, as imports fell and production was cut.

By spring 1941, the cost of clothes in the CLI was 68 per cent higher than in September 1939.[14]

Rising prices and demand for labour meant higher wages. By 1941, 2.5 million workers were on index-linked wage agreements, and increases in the CLI were the major source of wage demands in the first years of the war.[15] By July 1940, average wage rates were about 14 per cent higher than they had been in September 1939. They rose by about another 13 per cent of the pre-war figure during 1941, but continued to lag behind the rate of inflation.[16]

Increasing output and longer hours meant that actual earnings increased further than wage rates. In manufacturing industries as a whole, average male weekly earnings went up by about 30 per cent between 1938 and 1940, and by about 21 per cent for young women. By mid-1940, the average male weekly wage in the engineering industry was about £5 a week – enough to carry the recipient to the verge of what had been considered a middle-class income between the wars.[17]

During the summer crisis, when long hours became the norm, weekly earnings for some workers in the munitions and aircraft industries were much more than this, albeit at the cost of exhausting effort. For families with two or three members in war work, household incomes went up substantially. In Coventry, where labour was already in short supply and wages high, Madge's researchers found a 68¼-hour week earned a chargehand (an assistant workshop foremen) £10 16s.; while an unskilled male labourer got £5 13s. 11d. for a week in which he worked 73 hours – much more than he could have expected before the war.[18] With wage rates lagging behind the rise in the cost of living, however, most workers had to put in longer hours if they wanted to make ends meet, which adds a different perspective to the readiness with which employees returned to bomb-damaged factories in the aftermath of the Blitz.

Not everyone was earning big money. The way that these average wage rates were calculated left out wages paid to miners and agricultural labourers, whose work was critical for the war effort but who remained relatively poorly paid. In late 1940, basic weekly wages for farm workers were £2 8s. a week, and for miners about £2 18s.[19] Other groups were also left out of the boom. Pensions and service pay and allowances went up, but from rates that were already low. A private's wife with two children, for example, received £1 12s. a week in

1940 and £1 18s. a week in 1941. As before the war, old age and young parenthood remained the times when Britons were most vulnerable to cyclical poverty.

Increased earnings for many people did not immediately translate into improved health. In fact, during the first years of the war, the long-term decline in infant mortality temporarily reversed, climbing from 53 per thousand live births in 1939 to 60 per thousand in 1940 and 63 per thousand in 1941. This was not, as might be thought, primarily the result of bombing, but rather of increased rates of mortality from childhood diseases: whooping cough, measles and pneumonia. It denoted the combination of an exceptionally cold pair of winters, the deterioration of medical care available to the civilian population as doctors were called up and hospitals set aside for air-raid victims, and the vulnerability of those whose incomes remained static during a period of rapid price rises.[20] Significantly, the deterioration was most marked in Scotland and Northern Ireland during 1940, before either experienced heavy bombing. Deaths from bronchitis, most of them in the population aged over sixty-five, also shot up.[21]

In these circumstances, early war wage increases were not enough to make most workers feel better off. Some were certainly doing better – an aircraft worker explained to Madge that his family were 'not extravagant, but perhaps things that we had to go without before the war we get now'.[22] More common, however, were the feelings of a Geordie steelworker, speaking about his cost of living bonus in mid-1941: 'you'll never get anyone who knows anything about it to say that it covers anything like the increase in prices now, because it doesn't. It's nothing.'[23]

Nonetheless, the overall picture was of a relative improvement in working-class (and particularly unskilled male working-class) incomes relative to those of the middle classes. This was a long-term phenomenon – it had begun, concomitant with rearmament, in around 1935 – but it became really noticeable to contemporaries for the first time as the war economy took off in 1940–41.[24] In Nottingham, a deputy laboratory manager for Boots recorded a conversation about overtime pay and tax with his wife for Mass-Observation, in which she

said that at rock bottom the working class are entirely selfish and that they have really no thought for country, war or others, but only for themselves ... I answer that they have lived so near the margin of want that they are naturally after all they can get and have not had the opportunity to develop other characteristics. But I agree that the middle class are expected to work extra hours without any extra pay at all, let alone overtime pay, and to pay income tax without complaint, while the working class must be paid for everything they do.[25]

Yet the burden of wartime sacrifice and advantage was no more evenly borne among the middle classes than it was among the workers. The wealthy were subject to punitive rates of income tax and death duty, but some managed to make good money out of the war effort. Farmers and landowners benefitted from substantial state subsidies for agriculture. Businessmen who took up government contracts were guaranteed a profit: limited though they were by Excess Profits Tax, these were risk-free business opportunities, backed up by state investment and substantial allowances for depreciation and the establishment of reserves. Lower down the social scale, the construction of a high-tech war effort meant that factory managers, designers, scientists and technicians were more in demand: their salaries went up, which meant that they lost less ground relative to unskilled workers than the rest of the middle class.[26] Left behind was that stratum of the lower middle classes who were no use to the munitions industries and not rich or well-connected enough to profit from the war. Their incomes remained static as taxes and prices rose.

'THEY JUST DO WHAT THEY'RE TOLD AND CARRY ON'

Royal Army Medical Corps Depot, Leeds, December 1940. Henry Novy, formerly part of Tom Harrisson's paid team of Mass-Observers, has been called up to the army. As he completes his basic training, Novy reports back to Harrisson weekly on the morale of the men around him.

Everyone spends the first weeks exhausted by the apparently endless round of marching, PT, instruction and fatigues. Novy is irritated by the school-room discipline of the army, proud when his unit marches through the city and struck by how little his comrades seem to know about the war. When the papers come round, they are really only concerned about whether their own town has been raided, 'sometimes commenting thoughtfully "It's a bugger you know." '[27] 'As a topic of conversation', sport comes 'much before either war or politics.' Novy asked them what they missed most about their old lives: 'Home', 'my wife', 'Liberty to do what I like', 'money', 'Yes money, and a nice fireside, and a good table.'[28] When he asks soldiers at his next posting about their attitudes to the war, they reply:

> M25D: 'Oh it's a waste of time. They'll go on and on, but the lads'll get browned off, they'll all go home.'
> M20D: 'It's a fuck. It'll last years this war will.'
> M20D: 'It's bloody hell mate. I don't know what to think of it.'
> M35C: 'Aye, and it's worse when you're married.'[29]

In sum, Novy thought his comrades 'have few opinions, except that home is a better place, fatigues a "fucking nuisance", waiting in the cold a worse nuisance. They just do what they're told and carry on. Underlying it all is the firm belief that we cannot lose the war.'[30]

We might question whether men wanting to find out if their homes had been bombed, carrying on even though they hated the war and believing in victory were really signs of apathy. If Novy had been sampling opinion among volunteers in one of the newly formed commando or parachute battalions, he might have found a greater enthusiasm for military service than in his unit of the RAMC. For most soldiers in Home Forces, nonetheless, there were plenty of reasons to be 'browned off' with the army.

Since the start of the war, all three armed services had undergone very rapid expansion. By June 1941, there were 395,000 sailors in the Royal Navy, about twice the number in September 1939. More than 660,000 servicemen were in the RAF, three times the number twenty months before. The army too had tripled in size, to 2.2 million men.[31] Desperate to show that it was meeting the threat of invasion, in the summer of 1940 the government instructed the army to take in a flood of new recruits. Between June and August, more than 320,000 men were enlisted into the army – far more than the training system could cope with. Most of them went into new infantry battalions, because these were all that the army could equip.[32]

The strategy that Britain adopted to meet the German domination of Europe sidelined the army compared to the navy and the RAF. In September 1940, 92 per cent of the army was in the UK. This diminished somewhat as Britain's overseas positions were reinforced, but until late 1942, most of the fighting in the Middle East was done by troops from the Dominions and India, and until 1944, the majority of soldiers remained in the UK.[33] There, most of them spent the winter of 1940–41 preparing defences against a possible invasion in the following year. Troops were often seconded for other duties, including agricultural work and assistance with post-bombing clear ups in nearby cities. All of this disrupted attempts to train them to fight.

Swamped with new recruits, and often short of equipment, military trainers concentrated on the 'bull' of parade-ground drill and barrack cleanliness. Instructors often lacked aptitude for their job, and officers were often only a few pages ahead of their men in the training manual. Only from the summer of 1941 were large-scale offensive exercises held and 'battle schools' established in an effort to give soldiers greater preparation for combat. Even then, the army still struggled to ready its men for battle. This was partly because the UK was already a very crowded island that was trying to maximize its agricultural output, and getting enough space set aside for training was difficult. It was also because the hardest bits of fighting for tanks and infantry – sticking close to an artillery barrage and actually closing with the enemy – were very hard to practise without killing novice soldiers.[34]

The sudden expansion of the army and its deployment to man coastal defences in the summer of 1940 meant a deterioration in accommodation – particularly for detachments posted to isolated rural or coastal areas. Men had to live under canvas, with primitive sanitary provision and scant off-duty recreation. That September, an early survey of morale by the army recorded the complaints of a soldier in Scottish Command: 'The bell tent in which we sleep leaks . . . Haven't had clean clothes for 3 weeks or a bath . . . If we want a wash or shave we have to go half a mile to wash in a *ditch*.'[35] Soldiers who had been willing to put up with these conditions during the summer of 1940 became distinctly less happy as the weather worsened and the threat of invasion temporarily diminished. Simultaneously, they worried about their families, stuck in the big cities as the German bombers flew over, or trying to survive on meagre separation allowances. Few of them had wanted to join the army, even fewer burned with a fanatical desire to get to grips with the Hun, and while they accepted the burden of service, most wanted to get back to civilian life as quickly as possible. When Novy's commanding officer told his men that, if they measured up, they might be allowed to join the regular army, the response was derision:

> 'Fucking 'ell!! Did you see that Jim? Join the Regular army!! They must think we're fucking madmen. Who wants to join the fucking regular army anyway? Christ almighty, ain't it bad enough to have to wait for this bloody war to finish. I ask you! Join the bloody regular army!!'
>
> Everyone in the barrack room laughed and added a few swear words to his comment, much in the same spirit.[36]

By spring 1941, the desertion rate at home was at its highest of the whole war.[37]

Another effect of the rapid expansion of the army was to expose major problems in the way the army used its manpower. The technological war that the British wanted to fight demanded an army of specialists. By late 1941, more than a quarter of soldiers were meant to be in posts that required trade skills, but recruits were distributed across the army without much attention being paid to their past experience or aptitudes, or whether they were physically and mentally robust enough to cope with the rigours of military training. The growth of the army also created a huge demand for new officers. In choosing men for training as officers, the army establishment opted disproportionately for upper- and upper-middle-class young men from the right public schools, on the grounds that they had the natural leadership skills that working-class soldiers would follow. Accusations of bias and incompetence led to a rising tide of complaints in the press and in Parliament. By the middle of 1941, the war secretary was fielding up to thirty questions a week from MPs relaying their disgruntled constituents' anger at being denied the opportunity to rise from the ranks. At the same time, as the supply of men, and women, became tighter, the army was criticized for demanding more soldiers while wasting the talents of the personnel it already had.[38]

From a troopship steaming out to the Middle East – always a potent site for discontent because of the separation between officers in first-class cabins and other ranks crammed into hammocks below decks[39] – one gunner wrote back to his family:

We had a debate yesterday on 'marriage maketh man' . . . I would gladly have given a lecture on some subject or other but I see no reason why I should use what qualifications I possess in helping the army to fill up time when they refuse to utilise the same qualifications for more useful purposes . . . Actually at the debate I wanted to ask who the hell wants to be a man anyhow? When I joined the army I was told it would make a man of me – and look at me – the result of twelve months handiwork – an inefficient scullery maid cum lavatory attendant.[40]

Since 1939, some senior officers in the army had recognized that war-time expansion would require a new effort to address questions of morale and welfare. During 1940, a Directorate of Welfare was established at the War Office, the first time that such a central body had existed, and proposals were made to revive army education from the moribund state into which it had descended between the wars. The director-general of welfare, Major General Willans, conceived of his job in holistic terms: the army had to meet the needs of a serviceman's 'mind' and 'spirit' as well as his 'body', in order to create a 'contented soldier' and a 'contented Army'.[41] Very little progress had been made on achieving any of these by the start of 1941.

Things were given a significant boost in May 1941 by the appointment of a new adjutant-general (the senior officer responsible for the army's handling of its personnel), Lieutenant General Sir Ronald Adam. Adam was an Old Etonian career officer who had built a reputation as an intellectual high-flyer in the inter-war army and set up the defence of the Dunkirk bridgehead. He had the support of Dill and of General Brooke, with whom he had served since he was a subaltern. Adam held advanced views on the use of scientific man management and the need to improve soldiers' psychological welfare, which he had already tried to implement after he took charge of Northern Command in the summer of 1940. After he became adjutant-general, Adam oversaw a wide range of improvements in the way the army looked after and employed its soldiers. By the end of 1941, these included better recreational facilities in army camps, radio programmes and newspapers aimed directly at soldiers, and an array of educational provision, as well as a new initiative called the Army Bureau of Current Affairs (ABCA).[42]

ABCA was a scheme created in the summer of 1941 to address concerns that the British army lacked the 'crusading zeal' that was to be found among the soldiers of the Wehrmacht. The aim was to give soldiers more information about the course of the war and some instruction in the cause for which they were fighting, through a weekly group discussion session led by junior officers, following pamphlets issued by the army. As well as inculcating patriotic values, ABCA was also meant to give a training in citizenship – what was the difference between a colony and a dominion, say, or how did local government work – in order to prepare soldiers for the post-war world. It was run by W. E. Williams, formerly the secretary of the British Institute for Adult Education, the editor of the Workers' Education Association journal and an associate of Allen Lane at Penguin books.[43] By the end of 1941, it was estimated that about half the army units in Britain were holding ABCA sessions.[44] The idea that the army was being politicized and soldiers fed progressive propaganda infuriated more reactionary Conservative MPs, who went straight to the prime minister to get him to shut ABCA down. Churchill issued instructions that the scheme had to stop, but the War Office ignored him. He forgot: he had a few other things on his mind.

How seriously soldiers took the efforts of earnest education officers and nervous subalterns to turn them into better citizens depended a lot on the individuals involved. In their own little triumph for democracy, soldiers tended to be deeply suspicious and mocking of anything that looked like political indoctrination of any sort. For some men, any diversion from the monotony of military life was welcome. For others, this was just another boring duty that the army was making them endure. Some jumped at the chance to express their opinions, or to get one over on their officers in a debate, or to rekindle their interest in the world of talks, pamphlets and discussions that they had enjoyed in civilian life. Others were happy to have a break from PT, a snooze and a smoke. Among the reactions to an ABCA session collected by Novy in November 1941 were: 'A lot of bullshit . . .', 'all right, quite interesting, but I didn't like the bits about discipline . . . We're not kiddies', 'I don't like no bloody argument. I couldn't get to sleep, and I got no fags', and 'T'want bad. But why do they bloody talk about what they know fuck all about?'[45]

'THIS MIGHT HAVE BEEN A BOMB'

Newton Abbot, Devon, February 1941. The town is holding its War Weapons Week to promote the National Savings movement. It has been set the aim of increasing savings by £100,000 during seven days. To publicize the event, local organizers arrange a fly-over by RAF bombers from a nearby airbase. They drop 10,000 advertising leaflets on the town, with instructions about how to take part in the savings drive. Each is headlined 'THIS MIGHT HAVE BEEN A BOMB'. Whether this is a plea or a threat, it works: Newton Abbot smashes its target, with £216,000 invested by the time the War Weapons Week ends. This success is far from unique: during February 1941, purchases of National Savings Certificates alone amount to £21 million.[46]

Led by the banker Lord Kindersley, who had chaired the National Savings Committee during the previous conflict and was now the movement's president, National Savings was meant to combat inflation by persuading the public to forgo expensive luxuries and to lodge their wartime earnings with the state. The organization's mechanics were designed to allow small, regular investment in a form familiar from insurance schemes aimed at the working class. Minor sums bought savings stamps that could eventually be exchanged for 15s. certificates, which offered a return of 5s. 6d. if held for ten years. The idea was to encourage newly wealthy war workers to lock their money up, rather than splurge it on accelerating the inflationary spiral. Richer savers could also purchase £5 Defence Bonds, which offered a 3 per cent return with a small bonus if held for their seven-year term. In fact, since all banks, building societies and insurance companies invested their holdings in government bonds, any savings were not only minimizing inflation, but also being used to support the war effort.[47]

National Savings main means of securing deposits from small investors was the Local Savings Group. Members could expect a weekly visit from a local volunteer to collect their contribution. Between 1940 and 1942, savings groups proliferated in schools, factories, streets and villages. To inspire the formation of more groups, and to encourage existing savers to greater efforts, National Savings carried out special publicity campaigns. The first, National Savings Week, in June 1940, was the only time that one of these drives ran across the entire country for a single week. After that, Local Savings Committees chose a week within a longer national period. War Weapons Weeks, for example, ran from 14 September 1940 to 11 October 1941, and they were only the first of four more great wartime campaigns over subsequent years, with additional drives to recruit new members in between. As time went on, National Savings became increasingly difficult to escape.

Savings Weeks consisted of a rolling series of events of the sort seen in Newton Abbot. At their centre was the pursuit of targets and competition between different towns and cities. Those who raised the most money were rewarded with flags and trophies. During these weeks, funds were raised not only in the form of savings, but also in donations from a panoply of special activities: dances, rallies, variety shows, religious services, military parades and displays of British weapons or crashed German aircraft. In Stockport, for example, local trade union leaders toured the area with a National Savings cinema van, showing promotional films and speaking about the value of putting money aside. In Bridgewater, schoolboy volunteers stencilled 'LEND, LEND, LEND' in increasingly large white letters on all pavements leading into the town, while Royal Engineers nearby put pontoon bridges across the river and charged the public a fee to cross.[48]

Rooted as they were in the civic spectacles of pre-war life, Savings Weeks encouraged involvement from an even larger proportion of the population than that involved in regular weekly saving, but the consistent massive surpassing of apparently high local targets did not require an overwhelming response from individual savers. All money saved in an area during the week was counted towards the total, whether or not it went into National Savings certificates, and local banks timed their purchases of war bonds so as to contribute towards a week's success.

National Savings certificates were marketed on a mixture of military hardware and moral virtue. For Kindersley, their value went well beyond the part they would play in holding back inflation. As he explained to listeners in a 1941 appearance in the 'Postscript' slot:

Our weekly War Savings ought to be looked upon as a national barometer of abstinence for victory . . . So long as we put our own desire before the needs of the country, so long will victory elude us. But if, forgetting self, we realise that no sacrifice is too great for victory, then we shall have done our share in releasing a whole continent – perhaps a whole world – from the misery and degradation of slavery.[49]

Kindersley was not regarded as a successful broadcaster, but the values on which he called – sacrifice, communality, patriotism – were all staples of wartime life. As the war went on, the emphasis in National Savings' advertising shifted away from spiritual duty and towards a direct connection with the technology of modern war. Savings groups were given lists of equipment, from bullets to battleships, with the notional sums required to purchase them. This was financial nonsense (lack of *pounds* was never a problem for the British war effort) but advertising genius – supporting the armed forces proving easier than self-denial to sell to potential savers. Saving could also be a very public performance of patriotism, to which there was substantial pressure to conform. In the Reynolds Tube Company in Birmingham, for example:

> Among other things it was arranged that the foremen in each department should pay the wages personally to each man and should be accompanied by an attractive young girl with stamps for sale when the men were paid. The foremen and girls were provided with a list of non-members.[50]

By the end of March 1941, there were 230,000 Local Savings Groups in action across England and Wales: 84,000 of them in factories and other places of employment. About one in six of the population belonged to one: many more bought certificates outside the weekly savings round. In the year to that point, National Savings amounted to £195 million. Thanks to the immense quantity of money the state was pouring into fighting the war, this was nowhere near enough to hold back inflation, but savings were expected to increase as other opportunities for consumer spending diminished.[51]

If the reach of saving was broad, however, it was not uniformly deep. Having conducted more extensive research, Madge argued that patterns of saving were determined not only by disposable incomes but also by longer-held traditions of personal and family finance that varied by region and class. As their wages went up, lots of people could be persuaded to sign up to save a shilling a week in order to support the fight against Hitler. Half of those he spoke to in Coventry in 1940 gave 'patriotic' reasons for joining National Savings groups.[52] During this period, however, only a few working-class families built up substantial savings in a newly opened bank account or in National Savings certificates. In contrast, the middle classes invested much more sizeable sums in National Savings – partly because they were also more used to salting money away. With non-military production diminishing and bank lending at a halt, it was hard to spend money on the consumer goods of the 1930s – homes, cars and domestic appliances – but working-class savers in particular also wanted a buffer against the economic collapse and renewed unemployment that they presumed would follow the end of the war.[53] As one man in Bristol told Madge's researchers, he was expecting: 'Like it was in last war – terrible slump. Those who don't look after it'll have a hard do. They should buy clothes, bedding, and put a shilling or two away.'[54] Another recognized the importance of appearances: 'Well, I suppose I *ought* to be patriotic and save to help them win the war, but I *did* join to help my wife when I'm unable to help myself.'[55]

Just like war work, National Savings offered a chance to complain about those who weren't pulling their weight:

> A certain class of people are making every sacrifice, while other are just going along in the same way. I know one man walking about with £60 in his pocket. When I told him he should buy certificates with it, he said, 'What will the Government use it for if I do give? Probably for the Ministry of Information'.[56]

While it was common to put cash aside for emergencies, in fact very few working-class Britons were keeping this sort of money about their person. As prices went up and supplies were cut down, most of what they earned went on things they considered essential: clothes, tobacco and beer (both of which had become much more expensive, but which were under-weighted in the Cost of Living Index because they were such good revenue generators), and, above all, additional food to supplement the ration. While the boom lasted, it was best to make use of it: as a Glasgow riveter told Madge, he was not one of those who would 'starve their weans to put money in the bank'.[57]

'THE FOOD QUESTION'

Shotley Bridge, County Durham. May 1941. Henry Novy's wife, Priscilla, who has moved north to live close to her husband's military posting, notes down the conversation between two women in front of her on the bus on the way back from town:

> F35C: 'There's nothing in the shops is there?'
> F45: 'No, you'd think that you'd save a bit of money when there's not the stuff to buy, but you spend more, don't you?'
> F35: 'Yes, everything's so expensive.'
> F45: 'Oh, I wish this blinking war was over.'[58]

Over the winter of 1940–41, supplies of clothes, furniture and household goods for domestic consumption all fell sharply. What people noticed first, however, was the effect of the rapid change in imports on the availability of food. Meat was the biggest issue. In the early autumn, the expectation of future cuts in animal feed led farmers to send an unusually large number of animals for slaughter. The meat ration briefly went up to 2s. 2d.'s a person a week. The end of this glut coincided with a sudden drop in meat imports. By the start of 1941, the ration had fallen to 1s. 2d. worth, and that could only be fulfilled because offal and corned beef were brought within the ration for the first time. A campaign to get consumers to substitute oats for meat had to be abandoned when oatmeal-milling facilities proved unable to keep up with the increased demand. At the same time, the end of European imports of vegetables and eggs really began to hit home. With the European fishing grounds closed and fishermen and trawlers called up by the navy, fresh fish became all but unobtainable outside the coastal areas. Britons looked to other things to put on the table, and increased wartime earnings went on unrationed items that were in limited supply, including fresh vegetables, dried fruit, tinned meat and fish. Prices shot up. When the Ministry of Food tried to control them, these foodstuffs promptly disappeared from the shelves.

Given that during 1940 and 1941, famines ravaged Spain and Greece, it is important to note that the British were a long way from starvation. The price of essential food items within the Cost of Living Index was kept down with government subsidies. Even in its reduced state, the meat ration meant about a pound of meat a week. Bread and potatoes were never rationed during the war, because they remained cheap and widely available. Rations for the armed forces at home – which included almost 3 million people at the start of 1941 – were also cut back but remained much more generous than those available to civilians. Servicemen were also able to supplement their rations by purchasing their own food from NAAFI canteens. An unmarried, non-smoking private in the Royal Army Ordnance Corps recorded in May 1941 that he spent 60 per cent of his twenty-one shillings weekly pay on food and drink on top of his rations, including tea, cake, pies, chocolate and biscuits.[59] In the words of a wife visiting an army camp in early 1941 and seeing the food available to her husband: 'You're lucky yews are, we can't get that at home, we have to do without.'[60]

The sudden shortages of previously favoured foods, however, affected many people much more than the Blitz. During the first months of 1941, Home Intelligence repeatedly reported that food had become the number one topic of concern. In mid-February, for example, 'shortages and increased prices continue to form the main complaints. Queues are reported from many districts and are causing much inconvenience and hardship. Chief Constables remark on the time involved by the police in controlling some of them.'[61] In the same month, Mass-Observation mapped out 'food tensions':

> Shopkeepers are suspected of favouritism, and also occasionally blamed
> for not having food in stock or for the manner in which they announce
> the fact. In some reception areas evacuees are blamed for shortages.
> Those without facilities for leisured shopping resent those who have
> this opportunity for doing a round of shops for scarce goods, and
> there are a few cases of more specific resentment of rich people (who
> can get all they want) and those who evade rationing by eating in
> restaurants.[62]

In the BIPO poll for March, 49 per cent of respondents thought that food or shipping were the most important issues for the government to address that spring, compared to only 8 per cent who identified bombing, shelters or evacuation.[63]

In London, an upper-middle-class housewife explained the disappointment when the food order she had placed with the shops arrived:

A most depressing note awaited me when I went down to the kitchen this morning . . . 'No honey. No sultanas, currants, raisins, mixed fruit. No saccharine at present. No spaghetti or sage. No herrings, kippers, sprats smoked or plain. No matches at present, and no kindling wood. No fat or dripping. No tins of celery, tomato soup, salmon . . .'

No wonder that when her friend came to tea, their conversation 'was almost entirely devoted to the various shortages, of food in particular – to which it invariably returned before long, like a homing pigeon'.[64]

In contrast, shopping in Shotley Bridge was a rather different experience. Here too, people were obsessed with food – although they had to queue themselves to get it – but their discontents went further than an absence of spaghetti:

the food question, the difficulty of eking out rations with un-rationed foodstuffs, the high prices, particularly of perishable foods, shortages and the consequent queues, occupy the first place in the average working woman's present-day life. Moreover, it is beginning to become a major worry and topic of conversation with the men too, who are involved from the economic aspect, as well as the direct impact of having less to eat, and seeing their wives' struggle to get together adequate meals.

One of the men complained: 'It's a fact that if you've got the money you can buy anything you like, and you don't need rations. You can go out and buy chickens and game and fish, and you can afford the high prices for vegetables.'[65] As civilian supplies became increasingly restricted, bitterness at the ability of the wealthy to circumvent the shortages that everybody else had to endure became widespread. Calls for patriotic endeavour and official justifications for rationing created a language of equal sacrifice in which it could be expressed.[66]

'THE GO TO IT SLOGANS ARE HYPOCRISY'[67]

Clydeside, early March 1941. Six thousand apprentices in the shipyards have come out on strike against their low wages relative to wartime dilutees. The young men are angry with their employers, with the government and with the shipbuilding unions who have ignored their appeals for higher pay. Their action is illegal, and local newspapers allege that they have been incited by Communist agitators. All but one of their organizing committee are indeed members of the Young Communist League. Determined to present a united front, the apprentices vow to communicate with the authorities only through their appointed representatives. A Mass-Observation team, in Glasgow to investigate morale, tries to interview the strikers. It is a frustrating experience:

> The rank and file to whom inv. spoke during this period were intensely suspicious, and although he adopted several methods – such as making a statement to which a denial was expected – he was unable to extract from them even details of pre-war and present day wages and similar information that it is simply perverse to try to conceal, and was consistently referred to the Secretary or the Press Agent of the Clydeside Apprentice's Committee.[68]

For the first and only time, Mass-Observation's efforts were frustrated by an organized refusal to be observed.

The apprentices' strike was the first large strike of the war to extend beyond its original location – from the Clyde in late February, through west Scotland and thence to shipyards in Belfast, Barrow and Tyneside and the mills around Manchester. In all, 25,000 young men came out on strike for a few days. Both in its size and its spread, it was unusual. The number of days lost annually to industrial disputes during the early war stayed relatively low compared to the late 1930s: unsurprisingly so, given that wages were rising, that there was a reluctance to aid the enemy and that after May 1940, strikers were liable to prosecution under Bevin's Order 1305.

That did not mean that all was quiet on the industrial front, particularly in those sectors, including shipbuilding and dock-working, which were already characterized by poor relationships between employers and workers and which were now subject to new public scrutiny as a result of the strains of war. Although the number of days lost to industrial disputes was low, the number of stoppages was higher in 1941 than it had been at any point since 1920. Strikes, and even occasional lockouts, were frequent but brief.[69]

In the engineering sector in particular, industrial relations were unsettled by an influx of new recruits, the regrading of jobs and pay and the rearrangement of production lines. Calls for all-out effort found a willing response during the summer crisis, but they sat uneasily with employers' efforts to roll back existing workplace practices in pursuit of higher output, and workers' awareness both of the increased value of their labour and of the continuing rewards on offer to business owners. As the desperate mood of summer was replaced by the hard slog of the winter, the developing shortage of skilled labour encouraged increasing militancy from a workforce freed from the fear of dismissal. Anyone who was sacked would simply get another job.

The expansion of the engineering industries, and the discontent that often came with it, created a moment of opportunity on the factory floor. For trade unionists, it was a chance to recruit new members and to expand into factories that had previously been hostile to the organization of labour. Just like the disquiet over air-raid shelters, workers' grievances also offered welcome possibilities for Communists eager to recover the party's position after the Nazi-Soviet pact. Communists were prominent in the shop stewards movement, and in autumn 1940, claims that they were being victimized because they were standing up to the bosses led to lengthy 'holidays' from factories in Coventry and Glasgow.

From the summer, the CPGB had promoted the idea of a 'People's Convention': a new Popular Front that would press for a 'people's government' to nationalize industry and improve shelters and living standards, and a 'people's peace' that would inspire the workers of the world to stop the war. When the Convention gathered at the Royal Hotel in London on 12 January 1941, many of its 2,234 delegates were young male trade unionists. The Convention was derided in the newspapers as a defeatists' front, but the government took it seriously as a threat to morale.

This time, the home secretary had no qualms about intervening in the freedom of the press. On 21 January 1941, Morrison banned the *Daily Worker* for the 'systematic publication of matter calculated to foment opposition of the war to a successful issue'. Although his action received the support of the majority of Labour MPs in the Commons, a minority of left-wingers attacked Morrison for not giving the *Worker* a chance to state its case. They were led by a Welsh MP called Aneurin Bevan. A former coalminer and editor of *Tribune*, Bevan was another firebrand of the left who had been taken under Lord Beaverbrook's wing. During the war, he would make a name for himself as one of the most passionate and articulate critics of the government, who was willing to insult even Churchill to his face.[70]

Despite the banning of the *Daily Worker*, the government fought shy of acting against the Communists in the factories for fear of the labour unrest that might result, but the CPGB, worried about a more total crackdown, rapidly scaled back its public activities. In fact, official concerns had overstated the importance of the People's Convention, which though it captured a much broader sense of dissatisfaction, never found much popular purchase for its calls for peace.[71]

Similarly, though Young Communists provided the leadership for the Clydeside apprentices in the spring of 1941, they did not supply the underlying complaints. Apprentices had traditionally been paid much less than older workers while they served their five-year term – something that had led to strikes in 1937. Now the pay gap had widened as a result of wartime increases. Worse, apprentices had to help new workers in the engineering shops, some of them women, who, after six months' training, were paid at the rate of skilled men. Local trade union branches, dominated by older men, ignored the apprentices' complaints. As a result they took matters into their own hands – and their strike spread swiftly to other discontented young men in similar situations in Scotland and northern England. Yet these strikes too were swiftly resolved: a court of inquiry appointed by the Ministry of Labour found in the Clyde apprentices' favour and awarded them 50 per cent pay rises. When their comrades around Manchester held out against the settlement, Order 1305 was invoked for the first time to charge their leaders, while the rest of the men were warned that they would be called up if they did not return to work. The strikes, though not the discontent, quickly ended.[72]

The apprentices' circumstances were particular: their grievance rooted in the fact that they seemed to be the only people in their communities not benefitting from the wartime boom. Their antagonism towards their employers, however, who were 'bringing in girls on big wages and trainees', was far from unusual in workers to whom Mass-Observation did manage to speak in Glasgow that spring.[73] Summing up their findings, the Observers suggested that the problem lay not in an inevitable conflict between capital and labour, but rather in how problems with production were interpreted:

Serious aggravation came from the inadequacy and erratic flow of supplies in essential industries ... Many thousands of men were kept practically idle on high wages, with little work to do even where they wanted to work hard for the war effort. These supply deficiencies have been exaggerated in talk and time. They have had the effect of making the men feel that there is inefficiency from the management side and from the Government, that the GO TO IT slogans are hypocrisy, and that 'what's the good of compelling us, or of us sweating our guts out when everything's in a muddle with the bosses'.[74]

Most places in Britain were not Clydeside. Industrial disputes were much less common in southern England, or in the new government-owned munitions factories. Yet if the class divide between management and workforce was not always so antagonistic, its presence was nonetheless characteristic of British working life, and it was exacerbated by the conflict. Complaints about supplies being interrupted and eager workers being left with nothing to do reflected a much broader sense of concern about the organization of war production that gathered strength during 1941.

Arguments about production grew out of not only the endless struggle between workers and bosses, but also contemporary political debates about the ownership of property, national efficiency and who was sacrificing what for the war effort. In the circumstances of 1940–41, idleness in the workplace had to be explained, justified and complained about. After the *Daily Mirror* ran another spread about 'idle workers in factories, bad organisation, idle machines and so forth', Cecil King, the newspaper executive, noted in his diary that 'Such stories reach any newspaper office – I regret to say – by every post.'[75] In the BIPO's survey for June 1941, only 21 per cent of those questioned agreed that 'we are producing in our factories the greatest possible amount of war material'. Fifty-four per cent disagreed. Thirteen per cent of those questioned blamed inefficient management. Nine per cent blamed slack workers. Twelve per cent wanted more central control or the restriction of non-essential work. Only 2 per cent thought there was too much red tape and too many officials.[76]

23

Production and Reconstruction

After the formation of the Churchill Coalition Government, the war economy remained a political battleground. Ministers fought for the right to control resources. MPs criticized the government for mishandling national mobilization. The economic consequences of the war provided the momentum for a major extension of state intervention on the home front. From the start of 1941, pressure increased on the government to take greater control of munitions production. Talk of a production crisis gathered ground as a way to explain Britain's inability to achieve a quick victory over Germany. The belief in national inefficiency encouraged calls for the building of a new Britain before the end of the war.

'COMMITTEES TAKE THE PUNCH OUT OF WAR'

Vast though the remits of the supply departments were, being in charge of one of them did not automatically confer any great authority within the government. The supply ministers' job was to serve the war machine, not to shape it, and they had no seat as of right in the War Cabinet. Of the four men who held these posts from May 1940, Morrison got out of the Ministry of Supply as soon as possible, and his replacement, Sir Andrew Duncan, and the Labour first sea lord, A. V. Alexander, were competent managers rather than political high flyers. Lord Beaverbrook proved the exception, but he owed both his post and his wider power to his relationship with Churchill.

As minister of aircraft production, Beaverbrook embodied the spirit of desperate improvisation that was abroad in the summer of 1940. When he came to office, Churchill, whose belief in ministerial supermen stretched back to his admiration for David Lloyd George in the last war, thought that he had to replace the Air Ministry's production branch because it was failing to produce the aircraft necessary for national survival. In fact, the Ministry of Aircraft Production (MAP) simply took over the old department. Beaverbrook therefore inherited expert personnel, including Air Marshal Sir Wilfrid Freeman, who had overseen the RAF's rearmament since 1936, and their carefully worked out plans for the expansion of aircraft output, which were just about to come to fruition. Within a few months, the new minister had tried to get rid of all of them.[1]

Beaverbrook brought to his office all the things that had made the *Daily Express* a great success story: a manic sense of drive, a ruthless disrespect for propriety and a genius for self-promotion. He did not believe that specialist knowledge or past experience were prerequisites for organizing a supply ministry. On the contrary, any businessman with a track record of success would do better than the entrenched officials to accelerate production. Behind his desk hung banners reading 'Committees take the punch out of war' and 'Organisation is the enemy of improvisation'. When he met opposition, which was frequently, he went to Churchill and offered to resign, usually blaming his asthma. The prime minister would then persuade him to remain within the fold.[2]

By the time Beaverbrook arrived at the Ministry, deliveries of aircraft to the RAF had already begun to increase. They rose still further as the Battle of Britain got under way. The new factories ordered in the late 1930s were at last coming on line, production was temporarily focused on the output of whole aircraft rather than spares, the crisis aroused an intense effort from aircraft workers and a reinvigorated repair organization got damaged planes back into action more quickly. All of this would have happened without the new minister of aircraft production, but he claimed credit for it nonetheless, thus fulfilling Churchill's belief that his old friend had worked some sort of industrial miracle. In the autumn of 1940, the prime minister briefly contemplated putting him in charge of the Ministry of Supply as well as the MAP. Beaverbrook was the one person who Churchill was willing to contemplate fulfilling the role of a munitions supremo overseeing the whole of production.

Beaverbrook declined – a lucky escape for the British war effort. At the MAP, he imposed his own chaotic working methods on senior staff, and pursued a prolonged power struggle with the Air Ministry that drove out the RAF officers, above all Freeman, who had previously shaped aircraft policy. The 'Beaver's' obsession with the number of planes the MAP was turning out delayed progress on putting new aircraft – particularly the much-needed heavy bombers – into mass production. He rightly jumped at the chance, in July 1940, to place big orders from America, but he was furious when he realized that these represented an investment in US capacity rather than an actual schedule for the arrival of planes.

At home, his buccaneering approach gobbled up resources that were sorely needed elsewhere. Where the demands of the supply ministries for scarce raw materials, industrial capacity and skilled workers conflicted, they were meant to be resolved by discussion in the Production Council, the Cabinet sub-committee chaired by Arthur Greenwood. Beaverbrook attended only one of the Council's meetings. In the summer, aircraft manufacturing had been assigned priority status over other military supplies. It was soon clear that that would damage all the other arms programmes. By the autumn, the priority system was put aside, and resources allocated between departments on the basis of their long-term plans. Beaverbrook insisted that his ministry should have first call on whatever it wanted, and refused to negotiate with other ministers. At the end of autumn 1940, when the MAP developed a new production plan, he had output figures fixed well above what factories could actually produce as an incentive to greater efforts. Instead, the inevitable shortfalls disrupted planning across the aircraft industry, and the MAP demanded materials and manpower for planes it was unable to build.[3]

The winter of 1940–41 was particularly difficult for British aircraft manufacturers. Stockpiles of parts had been used up. Hours had to be cut back to protect an exhausted workforce. Bomb damage was limited, but the dispersal of factories in response to the Blitz further set back production. With the summer emergency over, firms moved to making new aircraft types, and assembly lines had to be reworked, imposing additional delays. Aircraft production fell back in September 1940, and stayed below its summer peak until the spring of 1941. A frustrated and bored Beaverbrook upped his rate of resignation letters to the prime minister. His methods had achieved all they could, he insisted, and it was time to move on. Churchill refused to let him go.[4]

Beaverbrook's individualist drive was simultaneously what appealed to Churchill and what put him out of step with the rest of the wartime state. He insisted on being 'the cat who walks alone'. In war, however, as in peace, committee work underpinned the operation of Whitehall. As the need to win a long war overcame the scramble of the summer, it was the organizers, not the improvisers, who would ultimately prevail.

From the moment he had been appointed, Beaverbrook's demands for skilled workers and stricter industrial discipline brought him into conflict with Ernest Bevin. The minister of labour detested Beaverbrook, not only with the antagonism of the trade unionist long-goaded by the Tory press baron, but also because Bevin recognized Beaverbrook as a charlatan. To Churchill's insistence that Beaverbrook was a magician, Bevin replied that 'the principal job of a magician is to create illusions'.[5] What really bothered Bevin, however, were Beaverbrook's attempts to control manpower. It wasn't just that this was a grab for powers that Bevin considered his own: it was also a fundamental disagreement about why it was worth fighting the war.

Although Beaverbrook's behaviour appalled many Conservatives, he shared with them a vision of how economic mobilization ought to work. An all-out effort was required to beat Germany. Everyone had a patriotic duty to serve. Workers should be subject to the same discipline as soldiers in the front line: working through air raids and being punished for absenteeism. Men of push and go were needed to take charge of the war effort, but the fight was to defend the Empire against totalitarianism, not to achieve social justice and democracy. Beaverbrook thought that the minister of labour's job was to conscript and deliver workers to the armed services and supply departments. Businessmen should be left to deploy them as they saw fit.

Bevin thought differently. No one could be expected to give their all for the war effort, he thought, unless they had decent working conditions. Controls on manpower must be applied with caution and used with restraint if industrial peace was to be maintained. Winning the war was inseparable from advancing the cause of democratic socialism. If he was going to manage the problem of labour supply, he could not just submit to the demands of service and supply ministers who were not using their existing workforces efficiently.[6]

These were issues over which Beaverbrook and Bevin would fight until the spring of 1942. Reluctant to see Labour dominating the home front, the prime minister had no desire for Bevin to emerge victorious, but in domestic affairs, the minister of labour always had the upper hand. Like Beaverbrook he was a bully, but he was also bureaucratically competent and he knew how to carry a committee. These were skills that Beaverbrook lacked. As importantly, whereas Churchill and Beaverbrook needed each other personally, Bevin's power with the trade unions made him indispensable nationally. As Chamberlain's fall had demonstrated, the war economy could not be mobilized without the co-operation of the Labour movement. Bevin's arrival in the War Cabinet in October 1940 was just part of his rise to become one of the most important figures on the home front.

'I . . . STILL PREFER TO BE A LEADER'

By the end of 1940, Beaverbrook wasn't the only person complaining that Bevin was doing too little to control the workforce. During the summer, the Production Council had commissioned an investigation into the labour demands posed by the forces' expansion programmes. Bevin selected Sir William Beveridge to head the investigation. A pioneering civil servant with a strong belief in the reforming power of the state, then an academic economist, Beveridge had struggled during the 1930s with how to reconcile liberal ideals with the organization of central planning. The approach of battle had shifted the balance, converting him fully to 'war socialism'.[7]

Beveridge was an autocratic character, always convinced that he was right and unwilling to seek compromises. He never left a job without his colleagues being glad to see him go.[8] Like all his reports, his investigation into manpower reflected strongly his own thinking at the time. As he calculated things, Britain was on the verge of a crisis. To fulfil the service programmes, another 3.29 million people would have to move into the armed forces, civil defence and the munitions industries over the coming year. That could only happen if large numbers of men whose jobs were currently reserved were brought into the military and women came into industrial work in much larger numbers. Beveridge saw one solution: conscript everyone, pay them a standard wage and introduce a massive welfare programme to look after their families while they were sent off wherever the country needed them. They would just have to accept that the 'motive of personal gain' must be replaced by the 'motive of service'.[9]

This was a bit too socialist for Bevin. He was much more cautious about extending conscription, and he also understood just how controversial issues such as skill dilution and the conscription of women – let alone wage-fixing, over which he had clashed with Beveridge during the last war – would be on the factory floor. Bevin believed strongly in exhausting the possibilities of 'voluntary-ism' before controls were extended. While shortages of machine tools, alloy extrusions and skilled workers held new factories back from full capacity, he was unwilling to conscript workers before there were jobs for them to go to. Public opinion must move ahead of government policy. As he told the Commons at the end of November 1940: 'Whatever may be my other weaknesses, I think I can claim that I understand the working classes of this country. I had to determine whether I would be a leader or a dictator. I preferred and still prefer to be a leader.'[10]

After Beveridge was appointed as an under-secretary at the Ministry of Labour in December, he continued to nag Bevin to make more use of his powers of compulsion. Beveridge thought his reluctance was down to an outdated trade union mind-set, and that Bevin was 'more anxious to revolutionise the wage system than to do his job of organising labour to win the war'.[11] For Bevin, these were not conflicting objectives. He didn't adopt Beveridge's solutions, but as the year came to a close he was grappling with the question of how to control manpower and meet the requirements of the armed forces.

'WE ARE NOT FULLY USING OUR INDUSTRIAL STRENGTH'

During the final months of 1940, the government's failure to take a closer grip on the economy became the subject of criticism in the press and in Parliament. On the Labour backbenches, the attacks were led by Emanuel 'Manny' Shinwell, a former clothworker and trade union militant, who had been secretary for mines in the Labour governments between the wars, and had taken his County Durham seat from

Ramsay MacDonald at the 1935 election.[12] Shinwell was still angry that he hadn't been offered the sort of ministerial job he thought he deserved when the Churchill coalition was formed, and he reached out to the disappointed on the Labour left by calling for much more radical economic reforms as a means of national mobilization. Shinwell took particular delight in goading Bevin, who had spent too much time reading out lengthy speeches to conference halls full of quiescent trade unionists to be comfortable making his case in front of a grumpy House of Commons.[13]

The government's handling of the war economy was also criticized from the right, in particular by the predominantly Conservative Select Committee on National Expenditure, which was chaired by Sir John Wardlaw-Milne. An influential Conservative businessman and MP, Wardlaw-Milne had been an advocate of financial retrenchment in response to the economic crisis of the early 1930s. 'National Expenditure' included the placing of government contracts and the organization of production: the Select Committee piled up instances of waste, inefficiency and hold ups in vital war industries. Another senior member of the Committee was the Conservative MP Herbert Williams, a businessman specializing in the manufacture of machine tools. Williams thought that, administratively speaking, the Churchill coalition was 'the most incompetent British Government ever'.[14]

Politically, there was a big gap between Labour critics of the government such as Shinwell, who wanted the government to nationalize industry and introduce central planning, and Conservative critics such as Wardlaw-Milne, who wanted it to direct workers and control pay. What they could both agree on – in a sign of how much things had shifted since the 1930s – was that the state had taken too little control. At the start of December 1940, Wardlaw-Milne asked the Commons:

> Do the Government really believe that this tremendous change-over in the lives and occupations of the people of this country can be carried through on a voluntary basis? . . . If we can get results on that basis, all well and good, but we are not getting them now. We are not fully using our industrial strength and we must use it if we are to win the war.[15]

The argument that Britain's strength was being wasted by inefficient production would be a defining feature of politics for the next two years.[16]

At the end of 1940, the ministerial machinery for managing both production and the wider wartime economy was reworked. The Production Council and the Economic Policy Committee were wound up, and Greenwood was sidelined to chair a new committee on post-war problems and reconstruction. The Production Council was replaced by the Production Executive – a smaller body, now chaired by Bevin – which was meant to work alongside the new Import Executive to co-ordinate demands for key resources. Bevin was a much more impressive chairman than his predecessor. Under him, the Production Executive held meetings in Beaverbrook's office to make sure he had to get involved, dealt quickly with issues of transport and distribution, and oversaw the allocation of construction work under the new Ministry of Buildings and Works. Despite the committee's title, however, he had no power over the supply ministries.[17]

Bevin's appointment indicated how important he was as the man best placed to mobilize British manpower. At the start of 1941, he got the approval of the War Cabinet for three new steps in labour policy, which he announced to the Commons on 21 January. All three would come into effect from March. First, all women and men over service age would be required to register with the Ministry of Labour for potential direction into work. Second, to make sure that skilled workers stayed where they were needed, Bevin would control employment rights in key industries. Once a factory was issued with an Essential Work Order (EWO), workers would not be able to leave their jobs and employers would not be able to fire them without permission from the Ministry of Labour. This would prevent high-paying competitors poaching skilled employees, but to be issued with an EWO, factories would have to meet minimum standards of cleanliness and welfare, and recognize workers' right to collective bargaining. Third, men would stop being reserved from conscription because of the sort of job they did, and instead be classified by the specific work on which they were employed. Only companies engaged on government contracts could expect to be allowed to keep their workforce.[18]

What stood out to Bevin's critics in Parliament was how limited these measures were. Shinwell lamented to the Commons that the year before, 'the changes in the Government' had 'imparted a fresh stimulus to the war effort and aroused expectations'. But now:

As the precious weeks go by our hopes have steadily diminished. Instead of active and unified policy, we have seen the Government resorting to a series of makeshifts, futile experiments and trifling devices, improvising without the vestige of a plan, living from hand to mouth and, what is worse, constantly waiting to be stimulated by this House and by pressure of public opinion.[19]

Behind, rather than ahead of, public pressure was exactly where Bevin wanted his policies to be.

To prepare for the looming shortage of unskilled labour, Bevin pushed the Board of Trade to find ways to release civilian workers for war industries. At the start of 1941, the Board cut permitted sales again, with cotton and linen goods reduced to twenty per cent of their previous level. In March, it instigated a concentration programme in which the remaining non-military production in consumer industries was allocated to 'nucleus' firms that would preserve the bare minimum of output, while other factories were shut down. By the start of summer 1941, Britain's workers and employers would be subject to an unprecedented level of compulsion from the state.

Bevin's hope that he could rely on 'voluntary-ism' to avoid conscripting women proved, however, to be misplaced. Parents, husbands and married women themselves often had strong prejudices against factory work – that it was monotonous, dirty and undertaken by rough girls of dubious moral reputation. Their feelings about the women's military services – particularly the Auxiliary Territorial Service (ATS), the women's branch of the army – were even worse: 'rather rough', and 'a load of whores', were two typical comments picked up by a Mass-Observation survey in 1941.[20] Employers were reluctant to take women because they thought they would be harder to train and less reliable than men, and would require the expense of providing separate bathroom facilities. Few factories offered the sort of part-time work that might have been attractive to women with young children.

Attempts to shame or tempt women into munitions work with 'War Work Weeks', in which parades of workers showed off their handiwork from the back of lorries bearing banners with titles such as 'Tanks for Women, Good for Slimming' and 'Don't Queue with the Shirkers, Join the Women Workers' failed to encourage many new recruits. Given the food shortages and other disruptions of wartime life, many women already felt that they were working flat out to look after their families. In a survey of a thousand women in October 1941, almost two-thirds referred to their domestic responsibilities or their inability to leave home as reasons that they would be unwilling to take up war work. Ministry of Labour officials proved reluctant to force women out of their homes and into the factories. By August, 2 million women had registered with the Ministry of Labour, but only half a million had been interviewed for possible direction into work, and of them only 87,000 had been placed in the auxiliary services or munitions factories.[21]

'JEHOVAH'

The growth of the war economy was not merely a matter of military forces and munitions factories: its consequences affected almost every aspect of civil life. Compared to the formation of military strategy, in these areas Labour secured more significant influence at the start of the coalition. Not only did Attlee and Greenwood chair Committees on Food, Home and Economic Policy, but Attlee also stood in for Chamberlain at the head of the Lord President's Committee during the latter's illness. Although Greenwood proved no more effective in directing discussions of economic policy than he did in matters of production, Attlee was a much more active presence, building up the Lord President's Committee as an important organizing body on the home front.[22] In terms of the tools being used to handle the civil economy, however, there was little to distinguish the first six months of the Churchill government from its predecessor's mixture of appeals for restraint, tax increases, government subsidies, control orders and limited food rationing. That would change during 1941.

When Greenwood was moved away from the seat of power at the end of 1940, the Economic Policy Committee was dissolved, and the remit of the Lord President's Committee, now chaired by Sir John Anderson, expanded. It was meant not only to co-ordinate the work of the other Cabinet committees, including the Production and Import Executives, but also to consider 'larger issues of economic policy'. As Churchill explained to Anderson, these were 'the most difficult and dangerous political issues. These issues were not solved in the last war and I cannot pretend they have been solved in this.' The prime minister expected the lord president to 'take the initiative over the whole field' and to 'take the lead prominently and vigorously'.[23]

Sitting at the centre of the administrative web of Whitehall suited Anderson's abilities very well. A scientist by education, he had had a stellar career as a civil servant. He played a major role in organizing the British chemical industry and shipping during the First World War, was a senior administrator in Ireland and at the Home Office during the troubled 1920s, then went out to India to govern Bengal before returning to oversee civil preparations against air attack in the late 1930s. Anderson was the embodiment of the inter-war British state, and he combined a vast experience of government with a scientist's logical rigour and facility with numbers and statistics.[24]

The lord president had no great departmental apparatus to help him, but he did have some important experts to hand. At the end of 1940, the academic economists assembled to assist Lord Stamp's inquiries into the war economy were divided between two groups, the Central Statistical Office, which gathered together information from across the departments of government, and the Economic Section of the War Cabinet Secretariat, which was deputed to provide analysis and advice on all aspects of the economy for the Lord President's Committee. Reams of detailed economic statistics and arguments were meat and drink to Anderson. In a characteristic memo to the Economic Section, just after Churchill had admonished officials to restrict all memoranda to a single side of paper, Anderson explained: 'I am not necessarily a foe to long documents if you think it is important that I should read them.'[25]

Anderson was dour and self-important, but he developed a remarkable overview of the entire economy and commanded considerable authority among ministers. His nicknames were 'Pompous John' and 'Jehovah'. As well as acting as a respected arbiter in disputes between departments, as lord president of the council he also took responsibility for a range of vital projects, including, from autumn 1941, British efforts to develop the atomic bomb.[26] Although he sat as an independent MP for the Scottish universities, Anderson's sympathies were Conservative. Crucially, however, he was seen as a bureaucrat, not a politician. Colleagues trusted that he was not trying to build an empire or launch a bid for the premiership in part because they knew that he lacked the skills to build up a following in the country.

During 1941, the Lord President's Committee (LPC) established a powerful position over domestic policy. Under Anderson, its key members were Attlee, Bevin, Morrison, Wood and Duncan. It was a serious-minded group that got through a lot of business: there was no room here for Churchillian monologues or Beaverbrookian histrionics. Although Anderson was now in the chair, Attlee remained a driving force. This was a place where he could push forward his favoured measures of 'practical socialism' – including an unsuccessful attempt to demand the nationalization of the railways – to promote wartime efficiency. As Churchill had noted, the issues that the LPC had to handle were politically 'difficult and dangerous'. It was little wonder that he placed such emphasis on Anderson taking personal control. Together with the lord president, the chancellor Kingsley Wood also took a leading role in trying to obstruct a total Labour takeover of the home front.

Nonetheless, the battleground on which the LPC was operating had shifted as a result of the war. Wood, the Conservative lawyer, and Duncan, the monopolist businessman, were both willing to contemplate extensive intervention in the economy for the purposes of victory. Anderson was no socialist, but given his background, he was not uncomfortable in using the power of the state. The experts on the Economic Section were mostly economic liberals who had opposed socialist planning before the war. As Lionel Robbins, the head of the Section from mid-1941, later explained, however: 'in conditions of total war, a degree of collectivist control which would be highly inappropriate for a would-be liberal community at peace, is a logical necessity'.[27] As the LPC established its power, it built a centrally directed and controlled economy much closer to the world Labour had imagined in the 1930s than to that idealized by inter-war Conservatives.[28]

TAMING THE DRAGONS

Nineteen forty-one saw major advances in the government's command of the domestic economy as it sought to manage the impact of the war. Although these were in part intended to equalize access to scarce resources, the primary target was to tackle inflation, which continued to rise as the state threw money at the fighting of the war and reduced supplies for civilian consumption. Here, John Maynard Keynes and

Kingsley Wood were crucial figures, but the Lord President's Committee also exercised a key role in shaping an anti-inflationary policy for the whole home front.

Keynes had taken up a seat on the chancellor's consultative committee in June 1940. That summer he became an expert advisor to Wood, with a licence to investigate any part of the economy that caught his attention. In May 1940, he'd had two severe episodes of heart trouble, and he was able to start work at the Treasury only with a strict regime of icepacks and injections. By the spring of 1941, however, he seemed to be flourishing as he grappled with the great issues of national finance.[29]

Over the autumn of 1940, Keynes sought to bring the Treasury round to his way of thinking on inflation. Officials knew that there was a substantial difference between what the government was spending at home and what it was bringing in from taxation and that this was inflationary. Keynes' great contribution was to define the 'inflationary gap' in terms of national income and expenditure rather than state finance: by working out how much money would be saved voluntarily and how much spent, it was possible to estimate how much should be extracted by taxation in order to keep inflation under control. Since the gap was entirely theoretic – it would always be closed by inflation – assessing its size was a matter of some difficulty, but the process was much aided by the drawing up, at the start of 1941, of new statistics for national income by James Meade and Richard Stone, two young (and subsequently Nobel Prize-winning) economists who worked for the Economics Section. The figure they eventually arrived at for the coming year was about £500 million.

While this was being established, discussions took place about how this excess spending power should be removed. Keynes initially proposed a 'war surcharge', graduated according to income and paid after tax, with a fixed sum set aside as 'deferred pay' to be returned to the payee after the war. Wood rejected the surcharge as too complex, but kept the deferred pay. What he liked about this was the chance to present a massive extension of the tax base in terms of enhanced saving. It did not mean that he had accepted the logic of Keynes' original 'compulsory saving' proposal in *How to Pay for the War* – that just as the state needed to drain inflationary pressure in the midst of a boom, it should also spend during a slump. Given that the lack of a long-term commitment to food subsidies was making it hard to restrain wage increases, Wood was already moving towards a formal statement on stabilizing prices. Keynes taught him that taxation and subsidy were connected parts of the battle against inflation. If the cost of living increased, so would wage demands, spending and the inflationary gap. If taxation didn't remove enough spending power, the cost of living would be driven up.

The budget Wood announced to the Commons on 7 April 1941 was the most important moment in terms of domestic financial policy of the entire war. In the previous year, Wood explained to the Commons, the government had spent a total of £3,884 million and got £1,409 million in tax. This year, he expected to spend £4,207 million. At the moment, £1,636 million of that would be recouped from tax. Crucially, he committed the government to stabilizing the cost of living where it now was, at about 135 per cent of its pre-war level, with subsidies extended to goods and services as well as food.[30]

As he now laid out, the chancellor assumed that about half of the inflationary gap of £500 million would be met by an increase in saving – partly because there were simply fewer things to buy, partly because of the successes of the National Savings movement. The rest would have to be met through increased taxation. In sum, Wood aimed to cover almost half the state's expenditure at home in the following year from taxation, and to raise a billion pounds more in taxes than the government had done in the last financial year before the war.

The basic rate of income tax would now go up to 50 per cent, and surtax to an extraordinary 97.5 per cent. In both cases, this was the highest they had ever been. Top-rate taxpayers would now give nineteen shillings in the pound to the state. This was a politically necessary counterpart to what would happen at the other end of the income scale, where Wood cut allowances to make enormous numbers of wage earners liable to income tax for the first time. In his budget speech, he estimated that 2 million more people than before would pay income tax in the fiscal year 1941–42. In fact, increased earnings meant that the actual figure for that period was 3.25 million new income taxpayers. Together with the implementation of Pay-As-You-Earn taxation to withdraw revenue direct from wages, this marked a revolutionary transformation in the fiscal reach of the modern British state.

Wood promised that a portion of the money taken from these new taxpayers would be repaid at the end of hostilities in the form of 'post-war credits', giving a 'substantial nest-egg' in the shape of deposits to accounts at the Post Office Savings Bank. In a sop to Conservative business interests, he also announced a similar scheme for the Excess Profits Tax. This would remain at 100 per cent, but at the end of the war, 20 per cent of the sum paid would be refunded to businesses to help them rebuild for peace.

This remarkable budget was the first to be organized primarily around the battle against inflation, and the first to be accompanied by a statement of national income, published simultaneously as a White Paper, which provided the evidence to back up Wood's case. It was another marker of how far things had come since the 1930s that Wood's extension of working-class taxation and partial relief of Excess Profits Tax were applauded as a triumph by Conservative backbenchers. It was almost Keynes' last contribution in person to issues of domestic finance: from now on, he would concentrate on the much trickier question of how to persuade the Americans to pay for the war. Home Intelligence's analysis of public reactions was that:

> The principle of compulsory saving is popular, but there is some doubt about whether the money will really be paid back after the war . . .
>
> The middle classes are glad that direct taxation is at last to affect the labour classes, whose income in munitions factories and on Government contracts the middle class regard as excessive. Little comment is reported from the working classes themselves, and it seems likely that many have failed to realise how they will be affected.[31]

Through the Lord President's Committee and the Economics Section, the April budget fitted into a much broader range of controls on the civilian economy, which included the extension of rationing and the stabilization of prices. The Board of Trade had been discussing how to ration household goods since November 1940. The Limitation of Supplies Orders were now successfully cutting back the quantity of goods available in the shops: now the question was how to make sure what was left was distributed properly across the country. A flat ration, as with sugar, was impossible given people's different household needs. A value-based ration was rejected as administratively impracticable. Instead, following the suggestion of the Economic Section, a points system was developed to cover clothes and footwear, which was approved by the Lord President's Committee in February 1941.[32]

Despite Churchill's doubts about a scheme that he thought would be 'unnecessary, unpopular and unworkable', the War Cabinet agreed to introduce points rationing for clothes in May. As well as paying for clothes, consumers had to surrender part of their points coupons from their ration books when they made a purchase. These were then passed back by retailers, through tailoring firms, to textile manufacturers, who were subject to detailed official control and who would in turn provide further supplies of cloth back down the chain. The new scheme, which had remained a closely guarded secret in an effort to prevent panic-buying, was announced on 1 June 1941, with spare margarine coupons from the existing ration book being used to provide the first issue of clothes points in order to avoid giving any prior warning of its introduction. The initial ration for adults was 66 coupons a year, which would permit about two-thirds of average pre-war consumption. Public reactions were mixed. One young diarist recorded all the right things that the government would have wanted him to say:

> Good work. Equality of sacrifice. Let me congratulate the Board of Trade on the marvellous way in which it has kept the whole matter secret . . . There is enough for all if we share and share alike. Rationing is the way to get fair shares. Fair shares – when ships must run the gauntlet with munitions and food rather than with wool and cotton . . . Rationing is not the same as shortage. Rationing, or fair shares, is the way to prevent a shortage without interfering with full war production.

Others worried that the allowance of coupons would not be enough for those who needed more clothes for work, or for growing children or for pregnant women.[33]

Food too was now subject to additional controls and rationing. During the winter of 1940–41, food shortages worsened as a result of disruption to imports and evacuation from bombed areas. When the Ministry of Food introduced price limits on goods that were scarce but unrationed, including rabbits, onions, turkeys, canned food and rice – they promptly disappeared from sale as retailers held them back out of sight for familiar, and higher-paying, customers. These foodstuffs could not be brought within the 'straight' ration, because demand for them varied widely across the country, and because they were not available in sufficient quantities to guarantee a universal supply. Against the initial reluctance of the Ministry of Food, the Lord President's Committee insisted that some foods also become subject to a points rationing scheme. It was first introduced for canned meat, fish and beans in December 1941. By April 1942, it covered dried fruits and pulses, canned fruit, tomatoes and peas, breakfast cereals and condensed milk.[34]

Points could be spent on a range of different rationed goods, thus preserving a vestige of consumer choice. They gave no guarantee of a minimum provision of any one item, although all points could always be spent on something. Unlike the ration of sugar or meat, customers did not have to register with one shop and could spend their points with any retailer. With prices for points-rationed goods centrally controlled, points effectively functioned as a substitute currency, and the Ministry of Food altered points values to reflect supply and influence demand.

Points rationing might have been sold as a matter of 'fair shares for all' – a slogan first used by the Board of Trade to advertise the clothes rationing scheme – but rather than giving everybody the same, it aimed to stabilize prices as well as regulate distribution for the wider good. Together with the subsidies to which Wood had committed the country in his April budget and controls on prices, it was meant to hold back increases in the Cost of Living Index. Since food formed a substantial part of the CLI and was relatively easily controlled, much of the micro-management of prices to keep things steady initially fell to the Ministry of Food. To counteract the increase in the cost of clothing items within the Index, for example – which were 91 per cent higher by the end of 1941 than they had been at the start of the war – the price of sugar had to be reduced by a penny a pound in December. From July, the Board of Trade acquired new powers to control sales and prices, and also began to institute 'Utility' schemes – first for the manufacture of clothes – which restricted production to approved specifications in an effort to ensure good quality at low prices with maximum efficiency in the use of resources. Only at the start of 1942 did Utility clothing start to become available in substantial quantities: until then, the Board just released sales restrictions on cheaper clothes in an effort to restrain price increases.[35]

The principal reason for curbing the Cost of Living Index was not to protect the least well off, but to try to restrict demands for wage increases that would further fuel inflation. Crucially, despite calls from Tory backbenchers and 'war socialists' such as Beveridge, this was one area of the economy in which the government did not institute direct controls. This was not for want of trying by Kingsley Wood. Whatever he had taken from Keynes, Wood was still eager to act as a Tory standard-bearer and he repeatedly pressed the idea of compulsory wage restrictions at the Lord President's Committee.[36] Bevin, however, made sure such proposals were rejected.

The minister of labour was determined to preserve the system he had established with employers and unions when he came into office – the extension of free collective bargaining across the working population, backed up with compulsory arbitration. Bevin wanted the state to set the context for industrial relations, not to get involved in determining them directly. Any attempt to restrict wages would, he argued, bring the government into conflict with the trade unions. Given the need to maintain production, ministers would have in the end to back down, with a consequent loss of authority that would wreck any call for restraint in the future. Only by trusting that union leaders would recognize the need for voluntary restraint in the national interest could co-operation be maintained. When new pay deals at the end of 1941 again raised the question of wage controls, Bevin promised his fellow ministers that he would 'resist to the uttermost and make it a real issue, that the State should say to one section of the community, you must work for another section at a maximum wage'. If this line were pursued, he would get the Labour Party to demand the immediate nationalization of industry. This proved a decisive argument.[37]

'NOT WORKING AT MORE THAN 75 PER CENT'

At the start of July 1941, Churchill carried out a minor reshuffle. Duff Cooper was removed from the Ministry of Information and replaced by Brendan Bracken. Rab Butler was moved from the Foreign Office to become President of the Board of Education and replaced with another Conservative, Richard Law. Churchill's son-in-law, Duncan Sandys, was brought in as the financial secretary to the War Office. This last appointment attracted a lot of attention as another example of Churchill finding government appointments for his cronies and hangers-on, but Butler and Bracken's moves were more significant. Butler was one of those younger Tories who was already looking forward to the task of post-war reconstruction; to Churchill's surprise, he jumped at the chance of moving out of the Foreign Office (which he loathed) to Education, where he knew that he could push through much needed reforms. Butler believed that this was the cause that would make his name and lay the path to his becoming viceroy of India, the ambition for which he had actually entered politics.[38]

As a pressman himself, Bracken proved a more successful minister of information than his predecessors. It helped that he had better news to report as the war went on. Under his leadership, the Ministry of Information (MoI) moved more towards explaining the war to the public than exhorting them to do better, encouraged service departments to be more open about defeats and tried to explain the rationale behind the new controls (and the penalties to be expected if they were contravened), in the expectation that people were more likely to obey controls they understood.[39] With Bracken at the MoI, however, Churchill lost his services as a parliamentary fixer. The enormous political capital that Churchill had built up with the British people in 1940 would ensure his safety at Number 10, but some of his toughest moments over the coming months would result from criticisms from the backbenches of the party of which he was leader.[40]

At the heart of many of these were issues of production. During the early summer, Wardlaw-Milne repeatedly stated that the country was 'not working at more than 75 per cent of our total possibilities of production' – a statement that attracted a lot of attention in the press.[41] Shortages of equipment were blamed for failures on the battlefield.

In a series of debates on supply during July 1941, MPs brought up a wide range of examples from their own constituencies of inefficiencies in design, ordering and manufacture that were supposedly holding back maximum production. Wardlaw-Milne lamented the fact that in 'the twenty-third month of the war, we are still behind in the supply of guns, tanks, aeroplanes and everything in the way of munitions of war that is required to bring us victory'. He argued that 'There are bottlenecks in connection with production which require clearance. There are efforts which are wanting in direction and there is a certain number of people, both in the managements and among the workers, who require discipline.'[42] Like many of the government's critics, he wanted the appointment of a minister of production to exert control. *The Times* argued for the same thing in a leader column that accused the government of 'breaking the hearts of producers, both managements and workpeople', by not intervening enough in industry.[43]

At the end of July, Churchill spoke out against these attacks in the Commons. No keener than his predecessors to appoint a munitions supremo who might take over his job, he refused to appoint a minister of production. Who, he asked MPs, 'is to be this superman who, without holding the office of Prime Minister, is to exercise an overriding control and initiative over the three Departments of Supply and the three Ministers of Supply'?[44] Churchill dealt with Wardlaw-Milne's accusations by asking, pertinently, for the baseline from which he was calculating his '75 per cent', and countered by showing an enormous increase in production in the past year even relative to the enormous effort that had been put in during the summer of 1940. He defended Bevin:

> He makes mistakes, like I do, though not so many or so serious – he has not got the same opportunities. At any rate he is producing, at this moment, though perhaps on rather expensive terms, a vast and steady volume of faithful effort, the like of which has not been seen before.[45]

The prime minister emphasized the extent of the transformation that had already taken place:

> There are no doubt a number of minor aspects of our national life which have not yet been effectively regimented. When as they are wanted, their turn will come. We are not a totalitarian State but we are steadily, and I believe as fast as possible, working ourselves into total war organisation.[46]

PROBLEMS IN PRODUCTION

Churchill had a point. British output of munitions during 1941 often fell below target, but this was in part because the targets themselves were unrealistically large and only theoretically related, if at all, to the country's industrial capacity. The effects of Beaverbrook's 'carrot' programmes have already been noted. Until the spring of 1941, the British were aiming for a maximum rate of annual shell production 35 per cent higher than in 1918, for an army that was smaller than its predecessor and not required to defeat the Germans on the Western Front. When the shell targets were scaled back in May 1941, the figures for tank requirements were increased – from 10,444 to 18,601 by the end of the year – a figure that would have involved the factories turning out about twelve times more tanks in the second half of 1941 than they had managed in the first.[47]

A different measure was to look, as Churchill did, at the improvement in production figures since 1940. Here, performance was more impressive. Total munitions output in the third quarter of 1941 was a third higher than a year before, during the extraordinary efforts after Dunkirk. Despite the difficulties posed by the Blitz, the UK had kept turning out more and more weapons, and it could look forward to further expansion over the coming year that would bring it closer to the targets originally set in the rearmament programmes.[48]

In terms of specific weapons, the picture was more complex. Deliveries of the heavy bombers, on which British strategy depended, had fallen well behind schedule. This was partly due to bottlenecks and inexperience within individual factories, but it also resulted from problems in planning by the Ministry of Aircraft Production, including shortages of propellers and engines. For the latter, as with the aircraft themselves, the slow arrival of the heavy bombers reflected the difficulty of developing new weapons at the cutting edge of technology: there was a lot of room for design failure, and it took time to develop the manufacturing techniques that would allow for mass production. Since incremental improvements in performance often had a big effect in aerial combat, aircraft were constantly subject to modification. In the UK, these improvements were incorporated, where possible, into the manufacturing process – which resulted in better planes but prevented the long, uninterrupted production runs that would allow the maximum output of aircraft. All three of the heavy bomber types that the British built in 1941 suffered from significant problems. The worst, the two-engine Manchester, performed so badly that it had to go back to the drawing board. Redesigned with four engines as the Lancaster, it would become the best heavy bomber of the war, but it would not enter operational service until 1942.[49]

Whereas improvements in aircraft output fell below expectations, the efficiency of the shell factories improved fast than had been anticipated. By the end of 1941, almost all the Royal Ordnance factories had been completed. Positioned as they were away from major industrial centres and with only a small pre-war workforce to draw on, it was expected that they would have significant problems integrating new workers. During the first half of 1941, however, a series of improvements in management and piece-rates resulted in rapid improvements in efficiency. By the end of 1941, the munition-filling plants were performing so well that, with the reduction in ammunition scales, the government was able to cancel plans for the construction of additional factories.[50]

Guns were more of a problem. Although the output of field artillery caught up with the programme during 1941, more complicated anti-aircraft guns lagged well behind target and only started to catch up in 1942. A dramatic expansion in the production of 2-pounder anti-tank guns – 211 were made in October 1940, 1,262 in October 1941 – was bought at the cost of a slower introduction of the 6-pounder gun, which had been planned to counter improvements in German tank armour. In the summer of 1940, the government had chosen to maintain 2-pounder production in order to re-equip the army as rapidly as possible with some form of anti-tank gun, rather than to reduce overall output by swapping over to the newer, heavier and much more effective gun.[51]

In tank production too, the numerical increase disguised problems of quality. At the end of 1940, 150 tanks had been made a month. By the end of 1941, the equivalent figure was 626.[52] Yet some of these vehicles had significant flaws. In an attempt to maximize tank output in 1940, a new infantry tank – the Churchill – had been rushed into production from the prototype stage. The Churchill would eventually become a good tank, but the first models were mechanically unreliable. They arrived at units with a list of the defects that were still being rectified by the manufacturer: not a measure that improved soldiers' confidence in the vehicle.[53]

Even worse was the Covenanter, a pre-war design that was recognized as a failure by the time the first models were delivered in 1940, but which was then kept in production rather than disrupt the flow of tanks to Home Forces. The Covenanter had the sleek lines of a speedboat, and was about as much use on the battlefield. Among its numerous design flaws was an inadequate lock for the turret hatch, which would, as a result, slam shut when the tank went over bumpy ground, braining the unfortunate commander. Units equipped with the Covenanter left a trail of broken-down vehicles behind them when they went out on exercise. It was used in large numbers as a training tank at home but never went into action overseas.

In contrast, the new tanks that were now being sent out to the Middle East – Valentines and Crusaders – were initially the equals of their opponents, but the Crusader had particular problems with its cooling systems, which showed up rapidly when it was deployed in the Western Desert. Despite the fact that the Germans were known to be up-armouring their tanks, both were still being fitted with the 2-pounder gun until early 1942 because of the delay in producing 6-pounders. Like other British vehicles, they were designed to a War Office specification that restricted their turrets, so they could fit on British railways, which made it difficult to fit them with bigger guns.

The manufacture of large numbers of tanks was not helped by the fact that the War Office changed its mind about what it wanted in response to experiences on the battlefield. After he became minister of supply in June 1941, Beaverbrook insisted that in order to maximize output, the same vehicles should remain in production until mid-1943. This would allow orders to be placed for another 10,000 tanks, but by the time they were produced, most of them would have been several years out of date.[54]

Inefficiency, mal-coordination, failed designs and misconceived programmes were part of every combatant country's experience of the early years of the Second World War. There is little sign that Britain was worse off in this regard than anyone else. Nor were British firms particularly inefficient in their use of resources, or British workers unproductive relative to the time they spent on the job: quite the contrary.[55] A comparison with Germany is very instructive. The Germans might have made better tanks than the British in 1941, but the British had mobilized their economy more extensively and were making better use of mass production. The result was that Britain out-built Germany – not just in planes and ships, but also in tanks and armoured personnel carriers. Relative to the size of their army – about a third the size of Germany's – in 1941 the British even made more heavy guns.

Judging on the output of the key weapons of mechanized war, it would be easy to mistake which of these countries was about to launch an invasion of the Soviet Union.

Table 5. Comparison of actual output of selected armaments, Germany vs. the UK, 1940–41

Armaments	Germany		UK	
	1940	1941	1940	1941
Military aircraft (structure weight million lbs)	59	64	59	87
Tanks (number)	1,600	3,800	1,400	4,800
Other armoured vehicles (number)	500	1,300	6,000	10,500
Heavy guns	6,300	8,100	2,520	6,040
Naval vessels over 1,000 tons (standard displacement)	NA	162*	222	346**

* submarines only; ** including 2 battleships, 2 aircraft carriers, 6 cruisers and 109 destroyers and corvettes, but excluding 1,156 merchant ships completed in 1941. Sources: C. Webster and N. Frankland, *The Strategic Air Offensive against Germany, 1939–45, IV: Annexes and Appendices* (London, 1961), pp. 469–70; CSO, *Fighting with Figures: A Statistical Digest of the Second World War* (London, 1995), pp. 151–3.

'HIS CABINET IS A LOT OF DUMMIES AND HE IS THE ONE SUPREME BOTTLENECK'

Churchill's defence of production in July made absolutely no difference to the belief that the government was failing to organize the effort necessary for victory. For the *Daily Mirror* executive Cecil King:

What it all boils down to is that the House and the newspapers are convinced that our production is not what it should be, and that this is due partly to bad organisation on the ministerial level and partly to the poor quality of minister responsible for this part of our operations. Churchill will not try and find better men outside his own little circle, and will not alter the arrangement by which his Cabinet is a lot of dummies and he is the one supreme bottleneck.[56]

The Conservative MP Cuthbert Headlam thought – as he often did – that Churchill's speech had fallen a bit flat:

Winston's oratory and make-up are not suited to such a subject as 'production' – you can't get away with it by phrases when you are called upon to explain why the supply of the most necessary and obvious things is terribly behindhand. Bevin who wound up for the Government ... made a kind of case for high wages and no compulsion. There is no doubt, I fear, that we are governed by the TUC industrially and God only knows what the mess will be after the war.[57]

As that suggested, concerns over production had a partisan dimension, as Jock Colville was told by the Conservative chief whip, James Stuart:

The Tories, conscious of the great sacrifices they are making financially and of the exceedingly high wages being paid to war workers, are cantankerous about the many reports of slackness, absenteeism, etc., in the factories. The Labour Party resent this criticism and blame the managers and employers for any shortcomings.[58]

As 1941 went on, Conservative backbenchers became more and more resentful about the amount of 'socialism' they were being expected to swallow for the war effort. They worried that Churchill and his cronies were far too bound up with fighting the war to stop Labour ministers taking advantage of their place within the Coalition Government to sneak in their policies by the back door. Meanwhile, Labour backbenchers grew more vocal in their disappointment at the lack of reward that Labour was getting for its ministers' service in government, and impatient for the economic reforms they believed would allow the country's resources to be properly mobilized for the war. Even as the country became organized on more socialist lines than ever before, Labour's leaders were castigated for their timidity and caution.

The LSE professor Harold Laski proved particularly determined to stir up the party's passions against the leadership. Laski was a prolific writer and broadcaster, and an inspiring teacher. By the time the war came, he was Labour's leading intellectual. He had a devoted following among the party's rank and file, who repeatedly voted him on to Labour's powerful National Executive Committee. Having adopted a liberal version of Marxism, Laski had spent the 1930s grappling with the question of whether democracy could withstand the inevitable change necessary to make the transition from a capitalist system. Now he argued that the moment was ripe for a 'revolution by consent', because the propertied classes would have to give ground in the face of the fundamental crisis posed by the war.

Laski thought that Labour's ministers were wasting their opportunity in the coalition. The moment was ripe, he believed, for them to press for the full implementation of the Labour Party manifesto, immediate nationalization of the means of production and all. With the aim of forcing the party's leaders into action, Laski attacked them both in the privacy of the NEC and in public in the pages of Labour-supporting newspapers. Attlee and Laski loathed each other, and feuded from 1940 until the end of the war. In summer 1941, Laski enlisted Herbert Morrison's help to set up a committee on Labour's reconstruction policies with himself as secretary. This, he hoped, would be the means by which Labour ministers could be forced to pursue much more dramatic economic and social reforms.[59]

'OUR MOST POSITIVE WAR AIM . . . THE COUNTRY WE ARE FIGHTING FOR'

For the moment, issues of production and strategy occupied the political centre stage, but 1941 was also an important period for discussions of reconstruction. These reflected an intellectual, cultural and political revolution that was taking place as the accumulated progressive thought of the early twentieth century reacted with the experience of the war. Alongside the new controls that were being introduced over the economy, a new middle ground was being staked out – anti-capitalist, pro-welfare, Christian, patriotic – that would shape British politics for decades to come.

This was a historical moment that left Churchill unmoved. He had little interest in promoting domestic reform, as was apparent in his appointment of Arthur Greenwood, the Labour minister without portfolio, to chair a new Cabinet Committee on Reconstruction and

Post-War Problems at the start of 1941.[60] Here, it might have seemed, was Labour's great chance to win the post-war rewards for its entry into office, and Greenwood started with grandiose plans to deal with every conceivable reconstruction issue at home and abroad. Yet his grand ambitions soon ran into the sand. Greenwood had lost his responsibility for the war economy because of his worsening drink problem, and he now struggled to chair a meeting or to master a brief. Churchill gave him no executive powers. In the year after it was created, the Committee on Reconstruction and Post-War Problems met only four times. At the end of January 1941, the prime minister also blocked fresh proposals for an official statement of British war aims. His argument, as Harold Nicolson noted in his diary, was that 'precise aims would be compromising, whereas vague principles would disappoint'.[61] That stymied the Ministry of Information's hopes of talking about post-war reconstruction as a means of bolstering popular morale.

Yet the work of reconstruction continued. At the start of 1941, the Labour academic G. D. H. Cole persuaded Greenwood to find the money from the Treasury to pay for a Reconstruction Survey, carried out by Nuffield College, Oxford. The Reconstruction Survey's volunteers fanned out from the provincial universities to investigate the location of industry, wartime changes in population, local government, social services and education, including the organization of the arts, so as to provide information to government departments too busy to collect it themselves. Professional bodies, including the British Medical Association and the Garden Cities and Town Planning Association, launched reconstruction investigations of their own in an effort to influence policy. Other interest groups, voluntary organizations and academic social researchers followed suit. Tom Harrisson, the director of Mass-Observation, who thought that most of those involved had little clue what people really wanted, called these projects the 'reconstruction racket'.[62] The government might have been dragging its feet, but change was in the air, and the experts all wanted to be in on the act.

In the leader columns of *The Times*, E. H. Carr kept up his campaign to persuade the political elite to plan against a return to the bad old days before the war. On 5 December 1940, in a celebrated piece on 'The Two Scourges' – war and unemployment – that had blighted a generation, Carr argued that the example of sacrifice in war must be followed when it came to building the peace:

> In 1940 the manufacturer foregoes profits, the worker foregoes trade union restrictions on conditions of employment, the consumer foregoes luxuries and lends to the government to finance expenditure from which no material return is asked or expected. In 1930 a small fraction of these sacrifices would have sufficed to avert the unemployment crisis of the ensuing year, and, at the same time, to bring the countries now involved in war better housing, more ample nutrition, better education, and more amenities for the leisure of the masses.[63]

Republished as a pamphlet in 1941, 'The Two Scourges' sold 100,000 copies.[64]

One of the ways in which the need for national reform became a central theme in wartime public life was via the plethora of articles, talks and pamphlets about the state of Britain which appeared in the aftermath of 1940. Sired out of the Slump by Hitler, they were the response of the progressive intelligentsia of the 1930s to the formation of the Coalition and the threat of German invasion. Their authors were a diverse bunch, but they had some common themes: a condemnation of the unbridled capitalism of the 1930s, the advocacy of broadly socialist solutions, and an underlying patriotism and optimism about the possibility of change.[65]

Back in November 1940, the director of the Ministry of Information's Film Division, Sir Kenneth Clark, had suggested that the magazine *Picture Post* – which sold a million copies a week, and claimed that it had 5 million readers – might run a special edition on 'the Britain we hope to build when the war was over'.[66] The resulting issue, 'A Plan for Britain', was published on 4 January 1941. It opened with a foreword that explained the necessity of working out schemes of reconstruction before it was too late. This was the time, it announced 'for doing the thinking, so that we can make things how we want them to be'. 'A Plan for Britain' sought to lay out a blueprint for 'our most positive war aim . . . the country we are fighting for'.[67] Across forty pages of short articles, expert contributors, including the economist Thomas Balogh (a protégé of Keynes), the scientist Julian Huxley and J. B. Priestley, laid out a prospectus for a 'new Britain': a universal welfare system, schemes of urban planning to sweep away the slums, and a planned economy to end the horrors of mass unemployment. *Picture Post* was always keen to create a dialogue with its readers, but the response to this issue was unprecedented. Over the weeks that followed, more than 2,000 letters poured into its offices. Most were enthusiastic. A few denounced the issue as socialist propaganda and cancelled their subscriptions.[68]

January 1941 also saw J. B. Priestley's return for a new series of talks in the 'Postscript' radio slot. Since his last appearance he had negotiated a pay rise to fifty guineas a programme, more than twice what any of the other 'Postscript' speakers got. In his first broadcast of this second run, Priestley insisted on the need for a new world order: 'The Nazis and the like are the festering sores on the diseased body of our world. Fight them? Of course we must fight them, but at the same time we must fight the diseased condition that produced them.' Priestley laid out no precise political agenda – indeed, his next 'Postscripts' dealt with much more prosaic issues – but when the BBC failed to extend his contract, he complained that he was being forced off the air because he was too radical. As before, the idea that he was being silenced by powerful vested interests had at least as important an impact on popular opinion as anything he actually said.[69]

In his book *Out of the People*, published later in 1941, Priestley suggested that 'the people feel, obscurely for most part, the need for many great changes. They want to have done with their pre-war life . . . It is this, just as much as their detestation of the Nazis, that made them ready to clear the decks for a truly gigantic war effort.' He called for an end to the class system and the nationalization of industry to liberate popular enthusiasm and imagination. 'The release of energy', he argued, 'will be terrific. We shall feel like a man throwing off a strait jacket.' As usual with Priestley, the book was big on calls for common sense, but short on practical details.[70] Commentators such as Priestley were frustrated with a government which seemed unwilling to rebuild Britain and unable to beat Hitler. Reconstruction was not, for them, a project that could be left until after the war. Before they got to a 'New Jerusalem', they wanted a New Leviathan: a democracy of citizens fighting for a state in which they had an equal share.

This sort of talk aroused a great deal of ire from more traditional Conservatives. Cuthbert Headlam was in many ways an unusual Tory MP: older and more reactionary than many, permanently grumpy because of his bitter disappointment at the stalling of his political career, but clever too, and very conscious of the way that the 1930s were now being rewritten as a period of failure. At the start of March 1941, he complained to his diary that:

> The amount of rubbish which is being spoken and written about this world to be is calculated to cause a deal of trouble later on and, of course, the people who are mainly responsible for all this prattle are the usual crew – the political intelligentsia and the good social workers. What always annoys me is that none of this crowd ever alludes to all that has been done within the last fifty years in the way of what is called 'social reform', or dreams of mentioning the vast sums of money which have been poured out to improve the condition of the people. From the way men like J. B. Priestley speak one might imagine that nothing was being done for the great mass of the population and that this country was preserved solely for an idle crowd of parasites who never lifted a finger for the public good . . . the foolish talk about equality can only lead to an increase in discontent and unrest when the peace comes again.[71]

As well as broadcasting and writing, Priestley also became chairman of the 1941 Committee, a body set up at the beginning of the year by Edward Hulton, the owner of *Picture Post*, to try to press more progressive policies on the government. A disparate umbrella group, it brought together a variety of journalists and intellectuals on the political left, many of them familiar from the days of the Popular Front, some of whom would play an important role in years to come. They included Tom Wintringham, Ritchie Calder and Victor Gollancz, the publisher who had founded the Left Book Club, but also Richard Titmuss, an up-and-coming writer on issues of population and health.

The son of a failed farmer, Titmuss was an astonishing autodidact, who had educated himself in statistics while working as a clerk in the offices of the County Fire Insurance Company. In his spare time, closely supported by his wife, he had written two books (and co-authored another two) and become a fellow of the Royal Statistical and Economic Societies. Since the start of the war, he had been helping the Ministry of Economic Warfare with its calculations of probable German mortality under the blockade. Titmuss was another former Liberal who was moving towards socialism. Deeply worried that inadequate welfare and a culture of acquisitiveness would doom the British population to eventual extinction, he argued that social reform was vitally necessary to decrease infant mortality among the poor and to encourage the wealthy to bear more children. In 1942, Titmuss would be appointed to join the team of academics who (in one of the more notable gestures of British self-confidence) were already writing the official history of the war. His volume on wartime social policy would become a key text in explaining how the conflict had created the welfare state.[72]

Another member of the 1941 Committee was the MP Sir Richard Acland. Acland came from a wealthy landowning family, and he was a former Liberal and campaigner for the formation of a Popular Front. In 1939, he had inherited his father's baronetcy and undergone a Damascene conversion to Christianity and socialism. In 1940, he wrote a best-selling title for Penguin called *Unser Kampf* ('our struggle', in contrast to Hitler's *Mein Kampf*), which set out his calls for an egalitarian spiritual revival in which 'the motive of service to our fellow-men' would take 'precedence over the motive of self-interest', and where 'great numbers of people' would find 'an entirely new faith in God'.[73] He had already founded a new political party, Forward March. A tall, sharp-featured man with a rasping voice, Acland practised what he preached: in 1943, he would make over all his family's estates to the National Trust.[74]

At the start of 1941, Acland attended a conference at Malvern College, Worcestershire, convened by William Temple, the archbishop of York, to consider 'the new society that is quite evidently emerging from the war'. Most of the papers that were read were theologically dense and tricky to understand. The speakers included some arch Tories, among them the poet T. S. Eliot, who were more hostile to socialism than to Fascism. If there was a unifying factor, it was a belief that the Church needed to offer a moral alternative to the materialism of the totalitarian ideologies that had plunged the world into chaos.[75] On the last day of the conference, however, Acland stood up and argued, simply, that 'the private ownership of the major resources of our country is ... the stumbling block which is making it harder for us to advance towards the Kingdom of God on Earth'. This electrified some of the more reform-minded delegates. When Temple decided to draw up a list of 'findings' for the gathering, Acland insisted that his argument was included. That generated a lot of press coverage and popular interest, and the two pamphlets containing the Malvern conference proceedings together sold more than a million copies.[76]

Temple was himself to become a figurehead of the reconstruction movement. His mix of privilege, Christianity and socialism was distinctively of Britain in the first third of the twentieth century.[77] Temple was the son of an archbishop of Canterbury, a brilliant academic and an ecumenical church leader. He had briefly been a member of the Labour Party, and he was president of the Workers' Educational Association. Temple firmly supported the war, but he was strongly against the generation of private wealth taking precedence over collective well-being, and in favour of improved welfare and better education. At the end of 1941, he would set out some of these ideas – alongside a call to restore the family to the centre of national life – in another Penguin Special, *Christianity and the Social Order*, which eventually sold 140,000 copies.[78] Temple was the first writer to use the term 'welfare state' in print, and he was widely acknowledged as the best leader the Anglican Church had. When Cosmo Lang, the archbishop of Canterbury, announced his retirement at the start of 1942, Temple was the only possibility to take his place.

As the audience and sales figures suggest, discussions of reconstruction plainly reached a large number of people. Yet they found their most receptive audience among the same group who had already been interested in these topics before the war: the largely middle-class members of the 'reading popular front' established by Victor Gollancz and Allen Lane in the late 1930s. These were also the people whose perceptions of morale were being canvassed by Home Intelligence, so it is perhaps unsurprising to find that, as early as February 1941, the Ministry of Information was able to report that the public had a clear set of ideas about what the country should look like after the war:

> On the home front, it is hoped that the extremes of wealth and poverty
> will be swept away, that there will be a greater degree of social security
> for all, and that what is loosely termed 'privilege' will also be got rid of;
> though many expect that 'privilege' will put up a stern fight.[79]

In practice, the impact on popular attitudes and expectations was less clear-cut than that. Hopes for the future had to compete with a deep cynicism about the prospect of change, born out of the folk memory of disappointments after the last Great War. Widespread though calls for reconstruction were, for the moment they were easily lost in the daily round of war news that filled most of the pages of the press.

Notwithstanding the changes wrought by the war, prescriptions such as the end of private property or the abolition of class seemed impossibly distant solutions to the problems that were confronting most people in the spring of 1941: inadequate shelters, queues, and the continuing disruption of mobilization into the forces and the factories.[80]

The experience of wartime life, however, also encouraged a radicalism of its own. Frustrations with the 'old gang' at the top were revived by the Blitz and the defeats in the Middle East, and they combined with a concern for fairness and a desire for equality of sacrifice that was further stoked by the Ministry of Information's repeated insistence that everyone had a part to play in the war. In the future, the growing popular desire for change would be a significant political force, but for the time being, it lacked a focus. The journalists, thinkers and writers who were calling for immediate reconstruction helped to set the wartime mood, but they were scarcely a coherent political movement, and all the major parties had committed themselves to the Coalition and the electoral truce.

So while in retrospect 'A Plan for Britain' and Priestley's broadcasts were steps along the path that led from 1940 to 1945, at the time the political outcome of the war was much less clear. As evidence of that, the first politician to enjoy some wartime by-electoral success against the government was not a liberal intellectual from the ranks of the 1941 Committee, but an extreme right-wing maverick – Noel Pemberton Billing – who, though he never won a seat, secured between 24 and 44 per cent of the vote (albeit on very small turnouts) in four contests against Conservative candidates in the summer of 1941.[81]

A vile bigot, and a self-publicist of epic proportions who toured constituencies in a bright yellow Rolls-Royce, Pemberton Billing stood on 'the urgent necessity of pressing on the Government a more vital war policy', including the massive and indiscriminate bombing of Germany. He attacked Conservatives who he claimed were plotting to remove the prime minister, with the slogan 'for Churchill and to hell with the Conservative party'.[82] As all this suggested, the bitter condemnations of *Guilty Men* still had some room to run. Yet 'P-B' also attempted to respond to the reformist mood, reassuring voters that although he was 'not a socialist', he had 'that resolve, shared today by every man of good intent, that out of this war we must build something better than the selfish chaotic world order that led to its outbreak'.[83] In the summer of 1941, even Pemberton Billing thought it was necessary to talk about rebuilding the peace as well as winning the war.

'YOU REMEMBER THIS 'ERE SOCIAL SECURITY BUSINESS?'

Churchill's lack of enthusiasm for thinking about the new world did not completely halt his colleagues' efforts to start building it. In practice, there were powerful reasons for presenting a vision of the future. As well as domestic demands for a statement of war aims, there was also a diplomatic need to impress the United States and Occupied Europe with an alternative to the Nazi 'New Order'.

This was what Anthony Eden did in a speech at the Mansion House on 29 May 1941. Drawing on Keynes' advice about how to respond to Nazi propaganda, Eden aligned the British Empire with the 'Four Freedoms' (of speech and worship, and from want and fear) that Roosevelt had identified in his State of the Union address in January 1941, and declared that 'social security' would be the 'first object' of Britain's policy at home and abroad when the war was finished. That would mean working with other countries to prevent the economic chaos that had contributed to the rise of the dictatorships and brought on the current war, but the foreign secretary made it clear that the strain of the conflict would also make it necessary for Britain to retain protectionist economic policies once peace was secured. In the same speech, Eden identified the key theme of policy for post-war Europe – a reconstructed Germany must be included in the continent's economic recovery, but it was essential to make sure that the Germans would never start another war again.[84]

This was an important moment, but not as significant as it might have been. Although the disaster in Greece had badly damaged his reputation, Eden remained a much more modern, forward-looking politician than Churchill, with a better understanding of the impact of the ideas that Roosevelt was unleashing on the other side of the Atlantic. His commitment to 'social security' was part of the emergence of a new sort of Conservatism: progressive, outward looking, and which trusted the state rather than the market. It was very different to Chamberlain's liberal unionism or Churchill's bombastic Toryism, and it would come to play a crucial role in the party's revival after 1945.

In 1941, however, Eden's vague espousal of social security was hardly a plan for the future. In the absence of a powerful minister driving on reconstruction at the centre of Whitehall, the momentum for reform came from individual departments conducting their own preparations for the period after the war.

The damage done by the Blitz made the physical reconstruction of Britain's cities a necessity, and the minister of works, Lord Reith, was determined to bring to the urban planning the same improving spirit that had so enlivened the airwaves when he was director-general of the BBC. Reith's outline plan for rebuilding Britain – including the compulsory purchase of land for development, the dispersal of industries, a national transport network and an overhauled electricity grid – was presented to the War Cabinet (and much hyped in the press) in January 1941. Reith asked two judges, Mr Justice Uthwatt and Lord Justice Scott, to chair committees investigating the future of the countryside and compensation for landowners respectively. He spent the whole of 1941 trying to secure approval to set up a central authority to oversee town and country planning. Reith and Churchill loathed each other: no sooner had Reith got his planning authority in early 1942 than he lost his job in favour of the prime minister's friend, the Conservative businessman Lord Portal.[85]

Meanwhile, at the Board of Education, officials decided that the time was ripe to dust off the 1938 Spens Report on secondary education. By summer 1941, they had developed proposals to raise the school leaving age to fifteen, to provide free secondary schooling for all, and to divide these schools into grammars, technicals and secondary moderns, between which pupils would be allocated on the basis of aptitude. When he became president of the Board of Education, Rab Butler was eager to carry through reforms. He also knew that this was an area of potentially great political controversy, particularly over religious schooling. Despite opposition from Churchill, Butler cautiously pressed ahead with plans for a new education Bill.[86]

Like Eden, Butler was now much influenced by Keynes, and he was also on good terms with Archbishop Temple. Unlike most Tory politicians, Butler was interested in formulating a philosophy of modern Conservatism that would provide an alternative to totalitarianism. Like other Conservative intellectuals, he now believed that social order, Christianity, individual freedom and economic recovery would only be preserved by the intervention of a much more active state. For that reason, Butler was willing to consider educational reforms that went well beyond those laid out by Spens in the late 1930s. Shortly before he joined the Board of Education, he had become chairman of a new Post-War Problems Central Committee that he hoped would prepare the Conservatives for a changed political world. He set up sub-committees on issues such as housing, town and country planning, and education. Yet it would prove extremely difficult to corral the different strands of Conservative thought into a coherent vision of the future. More diehard Tories condemned his project as an attempt to impose 'pink socialism' on the party.[87]

As Butler settled himself at Education, the Ministry of Health, then under the National Labour MP Malcolm MacDonald, was also working out plans for the future. By October 1941, it had committed itself to setting up a national hospital service after the war – largely because the expansion of the Emergency Medical Service, in anticipation of a flood of air-raid casualties, had left the voluntary hospitals so dependent on government finance that there would be major problems if state support were withdrawn. That May, the Ministry had already set up a committee 'to undertake, with special reference to the inter-relation of the schemes, a survey of the existing national schemes of social insurance and allied services, including workmen's compensation, and to make recommendations'. Despite his alcoholism, Greenwood, as chair of the Cabinet's reconstruction committee, still had enough sense for the political game to promote this to the papers as the first step on the path to social security for all.

Sorting out the confusing mess of welfare benefits that had been left by decades of partial reforms was a job that would keep even an expert in social policy tied up for ages. As it happened, Ernest Bevin had an ideal candidate. He rang up Greenwood: 'You remember this 'ere social security business? I've got just the man for you. I'm sending Beveridge round in the morning.'[88] Beveridge was less than amused at being handed what looked at first like a minor administrative job. His long-time secretary and future wife, Janet Mair, suggested to him that it might hold wider possibilities than he thought. Perhaps he could broaden his remit? Beveridge thought that indeed he might.

PART FIVE

Total War

On 19 June 1941, another official leaflet fluttered through the door of Richard Brown's home in Ipswich. It bore instructions to register his children for an evacuation scheme that would be implemented in the event of a German invasion. Did the authorities know more than they were letting on, he wondered, or was it just a routine precaution? In any case, it had re-awakened all 'the old distressing feelings which we had last July and August'. What would he do if the Germans stormed ashore? How would he get his family away? Could he bear to destroy his allotment to stop the Nazis enjoying it?

Three days later, he awoke with a start to hear the paper boys shouting in the street outside. Had they really said that Germany had declared war on Russia? There was nothing about it in his morning newspaper, but the nine o'clock news on the radio confirmed the truth. Straight away, the worries of the previous days eased. 'Invasion seems at least a month further away and now it all depends on how the affair goes as to how likely an invasion will be at all, but we hadn't better think like that just yet.'[1] That night he was so relieved that he gave his wife an extra kiss before bed.

'Operation Barbarossa', the German attack on the Soviet Union, was a crucial moment in the history of the war. It had significant consequences for life in Britain, and it dramatically altered the course of the conflict. Over the next six months, as Britain, America and Japan reacted to the opening of this new front, the European struggle that had started in 1939 was transformed into a truly global war.

24

The Widening War

In Eastern Europe, the war meant death on a scale that challenges our comprehension. The dismemberment of Poland had triggered a wave of annihilatory violence by both occupying powers. The Soviets sought to eradicate the middle class in occupied eastern Poland, massacring more than 20,000 military officers, policemen, landowners and professionals, imprisoning hundreds of thousands more, and deporting a million-and-a-half Poles to labour camps east of the Ural Mountains. By summer 1941, as many as a third of them were dead: more people than the total number of British service personnel and civilians killed by enemy action during the entire war. Meanwhile, to the west, the Nazis had begun a brutal campaign of racial reconstruction, driving out Poles from land intended for German settlers and terrorizing occupied Poland's 2 million Jews. Those who did not flee to the east were forced into ghettos where they were left to starve to death.[1]

The killing, on and behind the battlefield, only escalated after Hitler launched his invasion of the Soviet Union. It was an immense military operation. One hundred and fifty-three Axis divisions, nearly 3.6 million men in total, supported by more than 3,500 tanks, advanced into Soviet territory.[2] The vast battles on the Eastern Front killed and wounded huge numbers of soldiers on both sides. By the end of September 1941, the German army had suffered 400,000 casualties, and 2.75 million Soviet soldiers were dead, wounded or missing.[3] Following behind the advancing armies, the SS oversaw the murder of around half a million Jews by the end of 1941. Between June and December 1941, the Wehrmacht captured 3.35 million Red Army soldiers. By the end of the year, over 2 million of them were dead.[4]

This terrifying racial war might seem a different conflict to the struggle being played out between Britain, Germany and Italy in the west, but they were inextricably linked. Germany's strategic planning was based on depriving Soviet citizens of food so that the Wehrmacht – and ultimately West European civilians and livestock herds – could be supplied from the grain belts of the Ukraine. Germany's desperate need for food was a direct result of Hitler's decision in 1939 to fight the world's largest naval power, and Britain's subsequent implementation of an economic blockade.

In Britain, in contrast to Eastern Europe, the opening of the new front saved lives. The relief in terms of civilian casualties was immediate. From May 1941, Luftwaffe bombers were redeployed to Eastern Europe, Norway and the Mediterranean, and the substantial, regular air assaults on British cities that had characterized the previous eight months came to an end. In the first six months of 1941, there were 20,374 air-raid casualties. In the second half of the year, the figure fell to 1,467. The total casualties for 1942 and 1943 were 4,150 and 3,450 respectively. In those middle years of the war, more than twice as many Britons would die from road accidents as from air raids.[5] The fear and disruption that resulted from the prospect of air attack were not removed: German fighter-bombers continued 'tip-and-run' attacks around the coast, and there were substantial attacks on the cathedral cities – the so-called 'Baedecker Blitz' – between April and July 1942. Some of these caused what felt to Britons like heavy casualties. In Bath, for example, three nights of raids between 25 and 27 April 1942 killed more than 420 people. These attacks were no longer, however, part of a sustained attritional air campaign against the United Kingdom, and they had no impact on Britain's role as a formidable opponent of the Third Reich.[6]

During the middle years of the war, the bulk of the British army remained in the UK, and much of the fighting in the Middle and Far East was undertaken by soldiers from the Commonwealth and Empire. Certain groups – combat infantrymen, merchant seamen and bomber aircrew – still suffered terrible losses, but overall, the cost in death and wounding for Britain's participation in a total war during this period was astonishing light. Between September 1941 and September 1942, the British armed forces suffered just 26,268 fatal casualties. On average, in the year after the war on the Eastern Front began, the Red Army lost almost that many soldiers killed and missing every two days.[7]

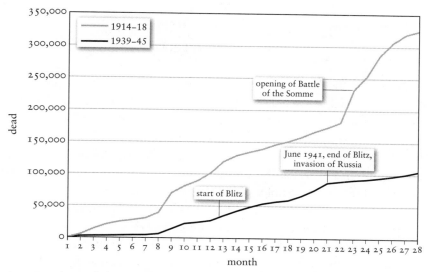

A comparison of the cumulative numbers of British dead in the first twenty-seven months of the two world wars

The difference the Eastern Front made to Britain can be seen by comparing the cumulative rate of military and civilian deaths suffered by the UK in both world wars. Once battle was joined in earnest, the rate of increase in deaths from enemy action in the two conflicts was initially not that dissimilar. Twenty-one months in, however, the lines sharply diverge – in the First World War, as the citizen army recruited in 1914 first went into combat en masse in July 1916; in the Second, as the weight of battle shifted towards the east from June 1941. One of the reasons that Churchill – and the rest of the British political and military elite – were so keen on fighting an ultra-modern, high-technology war of machines was that they hoped it would spare the country the slaughter of the Somme and Passchendaele. Yet the main reason that they were spared a higher casualty war was Germany's decision to launch a new war in the east and its failure to overcome the Soviet Union.

'RUSSIA WILL ASSUREDLY BE DEFEATED'

How should the British react to this new turn in the war? Most of the British ruling elite – including the leadership of the Labour Party and the churches, as well as the Conservative and Liberal parties, the armed forces, and the royal family – was hostile to Communism. The loathing for Stalin's regime had only been strengthened by the Nazi-Soviet pact, the assault on Finland and the economic aid that had allowed Hitler to withstand the economic blockade. The German invasion posed a question about the ideological nature of the war: should Britain just leave the two brutal totalitarian regimes to slug it out?[8]

Yet since the days of the Phoney War, British strategists had displayed a strong element of realpolitik in their attitudes to the Soviet Union. Even after September 1939, a strong consensus had formed between leading figures on the left and the right that favoured the construction of an Anglo-Soviet alliance. In 1940, Halifax and Rab Butler had fought hard to use Stafford Cripps as an envoy to Moscow on the basis that he might be able to build a connection with Stalin. With Germany triumphant, winning over the Soviets proved beyond even Cripps' considerable powers of argument, but the advocates of better relations with the USSR had never lost hope that it could be turned against the Nazis. In the summer of 1940, Butler bet his father-in-law, the industrialist Sam Courtauld, a case of champagne that Britain and the Soviet Union would end up fighting on the same side. On 22 June 1941, he cheerfully collected his winnings.[9]

When Eden took over at the Foreign Office at the start of 1941, he too accepted that an accommodation with the Soviet Union was a top priority. The problem was how this could be achieved. Churchill vetoed Eden's suggestion that he undertake a personal mission to Moscow. Even as evidence accumulated that Hitler intended to launch a major move in the east, Stalin seemed determined to keep placating Germany.[10]

Despite his well-known opposition to Bolshevism, Churchill's response to the possibility of a German attack on the USSR was clear. Contrary to Rudolf Hess's hopes, he showed no signs of wanting to conclude a peace with Hitler that would allow Germany to get on with fighting the Soviets. Rather, once he grasped the likelihood of an invasion, the prime minister insisted that Stalin must be told about the German threat. It was not his fault that the Soviet leader chose to ignore the warning.[11]

Between 21 and 22 June, as it became clear that a German invasion was inevitable, the prime minister cloistered himself at Chequers with Beaverbrook, Eden and Cripps, who had all already established themselves as strong proponents of improving Anglo-Soviet relations. Over the coming months all four would fight, alongside and against each other, about how to handle the new situation in the east.[12]

On the evening of 22 June, Churchill broadcast on the BBC to announce that the UK would stand alongside the Soviet Union. After stating that 'the Nazi regime is indistinguishable from the worst features of Communism', he nonetheless then conjured up the image of innocent Russians being crushed by an enemy to which Britons were already implacably opposed:

> Any man or state who fights on against Nazism will have our aid. Any man or state who marches with Hitler is our foe. The Russian danger is therefore our danger, and the danger of the United States, just as the cause of any Russian fighting for his hearth and home is the cause of free men and free peoples in every quarter of the globe.[13]

The prime minister carefully did not use the word 'ally' to describe Britain's relationship with the Soviet Union, but he did make clear that Britain would do what it could to keep the USSR in the fight.

Not least by acknowledging his own attitude to Communism, Churchill offered a lead to those who might otherwise have been willing to let the Germans and Soviets fight it out. In her diary for 22 June, for example, well-to-do middle-class housewife Clara Milburn described some satisfaction that

> now Russia will get a bit of what she gave Finland – and perhaps a lot more. Mr Churchill broadcast tonight and said we must stand by Russia. I suppose we must, as she is now against the enemy of mankind. But I wish we need not when I think of her ways.[14]

Not everyone was won over. The Catholic writers J. R. R. Tolkien and Evelyn Waugh, for example, both of whom had previously seen the war in terms of a defence of Western Christendom against the godless totalitarian hordes, now began to have serious doubts about what Britain was fighting for. Yet the reaction of most Britons to the opening of the Eastern Front seems to have been more like that of Richard Brown: relief that, at least for the moment, the focus of the war had moved elsewhere. Despite government fears of a right-wing backlash, over days that followed the press, the churches and Conservative MPs all fell into line behind the idea that beating Germany was so important that Britain ought to help the Soviet Union.[15]

In fact, Churchill, his military advisors and much of the press suspected that the Soviets would not hold out long enough for British aid to make a difference. 'Russia', the prime minister remarked over dinner on 21 June, 'will assuredly be defeated.'[16] There were good reasons to expect a quick German victory. The Wehrmacht's run of success since 1939 had lent it an air of invincibility, but the purged Red Army had struggled to beat even tiny Finland during the Winter War. Germany's initial victories on the Eastern Front seemed to confirm the diagnosis. If the Soviets were to go the same way as the French, the Germans would capture the resources they needed to sustain their war effort, and free their forces to attack Britain either with a cross-Channel invasion, or with a blow through the Caucasus Mountains against the Middle East. Yet Churchill, as ever, found reasons for hope. Germany's attack on the Soviet Union, he believed, made it still more likely that America would shortly enter the war. Once it did so, British victory would be assured, even if the Germans had already forced Moscow to surrender. To begin with, his attitude towards helping the Soviets was dominated by this mixture of pessimism and optimism. To his pro-Russian colleagues, the resulting caution looked suspiciously like a willingness to abandon the hated Bolsheviks to their fate.[17]

'NO ACTION OF ANY KIND'

Cripps, accompanied by a military mission, now returned to Moscow, where he signed, on 12 July, an Anglo-Russian alliance. Neither this nor Churchill's speech committed Britain to any specific action. Debates about what sort of aid could be provided to the Soviet Union would be a central feature of British strategic decision-making for the next eighteen months.

What the Russians wanted was immediate military help to open a 'second front' and distract the Germans from their onslaught. It was easy to see that the concentration of German forces in the east ought to have made it easier for Britain to take the offensive. Churchill was initially keen on a large-scale raid across the Channel. The chiefs of staff, however, were certain that any such operation was impossible. Home Forces had not yet begun to train for an invasion, the Luftwaffe still controlled the skies over France and the stock of landing craft was low. Any raid would be too small to make a difference, and its defeat would hand a propaganda victory to the Germans. As Soviet demands for help became more desperate, the chiefs became more insistent that the UK should stick to its existing plans: bombing, blockade and a new offensive in the Western Desert, then being prepared under Wavell's replacement, General Auchinleck.[18]

In the end, Churchill accepted that this was the only possible course of action. He remained deeply frustrated that Britain's growing forces in North Africa were so inactive. Aware, thanks to Enigma decrypts, that British naval attacks meant that Rommel's supply situation was worsening, he badgered Auchinleck to get a move on. 'It would be a very great reflection on us', he reminded the general, 'if, in this vital period when the Russians were bearing the full brunt of the attack, and when conditions were so favourable, we took no action of any kind.'[19] Auchinleck and Dill, however, were determined not to repeat Wavell's error of being bounced into action before the army in the Western Desert had been properly built up. The only joint action undertaken by Commonwealth and Soviet troops was the occupation of Persia, starting on 25 August 1941. This guaranteed that a pro-German regime would not take power in Teheran, secured the supply route to Russia through the Caucasus from the Gulf and made sure that the British could maintain their access to Persian oil. It was also an act of aggression against a neutral country, which was against international law.[20]

Throughout the summer, Eden advocated aid to the Soviet Union to the War Cabinet and pressed Churchill to do more to fulfil his promises of help. Despite his initial enthusiasm, this was another area where the prime minister actually proved very cautious. Eden placed more emphasis on the diplomatic importance of demonstrating that Britain would not leave the Russians in the lurch. He believed that this was the chance to bring the Russians into the international order, but he doubted that Churchill really wanted to help the Soviets, and he hated the fact that the prime minister now started swapping telegrams with Stalin. Just like his relationship with Roosevelt, Churchill didn't want to let anyone else control this crucial channel of communications.[21]

A belief in the potential of the Soviet Union was what connected Eden to Cripps. The ambassador hoped to put himself at the centre of a UK-USSR special relationship, in which wartime partnership would lay the grounds for agreement on how to construct the peace. Like Eden, Cripps had grasped what was going to become a central dynamic of Anglo-Russian diplomacy. If the Germans did not succeed in defeating Stalin, the British were going to have to come to some sort of agreement with him about the shape of post-war Europe.

As well as direct military assistance, the Soviets had also requested supplies, including raw materials, 3,000 fighter aircraft and 20,000 anti-aircraft guns. During July 1941, the British agreed to despatch 10,000 tons of rubber and 200 Tomahawk fighters that had recently arrived from the US and had been destined for the Middle East. This was the approach that the British would end up taking to the Eastern Front for the next year: offering up material help in lieu of more effective military activity. At the end of the month, Roosevelt ordered Harry Hopkins to Moscow to find out if it too should benefit from Lend-Lease. Stalin reassured Hopkins that Soviet forces could hold out if they got help. On 2 August, America and the Soviet Union signed a mutual aid agreement. Hopkins returned from Moscow to the UK, where he joined a prime ministerial party that was about to set sail in the battleship HMS *Prince of Wales*. Churchill was going to travel across the Atlantic to meet Roosevelt in person.

'THE LUNATIC PROPOSALS OF MR HULL'

He was not the only transatlantic traveller that summer. Since May, John Maynard Keynes had been in Washington, negotiating on the unfinished business left over from Lend-Lease: the fate of Britain's existing dollar liabilities, the possibility of a loan to cover British expenditure in the United States, and the 'consideration' that was meant to be offered in return for Lend-Lease.[22]

It was not Keynes' first time in Washington. In 1934, he had travelled to see the New Deal in action and met Roosevelt. Like most members of the British elite, however, he struggled to adapt to the turbulent atmosphere of American government. When it came to the negotiations, it didn't help that Keynes saw himself not as a supplicant but as an instructor. He managed to combine an obvious expectation that the United States had a moral duty to help the British Empire with a decreasingly ill-disguised frustration at American stupidity. In London, the Treasury had thought that sending their esteemed economist to Washington would help to win over the Americans. Ironically, Keynes tended to harden American convictions about the wily arrogance of their clients across the water.[23]

Keynes' belief in what the Americans *ought* to do, and his naivety about the impression he made in Washington, was apparent in his first proposals for dealing with Britain's continuing munitions contracts in the United States. He suggested that the Americans should take over these 'old commitments' and refund the down-payments Britain had already made, in order to rebuild Britain's dollar reserves. This would mean that the UK could buy (rather than be given) more of what it needed in America and allow it to retain more control of its own financial fate. This just confirmed American suspicions that the British were not quite as financially desperate as they pretended to be. The US Treasury remained absolutely determined to use the opportunity of the war to control Britain's foreign currency reserves.

When his proposal was rejected, Keynes switched back to the strategy that British Treasury officials had already been pursuing – trying to load as many British imports as possible onto Lend-Lease in order to minimize Britain's dollar expenditure, while getting a big loan from the American government's Reconstruction Finance Corporation, guaranteed on British assets in America, so that Britain could pay for the 'old commitments' without spending dollars or selling off any more of its investments in the United States. Since Britain was still earning dollars from the Empire's exports to America, these would allow it to run a trade surplus that would gradually rebuild its reserves to the $600 million that the British believed necessary for the basic operation of the Sterling Area. This position was more acceptable to the Americans, but ultimately it represented a defeat for Keynes because the decision about the size of Britain's dollar reserves remained in US hands.

The US State Department under Cordell Hull – an ardent free trader – had been given charge of the negotiations on the 'consideration' that the British would have to offer for Lend-Lease. Its aim was to get Britain to give up imperial preference and financial controls when hostilities ended. When Keynes was presented with US proposals for the elimination of imperial preference immediately after the war, he made it very clear that the imbalance between British imports and exports and the limitation of its reserves would mean that it had to retain some forms of discriminatory controls. The manner in which he did this was so strident that it convinced State Department officials that they needed to nail Britain down to specific action before it was too late. The draft of the Mutual Aid Agreement that they handed over to Keynes on 28 July had seven articles, most of them laying out the generous free transfer of goods under Lend-Lease. The sting was in the tail. Article Seven stated that after the war, Britain and America would agree to end all discrimination on all imports from the other. Keynes thought he had explained that forcing free trade on Britain at a point when it would have a massive export deficit would be bad for world trade as well as for the United Kingdom. Now he railed against 'the lunatic proposals of Mr Hull'.[24]

For the moment, however, the British did not have to sign anything to keep Lend-Lease going. Keynes returned to London at the end of July, but despite several reminders from the Americans, it took until the middle of October for the British to produce a response to the draft they had handed to Keynes. Meanwhile, British hopes of easing their currency position were disappointed. Over the summer, the Americans tightened the terms of the RFC loan, which lent Britain $425 million at 3 per cent interest, secured against $700 million of British-owned assets in America and serviced by the income from forty-one British insurance companies with branches in the United States.[25] Much to their discomfort, the British had to agree to the insertion of a 'War Disaster Clause' in the loan agreement, under which they would yield up all their US assets in the event of their military defeat. At the same time, the budget of the US War Department was cut, leaving it unable to take over the 'old commitments'. Yet the British hoped that by the time that Congress had to renew its approval for Lend-Lease at the start of 1942, America would be in the war, and talk of debts and considerations could be consigned to history. Only one of these wishes would come true.[26]

'THE ISSUE WITH JAPAN MUST BE FACED SOONER OR LATER'

Meanwhile, trouble was brewing in the Far East.[27] Since the Germans had not informed them of their plans, the Japanese had been taken by surprise by the Nazi-Soviet war, but they had used the opportunity to expand their power into South-East Asia. In July, Japanese troops occupied the southern half of Indochina, bringing their aircraft within range of Singapore. The Americans responded with economic sanctions that effectively introduced a total trade embargo.

Despite some trepidation that this would force Japan into war, the British followed suit. Churchill's determination to concentrate resources on the war that was being fought, rather than lock them up protecting the Empire against dangers that were only potential, meant that imperial defences remained very weak. The prime minister, the Defence Committee, the chiefs of staff and commanders in the theatre, however, all still shared the belief that the Japanese were inherently cautious. With their forces already heavily engaged in China, the threat of war with the United States would surely deter the Japanese from starting another conflict. That in turn encouraged British leaders to stick with the United States. Eden argued strongly that, though the Americans would give no firm commitment to defend European colonial possessions against Japanese attack, Britain had to follow the US lead if it wanted to rely on American help. As he put it: 'the issue with Japan must be faced sooner or later and the risk of the United States not intervening in a war between ourselves and Japan is small'.[28] If Britain didn't back the embargo, he warned, it would undermine American efforts at deterrence and damage Anglo-American relations: the one thing that the British could not afford in the summer of 1941.

With America, Britain and the Dutch East Indies all cutting off their trade, the Japanese were left in a critical position. As their oil supplies dwindled, they would have to choose either to capitulate to American demands or to attack southwards to seize the natural resources they needed to sustain their military might. At the same time as negotiating with the Americans, the Japanese also began to prepare for war. Meanwhile, America overhauled its strategic policy in the Pacific, launching an emergency programme to reinforce US bases in the Philippines so that they could be defended against any Japanese attack. At the heart of this new strategy was the belief that a force of long-range B17 bombers, based in the Philippines, would be able to strike decisively against a Japanese offensive anywhere in Asia. The new policy had knock-on effects on the war against Germany. Suddenly, the Americans reworked their production schedules of heavy bombers and cut the numbers they were willing to send to Britain. But the need to restrain Japan also encouraged Roosevelt to support the Soviet Union. By making sure that Hitler didn't defeat Stalin, he would be able to maintain a threat to Japan's northern flank.

The UK's backing for American sanctions left the Empire very exposed. During July, the Japanese began to pressure Thailand to give them bases and transit rights. That increased the threat to Malaya. The British response was to try to form a stronger defensive front. They wanted Britain, America and the government of the Dutch East Indies to issue a mutual guarantee of each other's territories, and a joint warning to Japan against future acts of aggression. This new effort to get the Americans to promise to defend the British Empire would have to be made in person. Churchill carried the proposals with him across the Atlantic.

As well as aid to Russia and deterrence against Japan, the question of American munitions production was also becoming increasingly urgent. The introduction of Lend-Lease had solved the problem of Britain's lack of dollars limiting its access to American arms and raw materials, but the United States was still a long way from turning itself into the 'arsenal of democracy'. In 1941, America produced a lot of weapons for a country that was still at peace, but it manufactured many fewer heavy bombers, tanks and pieces of artillery than Britain. The British needed US production to expand faster and further if it was to provide the tools of victory. Yet the industrial effort the British wanted was such that it would require the imposition of state controls over the economy that were politically impossible while America remained at peace. This was a crucial element in Churchill's determination to prioritize turning the United States into a belligerent. Effective support from the US armed forces would take a long time to develop: what Churchill looked forward to was the outpouring of materiel that could only come from the emotional furore of a nation at war.[29]

American officials, including the war secretary, the Republican Henry Stimson, were eager to make their government realize the extent of the effort that the war would require from US industry. For them, this was part of the preparation for their possible future involvement in the conflict. At the start of the summer, Roosevelt finally instructed his armed forces to come up with the figures for what equipment would be needed to defeat America's enemies if the country went to war, including the supplies that would have to be provided to their allies.

The first step was to sketch in the details of what production was already planned. From the start of June, British and American statisticians had begun to work together to draw up an overall statement of the munitions output that could be expected from Britain, America and Canada up to 1943. At the end of July, Churchill wrote to Roosevelt to suggest an Anglo-American conference on supply. Sir Arthur Purvis, the head of the British Supply Council in the United States, hoped that this would be the place where the British and Americans stated their strategic requirements, plotted them against existing capacity and worked out their plans to expand US production so that it could meet their military needs. By the middle of August 1941, with the joint statement on production coming together, Purvis was in excited mood. At last, he thought, he and his assistant, the French bureaucrat Jean Monnet, were making progress towards convincing the Americans of the colossal mobilization that would be necessary to win the war.

25

Atlantic Crossings

On 9 August the *Prince of Wales* anchored close to the American warship USS *Augusta* in Placentia Bay, off the coast of Newfoundland. The Atlantic Conference, the first of the great Anglo-American meetings that would punctuate the next three years, had begun.

'MOST IMPRUDENT ON OUR PART TO RAISE UNNECESSARY DIFFICULTIES'

Harry Hopkins had wanted Churchill and Roosevelt to meet for some time.[1] Knowing them both, he understood that a personal encounter would advance the Anglo-American alliance far more than any joint meeting of their advisors or the continued exchange of letters and telegrams. Roosevelt and Churchill were also keen to see each other face-to-face. They had been penfriends too long. Yet the arrangements had been delayed by the debate in America over Lend-Lease, then by the series of crises in the Middle East and Mediterranean.

For Churchill, the voyage over offered a brief relief from the pressure of work in London. He indulged his taste for Nelsonian melodrama by reading C. S. Forester's novel *Captain Hornblower, RN*, and by watching, for the fifth time, the film *Lady Hamilton*. Once again it moved him to tears. He played backgammon with Hopkins late into the night (seemingly better at calculating the stakes and the odds, Hopkins won £7 7s. from the prime minister over the course of the voyage); and enjoyed the caviar that the American had brought back from Moscow. It went well with the copious quantities of beef, butter and grouse that the party consumed: it was just a shame, as Churchill joked, that they had to be fighting alongside the Russians to get it.[2] Yet for all the fun and games, it was also a tense journey. Would Roosevelt like him in person, Churchill wondered, and would the president, as he hoped, finally commit himself to a precise plan to bring America into the war?

The encounter between the two great leaders was meant to be carefully choreographed. Yet when the *Prince of Wales* first entered Placentia Bay, the Royal Navy realized that it was operating on a different time zone to the Americans, and that they had arrived an hour-and-a-half too early.[3] The battleship put back out to sea while the Americans got into place.

The second time round, things went more smoothly. The British delegation went across to the *Augusta*, and the president and prime minister headed off for an intimate lunch together. It turned out that they had met once before, at a dinner in London in 1918. Roosevelt, then a junior naval minister, had been much impressed with Churchill, already a great political figure, and he still recalled the occasion fondly. Embarrassingly, Churchill had forgotten all about it. The two men now renewed their acquaintance. As Hopkins had suspected, they found they did get on. Their perspectives and their perceptions of their respective nations' interests were too different for them ever to become friends, but they shared a faith in their own strategic abilities, a conviction that war was far too important to be left to the generals and a belief that political life should be fun. Like a lot of people who met the president, Churchill left Placentia Bay impressed at the force of Roosevelt's personality and believing that they had forged a strong bond.

While the president and prime minister sniffed each other out, their officials and senior military officers chatted awkwardly over a dried up buffet in the wardroom of the *Augusta*. They too would take the chance of the Atlantic Conference to get to know each other a little better.

Churchill and Roosevelt were both deeply aware of the propaganda value of being seen to meet together. Although their meeting was kept secret while it was taking place, as soon as they were safely away it would be publicized around the world. Churchill personally vetted the order of service for the conference's emotional climax, a joint religious service on Sunday 10 August on the quarterdeck of the *Prince of Wales*, at which the president and prime minister, backed by intermingled ranks of American and British servicemen, prayed together and sang hymns that were familiar to both contingents: 'Onward Christian Soldiers', 'O God, Our Help in Ages Past' and 'For Those in Peril on the Sea'.[4] Caught by the photographers and the newsreel cameramen, it was a striking image of unity and co-operation in the face of a common threat.

The service done, the conference could get down to business. It was really three separate but connected sets of talks – the personal meeting between Churchill and Roosevelt; diplomatic discussions between Sir Alexander Cadogan (Anthony Eden had not been brought along) and the US under-secretary of state, Sumner Welles; and strategic conversations between the British chiefs of staff and the heads of the American navy and army. At all these levels, the British hoped that the conference would offer more than just a good photo opportunity.

Yet on their first meeting, the prime minister's hope that Roosevelt would set a date for an American entry into the war had been dashed. The president's reluctance to face the obloquy of leading his country into another global conflict had been compounded by the continued evidence of strong isolationist sentiment in the United States, where a Bill to continue the military service draft had only just scraped through Congress at the start of August. Instead, Roosevelt was willing to commit himself only so far as discussing plans for the US navy to start escorting North Atlantic convoys right across the western half of the Atlantic. Churchill took away the impression that the president would order escorts to start immediately and look for a clash with the U-boats that would allow him to bring America into hostilities. If this was what Roosevelt let him think, it was almost certainly not the president's preferred option. Rather, he hoped that by supporting Britain, the Soviet Union and China economically, he would be able to determine the outcome of the war against Fascism without having to involve America in the fighting.

Though Roosevelt would not promise to bring America into the war, he did offer to align his country still more emphatically against Hitler by making a statement of common purpose with the United Kingdom. The prospect of such a declaration had first been raised almost a month before, as Roosevelt sought to clarify that Britain was not secretly planning to adjust the boundaries of post-war Europe. Now he raised it again, and Churchill seized at the chance publicly to bind British and American interests.

Contrary to his previous reluctance to draw up war aims, the prime minister immediately had Cadogan rustle up a draft list of shared principles, based on the need for peace and international co-operation, the disarmament of aggressor powers, and the disavowal of any ambition for territorial aggrandisement. This became the basis for the document known as the 'Atlantic Charter', which Welles and Roosevelt then redrafted to reflect their own anti-imperialist agenda, inserting commitments to the universal right of self-government and the extension of free trade. They too wanted something concrete to take away from the conference.

Churchill knew what the Americans were doing, but he wanted the declaration agreed, and he thought he could control the dangers it posed. He always maintained that in their discussions at Placentia Bay, he and Roosevelt had discussed self-government purely in terms of liberating the nations of Occupied Europe. That distinction was not, however, incorporated in the wording of the Charter. Wary of the domestic political implications of abandoning imperial preference, Churchill also inserted a reference to the need to respect 'existing obligations' in promoting the spread of free trade. He believed that this would safeguard Britain's current trade and tariff agreements – and shield him from the wrath of the protectionist wing of the Conservative Party.

As the draft of the Charter developed, it became plain that it would require the approval of the government in London (despite its potential implications for the Empire, Churchill did not run it past the Dominions). On 11 August, the latest version was cabled back to London for urgent consideration by a late night meeting of the War Cabinet. The prime minister was plainly concerned that his colleagues would object to another round of concessions to the Americans. He told Attlee, chairing the meeting in his absence:

> It would be most imprudent on our part to raise unnecessary difficulties. We must regard this as an interim and partial statement of war aims designed to reassure all countries of our righteous purpose and not the complete structure which we should build after victory.[5]

In his cabin aboard the *Prince of Wales*, he waited nervously for the response.

In London, ministers wondered whether Churchill knew what he was about to sign. Convinced as he was of the need for US aid, Anthony Eden was also more suspicious than the prime minister of American intentions. Irritated as usual by Churchill's diplomatic efforts, Eden was concerned too about the implications of American meddling for the European settlement that Britain needed to reach with Stalin. As he told his private secretary, Oliver Harvey, he worried the joint declaration showed that Roosevelt intended to let Britain fight the war, then dictate the peace. In offering Churchill this 'terribly woolly document full of all the old clichés of the League of Nations period', Eden concluded, 'FDR has bowled the PM a very quick one'.[6]

Yet the War Cabinet also accepted the necessity for getting something from the summit. In fact, the Charter was just the sort of statement of war aims that many of Churchill's more progressive ministers – including Attlee – had been badgering him to make for the last year. If Churchill was now making pledges for the future, they didn't mind getting in on the act. The War Cabinet approved the draft, but at Bevin's suggestion, ministers also insisted on the insertion of a commitment to 'improved labour standards, economic advancement and social security' for all. In Placentia Bay, an anxious prime minister was relieved to find that this was all they wanted to change. Together with a Churchillian addendum foreseeing 'the final destruction of Nazi tyranny', the Atlantic Charter was now complete and ready to be released to the world.

Roosevelt and Churchill had agreed eight points:

First, their countries seek no aggrandizement, territorial or other;

Second, they desire to see no territorial changes that do not accord with the freely expressed wishes of the peoples concerned;

Third, they respect the right of all peoples to choose the form of government under which they will live; and they wish to see sovereign rights and self government restored to those who have been forcibly deprived of them;

Fourth, they will endeavor, with due respect for their existing obligations, to further the enjoyment by all States, great or small, victor or vanquished, of access, on equal terms, to the trade and to the raw materials of the world which are needed for their economic prosperity;

Fifth, they desire to bring about the fullest collaboration
between all nations in the economic field with the object of
securing, for all, improved labor standards, economic
advancement and social security;

Sixth, after the final destruction of the Nazi tyranny, they hope
to see established a peace which will afford to all nations the
means of dwelling in safety within their own boundaries, and
which will afford assurance that all the men in all lands may
live out their lives in freedom from fear and want;

Seventh, such a peace should enable all men to traverse the high
seas and oceans without hindrance;

Eighth, they believe that all of the nations of the world, for
realistic as well as spiritual reasons must come to the
abandonment of the use of force. Since no future peace can be
maintained if land, sea or air armaments continue to be
employed by nations which threaten, or may threaten,
aggression outside of their frontiers, they believe, pending the
establishment of a wider and permanent system of general
security, that the disarmament of such nations is essential
They will likewise aid and encourage all other practicable
measures which will lighten for peace-loving peoples the
crushing burden of armaments.[7]

Notwithstanding British disappointment that the Atlantic Charter
was not a US declaration of war, it was a powerful document, rooted
in notions of rights, freedoms, peace and international co-operation,
that not only set out Roosevelt's vision of a post-war world, but also
drew on a shared Anglo-American cultural heritage which went back
to Magna Carta. The Charter would form the basis for the assembly of
the wartime United Nations, and it committed Britain to a version of
the future that could be directly contrasted with the New Orders proposed by the Axis powers. The values incorporated in the Charter
would inspire people who would not have fought for the British Empire.
In retrospect, the British were very lucky that it was signed when it was,
and it was probably something they should have done sooner. Contrary
to Churchill's hopes, however, it would also unleash expectations that
he was unable to control.

THE ATLANTIC CONFERENCE:
STRATEGY AND SUPPLY

Churchill and Roosevelt had also been discussing policy towards Japan. The prime minister tried to persuade the president to join Britain in warning Japan that any further aggression in the South-West Pacific would spark counter-measures, even at the risk of war, and to extend a guarantee that America would come to the aid of Britain or Holland if the Japanese attacked their territories in the Far East. Roosevelt flatly refused to do the second, but under great pressure from Churchill, he did repeatedly promise that after he returned to Washington, he would issue a stern warning note to Japan in parallel with the UK.[8]

Finally, the president and the prime minister agreed to send a joint Anglo-American supply mission, headed by Beaverbrook and Averell Harriman, to Moscow, to find out what they needed to send to Stalin to keep the Soviet Union in the war. To start discussions on how Soviet demands could be co-ordinated with British and American production, Beaverbrook, who had arrived at the conference on 12 August, would head off from Newfoundland for talks in the United States. He was to be accompanied by Sir Arthur Purvis, who had returned to the UK on a brief visit. On 14 August, the plane carrying Purvis and his party crashed shortly after taking off from Prestwick airport en route back to the States. His grand plans for the mobilization of American industry would outlive him, but they would not be fulfilled in the way that he had intended.

While Roosevelt, Welles, Cadogan and Churchill had been conducting their diplomatic discussions, the senior officers of the British and American staff delegations had been talking about their plans for the future. The British laid out again their strategy for winning the war: bombing, blockade and the final arrival of a small expeditionary force in Europe to follow up a popular revolt and finish off an already defeated Wehrmacht. The Americans concentrated on explaining how weak their own armed forces were and how unready they were to enter the war. They also told the British that in order to build up their own air forces in the Philippines, they were going to have to cut back on the allocation of US-made heavy bombers to the RAF. The most the British could count on was another 1,100 aircraft between

August 1941 and June 1943, less than half the number they had been expecting.[9]

The two staff teams got on well enough – General Dill, the chief of the imperial general staff, and General George Marshall, the chief of staff of the American army, struck up the start of what was going to be a beautiful friendship – but the Americans openly disagreed with the extent of British commitments to the defence of the Middle East. Given that the closure of the Mediterranean had rendered the Suez Canal useless, they wondered, why were the British wasting scarce military resources defending Egypt and fighting in the Mediterranean, if not for outmoded reasons of imperial prestige? If Persian oil was so important, why not just withdraw to the Gulf? These were the start of what were to become long-running disputes between British and American strategists about the value of the Mediterranean theatre to the war against Germany.

They also demonstrated a more fundamental disagreement with British strategy that was less clearly articulated at the time, but which would also play a crucial role in the future. British plans were rooted in the particularities of the Empire's geo-strategic position and the contingencies of the first years of the war. To the American army, however, the emphasis on bombing, economic warfare, resistance movements and the Mediterranean all looked like peripheral dabbling designed to avoid the central issue. They thought that the only way to win the war was to go back into Europe and destroy Germany's military power. This was something about which British and American generals were going to argue for years to come.

'SHOULD BE GRATEFUL IF YOU COULD GIVE ME ANY SORT OF HOPE'

The Atlantic Conference ended on 12 August. As they returned to the UK, Churchill and Cadogan felt in good heart – helped, in Cadogan's case, by the fact that he was allowed to choose the films for the return voyage. Much to Churchill's disgust, Donald Duck and Laurel and Hardy now took the place of Emma Hamilton on the *Prince of Wales'* projection screen.[10]

The prime minister was disappointed that Roosevelt had not committed himself to battle, but he was never downhearted for long. He thought that he had secured pledges of American help in the Atlantic and the Far East, and together with the Atlantic Charter – announced to the world on 14 August 1941 – he believed that these represented important steps forward in Anglo-American co-operation. When he got back to London, however, he found the War Cabinet filled with gloom, convinced that the Americans were never going to join the fighting, worried that the Soviets might be defeated and concerned at the slow arrival of munitions under Lend-Lease. All this was politically dangerous for a man who had staked so much on making concessions to the United States. As so often, Churchill tried to ease the humiliation of submitting to America by promising that it wouldn't last for long. In his account of the Atlantic meeting for the War Cabinet, the prime minister talked up the prospects of imminent American belligerence. 'The President', he told his colleagues on 19 August, 'had said he would wage war, but not declare it, and that he would become more and more provocative. If the Germans did not like it, they could attack American forces.'[11]

The problem was that Roosevelt was already backing away from the promises Churchill thought he had made. No sooner had he returned to Washington than the president publicly asserted that the United States was no closer to entering the war as a result of the meeting at Placentia Bay. Whatever Roosevelt had intended to do about the Japanese, by the time Cordell Hull had had his say on the warning note that Churchill had persuaded the president to issue, it had become a much more anodyne affirmation of general principles, rather than a threat to go to war if the Japanese marched into Thailand. In the Atlantic, Roosevelt hung back from implementing the plans for the US navy to escort convoys. Contrary to Eden's comments about the speed of Roosevelt's bowling, on these points, Churchill could justly feel that he had been deceived not by the pace of the ball, but by the way it had deviated after it left the pitch.

Meanwhile, Halifax and Beaverbrook came back from the United States with depressing news about the administration's reluctance to go to war and the poor state of the American war industry. The 'Consolidated Statement' of war production, now being completed, revealed that if current plans were fulfilled, American munitions output by the end of 1942 would be little greater than that of Britain and Canada. This would be a huge quantity of materiel, but it would not be enough to meet what the British wanted for their own armed forces, let alone to meet the needs of American rearmament.[12] Worse, from Beaverbrook's point of view, the Americans were now planning to divert even the orders Britain had paid for before the introduction of Lend-Lease in order to supply Russia and China. In a difficult three-hour Cabinet meeting on 25 August, Beaverbrook spent a lot of time 'thumping the table and saying PM must do something "dramatic"' to force the Americans into action.[13] On 28 August, a worried prime minister cabled Harry Hopkins:

> I ought to tell you that there has been a wave of depression through Cabinet and other informed circles here about the President's many assurances about no commitments and no closer to war . . . If 1942 opens with Russia knocked out and Britain left again alone, all kinds of danger may arise . . . Should be grateful if you could give me any sort of hope.[14]

Hopkins warned the president that if the British stopped believing that America would eventually join them in battle, they might make a compromise peace with Germany.[15]

'ALL PEOPLES OF THE WORLD . . . ALL THE RACES OF MANKIND'

Meanwhile, the ripples started to spread out from the Atlantic Charter. On 14 August, while Churchill was on his way home, Attlee had announced the Charter in a radio broadcast. As secretary of state for India, Leo Amery was keen to hear the details.

For almost all of the past year, the Indian National Congress had been running a renewed civil disobedience campaign to protest against British rule in India. Gandhi, however, had not wanted to recommence the sort of mass campaign that might once again run out of control, encourage British repression of Congress and possibly spark a Hindu–Muslim civil war. Instead, he launched a closely controlled campaign of individual disobedience, in which carefully selected individuals deliberately violated the wartime restrictions on free speech. In the year from August 1940, there were 23,000 convictions under the Defence of India Act as Congress workers spoke out against the war and were arrested.[16] Of course, such a limited campaign did little to inconvenience the functioning of the Raj or to arouse popular support. Many people saw it as a failure, but Gandhi was content. Individual acts of civil disobedience kept the Congress occupied and unified, they didn't threaten to lead to a British defeat in the war against Germany and his supporters were given plentiful opportunity to test their spiritual strength by standing up alone against the police.

Nonetheless, Amery was keen to keep trying to forge some sort of constructive policy for the government of India, even in the face of the prime minister's opprobrium. In the middle of March, Sir Tej B. Sapru, an Indian Liberal, called publicly for the viceroy's Executive Council to be rebuilt with more Indian members as a provisional National Government. Though the Indian Liberals were not a powerful group, and despite some reluctance from the viceroy, Lord Linlithgow, Amery took the project up. When Churchill found out, he sent what Amery called 'a petulant protest . . . against stirring up the constitutional question'. 'The trouble is', Amery reflected in his diary, 'that Winston just dislikes the idea of anything being done in India at all and though he reluctantly drafted the Statement of August 8th he does not really believe in it and just hopes that we can sit back and do nothing indefinitely.'[17]

Yet Linlithgow was persuaded to change his mind, and after Amery rallied ministers in favour of Indian reform to the cause, at the start of June Churchill acquiesced in the changes too. A new Executive Council and National Defence Council were announced on 22 July 1941. These involved Indians – provincial politicians, well-known moderates and industrialists – more heavily than ever before in the central government and military policy of their country, but the viceroy retained his powers over defence, finance and home security. Congress, of course, was not involved, and Jinnah took the opportunity to assert his control over the Muslim League by insisting that its members too withdraw from the National Defence Council. That confirmed Linlithgow in his view that, since India was essentially quiet and the war effort was proceeding well, there was no need for further reforms. Nor was there any prospect of 'breaking away . . . from the party bosses' and their constitutional intransigence. As he told Amery: 'No individual is likely to be strong enough to stand up to the parties – nor do I see any marked anxiety on the part of prominent individuals to do so.'[18]

The new Executive Council's first decision was to release all those who were currently imprisoned for their part in Gandhi's individual civil disobedience campaign. Churchill disliked the idea of giving in to Congress, but the Cabinet supported the idea: a sign of just how ineffective the campaign had been as a blow against the British imperial war effort.

Then came the Atlantic Charter. Listening to Attlee's broadcast, Amery the campaigner for imperial preference was pleased. As he noted in his diary, the economic points 'might have been worse'. He was delighted to hear, among the 'meaningless verbiage', 'happily a phrase about "regard to our existing obligations" [, which] ought to enable us to save Imperial Preference'. But he also recorded that as soon as the Charter was announced, Burmese politicians had asked the governor, Reginald Dorman-Smith, to start fulfilling point three – the right for all people to choose their own form of government. For Amery: 'This is nothing more than we have told them already but it is a goal and can only be achieved by stages in accordance with circumstances. We shall no doubt pay dearly in the end for all this fluffy flapdoodle' (a rich point from a man well known for never using one word in a speech when fifteen and a Latin tag would do).[19]

The Burmese weren't the only ones who thought that point three of the Charter applied to them. Addressing the West African Students Union in London shortly afterwards, Attlee told his audience that the Atlantic Charter's principles 'applied to all peoples of the world . . . all the races of mankind'. The inhabitants of the Empire would not be excluded from its promises of self-government. He got a rapturous reception.[20] As the *Daily Herald* reported in its headline: 'THE ATLANTIC CHARTER: IT MEANS DARK RACES AS WELL.'[21] Attlee believed in the moral purpose of the Empire just as much as Amery, but for him, that meant spreading democracy while the conflict was still on. He believed that it ought to be a people's war abroad as well as at home.

When he got back to London, Churchill quickly moved to silence this interpretation of the Charter. At a War Cabinet meeting on 4 September, he got his colleagues to agree that the Atlantic Charter was not meant to apply to the British Empire. Attlee stayed quiet, but then, as Amery recorded:

Bevin butted in raising the whole policy as regards India and suggesting that there was something dramatic we could do immediately that would solve the whole problem. I am afraid he is chiefly concerned in this matter as in others, with his position in the Trade Union world and has not really got any clear ideas as to what could be done.[22]

In fact, a subsequent letter from Bevin to the India secretary suggested he did have some ideas – if no better sense than anyone actually dealing with the problem of how to break the deadlock that left Linlithgow so despairing of progress:

> We made certain definite promises in the last war and practically a quarter of a century has gone, and though there has been an extension of self-government we have not, in my view, 'delivered the goods' . . . It seems to me that the time to take action to establish Dominion status is now – to develop or improvise the form of Government to carry us through the war but to remove from all doubt the question of Indian freedom at the end of the war.[23]

Yet, notwithstanding Labour's power and influence on the home front, neither Attlee nor Bevin pushed really hard for a solution to the problem of India before the end of 1941. The block on a reform-minded approach from London that had been imposed when Winston Churchill became prime minister, remained.[24]

Churchill was, meanwhile, preparing to state his interpretation of the Atlantic Charter in the Commons. He sent a draft of his speech to the American ambassador, John Gilbert Winant, who warned him that any attempt to deny that Article 3 applied to India would 'simply intensify charges of Imperialism and leave Britain in the position of a "do-nothing policy" '.[25] The latter at least was very much what Churchill intended. As part of the preparation for a Commons statement about the Charter, Amery prepared a long paper for Churchill, explaining exactly what progress was being made towards Indian and Burmese self-government. However, when Churchill went to the House on 9 September, he preferred a simpler formulation:

> the Joint Declaration does not qualify in any way the various statements of policy which have been made from time to time about the development of constitutional government in India, Burma or other parts of the British Empire . . . At the Atlantic meeting, we had in mind, primarily, the restoration of the sovereignty, self-government and national life of the States and nations of Europe now under the Nazi yoke . . . So that is

quite a separate problem from the progressive evolution of self-governing institutions in the regions and peoples which owe allegiance to the British Crown.[26]

Having signed up to the Atlantic Charter in order to tie the United States more closely to Britain, Churchill now clarified it in terms that aroused American suspicions of British duplicity and antagonized even moderate nationalists across the Empire. Roosevelt, it appeared, was not the only one willing to row back from the promises he had made at Placentia Bay. That would not stop Britain being held to account on the pledges of the Atlantic Charter, but it would take a far bigger threat to the Empire to convince the prime minister to change his policy – though never his mind – about Indian reforms.

THE 1941 EXPORT WHITE PAPER

Meanwhile, British power continued to slip away, as the need to placate American fears of commercial competition handed the US government yet another lever with which to control the British economy. Over the summer of 1941, rumours had run wild in Congress that the British were using Lend-Lease materials to undercut American exporters in overseas markets. If the British could have done this, they probably would, but given the time lag between the granting of Lend-Lease aid, the delivery of supplies and their use in production, these accusations at this time were undoubtedly false. Their accuracy was less important than the way in which they reflected American suspicions that the British were taking them for a ride. To comfort the howling business lobby, the US government demanded a British commitment to restrict exports so as to ensure that Lend-Lease was not exploited for commercial purposes.

The British complied and hoped for the best: something that was already becoming a habit when it came to financial discussions with the United States. In some ways, it mattered less than it might have done. As a result of the concentration of effort on the war economy, British exports had already sunk so low that they were in effect already restricted, and many former export markets were in any case lost for the duration to enemy occupation. The British also hoped that the example of further sacrifice might persuade the Americans to reduce their own civilian output in order to increase military production. Convinced of their own moral superiority, the British were certain that the Americans would eventually recognize it too. When the US eventually entered hostilities, any such politically motivated restrictions would, they hoped, be swept away in an integrated Allied production effort.

On 10 September 1941, the government issued a White Paper stating that Britain would not use Lend-Lease supplies to manufacture goods for sale overseas, that Britain would reduce its exports to the minimum necessary to sustain the war effort and that even those materials acquired for cash would not be used for exports if they were in short supply in the US. Despite its name, the White Paper took on the status of a unilateral trade agreement with America, which was carefully policed by the US Office of Lend-Lease Administration. The American government could now decide what Britain would be allowed to export.[27]

THE 'VICTORY PLAN'

After Churchill issued his plaintive plea for hope at the end of August, Roosevelt finally fulfilled a little of his promise to get more involved in the Atlantic. On 4 September, a German submarine attacked the US destroyer *Greer* off Iceland. The president took the chance to announce that America would protect all shipping within 'US defensive waters', which were now defined as extending three-quarters of the way across the North Atlantic. On 17 September, the US navy escorted its first British convoy. During October, there were further clashes between American ships and German submarines in the Atlantic. On the last day of the month, a U-boat sank the US destroyer *Reuben James*, killing 115 American sailors.

Roosevelt did not take the opportunity of these naval incidents to declare war. During October and November, his efforts to repeal the Neutrality Acts to allow armed US merchant ships to sail into combat zones passed through Congress by only narrow margins. This helped to convince him that American political opinion would oppose a more active involvement in hostilities. He was also concerned that, if America were to go to war, the demand to rearm its own armed forces would be so great that he would be unable to keep up his flow of supplies to Britain, China and the Soviet Union.[28]

At the end of September, US army staff officers produced the 'Victory Plan', drawn up in response to Roosevelt's request to work out what would be needed if America had to win the war. A military and production programme of extraordinary ambition, the 'Victory Plan' set out the steps necessary to produce a 9 million-man army, 215 divisions strong, equip it with modern weapons and convey it to Europe to destroy the Wehrmacht. The earliest it could be achieved was mid-1943. Meeting that deadline would require holding back military aid to other countries so that the US army could concentrate on accumulating its own strength.[29]

Roosevelt hated the 'Victory Plan'. He did not want to tell American voters that 9 million of their sons were going to have to be conscripted in order to fight a bloody campaign in Europe. Roosevelt was himself a strong believer in air and sea power, and he found the tenets of British strategy much more attractive than most of his generals. He was worried that if the army's plans leaked (which they eventually did, at the start of December), they would add fuel to the fire of isolationism. During the autumn, he made the army stick to a much more limited mobilization programme and forced American generals to give up US munitions production so that more could be sent to Britain and Russia. The hope that the Soviet Union would be able to hold out meant that Roosevelt was now able to implement his own peripheral strategy: doing everything necessary to get supplies through to the countries that were fighting Fascism, but proceeding cautiously enough not to spark a political confrontation at home, or to put himself in a position where he had to declare war on the Axis powers.

Churchill thought that Roosevelt had promised to do his best to provoke a clash with Germany in the Atlantic. Although he was disappointed when the clashes came and went without America joining the war, he soon recovered his optimism. He was well aware of the political difficulties facing Roosevelt and remained confident that the Americans would become full belligerents before too long. They were, after all, an emotionally combustible people who would eventually be so infuriated by some action of the Germans that the president had to act. Yet Roosevelt's layer-by-layer peeling back of US neutrality did not whip up the sort of popular fervour that might have carried America into battle. On the contrary, it threatened to normalize naval clashes in the Atlantic, making it still harder to take the final step into open hostilities. An America at peace, however, would find it very hard to live up to the supply demands of a world at war.

'THERE IS A GENERAL FAILURE IN THE AMERICAN PRODUCTION PROGRAMME'

At the start of September, Stalin wrote to Churchill again to demand that the British establish a second front in Europe that would draw German forces away from the Soviet Union. Failing that, he wanted 30,000 tons of aluminium and at least 400 tanks and 500 aircraft a month with which to replenish the Red Army's defences. Still worried about Britain's own defences and the risk of invasion, the prime minister was inclined to dismiss the appeal. Beaverbrook and Eden, however, both argued that, in the absence of significant British military action, sending material support would be the only way to reassure Stalin of Britain's good intentions and persuade him to stay in the fight. At Beaverbrook's suggestion, the British promised to meet half the Soviet demands for arms. The rest they expected to come from the Americans.

The Anglo-American mission to Moscow that Churchill and Roosevelt had announced after the Atlantic Conference was scheduled for 25 September, and the Americans agreed to a supply conference in London on 15 September, before the combined delegation headed to the Soviet Union. The British hoped that this would be an occasion at which to pursue detailed production planning. Beaverbrook took charge of the negotiations. He wanted to insist to the Americans that they had to live up to the supply promises they had already made to Britain, despite Russia's entry into the war.

No sooner had the conference begun, however, than Averell Harriman, the head of the US delegation, made it clear that allocations were going to be issued, not discussed. Britain must regard America as a benefactor, not an ally, and be happy with what it got. Over the next year, the US planned to send thousands of tanks and planes to Britain and Russia, but most of the British supplies would come from orders placed before Lend-Lease. A large portion of the extra deliveries they had expected as a result of American financial aid would be sent to the Soviets instead.

The problem was not only that there were more claimants for American aid, but that US production had also fallen short of expectations. Without any central direction, and reeling under the effect of British contracts, Lend-Lease investment and American rearmament, the US arms industry was lagging well behind Roosevelt's repeated instructions to make more. The Americans were not able to match Britain's offer of tanks to Moscow, and Beaverbrook had to give up more American deliveries and British production in order to make sure that Soviet demands could be met. In fact, the people who did worst out of the deal were the US army, whose allocation of tanks was drastically cut at the president's instruction to make sure that the British didn't lose out too much. Nonetheless, Beaverbrook was bitterly disappointed. He reported to the Defence Committee that 'There is a general failure in the American production programme ... It is imperative that the Americans should organise rapidly a rapid increase of their production.'[30] The report was passed to Harriman in an effort to shame the Americans into doing more, but only after Churchill had changed 'failure' to 'retardation' – there was no point in antagonizing the Americans by suggesting they weren't coming up with the goods.

At the end of the conference, the British were given a chance to present figures for their production requirements until the start of 1943. These made clear just how much they wanted from the United States, including 12 auxiliary aircraft carriers, 150 escort vessels, 5 million gross weight tons of merchant shipping, 12,000 tanks and 13,000 aircraft. On land, they included the equipment needs of a hundred divisions: far more than the British intended to raise themselves, but enough to equip the forces of potential European allies.[31] There was no discussion of how these requirements fitted in to US strategy, but the conference agreed that the British statistics should be taken away, integrated with American and Russian requirements, and turned into an overarching production programme for victory.

This was what the British had wanted, but over the weeks that followed, progress in Washington slowed to a standstill. There were no further joint talks. The political situation was difficult. The threat of war with Japan as well as Germany started to loom. The biggest problem, however, was that there was no agreement on overall strategy, either between the British and American military, or between the US armed forces themselves. The US navy refused to provide details of its production needs to its own government, on the basis that it could not know what it wanted until it knew what sort of war it was going to have to fight. In the end, American civilian planners just came up with their own estimates of military requirements, added them to what America would need to provide for its allies overseas, and matched them to an assessment of 'national industrial potential'. Their report, delivered at the very start of December, foresaw that America would need to spend $150 billion in just under two years to ensure the defeat of Germany. This was about twenty-two times US defence spending in 1941 (and more than Germany spent on fighting the entire war).[32] Such an endeavour, however, would require economic controls and central direction of a sort that could not be contemplated while the country remained at peace. Until it was at war, America's full power was never going to be unleashed.

26

The End of the Beginning

During the final months of 1941, the transformation in the war that had begun with Britain's survival in 1940 and Hitler's consequent turn against the Soviet Union, became complete. Contrary to expectations, the Soviets survived the initial onslaught, turning what was supposed to have been a lightning campaign into a prolonged attritional struggle on the Eastern Front. As the industrial plans put into place at the start of the war started to bear fruit, British war production underwent another acceleration. On the far side of the world, rather than submit to Western sanctions, Japan launched a desperate grab for colonial resources in South-East Asia. Finally, America was dragged into the conflict, and the British Empire was thrown into a new and calamitous war.

'EVERY MAN AND WOMAN OF THE SOVIET MILLIONS'

Describing public reactions to the first reports of the titanic battles taking place on the Eastern Front in the summer of 1941, Home Intelligence identified 'great admiration tempered by some doubt' as well as a 'latent working-class sympathy for the "workers' republic".' The Ministry of Information faced the difficult problem of how to sell this new war to the people. Initially its main concern was to win over potential doubters by presenting Britain's co-combatant in a positive light. Britain's leading churchmen were mobilized en masse to declare that, whatever threat Communism might pose to the faith, it was nothing to the immediate danger from Nazi barbarism. In the much-publicized words of the moderator of the Church of Scotland, if his house were ablaze, he wouldn't stop to ask the firemen if they were all Christians.[1]

The MoI also wanted, however, to avoid advancing the cause of Communism at home. There was a controversy when the BBC (at Churchill's instruction) left the Communist anthem, the *Internationale*, out of its weekly programme of anthems from the Allied nations. As this showed, the Ministry had to walk a fine line between reactionary Conservatives, who saw any reference to Communism as further propaganda for socialism, and radical left-wingers who were convinced that the government intended to leave the Soviets in the lurch. Over the summer, the Ministry evolved a strategy of actively promoting the Soviet Union in order to 'steal the thunder' of the left. Newsreels and newspapers depicted Britain's new ally as a modern, egalitarian society in which everyone was committed to the fight.

In late July, for example, British Paramount's audiences were treated to footage of Red Army soldiers and civilians getting ready to resist the Nazis:

> The wounded ask to be quickly patched up to go back to the fight – typical of the Soviet's 180 millions, for whom this is the modern equivalent of a holy war. Army printing presses on all sectors produce newspapers, to tell the men in the front of the battle how the whole war is going. Intelligent soldiers intelligently treated are the best defenders of the Russian soil. Not only the soldiers; every man and woman of the Soviet millions is defending the soil . . . the land they love, the land that cares for them – to defend the soil, the good earth that nurtured them, whose riches are theirs – it must be defended though thousands die before the Nazis are hurled back.[2]

This was just the sort of place that British progressives had been insisting that their country ought to become before it could beat Nazism. The contrast between Britain – class-bound, old-fashioned and inefficient – and Russia – united by communal effort and economic planning – proved to be extremely appealing, and it fitted well with the rising tide of calls for domestic reform. In praising Russian resilience without mentioning the brutal dictatorship that underpinned it, British propaganda often ended up endorsing the Soviet political system.

Hitler's attack on the USSR transformed the position of the Communist Party. From defending the people from an imperialist struggle, it now moved to demanding an all-out effort to defeat Fascism, including the launch of a second front. The membership of the CPGB increased by about a third, from 15,000 to 20,000, over the second half of 1941.[3] In the engineering industry, Communist enthusiasm for increased production for the war effort invigorated the shop stewards movement. As far as Communists were concerned, Britain's military passivity proved that the bosses didn't want to help Russia, only to profit from the war. Management's apparent unwillingness to solve the difficulties of bottlenecks and delays in production demonstrated the same thing. Unlike some advocates of reform, however, the Communists did not want nationalization while the war was on, because they recognized that it would disrupt output. Instead, they called for workers to be allowed to sit on management committees so that they could sort out the hold-ups in production themselves. In October, the Engineering and Allied Trades Shop Stewards National Council held a huge conference on production in London. It was the largest gathering of shop stewards of the entire war, and the complaints it raised about delays and management inefficiency won extensive coverage in the press. In the engineering firms around Coventry, where the Communists were particularly strong, a major confrontation loomed between militant shop stewards and intransigent factory management.[4]

Despite terrible losses and repeated defeats, the Soviets kept fighting. By the autumn, as Home Intelligence described, this had aroused not only considerable public respect, but fascination with the 'moral strength of a country which was previously somewhat disparaged officially', and gratitude that 'Russia is not France' and 'the Battle of Britain is being fought on the Eastern Front'.[5] There was a real hunger for more information about the Soviet Union, and a concerted effort to fit the Soviets into the existing framework of British public life. This brought celebrations of Soviet achievements to the streets of Britain in a way unthinkable before the war. The prime minister's wife, Clementine Churchill, headed up a charity fund to buy medical supplies for the Red Army. In line with its efforts to 'steal the thunder of the Left', the Ministry of Information's regional officers headed off fellow-travellers' attempts to celebrate 'Anglo-Soviet friendship weeks' by setting up events of their own. In the East Anglian town of Stowmarket, for example, the Anglo-Soviet Week was started by a church service, followed by a procession through the town including the Salvation Army, the Boys' Brigade band, the Home Guard, the Air Training Corps and Civil Defence. Among the congregation at the church were the local Liberal MP, the lord lieutenant of Suffolk and his wife.[6] Probably not all of them had been converted to Communism.

Public demands for Britain to help Russia also grew, and not just from Communists following Moscow's line. From mid-July, calls for an attack to take advantage of German distraction began to appear in the press. Thirty per cent of respondents to the BIPO's August survey said that they were dissatisfied with the amount of aid being given to Russia. Seventy per cent of those who were unhappy favoured an offensive in the west.[7] By October, 48 per cent of those questioned felt that the government had not made enough of the opportunities presented by Russia's entry into the war, against only 29 per cent who thought it had.[8] Fears that Russia was being abandoned were stoked up by the press outcry after it was revealed that the minister for aircraft production, Colonel J. T. A. Moore-Brabazon, had argued at a private dinner that Germany and Russia should be left to fight each other to a standstill. As the Conservative MP Cuthbert Headlam noted to himself: 'It is what a good many of us think, but it is not wise to say so *coram populo* [before the people] – keep such opinions for a diary!'[9]

'TANKS FOR RUSSIA'

As September went on, and the Germans completed their conquest of the Ukraine, Stalin repeated his demands that Britain open an immediate second front, culminating in the suggestion that Churchill hurl thirty divisions (the equivalent of the whole British army at home) across the Channel, or send them through Persia to fight alongside the Red Army on the Eastern Front. These appeals were so far divorced from the military and logistic realities open to Britain that the chiefs of staff concluded that the Soviets were only interested in saving themselves, not in developing a combined strategy. Churchill was keener on an expedition to assist the Russians – perhaps to northern Norway, perhaps through the Caucasus – and to the possibility of using British aid to bring Turkey into the war. None of this offered the hope of any immediate succour on the scale the Russians wanted.

In Moscow, Britain's failure to provide military help provoked anger and disappointment, not least from Cripps, who backed up Stalin's appeals with a telegram warning London that if a 'superhuman effort' was not made to create a military diversion, Soviet resistance would probably crack. Churchill replied that if, by 'superhuman', Cripps meant 'an effort rising superior to space, time and geography', then 'Unfortunately, such attributes are denied to us.' In the absence of military action to help the Russians, material assistance became more important as a means to try to keep the Soviet Union in the war, and assure Stalin of British bona fides.[10]

Notwithstanding his disappointment with America's contribution, Beaverbrook advocated sending supplies even if it meant reducing the flow of equipment to the British army. He recognized the strategic importance of the Soviet Union, but he was also alert to the power of popular enthusiasm for the Russians to get him what he wanted at home: increased tank production and the power to do what he wanted on the industrial front. At the end of September, before he left for the supply summit in Moscow, Beaverbrook laid on a 'Tanks for Russia' week in British factories, calling for workers to up their efforts with the promise that every tank turned out would be despatched to the Eastern Front. Beaverbrook's *Daily Express* told readers: 'Next week we want you to work like men possessed . . . These tanks are going straight out to save lives and to KILL.'[11]

Beaverbrook arrived in the Soviet capital determined that he would return home with some concrete achievements. This was no time for hard bargaining with the Russians. Instead he and Harriman would hold a 'Christmas tree party' in a blaze of positive publicity. The Soviets would be given everything they wanted in an effort to convince Stalin that the Western powers would back him up. The question of what could actually be delivered could be left for a later date. The supply mission negotiated the First Moscow Protocol, an agreement that ran to June 1942, in which the British and Americans promised to provide 400 aircraft and 500 tanks a month, as well as large quantities of raw materials, machine tools and other military equipment.[12]

While the discussions continued in Moscow, Beaverbrook had no intention of sharing the spotlight with Cripps. According to Beaverbrook, when he badmouthed the ambassador to Stalin as a teetotal bore, the Soviet dictator replied that Cripps would be more fun if he'd leave off the earnest discussions about the meaning of Communism.

Excluded from the talks, the ambassador was disgusted by the supply minister's superficial grandstanding. This was just what he thought was wrong with the British government. Cripps resolved that this was the last time that he would ever work with Beaverbrook.

The minister of supply's ideas were also developing. Beaverbrook was a man who dealt in one big concept at a time, and who often ended up believing his own propaganda. In establishing himself as the figure-head for aid to the Soviet Union, he moved from advocating support for the Russians to the conviction that their continued resistance must become the sole and overriding objective of British strategy.[13]

Despite Cripps' fears, Beaverbrook actually did his best to defend the new commitments established by the Moscow Protocol. The quantities of materiel despatched never met the levels promised to Moscow, but they were significant. With the US unable to send as much as it had promised, until mid-1942 the UK played the leading role in providing military equipment. During that time, the British sent about 2,000 tanks and 1,800 fighter aircraft to the USSR. That meant delaying the re-equipping of British units, and Beaverbrook therefore had to fight off opposition from the British military. Carrying supplies to Russia also placed an additional maritime burden on the United Kingdom. Until the route through Persia was developed, 90 per cent of the aid had to be sent on convoys routed north along the edge of the Arctic. The fight to sustain this supply connection now shifted the surface war between the Royal Navy and the Kriegsmarine into the seas north of Norway.[14]

The effect of sending tanks and aircraft to Russia on British units in the front line was actually fairly minimal, mainly because of where the action was taking place. British forces in the Middle East were never short of tanks because they were going to Archangel. Units at home lost their vehicles, but for the moment they didn't have to fight. In fact, something of a supply merry-go-round developed, with American deliveries of tanks direct to the Middle East (on US ships through the combat-free Red Sea) allowing the British to send vehicles that might otherwise have been needed in the theatre through the perilous northern seas to aid the Russians. If America was the 'arsenal of democracy', then over the winter of 1941–42, Britain was an arsenal for totalitarianism. It was a very traditional expression of British power: an economic titan using its financial and industrial strength and control of the seas to allow a struggling ally to bear the brunt of the land fighting.

Churchill would later suggest that the sending of supplies to the Soviet Union was the reason that the British had not reinforced the Far East, but his desire to press the offensive in the Western Desert, the presumption that the Americans would deter the Japanese and the fears of an invasion of the UK were actually to blame. The decision to ignore Dill's warnings of weakness in Malaya back in May 1941 could not be put down to a desire to give some help to Stalin.[15]

During the first year of the Nazi-Soviet war, tank deliveries from Britain were equivalent to about 9 per cent of Soviet production. The tanks which Britain supplied were Matildas and Valentines, under-gunned, like most British tanks at this point in the war, but heavily armoured. They were not up to the standards of the tanks that the Russians would turn out in large numbers in 1942, but better than most of what they had in late 1941, when production had been badly disrupted by the German advance. The Hurricane and US-made Tomahawk fighter aircraft Britain sent (the equivalent of 8 per cent of Soviet production between June 1941 and June 1942) were not as effective as the best German and Soviet planes, but they were reliable and well made. Compared to the vast numbers of planes and tanks produced by the Soviet Union over the course of the war, and the huge quantities of food and trucks that the USA supplied to the Red Army during the last years of the conflict, British aid in 1941–42 was tiny, but at the time, it meant that Soviet forces were significantly better equipped than they would otherwise have been.[16] Holding his 'Christmas tree party', and insisting that British deliveries were kept up, was the one thing during the whole war that Beaverbrook got right.

'IF WE DO NOT HELP THEM NOW THE RUSSIANS MAY COLLAPSE'

Churchill's reluctance to stick to long-term plans, his sudden swings of mood and his well-known hatred of Bolshevism all meant that no one around him was sure about his strategy for the Soviet Union. After more than a year's experience of his premiership, ministers and senior officers feared that he might be just one late-night brainstorm away

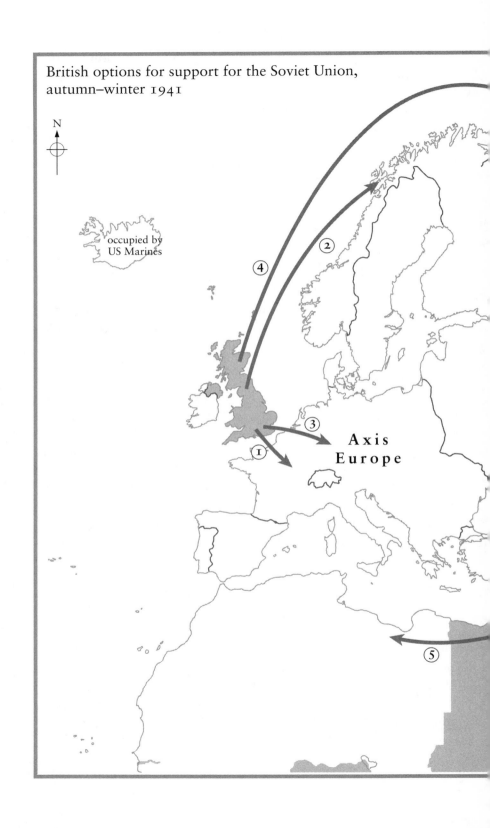

British options for support for the Soviet Union, autumn–winter 1941

N

occupied by
US Marines

② ④ ③ ①

**Axis
Europe**

⑤

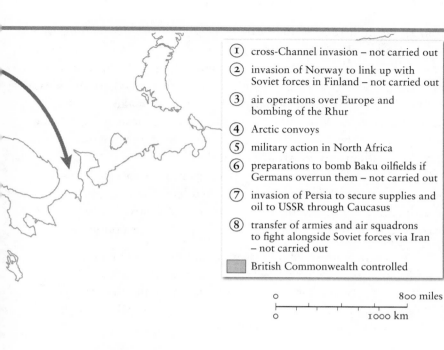

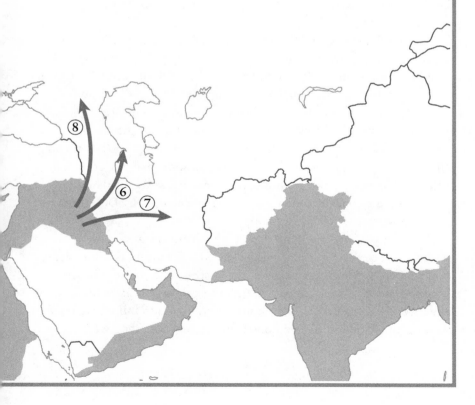

1. cross-Channel invasion – not carried out
2. invasion of Norway to link up with Soviet forces in Finland – not carried out
3. air operations over Europe and bombing of the Rhur
4. Arctic convoys
5. military action in North Africa
6. preparations to bomb Baku oilfields if Germans overrun them – not carried out
7. invasion of Persia to secure supplies and oil to USSR through Caucasus
8. transfer of armies and air squadrons to fight alongside Soviet forces via Iran – not carried out

British Commonwealth controlled

0   800 miles

0   1000 km

U S S R

from some radical new adventure – or even from abandoning the
Russians altogether. As a result, the members of his rolling strategic
seminar – Beaverbrook, Eden and the chiefs of staff – spent a lot of
time in late 1941 jockeying for position. As they pushed around ideas
and put forward different proposals, they tried to make sure that the
prime minister would back their preferred policy: or at least, that he
wouldn't adopt the options that they thought most dangerous. It was a
very Churchillian way for strategy to be made.

On 2 October, the Germans restarted their drive towards Moscow.
For most of the next two months, it looked like one more push would
take them into the Russian capital. Beaverbrook now insisted to the
Defence Committee that a 'second front' was the only option:

> The Chiefs of Staff would have us wait until the last button has been
> sewn on the last gaiter before we launch an attack. They ignore the pres-
> ent opportunity ... If we do not help them now the Russians may
> collapse. And, freed at last from anxiety about the East, Hitler will con-
> centrate all his forces against us in the West.[17]

This strident advocacy guaranteed that he would get the tanks and aircraft he wanted to send to Russia, but it also led to tension with the
prime minister.

Churchill had responded to the new German offensive by returning
to his earlier desire for British landings in northern Norway. This
would answer calls for a 'second front'; safeguard the convoys carrying
Russian aid; and threaten German supplies from Scandinavia. The
chiefs of staff thought this was lunacy: launching an ill-prepared force,
without adequate air cover, into the depths of an Arctic winter. Their
objections notwithstanding, Churchill pushed the proposals through
the Defence Committee, and ordered General Brooke, the commander
of Home Forces, to start planning the operation in detail. The chiefs of
staff refused to back down, and Brooke, forewarned by Dill, produced
plans showing the scheme was impossible.[18]

A furious Churchill refused to be put off. He also demanded an
earlier start to Auchinleck's much-delayed offensive in the desert, now
codenamed 'Operation Crusader'. To distract the prime minister, the
chiefs of staff dangled the suggestion of an invasion of Sicily, if 'Crusader' was successful. To their consternation, Churchill seized on this
as something that could be done immediately, but they were pleased

enough when he used it to face down Beaverbrook's demands for a cross-Channel attack. Only after this was achieved did the chiefs turn, with Admiral Pound arguing decisively that with shipping and escorts under strain, the attack on Sicily was also for the moment impossible. Instead, the chiefs convinced Churchill that a successful desert offensive should be continued westwards and combined with seaborne landings to bring French North Africa over to the Allied side.

This did not fit with proposals for direct military aid to Russia (nor, indeed, with Churchill's obsession with invading Norway). On the other flank of the Soviet line, the British explored the possibility of sending two divisions to assist with defence against a German break-through in the Caucasus. Here, their primary concern was to prevent an Axis thrust southwards towards the oilfields of the Middle East, and Churchill was keen to avoid British forces being dragged further north into the Soviet line. With uncertainty raging about how quickly the Germans might be able to advance and the state of the Soviet defences, and Britain building up to a big battle in the Western Desert, in November 1941 the prime minister tried to persuade Stalin to let British forces occupy all of Persia, and ordered plans to be laid to base heavy bombers in the north of the country. If the Russians collapsed, he hoped that these would at least ensure the destruction of the oil-fields north of the Caucasus, around Baku.[19]

These discussions led to the definite rejection of Beaverbrook's demands for an improvised, all-out cross-Channel assault. Britain's cautious strategy had been preserved. The debate had also, however, crystallized Churchill's determination to get rid of Dill – 'the dead hand of inanition' as he had called him to his face in Cabinet. He had never found 'Dilly-Dally' sympathetic, nor forgiven him for their row over the Middle East the previous May. During November, he decided that the chief of the imperial general staff should retire. Yet again, a distant posting would provide a useful dustbin. Dill, he decided, should become governor of Bombay. Eventually, at Dill's insistence, the prime minister selected General Brooke as his successor.[20]

Brooke's War Office nickname, 'Colonel Shrapnel', derived not only from the power of his personality, but also from his explosive force in argument. This was a key difference from Dill, his trusted friend and ally, with whom Brooke shared a strategic outlook and from whose work in establishing the relationship of the chiefs of staff with Churchill he benefitted. In debate, if not in strategy, Brooke instinctively took the direct approach.

Brooke's appointment as CIGS was a crucial moment for the higher direction of the British war effort, because he was one of the few men who proved capable of fighting Churchill on his own terms. As the prime minister put it, 'When I thump the table and push my face towards him what does he do? Thumps the table harder and glares back at me.' Where the prime minister took wing on flights of strategic fancy, Brooke would become Britain's strategic donkey, determined to plod on according to plan and administering a hefty kick at any attempted diversions. His diary, in which he poured out his frustrations with politicians, his colleagues and the Americans, became increasingly Eeyore-ish as the years of struggle went on. In his few moments of free time, Brooke restocked his powerful mental and physical reserves by indulging an obsessive interest in bird-watching. The quietness and stillness this required were not much drawn on in his professional life.[21]

Beaverbrook's calls for a 'second front' were never just a Whitehall gambit. From October, as his newspapers praised Russia as a 'workers' paradise' and lauded the shop stewards for their efforts to increase production, he courted Tory MPs with criticisms of Labour ministers' inefficiency and official inertia. By emphasizing public dissatisfaction with the war effort and presenting himself as the one dynamic force on the home front, he raised the prospect that he would turn his complaints about strategy into a challenge to the government. Beaverbrook was addicted to intrigues – he believed that his first achievement in British politics had been to make Lloyd George prime minister in 1916 – but he was never a systematic planner. He probably hoped that he could force his colleagues to recognize his demands for a change of strategy, but he also wanted to win supremacy over Bevin in their struggles over the war economy.[22]

It was never likely to work. Beaverbrook had no party following or cabal of ministers behind him, and he was always an unlikely leader for a workers' revolt. His place in office depended on Churchill's friendship – and in the end, the prime minister was not about to put that ahead of his continuing ability to fight the war. Yet Beaverbrook's scheming indicated the ways in which Germany's drive to the east had opened up not only new strategic vistas, but also fresh political opportunities.

As so often, Eden spent the autumn of 1941 aggrieved with the prime minister. He thought that, by dominating discussion with his unpredictable passions, Churchill was wasting the time of the chiefs of staff and avoiding the real issue of how to forge the Anglo-Soviet alliance. Eden believed that Soviet suspicions of British intentions were a key obstacle to the two countries' working properly together. He was also eager to take back control of Anglo-Soviet diplomacy from a prime minister who, he suspected, might suddenly abandon his promises of help because he had lost patience with Stalin. Eden argued that the British should do as the Soviet leader wanted, and declare war on Hungary, Finland and Romania, which had joined the German attack on Russia.[23] At the end of September, Eden was moaning about Beaverbrook's conniving and talking about what 'very decent people' Bevin and Attlee were, and 'whether he couldn't work with them after the war'.[24] By the middle of November, however, Eden was relying on Beaverbrook's support to get his pro-Soviet policies through the War Cabinet against the opposition of Labour ministers 'whose hatred of Communism blinded them to any other consideration'.[25] As had now become usual, Eden couldn't bring himself to fight it out with the prime minister. Churchill knew just the right amount of flattery to offer to manipulate his younger colleague. Now he told the Tory chief whip, in front of Eden, that if anything happened to him, the foreign secretary would have to take his place.[26]

As the Germans advanced towards Moscow, the foreign embassies had been evacuated from the capital to Kuibyshev, 500 miles deeper into Russia. That made it much harder to keep in touch with the outside world. From his new base, Cripps maintained a recriminatory commentary about the paucity of British aid to Russia. Churchill read Cripps' cables back to London, correctly, as a threat to come back and stir up trouble for the government at home. The prime minister, as ever, was up for the fight: if Cripps resigned, he decided, he would say that he had deserted the Russians in their hour of need. Cripps was willing to risk that in an effort to alter what he believed was a disastrous government policy.

Eden averted the crisis. He persuaded his colleagues to let him take up Cripps' suggestion that a leading minister should come to Moscow to persuade Stalin that the British took him seriously. That would also mean that Cripps had to remain at his post. Eden hoped that this was a chance to escape Churchill and undertake some proper diplomacy, but while the War Cabinet let him go, it also issued strict instructions about what he was allowed to discuss when he got to Moscow. There was to be no talk of territorial concessions or war aims other than the defeat of Hitler. Disappointed but energized by the prospect of being liberated from London, the foreign secretary got ready to leave at the start of December.[27]

'NO INTENTION OF CHANGING THIS POLICY'

Demands for a second front had been rejected in favour of continuing with Britain's existing strategy. At the heart of that strategy was the bombing offensive against Germany. Despite the revelation of severe problems with the bombing campaign, from the autumn, the British actually became more committed to it as the principal means by which they would carry the war to the enemy.

During the spring, while the bombers had been diverted to attacks on the Atlantic ports, the air staff had begun work on fresh plans. By July, these had crystallized into a new directive, instructing Bomber Command to strike at the transport system of the Ruhr when conditions were good enough, and for the three-quarters of each month when they were not, to bomb 'large working class and industrial areas in the towns', with the specific aim of destroying the German people's morale.[28] City bombing of this sort would require the Command to pack a much more powerful punch. For the moment, production delays and technical teething problems had delayed the arrival of a new generation of heavy bombers and set back plans for expansion, but the air staff had hopes that, having negotiated access to a portion of American aircraft production, they would by 1943 be able to build a front-line force of 4,000 heavy bombers, supported by deliveries of a thousand aircraft a month. The immense resources necessary to support this plan, however, soon raised objections from the other armed services.

The bomber force that was ordered back to attacking German cities in July 1941 was very far from a war-winning weapon. Its raids were carried out by aircraft numbering in the tens, not hundreds, let alone thousands. The four-engined heavies – Stirlings and Halifaxes, with bigger bomb loads – were just coming into operational use, but the Command was heavily dependent on the Wellington medium bombers with which it had started the war. Production of the heavy bombers remained behind schedule. Worse, between August and September, it had become apparent that the Americans – now set on their own massive rearmament programme – were not going to deliver all the heavy aircraft they had built since the spring, let alone give the British full access to their bomber production as it increased in the future.

In the meantime, Bomber Command's effectiveness had been called into question at the highest level of government. In July 1941, Professor Lindemann, Churchill's scientist, launched an investigation into the accuracy of British bombing, getting one of his assistants, David Bensusan-Butt, to analyse the results of hundreds of photographs taken by aircraft shortly after they released their bombs. Butt's report, produced in mid-August, was devastating. It suggested that only one in five sorties dropped their bombs within five miles of their supposed target. Of those despatched against the Ruhr that actually released their bombs, only one in ten got within the same distance. Although Sir Charles Portal, the chief of the air staff, and Air Marshal Peirse of Bomber Command fought back, the RAF's own analysis showed the same thing. The problems of night-time navigation and bomb-aiming were just too great. The crews often thought that they had bombed on target. Most of the time they were wrong.

Portal's response was to press for more resources. Just because bombing had not yet fulfilled its promise was no reason to stop. Instead, additional industrial support must be poured in to solving the problems of accurate target-finding and the supply of heavy aircraft. Churchill supported him. At the start of September, he told the Ministry of Aircraft Production to increase its bomber production for the next twenty-two months by a third in order to attain the numbers necessary to fulfil the planned British contribution to the 4,000-bomber programme. This objective was to prove well beyond the capacity of the aircraft industry, but it formed the basis for the MAP to extend its claims for materials and manpower at the expense of the other service and supply departments.

Notwithstanding his backing for Portal's demands for more resources, the prime minister had lost his faith in bombing as a war-winning weapon. At the end of September, Portal suggested that a

4,000-strong bomber force would win the war by laying waste to all
43 German towns with more than 100,000 inhabitants. Churchill
replied that it was 'very disputable whether bombing by itself will be a
decisive factor in the present war. On the contrary, all that we have
learnt since the war began shows that its effects, both physical and
moral, are greatly exaggerated.'[29] Yet when Portal asked whether this
meant that he wanted to rework the whole of British strategy, Churchill
backed down. He was unwilling to accept uncritically the claims of the
bombing enthusiasts, but he was in no position to give it up completely.
Similarly, the other chiefs of staff would challenge the bombing campaign's claims on resources without ever suggesting that it should be
wholly abandoned.

Bombing remained the only way out of Britain's strategic conundrum. Uncertain whether the USSR would survive, but convinced that
an early return to the European mainland was impossible, Britain's
strategists relied on the air offensive to solve the problem of German
domination of Europe. Churchill told Portal that he deprecated
'placing unbounded confidence in this means of attack', but he also
confirmed that: 'Everything is being done to create the Bombing force
desired on the largest possible scale, and there is no intention of changing this policy.'[30] During the autumn of 1941, as the prime minister and
the War Cabinet approved the programmes for the expansion of
Bomber Command and the direction of its destructive power against
the German civilian population, they increased their bet that bombing
would eventually prove an effective weapon.[31]

Meanwhile, however, the task of attacking Germany was becoming
more difficult. Improved defences, including night-fighters directed by
radar on the ground, exacted a growing toll on British bombers. New
crews arrived unprepared for the challenges of night-time operations
in the increasingly dangerous skies over Europe. Between July and
November, 414 aircraft on night sorties and 112 on day sorties were
shot down.[32] Peirse tried to keep up the offensive with smaller attacks
on less well-defended, less important targets, but that meant that little
progress was made towards the July directive's call for devastating city
attacks. His insistence that each aircraft should choose its own route to
the target was meant to protect his force, but because it spread them
out over space and time, it actually made it easier for the Germans to
pick them off.

With criticism of his leadership rising, Peirse attempted to redeem Bomber Command's reputation by launching a heavy raid on the German capital. On the night of 7–8 November, he despatched the largest raiding force Britain had ever sent – 392 aircraft – to attack Berlin, Cologne and Mannheim, choosing to persist with the operation despite predictions of bad weather. As they struggled through the storms, their aircraft icing up, the crews found it even harder than normal to reach their destinations. Only seventy-three got to Berlin, where the bombs they dropped killed a total of nine people. Over 9 per cent of the whole force failed to return. Among the aircraft sent to Berlin, the loss rate was more than 12 per cent. In the face of this disaster, Churchill told Peirse to suspend the offensive. In December, the air staff decided that he would have to be replaced. With casualties high, its command in crisis and its capabilities in question, Bomber Command's morale slumped. The gap between expectation and reality seemed as wide as ever.[33]

'CONSCRIPT EVERY ABLE-BODIED MAN AND WOMAN'

The much-anticipated labour shortage became evident in the summer of 1941.[34] In July the War Cabinet ordered the Ministry of Labour to undertake a new survey of available manpower. When the survey was complete, in October, it was presented first to the Lord President's Committee: a sign of the committee's growing importance for the direction of the war on the home front. The survey showed that another 2 million men and women would be needed for the armed services and war industries by June the following year.

That meant the government would need to find another 300,000 men for the services in addition to those who would be normally called up, and a million women for the auxiliary forces and the munitions industries. These demands confirmed Bevin's conversion to the need for the much greater compulsion of labour. Shortages of unskilled labour were increasingly widespread, public opinion had moved strongly in favour of compulsion and there had been extensive press discussion of the need to conscript women as well as men.[35]

Even before the manpower survey was ready, it was already out-of-date. To meet Churchill's demands for an increase in heavy bomber production, the MAP produced a new programme that would require another 360,000 workers, most of them women, by the end of June 1942, and another half a million over the following year. The scale of this demand marked the start of Britain concentrating more of its industrial effort on the strategic air offensive, and it would shortly force the Lord President's Committee to adopt a new method of allocating labour to the supply departments, rather than the Ministry of Labour just trying to fill their vacancies, so that production targets could be matched to manpower.[36]

After considering the manpower survey in October, the Lord President's Committee agreed that the only way to find the men and women who were needed would be to tighten the terms under which men were reserved from conscription, to make all men and women between eighteen and sixty liable for some form of national service, and to conscript younger women for the auxiliary forces (they were subsequently given the option of working in the munitions industries instead). When these proposals were taken to the War Cabinet, there was a long debate about the conscription of women. Churchill, with the support of the chiefs of staff, was opposed, on the basis that servicemen hated the idea of their wives being conscripted, and it would damage military morale. Agreement was eventually secured on the basis that female conscription would be tightly limited to single young women who did not have domestic responsibilities for invalid parents or male relatives. Younger married women without children would be liable to limited direction for employment. Mothers of children under fourteen would be exempt from any form of compulsory service.

By late 1941, after months of newspaper complaints about the failures of production, many people were in favour of the government taking more control on the home front. When the BIPO asked whether respondents were happy 'with the government's handling of the man and woman power problem' in October, only 27 per cent were content, against 53 per cent who were dissatisfied. In response to a question about the steps that could be taken to speed up production, the most popular answers were, in order: 'More efficient planning and supervision inside factories' (10 per cent), 'Conscript women for munitions work' (10 per cent), 'Conscript every able-bodied man and woman' (9 per cent), 'Conscript wealth and nationalise factories' (7 per cent), 'Comb out inefficient management' (7 per cent). Only 4 per cent said 'decrease government control and cut red tape'. In the same survey, 54 per cent of respondents wanted people who ate in restaurants to have to surrender food rationing coupons, most of them because 'At present rich have advantage over poor. Can get more for their rations. Would be fairer.'[37]

None of these changes included a minister of production, which was what many of the government's critics in the Commons had wanted. Moving the debate on the opening of Parliament on 12 November, Churchill announced that he would be making no changes in the structure of the government. On 2 December, when the National Service (No. 2) Bill, which would enact the new measures of compulsion, was moved in the House, MPs took it as an opportunity for another discussion of the problems in industry. On the opposition benches, the debate turned into the first serious Labour revolt against the government since the Coalition began.

Since the summer, the Labour Party had become increasingly concerned about what its leaders were doing in government. Labour MPs were disillusioned by their ministers' failure to implement a programme of socialist measures. Whether or not the radical literature calling for a new society reflected a popular mood, it certainly helped to convince some members of the Labour Party that the public would back dramatic reforms, if only their leaders would push them through against Conservative resistance. Nye Bevan and Harold Laski stoked Labour fires by insisting that the time had come to fight through the policies that the party had advocated during the 1930s. Attlee was sufficiently worried about dissidents starting an open fight with the Tories that he put in place new regulations to ensure that Labour members didn't stand in Conservative-held seats at by-elections.[38]

Labour anger came to a head when backbenchers realized that the new National Service Bill increased the compulsion of labour without demanding the nationalization of essential industry. Attlee and Bevin failed to talk them down. On 4 December, Labour MPs tried to move an amendment accepting additional conscription only on the basis that 'industries vital to the successful prosecution of the war, and especially transport, coalmining and the manufacture of munitions should be brought under public ownership and control'.[39] In the division on the bill, thirty-six Labour MPs, a fifth of the total party, voted against the government, and another third abstained. The revolt stoked party antagonisms on both sides of the House. Concerns that the failure properly to organize production was holding back Britain's military effort remained.

'EXTRAORDINARY SUPERIORITY . . . IN NUMBERS OF TROOPS AND EQUIPMENT'

With the bombing campaign on hold, the offensive in North Africa offered the only prospect of an immediate military success for the British Empire. During the autumn, the auguries for success looked good. Under the protection of the Navy's Force H squadron, stores, guns and troops were shipped in to transform Malta into a well-defended fortress. RAF fighters flown off the aircraft carrier *Ark Royal* reinforced the garrison, and used Malta as a staging post to reach Egypt. Meanwhile, submarines and bombers operating out of Malta struck at the Axis supply line from Italy. From June 1941, the British were able to read the Italian naval cipher, adding another layer of detailed intelligence that guided these attacks. Between January and August, they sank fifty-one Axis ships on the route between Naples and North Africa. During September and October, they sank another eighteen. At the end of October, the British established a raiding force (Force K) of two light cruisers and two destroyers at Malta for the first time since the start of the year. On 8 November, they fell on an Italian convoy on its way across the Mediterranean, sinking all seven merchant ships and two of the escorting destroyers.[40]

The threat that Axis forces in North Africa might be completely cut off convinced Hitler to act. Against Dönitz's advice, another twenty-one German submarines were ordered to transfer from the Atlantic to the Mediterranean, along with another Fliegerkorps from the Eastern Front. Typically, Hitler took his decision without consultation with Mussolini. On 13 November, one of the U-boats that had already passed through the Straits of Gibraltar sank the *Ark Royal* on its way back from another Malta reinforcement run. It marked the start of a much more closely fought contest for control of the central Mediterranean.

In the meantime, however, the shortage of supplies had delayed Rommel's planned assault on Tobruk, while Auchinleck's forces steadily accumulated in the Western Desert. Auchinleck was a careful and uncompromising soldier. He had spent most of his career in the Indian army, and had played a key role in its modernization and 'Indianization' – the replacement of British by Indian officers – during the late 1930s. When, as commander-in-chief of India in spring 1941, he had found troops to put down Rashid Ali's uprising in Iraq, Churchill had decided that 'the Auk' had the offensive spirit that was sadly lacking in Wavell.

Unlike Wavell, Auchinleck had a government minister resident in the Middle East, Oliver Lyttelton, appointed by the prime minister as a representative of the War Cabinet. Lyttelton had done a good job of standing up to Churchill at the Board of Trade (he later claimed, apocryphally, that he had only got the prime minister to agree to clothes rationing by waiting until he was distracted by the hunt for the *Bismarck*). Now, Churchill hoped that Lyttelton would give him a direct line to someone he could trust in the desert. The post gave Lyttelton a position of great power and potential significance at the heart of Britain's growing war effort in the Middle East.

The new minister resident was soon embroiled with trying to sort out the host of problems that the war had created in the region. In Egypt, the British worried that King Farouk was letting pro-Axis factions gain power in the palace and the government. In Syria and Lebanon, a major diplomatic crisis had blown up with General de Gaulle, over the terms of the armistice with the Vichy French. By the time it was resolved, de Gaulle had been so offensive that the officer Churchill had appointed to liaise with the Free French, General Louis Spears, had resolved personally to end French rule in the Levant.[41] Meanwhile, the whole Middle East was threatening to descend into economic chaos because of the shortage of civilian imports from Britain, the burdens of the huge forces now stationed around the theatre and the heavy flow of military equipment through the underequipped ports of the Red Sea. To try to address these issues, and to economize on imports, Lyttelton revived an organization called the Middle East Supply Centre (MESC). To run it, he appointed a brilliant young Australian officer, Robert Jackson. In early 1942, Jackson would use his control of shipping to impose a system of central co-ordination and controls on food that saved the Middle East from famine. In the years to come, the MESC would develop into a vast organization that kept most of the Middle East fed despite the disruption caused by the war.[42]

What Lyttelton didn't do was force Auchinleck into battle. Reinforcements were pouring into the Middle East, and by the end of the year there were about 750,000 Commonwealth servicemen in the theatre. 'The Auk', however, proved more obdurate than his predecessor about the preparations that had to be made before he could attack. Above all, he insisted that the troops that were being despatched to him needed time to train and acclimatize themselves to the desert before they could fight. The respite he won gave some units time to improve their training, but an influx of new weapons and soldiers meant that the renamed Eighth Army was still full of military novices at the end of 1941. To lead it, Auchinleck chose General Sir Alan Cunningham, who had commanded the step-by-step fight through the Eritrean mountains during the campaign in East Africa the previous spring.

Cunningham had command of the largest concentration of military technology assembled by the British Empire in the war to that point. By the time 'Operation Crusader' started, the Eighth Army could deploy more than 500 cruiser and infantry tanks, with substantial reserves, against 174 German and 146 Italian equivalents with no front line replacements. In the skies, the Desert Air Force enjoyed a similar advantage, with 554 serviceable aircraft against 313 Axis opponents when the battle began. Thanks to new systems for directing aircraft and quickly relocating squadrons, the Desert Air Force had also become better at providing support to units on the ground.[43]

Crusader got under way on 20 November. Cunningham's plan was based on using his armoured units to outflank the Axis defences to the south while the Tobruk garrison broke out from its perimeter. Rommel, however, refused to be pinned down. Communications within the attacking forces quickly broke down, and the battle degenerated into a series of confused confrontations, with units from both sides becoming isolated as they sought to outflank each other.

The Axis forces had much the better of these fights. A new Italian armoured division had arrived in the desert in September, and it helped to stop the British advance. German commanders dealt better with the chaotic clashes that followed, while the British struggled to co-ordinate their attacks. British cruiser tanks also suffered badly from mechanical breakdowns. Both tank and anti-tank units relied on the 2-pounder

guns with which they had started the war, while the Germans had reinforced their tanks' armour and were now making use for the first time
of longer-barrelled 50mm anti-tank guns, as well as the heavier 88mm
weapons. Since the 2-pounder only fired a shell suitable for penetrating
tank armour, not for killing gun crews, the British tanks had no way of
hitting back against them. Instead, British armoured units resorted to
desperate mass charges – not, as was sometimes thought, because they
were the last heirs of a cavalry tradition, but because this was the only
way to get close enough to their opponents to do them damage – either
with the tanks' machine guns or by running over the anti-tank guns
themselves.[44]

The casualties were very heavy. By 23 November it looked as if Cunningham had lost so many tanks that his opponents now outnumbered
his forces three to one. He thought the battle was lost. On 25 November, Auchinleck, believing victory was still possible, dismissed him and
replaced him with his deputy chief of general staff, General Neil
Ritchie. By 6 December, this confidence was rewarded when Rommel
was forced to withdraw. German and Italian troops had been worn
down by the prolonged fighting and the continued pounding from the
Desert Air Force. Their supply situation was now critical. Their generals believed they had been overcome by the enemy's 'extraordinary
superiority . . . in numbers of troops and equipment'.[45] An exhausted
Eighth Army pursued them first to the Gazala Line, south of Tobruk,
then, over the subsequent weeks, back across the desert to El Agheila.
By the time Operation Crusader was complete, however, the war had
undergone another dramatic change.

As the Crusader offensive began, the Germans were on the move
again in Russia. The onset of freezing winter weather made the muddy
roads passable and allowed them to attempt a final drive towards Moscow. By the end of November, it had ground to a halt, with its advance
troops within 15 miles of the city, fought to a standstill by the Red
Army's dogged defence. Hitler's attempt to win a quick victory over the
Soviet Union had failed. Of the 1.25 million Red Army soldiers involved
in the campaign, 660,000 had been killed, wounded or were missing.[46]
At the start of December, about a third of the heavy and medium tanks
of the Soviet forces guarding Moscow were British-provided Valentines
and Matildas.[47] On 5 December, just before Rommel retreated in the
desert, the Soviet high command began a counter-offensive against

German forces left strung out by their prolonged advance and ill-prepared for the bitter winter weather. Two days later, Anthony Eden and his party set off by train to board the ship that would take them to their meeting with the Soviets. En route, they noticed some excitement at a station. Japan had declared war on Britain and America.

'A CONFLICT BETWEEN JAPAN AND THE ENGLISH-SPEAKING WORLD'

Since the summer, Churchill and Eden had been in agreement about how deterrence would work in the Far East.[48] Britain needed not only to follow American policy towards Japan, but also to make it clear, both to Japan and to the US, that the UK was still a great imperial power whose belligerence ought to be taken seriously. That meant sending reinforcements to the Far East, not in the belief that they could safeguard the Empire if fighting broke out, but rather in the hope that they would help to stop a war. From the end of August, they pressured the Admiralty to send out a 'formidable, fast, high class squadron'[49] that included one of the new *King George V* class battleships.

This did not fit with the navy's plans. Since March, when it had become clear that the Americans were unwilling to protect Britain's colonial possessions by basing naval units at Singapore, the Admiralty had decided to gradually build up its own Far Eastern fleet. This was to be based on older battleships, it would come together in early 1942 and its initial aim would be to safeguard the Indian Ocean from a Japanese incursion in the event of war. Admiral Pound wanted to keep all Britain's more modern battleships in home waters, in case Germany's last remaining battleship, *Tirpitz*, broke out into the Atlantic convoy lanes.

Churchill and Eden thought this missed the point. They wanted ships that would send a message in the next few months, not a fleet of older vessels that would only come together after the Japanese had decided whether or not to go to war. As Eden argued in October, this would 'have a far greater effect politically than the presence in those waters of a number of the last war's battleships'.[50] This argument ultimately prevailed. While the Admiralty proceeded with its longer-term plans, on 25 October, the modern battleship *Prince of Wales* was despatched from the Home Fleet to form the basis of a new task force (Force Z) with the battlecruiser *Repulse*. They arrived in Singapore on 2 December.

The desire to match America's growing resolve in the Pacific also explains why the chiefs of staff decided in the summer of 1941 to ask Canada to provide two battalions of infantry to reinforce the garrison at Hong Kong. With Canadian troops bored and kicking their heels in Britain, and criticism of their inactivity rising at home, the government in Ottawa readily complied. Almost 2,000 Canadian servicemen (and 2 female nurses) arrived in Hong Kong on 16 November 1941. As they tried to get used to the heat and humidity, Canadian officers were struck by how confident everyone was in the colony's fortifications. They toured round the island and were shown the pillboxes defending the route along which the Japanese would advance. When they asked what would happen if the Japanese came from a different direction, discussion was rapidly moved on.[51]

Back in Britain, the prime minister sought to promote the idea of a common Anglo-American front. On 10 November 1941, in a speech at the Guildhall, he promised the Japanese that Britain would declare war if they attacked America, and warned them against 'a conflict between Japan and the English-speaking world'.[52] If this did not immediately elicit similar promises from Roosevelt in return, it did at least bolster a sense in Washington and Tokyo that Britain and America were acting as one when it came to dealing with Japan.

By then the Japanese, unable to escape the tightening economic pressure from the US, had already decided to gamble on war. On 16 October 1941, having failed to secure negotiations with the Americans, the government of Prime Minister Konoe Fumimaro resigned. Konoe was replaced by General Tojo Hideki, the head of a group of military hardliners. The Japanese planners had already devised quick campaigns in South-East Asia and the Pacific to establish an economically self-supporting defensive position that the Western democracies would be too weak to retake. They indeed took the US fleet at Pearl Harbor seriously – so seriously that knocking it out became an essential part of their first strike.

When, on 26 November, the Americans presented tough new demands before they would relieve the embargo, they knew it meant war. What they did not suspect was just how quickly it would come, or

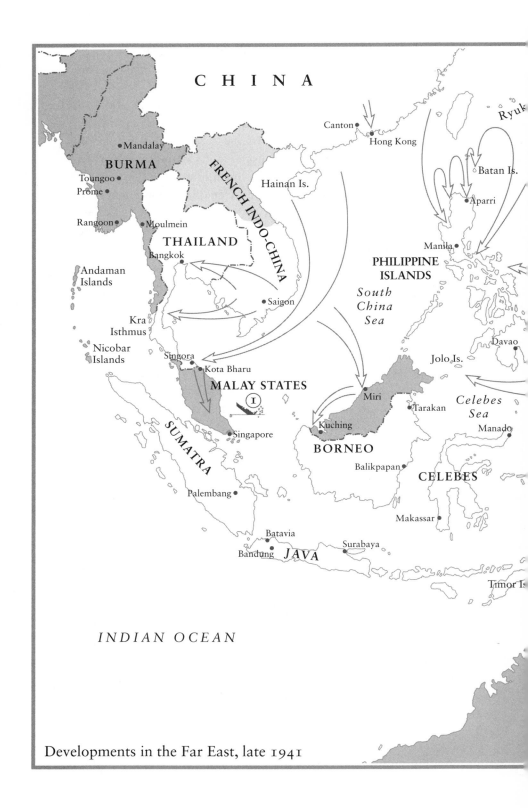

CHINA

Canton •

Hong Kong •

Ryuk

Batan Is. •

Mandalay •

BURMA

Toungoo •
Prome •

Rangoon •   • Moulmein

THAILAND

Bangkok •

Andaman
Islands

Kra
Isthmus

Nicobar
Islands

FRENCH INDO-CHINA

Hainan Is.

• Saigon

Aparri •

Manila •

PHILIPPINE
ISLANDS

South
China
Sea

Davao •

Singora •

• Kota Bharu

MALAY STATES
Ⅰ

• Singapore

SUMATRA

Palembang •

Jolo Is. •

Miri •

• Tarakan

Celebes
Sea

Kuching •

BORNEO

Balikpapan •

Manado •

CELEBES

Makassar •

Batavia •

Bandung • JAVA

Surabaya •

Timor Is

INDIAN OCEAN

Developments in the Far East, late 1941

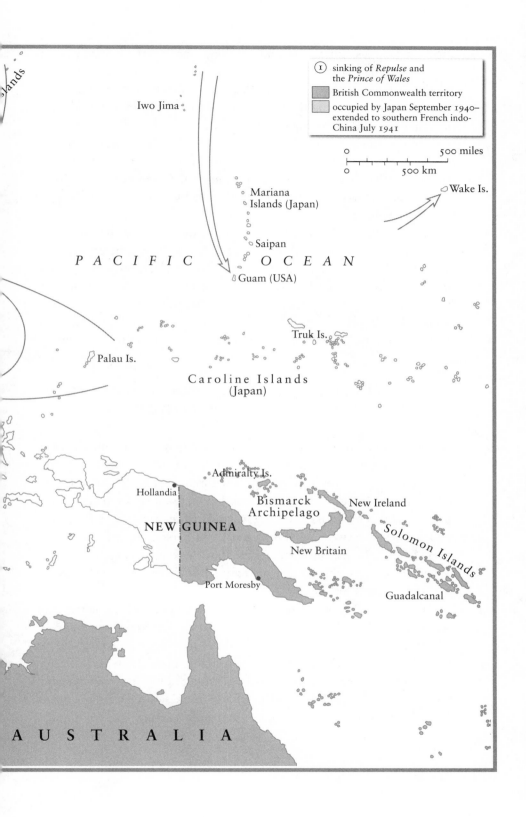

① sinking of *Repulse* and
the *Prince of Wales*

British Commonwealth territory

occupied by Japan September 1940–
extended to southern French indo-
China July 1941

0   500 miles
0   500 km

Wake Is.

OCEAN

Admiralty Is.

Hollandia

Bismarck
Archipelago

New Ireland

NEW GUINEA

New Britain

Solomon Islands

Port Moresby

Guadalcanal

AUSTRALIA

that the Japanese intended to hit Pearl Harbor. For the British government, a primary concern was to make sure that they did not end up at war with Japan without the US. With signals intelligence showing that Japanese forces were on the move, on 2 December Roosevelt told Halifax that in the event of a Japanese attack on the British or Dutch 'we should obviously all be together'.[53] In typical fashion, Roosevelt had finally given the assurance for which the British had been looking for so long. If they had been wrong to count on deterrence, they had been right to presume that in the end, the president intended to lead the fight against Japan.

Five days later, the Japanese took the Americans by surprise when they hit Pearl Harbor with a powerful attack from carrier-launched aircraft. This wrecked much of the US Pacific Fleet, but crucially not the American carriers that would subsequently play a key role in containing Japanese expansion in the Pacific. Meanwhile, Japanese troops attacked Malaya, Guam, Wake, Hong Kong and the Philippines. On 8 December, the United States and Britain both declared war on Japan.

'IN ALL THE WAR I NEVER RECEIVED A MORE DIRECT SHOCK'

America had entered hostilities, but not in the war that Churchill had wanted. American fury at the attack on Pearl Harbor raised the possibility that the US would abandon the fight against Germany in favour of an all-out effort to revenge itself on Japan. On 8 December, Churchill decided that he would have to travel to Washington to meet Roosevelt and confirm the two new allies' strategy in person. To Eden's frustration, Churchill insisted that rather than accompanying him to the American capital, the foreign secretary should proceed as planned to Moscow to meet Stalin.

Meanwhile, Britain's war in the Far East had got off to the worst of starts. In southern China, the Japanese quickly besieged Hong Kong. In Malaya, despite the weakness of the defending forces, the plan was to hold the Japanese as far up the peninsula as possible, with the army launching a pre-emptive strike into Thailand to block the route in from the north, while the RAF fought off any invasion fleet from the air. A Japanese task force had been spotted approaching the coast on 6

December, but the British held back from implementing the defensive scheme. Not knowing about the forthcoming attack on Pearl Harbor, they worried that the Japanese were trying to lure them into opening hostilities in order to isolate them from the United States. By the time the British got their act together, they were too late to forestall the Japanese advance from Thailand. The Commonwealth air forces in Malaya – outnumbered four-to-one – were rapidly destroyed, and the army was unable to hold Japanese landings on the beaches. The invaders had soon occupied airfields from which their aircraft could extend their reach further south.[54]

At the same time, Force Z had sailed into disaster. The *Prince of Wales* and *Repulse* were never meant to provide a viable defence for Singapore. Churchill, for all his usual combativeness, hoped after Pearl Harbor that they would sail to join the US fleet at Hawaii. Admiral Phillips, acting on his own initiative, chose to take his ships in search of the enemy. Force Z missed the invasion fleet, but on 10 December it was located by Japanese aircraft. Two hours later, after a devastating air attack, *Prince of Wales* and *Repulse* had both been sunk, and Phillips and 840 of his men were dead. Their loss reaffirmed what might have been apparent after Norway, Taranto and Crete – that airpower was now a crucial factor in naval warfare. With even the threat of action by the Royal Navy gone, Lieutenant General Percival's army was left to defend the Malayan peninsula alone.

Back in the UK, reports of rising tensions and recurrent crises in the Far East had been in the press for months, together with reassurances that the Japanese were going to have to back down.[55] The outbreak of hostilities came as a surprise. The soldier Henry Novy, a former full-time Mass-Observer, was visiting his parents when the news came in:

> Mother and Dad didn't seem to take much notice of the new war. We talked about it a great deal, and a surgeon friend of Dad's came in, we looked at the map of the world, and were amazed by the distances between Japan and the points attacked . . . On the whole for us it was just a new war, but not quite, the spread of the present war into something not very well known; expected, and less clearly excitable than the nearer issues. We got the impression . . . that the bloody world had gone mad, all mixed up, and it required an effort to think about it.[56]

The next day at work, he listened to other soldiers sounding off about the Japanese:

'The bloody little yellow monkeys', 'Bloody cheek isn't it'. They were all quite excited about it, a kind of excitement well expressed by one of the lads in the office: 'Christ, you can't go on a week-end without a new bloody war starting . . .'[57]

In a radio broadcast that evening, Churchill spent a lot of time explaining the way in which he and Roosevelt had co-ordinated the timing of the declaration of war. Then, being Churchill, he offered some hostages to fortune:

Although the imperative demands of the war in Europe and in Africa have strained our resources, vast and growing though they be, you and all the Empire will notice that some of the finest ships in the Royal Navy have reached their stations in the Far East at a very convenient moment. Every preparation in our power has been made, every preparation which our resources allowed – and you must not forget the many calls upon us – has been made. And I do not doubt that wherever we are attacked we shall give a good account of ourselves.[58]

The prime minister concluded with a plea for increased munitions production and a promise of eventual victory:

We have at least four-fifths of the population of the globe on our side. We are responsible for their safety – we are responsible for their future. And as I told the House of Commons this afternoon, in the past we had a light which flickered, in the present we have a light that flames, and in the future there will be a light which will shine calm and resplendent over all the land and all the sea![59]

It wasn't one of his more inspiring efforts. In Norwich, a married policeman recorded his reactions:

he didn't sound himself, he gave the impression of tiredness as well he might. The strain of the past few days on top of that of the past months must be telling on a man of his years. And I couldn't help feeling that however stimulating his broadcasts are (and they do buck us all up) . . . it is an unnecessary strain on an already overworked man.[60]

Somewhere in South London, a thirty-six-year-old female office worker felt the same way:

> It seems absurd that these places, Hawaii, Waikiki and Honolulu, associated in many of our minds with American films of singing girls and white-clad US marines, should be the scene of this most terrible of wars. We hear the speech of President Roosevelt to Congress and a fine speech it is too, such a contrast to that of Mr Churchill later in the evening, which is stilted and disjointed, but I suppose he is tired after his strenuous weekend.[61]

Two days later, news of the demise of Force Z almost turned her into another casualty of the war:

> I was in the middle of the road at lunchtime today when I saw the newspaperman writing on his board the terrible news 'Prince of Wales' and 'Repulse' sunk, and so surprised was I that a car nearly ran me down. The driver was furious until he saw my lapse. What a ghastly difference this will make to our power in the East and it seems that it will be some time before the Americans can do anything at sea there.[62]

Richard Brown recorded in his diary:

> The loss of those two ships has caused a big stir and lots of concern in the country. Undoubtedly it is a heavy blow . . . *Prince of Wales* was the pride of our Fleet and for her to be sunk by a nation like Japan in the opening days of the war, and by air attack too, makes one wonder just what we are up against.[63]

Henry Novy found his fellow soldiers in a state of patriotic bafflement:

> 'Christ, how did they do it! I wonder what they used. But it's always the same in the bloody start. It won't last long.'
>
> 'It's a big blow. But you wait, the Navy ain't beat. They'll teach the blighters . . .'
>
> 'I can't think how they did it. They say they bombed them. But that's hardly possible is it? I don't think they'll stand a chance when they meet our ships at sea . . .'
>
> 'The bloody Yanks have been jabbing and jabbing for years. Now they've got to fight their own bloody war. It'll do them good.'[64]

Churchill was as stunned as anyone else by the demise of Force Z. He would later recall that 'In all the war I never received a more direct shock.'[65] 'Poor Tom Phillips', his secretary heard him mutter.[66] Poor Churchill too, with the defences in the Far East crumbling, the ships that were meant to deter war sunk and the American industrial power that the British had paid so much to secure about to be diverted to the Pacific. Then came news to restore his optimism and reaffirm his belief that Providence was on Britain's side.

Since the Japanese had not informed the Germans about their plans, Hitler had been even more surprised about Pearl Harbor than Roosevelt and Churchill. He was not, however, taken aback. Ever since America had declared that it was backing both Britain and the Soviet Union at the Atlantic Conference, Hitler had become convinced that his long-predicted transatlantic war was not just inevitable, but imminent. By late 1941, the question had become not whether to fight America, but whether the Japanese could distract the US fleet long enough for him to complete the defeat of the Red Army and obtain the resources he needed for the battle to come. Notwithstanding his army's failure to capture Moscow, the Japanese seemed to have done critical damage to US naval power. Hitler spotted an opportunity. With the Americans occupied in the Far East, he could sever the supply lines by which they were sustaining the war against him. On 11 December, Germany declared war on America.

The next day, Churchill departed for Washington. Eden was already aboard ship on his way to Moscow. A truly world war had begun, and Britain's leaders were travelling to meet the men who were going to win it.

Acknowledgements

I would like to thank the following organizations and people for allowing permission to quote from material in their copyright or care: the Trustees of the Imperial War Museum, London; the London School of Economics and Political Science Library; Ronald Pountain; Michael Hall (grandson of General Sir Noel Mason-MacFarlane); Piers Mayfield (son of Guy Mayfield); Carole Jackson (daughter of J. E. Needham); Alex Mitchell (great-nephew of Mrs G. Cox); Jerry Cullum (nephew of Eileen Monk-Jones); Martin Howard (stepson of Captain G. E. Tapp); Trisha Staynes and Sir Edward Clay (the children of Colonel Ewart Clay); and Judy Avery (granddaughter of G. W. King). Quotations from the Mass Observation Archive are reproduced with permission of Curtis Brown Group Limited, London, on behalf of the Trustees of the Mass Observation Archive.

In the course of researching and writing this book, I have incurred many other debts of thanks. Natasha Fairweather, my agent, who first got me to write a proposal about Britain in the Second World War, has been both a wise, stalwart and patient advisor ever since. Simon Winder at Penguin sustained his and my enthusiasm, patience and faith while this book was coming to fruition, and provided invaluable commentary both on its overall shape and numerous points of detail. I am also grateful to Simon's assistant, Maria Bedford, and to Richard Duguid at Penguin for helping me as the book moved through to production. Charlotte Ridings not only provided masterful copy-editing, but also made me smile by being the first reader of the manuscript to suggest that I ought to add some more things in.

As *Britain's War* gestated, I benefitted greatly from my discussions with other historians. David Edgerton, Julian Jackson, Sir Hew Strachan, Jenny Macleod, David Reynolds, Pierre Purseigle, Gary Sheffield,

Lucy Noakes, Stefan Goebel, Matthew Grant, Alexander Watson, Jay Winter, Marcus Faulkner, Mark Connelly, Peter Martland, Jack McGowan, Victoria Carolan, Joel Morley, Eleanor O'Keefe and Ian Kikuchi will be just some of the people who may recognize things we have talked about. For their very detailed readings, and extensive corrections, comments and other suggestions for improvement, I am particularly grateful to Jonathan Fennell, Helen McCarthy, James Ellison and Patrick Higgins. Without their help this would not be the book that it is.

I am also very grateful to other of my colleagues in the School of History at Queen Mary University of London for their care and kindness: Miri Rubin, Julian Jackson (again), Thomas Asbridge, Catherine Merridale and Peter Hennessy all deserve particular mention for the guidance they gave at different stages. The late John Ramsden encouraged me to take on the project: hopefully he would disagree with some of what I have written but still see his influence upon it. John would have reminded me that one of the privileges of working at Queen Mary is the people you get to teach, so I offer my thanks also to the students on undergraduate and masters courses who have learned about the war alongside me for the past decade (or put up with me talking about it when we were meant to be doing something else).

My greatest thanks, however, must go to my family, which has expanded in ways more wonderful and powerful than I could have imagined since I started writing this book. I hope that they feel it does justice to our forebears: citizen soldiers of that titanic conflict. I am ever grateful for their love and support.

Notes

ABBREVIATIONS

BIPO | UK Data Service, 'British Institute of Public Opinion (Gallup) Polls, 1938–1946, http://discover.ukdataservice.ac.uk/catalogue?sn=3331

BUFVC | British Universities Film and Video Council, London, News on Screen Archive, http://bufvc.ac.uk/newsonscreen/about

CSO | Central Statistical Office

HC Deb | Hansard, House of Commons Debates: http://hansard.millbanksystems.com/

HIMR | Home Intelligence Morale Report, published in P. Addison and J. Crang (eds.), *Listening to Britain: Home Intelligence Reports on Britain's Finest Hour – May to September 1940* (London, 2010)

HIWR | Home Intelligence Weekly Report

IWM | Imperial War Museum, London

MOA | Mass Observation Archive, Brighton, University of Sussex

MOFR | Mass Observation File Report

NCDL IV | *The Neville Chamberlain Diary Letters, IV: The Downing Street Years*, ed. R. Self (Aldershot, 2005)

ODNB | *Oxford Dictionary of National Biography* (Oxford, 2004)

OHBE IV | *Oxford History of the British Empire, IV: The Twentieth Century*, eds. J. Brown and W. R. Louis (Oxford, 1999)

TNA | The National Archives, Kew, London

DIARISTS

Amery | J. Barnes and D. Nicholson (eds.), *The Empire at Bay: The Leo Amery Diaries, 1929–1945* (London, 1988)

Beardmore | G. Beardmore, *Civilians at War: Journals 1938–1946* (Oxford, 1986).

Brooke   A. Danchev and D. Todman (eds.), *War Diaries 1939–1945, Field Marshal Lord Alanbrooke* (London, 2001)

Brown   H. Millgate (ed.), *Mr Brown's War: A Diary of the Second World War* (Stroud, 1998)

Cadogan   D. Dilks (ed.), *The Diaries of Sir Alexander Cadogan, 1938–1945* (London, 1971)

Channon   R. Rhodes James (ed.), *Chips: The Diaries of Sir Henry Channon* (London, 1967)

Chuter Ede   K. Jefferys (ed.), *Labour and the Wartime Coalition: From the Diary of James Chuter Ede 1941–1945* (London, 1987)

Colville   J. Colville, *The Fringes of Power: Downing Street Diaries 1939–1955* (London, 2004)

Dalton   B. Pimlott (ed.), *The Second World War Diary of Hugh Dalton 1940–1945* (London, 1986)

Halder   A. Lissance (ed.), *The Private War Journal of Generaloberst Franz Halder, Chief of the General Staff of the Supreme Command of the German Army (OKH), 14 August 1939–24 September 1942*, Volume IV (online copy, Leavenworth, Kans., 2007), http://cgsc.contentdm.oclc.org/cdm/search/collection/p4013coll8/searchterm/War%20journal%20of%20Franz%20Halder/field/title/mode/all/conn/and

Ironside   R. Macleod and D. Kelly (eds.), *The Ironside Diaries 1937–1940* (London, 1962)

King   W. Armstrong (ed.), *With Malice Towards None: A War Diary by Cecil H. King* (London, 1970)

Harvey   J. Harvey (ed.), *The War Diaries of Oliver Harvey 1941–1945* (London, 1978)

Headlam   S. Ball (ed.), *Parliament and Politics in the Age of Churchill and Attlee: The Headlam Diaries 1935–1951* (Cambridge, 1999)

Nicolson   N. Nicolson (ed.), *Harold Nicolson: Diaries and Letters 1939–45* (London, 1967)

Mitchison   D. Sheridan (ed.), *Among You Taking Notes: The Wartime Diary of Naomi Mitchison 1939–1945* (London, 2000)

Musto   A. McCulloch, *The War and Uncle Walter: The Diary of an Eccentric* (London, 2009)

Pownall   B. Bond (ed.), *Chief of Staff: The Diaries of Lieutenant-General Sir Henry Pownall, Volume I, 1933–1940, Volume II, 1940–1944* (London, 1974)

Webb   London School of Economics and Political Science Library Collections, PASSFIELD/1/2/12, Beatrice Webb typescript diary, 4 January 1938–9 December 1940.

All websites accessed on 10 November 2015.

A NOTE ON MONEY

1. For this and the discussion and calculation that follow, see L. Officer and S. Williamson, 'Five Ways to Compute the Relative Value of a UK Pound Amount, 1270 to Present', www.measuringworth.com/ukcompare.
2. CSO, *Fighting with Figures: A Statistical Digest of the Second World War* (London, 1995), p. 266.
3. D. French, *Raising Churchill's Army: The British Army and the War against Germany, 1919–1945* (Oxford, 2000), p. 116.

1. STUDIES IN CELEBRATION

1. S. Bradford, *George VI* (London, 1989), p. 213.
2. Channon diary, 12 May 1937, pp. 125–6.
3. 'Marshalling the Troops', *The Times*, 12 May 1937, p. 17; H. Jennings and C. Madge, *May the Twelfth: Mass-Observation Day Surveys 1937* (London, 1937 [republished, 1987]), p. 8; 'Breakfast at any Time', *The Times*, 13 May 1937, p. 25.
4. 'London Travel Record', *The Times*, 14 May 1937, p. 7.
5. 'Controlling the Crowds', *The Times*, 12 May 1937, p. 17; 'Efficient Police Control', *The Times*, 13 May 1937, p. 25; 'Coronation Day Charges', *The Times*, 14 May 1937, p. 9.
6. Jennings and Madge, *May the Twelfth*, p. 112.
7. Ibid., p. 136.
8. Ibid., p. 153.
9. Ibid., pp. 162–3.
10. 'In the Provinces: Celebrations in the Country', *The Times*, 13 May 1937, p. 14.
11. J. B. Priestley, *Rain upon Godshill: A Further Chapter of Autobiography* (London, 1939), p. 41.
12. 'Messages from Abroad: An Empire's Devotion', *The Times*, 13 May 1937, p. 15.
13. 'America Stops to Listen' *The Times*, 13 May 1937, p. 15; 'Herr Hitler's Good Wishes', *The Times*, 12 May 1937, p. 12.
14. Bradford, *George VI*, p. 208, ch. 8 and p. 214.
15. *Radio Times*, 7 May 1937, pp. 28–30; *Radio Pictorial*, 7 May 1937, pp. 26, 28. The Corporation's regional stations for Wales and Scotland did not broadcast *Merrie England*, although that for Northern Ireland did. All the regional programmes carried that morning's *Children's Hour*, which had a special edition devoted to 'A Thousand Years of English Monarchs'.
16. Jennings and Madge, *May the Twelfth*, p. 283.

17. 'The King's Broadcast', *The Times*, 13 May 1937, p. 16.
18. MOA, Day Surveys, 12 May 1937, Correspondent No. 300.
19. Jennings and Madge, *May the Twelfth*, pp. 284–5.
20. Bradford, *George VI*, p. 210.
21. Any book such as this inevitably draws extensively on a wide range of secondary literature, and references are intended as an indication of sources and a guide to influences rather than a scholarly exploration of everything written on the subject. Throughout, notes on the first sentence of a new section indicate key works for the whole of what follows; notes within sections are for clarity, specific sources and arguments. Here: J. Hinton, *The Mass Observers: A History* (Oxford, 2013), ch. 1; T. Jeffery, *Mass Observation: A Short History* (Birmingham, 1978); N. Hubble, *Mass-Observation and Everyday Life: Culture, History, Theory* (Basingstoke, 2006), chs. 4 and 5.
22. Quoted in D. Pocock, 'Afterword' to Jennings and Madge, *May the Twelfth*, p. 418.
23. Hubble, *Mass Observation*, pp. 142–5; review quotations from C. Madge and T. Harrisson, *First Year's Work, 1937–38* (London, 1938), pp. 48–63.
24. Jennings and Madge, *May the Twelfth*, pp. 303–4.

2. ANCIENT AND MODERN

1. D. Edgerton, *Britain's War Machine: Weapons, Resources and Experts in the Second World War* (London, 2011), pp. 14–28; M. Pugh, *We Danced All Night: A Social History of Britain between the Wars* (London, 2009), pp. 302–22.
2. A. Root, 'Transport and Communication', in A. Halsey and J. Webb (eds.), *Twentieth Century British Social Trends* (Basingstoke, 2000), pp. 438–45.
3. A. Thorpe, *Britain in the 1930s* (Oxford, 1992), pp. 108–9.
4. J. Sedgwick, 'Cinema-going Preferences in Britain in the 1930s', in J. Richards (ed.), *The Unknown 1930s: An Alternative History of the British Cinema 1929–39* (London, 1998), pp. 1–36.
5. Thorpe, *Britain in the 1930s*, p. 108.
6. Ibid.
7. D. Fieldhouse, 'The Metropolitan Economics of Empire', *OHBE IV*, p. 102.
8. Thorpe, *Britain in the 1930s*, p. 64.
9. C. Feinstein, *Statistical Tables of National Income, Expenditure and Output of the UK, 1855–1965* (Cambridge, 1972), T140.
10. J. Lawrence, ' "Forging a Peaceable Kingdom": War, Violence and Fear of Brutalization in Post-First World War Britain', *Journal of Modern History*, 75, 3 (2003), pp. 557–89; M. Daunton, 'How to Pay for the War:

State, Society and Taxation in Britain, 1917–1924', *English Historical Review*, 111, 443 (1996), pp. 882–919; A. Gregory, *The Last Great War: British Society and the First World War* (Oxford, 2008); R. McKibbin, *Parties and People: England 1914–1951* (Oxford, 2010), ch. 2; idem, *Classes and Cultures: England 1918–1951* (Oxford, 2000); T. Kushner, *We Europeans? Mass Observation, 'Race' and British Identity in the Twentieth Century* (Aldershot, 2004), ch. 2; S. Pedersen and P. Mandler (eds.), *After the Victorians: Private Conscience and Public Duty in Modern Britain* (London, 1994); C. Brown, *The Death of Christian Britain: Understanding Secularisation, 1800–2000* (Abingdon, 2009); S. Szreter and K. Fisher, *Sex before the Sexual Revolution: Intimate Life in England, 1918–1963* (Cambridge, 2010), particularly ch. 3.

11. D. Butler and G. Butler, *British Political Facts, 1900–1985* (London, 1986), p. 224.

12. B. Harrison, *The Transformation of British Politics, 1860–1995* (Oxford, 1996), pp. 115–25.

13. J. Hinton, *Nine Wartime Lives: Mass-Observation and the Making of the Modern Self* (Oxford, 2010), pp. 7–11.

14. McKibbin, *Classes and Cultures*, chs. 1–3.

15. A. Thorpe, *Britain in the 1930s* (Oxford, 1992), p. 95.

16. H. McCarthy, 'Parties, Voluntary Associations, and Democratic Politics in Interwar Britain', *Historical Journal*, 50, 4 (2007), pp. 891–912.

17. McKibbin, *Classes and Cultures*, ch. 12.

18. R. McKibbin, 'Politics and the Medical Hero: A. J. Cronin's *The Citadel*', *English Historical Review*, 123, 502 (2008), pp. 651–78.

19. A. J. Cronin, *The Citadel* (London, 1937), pp. 376–7.

20. McKibbin, *Classes and Cultures*, chs. 4–5; S. Todd, 'Young Women, Work and Leisure in Interwar England', *Historical Journal*, 48, 3 (2005), pp. 789–809.

21. Thorpe, *Britain in the 1930s*, pp. 111–13.

22. G. D. H. Cole and M. Cole, *The Condition of Britain* (London, 1937), p. 74.

23. M. Swenarton and S. Taylor, 'The Scale and Nature of the Growth in Owner-Occupation in Britain between the Wars', *Economic History Review*, 38, 3 (1985), pp. 373–92.

24. C. Wrigley, *British Trade Unions since 1933* (Cambridge, 2002), pp. 7–12; Butler and Butler, *British Political Facts*, pp. 372–3.

25. Butler and Butler, *British Political Facts*, pp. 372–3.

26. J. B. Priestley, *English Journey* (London, 1934), p. 238.

27. McKibbin, *Classes and Cultures*, pp. 436–8.

28. D. Cannadine, *Class in Britain* (London, 2000), pp. 126–43; McKibbin, *Classes and Cultures*, pp. 98–101, 137–51, 198–205; idem, 'Class and Conventional Wisdom: The Conservative Party and the "Public" in Interwar Britain', in his *The Ideologies of Class: Social Relations in Britain,*

1880–1950 (Oxford, 1990), pp. 259–93; D. L. LeMahieu, *A Culture for Democracy: Mass Communication and the Cultivated Mind in Britain Between the Wars* (Oxford, 1988).

29. MOA, June 1939, Directive Response 1477, quoted in J. Hinton, ' "The 'Class' Complex": Mass-Observation and Cultural Distinction in Pre-War Britain', *Past & Present*, 199 (2008), p. 209.

3. POLITICS AND THE SLUMP

1. R. McKibbin, *Parties and People: England 1914–1951* (Oxford, 2010), ch. 2; P. Williamson, *Stanley Baldwin: Conservative Leadership and National Values* (Cambridge, 1999); R. McKibbin, 'Class and Conventional Wisdom: The Conservative Party and the "Public" in Interwar Britain', in idem, *The Ideologies of Class: Social Relations in Britain, 1880–1950* (Oxford, 1990).

2. Churchill College Cambridge, Halifax Papers, HLFX2, A4/410/14.2, Baldwin to Irwin, 20 June 1929, quoted in P. Williamson, ' "Safety First": Baldwin, the Conservative Party, and the 1929 General Election', *Historical Journal*, 25, 2 (1982), p. 387.

3. McKibbin, *Parties and People*, ch. 3; A. Thorpe, *The British General Election of 1931* (Oxford, 1991); P. Williamson, *National Crisis and National Government: British Politics, the Economy and Empire, 1926–1932* (Cambridge, 1992); S. Pedersen, 'From National Crisis to "National Crisis": British Politics 1914–1931', *Journal of British Studies*, 33, 3 (1994), pp. 322–35; Williamson, *Stanley Baldwin*, ch. 1; P. Williamson, 'Christian Conservatives and the Totalitarian Challenge, 1933–40', *English Historical Review*, 115, 462 (2000), pp. 607–42; D. Dutton, *Neville Chamberlain* (London, 2001), pp. 27–41; R. Self, *Neville Chamberlain: A Biography* (Aldershot, 2006), chs. 3–7.

4. To Hilda Chamberlain, 9–10 November 1935, *NCDL IV*, p. 159.

5. Quoted in Self, *Neville Chamberlain*, pp. 7–8.

6. A. Thorpe (ed.), *The Failure of Political Extremism in Inter-War Britain* (Exeter, 1989).

7. A. Thorpe, 'The Membership of the Communist Party of Great Britain, 1920–1945', *Historical Journal*, 43, 3 (2000), p. 781.

8. A. Thorpe, *Britain in the 1930s* (Oxford, 1992), pp. 54–6.

9. A. Thorpe, *Parties at War: Political Organization in Second World War Britain* (Oxford, 2009), pp. 126, 144.

4. POLITICS AND THE EMPIRE

1. Cmd 5482, Section X, quoted in R. Tamchina, 'In Search of Common Causes: The Imperial Conference of 1937', *Journal of Imperial and Commonwealth History*, 1 (1972), p. 97.
2. R. Whiting, 'The Empire and British Politics', in A. Thompson (ed.), *Oxford History of the British Empire, Companion Series: Britain's Experience of Empire in the Twentieth Century*, pp. 161–79; N. Owen, 'Critics of Empire in Britain', *OHBE IV*, pp. 208–10.
3. For this and the following paragraphs on Irwin, A. Roberts, *'The Holy Fox': The Life of Lord Halifax* (London, 1997), chs. 3–5.
4. G. Stewart, *Burying Caesar: Churchill, Chamberlain and the Battle for the Tory Party* (London, 1999), pp. 10–17 offers a useful overview of his career up to 1929; R. Toye, *Churchill's Empire: The World that Made Him and the World He Made* (London, 2010), pp. 162–88; A. Herman, *Gandhi and Churchill: The Epic Rivalry that Destroyed an Empire and Forged Our Age* (New York, 2008), pp. 354–81.
5. R. Adams, 'Hoare, Samuel John Gurney (1880–1959)', *ODNB*.
6. R. Pearce, 'Margesson, (Henry) David Reginald (1890–1965)', *ODNB*.
7. G. S. Harvie-Watt, *Most of My Life* (London, 1980), p. 31.
8. D. Low, *Eclipse of Empire* (Cambridge, 1991), pp. 132–3.
9. R. J. Moore, *Churchill, Cripps and India 1939–1945* (Oxford, 1979), p. 1.
10. This paragraph and the next, Low, *Eclipse of Empire*, pp. 70–73, 94–5.
11. Herman, *Churchill and Gandhi*, pp. 408–12.

5. PEACE AND WAR

1. G. Peden, *Arms, Economics and British Strategy: From Dreadnoughts to Hydrogen Bombs* (Cambridge, 2009), pp. 98–101, 125–31; D. Edgerton, *Warfare State: Britain, 1920–1970* (Cambridge, 2006), ch. 1; R. Boyce, *The Great Interwar Crisis and the Collapse of Globalization* (Basingstoke, 2009).
2. Edgerton, *Warfare State*, p. 23.
3. J. Maiolo, *Cry Havoc: The Arms Race and the Second World War 1931–1941* (London, 2010), for the UK pp. 88–101 and ch. 6; Peden, *Arms, Economics and British Strategy*, pp. 101–2; K. Neilson, 'The Defence Requirements Sub-Committee, British Strategic Foreign Policy, Neville Chamberlain and the Path to Appeasement', *English Historical Review*, 118, 477 (2003), pp. 651–84; C. Bell, *The Royal Navy, Seapower and Strategy between the Wars* (London, 2000), pp. 99–202; J. Maiolo, *The Royal Navy and Nazi Germany, 1933–39: A Study in Appeasement and the Origins of the Second World War* (Basingstoke, 1998), pp. 26–37.

4. TNA, CAB 23/70, Cabinet Conclusions, 10 February 1932, p. 9.

5. Maiolo, *Cry Havoc*, p. 44.

6. Quoted in B. Powers, *Strategy Without Slide Rule: British Air Strategy, 1914–1939* (London, 1976), p. 128.

7. R. Overy, *The Morbid Age: Britain and the Crisis of Civilisation* (London, 2010), pp. 219–28 and ch. 7; J. Hinton, *Protests and Visions: Peace Politics in 20th Century Britain* (London, 1989), chs. 8 and 9; P. Williamson, 'Christian Conservatives and the Totalitarian Challenge, 1933–40', *English Historical Review*, 115, 462 (2000), pp. 607–42; R. Griffiths, *Fellow Travellers of the Right: British Enthusiasts for Nazi Germany, 1933–39* (Oxford, 1983), pt. 1; D. Birn, *The League of Nations Union, 1918–1945* (Oxford, 1981), ch. 7; H. McCarthy, *The British People and the League of Nations: Democracy, Citizenship and Internationalism, c.1918–45* (Manchester, 2011); J. Stapleton, 'Resisting the Centre at the Extremes: "English" Liberalism in the Political Thought of Interwar Britain', *British Journal of Politics and International Relations*, 1, 3 (1999), pp. 270–92.

8. HC Deb, 10 November 1932, vol. 270, c. 632.

9. Birn, *The League of Nations Union*, p. 93.

6. PEACE AND PROGRESS

1. P. Williamson, *Stanley Baldwin: Conservative Leadership and National Values* (Cambridge, 1999), pp. 50–51 and ch. 10; G. Stewart, *Burying Caesar: Churchill, Chamberlain and the Battle for the Tory Party* (London, 1999), ch. 8.

2. HC Deb, 28 November 1934, vol. 295, c. 863.

3. M. Ceadel, 'The First British Referendum: The Peace Ballot, 1934–5', *English Historical Review*, 95, 377 (1980), pp. 810–39; R. Overy, *The Morbid Age: Britain and the Crisis of Civilisation* (London, 2010), pp. 229–34; T. Stannage, *Baldwin Thwarts the Opposition: The British General Election of 1935* (London, 1980); Williamson, *Baldwin*, pp. 309–11.

4. 'A Call to the Nation: The Joint Manifesto of the Leaders of the National Government', in F. Craig (ed.), *British General Election Manifestos 1918–1966* (Chichester, 1970), p. 81.

5. A. Bullock, *The Life and Times of Ernest Bevin, I: Trade Union Leader 1881–1940* (London, 1960).

6. 'The Labour Party's Call to Power', in Craig (ed.), *Election Manifestos*, p. 82.

7. R. McKibbin, *Parties and People: England 1914–1951* (Oxford, 2010), pp. 87–105, and see also Susan Pedersen's and Philip Williamson's reviews of McKibbin's book in *Twentieth Century British History*, 21, 4 (2010), pp. 560–67.

8. K. Harris, *Attlee* (London, 1982), *passim* and ch. 8; R. Crowcroft, *Attlee's War: World War II and the Making of a Labour Leader* (London, 2001) – one of the best books to be published on British politics in the Second World War in ages – lays out just what an expert leader Attlee became.
9. B. Donoghue and G. Jones, *Herbert Morrison: Portrait of a Politician* (London, 2001), ch. 14.
10. Ibid.

7. STATE AND SOCIETY

1. A. Thorpe, *Britain in the 1930s* (Oxford, 1992), pp. 70–85; R. Overy, *The Morbid Age: Britain and the Crisis of Civilisation* (London, 2010), ch. 2; D. Ritschel, *The Politics of Planning: The Debate on Economic Planning in Britain in the 1930s* (Oxford, 1997); R. Self, *Neville Chamberlain: A Biography* (Aldershot, 2006), chs. 9 and 10; R. Toye, *The Labour Party and the Planned Economy, 1931–1951* (London, 2003), pp. 9–33.
2. A term taken from J. Maiolo, *Cry Havoc: The Arms Race and the Second World War 1931–1941* (London, 2010), p. 145.
3. HC Deb 12 March 1937, vol. 321, c. 1574.
4. To Ida Chamberlain, 22 November 1936, in *NCDL IV*, p. 222.
5. R. McKibbin, *Classes and Cultures: England 1918–1951* (Oxford, 2000), pp. 114–18; J. Stevenson, *British Society 1914–45* (London, 1984), ch. 7; Thorpe, *Britain in the 1930s*, pp. 110–19.
6. Self, *Neville Chamberlain*, pp. 244–5.
7. M. Mayhew, 'The 1930s Nutrition Controversy', *Journal of Contemporary History*, 23, 3 (1988), pp. 445–64.
8. R. McKibbin, 'Politics and the Medical Hero: A. J. Cronin's *The Citadel*', *English Historical Review*, 123, 502 (2008), pp. 660–65.
9. J. Ramsden, *The Age of Balfour and Baldwin, 1902–1940* (London, 1978), pp. 356–7, 362–4.
10. McKibbin, *Classes and Cultures*, pp. 206–18.
11. P. Gosden, 'Spens, Sir William (1882–1962)', *ODNB*.

8. DIVISION AND UNITY

1. N. Crowson, *Facing Fascism: The Conservative Party and the European Dictators 1935–1940* (London, 1997), ch. 2; R. Self, *Neville Chamberlain: A Biography* (Aldershot, 2006), pp. 246–53.
2. D. Dutton, *Anthony Eden: A Life and Reputation* (London, 1997), pp. 51–5.
3. T. Jones, *A Diary with Letters* (London, 1954), 7 January 1936, p. 160.

4. Conversation of 29 July 1936, M. Gilbert, *Winston Churchill Companion, Volume 5: Part Three, The Coming of War, 1936–1939* (London, 1982), p. 291.

5. J. Maiolo, *Cry Havoc: The Arms Race and the Second World War 1931–1941* (London, 2010), ch. 8; R. A. C. Parker, 'British Rearmament 1936–9: Treasury, Trade Unions and Skilled Labour', *English Historical Review*, 96, 379 (1981), pp. 306–43; N. Rollings, 'Whitehall and the Control of Prices and Profits in a Major War, 1919–1939', *Historical Journal*, 44, 2 (2001), pp. 517–40; G. Peden, *Arms, Economics and British Strategy: From Dreadnoughts to Hydrogen Bombs* (Cambridge, 2009), pp. 137–43; idem, *British Rearmament and the Treasury, 1932–1939* (Edinburgh, 1979), pp. 73–9; R. A. C. Parker, *Churchill and Appeasement* (Basingstoke, 2000); G. Stewart, *Burying Caesar: Churchill, Chamberlain and the Battle for the Tory Party* (London, 1999), pp. 249–53; P. Williamson, 'Baldwin's Reputation: Politics and History, 1937–1967', *Historical Journal*, 47, 1 (2004), pp. 127–68; S. Ritchie, *Industry and Air Power: The Expansion of British Aircraft Production, 1935–1941* (London, 1997), pp. 44–6, 61–2, 75–85, 115–19, 156–68.

6. Peden, *Arms, Economics and British Strategy*, p. 127; TNA, CAB 23/83, Cabinet Conclusions, 25 February 1936, p. 2.

7. HC Deb, 23 April 1936, vol. 311, cc. 336–7.

8. TNA, T 161/720/S49175, Hopkins to Hamilton, 26 October 1936, quoted in Parker, 'British Rearmament', p. 310.

9. To Hilda Chamberlain, 14 November 1936, *NCDL IV*, pp. 219–20.

10. HC Deb, 12 November 1936, vol. 317, cc. 1111–18.

11. Ibid., cc. 1144–5.

12. Neville Chamberlain to Hilda Chamberlain, 14 November 1936, *NCDL IV*, p. 219.

13. B. Farrell, *The Defence and Fall of Singapore 1940–1942* (Stroud, 2006), pp. 40–61.

14. M. Kolinsky, *Britain's War in the Middle East: Strategy and Diplomacy 1936–1942* (New York, 1999), pp. 30–31.

15. For what follows on Palestine, see C. Townshend, 'The First Intifada: Rebellion in Palestine 1936–39', *History Today*, 39, 7 (1989); Y. Porath, *The Palestinian Arab National Movement: From Riots to Rebellion, II, 1929–1939* (London, 1977); W. F. Abboushi, 'The Road to Rebellion: Arab Palestine in the 1930s', *Journal of Palestine Studies*, 6, 3 (1977), pp. 23–46; K. Stein, 'Rural Change and Peasant Destitution: Contributing Causes to the Arab Revolt in Palestine, 1936–1939', in F. Kamezi and J. Waterbury (eds.), *Peasants and Politics in the Modern Middle East* (Miami, 1991), pp. 143–70.

16. M. Pugh, 'The Liberal Party and the Popular Front', *English Historical Review*, 121, 494 (2006), pp. 1327–50; R. Overy, *The Morbid Age: Britain*

and the Crisis of Civilisation (London, 2010), pp. 303–11; D. Blaazer, *The Popular Front and the Progressive Tradition: Socialists, Liberals and the Quest for Unity, 1884–1939* (Cambridge, 1992).

17. P. Clarke, *The Cripps Version: The Life of Sir Stafford Cripps* (London, 2002), pp. 55–65.
18. Quoted in Pugh, 'Liberal Party and the Popular Front', p. 1135.
19. T. Buchanan, *The Spanish Civil War and the British Labour Movement* (Cambridge, 1991), p. 28.
20. J. Fryth, 'The Aid Spain Movement in Britain 1936–39', *History Workshop Journal*, 35 (1993), pp. 153–64.
21. Quoted in Overy, *Morbid Age*, p. 305.
22. Buchanan, *Spanish Civil War and the British Labour Movement*, pp. 30–34.
23. Quoted in ibid., p. 59.
24. Ibid., chs. 1 and 2.
25. Overy, *Morbid Age*, pp. 245–61.
26. H. McCarthy, *The British People and the League of Nations: Democracy, Citizenship and Internationalism, c.1918–45* (Manchester, 2011), ch. 8.
27. P. Williamson, *Stanley Baldwin: Conservative Leadership and National Values* (Cambridge, 1999), pp. 326–29; Stewart, *Burying Caesar*, pp. 259–73; Crowson, *Facing Fascism*, pp. 126–130; Self, *Neville Chamberlain*, pp. 255–64; D. Dutton, *Neville Chamberlain* (London, 2001), pp. 41–3.
28. BUFVC, 'Premier Takes Stock, Finds Britain Best', British Paramount News, Issue No. 599, 23 November 1936, http://bufvc.ac.uk/newson screen/search/index.php/story/34850.
29. For this and what follows on Beaverbrook, see A. Chisholm and M. Davie, *Beaverbrook: A Life* (London, 1992); A. J. P. Taylor, *Beaverbrook* (London, 1972).
30. R. Cockett, *Twilight of Truth: Chamberlain, Appeasement and the Manipulation of the Press* (London, 1989), p. 14.
31. Quoted in Taylor, *Beaverbrook*, p. 339.
32. R. Pearce, 'Margesson, (Henry) David Reginald (1890–1965)', *ODNB*.
33. To Hilda Chamberlain, 25 April 1937, *NCDL IV*, p. 247.
34. B. Sabine, *British Budgets in Peace and War* (London, 1970), ch. 5.
35. To Ida Chamberlain, 22 May 1937, *NCDL IV*, p. 250.
36. R. J. Minney, *The Private Papers of Hore-Belisha* (London, 1960), p. 130.

9. 'MORE SUFFERINGS TO COME'

1. C. Madge and T. Harrisson, *Britain by Mass-Observation* (London, 1939), pp. 199–207, quotes pp. 201–2; for Storey's words see *NCDL IV*, p. 283, n. 102; for interpretations of Armistice Day and the importance of a

broken peace in understanding British responses to war, see A. Gregory, *The Silence of Memory* (Oxford, 1994), pp. 163–72.

2. To Ida Chamberlain, 30 October 1937, *NCDL IV*, p. 280.

3. M. Gilbert, 'Horace Wilson: Man of Munich?', *History Today* (October 1982), pp. 3–4.

4. G. Peden, 'Sir Horace Wilson and Appeasement', *Historical Journal*, 53, 4 (2010), pp. 983–1014.

5. D. Dilks, 'Introduction (1884–1938)', in idem (ed.), *The Diaries of Sir Alexander Cadogan, 1938–1945* (London, 1971), particularly pp. 12–15.

6. D. Dutton, *Anthony Eden: A Life and Reputation* (London, 1997), pp. 82–91.

7. R. Mitter, *China's War with Japan, 1937–1945: The Struggle for Survival* (London, 2013), pp. 10, 101–2, 141.

8. TNA, CAB 23/90A, CC 46 (37), 8 December 1937, p. 24, quoted in D. Reynolds, *The Creation of the Anglo-American Alliance, 1937–41: A Study in Competitive Cooperation* (Chapel Hill, NC, 1981), p. 10.

9. Reynolds, *Creation of the Anglo-American Alliance*, pp. 7–33; C. Witham, 'Seeing the Wood for the Trees: The British Foreign Office and the Anglo-American Trade Agreement of 1938', *Twentieth Century British History*, 16, 1 (2005), pp. 30–31.

10. R. Self, *Neville Chamberlain: A Biography* (Aldershot, 2006), pp. 298–300.

11. A. Roberts, *'The Holy Fox': The Life of Lord Halifax* (London, 1997), pp. 4–55.

12. R. Bernays, *Naked Fakir* (London, 1931), p. 51, quote p. 45.

13. Ibid., p. 70.

14. To Ida Chamberlain, 26 November 1937, *NCDL IV*, p. 297.

15. Dutton, *Eden*, pp. 98–111; G. Stewart, *Burying Caesar: Churchill, Chamberlain and the Battle for the Tory Party* (London, 1999), pp. 284–9; Self, *Neville Chamberlain*, pp. 284–9.

16. Cadogan diary, 20 February 1938, p. 52.

17. I. Gilmour, 'Butler, Richard Austin (1902–1982)', *ODNB*.

18. TNA, CAB 24/273, 'Defence Expenditure in Future Years', 15 December 1937, p. 3.

19. Ibid., p. 2.

20. G. Peden, *Arms, Economics and British Strategy: From Dreadnoughts to Hydrogen Bombs* (Cambridge, 2009), pp. 154–7; J. Maiolo, *Cry Havoc: The Arms Race and the Second World War 1931–1941* (London, 2010), pp. 208–13, 218–20.

21. TNA, CAB 24/274, 'Defence Expenditure in Future Years', 8 February 1938, p. 9.

22. Peden, 'Wilson and Appeasement', pp. 987–8.

23. Maiolo, *Cry Havoc*, pp. 227–8.

24. D. Dutton, *Simon: A Political Biography of Sir John Simon* (London, 1992), pp. 252–4.
25. Peden, 'Wilson and Appeasement', p. 988.
26. Maiolo, *Cry Havoc*, pp. 229–31.
27. S. Ritchie, *Industry and Air Power: The Expansion of British Aircraft Production, 1935–1941* (London, 1997), pp. 42–3, 95.
28. Cadogan diary, 16 March 1938, p. 63.
29. Stewart, *Burying Caesar*, pp. 292–4; Self, *Neville Chamberlain*, pp. 294–7, 302–6.
30. Maiolo, *Cry Havoc*, pp. 231–42; T. Imlay, 'Democracy and War: Political Regime, Industrial Relations, and Economic Preparations for War in France and Britain up to 1940', *Journal of Modern History*, 79, 1 (2007), pp. 10–20, 31–42; P. Jackson, *France and the Nazi Menace: Intelligence and Policy Making, 1933–1939* (Oxford, 2000), pp. 260–80.
31. J. Brookshire, ' "Speak for England", Act for England: Labour's Leadership and British National Security under the Threat of War in the late 1930s', *European History Quarterly*, 29, 2 (1999), pp. 251–87; B. Pimlott, *Hugh Dalton* (London, 1985), ch. 15; P. Ward, 'Preparing for the People's War: Labour and Patriotism in the 1930s', *Labour History Review*, 67, 2 (2002), pp. 171–85.
32. Quoted in Pimlott, *Dalton*, p. 227.
33. Quoted ibid., pp. 247–8.
34. To Hilda Chamberlain, 5 March 1939, *NCDL IV*, p. 390.
35. Self, *Neville Chamberlain*, pp. 261–6, 300–302; D. Dutton, *Neville Chamberlain* (London, 2001), pp. 41–8.
36. To Hilda Chamberlain, 9 April 1938, *NCDL IV*, p. 314.
37. House of Lords Library, London, Davidson Papers, DAV/258, Baldwin to Davidson, 11 April 1938, quoted in Self, *Neville Chamberlain*, p. 301; see also P. Williamson, *Stanley Baldwin: Conservative Leadership and National Values* (Cambridge, 1999), p. 357.
38. R. Griffiths, *Fellow Travellers of the Right: British Enthusiasts for Nazi Germany, 1933–39* (Oxford, 1983), pp. 260–87; I. Kershaw, *Making Friends with Hitler: Lord Londonderry and Britain's Road to War* (London, 2005).
39. M. Pugh, 'The Liberal Party and the Popular Front', *English Historical Review*, 121, 494 (2006), pp. 1337–41.
40. N. Crowson, *Facing Fascism: The Conservative Party and the European Dictators 1935–1940* (London, 1997), pp. 136–40.
41. Dutton, *Eden*, pp. 119–23.

10. CZECHOSLOVAKIA TO POLAND

1. For accounts of the high politics of the Sudeten crisis, see: R. Self, *Neville Chamberlain: A Biography* (Aldershot, 2006), pp. 309–26; A. Roberts, *'The Holy Fox': The Life of Lord Halifax* (London, 1997), chs. 12–13.
2. Churchill College, Cambridge, Diaries of 1st Lord Caldecote, INKP/1, Diary entry 17 September 1938, quoted in Self, *Neville Chamberlain*, p. 312.
3. Neville Chamberlain to Ida Chamberlain, 19 September 1938, *NCDL IV*, p. 348; G. Peden, 'Sir Horace Wilson and Appeasement', *Historical Journal*, 53, 4 (2010), p. 997.
4. Cadogan diary, 24 September 1938, p. 103.
5. Ibid., p. 104, emphases in original.
6. Ibid., quoted in editorial commentary, pp.105–6.
7. TNA, CAB 23/95/7, CC 43 (38), 25 September 1938, p. 5.
8. Peden, 'Wilson and Appeasement', pp. 1000–1001.
9. B. Collier, *Defence of the United Kingdom* (London, 1957), pp. 65–6.
10. J. Terraine, *The Right of the Line: The Role of the RAF in World War Two* (London, 1985), pp. 55–6.
11. C. Webster and N. Frankland, *The Strategic Air Offensive against Germany, 1939–45, I: Preparation* (London, 1961), p. 79.
12. R. Titmuss, *Problems of Social Policy* (London, 1950), pp. 28–31.
13. R. Overy, *The Air War 1939–1945* (London, 1987), pp. 20–24; W. Wark, *The Ultimate Enemy: British Intelligence and Nazi Germany, 1933–1939* (London, 1985), pp. 202–11; W. Murray, *The Change in the European Balance of Power, 1938–1939* (Princeton, 1984), pp. 219–52.
14. Self, *Neville Chamberlain*, p. 321.
15. Peden, 'Wilson and Appeasement', p. 1002.
16. To Hilda Chamberlain, 2 October 1938, *NCDL IV*, pp. 350–51.
17. J. Hinton, *The Mass Observers: A History* (Oxford, 2013), pp. 90–97.
18. C. Madge and T. Harrisson, *Britain by Mass-Observation* (London, 1939), p. 41.
19. Ibid., ch. 2.
20. Ibid., p. 43.
21. Ibid., p. 41.
22. Quoted in D. Dutton, *Neville Chamberlain* (London, 2001), p. 49.
23. Madge and Harrisson, *Britain by Mass-Observation*, p. 66.
24. B. Holman, *Post-Blogging the Sudeten Crisis: The British Press, August–October 1938* (e-book, www.airminded.org), pp. 65–6, 81.
25. Madge and Harrisson, *Britain by Mass-Observation*, pp. 76–7.
26. R. Cockett, *Twilight of Truth: Chamberlain, Appeasement and the Manipulation of the Press* (London, 1989), pp. 9–13.
27. Holman, *Post-Blogging the Sudeten Crisis*, pp. 65–6, 81.

28. Cockett, *Twilight of Truth*, pp. 12–13.
29. Ibid., pp. 56–8, 75–9.
30. Dutton, *Chamberlain*, pp. 53–4.
31. HC Deb, 4 October 1938, vol. 339, c. 194.
32. IWM, Private Papers of Miss W. D. Wareham, Documents 8528, letter from 'Bill', 2 October 1938.
33. HC Deb, 5 October 1938, vol. 339, c. 397.
34. HL Deb, 3 October 1938, vol. 110, c. 1308.
35. HC Deb, 3 October 1938, vol. 339, c. 45.
36. Ibid., 4 October 1938, cc. 258–9.
37. Ibid., 3 October 1938, cc. 87–8.
38. Ibid., 5 October 1938, c. 370.
39. Ibid., cc. 453–4.
40. G. Stewart, *Burying Caesar: Churchill, Chamberlain and the Battle for the Tory Party* (London, 1999), pp. 328–36.
41. I. Maclean, 'Oxford and Bridgwater', in C. Cook and J. Ramsden (eds.), *By-Elections in British Politics* (London, 1997); R. Eatwell, 'Munich, Public Opinion and the Popular Front', *Journal of Contemporary History*, 6, 4 (1971); M. Pugh, 'The Liberal Party and the Popular Front', *English Historical Review*, 121, 494 (2006), pp. 1341–2.
42. Diary entry, 20 October 1938, in R. Pearce (ed.), *Patrick Gordon Walker: Political Diaries 1932–1971* (London, 1991), p. 86.
43. J. Ramsden, *Don't Mention the War: The British and the Germans since 1890* (London, 2006), p. 168.
44. Self, *Neville Chamberlain*, pp. 344–5; Roberts, *'Holy Fox'*, pp. 128–9.
45. Pugh, 'Liberal Party and the Popular Front', pp. 1342–3.
46. D. Sutherland, 'Murray, Katharine Marjory Stewart-', *ODNB*.
47. Pugh, 'Liberal Party and the Popular Front', pp. 1344–5; N. Crowson, *Facing Fascism: The Conservative Party and the European Dictators 1935–1940* (London, 1997), pp. 104, 113.
48. Crowson, *Facing Fascism*, pp. 140–43, 154–63; Stewart, *Burying Caesar*, pp. 331–44.
49. Crowson, *Facing Fascism*, pp. 106–8; Bodleian Library, Oxford, Conservative Party Archive, CRD 1/7/35, H. Hanrott, 'Munich By-Elections', 25 November 1938, quoted in ibid., p. 113.
50. TNA, CAB 23/95, CC 48 (38), 3 October 1938, pp. 13–14.
51. G. Peden, 'Wood, Sir (Howard) Kingsley (1881–1943)', *ODNB*; A. Furse, *Wilfrid Freeman: The Genius behind Allied Survival and Air Supremacy 1939 to 1945* (Staplehurst, 2000), p. 80.
52. This paragraph and the next, Furse, *Wilfrid Freeman*, ch. 4.
53. Ibid., ch. 5; quote in G. Bulman, *An Account of Partnership – Industry, Government and the Aero-Engine: The Memoirs of George Purvis Bulman* (London, 2001), pp. 249–50.

54. TNA, CAB 23/96, CC 53 (38), 7 November 1938, pp. 10–11.
55. TNA, CAB 24/280, CP 247 (38), Appendix 1, 3 November 1938, quoted in R. Shay, *British Rearmament in the Thirties: Politics and Profits* (Princeton, 1977), pp. 239–41.
56. S. Ritchie, *Industry and Air Power: The Expansion of British Aircraft Production, 1935–1941* (London, 1997), p. 43; G. Peden, *Arms, Economics and British Strategy: From Dreadnoughts to Hydrogen Bombs* (Cambridge, 2009), p. 159.
57. Self, *Neville Chamberlain*, pp. 335–6.
58. Quoted in P. Dennis, *Decision by Default: Peacetime Conscription and British Defence, 1919–1939* (London, 1972), p. 163.
59. Self, *Neville Chamberlain*, pp. 338–43.
60. J. Maiolo, *Cry Havoc: The Arms Race and the Second World War 1931–1941* (London, 2010), pp. 258–9.
61. To Hilda Chamberlain, 5 February 1939, *NCDL IV*, p. 378.
62. P. Clarke, *The Cripps Version: The Life of Sir Stafford Cripps* (London, 2002), pp. 79–83.
63. Self, *Neville Chamberlain*, pp. 352–3.
64. Peden, 'Wilson and Appeasement', p. 1005.
65. Cockett, *Twilight of Truth*, pp. 113–15.
66. Peden, *Arms, Economics and British Strategy*, p. 157.
67. TNA, CAB 24/287, 'Ministry of Supply Bill', 19 May 1939, quoted T. Imlay, *Facing the Second World War: Strategy, Politics and Economics in Britain and France, 1938–1940* (Oxford, 2003), p. 325.
68. B. Bond (ed.), *Chief of Staff: The Diaries of Lieutenant General Sir Henry Pownall, I, 1933–1940* (London, 1972), p. 185.
69. B. Sabine, *British Budgets in Peace and War* (London, 1970), pp. 139–52; Shay, *British Rearmament*, pp. 217–18; G. C. Peden, *British Rearmament and the Treasury, 1932–1939* (Edinburgh, 1979), p. 67; Roberts, 'Holy Fox', p. 135.
70. Imlay, *Facing the Second World War*, pp. 330–33.
71. Ibid., pp. 237–42, 300, 343–5, 350; N. Rollings, 'Whitehall and the Control of Prices and Profits in a Major War, 1919–1939', *Historical Journal*, 44, 2 (2001), pp. 517–40.
72. Self, *Neville Chamberlain*, pp. 366–9; L. G. Shaw, *The British Political Elite and the Soviet Union, 1937–1939* (London, 2003), pp. 19, 188–9; R. A. C. Parker, *Chamberlain and Appeasement: British Policy and the Coming of the Second World War* (Basingstoke, 1993), pp. 225–50.
73. P. Mattar, 'The Mufti of Jerusalem and the Politics of Palestine', *Middle East Journal*, 42, 2 (1988), pp. 227–40.
74. This paragraph and the next two, see C. Townshend, 'The Defence of Palestine: Insurrection and Public Security, 1936–1939', *English Historical Review*, 103, 409 (1988), pp. 917–49; J. Norris, 'Repression and Rebellion:

Britain's Response to the Arab Revolt in Palestine of 1936–39', *Journal of Imperial and Commonwealth History*, 36, 1 (2008), pp. 25–45; M. Hughes, 'The Banality of Brutality: British Armed Forces and the Repression of the Revolt in Palestine, 1936–39', *English Historical Review*, 134, 507 (2009), pp. 313–54.

75. In a very good study of British behaviour during the revolt, Matthew Hughes details some instances where brutality crossed into atrocity. One of two examples where there is conclusive proof occurred near the village of al-Bassa in September 1938. After four British soldiers were killed by an explosive device nearby, their comrades forced twenty male villagers onto a bus, laid their own mine and then forced the bus over the mine, blowing all the occupants to pieces. Then they burned the village to the ground. No action was ever taken against the perpetrators.

76. M. J. Cohen, 'Appeasement in the Middle East: The British White Paper on Palestine, May 1939', *Historical Journal*, 16, 3 (1973), p. 575.

77. M. Kolinsky, *Britain's War in the Middle East: Strategy and Diplomacy 1936–1942* (New York, 1999), p. 2.

78. This is a key point in Norris, 'Repression and Rebellion'.

79. Hughes, 'Banality of Brutality', p. 349.

80. For this and the next four paragraphs, see Cohen, 'Appeasement in the Middle East'.

81. TNA, FO 371/23234, E 2955/6/31, meeting of 20 April 1939, quoted in Cohen, 'Appeasement in the Middle East', p. 591.

82. Mattar, 'Mufti of Jerusalem', p. 236.

83. HC Deb, 23 May 1939, vol. 347, c. 2132.

84. Ibid., c. 2175.

85. Ibid., c. 2178.

86. Ibid., c. 2194.

87. C. Behrens, *Merchant Shipping and the Demands of War* (London, 1955), pp. 24–34; Peden, *Arms, Economics and British* Strategy, p. 150.

88. Ritchie, *Industry and Airpower*, pp. 90, 110; CSO, *Fighting with Figures: A Statistical Digest of the Second World War* (London, 1995), p. 170; Collier, *Defence of the United Kingdom*, p. 73.

89. Furse, *Wilfrid Freeman*, pp. 86–98.

90. Maiolo, *Cry Havoc*, p. 277.

91. Ibid., pp. 278–9.

92. D. Reynolds, *The Creation of the Anglo-American Alliance, 1937–41: A Study in Competitive Cooperation* (Chapel Hill, NC, 1981), pp. 40–58.

93. R. A. C. Parker, 'The Pound Sterling, the American Treasury and British Preparations for War, 1938–1939', *English Historical Review*, 98, 387 (1983), pp. 261–79; Peden, *Rearmament and the Treasury*, p. 103; Peden, *Arms, Economics and British Strategy*, pp. 134–45.

94. A. Tooze, *The Wages of Destruction: The Making and Breaking of the Nazi Economy* (London, 2006), pp. 285–317; Maiolo, *Cry Havoc*, pp. 269–74.

95. To Ida Chamberlain, 23 July 1939, *NCDL IV*, p. 431.

96. Self, *Neville Chamberlain*, pp. 372–3.

97. S. Swann, 'The Tientsin Incident (1939): A Case Study of Japan's Imperial Dilemma in China', PhD, University of London, 1998; A. Best, *Britain, Japan and Pearl Harbor: Avoiding War in East Asia, 1936–1941* (London and New York, 1995), pp. 6–36, 193–201; Parker, *Chamberlain and Appeasement*, pp. 250–60.

98. E. Drea and H. Van de Ven, 'An Overview of the Military Campaigns during the Sino-Japanese War, 1937–1945', in M. Peattie, E. Drea and H. Van de Ven (eds.), *The Battle for China: Essays on the Military History of the Sino-Japanese War of 1937–1945* (Stanford, Calif., 2011), pp. 27–47.

99. C. Thorne, *Allies of a Kind: The United States, Britain and the War against Japan, 1941–1945* (Oxford, 1978), pp. 35–9.

100. Zhang Baijia, 'China's Quest for Foreign Military Aid', in Peattie et al. (eds.), *The Battle for China*, p. 532.

101. C. Bayly and T. Harper, *Forgotten Armies: Britain's Asian Empire and the War with Japan* (London, 2004), pp. 21–5.

102. B. Farrell, *The Defence and Fall of Singapore 1940–1942* (Stroud, 2006), pp. 49–52.

103. G. Kennedy, *Anglo-American Strategic Relations and the Far East, 1933–1939* (London, 2013), pp. 37–41.

104. Swann, 'Tientsin Incident', ch. 2.

105. Quoted in ibid., p. 114.

106. Quoted in Farrell, *Defence and Fall of Singapore*, p. 43.

107. Swann, 'Tientsin Incident', pp. 144–7.

108. Ibid., p. 178.

109. Pownall diary, vol. 1, p. 221.

110. Peden, 'Wilson and Appeasement', p. 1009.

111. C. Kohan, *Works and Buildings* (London, 1952), p. 25; C. Feinstein, *Statistical Tables of National Income, Expenditure and Output of the UK, 1855–1965* (Cambridge, 1972), T78.

112. Webster and Frankland, *Strategic Air Offensive I*, p. 84.

113. J. James, *The Paladins: A Social History of the RAF up to the Outbreak of World War II* (London, 1990), pp. 168–9; R. Higham, *Bases of Air Strategy: Building Airfields for the RAF and its Antecedents, 1914–1945* (Shrewsbury, 1998), p. 300.

114. P. Dennis, *The Territorial Army, 1906–1940* (London, 1987), pp. 147, 163–9, 181, 236, 249; A. J. Cooper, *Anti Aircraft Command, 1939–1955: The Other Forgotten Army* (Fleet, 2004), pp. 28–9; Peden, *Arms, Economics and British Strategy*, p. 157.

115. R. Overy, *The Bombing War: Europe 1939–1945* (London, 2013), pp. 36–8.
116. Ibid., pp. 134–5.
117. J. Meisel, 'Air Raid Shelter Policy and its Critics in Britain before the Second World War', *Twentieth Century British History*, 5, 5 (1994), pp. 300–319, quote p. 307; Overy, *Bombing War*, pp. 138–9.
118. MOA, A23 Special Report on ARP in Fulham, April–July 1939, pp. 18–20.
119. T. O'Brien, *Civil Defence* (London, 1955), pp. 120–25, 208, 216, 284; Overy, *Bombing War*, pp. 130–31.
120. A rough estimate based on adding together those already in the armed forces, reserves and associated part-time forces with those involved in civil defence.
121. J. Hinton, *Women, Social Leadership, and the Second World War: Continuities of Class* (Oxford, 2002), pp. 35, 51–5, 63–73.
122. Meisel, 'Air Raid Shelter Policy', pp. 307–16.
123. I am grateful to Dr Eleanor O'Keefe for this point. I. Mayer, 'Dollan, Sir Patrick Joseph (1885–1963)', *ODNB*.
124. J. Welshman, *Churchill's Children: The Evacuee Experience in Wartime Britain* (Oxford, 2010), pp. 24–5.
125. For this and the next three paragraphs, see M. Roodhouse, '"Fish-and-Chip Intelligence": Henry Durant and the British Institute of Public Opinion, 1936–1963', *Twentieth Century British History*, 24, 2 (2013), pp. 224–48.
126. Ibid., pp. 8–10.
127. Ibid., p. 13.
128. BIPO Surveys 53, December 1938, Q.4, and 54, January 1939, Qs.1, 4, 11–12, http://discover.ukdataservice.ac.uk/catalogue?sn=3331.
129. BIPO Surveys 57, April 1939, Q.5, 7; 60, June 1939, Q.4; 61, August 1939, Qs.6, 8.
130. Quoted in D. Hucker, *Public Opinion and the End of Appeasement in Britain and France* (Farnham, 2011), p. 159.
131. Editorial, *Daily Herald*, 16 August 1939, quoted in Hucker, *Public Opinion*, pp. 184–5.
132. Editorial, *Daily Mail*, 28 August 1939, quoted in ibid., p. 239.
133. M. Pugh, *State and Society: A Social and Political History of Britain since 1870* (London, 2012), pp. 238–41.
134. R. Overy, *The Morbid Age: Britain and the Crisis of Civilisation* (London, 2010), pp. 350–52.
135. MOA, Diarist 5046, 28 August 1939.
136. MOA, Diarist 5141, 29 August 1939.
137. MOA, Diarist 5342, 28 August 1939.
138. Musto diary, p. 58.

139. R. Griffiths, 'A Note on Mosley, the "Jewish War" and Conscientious Objection', *Journal of Contemporary History*, 40, 4 (2005), pp. 675–88, quote p. 677.

140. A. Thorpe, *Britain in the 1930s* (Oxford, 1992), pp. 56–7; J. Attfield and S. Williams, *1939: The Communist Party of Great Britain and the War* (London, 1984).

141. A. J. P. Taylor, *Beaverbrook* (London, 1972), pp. 379–95.

142. Overy, *Morbid Age*, pp. 352–4; M. Ceadel, *Pacifism in Britain, 1914–1945: The Defining of a Faith* (Oxford, 1980), pp. 276–8.

143. IWM, Private Papers of Mr and Mrs Monk-Jones, Documents 11582, A. Monk-Jones to E. Bellerby, 3 September 1939.

144. Ibid., E. Bellerby to A. Monk-Jones, 5 September 1939.

145. Self, *Neville Chamberlain*, p. 377.

146. Stewart, *Burying Caesar*, pp. 368–73, 379–80.

147. R. Crowcroft, *Attlee's War: World War II and the Making of a Labour Leader* (London, 2001), pp. 19–26; T. Burridge, *British Labour and Hitler's War* (London, 1976), pp. 17–24.

148. Self, *Neville Chamberlain*, pp. 378–9.

149. J. Lawrence, 'Labour and the Politics of Class, 1900–1940', in D. Feldman and J. Lawrence (eds.), *Structures and Transformations in Modern British History: Essays for Gareth Stedman Jones* (Cambridge, 2011), p. 260.

150. HC Deb, 2 September 1939, vol. 351, cc. 282–4.

151. Self, *Neville Chamberlain*, p. 380.

152. MOA, Diarist 5231, 1 September 1939.

153. MOA, Diarist 5426, 1 September 1939.

154. IWM, Private Papers of Major E. W. Clay, Documents 16117.

155. Ibid.

156. A. Wilkinson, *Dissent or Conform? War, Peace and the English Churches, 1900–1945* (London, 1986), p. 236.

157. Quoted Self, *Neville Chamberlain*, p. 381.

158. IWM, Private Papers of Captain G. E. Tapp, Documents 16041, diary entry 3 September 1939.

159. MOA, Diarist 5231, 3 September 1939.

11. LIMITED WAR

1. Contemporary listings of casualties at http://www.benjidog.co.uk/Athenia/Loss%20of%20Athenia%20-%20The%20Aftermath.html.

2. G. Peden, *Arms, Economics and British Strategy: From Dreadnoughts to Hydrogen Bombs* (Cambridge, 2009), pp. 165–7; I. Jennings, *Cabinet*

Government (Cambridge, 1959), pp. 306–9; J. Ehrman, *Cabinet Government and War* (Cambridge, 2003), pp. 120–25.

3. W. Philpott, 'The Benefit of Experience? The Supreme War Council and the Higher Management of Coalition War, 1939–1940', in W. Philpott and M. Alexander (eds.), *Anglo-French Defence Relations between the Wars* (Basingstoke, 2002), pp. 209–26.

4. T. Imlay, *Facing the Second World War: Strategy, Politics and Economics in Britain and France, 1938–1940* (Oxford, 2003), ch. 1 and 2.

5. Quoted in J. R. M. Butler, *Grand Strategy, II: September 1939–June 1941* (London, 1957), p. 10.

6. To Ida Chamberlain, 10 September 1939, *NCDL IV*, p. 445.

7. R. Self, *Neville Chamberlain: A Biography* (Aldershot, 2006), pp. 394–8.

8. Ironside diary, 10 September 1939, p. 106.

9. D. Reynolds, *The Creation of the Anglo-American Alliance, 1937–41: A Study in Competitive Cooperation* (Chapel Hill, NC, 1981), p. 84.

10. D. Dutton, *Simon: A Political Biography of Sir John Simon* (London, 1992), pp. 283–4.

11. A. Roberts, *'The Holy Fox': The Life of Lord Halifax* (London, 1997), p. 176.

12. Self, *Neville Chamberlain*, p. 387.

13. To Hilda Chamberlain, 17 September 1939, *NCDL IV*, p. 448.

14. C. Bell, *Churchill and Sea Power* (Oxford, 2013), pp. 160–73.

15. Quoted in Butler, *Grand Strategy II*, p. 2.

16. W. S. Churchill to N. Chamberlain, 18 September 1939, in M. Gilbert (ed.), *The Churchill War Papers, I: At the Admiralty, September 1939–May 1940* (London, 1993), p. 111.

17. Imlay, *Facing the Second World War*, p. 218; Dutton, *Simon*, p. 285; Ironside diary, pp. 102–6.

18. Bodleian Library, Oxford, Simon Papers, MS Simon 11, ff. 6–7, 23 September 1939, quoted in Dutton, *Simon*, p. 285.

19. TNA, CAB 65/1/23, WC 28 (39), 22 September 1939, p. 6.

20. M. Postan, *British War Production* (London, 1952), pp. 73–6.

21. Imlay, *Facing the Second World War*, p. 219.

22. T. Imlay, 'A Reassessment of Anglo-French Strategy during the Phony War, 1939–1940', *English Historical Review*, 119, 481 (2004), pp. 337–42.

23. Cadogan diary, 22 September 1939, p. 218.

24. TNA, CAB 65/1/9, WM (39), Cabinet Conclusions, 9 September 1939, p. 68.

25. Cadogan diary, 23 September 1939, p. 219.

26. TNA, CAB 65/1/9, WM (39), Cabinet Conclusions, 9 September 1939, p. 68.

27. To Hilda Chamberlain, 15 October 1939, *NCDL IV*, p. 458.

28. Roberts, *'Holy Fox'*, pp. 182–5.

29. K. Jeffery, *MI6: The History of the Secret Intelligence Service, 1909–1949* (London, 2010), pp. 382–6.
30. F. H. Hinsley, *British Intelligence in the Second World War (Abridged)* (London, 1994), pp. 13–17.
31. Imlay, *Facing the Second World War*, pp. 113–14.
32. Self, *Neville Chamberlain*, pp. 398–400; letter to Ida Chamberlain, 23 September 1939, *NCDL IV*, p. 451.
33. HC Deb, 12 October 1939, vol. 352, cc. 563–8.
34. To Ida Chamberlain, 9 October 1939, *NCDL IV*, p. 456.
35. A. Tooze, *The Wages of Destruction: The Making and Breaking of the Nazi Economy* (London, 2006), pp. 326–31.
36. Self, *Neville Chamberlain*, pp. 401–3.
37. Ironside diary, 14 September 1939, p. 107.
38. S. Roskill, *The War at Sea, 1939–1945*, I (London, 1954), pp. 62–82; C. Barnett, *Engage the Enemy More Closely: The Royal Navy in the Second World War* (London, 1991), pp. 74–82.
39. Roskill, *War at Sea I*, pp. 98–102, 124–9; P. Elliott, *Allied Minesweeping in World War Two* (Cambridge, 1979), pp. 33–40.
40. D. Edgerton, *Britain's War Machine: Weapons, Resources and Experts in the Second World War* (London, 2011), pp. 34–5; H. Herwig, 'The Failure of German Sea Power, 1914–1945: Mahan, Tirpitz and Raeder reconsidered', *International History Review*, 10, 1 (1988), pp. 92–101.
41. Roskill, *War at Sea I*, pp. 519, 614.
42. Ibid., pp. 44, 67.
43. Ibid., pp. 42, 151, 551–2; C. Behrens, *Merchant Shipping and the Demands of War* (London, 1955), p. 43.
44. Bell, *Churchill and Sea Power*, p. 170.
45. J. Buckley, 'Air Power and the Battle of the Atlantic 1939–45', *Journal of Contemporary History*, 28, 1 (1993), p. 144.
46. J. Terraine, *The Right of the Line: The Role of the RAF in World War Two* (London, 1985), p. 110.
47. R. Overy, *The Bombing War: Europe 1939–1945* (London, 2013), pp. 237–9.
48. Quoted in C. Webster and N. Frankland, *The Strategic Air Offensive against Germany, 1939–45*, I: *Preparation* (London, 1961), p. 136.
49. Overy, *Bombing War*, pp. 239–42.
50. Webster and Frankland, *Strategic Air Offensive I*, pp. 107–26; Terraine, *Right of the Line*, p. 85.
51. Webster and Frankland, *Strategic Air Offensive I*, pp. 192–201.
52. B. Bond, 'Introduction: Preparing the Field Force, February 1939–May 1940', in B. Bond and M. Taylor (eds.), *The Battle of France and Flanders 1940: Sixty Years On* (Barnsley, 2001), p. 6.

53. This paragraph and the next, see D. French, *Raising Churchill's Army: The British Army and the War against Germany, 1919–1945* (Oxford, 2000), pp. 12–47, 168–174; idem, 'Officer Education and Training in the British Regular Army, 1919–1939', in G. Kennedy and K. Neilson (eds.), *Military Education: Past, Present and Future* (Westport, Conn., 2002), pp. 119–23; B. Bond, *British Military Policy Between the Two World Wars* (Oxford, 1980), pp. 300–330; J. P. Harris, *Men, Ideas and Tanks: British Military Thought and Armoured Forces, 1903–1939* (Manchester, 1995), pp. 297–305; Bond, 'Preparing the Field Force', p. 4.

54. TNA, CAB 83/4, MC (40) 46, 7 February 1940, 'Target for the Second Year of War', p. 4.

55. French, *Raising Churchill's Army*, pp. 97–8; J. P. Harris, 'British Armour and Rearmament in the 1930s', *Journal of Strategic Studies*, 11, 2 (1988), pp. 220–44.

56. B. Bond, 'Ironside' and 'Gort' in J. Keegan (ed.), *Churchill's Generals* (London, 1991), pp. 17–33, 34–50.

57. Ironside diary, 24 October 1939, pp. 134–35.

58. Brooke diary, 28 November 1939, p. 20.

59. D. Fraser, *Alanbrooke* (London, 1982), p. 139.

60. French, *Raising Churchill's Army*, pp. 169–74, 178–79; H. Sebag-Montefiore, *Dunkirk: Fight to the Last Man* (London, 2006), pp. 8–25.

61. CSO, *Fighting with Figures: A Statistical Digest of the Second World War* (London, 1995), pp. 38–9.

62. Postan, *War Production*, pp. 112–13.

63. Ibid., p. 103.

64. C. Kohan, *Works and Buildings* (London, 1952), pp. 505–7.

65. S. Ritchie, *Industry and Air Power: The Expansion of British Aircraft Production, 1935–1941* (London, 1997), pp. 219–22; Behrens, *Merchant Shipping*, p. 44.

66. W. Hancock and M. Gowing, *British War Economy* (London, 1949), pp. 83–8.

67. R. Sayers, *Financial Policy, 1939–1945* (London, 1956), pp. 26–7, 31.

68. 'Blackout Budget', *Daily Mail*, 28 September 1939, p. 1; 'Opinion', *Daily Express*, 28 September 1939, p. 6; *Daily Mirror*, 28 September 1939, p. 1; HC Deb, 28 September 1939, vol. 351, c. 1542; B. Sabine, *British Budgets in Peace and War* (London, 1970), pp. 154–6.

69. Postan, *War Production*, pp. 76–80; Hancock and Gowing, *War Economy*, pp. 173–8; Behrens, *Merchant Shipping*, pp. 43–68; N. Rollings, 'Whitehall and the Control of Prices and Profits in a Major War, 1919–1939', *Historical Journal*, 44, 2 (2001), pp. 537–8.

70. H. Parker, *Manpower: A Study of War-time Policy and Administration* (London, 1957), p. 73.

71. Hancock and Gowing, *War Economy*, pp. 136, 140; CSO, *Fighting with Figures*, p. 172; Parker, *Manpower*, p. 73.
72. Ritchie, *Industry and Air Power*, pp. 220–23.
73. Tooze, *Wages of Destruction*, pp. 332–53.
74. Imlay, *Facing the Second World War*, ch. 5.
75. This and the next two paragraphs, ibid., ch. 6.
76. K. Jeffery, 'The Second World War', *OHBE IV*, pp. 307–9.
77. F. Wood, *Official History of New Zealand in the Second World War 1939–45: Political and External Affairs* (Wellington, NZ, 1958), p. 11.
78. Jeffery, 'Second World War', p. 309.
79. Ibid.
80. R. Fisk, *In Time of War: Ireland, Ulster and the Price of Neutrality, 1939–45* (Dublin, 1983), pp. 48–127; B. Girvin and G. Roberts (eds.), *Ireland and the Second World War: Politics, Society and Remembrance* (Dublin, 2000).
81. For what follows on Egypt and Iraq, see M. Kolinsky, *Britain's War in the Middle East: Strategy and Diplomacy 1936–1942* (New York, 1999); S. Wichhart, 'Intervention: British Egypt and Iraq during World War II', PhD, University of Texas, 2007, pp. 80–88, 95–104.
82. R. Moore, *Churchill, Cripps and India 1939–1945* (Oxford, 1979), pp. 18–19.
83. A. Herman, *Gandhi and Churchill: The Epic Rivalry that Destroyed an Empire and Forged Our Age* (New York, 2008), pp. 444–5.
84. Moore, *Churchill, Cripps and India*, pp. 20–21.
85. For this and the following paragraph, P. Clarke, *The Cripps Version: The Life of Sir Stafford Cripps, 1889–1952* (London, 2002), pp. 97–114.
86. Moore, *Churchill, Cripps and India*, p. 24.
87. Quoted in ibid., pp. 16–17.
88. Quoted in ibid., p. 26.
89. Quoted in ibid., p. 28.
90. This and the next paragraph, Herman, *Churchill and Gandhi*, pp. 453–5.
91. Colville diary, 12 April 1940, p. 79.
92. J. Beaumont, 'Europe and the Middle East', in Beaumont (ed.), *Australia's War, 1939–45* (St Leonards, NSW, 1996), pp. 3–7.
93. W. Murray, *Strategy for Defeat: The Luftwaffe 1939–1945* (Washington, DC, 1986), p. 254.
94. F. J. Hatch, *Aerodrome of Democracy: Canada and the British Commonwealth Air Training Plan* (Ottawa, 1983), ch. 1, figures pp. 16, 20; A. Stewart, *A Very British Experience: Coalition, Defence and Strategy in the Second World War* (Eastbourne, 2012), ch. 1.
95. C. Stacey, *Arms, Men and Governments: The War Policies of Canada, 1939–1945* (Ottawa, 1970), pp. 30–31.

96. S. N. Prasad, *Expansion of the Armed Forces and Defence Organisation, 1939–1945* (Calcutta, 1957), pp. 398, 400–407.

97. N. Sinha and P. Khera, *Indian War Economy (Supply, Industry and Finance)* (New Delhi, 1962), p. 147.

98. TNA, CAB 67/4/15, WP (G) (40) 15, 'Utilisation of the Manpower Resources of the Colonial Empire', January 1940, p. 2.

99. Sayers, *Financial Policy*, pp. 17–18; J. Hurstfield, *The Control of Raw Materials* (London, 1953), pp. 152, 161; S. Pollard, *The Development of the British Economy: 1914–1980* (London, 1983), p. 336.

100. W. N. Medlicott, *The Economic Blockade, I, 1939–41* (London, 1952), pp. 238–9, 332; Sayers, *Financial Policy*, pp. 443–7, 455; P. Cain and A. Hopkins, *British Imperialism: 1688–2000* (Harlow, 2001), p. 533, 538; Pollard, *Development of the British Economy*, p. 334; E. Hernández-Sandoica and E. Moradiellos, 'Spain and the Second World War, 1939–1945', and H. Kirchhoff, 'Denmark, September 1939–April 1940', in N. Wylie (ed.), *European Neutrals and Non-Belligerents during the Second World War* (Cambridge, 2002), pp. 246–8, 42–3.

101. Reynolds, *Anglo-American Alliance*, p. 76.

102. This paragraph and the next two, ibid., pp. 65–8.

103. J. Jackson, *The Fall of France: The Nazi Invasion of 1940* (Oxford, 2003), p. 20.

104. Reynolds, *Anglo-American Alliance*, pp. 69–82.

105. Duncan Hall, *North American Supply* (London, 1955), pp. 105–15.

106. Ibid., pp. 72–8, 86–93.

107. Reynolds, *Anglo-American Alliance*, p. 68.

12. BOREDOM

1. M. Gilbert (ed.), *The Churchill War Papers, I: At the Admiralty, September 1939–May 1940* (London, 1993), p. 193.

2. J. Welshman, *Churchill's Children: The Evacuee Experience in Wartime Britain* (Oxford, 2010), p. 68.

3. R. Titmuss, *Problems of Social Policy* (London, 1950), pp. 550–53.

4. Ibid., p. 101.

5. Ibid., pp. 543–9.

6. Ibid., pp. 102–7.

7. Ibid., pp. 110–12.

8. 'Castle and Cottage will Give Guests Warm Welcome', *News Chronicle*, 1 September 1939, p. 10.

9. 'Village Plans its Welcome', *Daily Express*, 1 September 1939, p. 5.

10. MOA, Diarist 5212, diary entry for early September 1939.

11. G. Field, *Blood, Sweat and Toil: Remaking the British Working Class, 1939–1945* (Oxford, 2011), pp. 20–24.

12. J. Hinton, *Women, Social Leadership, and the Second World War: Continuities of Class* (Oxford, 2002), pp. 147–54.

13. Field, *Blood, Sweat and Toil*, pp. 14–16.

14. MOA, Diarist 5212, 4 September 1939.

15. Ibid., 6 September 1939.

16. HC Deb, 14 September 1939, vol. 351, c. 822.

17. TNA, HLG 7/74, 'Preliminary Report on evacuation of children and others to Lindsey (Lincolnshire)', 11 September 1939.

18. HC Deb, 14 September 1939, vol. 351, c. 885.

19. Quoted in Welshman, *Churchill's Children*, p. 107.

20. Ibid., pp. 84–6.

21. Titmuss, *Problems of Social Policy*, p. 160.

22. Field, *Blood, Sweat and Toil*, p. 16.

23. Barnett House Study Group, *London Children in War-time Oxford: A Survey of Social and Educational Results of Evacuation* (Oxford, 1947), pp. 36, 34, 32, 37.

24. IWM, Private Papers of Mrs G. Cox, Documents 2769, diary entry 13 October 1939.

25. MOA, Diarist 5224, 19 September 1939.

26. Titmuss, *Problems of Social Policy*, pp. 116–19.

27. Quoted in Titmuss, *Problems of Social Policy*, p. 168.

28. Ibid., pp. 142–66.

29. Ibid., p. 172.

30. W. Boyd, 'Parents and Evacuation', in W. Boyd (ed.), *Evacuation in Scotland: A Record of Events and Experiments* (Bickley, 1944), p. 120.

31. Titmuss, *Problems of Social Policy*, pp. 193–7.

32. Field, *Blood, Sweat and Toil*, pp. 30–36.

33. To Ida Chamberlain, 17 September 1939, *NCDL IV*, p. 449.

34. Quoted in Welshman, *Churchill's Children*, p. 108, emphasis in original.

35. J. Macnicol, 'The Effect of the Evacuation of Schoolchildren on Official Attitudes to State Intervention', in H. Smith (ed.), *War and Social Change: British Society in the Second World War* (Manchester, 1986), pp. 3–31; J. Welshman, 'Evacuation and Social Policy during the Second World War', *Twentieth Century British History*, 9, 1 (1998), pp. 28–53.

36. A. Briggs, *The History of Broadcasting in the United Kingdom, III: The War of Words* (Oxford, 1970), pp. 71–93.

37. C. Madge and T. Harrisson, *War Begins at Home* (London, 1940), p. 201.

38. BIPO Survey 66, January 1940, Q.5.

39. M. Keep and T. Rutherford, 'Reported Road Accident Statistics', House of Commons Library, 24 October 2013, p. 4.

40. MOA, Diarist 5231, 18 September 1939.

41. CSO, *Fighting with Figures: A Statistical Digest of the Second World War* (London, 1995), pp. 26–8; R. Ingleton, *The Gentleman at War: Policing Britain 1939–45* (Maidstone, 1994), p. 83.

42. Cmd 7227, *Criminal Statistics 1939–45*, pp. 5–6, 12.

43. MOA, January 1940, Directive Response 1141. I am grateful to Dr Joel Morley for bringing this quotation to my attention.

44. C. Langhammer, *The English in Love: The Intimate Story of an Emotional Revolution* (Oxford, 2013), pp. 117–18; M. Houlbrook, *Queer London: Perils and Pleasures in the Sexual Metropolis* (Chicago, 2005), pp. 34, 43–67.

45. CSO, *Fighting with Figures*, pp. 6, 10.

46. Briggs, *History of Broadcasting III*, pp. 78–93, quote p. 98.

47. This and the next paragraph, see I. McLaine, *Ministry of Morale: Home Front Morale and the Ministry of Information in World War II* (London, 1979), pp. 24–45.

48. By 8 October, in fact, the Courage Brewery had brought out a poster based on the government's, proclaiming that 'Your Courage' had maintained its strength and was now, thanks to an increase in duty, contributing an extra 1½d. a pint to the Treasury. MOA, File Report, 'Government Posters in Wartime', 18 October 1939, pp. 97, 99.

49. Briggs, *History of Broadcasting III*, pp. 98–127.

50. McLaine, *Ministry of Morale*, pp. 40–46.

51. Madge and Harrisson, *War Begins at Home*, p. 191.

52. H. Parker, *Manpower: A Study of War-time Policy and Administration* (London, 1957), pp. 485, 488; R. Broad, *Conscription in Britain, 1939–1964: The Militarization of a Generation* (London, 2006), pp. 143–6.

53. J. Morley, 'The Influence of the First World War on Attitudes to Service in the Second World War', PhD, University of London, 2013.

54. Parker, *Manpower*, p. 488.

55. Ibid.; V. Carolan, 'British Maritime History, National Identity and Film, 1900–1960', PhD, University of London, 2012, pp. 125–33.

56. L. Noakes, *Women in the British Army: War and the Gentle Sex, 1907–1948* (London, 2006), pp. 105–9, membership figures p. 131.

57. This paragraph and the next, R. Barker, *Conscience, Government and War: Conscientious Objection in Great Britain, 1939–45* (London, 1982), pp. 13–23, 146.

58. IWM, Interview with Peter James Fishwick, Catalogue No. 31553, Reel 2.

59. IWM, Private Papers of B. C. F. Hooper, Documents 3290, undated letter, spring 1940.

60. IWM, Private Papers of Major E. W. Clay, Documents 16117, Ewart Clay to Dorothy Clay, 17 December 1939.

61. Field, *Blood, Sweat and Toil*, pp. 252–5.

62. BIPO Survey 68, March 1940, Q.7.
63. MOA, Worktown Papers, Box 52, 'Observations in Bolton in the Early Months of the War', File F, 'ARP and Soldiers', 'Soldiers' Conditions, 27/10/39 approx'; File A, 'Impact on outbreak of Second World War', 'Militiamen, Bolton, 16/11/39'; 'Conscription, Bolton, December 4 1939'.
64. J. Gardiner, *Wartime: Britain 1939–1945* (London, 2004), pp. 73–4; CSO, *Fighting with Figures*, p. 235.
65. Parker, *Manpower*, p. 501.
66. Ibid., p. 83.
67. Beardmore diary, 27 October 1939, p. 44.
68. Ibid., 2 November 1939, p. 45.
69. I. Zweiniger-Bargielowska, *Austerity in Britain: Rationing, Controls and Consumption 1939–1955* (Oxford, 2000), pp. 12–16.
70. TNA, CAB 65/1/63, War Cabinet Conclusions 39, 28 October 1939, p. 532.
71. Zweiniger-Bargielowska, *Austerity in Britain*, pp. 17–18, 69–70.
72. 'Opinion: Stop Food Rationing', *Daily Express*, 2 November 1939, p. 6; A. Chisholm and M. Davie, *Beaverbrook: A Life* (London, 1992), p. 373.
73. BIPO Survey 64, November 1939, Q.2.
74. MOA, TC Food Box 1B Introduction of Rationing: Autumn 1939.
75. Brown diary, 3 January 1940, p. 19.
76. MOFR7, 'Christmas Shopping in Wartime, 19/11/39'.
77. Ibid.
78. Harrisson and Madge, *War Begins at Home*, p. 415.
79. Ibid.
80. Ibid., p. 422.
81. Ibid., p. 417.
82. Ibid., p. 419.
83. MOFR10, 'Coordination of Social Research (During War), 2/11/39'.
84. J. Hinton, *The Mass Observers: A History* (Oxford, 2013), ch. 6.
85. BIPO Survey 62, September 1939, Qs.1, 8, 9.
86. A. Roberts, *'The Holy Fox': The Life of Lord Halifax* (London, 1997), pp. 178–80; S. Brooke, *Labour's War: The Labour Party during the Second World War* (Oxford, 1992), pp. 34–5.
87. J. Attfield and S. Williams, *1939: The Communist Party of Great Britain and the War* (London, 1984), p. 170.
88. BIPO Survey 64, November 1939, Q.3; BIPO Survey 67, February 1940, Q.7.
89. MOA, TC54, 'Police, Law and Invasion Reports 1939–41', Box 54-1-A, 'Police Reports 1939–41', 'Summary of Reports received from Chief Officers of Police and Regional Police Staff Officers, for the period from midnight October 15th to midnight October 29th, 1939'.
90. BIPO Survey 67, February 1940, Q.7; BIPO Survey 68, March 1940, Q.6.
91. BIPO Survey 62, September 1939, Q.5.

92. BIPO Survey 63, October 1939, Q.5.

93. MOA, Worktown Papers, Box 50D, 'Working Class War Questionnaire'.

94. Ibid., Box 52A, Impact on outbreak of Second World War, 'Bolton, 11ᵗʰ Dec '39'.

95. BIPO Survey 64, November 1939, Q.3; BIPO Survey 67, February 1940, Q.2.

96. BIPO Survey 63, October 1939, Q.10; BIPO Survey 64, November 1939, Q.10; BIPO Survey 65, December 1939, Qs.10, 3.

97. MOA, Worktown Papers, Box 50D, 'Working Class War Questionnaire'.

98. MOA, TC54, 'Police, Law and Invasion Reports 1939–41', Box 54-1-A, 'Police Reports 1939–41', 'Summary of Reports received from Chief Officers of Police and Regional Police Staff Officers, for the period from midnight October 15ᵗʰ to midnight October 29ᵗʰ, 1939'.

99. MOA, Worktown Papers, Box 52A, 'Morale, Bolton, 6/11/39'.

100. D. Edgerton, *Britain's War Machine: Weapons, Resources and Experts in the Second World War* (London, 2011), ch. 2.

101. K. Jefferys, *The Churchill Coalition and Wartime Politics* (Manchester, 1991), p. 16.

102. D. Dutton, 'Power Brokers or just "Glamour Boys"? The Eden Group, September 1939–May 1940', *English Historical Review*, 118, 476 (2003), pp. 415–19.

103. Nicolson diary, 6 September 1939, p. 26.

104. Amery diary, 5 September 1939, pp. 571–2.

105. This was a much repeated anecdote: L. Amery, *My Political Life III* (London, 1955), p. 330; E. Spears, *Assignment to Catastrophe, I: Prelude to Dunkirk* (London, 1954), p. 32; A. J. P. Taylor, *English History, 1914–1945* (Oxford, 1965); A. Calder, *The People's War: Britain 1939–1945* (London, 1969), p. 61. Amery also recalled it as part of the 1973 TV series *The World at War*.

106. L. Wetherell, 'Lord Salisbury's "Watching Committee" and the Fall of Neville Chamberlain, May 1940', *English Historical Review*, 116, 469 (2001), pp. 1134–45.

107. Cranborne to Violet Milner, 5 July 1938, quoted in K. Rose, *The Later Cecils* (London, 1975), p. 103.

108. Nicolson diary, 3 October 1939, p. 34.

109. Ironside diary, 11 January 1940, p. 196; Amery diary, 3 January 1940, p. 578.

110. R. Crowcroft, *Attlee's War: World War II and the Making of a Labour Leader* (London, 2001), pp. 28–31.

111. A. Thorpe, *Parties at War: Political Organization in Second World War Britain* (Oxford, 2009), pp. 1, 15–18, 33–6.

112. HC Deb, 3 September 1939, vol. 351, c. 294.

113. This and the next two paragraphs, see Crowcroft, *Attlee's War*, pp. 31–44.

114. HC Deb, 5 December 1939, vol. 355, c. 505.
115. R. Sayers, *Financial Policy, 1939–1945* (London, 1956), pp. 26–9.
116. This and the next paragraph, W. Beveridge, revised J. Harris, 'Stamp, Josiah Charles, first Baron Stamp (1880–1941)', *ODNB*; T. Imlay, *Facing the Second World War: Strategy, Politics and Economics in Britain and France, 1938–1940* (Oxford, 2003), p. 345.
117. Parker, *Manpower*, p. 82.
118. *Transport and General Workers' Record*, February 1940, pp. 242–3, quoted in A. Bullock, *The Life and Times of Ernest Bevin, II: Minister of Labour, 1940–1945* (London, 1967), p. 79.
119. TNA, CAB 68/5/2, WP (R)(40) 52, 'Tenth Report Submitted by the Minister of Labour and National Service Covering the Period 16 January–31 January 1940', p. 2.
120. R. Skidelsky, *John Maynard Keynes, III: Fighting for Britain, 1937–1946* (London, 2000), pp. 3–52.
121. For this and the next three paragraphs, ibid., pp. 52–6.
122. For this and the next two paragraphs, ibid., pp. 56–74; R. Toye, 'Keynes, the Labour Movement and "How to Pay for the War"', *Twentieth Century British History*, 10, 3 (1999), pp. 255–81.
123. R. Self, *Neville Chamberlain: A Biography* (Aldershot, 2006), pp. 407–8.
124. Ibid., pp. 404–7.
125. R. J. Minney, *The Private Papers of Hore-Belisha* (London, 1960), plate facing p. 273.
126. R. Cockett, *Twilight of Truth: Chamberlain, Appeasement and the Manipulation of the Press* (London, 1989), pp. 168–9.
127. To Ida Chamberlain, 27 January 1940, *NCDL IV*, p. 494.

13. ESCALATION

1. Mitchison diary, 16 September 1939, p. 40.
2. O. Sitwell, 'A War to End Class War', *Spectator*, 17 November 1939, in F. Glass and P. Marsden-Smedley (eds.), *Articles of War: The Spectator Book of World War II* (London, 1989), p. 69.
3. Quoted in D. Carlton, *Churchill and the Soviet Union* (Manchester, 2000), p. 71.
4. G. Cox, 'War on Babies in the Snow', W. Black, 'Children Hide in Ditches', *Daily Express*, 2 December 1939, p. 1.
5. P. Bell, *John Bull and the Bear: British Public Opinion, Foreign Policy and the Soviet Union* (London, 1990) pp. 33–4.
6. Quoted in Carlton, *Churchill and the Soviet Union*, p. 72, and see discussion, pp. 73–5.
7. HC Deb, 19 March 1940, vol. 355, c. 1836.

8. E. Roberts, 'The Spanish Precedent: British Volunteers in the Russo-Finnish War', *History Australia*, 3, 1 (2006), pp. 7.1–7.14.

9. See for example Chamberlain's account to the Commons, HC Deb, 14 December 1939, vol. 355, cc. 1337–40.

10. T. Imlay, 'A Reassessment of Anglo-French Strategy during the Phony War, 1939–1940', *English Historical Review*, 119, 481 (2004), pp. 343–8, 352–7.

11. C. Bell, *Churchill and Sea Power* (Oxford, 2013), p. 173.

12. TNA, FO 837/802, part I, O/81/1, 27 November 1939, quoted in G. Bennett, *Churchill's Man of Mystery: Desmond Morton and the World of Intelligence* (Abingdon, 2007), p. 205.

13. For this and the next four paragraphs, Imlay, 'Reassessment of Anglo-French Strategy', pp. 357–62.

14. TNA, CAB 66/4/12, WP (39) 162, 'Norway – Iron Ore Traffic', 16 December 1939, pp. 2–3; Bell, *Churchill and Sea Power*, pp. 173–5.

15. Ironside diary, 31 December 1939, 30 December 1939, pp. 176–7, 191.

16. TNA, CAB 66/4/29, WP (39) 179, 'Military implications of a policy aimed at stopping the export of Swedish iron ore to Germany', pp. 4, 21.

17. Bell, *Churchill and Sea Power*, pp. 176–9.

18. Imlay, 'Reassessment of Anglo-French Strategy', p. 355.

19. Ironside diary, 31 January, 1 February 1940, pp. 214–15.

20. The rescue of the British sailors, although much celebrated, was in fact rather more chaotic and less heroic than it was depicted at the time. See M. Docherty, 'The Attack on the *Altmark*: A Case Study in Wartime Propaganda', *Journal of Contemporary History*, 38, 2 (2003), pp. 187–200.

21. Ironside diary, 12 March 1940, p. 227.

22. Bell, *Churchill and Sea Power*, pp. 179–81.

23. J. Jackson, *The Fall of France: The Nazi Invasion of 1940* (Oxford, 2003), pp. 124–9.

24. Imlay, 'Reassessment of Anglo-French Strategy', pp. 362–6.

25. This paragraph and the next, ibid., pp. 366–9.

26. Ironside diary, 26 March 1940, p. 234.

27. T. Imlay, *Facing the Second World War: Strategy, Politics and Economics in Britain and France, 1938–1940* (Oxford, 2003), p. 229.

28. TNA, CAB 67/4/35, 'Survey of the National Resources in Relation to our War Effort', 30 January 1940, p. 8.

29. Imlay, *Facing the Second World War*, p. 352.

30. W. Hancock and M. Gowing, *British War Economy* (London, 1949), p. 117.

31. Imlay, *Facing the Second World War*, pp. 348–51.

32. This paragraph and next R. Sayers, *Financial Policy, 1939–1945* (London, 1956), pp. 31–44 (quotes p. 35), pp. 198–200; B. Sabine, *British Budgets in Peace and War* (London, 1970), pp. 160–73.

33. This paragraph and the next, Duncan Hall, *North American Supply* (London, 1955), pp. 116–27.

34. R. Crowcroft, *Attlee's War: World War II and the Making of a Labour Leader* (London, 2001), pp. 38–42.

35. HC Deb, 1 February 1940, vol. 358, c. 1313.

36. Ibid., c. 1933.

37. B. Pimlott, *Hugh Dalton* (London, 1985), pp. 269–72.

38. Quoted in A. Bullock, *The Life and Times of Ernest Bevin, I: Trade Union Leader 1881–1940* (London, 1960), p. 644.

39. 'War and the Consumer', *The Times*, 9 January 1940, p. 9, quoted in Imlay, *Facing the Second World War*, p. 230.

40. Sabine, *British Budgets*, pp. 164–5.

41. D. Dutton, 'Power Brokers or just "Glamour Boys"? The Eden Group, September 1939–May 1940', *English Historical Review*, 118, 476 (2003), p. 416; L. Wetherell, 'Lord Salisbury's "Watching Committee" and the Fall of Neville Chamberlain, May 1940', *English Historical Review*, 116, 469 (2001), pp. 1146–8.

42. Headlam diary, 1 February 1940, p. 180.

43. This paragraph and the next, J. Beavan, 'King, Cecil Harmsworth (1901–1987)'; A. Smith 'Bartholomew, (Harry) Guy (1884–1962)'; A. Howard, 'Cudlipp, Hubert Kinsman (Hugh) (1913–1998)', all *ODNB*; J. Curran and J. Seaton, *Power without Responsibility: The Press, Broadcasting and New Media in Britain*, 6th edn (London, 2003), pp. 39–53.

44. R. Cockett, *Twilight of Truth: Chamberlain, Appeasement and the Manipulation of the Press* (London, 1989), pp. 25–6.

45. King diary, 8 February 1940, p. 21.

46. Ibid., pp. 23, 22.

47. Ibid., pp. 21–2.

48. Ibid., p. 22.

49. Ibid., 12 October 1940, p. 82.

50. Ibid., 8 February 1940, p. 23.

51. R. Self, *Neville Chamberlain: A Biography* (Aldershot, 2006), pp. 413–14.

52. Wetherell, 'Salisbury's "Watching Committee"', pp. 1150–51.

53. Self, *Neville Chamberlain*, p. 415.

54. F. H. Hinsley, *British Intelligence in the Second World War (Abridged)* (London, 1994), pp. 18–20.

55. F. Kersaudy, *Norway 1940* (London, 1990), pp. 113–18; T. Derry, *The Campaign in Norway* (London, 1952), pp. 97–112.

56. Bell, *Churchill and Sea Power*, pp. 186–94.

57. M. Gilbert, *Winston S. Churchill, VI: Finest Hour, 1939–1941* (London, 1983), pp. 278–88.

58. Dutton, '"Glamour Boys"', pp. 419–20; Wetherell, 'Salisbury's "Watching Committee"', pp. 1153–7.

59. Channon diary, 3 May 1940, p. 244.
60. N. Smart, 'Four Days in May: The Norway Debate and the Downfall of Neville Chamberlain', *Parliamentary History*, 17, 2 (1998), pp. 218–21.
61. Ibid., p. 221.
62. HC Deb, 7 May 1940, vol. 360, c. 1093.
63. Ibid., c. 1150.
64. Dutton, ' "Glamour Boys" ', p. 421.
65. HC Deb, 8 May 1940, vol. 360, c. 1264.
66. Ibid., c. 1266.
67. Ibid., c. 1283.
68. Ibid., c. 1301.
69. Ibid., cc. 1361–2.
70. Smart, 'Four Days in May', pp. 222–6.
71. Ibid., pp. 229–37.
72. Ibid., p. 236; A. Roberts, *'The Holy Fox': The Life of Lord Halifax* (London, 1997), pp. 198–209.
73. Smart, 'Four Days in May', pp. 237–8.
74. Ibid., pp. 238–40.
75. Quoted in K. Harris, *Attlee* (London, 1982), p. 175.
76. Harris, *Attlee*, p. 178; S. Brooke, *Labour's War: The Labour Party during the Second World War* (Oxford, 1992), pp. 51–6; Crowcroft, *Attlee's War*, pp. 47–53.
77. MOFR95, 'Norway Crisis', 3 May 1940, pp. 14, 19, 7.
78. MOFR99, 'Political Crisis', 10 May 1940, p. 12.
79. MOA, Diarist 5205, 2 May 1940.
80. MOFR99, 'Political Crisis', pp. 12–13.
81. Ibid., pp. 23–4.
82. Ibid., p. 34.
83. MOA, Diarist 5231, 8 May 1940.
84. MOA, Diarist 5010, 10 May 1940.
85. MOFR103, 'Holland-Belgium Reactions (2)', 13 May 1940, p. 13.

14. THE BATTLE OF FRANCE

1. For accounts of the 1940 campaign see K.-H. Frieser, *The Blitzkrieg Legend: The 1940 Campaign in the West* (Annapolis, Md., 2005); L. Ellis, *The War in France and Flanders, 1939–1940* (London, 1953); J. Jackson, *The Fall of France: The Nazi Invasion of 1940* (Oxford, 2003).
2. R. Doughty, *The Breaking Point: Sedan and the Fall of France* (Hamden, Conn., 1990), pp. 155–6; Frieser, *Blitzkrieg Legend*, pp. 28–33.
3. Frieser, *Blitzkrieg Legend*, pp. 34–54, 211–13, 241–3, 283–6.
4. Ibid., pp. 339–41.

5. Jackson, *Fall of France*, pp. 151–82.

6. Frieser, *Blitzkrieg Legend*, pp. 89–90.

7. Ibid., pp. 90–92.

8. Ibid., pp. 140–44, and on the almighty traffic jam that developed in any case, pp. 109–18.

9. Doughty, *The Breaking Point*; see also his *Pyrrhic Victory: French Strategy and Operations in the Great War* (London, 2005); Frieser, *Blitzkrieg Legend*, pp. 336–9.

10. Jackson, *Fall of France*, pp. 79–100; P. Caddick-Adams, 'Anglo-French Cooperation during the Battle for France', in B. Bond and M. Taylor (eds.), *The Battle of France and Flanders 1940: Sixty Years On* (Barnsley, 2001), pp. 35–52.

11. Jackson, *Fall of France*, pp. 129–42.

12. Caddick-Adams, 'Anglo-French Cooperation', p. 41.

13. D. French, *Raising Churchill's Army: The British Army and the War against Germany, 1919–1945* (Oxford, 2000), pp. 165–7, 180–81; F. H. Hinsley, *British Intelligence in the Second World War (Abridged)* (London, 1994), pp. 27–31.

14. French, *Raising Churchill's Army*, pp. 176–7, 182–3.

15. Frieser, *Blitzkrieg Legend*, pp. 273–86.

16. French, *Raising Churchill's Army*, pp. 181–82.

17. M. Piercy, 'The Manoeuvre that Saved the Field Force', in Bond and Taylor (eds.), *Battle for France and Flanders*, pp. 53–71.

18. J. Buckley, 'The Air War in France', in Bond and Taylor (eds.), *Battle for France and Flanders*, pp. 109–26.

19. R. Broadhurst, 'The Navy's Role in the Campaign', in Bond and Taylor (eds.), *Battle for France and Flanders*, pp. 127–36; S. Roskill, *The War at Sea, 1939–1945*, I (London, 1954), pp. 217–28.

20. The best recent account of the experience of soldiers in the fighting around the Dunkirk pocket is H. Sebag-Montefiore, *Dunkirk: Fight to the Last Man* (London, 2006). See also R. Atkin, *Pillar of Fire: Dunkirk 1940* (London, 2000); M. Connelly and W. Miller, 'The BEF and the Issue of Surrender on the Western Front in 1940', *War in History*, 11, 4 (2004), pp. 424–41.

21. IWM, Private Papers of S. L. Wright, Documents 3964.

22. W. Harding, *A Cockney Soldier: Duty before Pleasure. An Autobiography 1918–46* (London, 1989), p. 132.

23. J. Langley, *Fight Another Day* (London, 1973), p. 39.

24. P. Hadley, *Third Class to Dunkirk: A Worm's Eye View of the BEF, 1940* (London, 1944), p. 137.

25. Quoted in Atkin, *Pillar of Fire*, p. 175.

26. 'Gun Buster', *Return via Dunkirk* (London, 1941), p. 245.

27. Quoted in Frieser, *Blitzkrieg Legend*, p. 302.

28. IWM, Interview with Lionel Tucker, Catalogue No. 32138, Reel 2.
29. Connelly and Miller, 'BEF and the Issue of Surrender'.
30. Quoted in Atkin, *Pillar of Fire*, p. 161, from his interview with Catt.
31. IWM, Interview with Ernest Lorne Campbell Edlmann, Catalogue No. 18735, Reel 6, quoted in Connelly and Miller, 'BEF and the Issue of Surrender', p. 434.
32. Hinsley, *British Intelligence*, pp. 35–6.
33. H. Koch, 'The Strategic Air Offensive against Germany: The Early Phase, May–September 1940', *Historical Journal*, 34, 1 (1991), pp. 126–8.
34. Cadogan diary, 15 May 1940, p. 283.
35. Koch, 'Strategic Air Offensive', pp. 128–30.
36. R. Overy, *The Bombing War: Europe 1939–1945* (London, 2013), pp. 243–51, 60–66.
37. W. Churchill, *The Second World War, II: Their Finest Hour* (London, 1949), p. 23.
38. TNA, CAB 65/13/20, 26 May 1940, p. 5.
39. TNA, CAB 65/13/21, 26 May, 2 p.m., pp. 2–6.
40. TNA, CAB 66/7/48, 'British Strategy in a Certain Eventuality', pp. 1–3, emphasis in original.
41. Lord Birkenhead, *Halifax* (London, 1965), p. 458.
42. TNA, CAB 65/13/23, 27 May 1940, pp. 4–6.
43. Birkenhead, *Halifax*, p. 458.
44. Amery diary, 28 May 1940, p. 619.
45. TNA, CAB 65/13/24, 28 May 1940, 4 p.m., pp. 2–6.
46. This paragraph and the next, D. Reynolds, 'Churchill and the British "Decision" to Fight On in 1940: Right Policy, Wrong Reasons', in R. Langhorne (ed.), *Diplomacy and Intelligence during the Second World War: Essays in Honour of F. H. Hinsley* (Cambridge, 1985), pp. 147–67; A. Roberts, *'The Holy Fox': The Life of Lord Halifax* (London, 1997), pp. 211–28; D. Edgerton, *Britain's War Machine: Weapons, Resources and Experts in the Second World War* (London, 2011), pp. 69–72, 321–2, n. 87 and n. 91.
47. G. Strobl, *The Germanic Isle: Nazi Perceptions of Britain* (Oxford, 2000), pp. 205–18.
48. This is the nub of Edgerton's argument, *War Machine*, p. 33, n. 91.
49. P. Bell, *A Certain Eventuality: Britain and the Fall of France* (Farnborough, 1974), pp. 45–7; Roberts, *'Holy Fox'*, pp. 220–22.
50. R. Self, *Neville Chamberlain: A Biography* (Aldershot, 2006), pp. 436–8.
51. J. Lukacs, *Five Days in London, May 1940* (New Haven, Conn., and London, 1999).
52. Bell, *Certain Eventuality*, ch. 4.
53. Pownall diary, June 1940, p. 359.
54. Cadogan diary, 2 June 1940, p. 293.

55. TNA, CAB 65/13/32, 4 June 1940, p. 1.
56. Brooke diary, 14 June 1940, p. 81.
57. Bell, *Certain Eventuality*, pp. 138–9.
58. Ibid., ch. 5.
59. Ibid., pp. 140–42.
60. This paragraph and the next, ibid., pp. 93–6.
61. Jackson, *Fall of France*, p. 180.
62. Ibid.
63. TNA, CAB 65/7/73, 24 June 1940, pp. 578–9.
64. Roskill, *War at Sea I*, p. 295, C. Bell, *The Royal Navy, Seapower and Strategy between the Wars* (Basingstoke and London, 2000), pp. 86–90.
65. Bell, *Royal Navy*, pp. 112–25; Roskill, *War at Sea I*, pp. 296–7.
66. Bell, *Certain Eventuality*, ch. 8.
67. Edgerton, *War Machine*, p. 72.
68. Bell, *Certain Eventuality*, pp. 148–9; J. Jordan and R. Dumas, *French Battleships 1922–1956* (Annapolis, Md., 2009).
69. Quoted in D. Porch, *Hitler's Mediterranean Gamble: The North African and Mediterranean Campaigns in World War II* (London, 2004), p. 62.
70. C. Smith, *England's Last War against France: Fighting Vichy 1940–1942* (London, 2009), chs. 4–6.
71. I. Playfair et al., *The Mediterranean and Middle East, I: The Early Successes against Italy (to May 1941)* (London, 1954), pp. 142–3.
72. Ibid., pp. 130, n.1, 141–3.

PART FOUR

1. IWM, Private Papers of G. W. King, Documents 3777, diary entry, 13 July 1940.
2. R. McKibbin, *Parties and People: England 1914–1951* (Oxford, 2010), pp. 118–24.
3. D. Reynolds, '1940: Fulcrum of the Twentieth Century?', *International Affairs*, 66, 2 (1990), pp. 325–50.

15. FINEST HOUR

1. For what follows, Dalton diary, 16 May 1940, p. 9; Colville diary, 12 May 1940, p. 89; R. Lowe, 'Wilson, Sir Horace John (1882–1972)', *ODNB*; J. Tomes, 'Bracken, Brendan Rendall, Viscount Bracken (1901–1958)', *ODNB*; G. Peden, 'Sir Horace Wilson and Appeasement', *Historical Journal*, 53, 4 (2010), p. 984.
2. Colville diary, 10 May 1940, p. 122.
3. Tomes, 'Bracken'.

4. A. Chisholm and M. Davie, *Beaverbrook: A Life* (London, 1992), pp. 384–97, quote p. 429.

5. J. Charmley, *Churchill: The End of Glory. A Political Biography* (London, 1993), pp. 42–4, 54–5.

6. R. A. Butler, *The Art of the Possible: The Memoirs of Lord Butler* (London, 1971), p. 85.

7. Colville diary, 13 May 1940, p. 103.

8. Ibid., 2 December 1940, p. 259.

9. Ibid., dedication to published volume and p. 95, fn. 5.

10. There is an excellent demolition job in A. Danchev, ' "Dilly-Dally", or Having the Last Word: Field Marshal Sir John Dill and Prime Minister Winston Churchill', *Journal of Contemporary History*, 22, 1 (1987), pp. 29–33, but a lot of insights can also be gathered from the extraordinary review by Alistair Forbes, 'Beyond the Fringes', *Spectator*, 11 October 1985, p. 32.

11. Colville diary, 19 May 1940, p. 108.

12. Ibid., 13 June 1940, pp. 125–6.

13. Dill to Gort, 24 April 1940, quoted in J. Colville, *Man of Valour* (London, 1972), p. 180, and requoted in Danchev, ' "Dilly-Dally" ', p. 24.

14. Danchev, ' "Dilly Dally" ', pp. 23–4.

15. B. Farrell, 'Yes, Prime Minister: Barbarossa, Whipcord and the Basis of British Grand Strategy, Autumn 1941', *Journal of Military History*, 57, 4 (1993), pp. 601–2; idem, *The Basis and Making of British Grand Strategy, 1940–1943: Was There a Plan?* (Lewiston, NY, and Lampeter, 1998), p. 47.

16. M. Postan, *British War Production* (London, 1952), p. 143; D. Edgerton, *Britain's War Machine: Weapons, Resources and Experts in the Second World War* (London, 2011), pp. 96–9.

17. A. Fort, *Prof: The Life of Frederick Lindemann* (London, 2003); G. Bennett, *Churchill's Man of Mystery: Desmond Morton and the World of Intelligence* (Abingdon, 2007).

18. R. Crowcroft, *Attlee's War: World War II and the Making of a Labour Leader* (London, 2001).

19. D. Dutton, *Anthony Eden: A Life and Reputation* (London, 1997), pp. 217–20.

20. TNA, CAB 66/7/42, 20 May 1940, 'Memorandum by the Lord President of the Council', Appendix 1.

21. TNA, CAB 65/7/28, WM (40) 133, 22 May 1940, p. 213.

22. HC Deb, 22 May 1940, vol. 361, c. 158.

23. E. Bevin, *A Survey of Britain's War Effort* (London, 1941), p. 12.

24. H. Parker, *Manpower: A Study of War-time Policy and Administration* (London, 1957), pp. 122–32.

25. Ibid., p. 132.

26. HC Deb, 27 June 1940, vol. 362, c. 634.

27. CSO, *Fighting with Figures: A Statistical Digest of the Second World War* (London, 1995), p. 41.

28. Ibid., p. 38.

29. H. Krabbe (ed.), *Voices from Britain: Broadcast from the BBC 1939–1945* (London, 1947), p. 39.

30. W. Hancock and M. Gowing, *British War Economy* (London, 1949), pp. 216–17.

31. Crowcroft, *Attlee's War*, pp. 61–5.

32. A. Briggs, *The History of Broadcasting in the United Kingdom, III: The War of Words* (Oxford, 1970), p. 144.

33. S. P. Mackenzie, *The Home Guard: A Military and Political History* (Oxford, 1995), pp. 22–3.

34. T. Kushner, 'Clubland, Cricket Tests and Alien Internment, 1939–40', in D. Cesarani and T. Kushner (eds.), *The Internment of Aliens in Twentieth Century Britain* (London, 1993), p. 84.

35. F. H. Hinsley, *British Intelligence in the Second World War (Abridged)* (London, 1994), pp. 35–8.

36. TNA, CAB 65/7/28 WM (40) 133, Annex, Ismay to Churchill, 21 May 1940.

37. Mackenzie, *Home Guard*, pp. 22–3.

38. 'Fifth Columns', *The Times*, 24 April 1940, p. 7; 'Parachutists', *The Times*, 11 May 1940, p. 7.

39. MOFR 103, 'Holland-Belgium Reactions (2)', 13 May 1940, p. 6.

40. Mackenzie, *Home Guard*, p. 34.

41. TNA, FO 371/25189, 'Fifth Column Menace', quoted in P. Gillman and L. Gillman, *'Collar the Lot!': How Britain Interned and Expelled its Wartime Refugees* (London, 1980), pp. 101–2, emphasis in original.

42. TNA, CAB 65/7/18, 15 May 1940, p. 139.

43. This paragraph and the next, R. Thurlow, 'The Evolution of the Mythical British Fifth Column, 1939–1946', *Twentieth Century British History*, 10, 4 (1999), pp. 477–98.

44. R. Griffiths, 'A Note on Mosley, the "Jewish War" and Conscientious Objection', *Journal of Contemporary History*, 40, 4 (2005), pp. 683–6.

45. C. Andrew, *Secret Service: The Making of the British Intelligence Community* (London, 1985), pp. 478–9.

46. Ibid., p. 480.

47. L. Sponza, 'The British Government and the Internment of Italians', in Cesarani and Kushner (eds.), *The Internment of Aliens*, pp. 126–7; P. Di Felice, 'Manchester's Little Italy at War, 1940–45: "Enemy Aliens or a reluctant foe?"', *Northern History*, 39, 1 (2002), pp. 116–18; T. Colpi, 'The Impact of the Second World War on the British Italian Community', in Cesarani and Kushner (eds.), *Internment of Aliens*, pp. 172–5.

48. Andrew, *Secret Service*, pp. 480–81.

49. Quoted in ibid., p. 478.

50. P. Summerfield and C. Peniston-Bird, *Contesting Home Defence: Men, Women and the Home Guard in the Second World War* (Manchester, 2007); B. Osborne, *The People's Army: Home Guard in Scotland 1940–1944* (Edinburgh, 2009), pp. 45–8.

51. Mackenzie, *Home Guard*, pp. 34–40.

52. Ibid., pp. 55–60.

53. B. Collier, *Defence of the United Kingdom* (London, 1957), p. 144; M. Marix Evans, *Invasion! Operation Sealion, 1940* (London, 2004), p. 64.

54. D. Newbold, 'British Planning and Preparations to Resist Invasion on Land, September 1939–September 1940', PhD, King's College London, 1998, pp. 206–7.

55. Ibid., pp. 152–4; Edgerton, *War Machine*, pp. 63–5, 320.

56. Newbold, 'British Planning', p. 207.

57. Essex Record Office, Chelmsford, D/P/292/6/39, 'Letter relating to precautions against invasion'. My thanks to former Queen Mary University of London undergraduate student Carly Hearn for highlighting this source.

58. M. Allingham, *The Oaken Heart* (London, 1941), pp. 176, 199.

59. H. Umbreit, 'Plans and Preparations for a Landing in England', in K. Maier et al., *Germany and the Second World War, II: Germany's Initial Conquests in Europe* (Oxford, 1991), p. 367.

60. P. Addison and J. Crang, 'Introduction', in idem (eds.), *Listening to Britain: Home Intelligence Reports on Britain's Finest Hour – May to September 1940* (London, 2010), pp. xi–xii; S. Adams, 'Adams, Mary Grace Agnes (1898–1984)', *ODNB*.

61. J. Hinton, *The Mass Observers: A History* (Oxford, 2013), pp. 143–62.

62. Addison and Crang, 'Introduction', pp. xii–xvi; Hinton, *Mass Observers*, pp. 166–9; P. Addison, 'Introduction', *Home Intelligence Reports on Opinion and Morale 1940–1944* (Microfilm) (Brighton, 1979), Reel 1.

63. I. McLaine, *Ministry of Morale: Home Front Morale and the Ministry of Information in World War II* (London, 1979), pp. 61–3.

64. HC Deb, 1 August 1940, vol. 363, c. 1515.

65. McLaine, *Ministry of Morale*, pp. 84–8; Hinton, *Mass Observers*, pp. 179–84.

66. HIMR, 22 May 1940, p. 19.

67. HIMR, 18 May, 19–20 May, 21 May, 23 May, 24 May 1940, pp. 5–10, 11, 16, 22, 24–5.

68. S. Badsey, 'British High Command and the Reporting of the Campaign', in B. Bond and M. Taylor (eds.), *The Battle of France and Flanders 1940: Sixty Years On* (Barnsley, 2001), pp. 140–51.

69. Badsey, 'Reporting of the Campaign', pp. 150–53.

70. HIMR, 29 May 1940, pp. 50–51.

71. IWM, Private Papers of Lieutenant General Sir Noel Mason-Macfarlane, Documents 12311, Reel 2, Item 12, quoted in Badsey, 'Reporting of the Campaign', pp. 152, 159 fn 70.

72. HIMR, 29 May 1940, p. 53.

73. MOA, Diarist 5352, 31 May 1940.

74. BUFVC, 'Gazette Special – War Latest – Dunkirk Evacuation', Pathé Gazette Issue No. 40/45, 3 June 1940, script, p. 1, http://bufvc.ac.uk/newsonscreen/search/index.php/story/97994.

75. MOFR215, 'Newsreels in Early June', 19 June 1940, pp. 3–4.

76. HC Deb, 4 June 1940, vol. 361, c. 791.

77. HIMR, 4 June 1940, p. 76.

78. V. Brome, *J. B. Priestley* (London, 1988), p. 244.

79. J. B. Priestley, *Postscripts* (London, 1940), pp. 1–4.

80. P. Addison, *The Road to 1945: British Politics and the Second World War* (London, 1975), pp. 107–8.

81. 'Please Kick Them Out', *Daily Mirror*, 6 June 1940, p. 7.

82. Crowcroft, *Attlee's War*, pp. 65–6.

83. To Hilda Chamberlain, 1 June 1940, *NCDL IV*, p. 535.

84. A. Roberts, *Eminent Churchillians* (London, 1994), pp. 162–3.

85. To Ida Chamberlain, 8 June 1940, *NCDL IV*, p. 538.

86. Roberts, *Eminent Churchillians*, p. 162; to Ida Chamberlain, 8 June 1940, *NCDL IV*, p. 538.

87. MOFR205, 'The Bow and Bromley By-Election', 18 June 1940, p. 24.

88. HIMR, 12 June 1940, p. 106.

89. HIMR, 13 June 1940, p. 110.

90. HIMR, 14 June 1940, p. 113.

91. Brown diary, 18 June 1940, pp. 52–3.

92. MOFR201, 'Report on French Surrender', 17 June 1940, p. 1.

93. MOFR181, 'Capitulation Talk in Worktown', 19 June 1940, p. 5.

94. Ibid., p. 6.

95. Ibid., p. 8.

96. Ibid., p. 10.

97. HIMR, 17 June 1940, p. 123.

98. http://www.winstonchurchill.org/learn/speeches/speeches-of-winston-churchill/1940-finest-hour/122-their-finest-hour.

99. MOFR242, 'Morale Today 1–2 July 1940', p. 2.

100. HIMR, 20 June 1940, p. 134.

101. D. Kynaston, *The City of London, III: Illusions of Gold, 1914–1945* (London, 1999), pp. 469–71.

102. McLaine, *Ministry of Morale*, pp. 62–82.

103. HIMR, 24 June 1940, p. 149.

104. Ibid., 27 June 1940, p. 157.

105. M. Ceadel, *Pacifism in Britain, 1914–1945: The Defining of a Faith* (Oxford, 1980), p. 299.

106. Thurlow, 'Evolution of the Mythical Fifth Column', p. 494.

107. Quoted in Ceadel, *Pacifism in Britain*, p. 297.

108. Parker, *Manpower*, p. 488.

109. Quoted in A. Calder, *Myth of the Blitz* (London, 1991), p. 82.

110. R. Croucher, *Engineers at War* (London, 1982), p. 114 quotes TNA, AVIA 22/1030, 28 May, 21 June 1940, quoted p. 91.

111. 'A Day of Prayer', *Yorkshire Post*, 25 May 1940, p. 4.

112. 'Diocesan News', *Church Times*, 31 May 1940, p. 403.

113. Quoted in C. Smyth, *Cyril Forster Garbett: Archbishop of York* (London, 1959), p. 254.

114. Musto diary, 26 May 1940, pp. 128–9.

115. HIMR, 21 June 1940, p. 141.

116. IWM, Private Papers of G. W. King, Documents 3777, diary entry, 23 June 1940.

117. Ralph Miliband diary, undated 1940, quoted in M. Newman, *Ralph Miliband and the Politics of the New Left* (London, 2002), p. 13.

118. HIMR, 25 June 1940, p. 155.

119. 'Sack the Munich Men – Union', *Daily Mirror*, 3 July 1940, p. 3.

120. HIMR, 18 and 19 June 1940, pp. 125, 128–30.

121. HC Deb, 30 July 1940, vol. 363, c. 1137; Summerfield and Peniston-Bird, *Contesting Home Defence*, pp. 30–39.

122. A. Smith, 'Wintringham, Thomas Henry (1898–1949)', *ODNB*; H. Purcell, *The Last English Revolutionary: Tom Wintringham 1898–1949* (Stroud, 2004), p. 200.

123. T. Wintringham, *New Ways of War* (London, 1940), p. 73.

124. Ibid., pp. 77–8.

125. Summerfield and Peniston-Bird, *Contesting Home Defence*, pp. 41–3.

126. Edgerton, *War Machine*, pp. 228–31.

127. Colville diary, 19 June 1940, p. 136.

128. R. Rhodes James, *Bob Boothby: A Portrait* (London, 1991), pp. 256–65.

129. C. Eade (ed.), *Secret Session Speeches: by the Right Hon. Winston S Churchill OM, CH, MP* (London, 1946), p. 16.

130. Dalton diary, 18 June 1940, p. 42.

131. Crowcroft, *Attlee's War*, pp. 56–61.

132. Nicolson diary, 3 July 1940, p. 96.

133. Crowcroft, *Attlee's War*, pp. 62–5, 72–81.

134. S. Brooke, *Labour's War: The Labour Party during the Second World War* (Oxford, 1992), p. 75; K. Jefferys, *The Churchill Coalition and Wartime Politics* (Manchester, 1991), p. 41.

135. TNA, PREM 4/68/9, ff. 954–60, quoted in M. Gilbert, *Winston S. Churchill, VI: Finest Hour, 1939–1941* (London, 1983), p. 428.

136. For what follows on the Prytz incident, T. Munch-Petersen, ' "Common sense not bravado": The Butler-Prytz Interview of 17 June 1940', *Scandia*, (1986), pp. 73–114.

137. Swedish Foreign Ministry Archive, Tel 723 from Prytz, 17 June 1940, HP39AXXXIII, printed in K. Wahlbäck and Göran Boberg, *Sveriges sak är vår. Svensk utrikespolitik, 1939–45 i dokument* (Stockholm, 1966), p. 120, quoted in Munch-Petersen, 'The Butler-Prytz Interview', p. 74.

138. Ibid.

139. Munch-Petersen, 'The Butler-Prytz Interview', pp. 74–88.

140. TNA, FO 800/322, Churchill to Halifax, 26 June 1940, quoted in ibid., pp. 78–9.

141. Ibid., pp. 79–80.

142. Ibid., pp. 101–9.

143. To Ida Chamberlain, *NCDL IV*, 29 June 1940, p. 545.

144. MOFR242, 'Morale Today 1–2 July 1940', p. 2.

145. HC Deb, 4 July 1940, vol. 362, cc. 1050–51.

146. Channon diary, 4 July 1940, p. 260; R. Toye, *The Roar of the Lion: The Untold Story of Churchill's World War II Speeches* (Oxford, 2013), pp. 62–3.

147. J. R. M. Butler, *Grand Strategy, II: September 1939–June 1941* (London, 1957), pp. 277–83; Hinsley, *British Intelligence*, pp. 36–8.

148. Colville diary, 12 July 1940, p. 159.

149. http://www.winstonchurchill.org/learn/speeches/speeches-of-winston-churchill/126-war-of-the-unknown-warriors.

150. N. Redfern, 'Anti-invasion Defences of Scotland, Wales and Northern Ireland, 1939–1945: Insights and Issues', *Defence Lines*, 12 (1999), http://www.britarch.ac.uk/projects/dob/dl12b.html.

151. W. Foot, 'The Impact of the Military on the Agricultural Landscape of England and Wales in the Second World War', in B. Short, C. Watkins and J. Martin (eds.), *The Front Line of Freedom: British Farming in the Second World War* (Exeter, 2007), p. 133.

152. Brooke diary, 19 July 1940 (post-war 'Notes on my life'), p. 93.

153. A. Roberts, *'The Holy Fox': The Life of Lord Halifax* (London, 1997), pp. 249–50.

154. HIMR, 5 July 1940, p. 192.

155. R. Overy, *The Bombing War: Europe 1939–1945* (London, 2013), p. 173.

156. S. Nicholas, *The Echo of War: Home Front Propaganda and the Wartime BBC, 1939–45* (Manchester, 1996), pp. 228–40.

157. MOA, TC Famous Persons Survey (1939–1952), 'Hitler Speech', 20 July 1940.

158. For the discussion of *Guilty Men*, P. Williamson, 'Baldwin's Reputation: Politics and History, 1937–1967', *Historical Journal*, 47, 1 (2004), pp. 134–7; D. Dutton, *Neville Chamberlain* (London, 2001), pp. 71–7.

159. 'Cato', *Guilty Men* (London, 1940), pp. 10, 16.
160. Ibid., p. 125.
161. Chisholm and Davie, *Beaverbrook*, pp. 380–83; A. J. P. Taylor, *Beaverbrook* (London, 1972), p. 435.
162. Dutton, *Chamberlain*, p. 74.
163. 'Cassandra', *Daily Mirror*, 4 July 1940, p. 4.
164. Addison, *Road to 1945*, p. 110.
165. Nicholas, *Echo of War*, pp. 240–42.
166. R. Self, *Neville Chamberlain: A Biography* (Aldershot, 2006), pp. 442–3.
167. W. Crozier, *Off the Record: Political Interviews 1933–1943*, edited by A. J. P. Taylor (London, 1973), interview with Beaverbrook, 24 August 1940, p. 199.
168. Headlam diary, 31 July 1940, p. 215.
169. B. Sabine, *British Budgets in Peace and War* (London, 1970), pp. 174–6.
170. Ibid., p. 177.
171. *The Times*, 25 July 1940, quoted in ibid.
172. Quoted in *The History of the Times: The 150ᵗʰ Anniversary and Beyond, 1912–1948, Part II* (London, 1952), p. 990.
173. J. Haslam, *The Vices of Integrity: E. H. Carr, 1892–1982* (London, 2000), pp. 81–6.
174. Quoted in ibid., p. 86.
175. N. Rose, *Harold Nicolson* (London, 2005), pp. 190–91, 244–5.
176. Nicolson diary, 16 July 1940, pp. 99–100.
177. TNA, CAB 65/8/45, 23 August 1940, p. 270.
178. McLaine, *Ministry of Morale*, pp. 105–7; Jefferys, *Churchill Coalition*, pp. 51–5.

16. 'WHAT WILL HAPPEN NOW?'

1. D. Edgerton, *Britain's War Machine: Weapons, Resources and Experts in the Second World War* (London, 2011), pp. 70–72, 78–81.
2. A. Tooze, *The Wages of Destruction: The Making and Breaking of the Nazi Economy* (London, 2006), pp. 402–3.
3. J. Charmley, *Churchill's Grand Alliance: The Anglo-American Special Relationship 1940–57* (London, 1995), p. 3.
4. W. Churchill, *The Second World War, II: Their Finest Hour* (London, 1949), p. 24.
5. D. Reynolds, *From Munich to Pearl Harbor: Roosevelt's America and the Origins of the Second World War* (Chicago, 2001), pp. 82–3; D. Hall, *North American Supply* (London, 1955), p. 134.
6. Hall, *North American Supply*, pp. 146–7; J. Hurstfield, *The Control of Raw Materials* (London, 1953), pp. 159–61, 263; W. Hornby, *Factories*

and Plant (London, 1958), pp. 309–26, 368, 335; Tooze, *Wages of Destruction*, p. 404.

7. http://www.winstonchurchill.org/learn/speeches/speeches-of-winston-churchill/1940-finest-hour/128-we-shall-fight-on-the-beaches.

8. D. Reynolds, *The Creation of the Anglo-American Alliance, 1937–41: A Study in Competitive Cooperation* (Chapel Hill, NC, 1981), pp. 112–13.

9. Hall, *North American Supply*, pp. 164–72.

10. Tooze, *Wages of Destruction*, pp. 405–6.

11. D. Hall, *Studies of Overseas Supply* (London, 1956), pp. 92, 110–12; M. Harrison, 'Resource Mobilisation for World War II: The USA, UK, USSR and Germany, 1938–1945', *Economic History Review*, 41, 2 (1988), p. 189.

12. Hall, *North American Supply*, pp. 146–7, 245–51; Reynolds, *Anglo-American Alliance*, pp. 147–8; B. Farrell, *The Basis and Making of British Grand Strategy, 1940–1943: Was There a Plan?*, (Lewiston, NY and Lampeter, 1998), p. 59, quoting TNA, PREM 3/483/3, Beaverbrook to Churchill, 12 August 1940.

13. C. Stacey, *Arms, Men and Governments: The War Policies of Canada, 1939–1945* (Ottawa, 1970), pp. 31–7.

14. R. Wigg, *Churchill and Spain: The Survival of the Franco Regime, 1940–1945* (Abingdon, 2005), pp. 4–24.

15. D. Porch, *Hitler's Mediterranean Gamble: The North African and Mediterranean Campaigns in World War II* (London, 2004), p. 18.

16. J. R. M. Butler, *Grand Strategy, II: September 1939–June 1941* (London, 1957), pp. 238–9.

17. Ibid., pp. 313–14.

18. R. Fisk, *In Time of War: Ireland, Ulster and the Price of Neutrality, 1939–45* (Dublin, 1983), chs. 6–7.

19. D. Killingray, *Fighting for Britain: African Soldiers in the Second World War* (Rochester, NY, 2012), pp. 58–75; A. Stewart, *A Very British Experience: Coalition, Defence and Strategy in the Second World War* (Eastbourne, 2012), pp. 54–5.

20. Stewart, *Very British Experience*, p. 48.

21. Quoted in V. Schofield, *Wavell: Soldier and Statesman* (London, 2006), p. 145.

22. S. Wichhart, 'Intervention: Britain, Egypt and Iraq during World War II', PhD, University of Texas at Austin, 2007, pp. 160–65; M. Kolinsky, *Britain's War in the Middle East: Strategy and Diplomacy 1936–1942* (New York, 1999), pp. 126–7.

23. D. Silverfarb, *Britain's Informal Empire in the Middle East: A Case Study of Iraq 1929–1941* (Oxford, 1986), pp. 115–16.

24. Wichhart, 'Intervention', pp. 110–16.

25. C. Bell, *Churchill and Sea Power* (Oxford, 2013), pp. 201–2.

26. Porch, *Hitler's Mediterranean Gamble*, pp. 42–3.

27. Kolinsky, *Britain's War in the Middle East*, pp. 132–4.

28. Schofield, *Wavell*, pp. 148–52.
29. D. Reynolds, *In Command of History: Churchill Fighting and Writing the Second World War* (London, 2004), pp. 190–93.
30. A. Danchev, ' "Dilly-Dally" or Having the Last Word: Field Marshal Sir John Dill and Prime Minister Winston Churchill', *Journal of Contemporary History*, 22, 1 (1987), p. 25.
31. Reynolds, *In Command of History*, pp. 191–3.
32. Schofield, *Wavell*, pp. 153–4, quote on p. 154.
33. Churchill, *Second World War II*, pp. 119–20.
34. L. Woodward, *British Foreign Policy in the Second World War* (London, 1972), pp. 141–2; Tooze, *Wages of Destruction*, p. 396; J. Maiolo, *Cry Havoc: The Arms Race and the Second World War 1931–1941* (London, 2010), pp. 352–4.
35. TNA, CAB 65/8/6, 5 July 1940, pp. 41–2; Cadogan diary, 5 July 1940, p. 311.
36. Quoted in Woodward, *British Foreign Policy*, p. 167.
37. P. Hasluck, *Australia in the War of 1939–45, Series 4 – Civil – I: The Government and the People, 1939–1941* (Canberra, 1952), p. 217.
38. Hasluck, *The Government and the People*, p. 231.
39. N. Taylor, *The Official History of New Zealand in the Second World War 1939–1945, The Home Front I* (Wellington, 1986), p. 161.
40. For what follows, B. Farrell, *The Defence and Fall of Singapore 1940–1942* (Stroud, 2006), pp. 63–81.
41. Quoted in ibid., p. 70.
42. R. Callahan, 'Churchill and Singapore', in B. Farrell and S. Hunter (eds.), *Sixty Years On: The Fall of Singapore Revisited* (Singapore, 2002), pp. 156–72.
43. N. Sinha and P. Khera, *Indian War Economy (Supply, Industry and Finance)* (New Delhi, 1962), pp. 147–97.
44. Quoted in R. Moore, *Churchill, Cripps and India 1939–1945* (Oxford, 1979), p. 40.
45. W. Roger Louis, *In the name of God, go! Leo Amery and the British Empire in the Age of Churchill* (London, 1992).
46. Quoted in Moore, *Churchill, Cripps and India*, p. 32.
47. Amery diary, 12 July 1940, p. 632.
48. Ibid., 25 July 1940, pp. 635–6.
49. Ibid., 26 July 1940, p. 637.
50. Ibid.
51. J. Darwin, *The Empire Project: The Rise and Fall of the British World-System* (Cambridge, 2009), p. 506.
52. Quoted in N. Mansergh, *Survey of British Commonwealth Affairs: Problems of Wartime Cooperation and Post-War Change, 1939–1952* (London, 1958), p. 83.

53. M. Glover, *Invasion Scare 1940* (London, 1990), pp. 82–3, 112, 121–2, 150–51, 196–200; P. Schenk, *Invasion of England 1940: The Planning of Operation Sealion* (London, 1990), pp. 223–33, 355–7; M. Marix Evans, *Invasion! Operation Sealion, 1940* (London, 2004), pp. 113–36.
54. For this and the following paragraph, H. Umbreit, 'The Return to an Indirect Strategy against Britain', in K. Maier et al., *Germany and the Second World War, II: Germany's Initial Conquests in Europe* (Oxford, 1991), pp. 408–15.
55. Halder diary, 31 July 1940, p. 244.

17. THE BATTLE OF BRITAIN

1. M. Glover, *Invasion Scare 1940* (London, 1990), pp. 109–10.
2. TNA, HO 191/11, 'Statement of Civilian Casualties in the United Kingdom (viz, Gt Britain and Northern Ireland), resulting from enemy action from the outbreak of war to 31 May 1945'.
3. CSO, *Fighting with Figures: A Statistical Digest of the Second World War* (London, 1995), p. 47.
4. H. Parker, *Manpower: A Study of War-time Policy and Administration* (London, 1957), pp. 504–5.
5. R. Croucher, *Engineers at War* (London, 1982), p. 86.
6. M. Postan, *British War Production* (London, 1952), p. 164.
7. CSO, *Fighting with Figures*, p. 172.
8. R. Overy, *The Bombing War: Europe 1939–1945* (London, 2013), p. 158.
9. H. Jones, *British Civilians in the Front Line: Air Raids, Productivity and Wartime Culture, 1939–45* (Manchester, 2006), pp. 42–6.
10. K. Maier, 'The Battle of Britain', in K. Maier et al., *Germany and the Second World War, II: Germany's Initial Conquests in Europe* (Oxford, 1991), p. 377.
11. W. Murray, *Strategy for Defeat: The Luftwaffe 1939–1945* (Washington, DC, 1986), pp. 39–43; R. Overy, *The Battle* (London, 2000), p. 49.
12. S. Cox, 'A Comparative Analysis of RAF and Luftwaffe Intelligence in the Battle of Britain, 1940', *Intelligence & National Security*, 5, 2 (1990), pp. 425–38; H. Boog, 'The Luftwaffe and the Battle of Britain', in S. Cox and H. A. Probert (eds.), *The Battle Re-thought: A Retrospective Study from Participants in the Battle of Britain* (Bracknell, 1991), pp. 22–24, 30.
13. R. Overy, *The Air War 1939–1945* (London, 1987), p. 74.
14. D. Richards, *The Royal Air Force, 1939–1945, I: Fight at Odds* (London, 1953), pp. 412–13; A. Tooze, *The Wages of Destruction: The Making and Breaking of the Nazi Economy* (London, 2006), p. 401.
15. Overy, *The Battle*, pp. 50–54; Murray, *The Luftwaffe*, pp. 6–18, 46; Boog, 'The Luftwaffe', pp. 27–8.

16. Overy, *Air War*, p. 77.
17. D. Wood, 'The Dowding System', in Cox and Probert (eds.), *The Battle Re-thought*, pp. 5–10.
18. A point made throughout J. Terraine, *The Right of the Line: The Role of the RAF in World War Two* (London, 1985).
19. IWM, 73 Sqdn Unofficial War Diary, Documents 9422, diary entry, 12 September 1940, p. 47. The identification of the planes involved as Heinkel 113s was a frequent one by RAF pilots, but in fact this plane was a propaganda invention created out of the He100, none of which flew during the battle.
20. P. Bishop, *Fighter Boys: Saving Britain, 1940* (London, 2003), p. 322.
21. Ibid., p. 305.
22. IWM, Private Papers of Venerable G. Mayfield, Documents 14311, 'RAF Duxford February 1940–December 1941: The Diary of The Reverend Guy Mayfield, MA (Hons) Cantab, RAFVR, Station Chaplain', p. 4.
23. IWM, Private Papers of R. Pountain, Documents 14379, 'Wartime Reminiscences of an RAF Armourer', pp. 16–19.
24. Overy, *Air War*, p. 89.
25. T. James, *The Battle of Britain: Air Defence of Great Britain, II* (London, 2013), pp. 322–3.
26. Cox, 'Comparative Analysis', pp. 431–4.
27. Overy, *Air War*, p. 89.
28. Murray, *The Luftwaffe*, pp. 52–3.
29. Overy, *Air War*, p. 89.
30. Cox, 'Comparative Analysis', p. 439.
31. Overy, *Air War*, pp. 82–7; Maier, 'The Battle of Britain', pp. 385–6.
32. 'RAF Battle of Britain Campaign Diary and Home Security Reports', http://www.raf.mod.uk/history/campaign_diaries.cfm; S. Broomfield, *Wales at War: The Experience of the Second World War in Wales* (Stroud, 2009), pp. 58–60.
33. TNA, HO 191/11, 'Statement of Civilian Casualties in the United Kingdom'.
34. MOA, Diarist 5231, 11 August 1940.
35. MOA, Diarist 5255, 19 August 1940.
36. Ibid., 16 August 1940, emphases in original.
37. HIMR, 19 August 1940, p. 343.
38. MOFR370, p. 4, emphasis in original.
39. MOFR382, 'Air Raids', 3 September 1940, p. 4.
40. MOFR370, p. 5, emphasis in original.
41. IWM, Private Papers of N. Cameron, Documents 06/80/1, diary entry, 24 August 1940.
42. G. Campion, *The Good Fight: Battle of Britain Propaganda and the Few* (London, 2008), p. 98.

43. *Daily Mirror*, 16 August 1940, p. 1; *Daily Express*, 17 August 1940, p. 1.
44. Campion, *The Good Fight*, pp. 97–114, figures, p. 99.
45. IWM, Private Papers of G. W. King, Documents 3777, diary entry, 25 August 1940.
46. IWM, Private Papers of C. G. King, Documents 3802.
47. 'The Front Line', *Daily Express*, 17 August 1940, p. 4.
48. https://www.winstonchurchill.org/learn/speeches/speeches-of-winston-churchill/113-the-few.
49. HIMR, 21 August 1940, pp. 349–50.
50. Quoted in C. Webster and N. Frankland, *The Strategic Air Offensive against Germany, 1939–45, I: Preparation* (London, 1961), p. 218.
51. Murray, *The Luftwaffe*, pp. 52–4; James, *Air Defence of Great Britain II*, pp. 324–5.
52. Overy, *Bombing War*, p. 88.
53. Ibid., pp. 89–93.
54. HIMR, 16 September 1940, p. 424.

18. THE MEANS OF VICTORY

1. D. Reynolds, *The Creation of the Anglo-American Alliance, 1937–41: A Study in Competitive Cooperation* (Chapel Hill, NC, 1981), pp. 114–30.
2. W. Churchill, *The Second World War, II: Their Finest Hour* (London, 1949), p. 361.
3. Reynolds, *Anglo-American Alliance*, pp. 134–8.
4. F. H. Hinsley, *British Intelligence in the Second World War (Abridged)* (London, 1994), pp. 51–2.
5. S. Roskill, *The War at Sea, 1939–1945, I* (London, 1954), p. 616.
6. CSO, *Fighting with Figures: A Statistical Digest of the Second World War* (London, 1995), p. 153.
7. Ibid., p. 184.
8. C. Behrens, *Merchant Shipping and the Demands of War* (London, 1955), p. 109.
9. K. Smith, *Conflict over Convoys: Anglo-American Logistics Diplomacy in the Second World War* (Cambridge, 1996), pp. 37–9.
10. Ibid., pp. 32–6.
11. Quoted in W. N. Medlicott, *The Economic Blockade, I, 1939–41* (London, 1952), p. 433.
12. Ibid., pp. 424–5.
13. Ibid., pp. 468–99.
14. Ibid., pp. 558–63.
15. W. N. Medlicott, *The Economic Blockade, II* (London, 1959), p. 668.
16. Medlicott, *Economic Blockade I*, p. 658.

17. A. Tooze, *The Wages of Destruction: The Making and Breaking of the Nazi Economy* (London, 2006), pp. 418–19.

18. Ibid., pp. 411–12.

19. For what follows, G. Peden, *Arms, Economics and British Strategy: From Dreadnoughts to Hydrogen Bombs* (Cambridge, 2009), pp. 208–9; B. Farrell, *The Basis and Making of British Grand Strategy, 1940–1943: Was There a Plan?* (Lewiston, NY, and Lampeter, 1998), pp. 58–73.

20. TNA, CAB 66/11/32, 'The Munitions Situation: Memorandum by the Prime Minister', 3 September 1940, p. 1.

21. TNA, CAB 66/11/42, 'Future Strategy', 4 September 1940, p. 5.

22. TNA, CAB 69/1/9, DO (40) 39, Confidential Annex, 31 October 1940, p. 233.

23. J. R. M. Butler, *Grand Strategy, II: September 1939–June 1941* (London, 1957), pp. 345–7; TNA, CAB 66/11/19, 'The Munitions Situation', 29 August 1940, p. 2.

24. TNA, CAB 66/11/42, 'Future Strategy', 4 September 1940, p. 8; Butler, *Grand Strategy II*, pp. 350–51.

25. C. Bell, *Churchill and Sea Power* (Oxford, 2013), pp. 200–201.

26. D. Reynolds, *In Command of History: Churchill Fighting and Writing the Second World War* (London, 2004), pp. 192–3; V. Schofield, *Wavell: Soldier and Statesman* (London, 2006), pp. 154–5.

27. Butler, *Grand Strategy II*, pp. 312–20; T. Benbow, ' "Menace" to "Ironclad": The British Operations against Dakar (1940) and Madagascar (1942)', *Journal of Military History*, 75, 3 (2011), pp. 769–809.

28. TNA, CAB 65/14, WM 40, Minute 2, Confidential Annex, 26 September 1940.

29. HIMR, 26 September 1940, pp. 454–5.

30. A. Roberts, *Eminent Churchillians* (London, 1994), pp. 179–80.

31. Channon diary, 26 September 1940, p. 268.

19. THE BEGINNING OF THE BLITZ

1. TNA, CAB 67/9/44, WP (G) (41) 44, 'Air Raids on London, September–November 1940', 5 May 1941, p. 2.

2. Mass Observation Archive, *The Blitz* (Brighton, 1987), p. 10.

3. TNA, HO 191/11, 'Statement of Civilian Casualties in the United Kingdom (viz, Gt Britain and Northern Ireland), resulting from enemy action from the outbreak of war to 31 May 1945'; R. Woolven, 'Civil Defence in London, 1935–1945: The Formation and Implementation of the Policy for, and the Performance of, the Air Raid Precautions (later Civil Defence) Services in the London region', PhD, King's College London, 2001, p. 144.

4. TNA, HO 186/2309, 'The Statistical Analysis of Mass Casualty Data', pp. 6-8.

5. R. Overy, *The Bombing War: Europe 1939-1945* (London, 2013), p. 100.

6. D. Edgerton, *Britain's War Machine: Weapons, Resources and Experts in the Second World War* (London, 2011), pp. 107-12.

7. TNA, CAB 65/9/33, War Cabinet 271 (40), 15 October 1940, p. 196.

8. G. Field, *Blood, Sweat and Toil: Remaking the British Working Class, 1939-1945* (Oxford, 2011), p. 43.

9. J. Hinton, *The Mass Observers: A History* (Oxford, 2013), p. 194; Woolven, 'Civil Defence', pp. 56-7.

10. Woolven, 'Civil Defence', p. 178; HC Deb, 9 October 1940, vol. 365, c. 441.

11. Field, *Blood, Sweat and Toil*, p. 45.

12. Ibid.

13. A. Calder, *The People's War: Britain 1939-1945* (London, 1969), p. 184.

14. T. Harrisson, *Living through the Blitz* (London, 1976), p. 111.

15. TNA, HO 186/2309, 'Analysis of (a) 590 cards relating to persons killed in the London area, (b) 1214 cards relating to persons injured in the London area but principally cases passing only through First Aid Posts'.

16. Overy, *Bombing War*, p. 146.

17. W. G. Ramsey (ed.), *The Blitz Then and Now, II* (London, 1988), p. 237.

18. Woolven, 'Civil Defence', p. 156.

19. R. Titmuss, *Problems of Social Policy* (London, 1950), pp. 276-7, and see his footnotes on the difficulties of estimating actual totals of housing damage.

20. TNA, CAB 67/9/44, WP (G) (41) 44, 5 May 1941, p. 9.

21. Titmuss, *Problems of Social Policy*, p. 293.

22. Ibid., pp. 251-6.

23. Woolven, 'Civil Defence', p. 153; Titmuss, *Problems of Social Policy*, pp. 259-262.

24. MOFR431, 'Survey of Voluntary and Official Bodies during Bombing of the East End 30 Sept 1940'.

25. HIMR, 10 September 1940, pp. 410-11.

26. MOFR392, 'Evacuation and other East End Problems, 10 September 1940', pp. 7-8.

27. Field, *Blood, Sweat and Toil*, p. 77; Nicolson diary, 17 September 1940, p. 112.

28. Overy, *Bombing War*, pp. 114, 181-5.

29. MOFR403, 'The Effect of Air Raids. The Isle of Dogs', p. 330.

30. Field, *Blood, Sweat and Toil*, pp. 46-8.

31. Lord Mayor's National Air Raid Distress Fund, *A Survey of the Work of the Fund, Sept 10th 1939 to June 30th 1946* (London, 1947), pp. 9, 14.

32. Woolven, 'Civil Defence', pp. 150-64.

33. Titmuss, *Problems of Social Policy*, pp. 263-7.

34. Woolven, 'Civil Defence', pp. 198-9.
35. J. Wheeler-Bennett, *John Anderson: Viscount Waverley* (London, 1962), pp. 251-7.
36. Webb diary, 15 September 1940.
37. MOA, TC 29 Men in the Forces, 1939-1956, Box 29-3-L, 'Impact of Blitz on East End'.
38. BUFVC, 'London Endures the Great Raid, 12 September 1940', Gaumont British News, Issue No. 698, http://bufvc.ac.uk/newsonscreen/search/index.php/story/60880.
39. Emrys Jones, 'I Saw What the Raiders Did', *Daily Mail*, 9 September 1940, p. 2.
40. Quoted in A. Calder, *Myth of the Blitz* (London, 1991), p. 216.
41. H. Marchant, 'The Cockneys are in it – Homes Shattered but not their hearts', *Daily Express*, 9 September 1940, pp. 1, 6.
42. J. B. Priestley, *Postscripts* (London, 1940), p. 74.
43. HIMR, 20 September 1940, pp. 438-9.
44. Calder, *Myth of the Blitz*, pp. 209-27, 231-3, quote p. 233.
45. 'The War in East London', *New Statesman*, 21 September 1940.
46. Field, *Blood, Sweat and Toil*, pp. 59-62.
47. R. Calder, *The Lesson of London* (London, 1940), p. 37.
48. See 'Sir John Anderson Gets Down to It!', *Daily Mirror*, 25 September 1940, p. 5; 'Scandal of Raid Homeless', *Daily Mirror*, 27 September 1940, p. 3; H. Marchant, 'They Can't Afford to Send Their Babies Away', *Daily Express*, 27 September 1940, p. 4; 'Thanks', *Daily Express*, 28 September 1940, p. 4.
49. *New Statesman*, 28 September 1940, p. 301. The edition was brought to Churchill's attention, and he questioned Anderson in the War Cabinet about what was being done to resolve it. A few days later, police cleared shelterers out of the unofficial part of the Tilbury shelter so it could be strengthened against the bombs (Hinton, *Mass Observers*, pp. 193-4).
50. MOFR431, 'Survey of Voluntary and Official Bodies', p. 85.
51. *Daily Worker*, 11 September 1940, p. 1.
52. TNA, CAB 65/9/12, WM (40), 250, 16 September 1940, p. 66.
53. BIPO Survey 72, October 1940, Qs.2, 5, 9, 7.
54. R. Self, *Neville Chamberlain: A Biography* (Aldershot, 2006), pp. 443-5.
55. K. Jefferys, *The Churchill Coalition and Wartime Politics* (Manchester, 1991), p. 51.
56. P. Murphy, 'Lyttelton, Oliver, first Viscount Chandos (1893-1972)', *ODNB*.
57. Overy, *Bombing War*, pp. 151-2.
58. 'Go to it Herbert', *Daily Herald*, 4 October 1940, p. 1.
59. B. Harrison, 'Wilkinson, Ellen Cicely (1891-1947)', *ODNB*.
60. Woolven, 'Civil Defence', p. 153.

61. Ibid., p. 178.
62. Ibid., pp. 199–207.
63. TNA, CAB 67/8/75, WP (G) 40 275, 'Air Raid Shelter Policy', 29 October 1940, p. 1.
64. TNA, CAB 65/9/42, WM (40) 280, 30 October 1940, pp. 269–70.
65. H. Morrison, 'We Have Won the First Round', *Listener*, 7 November 1940, quoted in Woolven, 'Civil Defence', p. 174.
66. Brooke diary, 12 September 1940, p. 107.
67. BIPO Survey 72, October 1940, Q.1.
68. TNA, CAB 65/9, WM 267 (40), 7 October 1940, quoted in B. Donoghue and G. Jones, *Herbert Morrison: Portrait of a Politician* (London, 1973), pp. 297–8.
69. King diary, 12 October 1940, p. 84.
70. Ibid., 11 October 1940, p. 80.
71. A. Roberts, *Eminent Churchillians* (London, 1994), pp. 191, 202–3; A. Thorpe, *Parties at War: Political Organization in Second World War Britain* (Oxford, 2009), pp. 61–9.
72. This paragraph and the next two, Jefferys, *Churchill Coalition*, pp. 52–6; Roberts, *Eminent Churchillians*, pp. 181–92.
73. MOA Famous Persons Survey (1939–1952), 'The Month Munich Died', p. 5.
74. Ibid.
75. Ibid., p. 3.
76. Priestley, *Postscripts*, pp. 98–100.

20. TAKING IT

1. S. Roskill, *The War at Sea, 1939–1945*, I (London, 1954), p. 616.
2. M. Milner, *Battle of the Atlantic* (Stroud, 2011), ch. 2; Roskill, *War at Sea I*, ch. 17; J. Buckley, 'Air Power and the Battle of the Atlantic 1939–45', *Journal of Contemporary History*, 28, 1 (1993), pp. 146–51.
3. Roskill, *War at Sea I*, p. 616.
4. C. Behrens, *Merchant Shipping and the Demands of War* (London, 1955), p. 184. Of course, all the armed forces contained large numbers of support staff, whereas all the merchant fleet was potentially in the front line. Compared to bomber aircrew or combat infantry, the merchant sailors got off lightly.
5. Ibid., p. 157.
6. Ibid.
7. T. Lane, *The Merchant Seamen's War* (Manchester, 1990), p. 27 and *passim*.
8. Figures from Arnold Hague's Convoy Database, http://www.convoyweb.org.uk.
9. Quoted in Milner, *Battle of the Atlantic*, p. 41.

10. G. H. Bennet and R. Bennet, *Survivors: British Merchant Seamen in the Second World War* (London, 2007), p. 73.

11. M. Page, 'All in the Same Boat', in J. Lennox Kerr (ed.), *Touching the Adventures ... of Merchantmen in the Second World War* (London, 1953), pp. 175–9, quoted in Lane, *Merchant Seamen's War*, p. 231.

12. Lane, *Merchant Seamen's War*, p. 155.

13. Behrens, *Merchant Shipping*, p. 128.

14. K. Smith, *Conflict over Convoys: Anglo-American Logistics Diplomacy in the Second World War* (Cambridge, 1996), p. 59.

15. Ibid., pp. 35–6.

16. Ibid., p. 37; Behrens, *Merchant Shipping*, p. 189.

17. http://www.leander-project.homecall.co.uk/Corvettes.html.

18. C. Bell, *Churchill and Sea Power* (Oxford, 2013), pp. 217–22.

19. Roskill, *War at Sea I*, p. 616.

20. This paragraph and the next, G. Field, *Blood, Sweat and Toil: Remaking the British Working Class, 1939–1945* (Oxford, 2011), pp. 71–2.

21. TNA, HO 191/11, 'Statement of Civilian Casualties in the United Kingdom (viz, Gt Britain and Northern Ireland), resulting from enemy action from the outbreak of war to 31 May 1945'.

22. B. Collier, *Defence of the United Kingdom* (London, 1957), p. 273.

23. Quoted in Neil Wallington, *Firemen at War: The Work of London's Fire-fighters in the Second World War* (Huddersfield, 2005), pp. 90–91.

24. R. Woolven, 'Civil Defence in London, 1935–1945: The Formation and Implementation of the Policy for, and the Performance of, the Air Raid Precautions (later Civil Defence) Services in the London region', PhD, King's College London, 2001, p. 183.

25. Ibid., p. 176.

26. R. Titmuss, *Problems of Social Policy* (London, 1950), pp. 299–300.

27. Ibid., pp. 293–4.

28. Woolven, 'Civil Defence', p. 156.

29. R. Overy, *The Bombing War: Europe 1939–1945* (London, 2013), p. 142.

30. Field, *Blood, Sweat and Toil*, p. 73.

31. Quoted in D. Thoms, *War, Industry and Society: The Midlands, 1939–1945* (London, 1989), p. 128. For rest, see Field, *Blood, Sweat and Toil*, ch. 7.

32. T. Harrisson, *Living through the Blitz* (London, 1976), p. 153.

33. Quoted in C. Smyth, *Cyril Forster Garbett: Archbishop of York* (London, 1959), pp. 264–5.

34. Swansea City Archives Office, P/SM 95 (County Borough of Swansea, ARP Miscellanea), 'Transcript of shorthand notes of the Air Raid Precautions Controller's Statement to the Council on the 18th March, 1941', quoted in J. R. Alban, *The Three Nights' Blitz: Select Contemporary Reports Relating to Swansea's Air Raids of February 1941* (Swansea, 1994), p. 150.

35. Thoms, *War, Industry and Society*, p. 133.

36. Overy, *Bombing War*, p. 143.

37. Harrisson, *Living through the Blitz*, p. 202.

38. Collier, *Defence of the United Kingdom*, p. 279.

39. B. Donoghue and G. Jones, *Herbert Morrison: Portrait of a Politician* (London, 1973), pp. 293–4, quote p. 293; Overy, *Bombing War*, p. 168.

40. Brown diary, 18 January 1941, p. 89.

41. IWM, Private Papers of Captain G. Watson, Documents 8610, Diana to Graham, 29 March 1941.

42. Donoghue and Jones, *Morrison*, pp. 294–6.

43. Titmuss, *Problems of Social Policy*, pp. 317–18.

44. Woolven, 'Civil Defence', ch. 6.

45. Donoghue and Jones, *Morrison*, pp. 290–91; T. O'Brien, *Civil Defence* (London, 1955), p. 528.

46. Titmuss, *Problems of Social Policy*, pp. 282–4; HC Deb, 6 June 1940, vol. 361, cc. 1011–14; D. Süss, *Death from the Skies: How the British and Germans Survived Bombing in World War II* (Oxford, 2014), pp. 155–7.

47. HC Deb, 12 February 1964, vol. 689, cc. 431–5.

48. Overy, *Bombing War*, p. 172.

49. J. Hinton, *The Mass Observers: A History* (Oxford, 2013), pp. 195–9.

50. MOFR495, 'Coventry', p. 2.

51. MOFR626, 'Second Report on Plymouth, 1.4.41', pp. 2–3.

52. Hinton, *Mass Observers*, pp. 199–205.

53. MOFR683, 'Third Report on Plymouth 4/5/1941', pp. 3, 4.

54. Hinton, *Mass Observers*, pp. 207–11.

55. Thoms, *War, Industry and Society*, pp. 108–17; Overy, *Bombing War*, p. 114.

56. B. Trescatheric and D. Hughes, *Barrow at War* (Chorley, 1979), pp. 4, 12.

57. Overy, *Bombing War*, p. 160.

58. C. Kohan, *Works and Buildings* (London, 1952), p. 320.

59. CSO, *Fighting with Figures: A Statistical Digest of the Second World War* (London, 1995), p. 172.

60. Kohan, *Works and Buildings*, pp. 317–18.

61. Overy, *Bombing War*, pp. 109–15.

62. H. Probert, *Bomber Harris: His Life and Times* (London, 2006), p. 116.

63. *Daily Express*, 16 November 1940, p. 1.

64. Overy, *Bombing War*, pp. 180–81.

65. BIPO Survey 72, October 1940, Q.6.

66. BIPO Survey 74, January 1941, Q.3.

67. BIPO Survey 77, April 1941, Q.6.

68. Ibid.

69. TNA, INF 1/292, HIWR, 19–26 March 1941.

70. Overy, *Bombing War*, pp. 175–6.

71. R. Calder, *Carry on London* (London, 1941), pp. 159–60.

72. IWM, Private Papers of Miss S. Curran, Documents 5531, Jim to Hilda, undated.

73. Ibid., Hilda to Jim, undated.

21. THE BATTLE OF THE BRITISH EMPIRE

1. Channon diary, 6 November 1940, p. 273; Nicolson diary, 6 November 1940, p. 123.

2. D. Reynolds, *The Creation of the Anglo-American Alliance, 1937–41: A Study in Competitive Cooperation* (Chapel Hill, NC, 1981), pp. 148–9.

3. J. Charmley, *Churchill's Grand Alliance: The Anglo-American Special Relationship 1940–57* (London, 1995), pp. 11–14.

4. W. F. Kimball, *The Most Unsordid Act: Lend-Lease, 1939–1941* (Baltimore, 1969), pp. 113–14, quote p. 108; R. Sayers, *Financial Policy, 1939–1945* (London, 1956), pp. 368–72.

5. Kimball, *Unsordid Act*, p. 235.

6. This paragraph and the next, Reynolds, *Anglo-American Alliance*, pp. 146–67.

7. 'Message to Congress, 1941', http://www.fdrlibrary.marist.edu/fourfreedoms, p. 9.

8. Ibid., p. 21.

9. TNA, PREM 4/17/1, Beaverbrook minute, 26 December 1940, quoted in C. Thorne, *Allies of a Kind: The United States, Britain and the War against Japan, 1941–1945* (London, 1978), p. 105.

10. Reynolds, *Anglo-American Alliance*, pp. 171–2.

11. Thorne, *Allies of a Kind*, pp. 101–6.

12. H. Umbreit, 'The Return to an Indirect Strategy against Britain', in K. Maier et al., *Germany and the Second World War, II: Germany's Initial Conquests in Europe* (Oxford, 1991), pp. 408–15.

13. G. Schreiber, 'Political and Military Developments in the Mediterranean Area, 1939–1940', in G. Schreiber, B. Stegemann and D. Vogel, *Germany and the Second World War, III: The Mediterranean, South-east Europe, and North Africa, 1939–1941* (Oxford, 1995), p. 181.

14. R. Wigg, *Churchill and Spain: The Survival of the Franco Regime, 1940–1945* (Abingdon, 2005), pp. 15–24.

15. A. Tooze, *The Wages of Destruction: The Making and Breaking of the Nazi Economy* (London, 2006), p. 398 and ch. 13.

16. F. H. Hinsley, *British Intelligence in the Second World War (Abridged)* (London, 1994), pp. 88–98.

17. S. Lawlor, *Churchill and the Politics of War, 1940–1941* (Cambridge, 1994), Part II.

18. I. Playfair et al., *The Mediterranean and Middle East, I: The Early Successes against Italy (to May 1941)* (London, 1954), pp. 263–98.

19. Dalton diary, 17 December 1940, p. 123.

20. TNA, INF 1/292, HIWR, 1–8 January 1941, p. 1.

21. BIPO Survey 74, January 1941, Qs.4, 5.

22. MOA TC11/1, Box A, 'Jokes About Italians', 27 December 1940.

23. R. Overy, *The Bombing War: Europe 1939–1945* (London, 2013), pp. 251–4.

24. Ibid., pp. 255–61.

25. Ibid., p. 92; C. Webster and N. Frankland, *The Strategic Air Offensive against Germany, 1939–45, IV: Annexes and Appendices* (London, 1961), Appendix 44.

26. J. Terraine, *The Right of the Line: The Role of the RAF in World War Two* (London, 1985), p. 274.

27. C. Webster and N. Frankland, *The Strategic Air Offensive against Germany, 1939–1945, I: Preparation* (London, 1961), pp. 302–3.

28. Overy, *Bombing War*, p. 262.

29. IWM, Private Papers of Wing Commander G. M. Brisbane, Documents 727, 'Observers and Air Gunner's Flying Log Book'.

30. Ibid., 'Operational Training in the RAF before and during the late war', pp. 12–13.

31. Overy, *Bombing War*, pp. 262–3.

32. D. Stafford, 'The Detonator Concept: British Strategy, SOE and European Resistance after the Fall of France', *Journal of Contemporary History*, 10, 2 (1975), pp. 193–208.

33. E. Harrison, 'The British Special Operations Executive and Poland', *Historical Journal*, 43, 4 (2000), pp. 1077–8.

34. TNA, INF 1/292, HIWR, 15–22 January 1941, p. 1.

35. A. Roberts, '*The Holy Fox': The Life of Lord Halifax* (London, 1997), pp. 272–80.

36. Halifax diary, 7 March 1941, quoted in Thorne, *Allies of a Kind*, pp. 97–8.

37. Quoted in Reynolds, *Anglo-American Alliance*, p. 180.

38. M. Hastings, *Finest Years: Churchill as Warlord, 1940–1945* (London, 2009), ch. 7.

39. A. Harriman and E. Abel, *Special Envoy to Churchill and Stalin* (New York, 1975), p. 28.

40. Colville diary, 11 January 1941, p. 284.

41. D. Reynolds, *From Munich to Pearl Harbor: Roosevelt's America and the Origins of the Second World War* (Chicago, 2001), pp. 110–15.

42. D. Hall, *North American Supply* (London, 1955), pp. 265, 270.

43. Reynolds, *Anglo-American Alliance*, pp. 167–75; A. Dobson, *US Wartime Aid to Britain 1940–1946* (London, 1986), pp. 35–57.

44. Taking £1 as equivalent to $7 to account for higher US production costs. As we will see, arms only made up a small proportion of Lend-Lease in 1941 – if it had all gone on raw materials and food, $7 billion would have been about half of British defence spending in 1941.

45. Hall, *North American Supply*, pp. 428, 430.

46. Reynolds, *Anglo-American Alliance*, pp. 270–72.

47. Ibid.

48. R. Skidelsky, *John Maynard Keynes, III: Fighting for Britain, 1937–1946* (London, 2000), pp. 194–7; P. Addison, *The Road to 1945: British Politics and the Second World War* (London, 1975), p. 168.

49. Quoted in Thorne, *Allies of a Kind*, p. 78.

50. Reynolds, *Anglo-American Alliance*, pp. 176–85.

51. For what follows on the Greek decision, Lawlor, *Churchill and the Politics of War*, pt. 3.

52. TNA, CAB 69/2, DO (41) 1, 8 January 1941.

53. For what follows on Eden, D. Dutton, *Anthony Eden: A Life and Reputation* (London, 1997), pp. 177–81.

54. Dalton diary, 4 February 1941, p. 150.

55. D. Day, *Menzies and Churchill at War* (Sydney, 1993).

56. Cadogan diary, 24 February 1941, p. 358.

57. Ibid., 28 February 1941, p. 359.

58. Ibid., 1 March 1941, p. 360.

59. Ibid., 6 March 1941, pp. 361–2.

60. Cadogan to Halifax, 18 March 1941, footnoted ibid., p. 361.

61. TNA, CAB 65/22/5, WM (41) 26, 7 March 1941, p. 4.

62. Playfair, *Mediterranean and Middle East I*, pp. 392–5.

63. Ibid., ch. 23.

64. Ibid., p. 423.

65. TNA, CAB 65/17/21, WM (41) 21, Conclusions, 27 February 1941, p. 107.

66. G. Prysor, *Citizen Sailors: The Royal Navy in the Second World War* (London, 2011), ch. 8.

67. IWM, Private Papers of J. E. Needham, Documents 1991, p. 3.

68. S. Roskill, *The War at Sea, 1939–1945, I* (London, 1954), p. 618.

69. C. Behrens, *Merchant Shipping and the Demands of War* (London, 1955), pp. 132–7; K. Smith, *Conflict over Convoys: Anglo-American Logistics Diplomacy in the Second World War* (Cambridge, 1996), pp. 52–4.

70. W. Hancock and M. Gowing, *British War Economy* (London, 1949), pp. 265–8.

71. R. Hammond, *Food, I: The Growth of Policy* (London, 1951), pp. 161–6.

72. TNA, CAB 66/15/42, WP (41) 69, Annex II, 'Naval Programme 1941', 27 March 1941, p. 6.

73. Contrast Smith, *Conflict over Convoys*, pp. 64–68, with D. Edgerton, *Britain's War Machine: Weapons, Resources and Experts in the Second World War* (London, 2011), pp. 210–11.

74. M. Carver, *Dilemmas of the Desert War: A New Look at the Libyan Campaign, 1940–1942* (London, 1986), pp. 19–23; D. French, *Raising Churchill's Army: The British Army and the War against Germany, 1919–1945* (Oxford, 2000), pp. 217–19; V. Schofield, *Wavell: Soldier and Statesman* (London, 2006), pp. 182–3.

75. TNA, CAB 69/2, Churchill to Eden, 3 April 1941, quoted in B. P. Farrell, 'Yes, Prime Minister: Barbarossa, Whipcord and the Basis of British Grand Strategy, Autumn 1941', *Journal of Military History*, 57, 4 (1993), p. 607.

76. J. Kennedy, *The Business of War: The War Narrative of Major-General Sir J. Kennedy* (London, 1957), p. 106.

77. D. Porch, *Hitler's Mediterranean Gamble: The North African and Mediterranean Campaigns in World War II* (London, 2004), pp. 152–5.

78. TNA, INF 1/292, HIWR, 16 to 23 April 1941, p. 2.

79. A. Whitfield, 'Stanley, Oliver Frederick George (1896–1950)', *ODNB*.

80. Dalton diary, 28 April 1941, pp. 189–92.

81. HC Deb, 7 May 1941, vol. 371, cc. 867–82, 944–5.

82. M. Kolinsky, *Britain's War in the Middle East: Strategy and Diplomacy 1936–1942* (New York, 1999), pp. 158–9.

83. TNA, CAB 69/2, DO (41) 25, 6 May 1941, Annex I, p. 4

84. This paragraph and the next, C. Smith, *England's Last War against France: Fighting Vichy 1940–1942* (London, 2009), pp. 174–80.

85. A. Beevor, *Crete: The Battle and the Resistance* (London, 1992), *passim* and pp. 87–94, 174; C. MacDonald, *The Lost Battle, Crete 1941* (London, 1993), pp. 169–281.

86. IWM, Private Papers of Captain T. C. T. Wynne, Documents 4821, 'Report from John Isdale Miller, 7 June 1941'. Miller was killed, with the rest of his crew, when his corvette, HMS *Salvia*, was sunk by a U-boat off Tobruk on Christmas Eve, 1941.

87. Smith, *England's Last War against France*, pp. 182–9.

88. Ibid., p. 192.

89. A. B. Gaunson, 'Churchill, de Gaulle, Spears and the Levant Affair, 1941', *Historical Journal*, 27, 3 (1984), pp. 697–701.

90. Smith, *England's Last War against France*, chs. 16–19.

91. W. Slim, *Unofficial History* (London, 1959), p. 162, quoted in Gaunson, 'Levant Affair', p. 706.

92. I. Playfair, *The Mediterranean and Middle East, II: The Germans Come to the Help of their Ally* (London, 1974), p. 171.

93. TNA, CAB 80/58, COS (41) 113 (O), 20 June 1941, quoted in Farrell, 'Yes, Prime Minister', p. 607.

94. IWM, Private Papers of Captain G. Watson, Documents 8610, Graham to Diana, 17 July 1941.

95. Reynolds, *Anglo-American Alliance*, pp. 197–204.

96. Ibid., p. 225.

97. M. Milner, *Battle of the Atlantic* (Stroud, 2011), p. 65; Roskill, *War at Sea I*, pp. 599–600.

98. W. Gardner, *Decoding History: The Battle of the Atlantic and Ultra* (Basingstoke, 1999), pp. 169–170.

99. Hinsley, *British Intelligence*, pp. 50–54.

100. Roskill, *War at Sea I*, pp. 395–418; Hinsley, *British Intelligence*, pp. 57–8.

101. Terraine, *Right of the Line*, pp. 248–9.

102. Gardner, *Decoding History*, pp. 169–70.

103. Smith, *Conflict over Convoys*, pp. 55–7.

104. C. Bell, *Churchill and Sea Power* (Oxford, 2013), pp. 219–20.

105. Smith, *Conflict over Convoys*, pp. 64–8; C. Webster and N. Frankland, *The Strategic Air Offensive against Germany, IV: Annexes and Appendices* (London, 1961), p. 508.

106. G. Schreiber, 'Politics and Warfare in 1941', in G. Schreiber, B. Stegemann and D. Vogel, *Germany and the Second World War, III: The Mediterranean, South-east Europe, and North Africa, 1939–1941* (Oxford, 1995), p. 567.

107. CSO, *Fighting with Figures: A Statistical Digest of the Second World War* (London, 1995), pp. 79, 81–2.

108. Smith, *Conflict over Convoys*, pp. 40–47.

109. J. R. M. Butler, *Grand Strategy II: September 1939–June 1941* (London, 1957), pp. 487–95.

110. TNA, CAB 69/2, DO (41) 20, 29 April 1941, p. 4.

111. TNA, CAB 69/2, DO (41) 12, 9 April 1941, p. 5.

112. Butler, *Grand Strategy II*, pp. 500–503.

113. A. Danchev, ' "Dilly-Dally" or Having the Last Word: Field Marshal Sir John Dill and Prime Minister Winston Churchill', *Journal of Contemporary History*, 22, 1 (1987), pp. 27–8; D. Reynolds, *In Command of History: Churchill Fighting and Writing the Second World War* (London, 2004), pp. 246–8.

114. R. Callahan, 'Churchill and Singapore', p. 159, and B. Farrell, '1941: An Overview', pp. 173–82, both in B. Farrell and S. Hunter (eds.), *Sixty Years On: The Fall of Singapore Revisited* (Singapore, 2002).

115. Quoted in Butler, *Grand Strategy II*, p. 506.

116. TNA, CAB 69/2, DO (41) 44, 25 June 1941, p. 1.

22. BRITAIN BEYOND THE BLITZ

1. D. Edgerton, *Warfare State: Britain, 1920–1970* (Cambridge, 2006), pp. 75–83; J. Lee, *The Churchill Coalition, 1940–1945* (London, 1980), ch. 4.
2. M. Postan, *British War Production* (London, 1952), p. 448.
3. W. Hancock and M. Gowing, *British War Economy* (London, 1949), pp. 321–2.
4. Which would be my take on the 'alternative classical' view laid out in S. Broadberry and P. Howlett, 'The United Kingdom: Victory at All Costs', in M. Harrison (ed.), *The Economics of World War II: Six Great Powers in International Comparison* (Cambridge, 1998), pp. 5–56.
5. CSO, *Fighting with Figures: A Statistical Digest of the Second World War* (London, 1995), pp. 54–6.
6. Ibid., p. 62; C. Kohan, *Works and Buildings* (London, 1952), pp. 74–81.
7. CSO, *Fighting with Figures*, pp. 67–9.
8. R. Hammond, *Food, I: The Growth of Policy* (London, 1951), pp. 161–2.
9. CSO, *Fighting with Figures*, pp. 214–15.
10. Ibid., p. 212.
11. B. Short, C. Watkins and J. Martin, 'The Front-Line of Freedom: State-Led Agricultural Revolution in Britain, 1939–45', in idem (eds.), *The Front Line of Freedom: British Farming in the Second World War* (Exeter, 2007), pp. 10–11.
12. C. Madge, 'Saving and Spending – A District Survey', *Economic Journal*, 50, 198/199 (1940), pp. 329, 331.
13. CSO, *Fighting with Figures*, p. 38.
14. Ibid., p. 237; H. Parker, *Manpower: A Study of War-time Policy and Administration* (London, 1957), p. 428.
15. Parker, *Manpower*, p. 428.
16. Ibid., p. 433.
17. CSO, *Fighting with Figures*, p. 237.
18. Madge, 'Saving and Spending', p. 331.
19. Parker, *Manpower*, pp. 429–31.
20. V. Berridge, *Health and Society in Britain since 1939* (Cambridge, 1999), pp. 18, 20.
21. CSO, *Fighting with Figures*, pp. 7, 13–18.
22. Madge, 'Saving and Spending', p. 337.
23. MOFR704, 'Report on Food and Rationing – Shotley Bridge, Newcastle District, 20 May 1941', p. 1.
24. R. McKibbin, *Classes and Cultures: England 1918–1951* (Oxford, 2000), pp. 66–7.
25. MOA, TC Budget, Money Matters and Household Budgeting, Box 1/F, Household Budgets and Saving and Spending, diary extract, 20 January 1942.

26. A. Atkinson, 'Distribution of Income and Wealth', in A. Halsey and J. Webb (eds.), *Twentieth Century British Social Trends* (Basingstoke, 2000), p. 356.
27. MOA, TC29 Forces. Men in the Forces 1939–1956, D – Army – Henry Novy, 'RAMC Depot Morale Report 1', 1 December 1940.
28. Ibid., 'Morale Report 5', 5 January 1941, p. 2.
29. Ibid., 'War in the East and Reactions, 2 April 1941', p. 1.
30. Ibid., 'Morale Report 2', 8 December 1940, p. 1.
31. CSO, *Fighting with Figures*, p. 39.
32. D. French, *Raising Churchill's Army: The British Army and the War against Germany, 1919–1945* (Oxford, 2000), pp. 185–6.
33. J. A. Crang, *The British Army and the People's War, 1939–1945* (London, 2000), p. 2.
34. Ibid., pp. 199–206.
35. Quoted in J. A. Crang, 'Army Morale Reports 1940–45', in P. Addison and A. Calder (eds.), *Time to Kill: The Soldier's Experience of War in the West, 1939–1945* (London, 1997), p. 62, emphasis in original.
36. MOA, TC29 Forces. Men in the Forces 1939–1956, D – Army – Henry Novy, 'War in the East and Reactions, 2 April 1941'.
37. S. Mackenzie, *Politics and Military Morale: Current Affairs and Citizenship Education in the British Army, 1914–1950* (Oxford, 1992), p. 86.
38. French, *Raising Churchill's Army*, pp. 64–74.
39. Crang, *British Army and the People's War*, p. 61.
40. IWM, Private Papers of Captain G. Watson, Documents 8610, Graham to Diana, 21 April to 1 May 1941.
41. Quoted in J. Fennell, *Combat and Morale in the North African Campaign: The Eighth Army and the Path to El Alamein* (Cambridge, 2011), p. 152.
42. Crang, *British Army and the People's War*, p. 9.
43. For ABCA, see Mackenzie, *Politics and Military Morale*, pp. 85–117.
44. Mackenzie, *Politics and Military Morale*, p. 113.
45. MOFR963, 'Report on Army Education: ABCA Scheme', 16 November 1941, pp. 4, 6.
46. TNA, NSC 7/78, 'War Weapons Weeks: Items of Special Interest'. Figures for national sales derived from figures published during the war in *The Economist*.
47. M. Cohen, *The Eclipse of Elegant Economy: The Impact of the Second World War on Attitudes to Personal Finance in Britain* (Farnham, 2012).
48. TNA, NSC 7/78, Campaign Notes 7, May 1941.
49. MOA, TC Budget, Money Matters and Household Budgeting, Box 2/B National Savings, 'Utmost Aid for Russia. Lord Kindersley's Call for Sacrifice', Postscript, 25 September 1941.
50. TNA, NSC 7/78, Campaign Notes 8, June 1941.

51. TNA, NSC 2/24, 'The Second War Savings Campaign', National Savings Committee 24th Report, 1939–45, pp. 34, 38.
52. Madge, 'Saving and Spending', p. 335.
53. C. Madge, *War Time Patterns of Saving and Spending* (Cambridge, 1943); P. Summerfield, 'The "Levelling of Class" ', in H. Smith (ed.), *War and Social Change: British Society in the Second World War* (Manchester, 1986), pp. 179–207.
54. C. Madge, 'The Propensity to Save in Blackburn and Bristol', *Economic Journal*, 50, 200 (1940), p. 434.
55. Madge, 'Saving and Spending', p. 335.
56. Madge, 'Blackburn and Bristol', p. 425.
57. Quoted in Summerfield, ' "Levelling of Class" ', p. 206.
58. MOFR704, 'Report on Food and Rationing', p. 2.
59. MOFR702, 'Report on Army Expenses', 16 May 1941.
60. MOA, TC29 Forces. Men in the Forces 1939–1956, D – Army – Henry Novy, 'RAMC Depot Report 8', 26 January 1941.
61. TNA, INF 1/292, HIWR, 19–26 February 1941, p. 2.
62. MOFR632, 'Food Tensions in Late February', p. 1.
63. BIPO Survey 76, March 1941, Q.7.
64. MOA, Diarist 5427, 1 April 1941.
65. MOFR704, 'Report on Food and Rationing', p. 2.
66. P. Addison, *The Road to 1945: British Politics and the Second World War* (London, 1975), p. 161.
67. G. Field, *Blood, Sweat and Toil: Remaking the British Working Class, 1939–1945* (Oxford, 2011), pp. 105–8.
68. MOFR604, 'The Scottish Shipbuilding and Engineering Apprentices' Strike', 13 March 1941, p. 1.
69. D. Butler and G. Butler, *British Political Facts, 1900–1985* (London, 1986), p. 372.
70. B. Donoghue and G. Jones, *Herbert Morrison: Portrait of a Politician* (London, 1973, 2001 edn), p. 298.
71. Field, *Blood, Sweat and Toil*, pp. 90–91; R. Croucher, *Engineers at War* (London, 1982), p. 115.
72. Croucher, *Engineers at War*, pp. 123–32.
73. Quoted in ibid., p. 130.
74. MOFR631, 'Glasgow', 3 April 1941, p. 2.
75. King diary, 26 July 1941, p. 136.
76. BIPO Survey 78, June 1941, Q.2; J. Hinton, *Shop Floor Citizens: Engineering Democracy in 1940s Britain* (Aldershot, 1994), pp. 27–9.

23. PRODUCTION AND RECONSTRUCTION

1. A. Furse, *Wilfrid Freeman: The Genius behind Allied Survival and Air Supremacy 1939 to 1945* (Staplehurst, 2000), ch. 8.

2. A. J. Robertson, 'Lord Beaverbrook and the Supply of Aircraft, 1940–41', in A. Slaven and D. Aldcroft (eds.), *Business, Banking and Urban History: Essays in Honour of S. G. Checkland* (Edinburgh, 1982), pp. 80–100.

3. M. Postan, *British War Production* (London, 1952), pp. 143, 160–61; A. Bullock, *The Life and Times of Ernest Bevin, II: Minister of Labour, 1940–1945* (London, 1967), pp. 34–5.

4. S. Ritchie, *Industry and Air Power: The Expansion of British Aircraft Production, 1935–1941* (London, 1997), pp. 228–40.

5. Chuter Ede diary, 3 February 1942, p. 45.

6. Bullock, *Bevin II*, pp. 19, 113–17; B. Farrell, *The Basis and Making of British Grand Strategy, 1940–1943: Was There a Plan?* (Lewiston, NY, and Lampeter, 1998), pp. 85–6, 192–3.

7. J. Harris, *William Beveridge: An Autobiography* (Oxford, 1977).

8. Ibid., pp. 194, 237.

9. TNA, CAB 67/8/84, 'Man-Power Survey', p. 16.

10. HC Deb, 27 November 1940, vol. 307, c. 284, quoted in Bullock, *Bevin II*, p. 43.

11. LSE Archives, Beveridge Papers, Beveridge/Supplementary/1/32, 'Letters from Beveridge to Mrs Mair, 1939–1941', Beveridge to J. Mair, 12 February 1941, quoted in Harris, *Beveridge*, p. 373.

12. K. Morgan, 'Shinwell, Emanuel (1884–1986)', *ODNB*.

13. R. Crowcroft, *Attlee's War: World War II and the Making of a Labour Leader* (London, 2001), pp. 79–81.

14. J. Tomes, 'Milne, Sir John Sydney Wardlaw- (1879–1967)', *ODNB*; King diary, 13 March 1941, p. 114.

15. HC Deb, 4 December 1940, vol. 367, c. 610, quoted in Bullock, *Bevin II*, p. 43.

16. K. Jefferys, *The Churchill Coalition and Wartime Politics* (Manchester, 1991), pp. 67–8.

17. Bullock, *Bevin II*, pp. 70–74.

18. Ibid., pp. 48–52.

19. HC Deb, 21 January 1941, vol. 368, cc. 125–6.

20. MOFR952, 'ATS Campaign', 7 November 1941.

21. P. Summerfield, *Women Workers in the Second World War: Production and Patriarchy in Conflict* (London, 1985), pp. 34–62; B. Coombs, *British Tank Production and the War Economy, 1934–1945* (London, 2013), p. 76.

22. Crowcroft, *Attlee's War*, pp. 63–5.

23. Quoted in W. Hancock and M. Gowing, *British War Economy* (London, 1949), p. 219.
24. J. Wheeler-Bennett, *John Anderson, Viscount Waverley* (London, 1962).
25. Quoted in ibid., p. 264.
26. Ibid., p. 271.
27. L. Robbins, *Autobiography of an Economist* (London, 1971), pp. 176–7, quoted in R. Toye, *The Labour Party and the Planned Economy, 1931–1951* (London, 2003), p. 115.
28. Crowcroft, *Attlee's War*, pp. 103–7.
29. For what follows on Keynes and the 1941 budget, R. Skidelsky, *John Maynard Keynes, III: Fighting for Britain, 1937–1946* (London, 2000), pp. 73–90.
30. For what follows on the budget, B. Sabine, *British Budgets in Peace and War* (London, 1970), pp. 181–201.
31. TNA, INF 1/292, HIWR, 9–16 April 1941, p. 3.
32. I. Zweiniger-Bargielowska, *Austerity in Britain: Rationing, Controls and Consumption 1939–1955* (Oxford, 2000), pp. 48–50.
33. MOFR756, 'First reactions to Clothes Rationing in MO Diaries', 24 June 1941, p. 1.
34. R. Hammond, *Food, I: The Growth of Policy* (London, 1951), pp. 194–203.
35. Hancock and Gowing, *War Economy*, pp. 333–7.
36. Crowcroft, *Attlee's War*, p. 104.
37. Bullock, *Bevin II*, pp. 84–92.
38. R. A. Butler, *The Art of the Possible: The Memoirs of Lord Butler* (London, 1971), pp. 90–91.
39. I. McLaine, *Ministry of Morale: Home Front Morale and the Ministry of Information in World War II* (London, 1979), pp. 243–57.
40. I am grateful to Patrick Higgins for this point.
41. HC Deb, 29 July 1941, vol. 373, cc. 1329–30.
42. HC Deb, 10 July 1941, vol. 373, cc. 335–6.
43. *The Times*, 11 July 1941, pp. 1, 8; J. Hinton, *Shop Floor Citizens: Engineering Democracy in 1940s Britain* (Aldershot, 1994), p. 32.
44. HC Deb, 29 July 1941, vol. 373, c. 1281.
45. Ibid., c. 1298.
46. Ibid., cc. 1276–7.
47. Postan, *War Production*, pp. 129–36.
48. M. Harrison, 'A Volume Index of the Total Munitions Output of the United Kingdom, 1939–1944', *Economic History Review*, 43 (1990), pp. 657–66.
49. Postan, *War Production*, pp. 123–6, 163–74; J. Zeitlin, 'Flexibility and Mass Production at War: Aircraft Manufacturing in Britain, the United States and Germany, 1939–1945', *Technology and Culture*, 36, 1 (1994), pp. 46–79.

50. Postan, *War Production*, pp. 174–82.

51. Ibid., pp. 182–3, 194.

52. Ibid., p. 185.

53. This paragraph and the next two, D. Fletcher, *The Great Tank Scandal: British Armour in the Second World War, Pt. 1* (London, 1989), pp. 57–66.

54. Ibid., pp. 66–8.

55. Contrast C. Barnett, *The Audit of War: The Illusion and Reality of Britain as a Great Nation* (London, 1986), pp. 55–183, with S. Ritchie, 'A New Audit of War: The Productivity of Britain's Wartime Aircraft Industry Reconsidered', *War and Society*, 12, 1 (1994), pp. 125–47; E. Lund, 'The Industrial History of Strategy: Re-evaluating the Wartime Record of the British Aviation Industry in Comparative Perspective', *Journal of Military History*, 62, 1 (1998), pp. 75–99; D. Edgerton, *Britain's War Machine: Weapons, Resources and Experts in the Second World War* (London, 2011), chs. 4 and 5.

56. King diary, 30 July 1941, p. 137.

57. Headlam diary, 29 July 1941, pp. 266–7.

58. Colville diary, 19 June 1941, p. 348.

59. Crowcroft, *Attlee's War*, pp. 82–90; I. Kramnik and B. Sheerman, *Harold Laski: A Life on the Left* (London, 1993).

60. P. Addison, *The Road to 1945: British Politics and the Second World War* (London, 1975), pp. 143–54, 183–9.

61. Nicolson diary, 22 January 1941, p. 139.

62. Hinton, *The Mass Observers: A History* (Oxford, 2013), p. 243.

63. 'The Two Scourges', *The Times*, 5 December 1940, p. 5.

64. J. Haslam, *The Vices of Integrity: E. H. Carr, 1892–1982* (London, 2000), pp. 89–90.

65. G. Field, *Blood, Sweat and Toil: Remaking the British Working Class, 1939–1945* (Oxford, 2011), pp. 304–12.

66. Quoted in R. Mackay, *Half the Battle: Civilian Morale in Britain during the Second World War* (Manchester, 2002), p. 229.

67. *Picture Post*, 4 January 1941, p. 4.

68. J. Stevenson, ' "Planners' moon?" The Second World War and the Planning Movement', in H. Smith (ed.), *War and Social Change: British Society in the Second World War* (Manchester, 1986), pp. 58–9; McLaine, *Ministry of Morale*, p. 175; Mackay, *Half the Battle*, p. 226.

69. S. Nicholas, *The Echo of War: Home Front Propaganda and the Wartime BBC, 1939–45* (Manchester, 1996), pp. 243–5, quote p. 243.

70. J. B. Priestley, *Out of the People* (London, 1941), pp. 9–10, 102–3.

71. Headlam diary, 8 March 1941, p. 243.

72. A. H. Halsey, rev., 'Titmuss, Richard Morris (1907–1973)', *ODNB*; A. Oakley, *Man and Wife: Richard and Kay Titmuss* (London, 1996); D.

Todman, 'Defining Deaths: Richard Titmuss's *Problems of Social Policy and the Meaning of Britain's Second World War*', in N. Martin, T. Haughton and P. Purseigle (eds.), *Aftermath: Legacies and Memories of War in Europe, 1918–1945–1989* (London, 2014).

73. R. Acland, *What it Will be Like in the New Britain* (London, 1942), pp. 9, 13.
74. A. F. Thompson, rev., 'Acland, Sir Richard Thomas Dyke (1906–1990)', *ODNB*.
75. P. Coupland, 'Anglican Peace Aims and the Christendom Group, 1939–1945', in T. Lawson and S. Parker (eds.), *God and War: The Church of England and Armed Conflict in the Twentieth Century* (Farnham, 2012).
76. Addison, *Road to 1945*, pp. 186–8.
77. A. Hastings, 'Temple, William (1881–1944)', *ODNB*.
78. Field, *Blood, Sweat and Toil*, p. 312.
79. TNA, INF 1/292, HIWR, 26 February to 5 March 1941, p. 2.
80. Field, *Blood, Sweat and Toil*, pp. 312–13.
81. Addison, *Road to 1945*, p. 155.
82. MOFR725, 'Hornsey By-Election', 5 June 1941.
83. Ibid.
84. 'Anthony Eden's, Secretary of State for Foreign Affairs of Great Britain, Speech on British War Aims', http://www.ibiblio.org/pha/policy/1941/410529a.html; E. Helleiner, *Forgotten Foundations of Bretton Woods: International Development and the Making of the Post-War Order* (New York, 2014), pp. 209–11.
85. Addison, *Road to 1945*, pp. 176–7.
86. Ibid., pp. 172–3. J. Harris, 'Political Ideas and the Debate on State Welfare, 1940–1945', in H. Smith (ed.), *War and Social Change: British Society in the Second World War* (Manchester, 1986), pp. 239–43.
87. K. Jefferys, 'British Politics and Social Policy during the Second World War', *Historical Journal*, 30, 1, (1987), pp. 123–44, quote p. 126; Butler, *Art of the Possible*, p. 134.
88. Quoted in Jefferys, 'Politics and Social Policy', p. 129.

PART FIVE

1. Brown diary, 19, 21, 22 June 1941, pp. 110–12.

24. THE WIDENING WAR

1. R. Evans, *The Third Reich at War* (London, 2009), pp. 28–66.
2. D. Glantz and J. House, *When Titans Clashed: How the Red Army Stopped Hitler* (Lawrence, Kans., 1995), pp. 49–50.
3. Ibid., p. 292.

4. Ibid., pp. 202, 209; A. Tooze, *The Wages of Destruction: The Making and Breaking of the Nazi Economy* (London, 2006), ch. 14, pp. 570, 482.

5. TNA, HO 191/11, 'State of Civilian Casualties in the United Kingdom'; Department of Transport, *Transport Statistics for Great Britain* (London, 1986), p. 201.

6. T. O'Brien, *Civil Defence* (London, 1955), pp. 419–39; http://www.bath blitz.org.

7. R. Titmuss, *Problems of Social Policy* (London, 1950), p. 336; Glantz and House, *When Titans Clashed*, p. 292.

8. P. Bell, *John Bull and the Bear: British Public Opinion, Foreign Policy and the Soviet Union, 1941–1945* (London, 1990), pp. 28–30.

9. I am grateful to Patrick Higgins for this point.

10. D. Dutton, *Anthony Eden: A Life and Reputation* (London, 1997), pp. 182–3.

11. D. Carlton, *Churchill and the Soviet Union* (Manchester, 2000), pp. 82–3.

12. P. Clarke, *The Cripps Version: The Life of Sir Stafford Cripps* (London, 2002), pp. 221–2.

13. M. Gilbert, *Winston S. Churchill, VI: Finest Hour, 1939–1941* (London, 1983), pp. 1120–21.

14. P. Donnelly (ed.), *Mrs Miburn's Diaries: An Englishwoman's Day-to-day Reflections, 1939–1945* (London, 1995), 22 June 1941, p. 101.

15. M. Kitchen, 'Winston Churchill and the Soviet Union during the Second World War', *Historical Journal*, 30, 2 (1987), pp. 418–19; Bell, *John Bull and the Bear*, pp. 37–8, 57–8, 61.

16. Colville diary, 21 June 1941, p. 350.

17. Carlton, *Churchill and the Soviet Union*, pp. 85–6.

18. J. Gwyer, *Grand Strategy, III, Pt 1* (London, 1964), pp. 93–8, 197–216; B. Farrell, 'Yes, Prime Minister: Barbarossa, Whipcord and the Basis of British Grand Strategy, Autumn 1941', *Journal of Military History*, 57, 4 (1993), pp. 604–5.

19. TNA, CAB 69/2, DO (41) 53, 1 August 1941, p. 3.

20. Carlton, *Churchill and the Soviet Union*, pp. 86–7.

21. Dutton, *Eden*, pp. 183–5.

22. R. Skidelsky, *John Maynard Keynes, III: Fighting for Britain, 1937–1946* (London, 2000), ch. 4.

23. D. Reynolds, *The Creation of the Anglo-American Alliance, 1937–41: A Study in Competitive Cooperation* (Chapel Hill, NC, 1981), p. 276.

24. Quoted in Skidelsky, *Keynes III*, p. 130.

25. R. Sayers, *Financial Policy, 1939–1945* (London, 1956), pp. 389–94.

26. Reynolds, *Anglo-American Alliance*, p. 277.

27. Ibid., pp. 233–8.

28. TNA, CAB 66/17 WP (41) 172, 20 July 1941, quoted in Reynolds, *Anglo-American Alliance*, p. 237.

29. This paragraph and the next two, D. Hall, *North American Supply* (London, 1955), pp. 308–35.

25. ATLANTIC CROSSINGS

1. D. Reynolds, *The Creation of the Anglo-American Alliance, 1937–41: A Study in Competitive Cooperation* (Chapel Hill, NC, 1981), pp. 213–18, 237–9.
2. Cadogan diary, 5–9 August 1941, pp. 396–7.
3. M. Gilbert, *Winston S. Churchill, VI: Finest Hour, 1939–1941* (London, 1983), p. 1158.
4. Ibid., p. 1159.
5. TNA, PREM 3/485/1, No. 11, Churchill to Attlee, 11 August 1941, quoted in Gilbert, *Churchill VI*, p. 1162.
6. Harvey diary, 12 August 1941, p. 31.
7. 'Atlantic Charter, August 14 1941', http://avalon.law.yale.edu/wwii/atlantic.asp.
8. Reynolds, *Anglo-American Alliance*, pp. 238–9.
9. This paragraph and the next two, Reynolds, *Anglo-American Alliance*, pp. 208–10; J. Gwyer, *Grand Strategy, III, Pt 1* (London, 1964), pp. 139–54.
10. Cadogan diary, 12 August 1941, p. 402.
11. TNA, CAB 65/19, WM (41) 84, 1, annex, quoted in Reynolds, *Anglo-American Alliance*, p. 214.
12. D. Hall, *North American Supply* (London, 1955), p. 330.
13. Cadogan diary, 25 August 1941, p. 402.
14. TNA, PREM 3/224/2, Churchill to Hopkins, 28 August 1941, quoted in Reynolds, *Anglo-American Alliance*, p. 215.
15. Reynolds, *Anglo-American Alliance*, p. 215.
16. A. Herman, *Gandhi and Churchill: The Epic Rivalry that Destroyed an Empire and Forged our Age* (New York, 2008), pp. 469–70.
17. Amery diary, 8 April 1941, p. 679.
18. Linlithgow to Amery, 30 August 1941, quoted in Amery diary, p. 664.
19. Amery diary, 14 August 1941, p. 710.
20. R. Toye, *Churchill's Empire: The World that Made Him and the World He Made* (London, 2010), p. 214.
21. Herman, *Gandhi and Churchill*, p. 475.
22. Amery diary, 4 September 1941, p. 713.
23. Quoted in R. Moore, *Churchill, Cripps and India 1939–1945* (Oxford, 1979), p. 47.
24. C. Thorne, *Allies of a Kind: The United States, Britain and the War against Japan, 1941–1945* (London, 1978), pp. 60–62.

25. Quoted in Moore, *Churchill, Cripps and India*, p. 42.
26. HC Deb, 9 September 1941, vol. 374, cc. 68–9.
27. A. Dobson, *US Wartime Aid to Britain 1940–1946* (London, 1986), pp. 130–32.
28. Reynolds, *Anglo-American Alliance*, pp. 216–19.
29. J. Maiolo, *Cry Havoc: The Arms Race and the Second World War 1931–1941* (London, 2010), pp. 372–5.
30. Hall, *North American Supply*, p. 333; TNA, CAB 69/2, DO (41) 62, 19 September 1941, p. 2.
31. Gwyer, *Grand Strategy III, Pt 1*, p. 154.
32. Hall, *North American Supply*, p. 335.

26. THE END OF THE BEGINNING

1. P. Bell, *John Bull and the Bear: British Public Opinion, Foreign Policy and the Soviet Union, 1941–1945* (London, 1990), pp. 50–51.
2. BUFVC, 'Russia in Action', British Paramount News, Issue No. 1086, 29 July 1941, http://bufvc.ac.uk/newsonscreen/search/index.php/story/37900.
3. A. Thorpe, 'The Membership of the Communist Party of Great Britain, 1920–1945', *Historical Journal*, 43, 3 (2000), p. 781.
4. G. Field, *Blood, Sweat and Toil: Remaking the British Working Class, 1939–1945* (Oxford, 2011), p. 92; J. Hinton, *Shop Floor Citizens: Engineering Democracy in 1940s Britain* (Aldershot, 1994), pp. 64–5.
5. Bell, *John Bull and the Bear*, pp. 61–3.
6. R. Brown, *East Anglia 1942* (Lavenham, 1988), p. 23.
7. Bell, *John Bull and the Bear*, pp. 58–9, 64–5.
8. BIPO Survey 80, October 1941, Q.1.
9. *Daily Mirror*, 3 September 1941, pp. 1, 7; Headlam diary, 6 September 1941, p. 271.
10. P. Clarke, *The Cripps Version: The Life of Sir Stafford Cripps* (London, 2002), pp. 226–8; G. Gorodetsky (ed.), *Stafford Cripps in Moscow, 1940–1942, Diaries and Papers* (London, 2007), pp. 155–63.
11. *Daily Express*, 20 September 1941, quoted in Bell, *John Bull and the Bear*, p. 54.
12. J. Beaumont, *Comrades in Arms: British Aid to Russia, 1941–1945* (London, 1980), pp. 52–60.
13. A. J. P. Taylor, *Beaverbrook* (London, 1972), pp. 487–93.
14. A. Hill, 'British Lend-Lease Aid and the Soviet War Effort, June 1941–June 1942', *Journal of Military History*, 71, 3 (2007), pp. 777–85.
15. Beaumont, *Comrades in Arms*, p. 210.
16. Hill, 'British Lend-Lease Aid', pp. 783–97.
17. Quoted in Taylor, *Beaverbrook*, p. 495.

18. This paragraph and the next, B. Farrell, 'Yes, Prime Minister: Barbarossa, Whipcord and the Basis of British Grand Strategy, Autumn 1941', *Journal of Military History*, 57, 4 (1993), pp. 610–20.

19. J. Gwyer, *Grand Strategy III, Pt 1* (London, 1964), pp. 206–16.

20. A. Danchev, ' "Dilly-Dally" or Having the Last Word: Field Marshal Sir John Dill and Prime Minister Winston Churchill', *Journal of Contemporary History*, 22, 1 (1987), pp. 23–6.

21. D. Fraser, *Alanbrooke* (London, 1986).

22. Taylor, *Beaverbrook*, pp. 496–501.

23. D. Dutton, *Anthony Eden: A Life and Reputation* (London, 1997), pp. 184–6.

24. Harvey, diary, 29 September 1941, p. 47.

25. Ibid., 11 November 1941, p. 63.

26. Ibid., 12 November 1941, p. 63.

27. Dutton, *Eden*, pp. 183–5.

28. Quoted in C. Webster and N. Frankland, *The Strategic Air Offensive against Germany, 1939–1945, I: Preparation* (London, 1961), p. 173.

29. Ibid., p. 183.

30. Ibid., p. 184.

31. B. Farrell, *The Basis and Making of British Grand Strategy, 1940–1943: Was There a Plan?* (Lewiston, NY, and Lampeter, 1998), pp. 142–3, 186–9.

32. M. Connelly, *Reaching for the Stars: A New History of Bomber Command in World War II* (London, 2001), p. 58.

33. R. Overy, *The Bombing War: Europe 1939–1945* (London, 2013), pp. 278–9.

34. H. Parker, *Manpower: A Study of War-time Policy and Administration* (London, 1957), pp. 109–15.

35. A. Bullock, *The Life and Times of Ernest Bevin, II: Minister of Labour, 1940–1945* (London, 1967), pp. 137–44.

36. Parker, *Manpower*, pp. 166–8.

37. BIPO Survey 80, October 1941, Qs.11, 2.

38. R. Crowcroft, *Attlee's War: World War II and the Making of a Labour Leader* (London, 2001), pp. 96–115.

39. HC Deb, 4 December 1941, vol. 376, c. 1305.

40. This paragraph and the next, Gwyer, *Grand Strategy III, Pt 1*, pp. 232–5.

41. A. B. Gaunson, 'Churchill, de Gaulle, Spears and the Levant Affair, 1941', *Historical Journal*, 27, 3 (1984), pp. 706–12; A. Roshwald, 'The Spears Mission in the Levant, 1941–1944', *Historical Journal*, 29, 4 (1986), pp. 897–919.

42. M. Wilmington, *The Middle East Supply Centre* (London, 1972).

43. I. Playfair, *The Mediterranean and Middle East, III: British Fortunes Reach Their Lowest Ebb* (London, 1960), pp. 29–31.

44. D. French, *Raising Churchill's Army: The British Army and the War against Germany, 1919–1945* (Oxford, 2000), pp. 217–39.

45. Quoted in J. Fennell, *Combat and Morale in the North African Campaign: The Eighth Army and the Path to El Alamein* (Cambridge, 2011), p. 60.

46. D. Glantz and J. House, *When Titans Clashed: How the Red Army Stopped Hitler* (Lawrence, Kans., 1995), p. 294.

47. Hill, 'British Lend-Lease Aid', p. 791.

48. C. Bell, *Churchill and Sea Power* (Oxford, 2013), ch. 8.

49. TNA, ADM 205/10, Churchill to Pound and Alexander, 25 August 1941, quoted in ibid., p. 240.

50. TNA, CAB 69/2, DO (41) 65, 17 October 1941.

51. K. Fedorowich, ' "Cocked Hats and Swords and Small, Little Garrisons": Britain, Canada and the Fall of Hong Kong, 1941', *Modern Asian Studies*, 37, 1 (2003), pp. 133–47.

52. R. Rhodes James, *Winston S. Churchill, His Complete Speeches, VI* (New York, 1974), p. 504.

53. TNA, FO 371/27913, F13114, Halifax to FO, 1 December 1941, quoted in D. Reynolds, *The Creation of the Anglo-American Alliance, 1937–41: A Study in Competitive Cooperation* (Chapel Hill, NC, 1981), p. 246.

54. For this paragraph and the next, B. Farrell, *The Defence and Fall of Singapore, 1940–42* (Stroud, 2006), the best account of why the efforts to defend Malaya failed.

55. *Change: Bulletin of the Advertising Services Guild, 3: An Enquiry into British War Production (in two parts). Part One, People in Production, prepared by Mass-Observation* (London, 1942), pp. 368–9.

56. MOA, Diarist 5165, 7 December 1941.

57. Ibid., 8 December 1941.

58. 'Prime Minister Winston Churchill's Broadcast on War with Japan, December 8, 1941', http://www.ibiblio.org/pha/policy/1941/411208e.html.

59. Ibid.

60. MOA, Diarist 5047, 8 December 1941.

61. MOA, Diarist 5443, 8 December 1941.

62. Ibid., 10 December 1941.

63. Brown diary, 11 December 1941, p. 138.

64. MOA, Diarist 5165, 10 December 1941.

65. W. Churchill, *The Second World War III: The Hinge of Fate* (London, 1950), p. 55.

66. Quoted in M. Gilbert, *Winston S. Churchill, VI: Finest Hour, 1939–1941* (London, 1983), p. 1273.

Index

Note: page numbers in bold refer to maps and tables

793

and enlistment 266–8
evacuation and 250, 252–3
preconceptions 36–7
and response to Blitz 523
and wartime incomes 596–7
Clay, Gunner Ewart 194–5, 267
clothing
points system for rationing 629,
630
price increases 594–5
Utility schemes 630–31
Clydebank 256
bombing raids 506, 509
shipyard apprentices strike
609–10
code-breakers, Polish 208
Cole, G. D. H. 103, 640
collective security 76–8, 91
failure of 93–4, 110, 120
Cologne, bombing raids 703
Colville, John 237, 364, 365–6,
404, 638
Combined Operations Headquarters
469
commentators (public experts) 21
Committee of Public Safety 396
Committee on Reconstruction
and Post-War Problems
639–40
Commonwealth
1937 conference on imperial
defence 50–51
see also British Empire
communications
convoy escorts 556
German army 329
revolution in 20, 30
see also radio
Communism
British view of 71, 72
change in Soviet strategy 103–4
and war on the Eastern Front
689–90

Communist Party of Great Britain
(CPGB) 43, 189
and effects of Blitz 490–91
and fall of France 391–2
and German-Soviet war 690–91
and Labour 104
and 'People's Convention (1940–41)
611–12
and Spanish Civil War 106, 107
companies, multinational 20
conscientious objectors 265–6
conscription 155, 222, 263–8
peacetime military 158
Conservative party
and 1940 criticism of pre-war
government 407–10
aristocracy and 28
and Chamberlain leadership
150–51, 157–8, 287–9
Churchill as leader 497
criticism of Churchill 386–7, 569,
632
criticism of economic management
620
dissent within 134–5, 307–8,
548–9, 565
and Empire 47
foreign policy 91, 92–3
and India 51, 54–6
and isolationism 61
and League of Nations 78
membership 44
and opposition to war 274
and plans for post-war
reconstruction 642–3, 647
and rearmament 73–4
and social reforms 410–11
and war aims 412–13
welfare reforms 39–40
construction industry 179, 591, 648
consumerism 27
Control of Employment Act (1939)
282

equipment 328
'halt order' before Dunkirk 333,
334
and invasion of Belgium 328–30
German navy 212, **213**
capital ship attacks in Atlantic 499,
555–6
see also U-boats
Germany 21, 120, 155
and Austria 125, 126–7
bilateral naval agreement (1935)
68–9
comparison of armament
production 636–7, **637**
declaration of war on America 718
economic pressure on 201–2, 465–6
economic problems 167–8, 169–70,
226
effect of bombing raids on 540–43,
700–703
invasion of Czechoslovakia 156
invasion of Denmark and Norway
311
invasion of Greece 533–4
and Italy 77
and Japan 169, 175
merchant shipping losses 214
oil supplies 466–7, 468, 542, 543
pact with Soviet Union 177, 426–7
'Pact of Steel' with Italy 157, 178
possibility of invasion of Britain
340, 362, 374–5, 436–7
rearmament 66, 67, 73, 98, 167
resources and shortages 465, 466,
656
Tripartite Act with Italy and Japan
460
and Versailles settlement 61–2, 63
war on Eastern front 519, 535, 653,
658–60, 687–90
western offensive (May 1939) 319,
323–5, 326–7
see also Hitler, Adolf

Ghazi, King of Iraq 230–31
Gibraltar 106, 355, 420, 437, 466
German plans for attack on 534,
564
Gillies, William 132
Gilmour, Sir John 310
Glasgow 12, 183
Glorious, HMS 313
Gneisenau cruiser 313, 555, 581
Gold Standard, sterling and 21, 22, 40
Gollancz, Victor 107, 186–7, 643, 645
and *Guilty Men* (1940) 407–8, 409,
646
Gordon Walker, Patrick 148–9
Göring, Hermann 436, 518
Gort, General John 'Tiger', VC, and
BEF 220–21, 331–2, 333–4
Government Evacuation Scheme 183
Government of India Act (1919) 52–3
Government of India Act (1935)
57–8, 59
Great Depression
effect on global security 61, 64
effect in UK 21–2, 40, 42–3
Greece 242
evacuation 564–5
expeditionary force to 551–5, 562–3
German invasion 533
Italian invasion 533
'W Force' 562
Greenland 420, 579
Greenwood, Arthur 82, 191, 281
and Beaverbrook 616
and Chamberlain 318
in Churchill's War Cabinet 319, 369
and Committee on Reconstruction
and Post-War Problems
639–40
and declaration of war 193, 280
and economic policy 623
and Lend-Lease 549
and Production Council 621
and social security policy 649

South Africa 100, 229
  contribution to war 238, 422
  gold exports 241
  gold reserves 530, 547
South-East Asia, Japanese expansion
    into 460
Southampton, bombing 485, 505,
    509, 510–11
Southport 12
Soviet Union 62, 83
  after fall of France 426–7
  Anglo-American supply mission to
      Moscow 674, 684–5, 691
  and Baltic States 426
  British aid to 660–61, 662,
      690–700
  British options for support 161,
      661, **662–3**, 688–90
  British view of 71, 72, 120, 658–60
  defence pact with France 69, 92,
      161
  exclusion from Tripartite Act 460
  German invasion 653, 655,
      657–8, 660
  Hitler's plans for 437–8, 534–5
  invasion of Finland 291–3, 295,
      300
  invasion of Poland 290–91
  and Japan 122–3
  military expansion 64–5
  mutual aid agreement with USA
      662
  pact with Germany 177, 426–7
  rearmament 427
  Red Army casualties 655, 656
  see also Eastern Front
Spackman, Frederick, war stories 2–3
Spain 103, 420, 534
Spanish Civil War 91, 105–7,
    109–10
Spears, General Louis 707
Spens, Sir Patrick, 1922 Committee
    307

Spens, Sir William, report on
    education 89, 648
stability, political 24, 38–40, 43–5
Stalin, Joseph
  demand for British second front
      661, 690, 696–7, 700
  demand for military assistance
      690–93
  relations with Hitler 534
  and United States 662
Stamp, Lord 160, 287–8, 624
  investigation into resources 301–3
  and wartime economic policy
      282–3, 287
Stanley, Oliver, MP 565, 568
Stark, Harold, US chief of naval
    operations 528, 550
state intervention 83–90
  education 88–9
  Emergency Powers Act 371–3
  health 87–8
  role in rearmament 99–100
  and war aims 413–14
  and war measures 224–5, 228,
      303–4, 614
  welfare 86–7
  see also post-war reconstruction
Statute of Westminster (1931) 50
Stepney
  Blitz 481, 490
  poor ARP preparations 477, 478,
      485, 513–14
  'Tilbury' air raid shelter 478, 482,
      489, 490
sterling bloc 22, 549
  wartime Sterling Area 240–41
Stimson, Henry, US war secretary 667
Stokes, Richard, MP 398, 496
Stone, Richard 626
Storey, Stanley 119
Strachey, John, and 'People's Front'
    movement 103
street parties, 1937 coronation 11–12